Sylvia Porter's
MONEY BOOK

UPDATED

Sylvia Porter's
MONEY BOOK

How to Earn It, Spend It, Save It, Invest it, Borrow It—and Use It to Better Your Life

UPDATED

VOLUME ONE

DOUBLEDAY & COMPANY, INC.
GARDEN CITY, NEW YORK

To G. Sumner Collins
My Husband

FOREWORD

The American market place is an economic jungle. As in all jungles, you easily can be destroyed if you don't know the rules of survival. You easily can fall into dangerous traps from which you cannot escape unharmed if you aren't alert and do not know how to avoid them. But you also can come through in fine shape and you can even flourish in the jungle—if you learn the rules, adapt them for your own use, and heed them.

This book's entire purpose is to prepare you to win in every sphere of your economic life. You may approach its contents in any way you wish, depending on your economic needs or desires at the specific time. Do you want a quick course in consumer economics? Scan the book from cover to cover, for it is designed to be your basic book in personal and family finance. Do you want help on buying or renting, furnishing or financing a home? Turn to Chapter 13, "A Roof Over Your Head," and I am confident you will find the information you are seeking. Are you concerned about investing your nest egg? In Chapters 20–25, on "How to Invest," you will find the fundamental guidelines on investing or speculating in stocks, bonds of all types, mutual funds, commodities, and even in the "far out" fields ranging from rare books and prints to art and antique cars. Do you need to know how to borrow money? Or plan your future financial security? Or finance a college education? Or do you want to know what are your rights in the market place and how to go about getting them? Out of a lifetime of dedicated study, I have tried to give you the fundamentals in each area.

Of course, all I—or anyone else—could give you in any book, no matter what its size or how great its goals, are the basic facts, the most accurate and complete guidelines available, an informed selection of subjects, and, in my case, a lifelong bias in favor of the consumer. You must carry on from here and translate all of it into whatever is right for you to do. In Chapter 6, "The Everyday Necessity of Food," for instance, you will find simple rules for using unit pricing to slash your food costs. But what help will unit pricing be if you ignore this technique when you go food shopping? In Chapter 11, "Your Job, Career, or Business," you will find the telltale signs of this era's most vicious "business opportunities" traps. But what purpose have I served if you refuse to heed the warnings? All of us must decide what and how much responsibility we will accept for the protection of ourselves and our families.

It was more than five years ago that I began this book with great confidence. It is with humility that I finish it. And it is with the hope that it will help make your own life as a consumer more rewarding in these closing decades of the twentieth century in America that I now submit it to you.

October 1974

Leading all acknowledgments must be mine to Lydia Lawrence Ratcliff, my associate for twelve years. She and I worked together on this book from start to finish. Whatever success it earns, I share with Lydia.

Also, my deep gratitude goes to:

Sylvia (Sally) Rosen, my executive secretary and friend for twenty-one years, who supervised the production of the book throughout;

Richard C. Andrews, who researched and reviewed thousands of facts with a reassuring respect for accuracy; and

Mary B. Williams, who organized and kept the files, thereby holding back chaos for five long years.

In the course of writing this book many organizations and individuals—all authorities in their respective fields—helped with essential research and correction of the manuscript. Their contribution has been enormous, and I acknowledge this too with profound gratitude. Among them:

American Automobile Association, American Bankers Association, American Dental Association, American Hospital Association, American Institute of Architects, American Legion, American Medical Association, American Movers Conference, American National Red Cross, American Psychiatric Association, American Society of Travel Agents, American Telephone & Telegraph Co., American Youth Hostels, Inc., Air Conditioning and Refrigeration Institute, Amtrak, Associated American Artists, Association of Home Appliance Manufacturers, Avis Rent-A-Car System, Inc.

The Bride's Magazine, Better Business Bureau of Metropolitan N.Y., Inc., Bicycle Institute of America, Blue Cross, Blue Shield, Bureau of Building Marketing Research, Car Tours in Europe, Inc., Celanese Corp., Chase Manhattan Bank, Chris Craft Industries Inc., College Entrance Examination Board, College Scholarship Service, Commodity Research Bureau, Consumer Education—Extension Service, Consumer Federation of America, Consumers Union, Credit Union x ACKNOWLEDGMENTS

National Association, Inc., Edmund Publications Corp., Electronics Industries Association.

Greyhound Lines, Inc., Group Health Association of America, Health Insurance Institute, Health Research Group, H. R. Harmer, Inc., Household Finance Corp., Institute of Life Insurance, International Association of Chiefs of Police, Inc., Insurance Institute for Highway Safety, Insurance Information Institute, Jewelry Industry Council, H. P. Kraus.

Litton Industries, Lightning Protection Institute, Manfra, Tordella & Brooks, Inc., Merrill Lynch, Pierce, Fenner and Smith, Mobile Homes Manufacturers Association, *Modern Maturity Magazine,* National Alliance of Television & Electronic Service Associations, National Association of Home Builders, National Association of Realtors, National Consumer Law Center, National Family Opinion Research, National Fire Protection Association, National League of Insured Savings Associations, National Live Stock & Meat Board, National Parking Association, National Safety Council, National Society of Interior Designers, New York State College of Agriculture and Life Sciences, New York Stock Exchange, No-Load Mutual Fund Association, Northeastern University, Planned Parenthood—World Population, Public Interest Research Group, Recreational Vehicle Institute, Research Institute of America, Rhode Island Consumers Council, Small Claims Study Group, Sotheby Parke-Bernet Inc., The Conference Board, The National Association of Food Chains, The Singer Corp., Village Music Studio, Vintage Cars of Rockland, Yale University, Zero Population Growth.

The United States Departments of Agriculture, Health, Education and Welfare, Housing and Urban Development, Transportation, and Treasury; the Internal Revenue Service; the Federal Housing Administration, General Services Administration, National Highway Traffic Safety Administration, Occupational Safety and Health Administration, Social Security Administration, and Veterans Administration; the Federal Bureaus of the Census, Customs, Labor Statistics, and the Women's Bureau; the Civil Aeronautics Board, Consumer Product Safety Commission, Federal Trade Commission, Food and Drug Administration, and the Interstate Commerce Commission; the Federal Deposit Insurance Corporation, the Federal Reserve Board, the Federal Savings and Loan Insurance Corporation, and the National Credit Union Administration; the Office of Education and the Office of Consumer Affairs.

Robert H. Bethke, Judith Burbank, Herbert Denenberg, Carol Brandt, L. W. Erickson, Karen Ferguson, Dave Gammill, Herbert Gilman, Dr. Eli Ginzberg, Leon Gold, Robert E. Harper, Richard Hesse, Dr. Milton J. Huber, Richard Huyler, Eugene Emerson Jennings, William L. Jiler, Walter Kolodrubetz, Ken McCormick, Ferris Mack, Harold I. Meyerson, Eugene Miller, Ernest Morgan, Franz Pick, Judge Morris Ploscowe, Walter Polner, Riva Poor, Betsy Rollason, V. Henry Rothschild, Larry Rothstein, Peter M. Sandman, Milton A. Schiff, Brooke Shearer, Elsa Sydorowich, Kacy Tebbel, Barbara Donovan Tober, Stan West, Graham V. Whitehead.

CONTENTS

FOREWORD   vii

ACKNOWLEDGMENTS   ix

VOLUME ONE

Part I EVERYDAY MATTERS

1   Your Personal Money Manager   3
2   Your Checking and Savings Accounts   44
3   How to Borrow Cash and Use Credit Wisely   85
4   How to Shop and Save on Everything   160
5   The Extra Cost of Being Broke   175
6   The Everyday Necessity of Food   177
7   The Now-and-Then Necessity of Clothes   244
8   The High Cost of Good Health   267
9   Your Transportation—By Wheels, Wings, and Water   335
10 A College Education and How to Finance It   434
11 Your Job, Career, or Business   472
12 How to Save on Vacations   600

VOLUME TWO

13 A Roof Over Your Head   625

CONTENTS

Part II MILESTONES

14 How Much Does a Husband and/or a Wife Cost?   793
15 The Economics of Children   801
16 The High Cost of Divorce   819
17 What You Should Know About Wills, Estates, and Trusts   829
18 Funeral Expenses and How to Control Them   858

Part III MANAGING YOUR MONEY

19 Planning for Your Financial and Personal Security   869
20 How to Invest in Stocks   932
21 How to Invest in Mutual Funds   1009
22 How to Invest in Bonds   1027
23 How to Speculate in Commodities   1067
24 How to Invest in Land   1079
25 How to Invest "Far Out"   1086

Part IV YOUR RIGHTS AND HOW TO GET THEM

26 Your Rights as a Consumer   1117
27 Your Other Basic Rights   1152
28 Where to Get Help   1177

    INDEX   1201

Sylvia Porter's

MONEY BOOK

Part I
EVERYDAY MATTERS

1

YOUR PERSONAL
MONEY MANAGER

THE CHARACTERISTICS OF CLASS   5
    "ERA OF ASPIRATIONS"   6
WHY BUDGET?   8
    WHICH SYSTEM OF MONEY MANAGEMENT FOR
      YOU?   9
    THREE PRELIMINARY NOTES ON BUDGETING   11
FOUR SIMPLE FORMS TO CREATE A PERSONAL
  MONEY MANAGER   11
    FORM I—FAMILY INCOME   12
    FORM II—FIXED EXPENSES   14
    INCLUDE YOUR SAVINGS!   16
    FORM III—WHAT YOU HAVE LEFT FOR DAY-TO-DAY
      EXPENSES   18
    FORM IV—BUDGETING YOUR DAY-TO-DAY EXPENSES   18
    DON'TS TO GUIDE YOU   20
WHAT ROLE DO YOUR CHILDREN PLAY?   21
    TEN RULES ON ALLOWANCES   21
IN CASE YOU'RE CURIOUS . . .   23
    HERE'S WHAT OTHER PEOPLE SPEND   23
    HOW MUCH CHEAPER ARE LARGE FAMILIES TO
      FEED THAN SMALL ONES?   24
BUDGETING IF YOU'RE IN COLLEGE   24
WHERE SHOULD YOU KEEP YOUR MONEY?   26
    THE JOINT CHECKING ACCOUNT   27
    SEPARATE CHECKING ACCOUNTS   28

WHERE SHOULD YOU KEEP YOUR MONEY? (*cont'd*)
    THE SAVINGS ACCOUNT   30
    THE COMBINATION OF SAVINGS AND CHECKING
      ACCOUNTS   31
    THE ALLOWANCE METHOD   32
    THE BROKEN SUGAR BOWL METHOD   33
HIS-AND-HER BUDGETS   34
    A BUDGET IF YOU'RE JUST LIVING TOGETHER
      ("MINGLES")   36
    WHO PAYS FOR WHAT?   37
HOW MUCH ARE YOU WORTH?   39
    HOW DOES YOUR NET WORTH COMPARE?   41
IF YOU'RE STARTING TO KEEP TAX RECORDS:
QUESTIONS AND ANSWERS   41

THE CHARACTERISTICS OF CLASS

Where does your income rank?

Are you rich?

You are if you have a household income of $50,000 and over. This is the class of the rich and there are only about half a million homes in it. But while you make up less than 1 per cent of our nation's population, you get 5 per cent of our entire personal income.

Are you affluent?

You are if your household income is $25,000 to $50,000, and if so, you are also in a skinny minority of 7 per cent of our households. But if you are in this class you have at your disposal some 18 per cent of our nation's total earnings and your per capita income is more than twice the nationwide average.

Are you upper-middle?

Your household income is $15,000 to $25,000 and some 15.5 million—or about one out of every four of the nation's homes—are in this class. Your per capita income exceeds $5,000, which is a third again as much as the national average.

Are you average?

Then your household income is $10,000 to $15,000 and you join nearly a quarter of all America's homes. What's more, in contrast to the affluent and the rich, many of you are thirty-four years of age or younger and less than 25 per cent of you are over fifty-five.

Are you below par?

That's you, if your household income is $5,000 to $10,000, and you represent one of every four homes. Your per capita income is only $2,600 a year and, despite the size of your group, only 14 per cent of all spending power flows to you.

In the United States in the mid-seventies, you qualify for this bottom class if your household income is under $5,000. In this bracket, including one of every six households, lie many of our social problems. Here are the retired, the widowed, the lone female, often over sixty-five years old, the less educated. But happily the importance of your "class" continues to shrink.

Where do you belong? In the past quarter century the distribution of incomes has undergone a dramatic upheaval and realignment. Each year more than a million of our households are moving from the middle into the upper income brackets, a process which has been fundamentally altering our social and economic life styles.

There are two characteristics of class inherent in this realignment which shout a direct personal message to you:

The first is that the higher the income class the higher the education. Among the below-average, only about 20 per cent of all household heads have had any exposure to college. In the $15,000 to $25,000 bracket, some 40 per cent of all household heads have had at least some college training. In the $25,000 to $50,000 bracket, this is up to 45 per cent with college degrees and an additional 15 per cent with some college training. In the class of the rich, an exceptionally high 54 per cent of all household heads have college degrees and 90 per cent are white-collar workers. You can't miss it! The tie is undeniable. The message is clear.

The second is the high incidence of the working wife in the upper-middle bracket—and in fact in well over half of all the $15,000 to $25,000 homes the wife is employed. There are relatively few working wives among the below-average; they rise to 45 per cent among average households and then up again.

The U.S. economy was an income "pyramid" a few generations ago, with most in the below-middle classes, a tiny few at the top. It has become "diamond-shaped," with most people in the middle, fewer at the bottom, still fewer at the top—and if incomes continue rising merely at the annual rate of the past twenty years, the average family income in the United States will top $15,500 by 1985. It remains, though, a far cry from the ideal "reverse pyramid," with most of us at the top and middle, virtually none at the bottom.

"ERA OF ASPIRATIONS"

You're a young family in the $10,000 to $15,000 income range—striving for the "surplus income" family status but still well below it.

You have a couple of elementary-school-age kids, you live in the suburbs, and the family breadwinner commutes to work in his car. Are two cars a luxury or a necessity?

Your children are in high school and you, their mother, want to go back to a full-time job to help finance their future education. Is a household employee, at least part time, a luxury or a necessity?

Is home air conditioning, for you who live in the very hot states, a luxury in this era? Is automatic transmission in a car still just an option or has it become "basic equipment"? Does anyone today consider a TV set an unqualified luxury?

We are into an "era of aspirations" in our economy. In this era, most of us will spend a shrinking share of our income on the traditional necessities of food, clothing, shelter, and transportation while we spend a steadily increasing share of our income for goods and services which reflect our hopes and wants.

The implications for our economy and for you are profound.

Even now, the proportion of our total buying power available for spending on the "aspirations" rather than the necessities of life is estimated at a record high 15 per cent. Every year our total "discretionary spending"—defined as "purchases resulting from decisions relatively free of pressure of necessity or force of habit"—soars to new peaks.

As Dr. Ernst A. Dauer, a consumer credit authority, put it, "The typical family no longer purchases only what it needs, it purchases what it would like to have, and its aspirations are continually expanding as rapidly as its income."

As Dr. George Katona, author of *The Mass Consumption Society,* elaborated: ". . . not just a thin upper class, but the majority of households have acquired discretionary purchasing power. In the new wants-or-aspirations economies, in contrast to needs-economies, many consumer expenditures may be postponed or may be bunched at a given time. Therefore, in addition to consumers' ability to buy, consumers' willingness to buy also exerts a great influence on economic trends."

But . . . does our ever rising capacity to buy most of the things we want, over and beyond the things we actually need, make us happier? Not by any means. Again, in Katona's words:

"If what you have today appears insufficient tomorrow, disappointment and frustration may become frequent occurrences. Stress, tension and anxiety may even grow far beyond what has prevailed in less affluent societies. Moreover, because of the persistent gap between the well-being of the affluent to very-affluent 85–90 per cent of our society and the other 10–15 per cent who remain outside the mass consumption society, deprivations are felt more strongly than ever before."

And the ironic clincher: "The higher the aspirations, the more chance that people will be disappointed."

WHY BUDGET?

As the previous analysis surely hinted, it's a virtual certainty that if you're a young couple in our country today you quarrel about money. How to finance not only your day-to-day needs but also your aspirations —that's the objective of people everywhere, in every income group, in every circumstance. And many of you are seeking help because you have an uncomfortable feeling that you ought to be able to manage better than you do.

You may be the rare one who does not need a budget at all, for you may have an instinctive sense of money management within the limits of your regular income. Or you may manage comfortably with only a loose outline of your living expenses and anticipated earnings.

But for the first time in a full generation, budget-keeping is coming back into style—as a result of the oppressively rapid rate of rise in living costs during the early 1970s and skyrocketing prices of many necessities and semi-luxuries. If, therefore, you feel you want or need a budget, you should have one. And if this is you, get this fundamental point straight now: your family's budget almost certainly will be radically different from that of families living near you. And it will without question differ in many key respects from any "average" spending-saving pattern of any "average" American family. The average family exists only on paper and its average budget is a fiction, invented by statisticians for the convenience of statisticians.

The shape of your own budget will depend directly on your own or your family's individual goals and priorities. Would you prefer to spend $4,000 on a new car or on a year of postgraduate education? Would $500 worth of color television mean more, or less, to you than $500 worth of, say, guitar lessons? There is no sense in attempting to fit into a ready-to-wear financial pattern which ignores your own personal wants and desires.

The budget you draw also will depend heavily on the composition of your family. A young working couple without children may have relatively low housing costs, relatively high entertainment and clothes costs, and a good opportunity to save substantial amounts toward future family goals. Drastically different will be the spending-savings blueprint of the young couple with growing children and a heavily mortgaged house.

In essence, there is no such thing as an average budget and you should not even look for a standardized format. Search instead for a simple, flexible financial outline to help you achieve the goals you truly want.

WHICH SYSTEM OF MONEY MANAGEMENT FOR YOU?

You can get your first basic guidance from the experience and methods of others. The shopkeeper on your corner has part of the answer in the way he handles his store's income and outgo and fits the two together with a margin left for "reserve." Your parents had part of the answer in the way they measured their earnings and their prospects for earnings, then divided their spending into so much for essentials, so much for savings, so much for luxuries. The giant corporation has much of the answer in the ways it keeps its books, prepares for bad as well as good times, and provides a cushion for the unexpected and unpredictable.

You may now be handling all your income and outgo on a basis of "Here's what's in my pocket, here's what has been spent." Income, in short, is what you actually have in your hands; outgo is what you are paying to other people. What's coming to you later isn't important this minute. What you owe later isn't important either. The big thing is what you have and what you spend now. Accountants call that operating on a "cash basis"—but, as millions discover, it doesn't go far enough.

It is obvious that what most people need is a system of money management which will:

(1) tell you what money is coming in during the next several weeks or months;

(2) tell you what has to be put aside today for future security and independence and for those big unavoidable bills due in the next several weeks or months;

(3) tell you what is left over for the day-to-day expenses, ranging from food to a new household gadget;

(4) tell you too how much is left, if any, for luxuries and semi-luxuries;

(5) relate your income and expenses to a reasonably long period of time so that you can avoid fumbling along from minute to minute and day to day;

(6) show you how to run your personal affairs the way most successful businessmen run their affairs;

(7) achieve your financial priorities.

This system, incidentally, is what accountants call operating on an "accrual" basis, but dismiss that fancy-sounding word right here. The important point is that no business can get anywhere unless it knows what money is coming in tomorrow as well as today and unless it knows also what is to be done with tomorrow's as well as today's cash.

A family or person cannot get far without this type of planning either.

Money is earned to be spent. When you spend, you buy more than material things such as bread or shoes; you make decisions which determine your whole way of life. Your decisions bring you closer to—or perhaps send you further away from—your ambitions, your aspirations, the things and non-things which are really most worth while to you.

Money never remains just coins and pieces of paper. It is constantly changing into the comforts of daily life. Money can be translated into the beauty of living, a support in misfortune, an education, or future security. It also can be translated into a source of bitterness.

It may seem that so many of your decisions are forced by circumstances that you have very little chance to control your own money. Perhaps, however, your income appears too small to go around only because you did not take into account the "nibblers"—the little items that nibble away at your income until there is nothing left. Perhaps you have debts left at the end of the year only because you ignored the "bouncers"—the big expenses that turn up a couple of times a year and make giant dents in your income. Or perhaps you're in trouble only because you haven't considered the "sluggers"—the unexpected expenses, such as sickness and major household repairs, that can throw even a good spending plan way off balance.

Start from the premise that no income you will earn will ever be large enough to cover *all* your wants. Accept the theory that the more income you have the greater will be your desires. Make up your mind that if you want something badly enough you will sacrifice other things for it.

Take the trouble to think out your own philosophy of living and your ambitions for the future. Develop a plan of control over your spending. Then you will make progress toward the kind of living which means most to you.

THREE PRELIMINARY NOTES ON BUDGETING

Although no system in itself can completely eliminate your money problems the following preliminary notes will certainly help:

(1) You must work together if you are married. Your plan must be a joint project and you must talk about a wide variety of things before trying to put down a single figure about income or outgo.

(2) You must provide for personal allowances in your plan—and let each person decide what to do with his or her own allotment. None of you should have to account for every cent of your allowance; that is a personal matter. Similarly, if you're a wife at home, you should not be asked to submit an item-by-item explanation of what happened to the food money. Never permit a budget to become a strait jacket—or it will surely fail. And most important, I repeat, do not try to fit yourself into other people's budgets or try to make the spending averages of other families solve your own problems.

(3) You must keep your records simple. Then they will be fun to maintain as well as helpful. All that is required from your records is a blueprint for each month's spending, a history of where money goes each month, and an over-all picture to help you whenever a financial emergency arises. You can get vital information from simple records, and the simpler the records, the more they will reveal.

Four Simple Forms to Create a Personal Money Manager

You are about to create a personal money manager that, no matter what your income, will do four things:

(1) tell you where your money is coming from—and when it is coming;

(2) provide for the necessities first, then the comforts and self-improvements, then the luxuries—when you have the money to spend for them;

(3) give you a means for saving—a plan to pay off debts or to keep out of debt;

(4) build good habits for spending—for today and tomorrow.

You can do this job very successfully if you, as a family, will learn to complete four simple forms.

Form I. Here is how I get my income.

Form II. Here is what I must put aside to cover my unavoidable expenses and my savings.

Form III. Here is where I find how much I have available for my day-to-day expenses.

Form IV. Here is how I will spend the money available for my day-to-day expenses during this period.

FORM I—FAMILY INCOME

The mistake most people make in beginning a money management plan is that they don't start at the beginning. The *beginning* surely is to find out how much money you have coming in to spend for all purposes during the year.

To reach this vital figure, take a sheet of paper and write down every item of income you expect during the year. Convert each total to a monthly basis. If you are a husband-and-wife working couple or are just living together under one roof, include the earnings of both.

(1) List not only the amounts of your regular take-home pay, translated into equal monthly totals, but also any income you anticipate from stock dividends, commissions, interest on bonds or savings accounts, yearly cash gifts from relatives, rent, bonuses, tax refunds due you, amounts owed to you by others. Also include profits from any sales of securities, your car, real estate, your home, assuming, of course, you sell any of these at a profit. Anything else? List it.

(2) Estimate each item of income as accurately and realistically as you can. When in doubt, put down the *minimum*.

(3) List only the net amounts of your regular paychecks—after subtracting withheld income taxes, your Social Security contributions,

union dues, company pension plan payments you make, any group insurance or other payments which your company automatically deducts from your pay check, etc.

(4) If your income is irregular—as it well may be if you are an artist, writer, teacher, small businessman, work part time or on a commission basis—divide the total you expect for the year by 12. Always keep your estimates low.

(5) If you are not certain how much your income will be for the entire year, list only the amounts you can accurately predict for a shorter period—again, converted to a monthly basis.

(6) If your income increases, don't get carried away: a pay raise always looks bigger than it really is. Before you start even to touch your raise, revise your budget income sheet to place the addition in accurate perspective. Add only the extra *net* (take-home) total—not the amount before taxes and other deductions.

(7) By the same token, if your income takes an unexpected dive, revise all your monthly totals downward as soon as the drop occurs. Remember, the amounts of money you'll have to spend will be based on the amounts actually coming in at any given time.

Form I Family Income

WHAT WE WILL GET FROM	JAN.	FEB.	MAR.	APR.	MAY	JUNE	JULY	AUG.	SEPT.	OCT.	NOV.	DEC.	YEARLY TOTAL	NOTES
Husband's job														
Wife's job														
Business Interests														
Interest														
Dividends														
Rent														
Gifts														
Company bonus or bonuses														
Tax refunds														
Moonlighting or jobs														
Profits from sales														
Alimony														
?														
?														
?														
Totals for the month														

Your inventory of income must reflect *facts*. On this sheet, there is little room for flexibility and *none* for fuzziness.

You have now broken down your income into 12 spending periods. You have taken the first step away from the "feast or famine" cash basis.

Knowing what you have available to spend each month, you will know how your expenses must be divided to match that real monthly income. When you have set up this kind of money manager, you'll be amazed how different your over-all income-expense picture will appear!

FORM II—FIXED EXPENSES

Now let's consider expenses.

There are three classes of outgo: (1) the unavoidable expenses—the big items such as insurance premiums, repayment of personal debts, real estate taxes—which must be paid no matter what the inconvenience; (2) savings and rainy-day reserves; and (3) day-to-day living expenses.

The key to a good system of money management lies in spreading your big expenses and your savings so that each month bears a share of them. When you put aside $20 every month to meet a $240 yearly insurance premium, for instance, you will not risk spending that insurance money on an unnecessary luxury.

Take a second sheet of paper. On it list all of your fixed expenses during the coming year and convert each of these to a monthly basis.

Among the more obvious fixed expenses to include on your monthly list are:

(1) Rent or mortgage payments.

(2) Predictable, regular household bills for such items as electricity, gas, fuel, telephone, water, garbage collection, cable TV, lawn mowing.

(3) Installment payments you make regularly for your car, washing machine, Christmas or Hanukkah Club, charge or credit card accounts, personal or education loan, etc.

(4) Big once- or twice-a-year obligations such as real estate taxes, payments for tuition and fees, auto, life, and homeowners insurance premiums, dues to your professional society, pledged contributions.

(5) Medical and dental expenses which can be accurately pinpointed for the year (e.g., costs of annual checkups, eye exams, orthodontia); health insurance premiums; predictable drug and vitamin bills.

Form II Fixed Expenses — Including Savings

WHAT WE MUST SPEND AND SAVE	JAN.	FEB.	MAR.	APR.	MAY	JUNE	JULY	AUG.	SEPT.	OCT.	NOV.	DEC.	YEAR'S TOTAL	NOTES
Rent or mortgage														
Fuel bills														
Telephone														
Electricity, gas														
Water														
Installment payment A														
Installment payment B														
Education (or other) payment														
Real estate taxes														
Income taxes														
Home and life insurance														
Auto insurance														
Medical, dental														
What we must set aside for savings alone														
Other														
Totals for each Month														

(6) Federal and state income taxes which have not been withheld.

(7) Automobile and commuting expenses which you can accurately estimate, such as commuter train tickets and car pool costs, monthly parking bills, car registration and inspection, average gas and oil bills for your car or cars.

(8) Membership dues—e.g., union, club, or professional association.

Among the less obvious fixed expenses to include are your monthly personal allowances for each family member. The amount of allowances you allot to each will depend partly on what expenses each person is expected to meet out of the allowance. Is the allowance supposed to pay for gifts? Lunches? Clothes? Music lessons? Charitable contributions?

Without a money management plan, if you have to pay a life insurance premium of $240, a property tax bill of $96, and a personal loan of $600—all in January—you would have to dig up $936 somewhere. And that might be tough indeed. But you probably know beforehand that in January you must meet those payments. When your money management plan is in full effect, you would set aside $78 out of each month's income and then you would be able to take the financial blows in stride.

Of course, when you start your plan, you might find it impossible to provide for those big expenses. For example, let's assume that the $936 is due in January and it is now November. You might have to get a loan or make the November, December, and January income bear the full brunt. But once that hurdle has been passed, you would divide the expenses by 12 to find out how much of the burden each month's income should bear.

Some of your large debts, such as loans from a member of the family, may be past due. Try to pay these as soon as possible and clear your slate.

INCLUDE YOUR SAVINGS!

At this point, let me back up and assure you that item (2) under the above "classes of outgo" was not a misprint. Rather a savings reserve is the least obvious—but still vital—expense you must include in your monthly list.

Put down a total you can reasonably expect to save each month. *Treat savings as an expense and budget for savings as you budget for rent or mortgage payments, and you will discipline yourself into building a nest egg.* "Pay yourself" first—as soon as you get your pay check—and your small monthly totals will become big totals over a period of time.

Include in your savings total an emergency fund equal to at least two months' income, to cover you should you be hit by big unforeseen expenses such as illness, unexpected home repairs, moving expenses. Note: The emergency part of your savings fund should be kept in a readily accessible ("liquid") form—for instance, a savings account.

As a starter, earmark 5 per cent of your total monthly income for savings, and boost the percentage from there if you can swing it.

If you have already saved the recommended equivalent of two months' income, freeze this amount as your emergency reserve. While you may want more or less than two months' income in reserve, be guided on this basically by the size of your other financial cushions: the amount of unemployment compensation for which you are eligible in the event that you are laid off or fired from your job and cannot find another one; the amount of your disability benefits which would be paid under Social Security or by your employer or through your health insurance policies; other health insurance benefits due you in the event of a medical crisis; your non-working wife's ability to take a job if an emergency arises or, if she has a job, to carry the family for a period; your credit-worthiness.

If you haven't the fund on hand now, figure how much more you will have to save before you reach the total. Then decide how long a time you'll need to save the amount necessary to lift your fund to the proper level. Don't try to save the extra amount too fast. Decide what you can put aside each month until the fund is assured and enter that amount on Form II as a fixed expense until your emergency fund is equal to the suggested level. Once it is there, keep it at that comfortable mark.

As for *how* you will save, you have many alternatives today.

(1) An automatic deduction plan from your checking account is offered by many banks. Under this plan, you authorize the bank to transfer to a simple savings account your specified sum at fixed intervals. You will receive the bank's stated interest rate on the amounts you accumulate in your savings account.

(2) Payroll savings plans are offered by many corporations under which a portion of your pay check is automatically deducted (by your authorization) and also is deposited in a savings account.

(3) Under other corporate employee savings plans now available to millions, a corporation may add its own contribution to the amount you authorize to be deducted regularly from your pay check. Your savings then may be invested in U.S. savings bonds, mutual funds, or company stock.

You'll find many other intriguing and important guides in Chapter 2, "Your Checking and Savings Accounts," pages 70–71, and in Chapter 22, "How to Invest in Bonds," pages 1028–66.

Whatever method you choose, these fundamentals will remain unaltered:

The "secret" to saving is to put aside little amounts regularly and let the little amounts mount up to big totals.

The great value of your emergency reserve is protection for you against the unexpected and thus preservation of your peace of mind when the unexpected comes.

FORM III—WHAT YOU HAVE LEFT FOR DAY-TO-DAY EXPENSES

Now that you have taken care of your inflexible expenses—which you must regard as already spent from each pay check—you are ready to begin work on budgeting for day-to-day expenses.

Take a third sheet of paper for Form III. As illustrated, put down your total income divided into 12 equal parts. Put down your unavoidable expenses and your savings, divided into 12 equal parts. The difference is what you have available for day-to-day living expenses.

This much is easy.

Form III Day-to-Day Expenses

	JAN.	FEB.	MAR.	APR.	MAY	JUNE	JULY	AUG.	SEPT.	OCT.	NOV.	DEC.
From Form I, your monthly income	$											
From Form II, the total of your unavoidable expenses and savings for the year, divided by 12.	$											
What you have available for your day-to-day living expenses	$											

FORM IV—BUDGETING YOUR DAY-TO-DAY EXPENSES

Form IV will show you whether you will have to do some major juggling to make ends meet. You can't argue with the fixed figures on Form II, but you can juggle the items you will list on Form IV.

This is important: on Form IV, don't try to figure ahead for a full year. That's too difficult. Simply plan your regular day-to-day living expenses for a month or two ahead.

These will vary considerably but they are a substantial and crucial part of your budget. They also are expenses over which you have the most control.

Because you probably won't even be able to remember many of the little items when you begin your list, keep a detailed record of *all* your living expenses just for a couple of weeks. From this, you'll get an accurate idea of how much you're spending and for what. After you've obtained this guide, stop keeping records in such stultifying detail.

Here are the main categories of day-to-day expenses:

(1) *Food and related items:* the amounts of your regular grocery bills; what you spend to eat out in restaurants (including tips); candy and snacks from vending machines; soft drinks, beer, wine, and liquor; cigarettes; pet foods and supplies; personal and household items such as toothpaste and cosmetics which you buy at the supermarket.

(2) *Household services and expenses:* home repairs and improvements; any maintenance costs not counted in your fixed expenses; cleaning supplies; household help.

(3) *Furnishings and equipment:* what you buy outright for cash and down payments for large and small appliances, glass, china, silverware, curtains, rugs, upholstering, accessories, other items.

(4) *Clothes:* everything, ranging from repairs and alterations through laundry and dry cleaning to the seemingly insignificant accessories which can mount up to alarming totals.

Form IV Budgeting Day-to-Day Expenses

WHAT WE WILL SPEND FOR DAY-TO-DAY LIVING THIS MONTH	JAN.	FEB.	MAR.	APR.	MAY	JUNE	JULY	AUG.	SEPT.	OCT.	NOV.	DEC.	NOTES
For food and related items	$	$	$	$	$	$	$	$	$	$	$	$	
For household services and expenses													
For furnishings and equipment													
For clothes													
For transportation													
For medical care													
For personal care													
For education and recreation													
For gifts and contributions													
For other things and non-things													
TOTAL													
Total available for the month (from last line of form III)	$	$	$	$	$	$	$	$	$	$	$	$	

(5) *Transportation:* car repairs, tune-ups, oil changes, new tires; bus, train, taxi, and air fares, parking charges; bridge tolls.

(6) *Medical care:* doctor and dentist bills not listed under your fixed expenses; drugs; eyeglasses; hospital and nursing expenses not covered by medical insurance; veterinary bills for your pets.

(7) *Personal care:* the barber and hairdresser; toilet articles; cosmetics and other items not paid for by each family member's personal allowance and *not* in your supermarket bills.

(8) *Education and recreation:* books; theater, movie, and concert tickets; entertaining friends; newspaper and magazine subscriptions; musical instruments and music lessons; hobby equipment; vacation and holiday expenses; the upkeep of your pleasure boat, swimming pool, or riding horse; tuition and fees not included on Form II.

(9) *Gifts and contributions:* what is not paid out of personal allowances.

(10) *Other things and non-things:* Only you can fill out this item.

DON'TS TO GUIDE YOU

Just a glance at the list on Form IV shows why it is futile to attempt a precise budget at the start. Unless you are the exception who always has kept exact records of your spending, you will have to estimate the totals. Later it will be possible to be more accurate.

Don't set spending limits which are impossible to meet. It may be hard to fix a range until you've tried this money management system for a few months. That's expected. You'll learn by experience what the limits are and what they should be.

Don't start out by slashing one classification arbitrarily, "on paper." A major expense category cannot be cut just because the figure appears so big when listed. "Food" is the category that most of you will try to slash first. But if you cut this too low, you'll discover you've set an impossible limit.

Don't forget that the big expenses are on Form II. The classifications on Form IV cover only the usual day-to-day expenses. Major costs, such as orthodontia for your child, may be spread over a whole year of income periods. If "spreading" is easier for you, transfer other big items from Form IV to Form II.

Don't ignore your wants and don't try to kid yourself. When you're setting your allocations, be realistic. If your menu says steak, don't put down a figure for stew.

Don't fail to leave room for unexpected expenses. These are certain to arise and you never know in advance what they will be. They may range from a flat tire to an office contribution for a wedding gift.

Don't underestimate the importance of detailed records during the first month of your money management plan. When the next period rolls around and it turns out that your guesses weren't right, cross out the inaccurate estimates and put down what was really spent for each item.

With these hints to help, you can fill out Form IV, marking down your estimates, adding them up for each month, and comparing them with the total amount available. The result easily could be a big minus, indicating that you're spending or planning to spend more than your projected income. If your expense total, including savings, comes out way above your income total and the tally indicates you're heading into a flood of red ink, some items here must be cut.

But you can't cut unless you vow to make the cuts good. This money management plan is more than a pencil-pushing game.

What Role Do Your Children Play?

TEN RULES ON ALLOWANCES

In any successful family spending plan, your children must play some part—especially when the things *they* want are to be considered. Although the responsibilities to be given children will undoubtedly vary from family to family, here are ten widely accepted rules:

(1) Begin giving your child an allowance just as soon as he or she understands the use of money for getting the things he or she wants.

(2) Have an understanding on what the allowance is to cover. At first it can relate only to such things as toys and special treats, but adjustments should be made from time to time in the size of the allowance and hence in its use. Many teen-age boys and girls can handle allowances that cover their clothing. By the time they are mature, they will have had some experience in looking ahead and in saving for special things.

(3) In addition to having a clear understanding with your child

on just what an allowance is or is not supposed to cover, renegotiate the contract at least once a year to take new obligations into account.

(4) Make your child's allowance a fair share in terms of your family's consumption in general.

(5) Take into account what your child's friends and schoolmates have. The allowance should certainly not be so markedly less that the child feels constantly deprived; but it should also not be greatly in excess of what others get; that's just as bad.

(6) As your child gets older, give him a voice in deciding what his allowance should be. Let him share in a family round table on the spending plan. He will thus gain a greater appreciation of fair sharing.

(7) Give your child full responsibility for spending his allowance, although your advice may be required for some things and should be available at all times. If he makes mistakes, he should come to recognize his responsibility for them and put up with the results. In unusual situations you might, perhaps, help him out by an advance from the following week's allowance.

(8) While your child is learning to plan ahead, give him the allowance only for short periods. Perhaps give first for the day, then for the week, and only later for somewhat longer periods. Very early in their lives, your children should learn where the family's money comes from and the effort that goes into earning it. A child's spending should, therefore, be made in part dependent on his own efforts. Children often can be taught the simple lessons of earning and spending by being paid extra for special household tasks. But *do not* carry this too far; your child may acquire the habit of putting all helpfulness on a "pay me" basis. Pay only for exceptional—and not for routine—household chores. Do not confuse this sort of payment with the allowance.

(9) As for saving, teen-agers are notorious non-savers. They tend to spend income as fast as possible and often on apparently frivolous things. But at the same time they are deeply attracted by such big-ticket items as motorcycles, autos, stereos. Once a teen-ager sets an expensive item as a goal, the message usually seeps through that the purchase requires saving over a long period. Encourage your youngster to keep a savings goal within reasonable limits and not to make it prolonged drudgery. Encourage your youngster also to learn how to manage a checking and/or savings account.

Here are some rough guides, developed by Household Finance

Corporation, on what children in various age brackets might be expected to buy and pay for out of their allowances:

Under 6: candy, gum, ice cream, small toys, gifts for others, books, playthings, paints, crayons, blocks, and dolls

Ages 6–9: movies, amusements, toys, books, magazines, hobbies, club dues, special savings for sports equipment, carfare and lunches at school, school activities and school expenses, gifts for birthdays and holidays, and contributions

Ages 9–12: fees for skating rinks, pools, etc., club dues, hobby materials, sports equipment and repairs, games and special events, carfare and lunches at school, gifts for birthdays and holidays, contributions, trips, school supplies, clothing and upkeep

Ages 12–18: the above, plus money for dates, grooming, cosmetics, jewelry, clothing, school activities, savings for special purposes such as travel and a future education

Finally, on charge accounts, expert opinion divides violently—with one side warning that it is extremely reckless to give a teen-ager a charge account and the other arguing that, since charge accounts are so much a part of American life, a youngster should learn early how to buy on credit.

My compromise rule would be to teach your teen-ager to use credit modestly and wisely and to pay bills promptly. As an allowance is "learning money," so installment buying is vital financial education. The crucial point is that the earlier a youngster learns to live within a fixed income the better prepared he or she will be to manage money soundly as an adult.

These guides may seem no more than simple common sense—but isn't that fundamentally what proper money management always is?

IN CASE YOU'RE CURIOUS . . .

HERE'S WHAT OTHER PEOPLE SPEND

I repeat: an "average" family living on an "average" budget does not exist. Even if you and your neighbor lead very similar lives on very similar incomes, your budgets may be radically different. Your own ages, your children's ages—not to mention your hobbies or jobs or dozens of other aspects—would make this so.

But, if you're merely normal, you're still curious about the spending patterns of others.

So to start with, here's what the *average* Americans were spending in the mid-seventies of each after-tax dollar in each major category:

For	AMERICANS WERE SPENDING OF EACH DOLLAR
Food, alcohol and tobacco	22.3¢
Housing	14.5
Household operation	14.4
Transportation	13.6
Clothing	10.1
Medical care	7.7
Recreation	6.5
Personal business	5.6
Private education	1.7
Personal care	1.5
Religious and welfare activities	1.4
Foreign travel	.7

HOW MUCH CHEAPER ARE LARGE FAMILIES TO FEED THAN SMALL ONES?

In a family of five, it costs 5 per cent less to feed each person than it costs to feed each person in a family of four.

In a family of six, it costs 10 per cent less to feed each person than in a family of four.

In contrast, it costs 20 per cent *more* to feed an individual living alone than it costs to feed each member of the four-person family.

BUDGETING IF YOU'RE IN COLLEGE

Now let's assume you're a college student living—or trying to live —on an allowance. How can the money management plan help you?

Some of you are at home during school years and are on weekly allowances; many others of you live away and receive your checks every month. But for all of you the problem is identical: college years are a constant—and usually losing—battle to make financial ends meet.

Halfway through the week or month, most of you are either broke or on the brink. Some of you live high the first few days you get your money, then scramble for help toward the end. Some of you have only far-apart intervals when you are out of debt. The vast majority of you are either flush or frantic.

But your allowance is a pay check. It deserves the respect and care you will give a pay check after graduation. Just as your parents get the most for their dollars by living by certain financial rules, so you in college can get the greatest satisfaction out of your allowance if you live by certain financial rules.

Whether you live at home or away from home, whether you're at the fanciest of schools or on a scholarship or working your way through, the fundamental principles of money management apply equally.

Here are your "Allowance ABCs." Try them for size.

(1) Plan the spending of your allowance with your parents before you leave for college, and then keep planning on your own from the day you arrive at school.

It's nonsense to say that $20 a week will be fine when $20 a week won't do at all for what you have to cover. Plan realistically and with a clear understanding of what your allowance is to take care of. Then, when you arrive at school, work out your day-to-day budget to cover your necessities and luxuries. Be honest with yourself. (If Cokes and coffee are going to cost X cents a day, plan for X cents a day.) If your allowance is supposed to cover such items as new panty hose, dry cleaning, shoe repair, oil, gas, auto maintenance, and so forth, budget these costs—don't ignore them. This is *your* budget; it should fit *you*.

(2) Deposit your money in a bank account and draw on it only as you need the money. If you carry a wad of cash with you, you'll risk being mugged and the temptation to spend it recklessly may become irresistible. Discipline yourself via your bank account; the lessons you learn now will be valuable throughout your life.

If your school has banking facilities, use them. If not, a nearby bank will accept your deposit even if it's just a few dollars. While you may be slapped with service charges, the bank's advantages could far outweigh the disadvantages; check it out. And while you are learning how to make deposits, to draw checks, to balance a checkbook, etc., you are getting excellent training in personal financial management.

(3) If you and your parents can manage it, also start an account in a nearby savings bank, or try to build one through the term.

There always will be large extra expenses—a special event or a crisis—for which you'll need or want to spend money. Your savings account should be earmarked for your tuition, rent, and extraordinary expenses only. If you can't start with this savings nest egg, try to juggle your seven-days-a-week spending plan so you can save a bit and build one yourself.

(4) Don't figure down to pennies. No money plan ever should be that precise. For your protection and pleasure, give yourself a margin of safety.

(5) Keep some simple records to show you where your allowance is going and why. A record for one week alone would be enough to reveal your errors of omission and commission. For one week, list on a sheet of paper what you spend and where and when you spend it. See how this week's total fits into the monthly total allotted to you. If need be, push your spending around to make it fit. When you've found the right pattern, stick with it. Keep your list in a convenient spot where you will see it from day to day.

(6) Stretch your dollars by learning how to buy items you must have (toiletries, for instance) during special sales or in economy sizes, etc. If you're buying your own wardrobe, stretch your dollars further by buying simple basic styles which will last longer and cost least in upkeep. Also investigate ways you can save by pooling purchases with your friends as you can buy in bulk at bargain prices.

(7) If your evidence is clear after a trial that your funds are too limited, renegotiate your allowance. Your records will be your evidence.

WHERE SHOULD YOU KEEP YOUR MONEY?

You have established a budget to make sure your income covers your expenses each month. You are now ready for your next step in money management: a system to control your money in real life as well as on paper.

For your careful plans can easily blow up into chaotic confusion unless you do have a system to help you put your money where it is supposed to be. There are six basic systems from which you can choose:

(1) the joint checking account;
(2) separate checking accounts;
(3) the savings account;
(4) the combination of savings and checking accounts;
(5) the allowance method;
(6) the broken sugar bowl method.

Whichever control system you choose, it must be:

Efficient. Your "control" should direct your cash where you want it to go.

Easy to operate. This is a "must." The major objection to most financial advice is that it is too complex. If a method is complicated or burdensome, you will abandon it in less than a month.

Suited to your income. How much money you have to manage should guide you on how to control the management.

Your problem is not simply a question of managing your income and outgo "on paper"; it is also a matter of controlling your cash income and cash outgo so that the money goes where it is scheduled to go.

The four budget forms can be of immeasurable help in showing you how to match your income to your outgo but they cannot give you the complete control over your actual spending which will come from intelligent use of one or more of the following six systems.

THE JOINT CHECKING ACCOUNT

If you're a young husband-and-wife team and you decide on the joint checking account method, you'll establish a checking account at a neighborhood bank in both your names. Into that account will go all your earnings. Each of you may write checks on that account to meet your expenses. When this system is adopted, the husband usually writes the checks for the big fixed expenses and for the savings (Form II). The wife writes the checks for the day-to-day and week-to-week expenses (the items on Form IV).

Advantages

Since each of you has a definite responsibility to meet specific expenses you develop a co-operative spirit. Similarly, since each of you has a sense of "owning money," you develop a keener understanding of the value of money.

With a *joint* checking account your average monthly balance will be higher than the balances in two *separate* checking accounts and thus you will have a better chance of avoiding or minimizing bank service charges.

With only one checkbook, you'll find it easier to keep records and file your income tax returns. (If you do have two checkbooks, be sure you tally your stubs every month to prevent overdrawing.)

In an emergency, either of you can sign checks and get money.

Disadvantages

This method can be a success only if both of you are careful about drawing on the joint account. And even then you may get into trouble unless you constantly watch the balance in your account and keep each other thoroughly informed about the checks each is drawing. Monthly tallies of stubs are important.

SEPARATE CHECKING ACCOUNTS

The separate checking account method is fairly satisfactory if you have a moderate to high income and many expenditures. When you use this control system, all the salary or income of the family will generally be deposited in one account in the husband's name. He then will deposit an agreed-upon sum in the second account, which will be in the wife's name.

The husband's account will be used to meet the major, fixed-expense items and to cover savings (Form II). The wife's account will be used to pay for the day-to-day or week-to-week expenses (the items on Form IV).

The main control in this system is the husband's account—for from it will come not only the amounts for fixed expenses and for the wife's account but also the totals for savings.

Usually the wife will cash a check on her account each week or at another regular interval to pay for food and household operation expenses. Expenditures for food and for operation of the house will thus be controlled automatically by the amount of money deposited in her account.

Advantages

The portion of your income determined as necessary for food and clothing expenditures is automatically separated from other funds. Also, by cashing weekly, semimonthly, or monthly checks for food expenditures, you, the wife, automatically control the family's food costs for the period.

Since clothing allowance will be regularly deposited in the wife's account, you'll allow funds to accumulate as desired and this will permit you to take advantage of special sales and bargains. You might leave the clothing allowance mostly untouched for two or three months, then use the funds at a pre- or postseason sale to achieve important savings. The money will be available: that is the key point.

Your checkbooks will contain all the information necessary for a complete summary of your purchases and expenditures, assuming you fill out the stubs conscientiously.

Control of your income is divided between the two of you. Each of you has responsibility for your portion of your income and expenditures. Your separate accounts can give you better control of your income and outgo than a joint banking account.

Disadvantages

The separate account control system isn't practical unless your family income is fairly large. You must have sufficient money at your disposal to permit the establishment of separate bank accounts and justify what service fees may be involved.

Unexpected expenditures may cause considerable mix-ups in your accounting. In fact, a key difficulty with this system—and, indeed, with the joint account method, too—is in the handling of miscellaneous expenditures.

A reasonable solution to this problem is a petty cash fund to meet the "extras" that arise in every household. This fund should be operated on the same principle as the petty cash fund in a business office. A specified amount—say $100—might be deposited in the fund. Each time you have to draw on this fund—as when you have to buy extra food for guests —you'll put a slip of paper with a notation describing the expense into the cash box in place of the money taken out. If you, the wife, take out $25, you'll put in a chit: "Entertainment—$25." Thus the total of cash in the fund plus the total of notations on the slips always ought to equal the amount of the original fund.

The chits furnish a record to show where the money went, so that if the petty cash fund is being used to stretch the other funds, the situation can be remedied—either through stricter control of your expenditures or by revision of your spending plan to raise the inadequate fund to the necessary level. Each month or pay period, refill the emergency fund and bring it back to its original mark.

THE SAVINGS ACCOUNT

If you don't have a fairly substantial income and you don't write many checks each month, the savings account method may be the best spending control for you. Savings accounts can serve you best if:

(1) You deduct from your monthly income or your regular weekly pay check the totals needed for your fixed major costs and for savings —Form II of your record—and place them in a savings account for safe-keeping.

(2) You deduct for your monthly allowances out of your remaining cash and keep those funds at home or in another account. Savings accounts pay interest, and since these accounts can be set up to permit joint withdrawals, either of you can use them freely. Many institutions will help you pay large bills by giving you bank checks made out exactly the way you want them for the now-and-then expenses.

Some savings institutions also will help you control your spending and savings by encouraging "special purpose" accounts—for vacation funds, travel funds, insurance funds, tax funds, etc. The purpose of each fund will be marked on the deposit books, and these books will give you a complete picture of your savings for each objective. A combination of these "special funds" with a rainy-day savings account for unexpected expenses thus can provide both a system of control and a detailed record of your savings.

This idea of using separate accounts for special purposes is becoming increasingly popular, though it is really nothing more than an extension of the long-used Christmas Club plan. The value of these special funds lies simply in the fact that they encourage setting aside a stipulated sum each week (no matter how small) so that the regular saving of little amounts builds toward the stated goal.

Advantages

Like any form of "forced savings," the scheme has the great advantage of earmarking your funds before you receive them—and before you are tempted to spend them elsewhere. It can be an excellent control over the money that must be set aside to meet the items on Form II.

Your money is placed in a thrift account on which interest is paid and compounded. As the account grows, there is a real psychological spur to save more.

Disadvantages

The savings account method is not suitable if you must write many checks every month.

You must have sufficient savings funds to justify the opening of several "special purpose" accounts.

You may earn next to nothing in interest if you keep depleting your account or accounts. Also some of the special savings accounts may pay little or no interest.

Although you may deposit funds by mail to your savings account, you must visit the bank personally each time you make a withdrawal. Another inconvenience is that you must pay many bills with cash if you make a savings account the sole "home" for your income.

THE COMBINATION OF SAVINGS AND CHECKING ACCOUNTS

Or your best method of spending control may be a combination of several methods. One such combination is:

(1) the establishment of a checking account from which you draw funds each week or month to pay for all regular and recurring expenditures (some of the items on Form II and all on Form IV); and

(2) the establishment of a savings account in which you accumulate cash for the major expenses that come up only occasionally during the year and for savings (the rest of the items on Form II). You'll maintain your "emergency fund" in this separate savings account.

Advantages

Your income is divided and your day-to-day expenses are separated from your other expenses. Through your checkbook stubs, you can keep an accurate and up-to-date record of your spending.

Through your savings account, you can accumulate cash to take advantage of sales and other bargains when they are available. Also the savings account part of this system will help you develop the savings habit which is so essential to achieving financial security. You will take pride in watching your nest egg grow and, hopefully, will make a real effort to meet more of your expenses from your regular checking account.

Disadvantages

Fees well may be charged for maintenance of a no-minimum account or for a regular checking account if the balance falls below the bank's established minimum.

Separation of your savings from your checking account may push your average balance in your regular account way down.

THE ALLOWANCE METHOD

The allowance method of money management is used by millions of couples in America, many of them, probably, having adopted it automatically when they married.

Admittedly, it is a simple system. The husband of the non-jobholding wife usually controls the distribution of the money. Every payday he makes an allowance to his wife for the day-to-day living expenses—the items that are primarily on Form IV. After making this allowance, the husband uses the balance to meet all the major items—those on Form II.

The wife may deposit the allowance in a separate account or draw checks on a joint account up to the limit of the allowance—or just keep the money in a strongbox at home.

Advantages

The allowance method is simple, involving merely the distribution of a set allowance to the wife every payday or week or month.

Disadvantages

The allowance made to the wife is often too small, and she takes only a minimum of responsibility for management of the family income. She is often forced to ask for more money to cover essential or luxury expenditures. Such an arrangement discourages co-operative management.

If the allowance is not carefully calculated to cover all the items on Form IV, the control will be too loose.

THE BROKEN SUGAR BOWL METHOD

Many young couples—particularly those still in school or just out of school—use envelopes, marking one "for rent," another "for clothing," a third "for food," and so forth. Or they may have a cash box at home which is divided into compartments labeled "rent," "clothing," "food," and the like. Or it may be that they label small glass jars.

This is nicknamed the "broken sugar bowl method" because many older people remember that when they were children there were always a few old sugar bowls hidden behind the other dishes in the kitchen closet or pantry in which there were always a few dollars for specified expenses.

But the name applied to this money management arrangement doesn't matter. The point is that under this system you'll divide your cash income into fixed amounts to meet the regular and now-and-then expenses. Into each labeled bowl, jar, envelope, or compartment you'll put the dollars agreed upon as necessary to meet that particular living expense.

Both husband and wife will have equal access to the bowls or jars or envelopes. Generally, as in other systems, each will take on the responsibility for meeting certain expenses. This method is designed for very small incomes.

Advantages

When you use the sugar bowl method, presumably the money is always where it is supposed to be—and in cash to cover any specific expense. The system may be used just as separate bank accounts are used to apportion responsibility. And how simple can you get?

Disadvantages

Obviously, it is a risk to keep money in the house—even comparatively small amounts. While the cash is conveniently available for easy spending, it may be too available. When the money is there, the temptation to use it carelessly also is there. And when a sudden shortage develops, the obvious short cut is to shift money from one bowl or envelope to another. While the utter simplicity of the broken sugar bowl method of spending control may be commendable, it is hardly a "control."

HIS-AND-HER BUDGETS

America is a land of working couples. Tens of millions of you who are and will be brides will continue working long after the wedding. Millions of you will quit working for pay only during the years your children are babies. Most of you will return to work when your children go off to school.

Money management takes on a special aspect in today's two-pay check American homes. For with both of you earning salaries, specific questions are bound to come up:

How do you divide the money you bring in? Who pays for what around the house? If you had an ideal partnership, who would pay for what—how and why?

Here are ten basic rules I've worked out over years of discussions with experts on family finance, interviews with husbands and wives in every income bracket across the country, my personal experience as a working wife through my entire adult life. These are *my* rules, no one else's, but I'm sure all of you can benefit from some of them, some of you can benefit from all of them, and any one of them can be revised to fit your individual circumstances.

(1) Make your marriage a *financial partnership;* discuss your income and plan your spending as a husband-and-wife team.

The wife who insists she should pay for only the part-time housekeeper and put the rest of her pay check in her savings account is selfish and wrong. If you're a team in other ways, be a team financially as well. If your mutual decision is that the wife's pay check should be saved, excellent—but make the decision as a couple. Otherwise, deceit and suspicion are virtually inevitable. This is a fundamental rule.

(2) Pool part of your individual pay checks in a family fund which is to be used to cover essential household expenses.

In many households, the pooling will be automatic, for both pay checks are being used to buy things and non-things the family wants. *It should be automatic.* How much of the wife's pay checks will go into the pool may vary from home to home, depending on the wife's income and the family's circumstances, but the key point is that there should be a pool.

(3) Decide which of you will be responsible for paying specific bills out of the pool. As a husband you might take over payment of the "big bills"—rent, mortgage, insurance, taxes, the like. As a wife, you might take over management of the "household bills"—food, entertainment at home, ordinary household overhead. To me, this is a logical division of responsibility. It's entirely okay if you have other ideas, but talk them out to your mutual satisfaction.

For instance, some experts say a woman who has been accustomed to her independence for a long period may be actively unhappy unless, as a working wife, she continues to have "my" telephone, "my" bank account, etc. So be it—as long as she and her husband agree on the division and there is no secret resentment of the situation.

(4) Use the combination savings account and checking account method as your money control.

If you don't carefully separate your savings from your regular checking account, your savings easily can dribble away without your knowing just how or why. For most couples, the two-account "control" works best.

(5) If the wife's job necessitates the added expense of household help, the wife's pay check should cover it. This is a rule I came to instinctively, for in most homes, if the wife did not hold an outside job, she could, if she had to, get along without any extra help. Thus, this is "her" expense which she should handle. If the expense is to be paid out of the family pool, the wife should directly make the payment. Or the wife may withhold a specified part of her earnings for this expense. Whatever the details, it should be understood that this expense is in the wife's department.

(6) Extra expenses for entertainment at home should be handled by the wife, but when you go out, it's the husband's deal. Again, this is my viewpoint only.

(7) If you're a young couple planning to have children, the husband's pay check should cover all basic household expenses, and part of the wife's earnings should be earmarked for the initial expenses of a baby. You must be prepared for the time when, for a while at least, you'll scale down to one pay check. You may decide to share this planning by

earmarking funds out of each pay check—but at least *plan*. A couple without the financial responsibilities of children obviously has more leeway to shift spending and saving.

(8) Follow faithfully the budget rules for Form II. With both of you earning money, you'll really benefit from spreading payment of your big bills so that each month bears a share.

In addition, plan your installment buying as a team and with caution so that even if you're hit by an emergency your total monthly bills will be well within your capacity to repay. Under no circumstances take on *any* installment debt without a joint agreement.

(9) The rules on personal allowances are particularly vital for you. If you want to do something absurd with your personal allowance, that's your business. Your allowance is yours alone.

(10) Make a pledge to each other today that when you get into a squeeze in the future—which you will, for nearly everyone does—you'll choose a quiet evening alone to argue it out and decide how to escape from it. And when you talk about it, call it "our" squeeze, not "yours."

A superficial point? Oh no. The wife who in the heat of a money fight says, "We wouldn't have any savings at all unless I worked," is begging for resentment and the retort that she wouldn't have any home unless he paid for the rent or mortgage. It's imperative to avoid discussing your money mess when you're both frantic. If you can't figure a way out, take your problem to the service department of your bank or savings institution and ask for guidance on where and how you might get help.

Here is a chart which you can use as a starter for building your own his-and-her budget. Add to it as you wish; switch it around as you see fit; make it yours.

A BUDGET IF YOU'RE JUST LIVING TOGETHER ("MINGLES")

What if you're among the millions of young Americans who today are just living together under one roof ("mingles")—with no legal ties, no established rules for behavior except those you and your peers agree are okay, and certainly no guidelines for management of your individual incomes and expenses?

You could easily and successfully follow the rules in the preceding pages for a working man and wife. But you may be far more fascinated by the following real-life system of budgeting created over the past two years by a young technical consultant and his schoolteacher living com-

WHO PAYS FOR WHAT?

WHO PAYS FOR:	HE	SHE	BOTH
Rent or mortgage, home repairs, utilities			
Food at home			
Clothing			
Household help			
Auto loan, repairs, maintenance			
Recreation (outside)			
Entertainment (at home)			
Entertainment (outside home)			
Life and health insurance			
New baby			
Education (adult, college)			
Gifts and contributions			
Vacations, recreation			
Income and property taxes			
Savings			
Other expenses			

panion. The two insist that, once their system was perfected, it ended two years of destructive fighting about money (an even more brutal cause of split-ups among the non-married than among the married).

"Basically," says Dick, "the system consists of four (yes four) checking accounts which we call 'yours,' 'mine,' 'ours,' and 'car.'"

"In addition, we have savings accounts. We keep a minimum balance of $100 in each checking account to avoid service charges, which would run between 12 and 18 per cent for us, but higher for frequent check writers. To reduce the temptation to dip into the $100 minimums, we delete the balances from our records and pretend they don't exist."

Here are details which are provocatively similar in many ways to the his-and-her budgets:

• All income from both individuals goes into the "ours" account. Each has a checkbook and the money deposited is arbitrarily split in half between each checkbook as a hedge against overdrawing. If either book runs dangerously low, temporary transfers are made. Then, at the end of each month, the books are balanced and the joint bank statement reconciled.

• Out of this "ours" account come virtually all living expenses—food, rent, utilities, etc.—which these two have agreed to share on a regular basis.

• Once a month, $50 is transferred from the "ours" account to each individual account ("yours" and "mine") as each person's personal allowance. "This figure was chosen arbitrarily and is still experimental," says Dick. "We expect to adjust it after we have had more experience with it." The personal allowance covers clothes and other items "which have a large potential for conflict over what is or is not extravagant" and for "simply spending as we please." Neither accounts to the other for what happens to each month's personal allowance.

The special account for the car is an ingenious twist. "This is the largest single expense we have, costing more than rent and food combined," says Dick. "And we feel that it's important for us both to be conscious of what cars really cost." They are making a vital point. Also, watching the real costs of their car tends to discourage excessive driving.

A simple record is kept of the number of miles driven and deposits of 10¢ per mile are regularly transferred from the "our" account. The 10¢ covers all operating expenses, plus a margin of 5¢ a mile for depreciation. (This figure is subject to revision upward as costs dictate.) The "car" fund includes forced savings for a new car in the future.

Another ingenious system for food shopping involves the initialing of all store register tapes or chits and periodic checking and reconciling of the records.

There are many gaps in this couple's system—but if you add their hints to all you've read in "Your Personal Money Manager," you will be way, way ahead of the vast majority of budget-keepers.

Without any difficulty, you can shift the details to fit your own situation. You, for instance, may prefer to contribute equal amounts—rather than all—of your income to your joint checking and savings accounts. Whether you're a married couple or merely living together, you may feel it's unfair for both of you to bear an equal share of the food costs if the man regularly eats far more food and far more expensive food than the woman. Or you may argue that it's unfair for both of you to bear an equal share of the phone bills if the woman does most of the long-distance talking.

Whatever your own decisions, I guarantee that personal budget-keeping will help you curb your living costs—and help bring you peace of mind.

(Like the working husband and wife, use the chart "Who Pays for What?" as a basic guide and switch it around to fit your own needs and desires.)

How Much Are You Worth?

You easily may feel flat broke or, at a minimum, painfully squeezed when you are creating a budget and a system to manage your money. But I'll wager that if you figure your "net worth" even at this sticky stage you'll be happily surprised by the outcome. Try it right now—and see if you don't discover you're richer than you think in many ways!

Here's a simple method to put a specific figure on your worth. Take a pencil and three sheets of paper. Mark the first sheet "Assets" and list:

(1) The amount of money you have in checking and savings accounts, in savings and loan associations, in credit unions, in time deposits, in cash on hand, in a strongbox at home or elsewhere.

(2) The cash value of your life insurance. This is the amount you actually could borrow back on request.

(3) The cash value of your United States Savings Bonds. This is not the maturity value but the amount you would get if you turned in your bonds now.

(4) The amount of cash or its equivalent you could withdraw tomorrow from profit sharing employee savings, retirement programs, etc. A rough calculation will do.

(5) The current market value of stocks and mutual fund shares you may own. Not the purchase price, but what you'd get if you sold the stocks tomorrow.

(6) The current market value of other securities you may own—

marketable federal government, municipal, or corporate bonds—and the market value of other investments you may have, such as mortgages you have extended to others.

(7) The price you would get if you put your house and land, summer house, or other real estate on the market this week. Get a conservative estimate from a reliable real estate agent.

(8) The price you would get if you offered your car (or cars) to a used-car dealer or sold it privately for cash right now. Be cold-blooded about it. Also, your boat, motorcycle, airplane, trailer, snowmobile, the like.

(9) The market value of your household goods—furniture, rugs, appliances, TV, stereo, linen, silverware. Make your own *conservative* estimate, then *slash* it by 75 per cent and you'll be on safe ground.

(10) The market value of your other personal assets, such as jewelry, paintings, furs, rare books, art objects, coins, stamps, antiques, clothes, etc. Cut your own conservative estimate here, too, by 75 per cent.

(11) The price you'd get if you sold out your investment in any unincorporated business, farm, or other ventures.

(12) Amounts of money other *responsible* people owe you.

(13) A conservative estimate of the value of any other asset you can think of.

Add the totals.

Take a second sheet, mark it "Liabilities," and list:

(1) The total amount you owe on your mortgage or mortgages and on your car, boat, motorcycle, etc.

(2) The amount you owe on other installment debts, charge accounts, credit cards, other personal debts and bills.

(3) The amount you owe for taxes which have not been withheld.

(4) Sums you've committed for college education, etc.

(5) Any other liability you can think of.

Add these totals.

Take a third sheet, mark it "Net Worth," and:

simply subtract the total on your second sheet from the total on your first. *The difference between what you own and what you owe is your net worth.*

You should be unexpectedly pleased by the outcome, for you are only average if your net worth runs into many thousands of dollars. You are part of the vast majority of Americans if you have some cash in the bank and in savings accounts and own a car. And while you have debts, you also have substantial assets to offset the debts. This is the norm in no other nation in the world.

HOW DOES YOUR NET WORTH COMPARE?

When you have tallied your net worth, break it down into the ratio of your assets to your debts. Now, just for fun, compare your balance sheet to that of the mythical "average" American consumer.

As the mid-1970s neared, John Doe had $11.40 in assets for every $1.00 of debt—not counting his home mortgage.

If you included his mortgage, John Doe's ratio was $5.70 in assets for every $1.00 of debt. And for every $1.00 of his mortgage debt, John Doe had $2.40 in equity in his home.

IF YOU'RE STARTING TO KEEP TAX RECORDS: QUESTIONS AND ANSWERS

Q. *What records should you keep?*

A. Preserving the right kind of records for tax purposes can be vitally important if your income tax returns are examined later and if you're to be able to prevent a budget-busting disallowance of your deductions because you can't prove their validity. Here, therefore, are key record-keeping points from the Internal Revenue Service:

• Keep a permanent record of your earnings—including W-2 forms provided by your employers and precise statements from others contributing to your income. Vague estimates of income are *not* acceptable. Also, keep copies of all previous tax returns.

• If you use your car for business purposes and intend to deduct a part of the expenses, keep records of the original cost of the car, annual total and business mileage, gas and oil, repair costs, garage rent, license and registration fees, tolls, chauffeur's salary.

• If your job involves travel for business purposes, keep a diary of all expenses involved—including hotel bills, transportation costs, taxi fares, meals, tips, telephone and telegraph charges, stenographer fees. Also keep receipts, paid bills, and canceled checks to document all lodging expenses and any other sizable expenses. However, says the IRS, you are *not* required to keep receipts for transportation costs, such as taxi fares, bus fares, "if they are not readily available."

• If you use your home as an office keep a full record of costs attributable to the office space alone, including the percentage of depreciation on the house or rent paid, of utilities, and of household maintenance costs that can be allocated to the office space. If business entertainment is done in your home, keep records of entertainment expenses such as catering costs and food and liquor bills. Also keep guest lists and other evidence to show that the entertainment was for business rather than social purposes.

• If you have made charitable contributions, keep records of the cash or fair market value of any contributions of property as well as to whom and when made.

• If there is any chance your annual medical expenses will exceed the per cent of your adjusted gross income stated in the tax law, keep copies of all doctor and hospital bills and other allied costs.

All these records should be kept at least five years.

For longer periods:

• If you buy or sell securities, keep full records of the purchase date and price of each stock or bond you buy, the number of shares bought at each price, amounts of commissions, and records of any and all stock splits, swaps, and dividends along the line. Also, keep records of dates, prices, commissions, etc., at which you sell each block of securities. Otherwise, when you sell a batch of stock at a profit, IRS will assume you sold the first batch you bought—for which you probably paid the lowest price, and on which you would be liable for the biggest capital gains tax.

• If you buy a home, keep full records of the date and purchase price, plus all other costs such as commissions, legal fees, etc. Also keep full records of major improvements or additions to the house. When you sell the house, keep records of all costs involved in the sale.

Q. *How long should you keep your tax records?*

A. If you ask the Internal Revenue Service how long you should keep various records for tax purposes, here is the answer you will get: "As long as their contents may become material in the administration of any internal revenue law." Period.

Does this mouthful of mush translate into "You must keep piles of tax records indefinitely?" Generally no, says the IRS. But there are important exceptions. And although there are no hard rules, there are rules of thumb which, for all practical purposes, apply to the majority of ordinary taxpayers. Here they are:

Ordinarily, the statute of limitations for the IRS to demand additional taxes from you or for you to demand additional refunds from the IRS is three years after the return was due or was actually filed, whichever was later. In cases of substantial omission of income or fraud, the statute of limitations may be longer or there may be no limitations at all.

2

YOUR CHECKING
AND SAVINGS ACCOUNTS

GETTING THE MOST OUT OF YOUR CHECKING AND
   SAVINGS ACCOUNTS   45
WHAT EACH FINANCIAL INSTITUTION IS   47
   FULL SERVICE BANKS   48
   SAVINGS AND LOAN ASSOCIATIONS   48
   MUTUAL SAVINGS BANKS   49
   CREDIT UNIONS   50
SHOPPING GUIDE TO BANKS   51
YOUR CHECKING ACCOUNT   56
   RULES FOR WRITING AND ENDORSING CHECKS   59
   KEY QUESTIONS ABOUT WRITING CHECKS   61
   GUARDING AGAINST CHECK FORGERIES   62
   HOW TO BALANCE YOUR CHECKBOOK   63
YOUR SAVINGS ACCOUNT   65
   HOW MUCH SHOULD YOU KEEP IN A SAVINGS
      ACCOUNT?   65
   KEY FORMS OF SAVINGS ACCOUNTS   67
   WHICH TYPE OF SAVINGS ACCOUNT IS BEST FOR
      YOU?   70
   HOW CAN YOU FORCE YOURSELF TO SAVE—
      GRACEFULLY?   70
   WHAT IS "HIGHEST" INTEREST ON SAVINGS?   72
   HOW DOES A SAVINGS ACCOUNT GROW?   73
HOW TO SAVE ON BANK SERVICE CHARGES   77
HOW "SAFE" IS YOUR MONEY?   79
SHOULD YOU RENT A SAFE DEPOSIT BOX?   83

Getting the Most out of Your Checking and Savings Accounts

When you start looking for a financial institution in which to open your checking account or savings account—or both—you may not be able to escape the extraordinary gift-gimmick war waged in recent years by our nation's financial institutions via newspaper ads and radio commercials for your checking and/or savings dollar. Never has the competition among financial institutions, for your savings dollar particularly, seemed so frantic. All the institutions are in it: commercial banks, savings and loan associations, mutual savings banks, other lesser ones. All are using lures which can befuddle as well as bewitch you.

Obviously it would be utterly senseless for you to channel your family's entire banking business to institution A simply because it offers you a pair of free football tickets while B offers no such gimmicky prize.

Before you even start shopping for a financial institution, familiarize yourself with the basics about today's array of bank services, different types of savings and checking accounts, varying charges for each service. Before you even consider changing institutions, make sure you're using your present one to its very best advantage.

Let's say you have just moved to a new home in a new town. You urgently need the services of a bank so you can get checks cashed, pay bills, start a savings account, arrange for a small loan to buy a needed household appliance. Where do you start shopping? How do you weigh the virtues of bank A against those of bank B?

Or let's say you're not sure you are now getting the most economical deal with your present bank, in terms of services offered, service charges, or the frequency with which interest on your savings is compounded. How do you compare the services offered by other local banks in these areas?

In short, how do you find your way around the financial market place?

By comparing institutions on each of the following points and then deciding which are the most important to you.

Savings: Does the bank offer a range of various savings plans? Does it offer time deposit plans and savings certificates in addition to the straight passbook account? Will it automatically transfer funds from your checking to your savings account if you choose?

Interest: Is the institution's rate of interest on savings competitive? How frequently is interest compounded and credited? What about the grace periods at the beginning and end of each quarter during which you can make deposits or withdrawals without losing full interest for the quarter? Most banks today compound interest at least quarterly: the more frequently interest is compounded, the greater your financial advantage. Also, it's to your advantage if interest is paid on your average balance instead of on your minimum balance during the interest period.

Availability: Are there any restrictions on withdrawals in case you require your money in a hurry? Could your deposit be "frozen" without your being aware of it? What are the legal restrictions on withdrawals—if any?

Insurance: Are your deposits federally or state insured? With more than 99 per cent of all deposits in commercial banks covered by the FDIC, for example, they almost surely are. But make certain.

Checking: Is the minimum required balance on regular checking accounts about as low as you can get in your area? Also, what are the service and maintenance charges, the fees for checks? Does the bank offer an automatic line of credit with checking? What are the charges on special checking?

Charges: In addition to charges on checking accounts, what about the exact charges on such other bank services as safe deposit boxes? In these charges is a key to saving—and so here, compare each institution with extreme care. Many banks offer safe deposit boxes at a low monthly rate as part of a package of services.

Loans: How does the bank compare on availability of installment loans—ease, lack of red tape, speed? And how does it compare on interest rates, other terms, and availability of auto and similar loans?

Mortgages: Are mortgages easy to get? On what terms? Are mortgages available for co-ops, condominiums, summer homes?

Trust Department: Has this department a good junior as well as senior staff so that there will be continuity of trust services you want? Can you check the department's record with investments to find out how it has performed for clients over a long period?

Proximity: Is the bank—or at least a branch office—convenient to your house or office or both? If you're in business and much on the move, a bank with lots of branches might be the best, provided its other services measure up.

Banking Hours: Are they convenient for you—late on Friday or early Saturday, for instance? If the hours are limited, does the bank provide off-hour services to assist you?

Teller Service: Courteous? No congestion and long waiting times? If you want to bank by mail, does the bank supply stamped, self-addressed envelopes? Are there automated teller services?

Extra Services: Do you need or want these? Comprehensive monthly statements? Superchecks? Charge cards? Interest-paying Christmas Clubs? Help with your income tax forms? A travel service? Automatic bill paying?

Continuity: If you do stay with the institution with which you've banked a long time, will you receive preferential treatment—mortgage money when mortgages are tight, other special and valuable favors of this nature?

What Each Financial Institution Is

As the second half of the decade of the 1970s began, the trend among America's financial institutions was clearly toward over-all similarity in services offered. Savings institutions and credit unions were finding ways to provide checking accounts in mounting numbers; commercial banks also were finding ways to become directly competitive with other institutions in both the interest rates they paid and in the forms they offered on savings mediums. It appeared increasingly probable that by the start of the 1980s, an entirely overhauled and unprecedentedly "homogeneous" financial system would be serving the United States. However, in mid-decade, the following is the way the institutions were still set up and these were the major services each type offered.

FULL SERVICE BANKS

(also known as commercial banks, trust companies, and community banks)

Structure: Federally or state chartered corporations owned by stockholders, organized for profit.

Deposits Insured By: Federal Deposit Insurance Corporation (FDIC) in Washington. (Virtually all banks are insured.)

Services: The widest range, including:

> Checking accounts
>
> Savings and time deposits
>
> Mortgage and home improvement loans
>
> Consumer credit loans for automobiles, appliances, the whole range of big-ticket and small-ticket items
>
> Personal, farm, and business loans
>
> Student loans
>
> Trust, investment, estate, and custodian services
>
> Financial counseling
>
> Letters of credit
>
> Safe deposit boxes
>
> Traveler's checks
>
> Christmas and vacation clubs, many of which now pay interest
>
> A variety of travel and miscellaneous financial services
>
> Sale and redemption of U.S. savings bonds
>
> In mid-seventies, paid, in general, the lowest interest rates on savings accounts, but the situation was changing

SAVINGS AND LOAN ASSOCIATIONS

(also known as building and loan associations, co-operative banks, savings associations, and homestead associations)

Structure: Specialized financial associations, either federally or state chartered, operating in every state. Mainly mutually owned by their shareholders. When you open an account, you become a member of the association and thus a shareholder. Dividends paid on the money you put in your account.

Deposits Insured By: All federally chartered associations insured by the Federal Savings and Loan Insurance Corporation (FSLIC). State-chartered associations also insured by FSLIC and most of them are. Some other state-chartered associations are insured by state-chartered savings account insurance organizations.

Services:

> Savings accounts and time deposits
>
> Finance home building, home buying, and remodeling and thus play a key role in the housing field
>
> Passbook loans to customers with money on deposit
>
> Personal loans
>
> Sale and redemption of U.S. savings bonds
>
> Guaranteed student loans
>
> Provide safe deposit boxes, sell money orders, traveler's checks, etc.
>
> In mid-decade, in general, did not offer checking accounts and did not make business loans, but the situation was changing
>
> Also, in mid-seventies, paid in general, higher interest rates on deposits than full service banks. (In mutually owned savings associations, share owners receive "dividends," not "interest.")

MUTUAL SAVINGS BANKS

(operate in 18 states)

Structure: Non-profit specialized savings institutions, organized and operated for their depositors on a mutual basis with no stockholders; administered by trustees.

Deposits Insured By: Federal Deposit Insurance Corporation (FDIC) or by state deposit insurance funds.

Services:

Savings accounts

Home mortgage loans and home improvement loans

Safe deposit boxes

Student loans

Personal money orders

Passbook loans

Traveler's checks

Sale and redemption of U.S. savings bonds

Low-cost life insurance policies in some states

In mid-decade, began offering checking account services in increasing numbers

Generally paid higher interest rates on deposits than full service banks, but gap was closing in mid-decade. (Since savings banks are "owned" by their depositors, savings also actually receive "dividends," not "interest.")

CREDIT UNIONS

Structure: Co-operative associations of people with a common bond, such as place of employment, professional association, place of residence, membership in a union, religious group, etc. Governed by the member-users on a one-member-one-vote basis, they basically accept savings from the members and make loans at low cost to the members. The member is a "shareholder," not a depositor, and holds "shares" rather than makes deposits.

Deposits Insured By: National Credit Union Administration (NCUA) in Washington; various state insurance programs; some private insurance programs too.

Services:

Savings accounts

Loans (mortgage and home improvement, student)

Credit counseling

Traveler's checks, money orders

Payroll deductions

Interest refunds

Check cashing

Sale and redemption of U.S. savings bonds

Borrowers' protection insurance and life savings insurance

Group discount buying

Consumer education

On checking accounts the trend in recent years has been for more and more credit unions to offer accounts, in collaboration with commercial banks, with the balance kept in such accounts earning the regular rate of interest.

SHOPPING GUIDE TO BANKS

You probably take for granted such "routine" bank services as free parking, conveniently located branches, evening or Saturday banking hours, stamped banking-by-mail, personal money orders, night deposits, drive-in banking facilities. Some banks are even open twenty-four hours a day, frequently using "robot tellers," capable of dispensing cash, making deposits, and transferring funds at any hour.

Increasingly, banks are offering such services as automobile rentals and computer leasing and are even serving as part-time employment agencies.

If you are a doctor, many banks will take over all your patient billing and fee-collecting problems.

If you are a landlord, you might find your bank is set up to serve as your rent collector.

If you are a share owner, you may find that you can have your dividend checks sent directly to your bank to be deposited and acknowledged—via a receipt to you—without charge.

If you wish to reinvest your dividends in the same company's stock, automatic reinvestment-of-dividend plans also are available.

If you want to invest in stocks, many banks offer monthly stock investment plans which are automatic and which can be tailored to meet a limited budget.

If you are planning a vacation, you may discover that your bank offers you a wide range of travel services—from hotel and airplane reservations to traveler's checks—in addition to a savings plan or a special loan to pay for your holiday.

But let's say you are *not* a doctor or a landlord or a stockholder, you *don't want* to rent a computer, and you are *not* planning a vacation. What types of special services does today's *typical* bank offer you, a typical customer?

Here's a sampling (in alphabetical order) of 11 increasingly common bank services, including some which go way, way beyond the traditional savings and checking account.

(1) *Automatic Bill Paying*. Many banks today will pay at least a few of your routine bills and some will, if you authorize them to do so, automatically deduct your insurance premiums, your monthly automobile installment loan payments, and a variety of other types of regular payments from your checking account. Hundreds of banks will allow customers to pay such regular monthly bills as utilities, telephone, and water directly at the bank—thereby saving cost of writing and mailing out checks. In mounting numbers, savings institutions too permit automatic deductions from accounts to pay certain bills—such as insurance premiums, mortgage payments, the like.

(2) *Automatic Line of Credit*. On your application, a specified maximum amount of credit (depending on your credit rating) will become available to you either through your regular checking accounts or through a separate checking service which goes by various names, such as Executive Credit. In cases where the credit line is pinned to your own checking, you are able to write checks for more than your balance, up to a certain specified level. With the Executive Credit-type plan, you receive a special book of checks to write against a predetermined credit maximum. As you write the checks, you will receive notices from your bank as to when you must start repaying the total in monthly installments. This is one way to take advantage of special sales on big-ticket items, and the amount you may save may more than offset the high interest charges you'll have to pay on this type of loan.

But beware! "Tap credit" also is an invitation to overspend, so if you're the type who is constantly tempted to live beyond your means, steer clear of all types of revolving loan accounts.

(3) *Automatic Savings*. On your request, the bank will transfer at regular intervals given amounts of money from your checking account to your regular or special savings account. Or the bank will invest such funds every month or quarter in U.S. savings bonds or specified mutual funds. Or, if you have a trust account with the bank, you can have any dividends or interest from your investments automatically deposited to your savings account.

(4) *Bookkeeping Services*. A few banks are beginning to expand the automatic bill-paying idea into a full range of accounting and other financial services for their customers. Included among these services are tax accounting, financial counseling, bill paying for purposes ranging from credit card accounts to parking tickets to taxes and health insurance premiums—plus detailed record keeping for all of these expenses. Of course, any bank offering this type of personally tailored service will charge you for it. However, as one appealing alternative, some banks keep an adding machine in the lobby for customers to use.

(5) *Comprehensive Checking*. A few banks are trying out a comprehensive checking technique which one institution calls Phase II checking. In one package, the customer gets a cash reserve, automatic monthly payments on consumer loans and the mortgage, automatic monthly transfer of funds to savings or the Christmas Club account.

(6) *Investment Services*. Many commercial banks offer across-the-board investment counseling for specified fees and also handle the details of purchases, sales, reinvestment of dividends in selected stocks and safekeeping of securities.

(7) *Money Substitutes*.

(a) *Cashier's checks*. Also called "official checks," these are bank-guaranteed checks written against the bank's own account which you buy by giving the bank the amount of the check plus a small service fee. Cashier's checks are a far safer way to transfer major amounts of money from one place to another than cash itself and, since they are bank-guaranteed, will be accepted by a stranger. You may ask the bank to give you a cashier's check when you withdraw a relatively large sum from your savings account or when you borrow a sizable sum of money which you intend to turn over to another individual or company.

(b) *Certified checks*. These are simply regular checking account checks which the bank stamps to certify that the amount of the check has been deducted from your checking account and that the bank guarantees the payee that the check is good. Banks will make a small charge for this service.

(c) *Traveler's checks.* Probably the most familiar form of money substitute, available from most banks in denominations of $10, $20, $50, $100, and more, and widely used by travelers because they can be cashed throughout the world. You pay the total amount of the checks you want to buy, plus a small fee (except for the Barclays Bank checks, sold in some major cities at no fee), and establish your identity by signing the checks when you buy them and again when you cash them. With most types of traveler's checks, you are protected in the event you lose any checks—so long as you report the loss promptly to the issuing company. (Incidentally, you lose money if you hold your un-used traveler's checks after you have returned from your trip, for you get no interest on the money the checks represent until you cash in your checks, redeposit the money in an interest-bearing account, and put your funds to work for you.)

(d) *"Do it yourself" traveler's checks.* Some banks will give you a supply of "free" do-it-yourself traveler's checks which you can write anywhere in the country instead of regular checks. Like traveler's checks, these checks are accepted far more readily than ordinary checks because the issuing company—your bank—guarantees them. You pay a small service charge only on the checks you actually write and, if you write a check for more than the amount of your account balance, this automatically becomes a loan. The key advantage of this type of check is that you don't tie up a large sum of cash in purchasing the checks, as you do with regular traveler's checks.

(e) *Letters of credit.* Similarly, banks will issue to you letters of credit, along with letters of identification which you can present to the bank's branches or correspondents elsewhere in the United States or abroad, to open up reserves of cash for use in your travels.

(f) *Bank drafts.* Banks also will issue "drafts" transferring funds from your account to someone else in another state or country in a matter of hours. You can, in effect, overnight wire your cash to any payee you wish and have it converted into the currency of the country —a tremendous help in an emergency.

(8) *No Checks at All.* In areas throughout the United States, banks are experimenting with the ultimate in checking sophistication—

no checks at all. Funds are electronically transferred via computer terminals among consumers, merchants in giant shopping centers, and the banks. Look, Ma, no hands. . . .

(9) *One-check Payroll System.* Corporations across the country are sending their banks lists of their employees with the amount of salary due each, the amount of each individual's federal income and Social Security taxes to be withheld, plus all other regular deductions. The corporation issues one check each pay period for the entire operation. Then the bank takes over, deposits each employee's check to his or her own account at the bank or to his or her account at another bank.

The employee receives no pay check—only a deposit slip indicating the money has been credited to his account. The company receives a periodic statement showing the cumulative pay to each employee, his total tax and other deductions.

The success of the one-check payroll system in reducing a company's payroll department costs and in assisting employees has encouraged a few banks to go beyond this to a "no-check payroll" system. Here payroll funds are simply deducted by the bank from a company's account and credited directly to each employee. Thus payday becomes just a computerized paperwork transaction. In sum, "the modern pay check is rapidly becoming as obsolete as the old pay envelope stuffed with bills and coins," says one banking official.

(10) *One-statement Banking.* This is an expansion of your monthly checking statement to include your savings account balance, cash reserve, the balance of any installment loan and any mortgage you have outstanding. Some banks today also list your checks not in the order they clear but in the exact order you wrote them, thereby giving you a great assist in keeping your checkbook records in order.

(11) *Superchecks.* More and more banks are offering the monthly "multipurpose check" or "supercheck"—an oversized check which you can use to pay as many as 45 regular monthly bills. Some 500 banks from coast to coast offer this service, usually for 50 cents a supercheck —which amounts to a substantial saving considering the number of individual checks and stamps you'd use otherwise. On that one check, you write the figures you want the bank to pay each of several merchants, up to 45, attach the bill stubs, send the whole thing to the bank to handle.

Imaginative as some of these innovations are, they are just a sampling of the changes under way.

In the offing is an "electronic fund transfer system" in which you will be able to pay your bills simply by inserting a plastic card coded to identify your checking account in a special slot in your home telephone, dialing the bank's computer number, and then dialing also the amount of the check you wish to "write." Within seconds, an electronic voice informs you, let's say, that $18.43 has been transferred out of your checking account into the payee's account—and that is that. Ultimately, banking by telephone could mean the elimination of as much as 75 per cent of all your check writing.

And what if the computers spin out more "checks" than you have money in your account to cover? The overdraft total would simply become a loan—until you replenished your account—at the going interest rates, of course. The extent of the damage would become evident only when you received your comprehensive computerized monthly bank statement.

Even farther out—but still *not* off the edge of the horizon—is your future "shop at home" plan. In this scheme, you would tune in a supermarket display on your home Picturephone and dial, for example, "vegetables." The store's current stock of spinach, beans, carrots, etc., would then be displayed on your home phone screen, along with prices and identification numbers. You would next punch numbers on your telephone to indicate exactly what you wished to order. The supermarket would then assemble your order and dispatch it to you in a delivery truck. As for paying? Why, of course, the store—via a telephone hookup with the bank—would just automatically charge your bank account for the total you owed.

YOUR CHECKING ACCOUNT

I remember—and I'm sure you do too—when a checking account was just that and nothing more, so basic that about your only option was to choose between a regular and a special account. But now the alternatives have become so numerous that it's actually unfair to compare today's checking account with that of as recently as the 1960s.

The reasons are apparent: our rising pay checks, the ever continuing uptrend of American families into middle-income ranges where checking accounts are commonplace, our increasing familiarity with financial services, the banks' hard sell, and the steady growth of the two- or three-checking-account family.

Visibly, the checks are different, too. For ladies, the pattern may be several shades of tweed or herringbone. Many banks offer checks with scenic illustrations across the check's face. A few have special left-handed checkbooks for southpaws.

The purpose of a checking account, of course, is to give you a convenient and safe way to handle relatively large amounts of cash and to transfer money to other people. Your checkbook serves as an excellent personal financial record and your canceled checks are among the best forms of proof of to-whom-you-have-paid-how-much-and-when.

As of the mid-1970s, well over 24 billion checks worth more than $12 *trillion* were clearing annually through the U.S. banking system and the number of checks we write is due to cross the 50-billion mark during this decade. This despite all the talk about our becoming a "checkless society"!

Four out of five American families have at least one checking account. Today, more than 90 per cent of payments in this country are by check. In some states, you must be at least eighteen, or twenty-one, to open an individual checking account. Otherwise, you may open a joint account with a parent or relative.

To open an account, you simply go to your bank's New Accounts Department, fill out a signature card, decide what type of checking account you want (or can afford) to open, and make your initial deposit.

There are two main types of checking accounts—regular accounts and special accounts.

In a regular checking account, you normally must keep a certain cash minimum—which usually is at least $100 and quite possibly $200 or more. As long as you maintain the required minimum at all times, many banks will permit you to write as many checks and make as many deposits as you please without paying any monthly service charge.

However, as of the mid-seventies, generally if the amount in your regular checking account falls below the minimum, you may have to pay a monthly charge of $2.00 to $3.00. Or the bank may levy a maintenance charge for your account each month, in addition to the required minimum balance. Or still other banks will let you write a certain number of checks each month before any service charge is made.

And in many parts of the country banks in the mid-seventies were offering free checking accounts requiring no minimum balance.

A regular checking account will be the best for you if you write a relatively large number of checks during the month and you are also able to maintain the required minimum balance in your account. But the key point about *any* checking account involving a required minimum balance is that this money is not earning interest. So before you decide which type of account is best suited to you, make at least a rough calculation of the interest you would not earn on whatever minimum balance is required over the span of a year.

One calculation is to count your checks for the last year. The average person uses 22 checks per month. Multiply the total by the figure the bank charges per check on special checking. Multiply the monthly maintenance charge by 12 and add this to the check charges. The total shows the *annual cost of special checking*.

Then take 5½ per cent of the minimum balance required by the bank for regular checking, which is about the least interest a person would earn by keeping that amount in a savings program rather than tying it up in a minimum balance. On a $300 minimum, for example, it would come to $16.50 a year. Multiply by 12 the bank's monthly maintenance charge on a regular account. Add any charges the bank makes for deposits on regular checking. Add the interest total, maintenance total, and any per check and deposit charges on regular accounts to get the annual cost of regular checking.

In a special checking account (or "economy account") you do not have to keep a minimum balance. However, you usually must pay a flat monthly service charge plus another 10¢ or 15¢ charge for each check you write.

This type of account is probably the more economical for you if you are a young individual or couple whose balance tends to dip way down at the end of each pay period and if you write only a few checks during the course of a month.

A third type of checking account which has exploded onto the banking scene in recent years is the automatic line of credit or overdraft account—or whatever its name—mentioned in the previous section, "Shopping Guide to Banks." Some banks simply tack the "overdraft" feature on to your existing regular checking account; others will issue a special set of overdraft checks.

In recent years, more and more banks have begun offering free checking accounts with no minimum balance. Assuming other bank services are generally equivalent, of course it makes sense to take advantage of free checking if a bank in your area is offering it.

To repeat and emphasize: the type of checking account you choose will depend on the cash balance you are able to keep in the account, the number of checks you normally write, and whether you have the discipline to avoid the temptation of instant loans at relatively stiff interest rates.

RULES FOR WRITING AND ENDORSING CHECKS

Millions of Americans do not know the basic rules for writing, endorsing, and depositing a check. Do not permit yourself to be among them—for you may be unwittingly courting the bank's refusal to honor your checks—or even inviting costly check-doctoring by a professional earning a living in this craft.

Heed these main do's and don'ts on writing checks:

Do date each check properly. A bank may refuse to accept a check which is dated ahead, or hold it until its date is reached. The bank's reasoning is that, if the check were charged to your account before you expected it to be, it might cause other checks you wrote to bounce.

Don't leave any spaces between the dollar sign and the amount of the check you are writing, or between the amount you spell out in the middle line and the word "dollars" at the end of that line. Or, if you do leave such spaces, draw lines across them.

Do make sure each check is numbered properly—for your own bookkeeping purposes.

Don't alter the way you sign your checks (e.g., by adding your middle initial) once you have decided on a standard signature.

Do, if you are a married woman, sign checks with your own first name, plus your married name—"Mary Dowd," *not* "Mrs. Jack Dowd."

Don't use "Mr.," "Miss," or "Mrs." as part of your signature.

Do fill out the middle line ending with the word "dollars" in this format: "Five and 50/100," or "One hundred and fifty and no/100." If you write a check for less than $1.00 be sure to put a decimal point between the printed dollar sign and the amount of the check—followed by the word "cents." On the line where you write out the amount of the check, write, for example, "Only 95 cents," and cross out the word "dollars."

Don't use somebody else's check unless you cut out the special magnetic code number which usually appears at the lower left-hand corner of the check. Inking it out won't do the trick with today's electronic check-"reading" devices; if you don't actually cut out this account number, you risk having the check charged against your friend's account. (Technically, you can write a check on any surface from a paper bag to an eggshell, but banks shudder at this sort of eccentricity for obvious reasons.) For the identical reasons, don't lend anyone one of your checks. Because of the indelible symbols, your pre-imprinted check will be sorted according to its magnetic coding and charged to your account even if someone else, with no dishonest intentions at all, has crossed out your identifying number and name and written in his own.

Do endorse a check only on the back of the left-hand side (the perforated side, in one type of checkbook), *exactly* as your name appears on the front of the check. If this is not your usual signature, add the correct signature below your first endorsement. Of course, if your address is on the check too, you need not include this—or the "Miss," "Mrs." or "Mr." which may also be included.

Don't ever underestimate the importance of your endorsement or forget that your endorsement on someone else's check means you would be willing to cover the check yourself should the bank for any reason refuse to honor it.

A blank endorsement—your signature only—means you transfer the ownership of the check to the person holding it at the time. This person may then cash it.

An endorsement in full—or special endorsement—means you sign a check over to someone else by writing on the back of a check "Pay to the order of" this person or organization.

A *restrictive endorsement* should be used on checks you wish to deposit by mail. You write "For deposit only" over your signature. Or, if you give someone a check which has been made out to you or cash, you write "Pay to the order of ———" and sign your name beneath this.

Do deposit all checks you receive as soon as you get them. Not only is it a big bookkeeping nuisance for the person who has issued the check if you keep it for a month or more, but many banks refuse to honor checks which are two or three months old—unless they are "re-authorized" to do so by the payer.

Don't write checks out to "cash" unless you yourself are cashing them at a bank, supermarket, or elsewhere. Such checks are negotiable by any bearer and leave you with no record of how the money was spent.

Do record on your check stub the key facts about every check you write. This includes the date, check number, payee, amount, and the purpose of the check if the "payee" notation doesn't make that evident. The best way to make sure you don't forget to record this information is to do so *before* you write the check itself.

And *don't* ever, ever give signed blank checks to anybody whom you do not trust completely; blank checks are as good as cash—unlimited amounts of it, for that matter. As a matter of fact, it's risky to ever sign a blank check!

KEY QUESTIONS ABOUT WRITING CHECKS

Now here are additional questions you almost surely would like to have answered—leading logically from the rules covered in the preceding pages.

Q. *When you deposit a check from another bank, how long should you wait for it to be cleared before you can safely draw checks against your deposit?*

A. If the other bank is in the same city, allow two or three more days for the check to be collected. If the bank is out of town, allow five to ten days depending on its location. When it's important for you to know exactly when a check will actually be credited to your account— so you won't risk having any of your own checks returned—ask one of your bank's officers about the particular check.

Q. *Is it legal to write a check in pencil?*

A. Yes. But it's obviously dangerous since anyone could erase the amount and substitute a larger one. Write all checks in ink.

Q. *May a check be dated on Saturday, Sunday, or a holiday?*

A. Yes. The folklore to the contrary is wrong. However, since some people who believe the folklore may refuse to accept the check, it's generally safer to date it on a previous day.

Q. *What happens when you make the mistake of writing one amount in words and another amount in figures?*

A. Most banks pay the amount which is spelled out. If they don't pay this amount, they return the check.

Q. *Should you ever erase or cross out anything on a check?*

A. No. Even if you initial the change, the bank will not honor an altered check. And knowing this, you should never accept or cash an altered check yourself.

Q. *How long does a check remain valid?*

A. Technically, a check is good for six years. In actual practice, though, most banks consult with the payer before honoring a check which is more than six months old and many, I repeat, do this after only two or three months.

Q. *Will your bank give you a new check if you spoil one for which you've already paid?*

A. Yes.

Q. *How do you stop payment on a check?*

A. You can, for a small fee of about $1.00, stop payment on any check you have written simply by *telephoning* your bank's stop payment department and giving the details, including: the date, amount, name of payee, check number, and the reason for stopping the payment. Then immediately confirm the order in writing. The bank will issue a stop payment form which you must complete and which the bank will keep on file—to be sure your intention *not* to have the bank honor your check is properly carried out.

When you stop payment, be sure you notify the payee—the person, company, or organization who was to have received the amount of money you specified on the check.

As a general rule, *don't* send a check in payment unless you are willing to have it honored. Stopping payment may damage your credit rating.

GUARDING AGAINST CHECK FORGERIES

What would you do if you suddenly discovered your checkbook had been stolen and that a professional forger was using *your* name to write check after check against your account?

Do not dismiss the question, for check forgeries have been climbing at an alarming pace in recent years. As a simple precaution against becoming another victim, you should at least be aware of a few of the forger's favorite techniques.

Typically, the forger will find out when your bank mails out monthly statements and will loot your mailbox at that time. Armed with samples of your signature, a good idea of the amount of money you keep in your account, and the number of checks you usually write during the month, he will start raiding your account. You may not discover the damage until *his* canceled checks start coming home to you.

Or the forger may simply "raise" a carelessly written check of yours, by hiking the amount from "one" dollar to "one hundred" or "six" dollars to "sixty," or "twenty" to "seventy"—at the same time subtracting this amount from your account.

Here are a few key rules to protect yourself against check forgery:

• Guard your checks as if they were cash. I re-emphasize, in many ways, they're *better* than cash, since they can be written out for any amount.

• Notify your bank *immediately* if you lose even a single check, not to mention your entire checkbook. Note: Forgers frequently will steal checks from the *back* of your checkbook to postpone detection, so flip through your whole checkbook now and then as an added precaution.

• Notify the bank if you fail to receive your bank statement within a couple of days of the usual time.

• Reconcile your bank statement promptly each month and glance at each returned check for evidence of any tampering or forgery.

• Report any such evidence to the bank immediately. Banks normally are insured against such losses.

• Learn and obey the rules I've already given you for writing checks.

• Destroy all old checks if and when you change your name, address, account number—or become formally separated or divorced.

• Avoid the sweeping illegible "executive" signature—or a handprinted signature. This is much easier to forge than a clear, freely written two-name signature with connected letters.

HOW TO BALANCE YOUR CHECKBOOK

As Chapter 1, "Your Personal Money Manager," stressed, the monthly ritual of checkbook balancing should be assigned to whichever member of the family is the more deft at it and the more willing to do it *as soon as possible* after each bank statement comes in. An arbitrary decision that this chore should automatically go to the man in the family is downright foolish—if he has neither a flare for nor an interest in it. Whoever of you gets the job can use the chart illustrated to guide you on the key steps to balancing a checkbook.

1. Your own checkbook balance	
2. Minus service charges appearing on your bank statement	
3. Your own new checkbook balance	
4. Balance in the bank's statement	
5. Plus recent deposits not yet recorded in bank statement	
6. Minus value of all outstanding checks — those not appearing on bank statement	
7. New bank statement balance	

This last total—item 7—should agree with item 3, your own "new checkbook balance." If it does not, go back and follow these steps:

(1) First compare the amount of each canceled check with the amount appearing in the bank statement. Make a notation after each check on the bank statement as you go.

(2) Now arrange the stack of checks in order of check numbers—which will permit you not only to recheck the amounts against those appearing in your own check records but also to tell immediately which ones are missing.

(3) Compare the amount of each check with the amount you have written on each appropriate stub—and check off each entry in your record as you go.

(4) Compare, and verify with a notation, all the deposits you have made and recorded with the deposits recorded on the bank statement.

(5) Add up, in the appropriate space provided on your bank statement, the amounts of all checks you have written which have not yet appeared on your statement and subtract this total from the balance appearing at the end of your bank statement. Make sure the amounts on the checks agree with the amounts recorded on your check register.

(6) Add to the statement balance the total amount of deposits

you have made to your account which do not appear on the bank statement.

(7) Subtract any bank service charges appearing in your statement from the balance which appears in your checkbook. Do this in your checkbook as well.

The revised totals for the bank statement and for your checkbook balance should agree to the penny.

But don't panic if they still don't agree. Here's what to do:

Recheck your original math in your checkbook. The bank's math is usually correct since it was probably done by a machine. However, errors of other sorts are entirely possible.

Recheck the balances you carried forward from page to page in your checkbook.

Double-check to be certain you have subtracted *all* outstanding checks from your bank statement balance—including those still missing from previous statements.

Double-check to be certain all of the canceled checks which came with your statement are included in your checkbook record—and that you haven't forgotten to note *any non-checkbook checks* you may have written during the period of the statement.

If your accounts *still* don't balance, and you're completely stymied as to why, take the whole business to the bank and ask for help. You'll almost surely be given this help freely and without charge—but don't delay. There is always the possibility, although remote, of sleight of hand with your bank balance—and the sooner any type of thievery is pinned down, the better your chance of avoiding financial losses. Most banks expect to be informed of a possible error within ten days.

YOUR SAVINGS ACCOUNT

HOW MUCH SHOULD YOU KEEP IN A SAVINGS ACCOUNT?

How much money should *you* keep in a savings account?

• The average amount of money kept in a regular savings account in a U.S. financial institution in 1975 was close to $2,000.

• The rule of thumb I gave you in Chapter 1, "Your Personal

Money Manager," is that your emergency fund should equal at least two months' income.

• Many of the major financial institutions of the country would call my total far too low, would recommend your reserve in the form of "liquid assets"—cash or its equivalent—should total three to six months' income.

• But the vital point which erases any apparent disagreement is that your own special financial circumstances must be the crucial factor deciding whether your emergency reserve can safely be as low as two months' income or should properly be equal to six months' earnings.

So how much should *you* keep in an emergency fund? Let me answer by asking you these questions:

How many circumstances can you think of in which you might require really large sums of cash, literally at overnight notice?

What types of unexpected financial emergencies might conceivably befall you or your family? (A disabling accident, job layoff, big auto repair job.)

What share of the estimated costs of such emergencies would be covered by your other forms of financial protection such as major medical insurance, life insurance, other types of insurance, disability and survivor's benefits under Social Security, U.S. savings bonds you might have stashed away, stocks, mutual fund shares, bonds, other investments, benefits from your employer?

What emergency financial help could you realistically expect from parents, other relatives, or your employer?

Could you, the non-working wife, move into a paying job fairly readily—if need be?

If the family breadwinner should lose his or her job tomorrow due to a layoff, merger, or other development, how long would it probably be before he or she could find a comparable job in his or her field of training?

How big a financial nest egg in cash do *you* need to *feel* financially secure?

Are you preparing for big-ticket expenses and purchases in the months ahead—e.g., a down payment on a house, a new baby, a long-planned vacation, a big outlay to go into business for yourself?

The amount you really need as an emergency reserve will depend on your honest answers to these questions.

It well may be that *if* you're a young couple with no children and a modest income, the *maximum* you should keep is $1,000 to $1,500 in a regular savings account. And in some cases even less would be realistic if you have other safe financial reserves which you could readily tap.

For your emergency cash reserve—whatever its amount or wherever you deposit it—should be precisely what its name implies. It should be protection against unexpected financial emergencies. It should be no more nor less than that.

KEY FORMS OF SAVINGS ACCOUNTS

Within any single financial institution, you may choose between a variety of savings accounts, each one tailored to fit particular needs, each account with special advantages, and each with disadvantages. You must select the one which best fits your requirements.

In general, these will be offered to you:

Passbook Savings Accounts

Have complete flexibility. Your money is always instantly available. You may deposit or withdraw any amount at any time.

Interest you earn on this type of "liquid" savings will be the lowest among the major types of accounts. Commercial banks by law paid the lowest rates on passbook savings accounts in the mid-1970s—one of their key disadvantages.

"Liquidity" of this type of account is the highest, the best of all types of savings outside of your checking account or cash in your hand. Liquidity denotes the ease and speed with which you can convert your funds into cash, and the amount of interest you can earn on your savings tends to be lowest where the degree of liquidity is highest.

Interest is usually compounded annually, semi-annually, or quarterly and in some cases daily.

Federally insured or state insured in almost all cases up to $40,000 for each account held in a different name (a joint account can be insured separately from the individual accounts of those sharing the joint account).

Funds in this type of account can be used as collateral for personal bank loans.

Tally of your savings balance may be kept in a passbook or reported periodically to you in computerized statements mailed by the

financial institution holding your account. The passbook itself is being
gradually phased out.

Time Deposit Open Accounts

Form of savings account in which you must leave your savings with
the institution for a specified period of time in order to obtain the higher
interest rate offered on these deposits. (Has many names. The trick
name depends on the institution.) Note: you can withdraw the interest
but not the principal.

Minimum initial deposits required, usually ranging from $500 to as
much as $5,000.

While you can add funds to this type of account or withdraw
interest at any time, notice of thirty to ninety days frequently required
for withdrawal of the principal, with the actual interest you receive depending on how long you maintain your account.

Insurance features the same as for Passbook Savings Accounts.

Consumer Certificates of Deposit

• These are the certificates of deposit for individuals with savings
of under $100,000. They are a medium for your most liquid funds—
assuming you are confident you will not need to cash in your certificates
before they mature.

• In the mid-1970s, consumer CDs were available in denominations from $100 to as high as $5,000 to $10,000.

• Maturities ranged from two to four years or more with the interest
rate the highest paid on any savings account.

• Notice of withdrawal was required and penalty imposed—in form
of reduction of interest—in event of prior withdrawal.

• Insurance features and all the rest identical with other forms of
savings accounts.

On top of these basic forms of savings accounts, financial institutions are developing new savings programs or variations of older ones.
As a banker remarked, "In my Midwestern youth, our small-town bank
had only two different devices to help me save. Today, that bank has
nine variations and larger banks have still more." Just to indicate the
scope, ponder these variations:

• Monthly memo savings. The full service bank lets you set a goal
in total dollars, then it develops a savings plan to fit and determines

what monthly deposits you need to make to meet the goal. Every month the bank sends a statement to the depositor reminding him that he "owes" the account a deposit of X dollars. The top of the statement can be detached and used as a deposit slip, with an attached prestamped envelope.

• Assorted interest. On many savings accounts, especially higher-interest time accounts, larger banks offer several options on payment of interest: interest can be credited to the time account, the regular savings account, the checking account, or mailed out on a quarterly basis.

• Special savings withdrawal. In one Midwestern city, several banks have together installed a special-purpose computer system to provide instant savings withdrawal transactions for customers. Through an on-the-line system of 90 keyboard terminals, the teller keys in a savings account number and dollar amount any time a customer wants to make a withdrawal and gets a green, yellow, or red light response for Yes, Maybe, or No.

• Quick deposits. More and more banks have quick deposit boxes for savings so customers needn't stand in the teller line. There also has been great improvement in teller line traffic, drive-in and walk-up windows, expresslines, etc.

• Safe deposit boxes. Some banks give customers free use of safe deposit boxes if their savings accounts run a certain size. Other special promotions are widespread.

• Insurance. Based on the depositor's age and the size of his account, this program makes term insurance available at what amounts to a group policy rate or less.

The mutual savings banks in New York, Massachusetts, and Connecticut also sell low-cost life insurance over the counter. It is inexpensive insurance because it is sold directly to you—at the bank itself or by mail—and there are no salesmen's commissions to add to its price to you. Many savings banks now also sell shares in a no-load, no-redemption-fee mutual fund. (See Chapter 21, "How to Invest in Mutual Funds," for details on no-load funds.)

Most credit unions provide life insurance without charge to you if you put your savings in the credit union.

WHICH TYPE OF SAVINGS ACCOUNT IS BEST FOR YOU?

You can decide which savings account is best suited for your personal needs and goals only when you know the variety of accounts available. In brief, you may choose among these major types:

(1) *An individual account.* This may be opened by only one person—adult or minor—and you are the sole owner, the only person who can draw on the account. You can open this type of account with a small deposit.

(2) *A joint account.* Two of you may open this type—usually a husband and wife. Either of you may deposit funds in the account and either of you may withdraw funds from the account. In the event that one of you dies, the balance will be payable to the survivor.

(3) *A voluntary trust account.* You may open this type in trust for your child or another person. You will control the account during your life—after which it will be payable to the person you name as beneficiary. You have the right to change the beneficiary of this account at any time.

(4) *A fiduciary account.* If you are appointed an administrator, executor of an estate, or a guardian of another person, you may open a fiduciary account for the funds entrusted to you.

(5) *An organization account.* If you belong to an organization which collects dues or fees and which therefore has funds to safeguard and if you are in charge of the funds, you can open an organization account. The organization might be a club, your church, your lodge, a mutual benefit society, or any other non-profit organization.

(6) *A school savings account.* Your child may open a regular school bank savings account with insignificant deposits—and as he or she learns how to save and the virtues of saving, this tiny account may grow to become your child's regular savings account with a respectable deposit balance.

HOW CAN YOU FORCE YOURSELF TO SAVE—GRACEFULLY?

One way to save money is through a "loose money" system. Put aside at the end of each day all the change you have left in your pocket— or only all your quarters, or even all your single dollar bills. Once every week, faithfully deposit your little hoard in a nearby bank or savings association. In just over eighteen months, the dollar-bill approach helped one family make the first payment on a piece of land in the exurbs for a weekend cabin.

Another way to build a nest egg is to save all windfall money—dividends, inheritances, bonuses, cash gifts, tax refunds. Put this money in your savings account the instant you get it. Don't even cash the check or do more than peer at the amount of cash in a gift envelope. Don't give the temptation to spend the windfall the slightest edge.

A third excellent way to save is to authorize your bank to deduct a specified percentage from your pay check automatically when you deposit the pay check in your checking account and to transfer this percentage to your savings account. Make it 10 per cent, if you can manage, or 5 per cent—but make the transfer automatic and regular. The automatic, regular feature is the secret, as I stressed over and over again in Chapter 1, "Your Personal Money Manager."

Or maybe you will decide the best approach for you is an automatic deposit of X number of pay checks each year entirely in the savings account. For instance, you might decide to save every tenth weekly pay check or the first check of every quarter of the year. Or if you're paid on a semi-monthly basis, you might decide you can manage to put away two or three full pay checks a year.

Or you might find a periodic "Nothing Week" is your best deal. During this week you would not spend any money on dinner out or stop at the bar on the way home from work or go out to the movies or go bowling—or whatever. You would eat inexpensive foods at home, read books, or look at TV—and add at least $25 to your nest egg.

Or surely you could save the money you formerly used for, say, cigarettes. I, for one, am saving more than $300 a year on this item alone since I quit.

And there are all sorts of tricks, of course. You might put, say, $50 in your savings account on every national holiday or family birthday. Or you might add an agreed-upon amount whenever you break a family rule. Or add that agreed-upon amount whenever you enjoy a particular pastime.

You can easily figure out your own approach, once you make up your minds to adopt one.

You'll save if you force yourself to by some method. Then you'll build your nest egg if you'll put the program on an automatic basis. You can't lose by trying this. You can only win.

WHAT IS "HIGHEST" INTEREST ON SAVINGS?

By law, banks and other financial institutions must state clearly in their advertisements the *true* annual interest rate they pay on savings—if they make any reference at all to interest in their ads—as well as any special conditions for getting the full interest rate.

But clear as this seems, it still leaves plenty of room for befuddlement. In fact, in this area of interest earned on savings, "highest" may not be highest at all—and the institution which advertises the top stated rate of interest on your funds may not be actually paying you the top total of dollars on your funds.

So much more than the stated rate of interest is involved. Far more revealing than the percentage which stands out in the ad may be what is not even included in the ad. For instance, how often is the interest promised you compounded—so that your interest earns interest? When does your deposit start to draw interest? Is there any penalty for frequent withdrawals or any bonus for no withdrawals for a specified period?

To underline my point, a while ago, as an experiment, I surveyed a couple dozen of employees in my newspaper office who had savings accounts nearby. With two exceptions, all were fuzzy about every aspect except the stated interest rate.

This ignorance is self-defeating. You may think you are getting the best interest deal but you might be able to do significantly better at another institution a block away. You may think you are handling your savings sensibly, but you actually may be cutting your own return by the way you deposit and withdraw funds. Here are five questions you should be able to answer:

(1) What is the institution's policy on the compounding of interest? The more frequently interest is compounded the more interest your savings earn. A rate of 6 per cent paid once a year is a straight 6 per cent—or $60 per $1,000 of savings. But a rate of 6 per cent paid to you every quarter is higher, because the interest credited to your account is added to your original amount every quarter and then the stated rate is paid on the bigger sum. A rate compounded every month comes out to still more and a rate compounded every day is most. The larger your savings and the longer you maintain your account, the more the factor of "compounding" matters.

(2) When does your savings account start to earn interest (or dividends)? Under a policy most favorable to you, the institution will pay interest on your account from the day of deposit to the day of withdrawal. Also, under a most favorable policy, the institution will pay interest on all funds you keep in your account during the interest period. Under a least favorable policy, the institution will pay interest only on the smallest balance you have in your account during the interest period.

(3) When is interest credited to your account? On the first of each month? At the end of each quarter? At the end of June and December? Or just at the end of December? This is of major importance, for under the policies of many institutions, if you withdraw funds before the stated interest payment date, you will lose all the interest owed to you on these funds, for the interest period. When you withdraw funds, try to schedule the withdrawal immediately after the date for crediting interest.

(4) Is there any "grace period" during which you can withdraw funds around the interest payment date without being penalized by loss of interest? If so, how many days of grace are you allowed in which to withdraw funds and still be entitled to the interest the funds had earned? Also find out if there is a grace period after each interest payment date during which you can deposit funds and have them earn interest from the payment date. Pertinent too is whether the period of grace includes every calendar day or just business days. A period of grace which includes only business days will be longer than it appears offhand.

(5) What about penalties for frequent withdrawals? And what about payment of an interest bonus if you make no withdrawals for a specified period—say none for one year? Both penalties and bonuses are fairly commonplace.

Any reputable financial institution should automatically answer these questions (and others which may bother you). With the answers, you then may make an intelligent decision on where to keep your cash nest egg.

HOW DOES A SAVINGS ACCOUNT GROW?

Compound interest means that you are earning interest on the interest paid to you as well as interest on your own deposits.

Say you deposit $5.00 a week in your savings account at a local bank and you earn 5 per cent interest from the day of deposit. Say your bank compounds your interest quarterly.

Here is how much your account would grow *without* the compound interest and *with* compound interest—at 5 per cent.

$5.00 a Week at 5%

NUMBER OF YEARS	SAVINGS WITHOUT COMPOUND INTEREST	SAVINGS WITH COMPOUND INTEREST	SAVINGS INCREASE REPRESENTED BY COMPOUND INTEREST
1	$ 260	$ 266.45	$ 6.45 (2.5%)
2	520	546.48	26.48 (5.10%)
3	780	840.77	60.77 (7.8%)
5	1,300	1,475.10	175.10 (13.5%)
10	2,600	3,366.23	766.23 (29.5%)
15	3,900	5,790.74	1,890.74 (48.5%)
20	5,200	8,899.04	3,699.04 (71.1%)

Or say you can deposit $5.00 to $50 a month. How will your savings grow at 5 per cent a year interest, compounded semi-annually? Here's how much:

How SAVINGS GROW	$5 MONTHLY	$10 MONTHLY	$15 MONTHLY	$20 MONTHLY	$25 MONTHLY	$50 MONTHLY
6 months	30.44	60.88	91.31	121.75	152.19	304.38
1 year	61.64	123.28	184.90	246.54	308.18	616.37
2 years	126.40	252.81	379.17	505.57	631.97	1,263.94
3 years	194.44	388.89	583.26	777.71	972.15	1,944.30
4 years	265.93	.531.85	797.69	1,063.62	1,329.55	2,659.10
5 years	341.03	682.06	1,022.98	1,364.01	1,705.04	3,410.09
10 years	777.58	1,555.16	2,332.48	3,110.06	3,887.64	7,775.28
15 years	1,336.40	2,672.80	4,008.76	5,345.15	6,681.55	13,363.10
20 years	2,051.73	4,103.47	6,154.53	8,206.26	10,257.99	20,515.99

Or say you have $5,000 in cash to deposit in a savings account. How much will this sum grow at varying interest rates over the years, if compounded quarterly?

Here's that answer:

How a $5,000 Deposit Will Grow

INTEREST RATE	AFTER 1 YEAR	AFTER 3 YEARS	AFTER 5 YEARS	AFTER 10 YEARS
4.50%	$5,229	$5,718	$6,254	$7,822
4.75	5,242	5,761	6,332	8,018
5.00	5,255	5,804	6,410	8,218
5.25	5,265	5,848	6,491	8,425
5.50	5,280	5,890	6,572	8,636
5.75	5,294	5,934	6,652	8,851
6.00	5,306	5,978	6,734	9,070

Or say your objective is to save a specific sum—anywhere from $2,000 to $20,000. If you save X dollars a month, how many years will it take you—at Y interest compounded continuously—to achieve your goal?

The following compilation answers this one.

Start by setting your savings target in total dollars and years (the left-hand column). Follow across to one of the other columns and see how much you should save each month in order to reach your goal—at varying interest rates.

Or start with a rough idea of how much money you can put aside every month. Then look in the left-hand column to see what size nest egg you're aiming for.

Savings Time Table

If you want this amount:		Save this much each month at the interest rate of:		
		4½%	5%	5¼%
$ 2,000 in	1 year	$162.64	$162.20	$161.53
	3 years	51.79	51.39	50.78
	5 years	29.67	29.28	28.70
$ 4,000 in	1 year	$325.28	$324.40	$323.06
	3 years	103.58	102.78	101.56
	5 years	59.34	58.56	57.40
$ 6,000 in	1 year	$487.92	$486.60	$484.59
	3 years	155.38	154.17	152.34
	5 years	89.00	87.84	86.10

If you want this amount:		Save this much each month at the interest rate of:		
		4½ %	5%	5¼ %
$ 8,000 in	5 years	$118.67	$117.12	$114.80
	10 years	52.69	51.28	49.21
	15 years	31.06	29.78	27.93
	20 years	20.51	19.36	17.72
$10,000 in	5 years	$148.34	$146.40	$143.50
	10 years	65.86	64.10	61.51
	15 years	38.83	37.23	34.91
	20 years	25.64	24.20	22.15
$12,000 in	5 years	$178.01	$175.68	$172.20
	10 years	79.03	76.92	73.82
	15 years	46.59	44.67	41.90
	20 years	30.77	29.04	26.58
$14,000 in	5 years	$207.68	$204.96	$200.90
	10 years	92.21	89.74	86.12
	15 years	54.36	52.12	48.88
	20 years	35.89	33.88	31.01
$16,000 in	5 years	$237.35	$234.24	$229.60
	10 years	105.38	102.56	98.42
	15 years	62.12	59.56	55.86
	20 years	41.02	38.72	35.44
$18,000 in	5 years	$267.01	$263.52	$258.30
	10 years	118.55	115.38	110.72
	15 years	69.89	67.01	62.84
	20 years	46.15	43.56	39.87
$20,000 in	5 years	$296.68	$292.80	$287.00
	10 years	131.72	128.20	123.03
	15 years	77.65	74.45	69.83
	20 years	51.28	48.40	44.30

NOTE: This table was prepared by the Continental Bank of Chicago. It is based on three assumptions: (1) Deposits monthly are made at the first of the month; (2) periodic deposits are monthly and are the same amount as the initial deposit; and (3) interest is compounded continuously.

How to Save on Bank Service Charges

Do you know how much you are now paying in bank service charges to maintain your checking and savings accounts? Probably you don't. But these charges often run $35 to $50 or even more a year, depending on the number of services you use. This is a possible leak in your budget which you should not ignore—particularly in view of the fact that you're using an unprecedented variety of bank services today, are likely to use more and more in the future, and the long-term trend of charges for these services is relentlessly up.

Here, therefore, are guides on the amounts you well may be paying without realizing it and ways to reduce your charges. At one Midwestern bank, the service charges on a regular checking account with a minimum balance of $300 are 5¢ for each bookkeeping entry, 4¢ for each deposit, 75¢ a month for maintaining a regular checking account, and $3.00 for each overdraft. Thus, this bank's typical net monthly charge is $1.00 to $2.00.

Some banks charge you for any checks you write over a certain maximum number as well as the monthly maintenance charge. Typical charges in the mid-1970s on a special checking account with no minimum balance were 50¢ to 75¢ a month plus 10¢ for each check you wrote. Some banks charge less per check but add a charge for each deposit. But using this example, if you wrote 20 checks a month, the service charge would run $2.50 to $2.75—or $30 to $33 a year.

Most banks also impose a "late charge" if you fail to make a payment on an installment loan within five to ten days of the due date. This "grace period" is not advertised, but most banks which extend home mortgages provide for several days of grace on loan repayments. A typical charge is 5 per cent of the payment, up to a maximum of $5.00 in any one month and $25 over the life of the loan—or 2 per cent of the original loan amount, whichever is less.

Usually there is no service charge on savings accounts. However, many banks charge "activity fees" for frequent withdrawals.

If a bank pays no interest on Christmas Club or Vacation Club accounts, this adds up to a "hidden" service charge of sorts. Even banks which do pay interest on such accounts generally pay less than the going rate for regular savings accounts. (A few do pay full savings rates.) Similarly, on regular savings accounts, some banks pay no interest on balances below a certain amount.

Here are basic rules to help you save on bank service charges:

• Generally, a regular checking account is the most economical type, for on this type of account, you can often eliminate *any* service charge simply by keeping the required balance in the account—and as I reported in the section "Your Checking Account," many banks now offer completely free checking accounts.

But keep in mind that if you maintain a large minimum balance you are losing a substantial amount of interest on these funds. A $500 minimum, for example, translates into a loss of about $25 in interest during one year.

• If you have a regular checking account and there is a minimum balance requirement, make sure you don't dip under the minimum balance and invoke a monthly penalty charge.

• If you are being regularly charged for drawing beyond the minimum balance in your checking account, consider transferring money from your savings account. You might be able to save more in charges than you'll lose in interest.

• If you, a young couple, have two separate accounts (one individual and one joint account), consider consolidating them—to increase your combined minimum balance and thus shave service charges you might be piling up for dipping below this minimum.

• If yours is a special checking account and you find that you are writing a rising number of checks, perhaps it would be cheaper to switch to a regular checking account. Normally, a special checking account is the more economical only if you write fewer than ten checks a month.

• In either type of account try to limit the number of checks you write. Just by writing a single check for $60 in cash instead of six checks for $10 each, you could save 50¢ or more in service charges. Or hold out a fairly large sum of cash when you deposit your pay check. Also, pay as many little bills in cash as you conveniently can unless you need the canceled checks for your tax records—and find out if you can pay your utility bills at the bank, without using any checks.

• Check your bank statements immediately when you receive them to make sure that you're not about to make a costly overdraft. And *don't* get into the habit of sending out a deposit in the same mail as you send out a slew of checks drawn against that deposit. An out-of-town check you deposit may not be credited to your checking account until it is actually cleared—which may take from a day to a week. On the other hand, the amount of each check you write is deducted from your balance the minute your bank receives the check. In this era of erratic postal service and computerized check-clearing techniques, what this means is that your checks easily might beat your deposits to the bank. Quite aside from the fact that this practice is illegal, it could leave you with both a fistful of rubber checks which reached the bank before your deposit got there and overdraft penalties of $2.50 to $5.00 or more *per check*.

• Make installment loan payments within the period of time your bank specifies in order to eliminate late charges.

• Avoid asking for a statement of your checking account balance. A growing number of banks are now making extra charges if you ask for such statements before they are automatically sent to you. Charges range from 25¢ to $4.00 for an itemized supplementary statement, and the typical cost of a simple verbal report on your balance is 50¢.

• And try to avoid requesting a special search for a "lost" deposit you may have failed to record properly. You may find that your bank makes a charge of $1.00 or more for such a search.

How "Safe" Is Your Money?

It is almost impossible for most Americans to conceive of what it must have been like before federal government insurance of bank and savings association deposits—to imagine the tragedy when an innocent family's lifetime savings disappeared in the crash of the trusted bank on the corner.

But ponder what it is like now:

In recent years a fair number of banks have failed—several of them frighteningly large but *in no case did a depositor lose a single penny of his or her insured deposits*. The system has worked superbly well, there has been no worry—much less panic.

In recent years a fair number of savings and loan associations also have failed—*but not one depositor in an institution federally insured lost one penny of his or her insured funds either*.

Today, 98 per cent of our banks are insured by the Federal Deposit Insurance Corporation in Washington. The insurance fund, paid in by nearly 14,000 member banks throughout the nation, totaled an awesome $5 billion-plus in the mid-seventies. On top of that, the FDIC has authority to borrow as much as $3 billion additional from the U. S. Treasury.

As for us, 99 per cent of all bank depositors' savings and checking accounts are FDIC-insured, and as of the mid-1970s most of the funds we had on deposit in insured banks were covered up to a $40,000 limit.

In a recent year, too, about 4,200 federal and state-chartered savings and loan associations—out of a total of roughly 5,400—were insured by the Federal Savings and Loan Insurance Corporation in Washington. The FSLIC's fund totaled $3.1 billion and covered more than 96 per cent of the savings in insured associations. The vast majority of associations not covered by the FSLIC are backed by state insurance funds.

In 1974, all federally chartered credit unions were insured by the National Credit Union Administration—a total of approximately 12,700 —and 1,705 of the 11,000-plus state-chartered credit unions were also federally insured. Many of the credit unions not protected by federal insurance have opted for other insurance alternatives and some states have mandatory laws for federal insurance.

It's not a perfect system for depositors, but it's coming close, and the performance record has been great.

Q. *What are the chances your bank might fail?*

A. Very slim indeed. In contrast to an average of 588 bank failures a year in the 1920s and an average of 2,277 in the 1930–33 period, bank failures averaged only 5 a year between 1943 and 1973 among all banks, and only 3 a year for insured banks. The record has been similar for insured savings and loan associations.

Q. *Are only savings and checking accounts insured?*

A. No. These other types of deposits also are insured: Christmas savings and other open-account time deposits, uninvested trust funds, certified checks, cashiers' checks, bank traveler's checks, and all other deposits "received by a bank in its usual course of business."

Q. *If you have both a checking and a savings account, is each insured up to $40,000?*

A. No. All deposits under your own name are added together and this total is insured up to $40,000.

Q. *What if you have, in addition to your own accounts, a joint account with your husband?*

A. Your joint account, with your husband or your child, is insured separately for up to $40,000.

Q. *Are accounts kept at different banks insured separately?*

A. Yes. However, if you keep separate accounts at separate branches of your bank, all of these are considered as a single bank for the purposes of deposit insurance.

Q. *Are certificates of deposit covered?*

A. Yes. But they are not insured separately if they are held in the same bank at which you have other deposits in the same name.

Q. *How and when would you be paid in the event your bank failed?*

A. You might be paid, probably within a week of the date your bank closed, by an FDIC check which you could then either cash or have deposited in your name in another insured bank. Or, more likely, your funds would be transferred to a new bank under new management, and become available to you within a few days. The payment period might be more prolonged in the case of a savings association failure but the payment period of the FSLIC has generally been comparable to that of the FDIC.

Q. *Who pays for the insurance coverage on deposits?*

A. FDIC member banks, which are assessed approximately 1/30th of 1 per cent of their total deposits. Savings and loan associations pay higher assessments.

Here's a brief table to give you an idea of how much money you, a couple with one child, could keep in a single bank or savings and loan association, fully insured:

INDIVIDUAL ACCOUNTS

Man:	$40,000
Wife:	40,000
Child:	40,000

JOINT ACCOUNTS

Man and wife:	40,000
Man and child:	40,000
Wife and child:	40,000

TESTAMENTARY REVOCABLE TRUST ACCOUNTS

Man (as trustee for wife):	$40,000
Man (as trustee for child):	40,000
Wife (as trustee for husband):	40,000
Wife (as trustee for child):	40,000

IRREVOCABLE TRUST ACCOUNTS

Man (as trustee for wife):	40,000
Man (as trustee for child):	40,000
Wife (as trustee for husband):	40,000
Wife (as trustee for child):	40,000
TOTAL	$560,000

It's most unlikely anyone would keep this total in cash in a financial institution, but you can actually have *insured* savings of as much as $560,000 in one institution!

To get 100 per cent protection against the remote possibility of a bank failure, follow these two fundamental rules:

1. *Don't* keep more than the legal maximum in your individual accounts of all types in any one financial institution or its branches.

2. *Do* bank only with a federal- or state-insured institution. All insured institutions advertise this fact, so take the time to make sure your institution is properly insured.

But be reassured. Banking is among the most tightly regulated and closely scrutinized industries in the nation. And legal steps are continually being taken by federal and state regulatory agencies to make the system ever more failureproof.

Should You Rent a Safe Deposit Box?

You almost surely own a collection of records and valuables which *should* be stored in a bank safe deposit box—particularly in this period of soaring numbers of home burglaries and in view of the fact that many types of documents are very difficult if not impossible to replace.

Today, it costs only $5.00 to $15 a year to rent the small (typically 2 or 3 by 5 by 22 inches) safe deposit box most people find adequate. In some areas the cost is under $5.00. And, assuming you use the box to store such income-producing property as stocks or bonds, the rental charge is deductible from your federal income tax.

To be specific, you *should* rent a safe deposit box and put into it your valuables, hard-to-replace or irreplaceable items, including:

Any stock or bond certificates or bank savings certificates which you do not keep at your bank or with your stockbroker.

Insurance policies—except life insurance policies, which should be kept in a more accessible place in the event of your death.

Property records, including mortgages, deeds, titles.

Personal documents such as birth certificates, marriage licenses, divorce papers, citizenship papers, adoption papers, diplomas, business contracts and agreements, important legal correspondence and income tax records, passports, military discharge papers, and trust agreements.

An inventory of all household items of any value, giving the cost and purchase date of each item as a reference in case of fire or theft. This inventory should include photographs of furs and jewelry and fine pieces of art and furniture; serial numbers of TV sets, stereo sets, etc.; details about valuable coin or stamp collections you keep at home; jewels, collections of stamps or coins, heirlooms which you seldom wear or use or refer to.

A copy of your will—but *not* the original, which should be filed at your lawyer's office, kept in the hands of an executor, or in some similar protected but accessible place. Frequently a bank safe deposit box is sealed by state law for a specified period after the box owner's death.

Should you, as a married couple, own a safe deposit box jointly? How do you arrange for someone besides yourself to get in the box if need be?

The advantages of joint ownership of a safe deposit box are strongly offset by the disadvantages. You may squabble—when it comes to removing the box's contents—over which of you owns what. Or if a lawsuit is brought against one of you, this would tie up the property of the other —if it's in a jointly owned safe deposit box. As for what happens when *one* of two joint renters dies, ask your lawyer what are your own specific state laws covering this aspect.

Instead of joint ownership, you might authorize the other (or a lawyer or trusted relative) to serve as his or her "agent" if necessary. The first spouse keeps the keys and, technically at least, owns the entire contents of the safe deposit box. If the second spouse has valuables or important records of her or his own, there is no reason why this partner shouldn't have a separate box.

Once you make the decision to rent a safe deposit box, here are further rules for you to follow:

Make a list of what is in your box and put the list in a safe place at home. Your list should include: an identification of each valuable in the box; serial numbers and dates of stock or bond certificates, insurance policies, etc.; written appraisals of jewelry; the date you put each item in the box; the date you remove any item; the date of your most recent inspection. Keep this inventory up to date.

Collect receipts or other papers which prove you own the items in the box and put them in a safe place outside the box. Then you will have the essential papers should the box ever be destroyed or burglarized (most unlikely but possible).

Check your homeowner's insurance coverage to find out if it covers the contents of your safe deposit box and, if so, to what extent it insures you against loss. Also, check the agreement you sign or have signed with the institution from which you rent your box to find out if the agreement includes clauses which limit your protection. For instance, are you prohibited from putting cash or diamonds in the box?

Keep each other (husband and wife) informed about the location of your safe deposit box, the number of the box, the contents of the box, the place you keep the keys.

Of course, the odds are overwhelmingly against any loss of the contents of your safe deposit box due to a robbery or some other catastrophe. This is obvious from the way boxes are built and the location of the vaults. And remember, *nobody* but you, the box holder (and any agent you may name), has keys which can open the box.

3

HOW TO BORROW CASH AND USE CREDIT WISELY

INTRODUCTION   87
THE RIGHT AND WRONG REASONS FOR BORROWING   89
THE BASIC DO'S AND DON'TS OF CREDIT   92
HOW DO YOU ESTABLISH A CREDIT RATING?   95
   HOW TO MAINTAIN OR RESTORE A GOOD CREDIT
     RATING   98
   WHAT IS THE DIFFERENCE BETWEEN CREDIT
     REPORTS AND INVESTIGATIVE REPORTS?   99
THE BASIC TYPES AND MATURITIES OF LOANS   99
   THE SINGLE-PAYMENT LOAN   99
   THE INSTALLMENT LOAN   100
   A SHORT-TERM LOAN   100
   AN INTERMEDIATE-TERM LOAN   100
   A LONG-TERM LOAN   101
YOUR SOURCES OF LOANS IN CASH   101
   PARENTS OR OTHER RELATIVES   102
   FRIENDS   103
   ADVANCE AGAINST SALARY OR LOAN FROM
     EMPLOYER   103
   FULL SERVICE COMMERCIAL BANK   105
   LICENSED SMALL LOAN COMPANY   109
   CREDIT UNION   111
   SAVINGS BANK OR SAVINGS AND LOAN ASSOCIATION 112
   LIFE INSURANCE COMPANY   113
   INDUSTRIAL LOAN COMPANY   114

YOUR SOURCES OF LOANS IN CASH (*cont'd*)

BANK CREDIT CARD   115
SECOND MORTGAGE COMPANY   116
YOUR OWN HOME MORTGAGE   117
RURAL FAMILY LOANS   119
PAWNBROKER   119
LOAN SHARK   121

YOUR SOURCES OF CREDIT FOR GOODS AND SERVICES   122

SERVICE CREDIT   123
CHARGE ACCOUNT   123
RETAIL INSTALLMENT CREDIT   124
CREDIT CARD   124

INTEREST RATE CHARGES SIMPLIFIED   125
CREDIT CARDS   131

DIFFERENCES BETWEEN TYPES OF CREDIT CARDS   131
HOW DO YOU USE CREDIT CARDS?   133
SHOULD YOU USE A CREDIT CARD?   134
HOW TO PROTECT YOUR CREDIT CARD   135

HOW TO HOLD DOWN YOUR BORROWING COSTS   137
THE GREAT PITFALLS OF CREDIT   138

"DEBT POOLING"   139
"SEWER SERVICE"   140
"INCONVENIENT VENUE"   141
"CONFESSION OF JUDGMENT"   141
HARASSMENT   141
REPOSSESSION   142
"HOLDER IN DUE COURSE"   144
AND ALSO BEWARE THESE TRAPS!   145

HOW MUCH DEBT IS TOO MUCH DEBT?   146
BUT WHAT IF YOU FIND YOU'RE OVER YOUR HEAD
IN DEBT?   148
HOW TO GO BANKRUPT   150
THE BAFFLEGAB OF BORROWING   151

INTRODUCTION

Should you borrow money NOW?

Of course you should—*if* you have sound (to you) reasons for doing so.

Is this the RIGHT TIME *for you to borrow money?*

Of course it is—*if* your reasons for borrowing are sound and your chances of repaying your debt within a tolerable period of time are good.

"Of course" always will be the answer to both these questions assuming your debt is for goods or services you feel you need or want, your loan is in line with your income, you have a plan for regular repayments.

There are two distinct sides to the possession of money: one is saving it, the other borrowing it. In our economy, both sides are crucially important to our financial health as a nation and as individuals. And both sides make vital contributions to our financial well-being as a nation and as individuals.

It is no exaggeration to say that almost uninterrupted buying on the installment plan has become a way of life in American homes to a point where a hefty percentage of the families we consider as representing the "ideal" in our nation are never out of debt and another hefty proportion seldom are.

That was, in fact, one of the most provocative findings which emerged from a survey I made a few years ago of the finalists in the "Mrs. America Pageant"—all outstanding women, bright, talented, good-looking, superb homemakers. What leaped first from their answers was how knowledgeable the women were, how acutely aware they were of money management, how devoted they were to budgeting, even "strict" down-to-the-penny keeping of the household accounts. And what leaped next from their answers and impressed me even more was the extent to which installment buying was an essential part of their family lives.

As one contestant put it to me: "We find that the best way to obtain major items is to maintain planned debt, purchasing one major item at a time for a cost which will fit into our budget and including interest as part of that cost." In the words of another, "We consider it worth the interest cost to use someone else's money and have earlier use of a product."

The statistics underline this further. More than one out of every two U.S. families today owes installment debt. And it's a virtual certainty that you have installment debt *if:* you are married and the head of a family; you are between eighteen and thirty-five years of age; you have children, teen-agers or younger; your income is between $5,000 and $25,000 a year. Nine of every ten families with these four basic characteristics have installment debts.

I do not find the modern attitudes toward debt any cause for alarm. I see nothing wrong with paying money to use "someone else's money." I approve of "planned debt" which really is a kind of thrift. And, to an important degree, payments on an installment loan are merely replacing many old-time cash payments—like the money Americans used to dole out to the ice man or the cash we paid to the corner laundry.

In fact, I'll go beyond this and submit that the fundamental reason Americans have been borrowing so much today is precisely because they have had so much. This has intensified your desire to satisfy your aspirations rather than simply to finance your needs. And this in turn has led to unprecedented borrowing to achieve your aspirations at once.

Another factor is your increased financial security—through health insurance, Social Security, unemployment compensation, retirement pensions, employee savings and stock plans, ownership of stocks and mutual funds, life insurance, etc.—and, very importantly, the income of the working wife. All these economic cushions are helping to make obsolete the traditional goal of protection against a "rainy day." (See Chapter 1, "Your Personal Money Manager," and Part III, "Managing Your Money.")

A third similarly subtle factor is the increased *regularity* of your income, which strengthens your capacity to take on responsibility for repaying installment debts. This development stems from the fundamental fact that our economy is now dominated by the service industries —and employment is much steadier in a service-oriented economy than in a predominantly industrial society.

Other factors include: the huge amounts of financial assets you as families are building up, primarily in your homes; the dramatic extension of credit to include unsophisticated as well as sophisticated borrowers; the youthful hunger to acquire, instantly, all the things that other families have; and finally, the tendency of lenders to extend credit to borrowers at much younger ages than ever before.

And, of course, behind all the factors is the basic change that inflation has created in your attitudes toward being in debt and toward the goods and services which you appropriately may buy on time.

Perhaps as fundamental as any point is this: You, today's American, are far less interested than past generations in your legal total ownership of your toasters or automobiles or refrigerators. Instead, you are far more interested in the toasting services of that toaster, the transportation services of that automobile, the cooling services of that refrigerator. You are less and less impressed with *owning things,* more and more interested in the proper *use of things*.

THE RIGHT AND WRONG REASONS FOR BORROWING

The cheapest way to buy any thing or non-thing is to buy it for cash. You *always* save money when you do this, for there are no extra charges added to your purchase price. As a buyer for cash, you can shop around for the best buy. Also, as a buyer for cash, you don't tie up future income, you are well aware of how many dollars you actually are spending, and you are not tempted to overbuy. The reason that retailers dangle the lure of "easy credit terms" before you is that the lure does work. It does encourage you to buy more. It does increase the retailer's sales.

But when you borrow to buy some things or non-things, you get the privilege of enjoying the purchase while you pay for it. You can start using at once something you need or want instead of being forced to wait until you can accumulate the savings to finance its purchase. Your buying on credit can teach you thrift. The discipline forced on you by your installment payments can spill over and encourage you to develop excellent saving habits. Many types of credit charge accounts are more convenient than cash or checks. Credit can be a crucial assist in a financial emergency.

To me, the advantages of buying on credit far outweigh the disadvantages of the cost of credit and the possible extravagance.

THE RIGHT REASONS FOR BORROWING

Regardless of whether you are equally convinced at this point, for the moment assume you agree that borrowing money is right for you if your reasons are right.

What might those reasons be?

(1) You are establishing a household or beginning to have a family. Either of these major events in life will take a lot of money—and it's in these, your early years, that you should learn how to use credit wisely and to the best advantage for yourself.

(2) You must make some major purchases. Few Americans can buy a car out of cash on hand and few can buy furniture or appliances that way either. These big-ticket items are traditionally bought with credit. As for a house, virtually all of us borrow to finance that key purchase of our lives. (See Chapter 13, "A Roof Over Your Head," for details.)

(3) You are faced with a genuine emergency and have not as yet had the opportunity to accumulate a sufficient emergency cash fund. Borrowing to meet emergencies is about as valid a reason as there can be.

(4) There are attractive seasonal sales or specials on which you can save money if you can use a charge account or a time-payment plan or get a low-cost loan from a financial institution. This assumes that the items on sale are ones you really want or need.

(5) You need money for college or other education expenses. This also is a top-notch reason for borrowing either by the student or by the parents. In fact, borrowing for college is the normal thing in America in this era. See Chapter 10, "A College Education and How to Finance It," for details.

(6) The price of an item you will need in the future is heading sharply higher and it is ridiculous for you not to try to beat the price rise by borrowing the money to buy it now.

THE WRONG REASONS FOR BORROWING

(1) You haven't a reasonable prospect of repaying the loan but you are going ahead anyway and borrowing because you need the money or want the goods or services. Or you are borrowing to the very hilt of your capacity to repay, which means that even a minor miscalculation on your part could force you to default.

(2) You are buying something impulsively and are primarily attracted to the purchase, not because the product is of good quality and reasonably priced, but because the payment terms seem so easy and you are offered a long time to pay up. This is self-deception of the most dangerous kind from your personal financial point of view.

(3) You are charging purchases solely to boost your morale. Some individuals try to beat the blues with an extravagant shopping spree. Doing this on credit can bring on an even bigger attack of melancholy when the bills—with interest—finally come due.

(4) You are using credit to increase your status. Charging a purchase does allow you to pay for things while you're enjoying them. But credit alone can't raise your standard of living. Over the long run, if you "can't afford" certain items on your present income, you can't afford to buy them on credit.

(5) You are overusing credit generally and failing to maintain an adequate cash reserve. People who do this also tend to live hand to mouth with their cash. They build up little or no savings fund to use during medical or other emergencies. So even if they are able to repay regular debts on schedule, any unexpected financial reversal can be their complete undoing.

(6) You are using credit against the expectation of future salary increases or windfall cash. When your income is on the rise, it's tempting to figure that your next raise is a cinch. But if you go ahead with major credit expenditures and then don't get the extra money, your budget can get very, very tight in a hurry.

(7) You are borrowing to gamble on some exceedingly risky venture—as distinct from borrowing to invest in a worthy enterprise you have thoroughly investigated. Borrowing to buy stocks or real estate or invest in a small business deal is entirely in order, particularly if you are young enough to recoup if you lose. But borrowing to gamble

is begging for trouble—and the very fact that you have to borrow means that this is not extra money you can afford to lose.

(8) You are living so far beyond your income that you have to borrow to meet your current bills. In Chapter 3, in the section entitled "How Much Debt Is Too Much Debt?" you'll find several guidelines on the safe limits for borrowing. Suffice it to say here that when you must pile up debts just to manage your day-to-day living you are headed for financial disaster.

(9) You are borrowing to buy something that will be used up or worn out long before you have made the final payment for it. This caution is exceedingly flexible, though, and you must use your common sense in applying it to yourself.

For instance, it might make sense to take out a twelve-month installment loan to pay for this year's vacation, for even though you would still be paying off the loan after the vacation is a memory, it could be worth it if you wouldn't have any vacation otherwise. But it would not make sense to take out a two-year loan for this year's vacation, for in this case you would still be paying off this year's vacation when next year's vacation time rolls around.

Another illustration of this point (9) is borrowing to pay for college education or special training courses. You well may be paying off a loan years after you've completed your education but the value of your education will endure years and years after that. In this case, the value of your purchase is without time limit and cannot be measured by the yardsticks which we use for material goods. But precisely the opposite is borrowing to pay for an exceedingly expensive gown. Buy this sort of gown for cash if you have it, and if this is your deep desire. But *borrowing* to buy it? That's financial stupidity.

The Basic Do's and Don'ts of Credit

No matter where you go for credit and no matter how many different types of loans you take out in the years to come, the basic *do's* and *don'ts* of credit will remain the same. Below you'll find them in the form of a simple check list to which you can refer again and again to make sure you are obeying these most fundamental of all credit rules.

Do always keep in mind that credit costs money. When you borrow you are, in essence, renting money—and just as you must pay when you rent an apartment or a car, so you must pay when you rent money. Anything you buy on credit will cost you more money than the identical item bought for cash.

Do shop for credit as you shop for any other important purchase and buy your credit on the most advantageous terms to *you*. You can compare credit terms much more easily today than before the Truth in Lending law went into effect in 1969. Compare the price of any item bought for cash or bought on the installment plan. Find out whether it's cheaper for you to borrow from a bank or credit union and then buy the item you want for cash—or whether it's better for you to finance the purchase at the store or dealer's.

Do check with care the maximum amount of credit you can soundly and safely carry. You can do it against the guidelines you'll find in this chapter and you also can check your credit status with a responsible loan officer at your local bank, consumer finance office, credit union, other lending source. This officer is in the business of "selling" money —and nothing else—and he will want to make sure the person to whom he is selling the money is in a sound position to pay back.

Do ask lots of questions about the credit deal you are being offered, if you have any doubts at all. Insist on a written statement from the salesman showing you all charges plus the cash cost *before* you decide on buying.

Do ask yourself: would you buy the item for this amount of money in cash if you had the cash in your wallet or purse right now? Would you buy as expensive an item as the one you are considering if you had to put down the entire sum in cash now? In short, have you taken the proper *time* to make sure that this is a good purchase for you in view of the *time* it will take you to pay for it?

Do study your installment contract with utmost care and be sure you understand it before you sign it. When you sign, get a copy of the contract and keep it in a safe place.

Do keep receipts of your payments in a safe place.

Do pay off one major installment debt obligation before you take on another. Stagger your debts; don't pile them one on top of another.

Do make sure that, in the installment deal you sign, all your monthly payments are roughly equal and make sure this applies particularly to your last payment. Avoid the danger that you'll be faced with a very big final installment ("balloon" payment). (See "The Great Pitfalls of Credit" later in this chapter.)

Do have the courage to say *No!* to an installment deal if any of the above warning signals are flying—any of them.

And *do* continue saving regularly as you buy on credit. Even if you can save only a small amount each week, save it. For it's the regularity of savings and the discipline of the installment payments which will be the foundation of your own and your family's wealth.

Don't buy any item or service from any seller unless you have checked his reputation and have confidence he is a responsible retailer or dealer or whatever. Before you pledge to pay a specified part of your earnings for a protracted period, use your common sense and make sure you are dealing with a reputable businessman conducting a reputable business at a reputable place and that you can come back to him should your purchase turn out to be a lemon.

Don't buy anything you don't need or want—certainly not for credit. Learn how to handle high-pressure selling.

Don't carry several charge accounts which are seldom or never paid up. Revolving accounts make it very easy to maintain a permanent debt. But pay off each account periodically, for without this kind of self-discipline, revolving balances tend to grow ever larger (and more expensive) over periods of time.

Don't use your debts to establish your budgeting "system." Although some people would have no financial system at all if it weren't for their stack of bills, wise use of credit means month-by-month planning—not this sort of upside-down method.

Don't ever buy any thing or non-thing on credit without consulting your spouse or other person with whom you may be sharing financial responsibility and making sure that the two of you think the purchase is worth while. You must agree on any major purchase or you'll have great difficulty meeting the discipline of installment payments.

Don't be in any hurry to sign any installment contract or agreement.

Don't make the mistake of thinking you can get out of an installment debt simply by returning the merchandise you bought to the seller. What you almost surely have done when you bought the item is sign two contracts: one for the actual purchase and the second for the money to finance the purchase. In most cases, your loan contract will be sold by the retailer at once to a bank or finance company and it is to this bank or finance company that you will have to continue making your payments in full—even though your TV set may not show a picture or your dishwasher may not wash a dish or your automobile may not move a mile.

Don't rely on verbal warranties or pledges of the salesman or his boss. Get the warranties and pledges in writing.

Don't buy any item on credit which does not have a value that will outlast the installment payments. This is an extension of the flexible wrong reason No. 9 for borrowing. The key word in this rule is "value."

Don't buy anything on credit of which you will tire before you finish the installment payments. You might really ponder this "don't" when buying your four-year-old an expensive and easily breakable toy game on a twelve-month payment plan.

Don't ever borrow money from a loan shark—even if you are desperate for the cash. In fact, the more desperate you are for the money, the more insane it is for you to commit yourself to pay back interest rates ranging to 1,000 per cent a year and more for the money. This way lies financial disaster.

Don't sign any loan contract which contains blank spaces that could be filled in to your disadvantage.

And *don't* co-sign a loan for anyone unless you have complete faith in that person's ability and willingness to repay the loan. For, if the borrower whose note you co-sign defaults on the loan, *you* are responsible for paying off the entire indebtedness.

How Do You Establish a Credit Rating?

A young Army veteran, with a wife and two babies, was recently turned down for an FHA mortgage which he needed to buy a new home in eastern Texas. The reason: information at the local credit bureau showed him to be a bad credit risk. Astonished, the veteran visited the credit bureau and discovered that the reason for his credit troubles was that his former wife had run up a lot of unpaid bills just prior to their divorce. The veteran explained that under the separation agreement his estranged wife had signed a full year before she ran up the bills, she was legally responsible for all her debts and his credit record had been wrongly damaged. His credit record was cleared and he got the mortgage he needed.

The ease with which Americans can open a charge account, get a new credit card, or take out a bank loan is directly dependent on the voluminous dossiers in the files of 2,500 credit bureaus throughout the United States and of large numbers of local merchants' associations on virtually every borrower. The bureaus freely exchange this information. They sell it to retailers, banks, other lenders, credit card companies, corporations, etc.—and a credit report almost surely will be obtained on you when you apply for a job or insurance or credit.

The consumer credit reporting industry processes from 125 to 150 million credit reports each year. Just one computerized credit reporting company says it maintains 30 million files, enters 4 million "pieces of information" on individuals each month, services 14,000 subscribers, and maintains on some individuals as many as 35 to 40 open accounts on which credit performance is reported.

Credit bureaus do *not* "rate" how good or bad a credit risk you are. They simply collect, from merchants with whom you have credit, public records, other sources of information on you which can be used in turn by banks, merchants, etc., to decide whether to grant you credit. The information ranges from your name, address, occupation, employer, and earnings to your former employment and earnings record, your marital history, your moving habits, your repayment patterns on previous loans, and records of any court proceedings against you.

The lenders then decide, on the basis of information provided by the credit bureau, whether or not you are a good credit risk. The guidelines vary from lender to lender, of course. A department store may be satisfied if you are in the habit of repaying charges within thirty to sixty days, while a bank may demand that, with very few exceptions, you repay bank loan installments on the due dates.

Or lenders may summarize their policies by telling you they are rating your application in terms of the "Three C's" of Credit. These Three C's are *your:*

Character: Your personal characteristics, revealed through factual records, which indicate how you are likely to perform as a borrower. These would include your honesty, sense of responsibility, soundness of judgment, your trustworthiness.

Capacity: Your financial ability to repay your loan. Your capacity would be judged on the basis of the job you hold, the amount of money you earn, the length of time you have held this or a previous job, your prospects in this or another job.

Capital: Your assets which can serve as backing—collateral—for your loan. These assets would include your home, bank accounts, stocks and bonds, a car or cars, jewelry, valuable paintings, other tangible property.

These three qualities of Character, Capacity, and Capital form the foundation of any credit rating for you, as an individual or as a family.

To get even more specific, here are points which every lending officer will tick off when considering your application for a loan and your rating as a credit risk.

Your Employment Record: How long have you worked for the same company—although not necessarily in the same office or plant of the company?

A prime consideration is the stability of your employment. It is up to you to prove your trustworthiness by showing you have not been a job-hopper who might once again leave for a job far away from your present one when, say, less than half your loan payments have been made.

Your Previous Loans: Have you ever paid off a loan before? The theory is that, if you have repaid a loan on time before this one, you will repay this loan too. If you have defaulted on any previous loan, the danger is you'll default again. You'll almost certainly have a poor credit rating if you have any record of defaults or of repossession of items you have bought because you didn't maintain your payments or of suits for being delinquent in payments.

Your Home: Do you own your own home? Or have you lived in the apartment in which you now live for some time? If the answer is "yes" to either question, it's a sign that you probably are trustworthy.

Your Charge Accounts: Have you a record of paying your charge accounts regularly? If so, this will be a plus mark for you because it will indicate your sense of responsibility and your ability to repay.

Your Checking or Savings Accounts: Do you have either? If so, and particularly if they are at the bank to which you may be applying for a loan, this will be a great help.

Now here are six potential black marks on your credit rating:

(1) If you can't identify yourself. Surely you will have one or more of these: a driver's license, birth certificate, Social Security card, draft card, union card.

(2) If you have a "floating" address. This might be a furnished room in a rooming house or a transient hotel, a post office box number, a mail address in care of a friend. You might offset this, however, if previously you had lived in one place for a long time.

(3) If your employment is in an exceedingly unstable industry or profession and your own job is also basically volatile. If you're a ballet dancer . . . have a strictly seasonal job . . . are in a very restricted field. . . .

(4) If, in some states, you are under twenty-one or eighteen and have no adult to co-sign for you. However, many stores do extend credit to teens without a co-signer anyway, for as a group they have turned out to be good credit risks.

(5) If you apply for a loan at a bank or small loan company or other financial source far from your residence or if you have a record of dealing extensively with numerous small loan companies.

(6) If you are planning to go into the armed services before your loan is repaid. Under these circumstances, the lender almost surely will demand that a co-signer guarantee your loan repayment.

HOW TO MAINTAIN OR RESTORE A GOOD CREDIT RATING

How do you keep up a good credit record? Or *restore* one if it has gone bad? Here are the key rules:

• Avoid overloading yourself with installment debt. Note those guidelines on how much debt is too much debt for you and abide by them!

• Aim for and maintain a rainy-day fund in cash or its equivalent equal to two to three months' pay.

• Be truthful when you apply for credit and repay all your debts as agreed. But if you find you are unable to meet one or more payments on time, go to the creditors involved, explain your circumstances, and try to work out a more practical repayment schedule. The problem could be merely that payments on a loan or a purchase fall due on the twelfth of the month, though your pay check doesn't arrive until the fifteenth.

• Do everything possible to avoid such extreme measures as repossession, litigation, or having your account turned over to a collection agency. However, if any of these is threatened, go to your credit granters first, explain what happened, and in many cases they will be willing to extend your payment schedule. Or they may refer you to a reliable local credit counseling service.

But what if you are turned down for credit and believe the turndown is unwarranted? Turn to Part IV, "Your Rights and How to Get Them," Chapter 27, for details on what to do.

WHAT IS THE DIFFERENCE BETWEEN CREDIT REPORTS AND INVESTIGATIVE REPORTS?

A regular *credit report* is compiled and maintained by a credit bureau for the purpose of helping consumers obtain credit. The credit bureaus do not make use of outside investigators, who are sometimes used in insurance reporting.

The information normally accumulated in your credit record consists of identity information, including your name, address, marital status, and Social Security number; present employment, which includes the position you hold, length of employment, and income; your personal history, such as date of birth, number of dependents, previous address, and previous employment information; credit history information including your credit experiences with credit granters; and public-record information which credit granters feel is important to know.

An *investigative report* consists of much more information—including data about a consumer's character, general reputation, personal characteristics, or mode of living. The information usually is obtained through personal interviews with the consumer's neighbors, friends, or associates or with others with whom the consumer is acquainted.

Credit bureaus do not normally compile this type of report, although an employment report made by a credit bureau will often contain some investigative information.

THE BASIC TYPES AND MATURITIES OF LOANS

THE SINGLE-PAYMENT LOAN

This is precisely what its name implies: a loan you must repay in one lump sum. A single-payment loan may be a demand loan, meaning there will be no set time when you must repay but you will be obligated to pay back what you owe when the lender asks you to. Or the single-payment loan may be a time loan, meaning your loan will have a fixed maturity date and you'll have to pay back every penny on that prefixed maturity date.

A single-payment loan is usually made against collateral, meaning that you must put up certain valuable assets, such as your stocks, bonds, insurance policies, etc., to guarantee the loan repayment. The primary drawback of the single-payment loan is that you do not have to make periodic payments on it and thus you are not disciplined into reducing the loan month after month until it is all paid off. Instead you are faced with the entire repayment on a single date.

THE INSTALLMENT LOAN

This also is precisely what its name implies: a loan you must pay off in specified amounts at periodic intervals.

Usually you repay an installment loan in equal amounts every month over a period from twelve to sixty months. Usually, too, the interest cost is figured on the total amount of your loan.

In addition to these two basic types of loans, there are three major *maturities* on loans.

A SHORT-TERM LOAN

This is the type of loan you use most frequently either to buy goods or to obtain cash or to finance everyday services.

For instance, you're using short-term credit when you buy a big-ticket appliance on the installment plan and promise to pay off within twelve to thirty-six months. You are also using short-term credit when you get a cash loan—single-payment or installment payment—and promise to pay off within three years. Whether it's "cash" credit or "sales" credit, whether it's "installment" credit or "non-installment" credit, whether it's a "demand" loan or "time" loan, you're using short-term credit if you pledge to repay within a period ranging from as little as thirty days to three years.

AN INTERMEDIATE-TERM LOAN

This is the type of credit you use most often when you are financing major improvements or major repairs on your home. The maturity of this type of loan ranges from five to seven or even to ten years.

A LONG-TERM LOAN

This type is implicit in its name. A familiar example is the real estate mortgage, extended over a period ranging from twenty to thirty years or even more—and repayable in regular installments at fixed intervals, usually monthly, during the life of the loan. Of course, you may get a long-term loan for other purposes but the mortgage is the best illustration of this category.

Your Sources of Loans in Cash

If you want to buy a new TV set you don't just walk into the first TV store you pass and buy it. You look around, decide which model you prefer, then shop for the dealer who offers the set you want at the most favorable price to you.

Okay, *you* want to buy *money*.

Whatever the reasons why—whatever goods or service you want to buy or whatever you want to build or finance—you need more money than you're earning each week or are able to commit for this single purpose. Whatever the amount—$500 or $2,500 or $5,000 or whatever—you are about to borrow (buy) money and pay the interest rate (price) asked by the lender (seller).

You live in a highly competitive economy, though, and the price of money in this competitive economy, like the price of everything else, will vary considerably. There are many sources for cash loans. Many compete for your patronage on the basis of price, convenience, service. Many also compete by specializing in specific types of loans. Many of them—such as your parents, other relatives, or friends—are simply "there." But never forget this key point: you easily can pay a price (interest rate) hundreds of dollars a year *more* than you need to pay by going to a lender who is not the best for you. You easily can cheat yourself disgracefully by not shopping for your money.

Let's approach this vital aspect of your financial life in the simplest way possible. To begin with, here are your sources of loans in cash.

PARENTS OR OTHER RELATIVES

Your parents or other relatives could be your best, easiest source of low-cost or no-cost loans. Assuming they have money available and are eager to help, your search for a cash loan may end right here.

Typical maximum you may borrow:

That depends on your relatives' affluence, their attitudes toward lending you money, your needs, your relationships, etc. In short, obviously there is no "typical" maximum.

Typical annual interest rate:

Yours could be a no-interest loan or you could insist on paying the same interest rate you would pay another lender (say, what you would pay the bank on the corner). I opt strongly for paying an interest rate and also for matching at least the minimum you might be charged by an outside source of credit. But this is your loan negotiation and again the obvious point is there is no "typical" charge.

Typical maximum maturity:

There is no typical maximum maturity and, just because most loans made by the parents would have no maturity date, the loan might drag on and on. This lack of a definite maturity can be both an advantage and a disadvantage.

Advantages:

There is no legal pressure on you to meet regular monthly payments, even if you do have a moral, if not contractual, responsibility to try to pay back the loan as soon as you can.

Your parents may have a sympathetic understanding of the reasons you are borrowing and be eager to help you.

Disadvantages:

The embarrassment of having to ask your parents or other relatives for financial help.

The very lack of pressure on you to repay may make you lazy about repaying and the debt could continue hanging over your head much longer than it need to or should.

The amounts you borrow may be too large or too small, because the personal relationships will affect your judgments on both sides.

FRIENDS

A loan from a close friend or a group of close friends with sufficient extra cash and interest in you to be your loan source is in the same general category as a loan from your parents or other relatives.

This applies even though your friends may be backing you in a venture they think is as exciting and promising as you do and even though there is a stated or implied pledge on your part to let them share liberally in any profits you make, for presumably you are also making the same explicit or implied pledge to share the profits with your own relatives. And if you aren't, you should.

Typical maximum you may borrow:

None. See above.

Typical annual interest rate:

Also none. But I repeat it's only common sense to insist on paying roughly the same interest rates you would pay the local bank.

Typical maximum maturity:

None. However, again I suspect your friends will work out a maturity date of some sort—and if they don't, *you* work it out.

Advantages:

In general, the same advantages that apply to a loan from parents or other relatives apply to loans from close friends. But I warn you: a loan from friends easily can corrode your friendship even if you pay it off promptly.

Disadvantages:

The same disadvantages apply to these loans as to loans from relatives.

ADVANCE AGAINST SALARY OR LOAN FROM EMPLOYER

Most employers are reluctant to advance a salary pay check or to make a personal loan. This generality, though, by no means applies to all employers, and in fact many corporations have special departments through which employees may borrow money with a minimum of red tape. Also your boss may be an acceptable loan source for you if yours is a close friendly relationship in a small office.

But an advance against your future salary—say your next two pay checks delivered right now—means you will face two empty pay periods some days hence.

Typical maximum you may borrow:

This varies so widely from corporation to corporation and small business to small business that it would be a disservice to be specific. Also, in a small business, the maximum will depend on the business' profit picture, the employer's financial position, your relationship with the employer, your reasons for borrowing, and on and on.

Typical annual interest rate:

Usually the same interest rate that you would be charged if you went to a bank for a loan. However, I know of no employer who charges interest on a salary advance. Other conditions of the salary advance are subject to private negotiation between the employer or the corporation personnel manager and the employee.

Typical maximum maturity:

Usually six months to a year although, again, this maximum varies widely among both large and small businesses.

Advantages:

The money is there.

Your employer may be a most sympathetic lender if he knows and approves the reasons you are borrowing.

The interest rate and repayment period will be among the best available from all sources.

An advance on your salary is simply borrowing in advance money due you in the future and involves no more than that.

Disadvantages:

Borrowing money from your boss can hurt your relationship with him and place you in a sticky position.

This loan may permit him to ask and find out things about your personal financial life which you would prefer he not know.

If you take an advance on your salary, you may not be able to swing the payless pay periods and you may have to go to outside sources for cash after all.

FULL SERVICE COMMERCIAL BANK

For most of you a commercial bank will be the most convenient loan source of all. For at this bank, which is probably a mere city block or two from where you live in town or only a couple miles away if you live in the suburbs, you may get the widest variety of loans including:

Personal loan

You may apply for a personal loan, repayable in one lump sum at its due date, or you may apply for an installment loan repayable in regular monthly installments over a period of twelve, eighteen, twenty-four, or thirty-six months.

Automobile loan

You may apply for an automobile loan to finance your new or used car. These loans usually are repayable in installments ranging from twelve to forty-two or even forty-eight months. Many automobile dealers as well as other merchants help the customer arrange for bank installment financing right in their showrooms.

Check loan

You may get money simply by writing a check, assuming you qualify. Your bank automatically enters the "loan" on your monthly statement of checking account transactions.

Mortgage and home improvement loan

You may get home improvement loans with intermediate maturities under which you can repair, remodel, expand, and generally improve your home. And you may get a long-term mortgage through which you may finance the purchase of your home in the first place.

Secured loan

You may get a loan quickly and comparatively inexpensively simply by putting up collateral to back your pledge to repay the loan. You can arrange to repay this loan in monthly installments. Your collateral may include your stocks or bonds or mutual fund shares or savings account passbook or the cash surrender value of your life insurance policy.

Student loan

Banks offer several types of student loans—some government subsidized, some not.

Credit card loan

You, the owner of a bank credit card, may use your card to buy goods at stores participating in the bank's credit card plan. The bank bills you monthly, and you, the borrower, pay interest on the unpaid balance you owe on your purchases. There is no interest charge, typically, for the first twenty-five or thirty days of your unpaid balance.

Or you may use your bank credit card to borrow a limited amount of cash.

Typical maximums you may borrow:

$5,000 on a personal loan; auto loan.*
$50,000 on a mortgage loan.*
$10,000 on a home improvement loan.*
$2,500 a year on a federal-state-guaranteed student loan.
$1,000 on a check loan.
$500 to $750 on a bank credit card plan.*

Up to the amount in your savings account on a passbook loan and up to a specified proportion of the estimated value of the collateral you put up to back a secured loan.

Typical annual interest rates:

So flexible and variable from year to year and loan to loan and area to area that no "typical" figure has meaning to you for long. However, here were typical rates as of 1974.

Personal loan:	10.5 to 13%
Automobile loan:	
New car	9 to 12
Used car	11 to 16
Check loan:	12 to 18

* Although these are typical amounts in most cases, banks are *not* in any way limited to making loans in these amounts.

Mortgage loan:	8	to	11
Home improvement loan:	10	to	15
Passbook loan:	9	to	10
Secured loan:	10	to	13
Federal-guaranteed student loan:			7
Credit card loan:	12	to	18
Education loan:	9	to	12

Typical maximum maturities:*

Three to four years on personal loans, auto loans, secured loans. Five to seven years on home improvement loans.

Up to thirty or thirty-five years on first mortgages and three to ten years on second mortgages.

Up to twenty-five to thirty years on refinancing mortgages.

By regulation, up to ten years after graduation on student loans.

Advantages:

Simplicity: you fill out an application and a financial statement, have an interview with the bank loan officer, and quite likely your cash loan is approved within twenty-four hours.

Objectivity: you can get a loan whether or not you are a depositor at the bank and, although of course bank practices vary widely, generally you will qualify for a loan if your credit rating is okay and your income will enable you to handle the monthly payment.

Relatively inexpensive: rates on bank loans compare favorably with rates from most other loan sources and so do bank loan maturity terms.

No extra or hidden fees or charges; under the law, there must be full disclosure of terms.

Since co-makers are not usually required, you need not appeal to friends or business acquaintances to endorse your note.

When you have fulfilled the terms of the loan, as prescribed, you have established a valuable credit reference.

The insurance the bank may take out on your life protects your family, for should you die before the loan's repayment the insurance will repay the loan. (Note: This insurance may be comparatively costly, though.)

* Typical but actual maximums set by bank policy.

Even in instances where the insurance is optional, banks generally make it most convenient for you to obtain credit life insurance plus health and accident insurance at the time the loan is made.

Disadvantages:

The requirements—your personal financial standing, credit rating—are sometimes more rigid than other lenders may demand.

You will be penalized if you take out an installment loan and don't meet your monthly installments on schedule. The penalty is often a flat fee of 5 per cent, plus interest, for each delinquency. State laws generally prescribe allowable charges for delinquency.

How to use "ready credit":

How does this form of credit work? Who qualifies for it? When is it economical to use it and when not?

Ready credit is an automatic line of credit offered by your bank. In some cases its reserve is an extension of your checking account. In others the reserve may be kept in a separate account involving special checks. Usually the reserve is between $500 and $1,000, but it may run up to $5,000.

In either case, the overdraft check or special check you may write becomes a loan as soon as it reaches your bank. In either case also, the typical interest rate, including credit life insurance, is 1 per cent a month on the basis of the daily outstanding balance, which works out to a true annual interest rate of at least 12 per cent. Typically, no interest charge is made unless and until you actually use your special line of credit, and the interest charge stops when you repay the amount you have withdrawn from your reserve.

"Ready credit" is granted by a signed agreement to qualified customers and the requirements for eligibility are generally stricter than those for ordinary bank loans because it is unsecured credit and, once granted, is available year after year to the responsible borrower.

As an illustration of the costs involved at 1 per cent a month interest, let's say you overdrew your checking account by $100. If you repaid the amount one month later, the cost to you would be $1.00. If you repaid the total after one week, the cost would be 23¢. If you repaid it in one day, the cost would be 3¢.

Under what circumstances is it to your advantage to use this type of credit and when is it a disadvantage? Here are the answers:

• If you spot a major bargain, an appliance selling at a big discount, for example, you probably would save by using the overdraft plan. Here, the amount of interest you would pay would be comfortably covered by your savings on the appliance, assuming you repaid the special loan within a few weeks or even a few months.

• If an emergency arises on a weekend, or when you are far from home, a reserve credit line may be the easiest and surest way to raise emergency funds.

• If you are a chronically bad bookkeeper, the interest on a reserve credit line might be less costly to you than a pile of service charges for department stores or for overdraft checks. It might also save you the tremendous embarrassment of bouncing checks.

• If you are self-employed or if your income goes into sharp but temporary dips, this credit may provide you with enough peace of mind to make it worth the interest you pay.

To save on interest expense, a fundamental guide is that your line of ready credit should be strictly for short-term purposes and your over-drafts should be repaid as quickly as possible. Thus, "ready credit" is *not* usually the right type for you when you're paying longer-term debts —financing a car, a planned home improvement, your college education. Banks offer other types of loans more appropriate for these purposes and generally at lower interest rates.

LICENSED SMALL LOAN COMPANY

Over the years, leading small loan companies the nation over have spent countless tens of millions of dollars to advertise their willingness and readiness to extend financial aid to you, the little fellow. They have boasted that they exist to help solve your emergency problems and the littler you are the more welcome you are. Their very name—small loan company—inspires the trust of the would-be borrower. (Other well-known names are "consumer finance company" and "personal finance company." All have the same appeal.)

There is no doubt that these companies have filled and do fill an important place in our financial structure. You will note from the interest rate range below that the small loan companies charge a comparatively high rate of interest—but there are explanations. For one thing, they borrow part of their own capital from banks so they themselves are paying a high rate of interest to get the money to lend in turn to you.

For another, small loan companies lend to individuals who do not have top credit ratings and who well might receive a flat "no" from a local bank. Inevitably, they have to write off a number of these risky loans or spend considerable money and time collecting the money due them.

Small loan companies specialize in personal and automobile loans and offer both single-payment and installment loans. As for security, the usual requirement of the small loan companies is nothing more than your promise to pay: i.e., your signature. Under certain conditions, they also ask additional security in the form of a chattel mortgage on your household furniture, to make sure that you will honor your debt.

If, though, you have a questionable credit rating and do not have a regular source of income, the small loan company may demand that a qualified friend co-sign for your loan. If you, the borrower, then fail to meet your payments, your co-signer will become responsible for the unpaid balance of your loan.

Typical maximum you may borrow:

$500 to $1,000—with the actual limits (some are higher) depending on state law.

Typical annual interest rate:

State laws generally prescribe interest rate ceilings but rates often are two to three times higher than bank interest charges.

Typical maximum maturities:

One to three years.

Advantages:

Frequently you can obtain a smaller loan from a small loan company than from a bank. You may even borrow just a few dollars if that is all you need.

The small loan companies are not as selective as banks. They can take greater risks just because they charge higher rates.

As the charge is based on the unpaid balance of your loan, you pay only for the credit you actually use.

Suits for collection are relatively infrequent and lawyers' fees are rarely imposed on a delinquent borrower.

If you have a grievance against a small loan company, you may take it to the state banking department and get advice and help at no expense.

You also may take a gripe about a small loan company to the Consumer Affairs Center of the National Consumer Finance Association, 1000 16th Street, N.W., Washington, D.C. 20036. Telephone (202) 638-1340.

Disadvantages:

The interest rates are much higher than those charged by full service commercial banks.

The maximum amount you can borrow is often less than you can get from banks and less than you need.

You may not be able to get the loan without a co-signer.

CREDIT UNION

A credit union may be the ideal answer to your borrowing problem if you have access to one and the union is efficiently managed.

Few, if any, regular lending agencies have the credit union's advantages of low operating costs, tax exemption, and often free office space, clerical and managerial help too. Thus naturally no other type of lender can afford to make loans at the low rates credit unions charge or can compete with the credit unions on service to borrowers.

Credit unions usually are formed by members of a closely knit group—such as employees of a business firm or members of a labor union, club, or lodge—and their purpose is implicit in their name. The union extends credit to its members when the members need the help.

There are now more than 22,500 credit unions operating in offices, churches, professional organizations, and communities across the country, chartered under federal or state laws. Moreover, if there isn't one around and you are part of a well-defined group, it is not too difficult to form one of your own. You can get help and precise rules for creating a credit union with either a federal or state charter by writing to CUNA International, Inc., P.O. Box 431, Madison, Wis. 53701.

Credit unions specialize in small personal loans, particularly to a member faced with a sudden emergency. Credit unions also make automobile and home improvement loans.

Typical maximum you may borrow:
Up to $2,500 on your personal signature.

Typical annual interest rates:
Maybe as little as ¾ of 1 per cent per month. Usually the lowest of any major category of lender.

Typical maximum maturities:
Two to three years.

Advantages:
The interest rates may substantially undercut rates charged by other lenders. A credit union is probably the cheapest borrowing source available to you.

You pay no extra fees and credit life insurance usually is automatically included in the stated interest rate.

You are dealing with fellow workers or friends or lodge members who have in common a special interest in the financial welfare of all credit union members.

Disadvantages:
You must be a member to borrow. This means not all of us have the opportunity to borrow through one of these co-operatives.

You may hesitate to reveal your borrowing needs and financial problems to the committee of fellow workers who must approve your loan request.

SAVINGS BANK OR SAVINGS AND LOAN ASSOCIATION

Savings banks exist in only seventeen of our fifty states, mostly in the Northeast. Savings and loan associations exist in all states, but in most they are given power to lend primarily for the purchase of home and for home improvements.

Both types of savings institutions specialize in mortgages and home improvement loans. (Savings and loan associations are authorized to make mobile home loans and educational loans too.) Savings banks also frequently make personal loans.

Typical maximum you may borrow:

Up to 90 per cent of your passbook savings total for passbook loans.

Up to $3,000 for personal loans.

Up to $30,000 for mortgages.

Up to $10,000 for home improvement loans.

Typical annual interest rates:

Slightly less than a commercial bank for passbook loans and home improvement loans; about the same for other types of loans.

Typical maximum maturities:

One year for passbook loans and up to three years for personal loans.

Up to twenty-five to thirty years for mortgages.

Up to ten years for home improvement loans.

Advantages:

Although you are borrowing your own money when you make a passbook loan, your net cost is far less than on any regular installment loan and you are disciplining yourself into maintaining your savings.

Savings institutions specialize in mortgage and home improvement financing. Their rates are competitive and their services superior.

Disadvantages:

Really none.

LIFE INSURANCE COMPANY

This may be your indisputably number *one* source for money. In fact, it is a source I suggest you check *before* you turn to any other. After a period of two or three years the premiums you have paid on a regular life insurance policy (not a term policy) become a prime cash asset. Your insurance company will then lend you your cash surrender value directly at a specified and relatively very low interest charge.

Typical maximum you may borrow:

Generally up to 95 per cent of your life insurance policy's cash surrender value. And since every year the cash value of your policy increases, every year the total you may borrow increases too.

Typical annual interest rates:

Five per cent simple interest in New York, 6 per cent simple annual interest in other states; only 4 per cent on a veteran's life insurance policy. The interest rate will be specified in the policy.

Typical maximum maturities:

None.

Advantages:

The loan is a cinch to get. You merely ask your company to send you the loan forms, fill them out, return them, and the cash is yours.

The interest charged is very low by today's standards—a flat rate on the unpaid balance of your loan without any extras or hidden charges. Usually the company will collect the interest you owe at the time you pay your premiums: quarterly, semi-annually, or annually.

You are not held to any specified time for repayment. This may be an advantage if you cannot take on the burden of regular payments right away.

Disadvantages:

The amount of your loan decreases the face value of your life insurance policy—which means, of course, that you're temporarily undercutting the protection of your family.

The absence of a specified time for repayment might lull you into maintaining the loan indefinitely, thus continuing to pay interest indefinitely and decidedly increasing the over-all cost of your loan.

INDUSTRIAL LOAN COMPANY

The "industrial" part of this source's name stems from the fact that the companies make loans mostly to industrial workers—not to the industrial corporations employing them.

Industrial loan companies fill a gap between the commercial bank and the small loan company. They make a wide variety of loans, ranging from a regular personal or auto loan to a second mortgage on your home.

Typical maximum you may borrow:

Up to $5,000 on personal loans.
State laws prescribe limits on second mortgages.

Typical annual interest rates:

Comparatively high compared to banks but the companies *may* make loans at lower interest rates than small loan companies.

Typical maximum maturities:

One to three years on personal or auto loans.
Ten years on second mortgages.

Advantages:

They can make larger loans than small loan companies and might charge lower interest rates.

They will accept a wide variety of your possessions as collateral, ranging from your home to pieces of your furniture.

They might lend you money when you do not have a sufficient credit rating to get a loan from a bank.

Disadvantages:

Interest rates are higher than charged by banks.

Industrial loan companies frequently insist on co-signers—which means you must ask your friends or business acquaintances to guarantee the repayment of your loan and this you well may hate to do.

BANK CREDIT CARD

With your bank credit card you may not only charge items ranging from hotel bills and air travel to TV sets and fur coats; you also may get "instant" cash loans. At a few banks you even can get an instant $50 to $100 loan simply by slipping the bank's magnetically coded plastic card into a machine.

Typical maximum you may borrow:

$400 to $5,000 at any bank honoring the card.

Typical annual interest rates:

Interest is not charged on any balance if paid within normal cycle from purchase date-billing date to repayment time—usually a span of twenty-five to thirty-five days from the date of billing.

Then interest accrues only on balances "rolled over" or unpaid after fee billing time allowance.

Annual rate of interest charged at that time ranges from 12 to 18 per cent (as of 1974).

Typical maximum maturities:

One to two years.

Advantages:

It's quick, "easy" convenient credit.

You don't have to ask anyone directly for a loan; you just use your own previously established line of credit and get it.

Disadvantages:

That interest rate of up to 18 per cent a year if you are not careful about paying.

The temptation to overuse this source of credit just because it's so easy.

SECOND MORTGAGE COMPANY

These companies do precisely what their name implies: lend you money against your home on a second mortgage so you can meet your pressing obligations. On top of the first mortgage you are carrying to finance your original home purchase, you take out a second mortgage for a given period of time and then use the money raised from the second mortgage for purposes which may have nothing whatsoever to do with your home.

But this can be an exceedingly expensive source for money—and an unsound borrowing method too. The interest stated on your mortgage may not seem high but the extra charges can multiply the actual rate you are paying. At the same time, your second mortgage may run for years—meaning you'll be paying for the money long after you have

forgotten the purpose for which you borrowed. And this, you will recall, breaks one of the cardinal rules for borrowing.

Typical maximum you may borrow:

Up to $10,000.

Typical annual interest rates:

The legal maximum in the state plus "charges" which, I repeat,
can build up to startlingly high percentages.

Typical maximum maturities:

Three to ten years.

Advantages:

Quick way to raise funds for just about any purpose.

Repayment can be strung out over a number of years.

Disadvantages:

A second mortgage can add a financial burden undermining your
entire investment in your house in bad times.

You take on a relatively long-term debt—three to ten years—to purchase a product or service which may have a much shorter life.

You could, without realizing it, commit yourself to paying an excessively steep rate for the money.

YOUR OWN HOME MORTGAGE

You may get a second mortgage on your home and raise substantial sums from other lenders besides a second mortgage company, of
course. Or you may refinance your mortgage, take out a new mortgage
with a new long-term life and new interest rate, to raise hefty sums. This
you may do through the institution which gave you your first mortgage
or through another bank, savings association, or an individual investor.

The trend toward borrowing on your own home to raise money for
non-home purposes exploded in the 1960s and the trend is apparently
here to stay. What this represents, in effect, is the dramatic development of a *twenty- to thirty-year installment loan* as against the familiar
two- to three-year installment loan. The long-term mortgage is the ve-

hicle through which money is raised for everything from college costs to pleasure boats.

Typical maximum amounts you may borrow:
Depends on your deal.

Typical annual interest rates:
The going rate for first mortgages.

Typical maximum maturities:
From ten years up to original life—twenty, twenty-five, thirty years —of first mortgage, depending on age of the property.

Advantages and disadvantages:
This trend toward using the home mortgage for purposes far removed from the original purchase of the home is so powerful that it demands more than a few short sentences stating the pros and cons. Thus read the following real-life illustration with care:

Mr. H.B.A. is a successful lawyer in his forties who bought a $50,-000 house in a suburb near New York fourteen years ago with the help of a 6 per cent mortgage. H.B.A. now has one son in college, another entering this fall, and an extremely popular teen-age daughter. In addition to tuition fees, he therefore has suddenly developed a wallet-emptying list of new "necessities": a car for the boys, a swimming pool, new terrace furniture, etc.

So H.B.A. recently refinanced his mortgage and raised $12,000 in new cash to be repaid over a twenty-year period. He has bought the car for his boys, he is decorating the terrace, and he is about to build the swimming pool. To him, this is an excellent deal—a way to borrow "instant cash" on the most painless repayment terms.

But right as the deal seems to H.B.A., it's wrong from a strictly dollars-and-cents viewpoint. For H.B.A. is breaking that fundamental rule of sound finance: he is "borrowing long to buy short." Years after his son's auto will have been junked, he'll be paying interest on the loan to purchase it. By committing himself to pay interest over a twenty-year period, he'll end up paying far more on this loan than he would have paid on a two- or three-year loan at twice his borrowing rate.

That's H.B.A. Now let's take *you* as an illustration. Say you borrow $3,000 on a conventional installment loan, pay 6 per cent interest in advance, agree to repay over a two-and-a-half-year period. Your true interest rate is roughly double 6 per cent. Your monthly repayment will be $115. Your total interest cost will come to $450 ($3,000× .06×2.5=$450.)

Or say you borrow $3,000 by refinancing your mortgage over a twenty-year period. Your interest rate is a simple 6 per cent a year. Your monthly repayment will be only about $21.50. But over the twenty years the 240 monthly payments will total $5,160—an out-of-pocket interest cost to you of $2,160. In addition, you'll pay at least $250 for closing costs.

In the first case, your interest cost is $450. In the second, it's $2,285 to $2,410—about five times more.

Now I can summarize the pros and cons, confident that you grasp the nuances. The easy appeal of refinancing a home mortgage to obtain cash for non-home equity purposes is undeniable but it glosses over the tremendous difference in interest costs. Like other financing methods which on the surface seem easiest and least expensive, this one turns out to be among the hardest and most costly.

RURAL FAMILY LOANS

If you are a farm family living in a rural area, you may be able to get a rural family farm or home loan at a comparatively low interest rate through a nearby production credit association. These are co-operative associations created to assist in providing credit for people living in rural regions—and you also may be able to get a loan to finance your farm or farm-related business or other enterprise.

You'll get details on these loans and your possible eligibility for them from the production credit association serving your area or from the Farm Credit Administration, 490 L'Enfant Plaza, N.W., Washington, D.C., 20578.

PAWNBROKER

The pawnbroker is not the worst of all loan sources but he's close to it. He certainly must be classed as a source of last resort for the desperate borrower. You'll not only pay an enormous annual interest rate on small loans; you'll also be able to borrow only a fraction of the auction value of the asset you pledge as collateral. And to get your funds, you'll have to turn over your property (which you may badly need) to the pawnbroker for the life of the loan.

Your loan usually will have a very short life and in many parts of the country you must redeem your collateral within thirty to sixty days or it becomes the property of the pawnbroker, who may then offer it for sale. A pawnbroker's terms underscore how limited are the options of the desperate borrower. The person least able to afford horrendous interest rates always is the one who pays them.

Typical maximum you may borrow:

Up to 50 per cent (but possibly 60 per cent) of the auction value of the asset you pledge.

Typical annual interest rates:

Three to four times higher than rates on personal loans charged by most major lending institutions.

Typical maximum maturities:

180 days, possibly with the privilege of a 180-day extension.

Advantages:

You have complete privacy, need not give any information about yourself or your financial circumstances. The pawnbroker doesn't care who you are so long as he's assured the asset you are pledging isn't stolen property.

You can borrow money at once against your possession and, if you need the cash in a matter of hours, this can be a crucial factor.

If you are in a very volatile profession—the theater, say—you can get periodic loans by pawning and redeeming the same asset over and over again.

Disadvantages:

It's an excessively expensive way to borrow.

You do not have the use of your asset while the loan is outstanding —and you might need that asset to earn an income. (A musical instrument, for instance, or a typewriter or special tools.)

You can borrow only a small percentage of the value of your assets.

LOAN SHARK

Absolutely at the bottom of any list of loan sources is the loan shark—in every way an evil source, lending money to the desperate, innocent, and ignorant at sinfully high and openly illegal rates. He is a racketeer charging usurious rates for money and threatening punishment if the repayment is not on schedule.

A typical deal might be "7.50 for 5"—$7.50 for $5.00 borrowed until payday next week. That may seem only $2.50 in interest on your $5.00 loan, but it's actually 2,600 per cent a year, and that's a hellish rate by any yardstick. Moreover, the loan shark usually will try to keep you from repaying the entire sum you owe, for if part of your loan remains outstanding at all times, he can build up the interest you owe to ever higher totals. At the same time, he threatens you with punishment ranging from broken bones to death itself for failure to repay.

Yet the brutal fact is that the loan shark continues to thrive. Even though the Truth in Lending law forbids the collecting of debts by violent means, loan-sharking is a multibillion-dollar business dominated by organized crime. Even though there are many alternative sources for loans, these crooks can and do get away with charges running 1,000 per cent, 2,000 per cent, or more a year and a conservative estimate is they are bilking the poor out of more than $350 million each year.

How do you spot a loan shark? Be suspicious *if* he:

does not show his state license prominently;

dates a loan prior to the time you get the money;

asks you to sign the papers before the figures are filled in;

requires more than one note for one loan;

refuses to give you a copy of the papers you signed or receipts for payments;

requires you to buy expensive insurance.

Get legal advice immediately if, when you attempt to repay part of a debt, the lender says you must repay the entire principal or none.

Appeal to local or state legal authorities at once if, when you admit to the lender that repayment is difficult, he sends you to someone else who seeks another fee in addition to the interest owed.

If a reputable lender's plan for repayment seems too difficult for you, turning to a disreputable lender will only intensify your problems.

Typical maximum amount you may borrow:

None.

Typical annual interest rates:

500 to 2,600 per cent.

Typical maximum maturities:

None.

Advantages:

None.

Disadvantages:

Endless. The loan shark as a source for money is truly unspeakable.

YOUR SOURCES OF CREDIT FOR GOODS AND SERVICES

When you have a telephone installed in your apartment or house, make a number of phone calls, receive a bill, and pay the bill *after* you have used the phone, you have been using credit. Only instead of a loan in the form of cash, you are getting credit in the form of the service provided to you by the telephone company. The same goes for an electric light bill or a gas bill or doctor bill or dentist bill.

You receive the service. The service is unmistakably, indisputably worth money. You do not, however, pay for the service until usually thirty days or more after you've taken advantage of the service. This is credit.

When you open a charge account at a local store, buy goods you want or need, use the goods, receive a bill the month after your purchase—and pay the bill usually at least thirty days later, you have been using credit too. This time the credit is in the form of the goods provided to you by the store. This is credit just as much as a loan in cash is —with the vital distinction that the loan comes via goods given to you with the clear understanding that you will pay later under an agreed-upon schedule.

When you sign a charge account agreement, you have applied for credit. When you have filled in the lines of the application form asking about your income, outstanding debts, assets, family responsibilities, etc., you have in effect done the same thing you do when you fill out an application for a cash loan.

Similarly, when you sign a retail installment contract to buy an important product—TV set, furniture, kitchen appliances, a car—this too is a loan in the form of credit for the merchandise you are buying on time. The contract spells out the terms you, as buyer, and the merchant, as seller, agree upon. You, the buyer, do not own the goods until *after* you pay for them and if you do not meet the terms of your contract the seller may take back (repossess) the goods.

After you've signed an installment contract, you may receive instructions in the mail that you are to make your payments not to the merchant who sold you the TV set or auto or furniture, but instead to a bank or finance company. This means simply that the merchant has sold your contract or "paper" to the financial institution named in order to replenish his cash so he can continue offering installment contracts to other customers. That's all it means—just that you must make your payments to the financial institution which took over your contract.

Here are the types of credit you can get today in the form of goods and services and examples of these credit sources.

SERVICE CREDIT

Sources: Utility companies; physicians; dentists; hospitals.

What it is: This is the free credit you use to get vital services such as utilities and professional help. You pay for the services only after you have taken advantage of them. Your debt is usually payable within thirty days after the service has been rendered.

CHARGE ACCOUNT

Sources: Department stores; other types of retail stores.

What it is: An *open* (*thirty-day*) *account* is an account in which the store accepts your promise to pay for the goods you buy, usually within thirty days of your purchase.

A *revolving account* is one in which the store states a maximum amount of money you may owe the store at any one time. The limit is decided when you open the account and is based on your income and credit rating. You in turn agree to pay a stated amount on your balance every month and to pay interest on the unpaid balance you owe.

A *budget account* or *flexible account* is an account in which your monthly installment payments to the store are based on the size of your account balance and interest is charged on the unpaid amount. For instance, if your account balance is $100 you might be expected to make monthly installment payments of $25 each.

A *coupon credit plan* is an account in which you are given "credit coupons" which you may use in the store as cash while you pay for the coupons over, say, six months. This eliminates a monthly billing to you and the nuisance of detailed bookkeeping by the store.

RETAIL INSTALLMENT CREDIT

Sources: Department stores; appliance stores; furniture stores; automobile dealers; hardware stores; sales finance companies; door-to-door salesmen of big companies selling books, magazines, cosmetics, hardware items, etc.

What it is: This is the credit you use when you buy such big-ticket items as automobiles, vacuum cleaners, other household appliances, encyclopedias, the like. You usually make a down payment and then sign a contract to pay off within a period ranging from a few months to as much as five years in regular weekly or monthly amounts which you and the seller agree upon and which are stated in your contract. The retailer adds a finance charge to the cash price of the article and you, the buyer, do not own what you have bought until you have completed your payments.

Sales finance companies specialize in auto loans but also finance such big items as boats, mobile homes, major home appliances.

CREDIT CARD

Sources: Issuers of travel and entertainment cards; airlines; oil companies; banks.

What it is: This is an identification card permitting you, the holder, to charge a wide variety of goods and services simply on your signature.

You agree, in most cases, to pay for all you charged once a month. If you make only a partial payment on your account, your account is automatically treated as a revolving account and interest is charged accordingly.

If you have an airline card, you use it to charge air trips; an oil card, to charge gas and other purchases at a gas or service station; a travel and entertainment card, to charge travel and all sorts of hotel, restaurant, and entertainment bills the world over. This card is an automatic charge account at all the participating businesses in the plan to which you belong and may give you charge accounts at thousands of places.

If you have an all-purpose bank credit card, you also have automatic charge accounts at all the businesses participating in the bank's plan, which can include thousands of places all over the world.

The card issuer gets a record of what you have charged from the business at which you have charged a purchase of goods or services. The issuer then bills you, the holder of the card, once a month for the total of your charges. You write one check a month covering what you owe. If you don't pay off within twenty-five days on a bank credit card, your account also is automatically treated as a revolving account and interest is charged accordingly. You are expected to pay for charges on travel and entertainment cards upon receipt of a bill unless it is a major item which may be paid for in installments set up at time of purchase. If you haven't paid your debt within sixty days after receipt of your bill, you must pay a late charge and your card may be revoked.

INTEREST RATE CHARGES SIMPLIFIED

The primary purpose of the Truth in Lending law is to help you understand just how much it costs you to borrow money either in the form of cash or in the form of goods and services.

That is why the law makes it mandatory for the lender or merchant to provide complete information to you. For the theory is that, once you have this information and you know how much the credit costs, you will be in a position to judge whether or not it is worth while for you to borrow—and if you decide it is, you will be able to compare the costs at various sources.

Despite the law, though, most borrowers are still in an interest rate labyrinth. Even sophisticated borrowers admit they are still befuddled by the various ways interest charges are stated. As for most amateurs, they readily confess they are lost in the maze. Shockingly, a study made years *after* Truth in Lending became law disclosed that only two out of three borrowers knew what interest rate they were paying on their used car loans. Even more shocking, one in seven didn't even know the rate of interest they were being charged on their home mortgages! This is something like buying a house without bothering to inquire about the price.

Thus, I think the easiest way to guide you through this labyrinth is to pretend the law doesn't compel disclosure and to take you through a series of fundamental questions and their answers.

Q. What is the annual percentage rate?

A. The annual percentage rate (APR) is the key yardstick by which you can measure and compare the costs of all types of credit. It is the basic interest rate you pay when you borrow—essentially a simple annual rate which relates the finance charge to the amount of credit you get and to the amount of time you have the money. With this information, you can compare financial terms offered by competing lenders, regardless of the terms of the loan or the amounts of credit offered or the difference in state laws.

When you know the annual percentage rate and the finance charge, you know the cost of borrowing money.

Q. What is the finance charge?

A. This is the total of all charges you are asked to pay to get credit. Among the charges which must be included in the finance charge are interest, loan fees, finder's fee, service charge, points, investigation fees, premiums for life insurance if this is required, amount paid as a discount.

Some costs are *not* part of the finance charge, though: for instance, taxes, license fees, certain legal fees, some real estate closing costs, other costs which you would pay if you were using cash instead of credit.

Q. If I borrow $1,200 for twelve months at a dollar cost of $6.00 per $100, or $72 for the year, what rate of interest am I paying?

A. That depends on your terms of repayment. If you repay the total amount of $1,200 plus $72 at the end of the year, your interest rate is a simple 6 per cent.

But if you repay in twelve monthly installments of $106 each, your interest rate is almost double 6 per cent, or 11.08 per cent, to be precise.

Your dollar cost is still $72 but, because you are paying off steadily throughout the year, you don't have the use of your $1,200 for the full year. In effect, you have the use of only about half the original amount for the full year.

This table explains it clearly:

DETAILS	SINGLE PAYMENT LOAN	INSTALLMENT LOAN
Amount of loan	$1,200	$1,200
Term of loan	1 year	1 year
Charge for loan	$72	$72
Dollars per $100	$6.00	$6.00
Monthly payments	None	12 @ $106
Simple annual interest rate	6%	11.08%

It is the very easy payment method of an installment loan which increases an apparent 6 per cent interest rate to an annual percentage rate of almost 12 per cent.

Q. What is an "add-on" rate?

A. It is one of two major ways (the other is directly below) you may pay interest on an installment loan. When you pay the *add-on* rate, your finance charge is added to the principal at the time you take out the loan and you pay the total of the two. In the preceding illustration, for instance, you borrow $100; 6 per cent is your add-on finance charge; you pay back $106; your true annual interest rate is 11.08 per cent.

Here is a further translation of the add-on rate:

IF YOU'RE CHARGED		THE TRUE ANNUAL INTEREST RATE IS
$4.00 per $100	or 4% per year	7.4%
$4.50 per $100	or 4½% per year	8.31
$5.00 per $100	or 5% per year	9.23
$5.50 per $100	or 5½% per year	10.15
$6.00 per $100	or 6% per year	11.08
$8.00 per $100	or 8% per year	14.8
$10.00 per $100	or 10% per year	18.5
$12.00 per $100	or 12% per year	22.2

Q. What is the "discount" rate?

A. Under the discount method, the second major way you may pay interest on an installment loan, the finance charge is deducted from the principal of your loan at the time you get the money. Again using the preceding illustration, you borrow the $100; 6 per cent is your finance charge discounted in advance from the loan; you receive $94; your true annual interest rate is 11.58 per cent.

In this case you also begin paying back your loan within a month and don't have the use of your $94 for the entire year.

Here is a further translation of the discount rate.

IF YOU'RE CHARGED	THE TRUE ANNUAL INTEREST RATE IS
$5.00 per $100 per year	9.57%
$6.00 per $100 per year	11.58
$7.00 per $100 per year	13.61
$8.00 per $100 per year	15.68

Q. Is a 6 per cent interest rate ever a simple 6 per cent annual rate (or 8 per cent or 9 per cent)?

A. A 6 per cent annual rate is 6 per cent simple annual interest if you borrow the $100 for one year and repay it one year later with the $6.00 added on—or a total of $106 in a *single payment*. (Or $108 or $109.)

A 6 per cent mortgage also is a true 6 per cent a year, for you are paying the 6 per cent on the *declining balance* of your mortgage, not on the original total.

Q. What if I'm charged interest monthly on my unpaid balance?

A. If you're charged monthly on the unpaid balance you owe, then:

¾% per month	is 9% simple annual rate
⅝	is 10
1	is 12
1¼	is 15
1½	is 18
2	is 24
2½	is 30
3½	is 42

Q. How can I compare the dollar cost of different ways of charging interest?

A. Take as an example a $500 loan to be repaid in twelve monthly installments. If the rates charged are:

• 1 per cent per month on the unpaid balance, the dollar cost will be about $32.

• 6 per cent annual interest on the unpaid balance, the dollar cost will be about $16.

• 6 per cent annual interest "add-on," the dollar cost will be about $30.

If the payments are spread over eighteen months, each payment would be smaller, but the total dollar cost would of course be higher. For example, at 1 per cent per month on the unpaid balance, the cost over eighteen months would be about $47 compared to $32 for twelve months.

Q. Why does the percentage rate on an installment loan for twelve months sound so much higher than the dollar charge?

A. Because the dollar charge is applied to the total amount of money you borrow, but on an installment loan you do not have the use of the money for the twelve months and this increases the percentage rate charged.

Q. If I pay back a twelve-month installment loan in six months, will I get back half the interest added to my loan?

A. No. You will get back less because in the first six months you've had the use of most of the loan funds, so it is only fair that you pay more of the interest in the first six months than in the last.

To illustrate, in the first month of your twelve-month loan, you have the use of 12/12ths of the money. In the final month of your twelve-month loan, you have the use of only 1/12th of the money.

Your rebate of interest on your installment loan will be figured on the basis of the "Rule of 78s" formula. In this formula, the total of the number of months for the loan equals 78: 100 per cent of the interest due on a twelve-month loan thus equals 78/78ths.

In the first month of your twelve-month loan, you pay off 12/78ths of the interest; in the second, 11/78ths of the interest; in the third, 10/78ths of the interest and so on to the last month, when you pay 1/78th of the interest.

Now say you pay off your twelve-month loan at the end of the sixth month. You have already paid off 12/78ths, 11/78ths, 10/78ths and on through 7/78ths. The total of 12+11+10+9+8+7 equals 57. What's left is 21/78ths—or about 27 per cent of the interest initially added on to your loan. And that 27 per cent, not 50 per cent, is what your rebate would total.

It *is* a complicated formula and you need not puzzle over it. But should you ever ask for a rebate of loan interest and question why it is less than you think is due you, refer to the "Rule of 78s" for the explanation.

Q. What about the charges on bank credit card and revolving credit accounts?

A. Finance charges on these accounts are usually expressed as a percentage of the unpaid balance per month, as of the billing date. This is a simple monthly rate, which is then multiplied by 12 to give you the annual percentage rate. Thus:

A monthly rate of 1½ per cent becomes an annual percentage rate of 18 per cent.

A monthly rate of 2 per cent becomes an annual percentage rate of 24 per cent.

A monthly rate of 2½ per cent becomes a yearly 30 per cent.

3 per cent becomes 36 per cent.

And so it goes. . . .

Q. Why is the rate on credit card accounts higher than the rate on a simple installment loan?

A. The main reason, say the banks, is that the amounts are smaller and the monthly processing expenses are higher. Generally, the monthly processing on a regular installment loan involves only one operation— recording the monthly payment. With a credit card account, the bank or retailer, etc., must make a record of the charge every time the card is used, total the charges at the end of the billing period, compute the interest on any unpaid balance, make up a bill, mail it, and record your payment.

Q. How are mortgage rates quoted?

A. Mortgage rates have been traditionally described in terms of simple annual interest rates. However, if points, a finder's fee, or certain other charges are required, these now—under the Truth in Lending law— must be included in the finance charge. These "extras" make the true annual rate appear slightly larger than before the law went into effect.

Q. Why are mortgage rates lower than rates on installment loans?

A. The average cost to the lender per dollar loaned is lower for a mortgage loan because mortgage loans are substantially larger than most other types. Their sheer size helps to offset the monthly processing expenses, permitting the lender to pass the saving on to the borrower in the form of a lower interest rate.

Q. What can I do when no credit charge is quoted at all?

A. This is illegal. But, for illustration, let's say a sewing machine is offered to you at $100 and you can pay for the item in twelve monthly installments of $9.00 for a year. Multiplying the monthly payment by twelve will give you $108. You are therefore paying $8.00 or a 15.8 per cent true interest rate for the equivalent of an installment loan of $100.

CREDIT CARDS

DIFFERENCES BETWEEN TYPES OF CREDIT CARDS

You can now use credit cards to pay for:

tooth extractions, tombstones, and taxi rides;

driving lessons, diamonds, and dog kennel fees;

ambulance service, apartment rent, and auto license fees;

music lessons, movie admissions, and marriage costs;

and savings bonds and scuba diving instructions, church tithes and college tuition, garbage removal and psychiatric care . . .

In 1975 nearly 12,000 banks were participating in credit card plans and more than 65 million bank credit cards alone were in circulation. About 6 million travel-entertainment cards are in use. So it goes, for we are far into the era of plastic credit.

If you know how to handle your credit cards, they can be a tremendous convenience. They can help you keep detailed tax records for your travel and entertainment expenses. They can allow you to charge these costs anywhere in the world—without paying any interest. They can be a magnificent substitute for cash everywhere, a major benefit if you travel a lot. (And Americans lose more than $2 billion a year in cash, says the American Express Company.)

Or if you are among the millions who have all-purpose bank charge cards, you can greatly simplify your budgeting problems by paying for hundreds of dollars' worth of purchases of every kind with a single check at the end of the billing period. You can achieve substantial savings by buying an item on sale even if you're low on cash. You can order goods easily by mail or telephone—and also return merchandise with a minimum of trouble. And *any* arrangement which can give you the use of big amounts of cash for as long as twenty-five days without interest (from date of billing), as with bank charge cards, is advantageous to you.

To use credit cards to your maximum advantage, you must first learn the differences between the various types in use. There are:

Single-purpose cards issued by all kinds of businesses—oil companies, motel chains, telephone companies, car-rental agencies, department stores, and the like. You pay nothing for them, and they allow you to charge merchandise or services, paying when billed. If you don't pay promptly, you will be charged interest, typically amounting to 1½ per cent a month. The aim of this kind of card is to encourage you to buy only from the company that issued the card to you.

Food, travel, and entertainment or multipurpose cards, like Diner's Club, Carte Blanche, and American Express. These are used mostly by businessmen, although anyone may apply. Holders of these cards pay a yearly fee—usually $15 to $17—to the issuer, and can then use the card in thousands of business places. Bars, restaurants, hotels, and expensive shops are this kind of card's best customers. Usually cardholders are billed within thirty to sixty days and are expected to pay on receipt of the bill. No interest is charged if payment is prompt.

Bank credit cards, of which BankAmericard and Master Charge are the best known. All operate in much the same way. The bank issues you a card after checking your credit rating. There is no fee. You may then use the card in place of cash at any shop, restaurant, service station, or other business participating in the plan. The shop will turn the charge slips over to the bank, which will accumulate them until the end of the billing period. If you pay the bill within the time specified—usually twenty-five days from the date of billing—the use of the credit card is free. After that a service charge of 1 per cent to 1½ per cent a month is levied against the balance.

HOW DO YOU USE CREDIT CARDS?

Do you have at least three credit cards, most of them good only at a particular store or chain of stores?

Do you use at least one of these cards regularly?

Do you think of your card or cards primarily as a source of credit, and in only a secondary way as a convenience?

Do you write more checks than you used to, despite your use of the cards too?

Do you have a basic, nagging fear that credit cards make it too easy for you to buy things you do not really want or cannot honestly afford?

Do you, as a result of this basic fear, tend to think of your cards as an evil—a necessary evil, but still an evil—and not as a good thing?

If you answered yes to every one of these probing questions, you are typical of today's credit card user, according to "Credit Card Use in the U.S.," the first comprehensive study of the subject ever made, published by the University of Michigan Institute for Social Research. "Few Americans tend to think of credit cards as a good thing, whether they use them or not," says Dr. Lewis Mandell, who directed the ISR study. "Fully 75 per cent of all respondents said that credit cards made it too easy to buy things."

Now check where you, a credit card owner, fit in the wide range of users analyzed.

• If you have a higher-than-average income and higher-than-average education, you're more likely to be a card user than those with lower incomes and educations. Income is the major determinant of credit card use.

• If you are a young family and have children, you are more likely to use cards than other groups and more likely to incur debt on your cards than other groups. Another determinant of credit card use is related to the age of the family head.

• If you live in the suburbs, it's probable that you are an active credit card user, while families living in central cities or rural areas are least likely to use such cards.

• If you use your cards to buy clothing more than any other category of goods, you're typical. On both bank and store credit cards, clothing is the most frequent type of purchase.

• And if you're in any income group below the very top, you use your card to obtain credit, and this is the most important use you make of the card. You see your card as another instrument for taking on installment debt and you treat your card debt like an installment loan—paying a little each month, generally the minimum allowable monthly payment.

• But if you're in the highest income group you use your card as a convenience—and whatever debt you incur on the card you attempt to pay off as quickly as you can.

• And no matter what your special group, you write more checks than families who do not use cards.

What are some of the fundamental implications of all this? One prime implication is that, although all credit cards are substitutes for money or checks in transactions, they are *not* pushing us toward a "checkless society"—as was so widely forecast and is still so widely believed.

Another prime implication is that our consumer debt pattern is being changed by the addition of credit card debt to other types of consumer debt.

The use of credit card debt is most pronounced among higher-income families, who often have no other consumer debt and certainly could borrow at less than an 18 per cent annual rate. But these families aren't taking on long-term debt; they're using the cards as convenience and they pay off the debts quickly.

And a third implication is that most of you are using your eminent common sense in handling your credit cards—recognizing their dangers as well as their allure. Most Americans are indeed their own best money managers.

SHOULD YOU USE A CREDIT CARD?

As a general rule, you should—at any income level—if you have shown in the past that you can handle credit responsibly and that you will use your card as a convenient budgeting and record-keeping tool rather than a license to overspend.

As a general rule, though, you should not use cards *if* you're a habitual impulse buyer who frequently buys unnecessary things; *if* you're habitually late in meeting payments; *if* you've never managed to live comfortably within your income. And you should certainly shy away *if*, on top of all these characteristics, you do not have a steady income.

Here are the ways to use any credit card to *your* best advantage.

• Accept only those cards which you actually need and want and will use fairly regularly. For most of you in the middle-income bracket, one bank charge card and maybe a couple of oil company cards for gas are enough—although if you are in business you may find a travel-entertainment card helpful as well.

• Treat every purchase you are planning to charge as you would a cash purchase. Ask yourself: Do you really want and need the item? Can you really afford it? Can you repay the charge comfortably and on time?

• At the beginning of each month, decide on a maximum total of charges you'll be able to repay easily. Stick within that limit and repay the charges promptly to avoid any finance charges.

• Keep all your receipts until you receive your statement to check your spending and your totals against the statement for errors, which can easily occur (due, say, to no more than a clerk's bad handwriting).

HOW TO PROTECT YOUR CREDIT CARD

In just a matter of days a while ago:

• Three Long Island housewives went on a shopping spree, billed $16,000 worth of merchandise to stolen credit cards.

• A Pittsburgh gambler was arrested with $10,000 in his pocket—most of it refunds from airline tickets he had bought with other people's credit cards.

• A credit card thief posing as a health center operator ran up bills of more than $10,000 at gas stations by promising attendants health courses in his non-existent health center if they would make out phony bills against the credit card and give him cash.

These are *not* extreme examples, and the warning to you is implicit if you own a credit card or department store charge plate. Criminals have invaded the credit card field. Millions of cards are now being lost or stolen each year and are being used by thieves and other fraudulent operators to run up millions of dollars in unauthorized charges.

Fraudulent use of credit cards on sizable amounts is now a federal crime and the Truth in Lending law forbids the mailing of unsolicited credit cards.

The Truth in Lending law now also provides that a cardholder is not liable for charges on a stolen or lost card if the issuer has failed to inform him that he is otherwise liable for up to $50 per card, or has failed to supply the holder with a self-addressed, pre-stamped notice to use if a card is lost or stolen. Your maximum liability in the case of unauthorized use of any credit card which has been stolen from you is $50 for each card. This maximum holds even if you fail to discover the loss for a considerable period of time and even if you fail to notify the issuer promptly. The law also provides that all cards must bear your signature, photograph, or similar means of identification.

But you also must take steps on your own to protect yourself. Here's what to do:

• As soon as you've finished reading this, go over every card you own. Make sure you have destroyed all you do not need. Cut unwanted cards in half and throw them away.

• Make a list of all credit cards you decide to keep with the names and addresses of the issuers and the account numbers. Keep this list in a safe place but *not* in your wallet.

• Sign each new card you decide to keep this minute. This will force anyone trying to use the card fraudulently to forge your signature on store bills, restaurant checks, etc.—no problem for the professional card-abuser, admittedly, but a definite deterrent to an amateur.

• Check your credit card collection every couple of weeks. If any card is missing, inform the issuer immediately—first by phone, then by letter or telegram in which you refer to your call. Some issuers now have twenty-four-hour answering services for just this purpose. Although there is a federal $50 limit on your liability, it applies to *each card* you own.

• Never lend your card to anyone else. This is a violation of your contract with the issuer.

• Make sure your card is returned to you each time you use it. Among the major suppliers of credit cards to fraudulent users are dishonest employees of legitimate establishments.

• Don't leave your credit card in the glove compartment of your car. This is one of the first places a professional credit card thief looks.

• Don't underestimate the value of your card because it's made of plastic. Consider it the equivalent of cash and at least as tempting to a thief as cash.

• Don't leave credit cards lying around in your office or hotel room any more than you would leave a stack of cash lying around. Instead, keep your cards securely in your wallet or purse.

In sum, either give up the advantages of owning credit cards and return to cash-check living or treat these cards with the respect which they—as the equivalent of cash in your wallet or purse—deserve.

How to Hold Down Your Borrowing Costs

How can you, an attractive credit risk, hold down your cost of borrowing?

Throughout this section I have dropped in rules on this and you will find more hints for mortgages in Chapter 13, "A Roof Over Your Head," and more rules for automobile loans in Chapter 9, "Your Transportation." But the guides below are the most fundamental of all and go across the board for all types of credit. Whatever repetition you note can only help underline their value to you.

(1) On any type of purchase on time, always keep in mind that the most expensive way to borrow money is to make a small down payment and to stretch out the life of the loan for the longest possible period.

(2) Thus, to save interest on any type of loan—from appliance to auto or mortgage—make the largest down payment you can manage and repay in the shortest period that's feasible for you. Unless you buy the pessimistic argument that we're in for a never ending period of galloping, utterly ruinous inflation, in which the only way to protect yourself is to borrow as much as you can so you can pay back in dollars of dwindling value, you cannot dispute this rule's logic.

(3) Try to include a clause in any long-term loan contract giving you the privilege of prepayment of your loan at no penalty to you or at the lowest possible penalty. This will give you leeway to renegotiate your loan at more favorable rates when and as interest rate levels decline or to pay it off entirely. (Note, though: Refinancing costs must be considered and minimum loan charges are often set by policy and sometimes law.)

(4) On the other hand, don't pay off loans you might have outstanding at dramatically lower rates than now prevail. Just keep up your regular required payments and invest your extra cash so it earns more money for you than you're paying out on your old loans.

(5) Beware of ads for big-ticket items on "easy" repayment terms, and if the ads are befuddling despite Truth in Lending law requirements,

use the formulas I've given you for determining how much you are paying on a true annual basis.

(6) Always keep in mind that any "instant cash" plan will be comparatively *expensive* to you. Whether it's a multipurpose credit card or an automatic line of credit at your bank, or any newer plan, the point is you'll almost surely end up paying *more* for this instant cash than you would for a traditional loan.

(7) In general, during periods of high interest rates, borrow only the exact amount you need. Borrowing more will mean paying peak interest rates for the extra cash. Borrowing too little will mean returning for another loan and paying extra processing costs.

(8) Offer the best security you can. A loan secured by top-notch collateral almost always may be obtained at a cheaper rate than a loan backed only by your signature. You lose nothing. You get back full possession of your asset when you pay off your debt.

(9) Before you borrow or buy on time, use whatever free credit you can get. For instance, use your regular thirty-day charge account as much as you can. If you buy at the start of the billing cycle, you won't be billed for about thirty days, and then you have another thirty days to pay.

(10) In shopping around for bargain credit, don't overlook the occasional "money sales" or similar features offered by full service banks. For regular bank customers who already have savings, checking accounts, and the bank's charge card, installment credit may be offered at a full per cent less than the normal interest rates. And if you have a number of small loans outstanding, ask your bank whether you would qualify for a "cleanup" type of loan at a lower rate. If so, by all means take advantage of the lower rate.

THE GREAT PITFALLS OF CREDIT

Truth in Lending has not eliminated the credit tricksters and racketeers—and the likelihood is no law ever will wipe them out. As for us, it would be ridiculous to claim that even an excellent education on credit would be sufficient protection for the vast majority of Americans —particularly since eight out of ten Americans admit they are unable to find their way through what one observer once called the "wonderland of credit where percentages multiply and divide at will, where finance charges materialize on command and fees are collected on the way out."

Do you know how to read the fine print on a complicated installment sales contract? Do you even understand the bold-type statement of interest charges required under the Truth in Lending law? How, then, can you, the ordinary borrower, detect hidden interest charges, protect yourself against unsuspected loan costs? One very good way is by becoming aware of the great pitfalls of credit—and, by this awareness alone, learning how to avoid these yawning traps.

"DEBT POOLING"

No matter what your plight, avoid commercial debt poolers, who simply lump your debts together, collect one regular payment from you —then charge you as much as 35 per cent of your debts for this "service."

Debt pooling, or "pro-rating" or "debt adjusting" or "debt liquidating," for profit is now barred in a majority of our states and the District of Columbia. But it still thrives in many parts of the country, and you must be on guard.

Specifically, a "debt adjuster" may say to you: "If installment payments or past-due bills are troubling you, let us consolidate and arrange to pay all your bills, past due or not, with one low monthly payment you can afford." If you accept this offer, you will turn over part or all your income to a firm and your debts supposedly will be paid out of the income on a pro-rated basis. The basic difficulty with the arrangement is the fact that almost never is the plan carried to fruition. Either the creditors won't accept the plan or you, the debtor, find it impossible to live with the expected payments. Some "consolidators" simply pocket the money and never pay your creditors. As a consequence, the only thing you, the debtor, obtain is an expansion of your original debt because of the fee you must pay to the adjuster. The service charges are steep in debt consolidation and, typically, your whole first payment may be taken by the company for these charges—without a penny going to your creditors.

Debt adjusting or debt pooling has nothing to do with legitimate credit counseling services—nor should it be confused with legitimate bank or credit union debt consolidation loans. The debt adjuster merely takes the debtor's money with the understanding that he will make the payments to the creditors—after absorbing a substantial portion of the debtor's funds as payment for his services. He adds to the debtor's problems with excessive charges and makes no effort to offer financial counsel or budget guidance. In some cases, he leaves the debtor with far too little money to live on.

"SEWER SERVICE"

Let's say that you, a consumer committed to periodic payments on an installment loan, lose your job and subsequently default on a payment. Under the law, if a creditor wishes to sue you for payment, he is required to serve you a formal notice of the impending lawsuit.

But let's say you never receive the notice—quite likely if you are among the nation's millions of unsophisticated borrowers. If so, the next blow well may be a "default judgment" against you, the equivalent of a decision that you, the debtor, are at fault before you consult a lawyer and find out your rights, not to mention go to court.

"Sewer service" is the colloquial name for this technique, which is widely used by unscrupulous debt collectors to deprive the gullible low-income borrower of his or her legitimate rights. To summarize what happens: the summons or other legal document which the creditor is supposed to deliver to the debtor is simply chucked into any dead-end receptacle (thus, "sewer" service). Unless you manage to get the judgment set aside, you are automatically stamped as liable and may be legally bound to pay whatever the creditors say you owe and you may lose your right to defend yourself in court, no matter what the facts may be.

Sewer service is the least expensive way for an unprincipled creditor to force payment of a debt. It is used not only to collect payments on installment debts but also to deprive tenants of their rights to contest eviction by landlords.

This is a flagrant attack on your most basic rights. If it happens to you, complain immediately to a law enforcement agency and also to the court where the judgment was entered. Get a lawyer to move to set the judgment aside. If you can't afford a lawyer, tell the clerk of the court you want to make a motion to set aside a default judgment for lack of service and ask him for advice on how to file the necessary papers.

Don't take this lying down!

"INCONVENIENT VENUE"

"Inconvenient venue" is another technique designed to deprive debtors of their legal rights. Under this procedure, the creditor simply files suit against his victim from a branch, affiliate, or lending institution hundreds of miles away from the debtor's home. Again, the victim has no feasible means of defending himself against the suit.

Pressure is now mounting steadily for state and federal laws to ban inconvenient venue as a means of obtaining default judgments against debtors, guilty or not guilty.

"CONFESSION OF JUDGMENT"

Ranking with the most vicious of all ways in which debtors are being trapped is the "confession of judgment" clause appearing in so many installment sales contracts. In effect, this clause is a built-in confession of guilt should the borrower miss a single monthly payment unless, in many instances, he can come up with the entire amount he still owes. By signing the contract he has waived whatever legal rights he otherwise may have had in advance—and the creditor can move in to collect at once. Frequently, too, the first a debtor knows that such a judgment has been made against him is when he receives a notice that his property is being put up for a sheriff's sale within days.

Confession of judgment is legal in only a few states, but this technique is still being illegally used to some extent against consumers in many other states as well.

Of course, it is reasonable for lenders to insist that they be protected against default and, of course, there are explanations for each of these clauses. But this technique is an outrageous deprivation of the rights of the individual.

Even if you signed a confession of judgment, under recent Supreme Court decisions you may be able to have it set aside if you can show that you didn't understand the clause when you signed it and didn't have legal advice.

HARASSMENT

Harassment is the "normal" means, in countless cases, of collecting small debts and past-due installment payments. And you need not be a ghetto resident to come up against this: it can happen to you, whoever and wherever you are.

• A typical cornered debtor may first receive a flood of dunning notices from debt collection agencies with names which sound in some cases very like those of government agencies. The letters will threaten legal action and serious damage to the debtor's credit rating.

• In addition, the debtor may be subjected to repeated telephone calls at all hours of the day and night, not only at his home but also at his job.

• The caller may falsely represent himself as a lawyer, a policeman, a private detective. Or he may hint that he works for a government agency.

• He may call a debtor's neighbors, relatives, wife, even his children. He also may call the debtor's employer, a tactic which easily can lead to the debtor's losing his job.

Whatever the tricks, the harassment usually succeeds in frightening a debtor into "settling" his debt—even though the debt may have been imposed on him through fraudulent, illegal means and even though he may have a sound, legitimate, legal defense against the creditor who is harassing him.

As you might expect, laws are being passed to control this sort of viciousness. The Federal Trade Commission has proceeded against some unfair debt collection methods. In Massachusetts debt collectors are licensed by the state and a collector may lose his license if he calls you late at night, informs your employer that you owe money, or indicates on an envelope that you have not paid your bills. In New York City a regulation forbids creditors (or their lawyers or collection agencies) to "communicate or threaten to communicate with an alleged debtor's employer" without first obtaining a court judgment against the debtor. And the Federal Consumer Credit Protection Act makes it a federal crime for a creditor or his representative to use violence or threats of violence to collect debts.

But none of it is enough. Neither the new laws nor regulations are curbing, much less wiping out, the problem of debtor harassment.

REPOSSESSION

You buy a slightly used car loaded with options for $3,600, including 18 per cent interest on your auto loan, fees, insurance, etc. You pledge to pay $100 a month for three years.

After one year and $1,200 in payments, you fail to meet a due date. A while later your car disappears from your driveway. A lending company which bought the note for your car from your used car dealer has simply sent his "repo" man to your home. He has crossed the wires of your car to get it going and has driven off.

Repossession of automobiles, as well as of many other personal items, is a widespread and entirely legal practice used against the delinquent—particularly low-income—debtor in the U.S. today.* It also may be only the beginning, for the lender may then turn around and sell your repossessed car back to the original dealer for an amount to be credited to you. This resale price, if the participants are unprincipled, may be a rigged bargain sum of, say, $500 for your car. You are now sued for the remainder you still owe: $2,400 minus $500, or $1,900. You're also liable for extra charges.

You thus not only have no car but you also have a debt equal to nearly two more years of payments. And now the used car dealer may in turn resell your repossessed car to another buyer for $1,500. Of course, cars are repossessed without such tactics—but a shocking number do involve deceit, fraud, perjury too.

Automobiles are only one category of consumer goods subject to repossession today. Another not untypical situation is repossession when the consumer buys a set of furniture on time, then defaults on a single payment. The seller or the holder of the installment loan contract may confiscate the entire set and then sue to collect the remainder of the debt, plus charges and fees. Many corrupt ghetto merchants, in fact, make a living selling goods over and over in this manner. Their profit depends on default in payment and a chance for resale—not on the original sale itself.

To crack down on these practices, laws are being urged at both federal and state levels which would permit creditors either to repossess their goods or to sue for payment of the debt—but not both. Meanwhile, the only protection you, the debtor, have is your own awareness of the pitfall.

* However, the U. S. Supreme Court recently ruled that certain repossession practices which have been widely used violate constitutional guarantees. The Court ruled that no item may be repossessed unless the buyer is notified that the matter is in court and given a chance—in formal hearings—to tell his side of the story.

"HOLDER IN DUE COURSE"

An elderly woman bought a hearing aid for her son, involving a fat down payment and an installment loan for the balance of her purchase. When the device failed to work, she took it back to the seller, who agreed to send it to the factory for repair. But when she returned again to pick up the hearing aid, she found that the seller had gone out of business—and had sold her installment loan contract to a local lender.

Incredibly, this woman remained under legal obligation to repay the loan plus stiff interest charges—despite the fact that her son still had no hearing aid.

This legal quirk—called the "holder in due course" doctrine—was, until May 19, 1976, one of the biggest and costliest loopholes remaining on our consumer lawbooks, with "literally millions of dollars lost every week because of this doctrine," said the Consumer Federation of America in Washington.

Under the holder in due course doctrine, an unscrupulous used car dealer or other retailer could lure naive consumers into buying a long list of products or services on time. He would then immediately sell the contract to a finance company. The product might have turned out to be a lemon, badly damaged, or have needed servicing under the warranty, or it might not even have been delivered. And the seller might have flatly refused to replace or repair the product. Nevertheless, the financial institution which owned your loan contract would sternly remind you that he was "in the business of financing, not repairing furniture or cars." If you refused to make payments as they came due, you might be sued for the remainder of the loan, payable at once. Or, as an alternative, the finance company might have repossessed not only the item in question but also other personal goods. It was indisputably one of the most vicious of all consumer traps.

Among the goods and services most frequently involved in holder in due course problems were: vacuum cleaners, furniture, carpeting, sewing machines, "lifetime" series of dancing or judo lessons or health spa visits, major appliances, home improvements.

But now as the result of a '76 Federal Trade Commission rule, the holder in due course loophole has been plugged. You have the right to assert claims and defenses against a creditor as you might against an unscrupulous seller. You may, for instance, stop payment to a creditor on a defective dishwasher or a car that turns out to be a lemon. You may refuse to pay a financing company for a set of encyclopedias that doesn't arrive or may sue for refund of payments already made to a health spa that has gone out of business.

Furthermore, all consumer contracts now must carry a notice informing you of your rights of action against creditors as well as sellers. The rule applies to merchants who offer you installment sales contracts or arrange direct loans with finance companies or engage in "referral" schemes in which you are led to believe you will get a product free if you refer a specified number of other customers to the seller.

You no longer must bear the burden of a seller's wrongdoing; your lender must either absorb the costs of unfair or fraudulent practices or take the seller to court and force him to pay up. At last, this utterly unfair credit practice that in the past has compelled so many consumers to pay for broken or worthless merchandise has been outlawed. But be on guard! Some sellers still will try to pull you into the trap.

AND ALSO BEWARE THESE TRAPS!

The *add-on clause*. Avoid the contract in which the seller keeps title to a whole list of items you are buying on credit until all payments have been completed (for instance, a 14-piece set of furniture). A single delinquent payment could permit the seller to repossess the entire set, even though you have paid all but a few dollars of the total. This gimmick also permits the installment seller to add purchase after purchase to your original installment contract. Then just one delinquent payment could permit the seller to repossess your whole collection of purchases.

The *balloon contract,* which provides for a final payment which is considerably larger than the previous monthly payments. If you are not aware of this and are not prepared to meet the final payment, your purchase may be repossessed before you can produce the money. Or you may be compelled to refinance at disastrously disadvantageous terms to you. Balloon payments are illegal in some states today because they are widely used to trick you into buying—at low initial monthly costs—things or services you cannot afford.

An *acceleration clause*. In this case, default in one single payment —or in some instances, the fact that you have lost your job—can make all other payments due at once. If you are unable to pay the total balance, your purchases could be carted away for resale and you still may not be absolved of all future liability.

Obscure provisions in your credit contract which stipulate you must buy extra items you may not want. These clauses are frequently buried in the contract so you don't realize they are there until after you have signed.

Exorbitant extra charges and "processing fees," adding substantially to your borrowing costs. A lender might list such charges separately to deceive you with seemingly very low loan rates.

How Much Debt Is Too Much Debt?

Who are the individuals and the families who get caught in an intolerable debt squeeze? Can we draw a fine but critical line between a healthy, bearable load of loans and an unhealthy, unbearable load?

The overextended credit individual is usually a faceless vexation in our society, according to a revealing study by a University of Wisconsin professor some years ago, who then drew this detailed portrait of the overextended credit family:

• The family is young, has more than the average number of children and an average income.

• The parents are easygoing, carefree, and impulsive, have "limited pleasure postponement mechanisms" and rubber wills when confronted with high-pressure salesmen.

• Although the husband, in most cases, is satisfied with his job, one in three wives is dissatisfied with her husband's pay.

• The family doesn't read anything, not even the daily newspaper. TV is the major communications medium in the family's life and TV disproportionately influences the couple's buying decisions.

• The parents tend to blame their plight on vague, unavoidable "circumstances" or superficial backbreaking straws such as pregnancy, temporary loss of job, buying a car—and thus they feel their troubles are not really their fault.

• Neither husband nor wife assumes clear responsibility for managing the family's finances. Even among the couples who think they are sharing money management responsibilities, there is little indication of joint decision making. As one husband remarked, "We don't quibble about it. If either one of us wants to buy, we buy!"

• The family moves from house to house more often than the average U.S. family.

Most consumer debts are adequately cushioned by our incomes and savings, our financial assets, and our earnings potentials. But there is a minority always in deep financial trouble—in the eighteen-to-twenty-four age bracket, and in the under $10,000 bracket, particularly.

The crucial difference between sound and unsound borrowing is whether or not *you* are carrying too much debt at any one time. Okay, then, *how much debt is too much debt?*

Deep and prolonged study has gone into this question—and there is considerable disagreement on the conclusions. However, the following are clear warning signals that you're moving dangerously close to the debt borderline and may be crossing it.

• You are continually lengthening the repayment periods on your installment purchases and putting down smaller and smaller initial payments. At the same time, your interest charge load is mounting just because you are sinking deeper and deeper into debt for longer periods.

• What you owe on your revolving charge accounts also is climbing steadily. You're never out of debt to the local stores at which you have revolving charge accounts.

• Before you have finished paying last month's bills this month's are piling in. You're always behind these days in your payments and you're now regularly receiving notices that you're delinquent. You might even get an occasional notice threatening repossession or legal action against you—something that has never happened to you before.

• Slowly but unquestionably, an ever increasing share of your net income is going to pay your debts.

• You are so bedeviled by so many separate bills coming at you from so many sources each month that you turn to a lending institution or lending agency for a loan to "consolidate" and pay off all your debts and leave you with just this one big consolidation loan to meet. But you continue to buy on credit—thereby adding more new bills on top of your one big debt you must pay each month.

Here are more specific guidelines on how much debt is too much debt:

Do not owe more than 20 per cent of your yearly after-tax income (not including your home mortgage, though). This means that if you earn $800 a month in take-home pay or $9,600 after taxes a year, your debt limit would be about $2,000.

Do not owe more than 10 per cent of the amount you could pay for out of your income within the next eighteen months. Again, say your take-home pay is $800 a month; that gives you 10 per cent or $80 for debt repayments each month. With this monthly sum you could pay off $1,500 over eighteen months. Your safe debt limit would be about $1,500.

Do not owe more than one third of your discretionary income for the year—meaning the income you have left after you have paid for the basic needs of food, clothing, and shelter. Once again, say you earn $9,600 in take-home pay a year and you spend an average of $200 a month for shelter, $280 a month for food, $50 a month for clothing. Your basic living costs are $530 a month or $6,360 over the year. Your discretionary income is, therefore, $3,240. By this measurement, your debt limit is $1,080—or one third of your discretionary income of $3,240.

Also, in deciding how much debt your family can handle, ask yourself: How stable is your family breadwinner's job and income?

What is the chance of a layoff in his occupation and in your area? Is he eligible for unemployment compensation? How much? How long would this finance your needs? How many protections does your family have against other disasters besides unemployment—insurance coverage for your home, health and life pension credits, savings and investments, equity in your home, etc.?

BUT WHAT IF YOU FIND YOU'RE OVER YOUR HEAD IN DEBT?

In South Bend, Ind., a young couple with three children accumulated debts of $4,200. This couple's monthly take-home pay amounted to only $328, and monthly payments on installment debts to eighteen creditors amounted to $148.73, nearly half their take-home pay.

The couple finally appealed to a Consumer Credit Counseling Service, which advised them to trade in the expensive new car they were buying for a lower-priced car involving lower monthly payments. The service also arranged for the couple to make small monthly payments to two hospitals and seven doctors to whom they owed substantial amounts. Within nine months the couple had reduced their debt by nearly $1,400, and within eighteen months all of their debts had been completely paid off. This case history is just a single illustration of how one family out of hundreds of thousands was saved from personal bankruptcy.

It's estimated only about one in six families cannot be helped by credit counselors, because their problems are psychological or legal or because they are "credit drunks" who simply are not willing to try to solve their problems. However, without counseling service, today's huge annual personal bankruptcy toll easily might be 50 per cent higher than it is.

The fact is, says the Family Service Association of America, "People do want help—desperately—but they don't know where to go, and until recently there hasn't been anywhere to go."

So what if *you* find you are over your head in debt?

Start at your local bank: more and more banks are offering formal or informal debt counseling to overburdened customers.

If your bank (or credit union or consumer finance company) can't or won't help, write to the National Foundation for Consumer Credit, 1819 H Street, N.W., Washington, D.C. 20006, for the address of one of the 150 Consumer Credit Counseling Services nearest to you. These non-profit organizations, backed by local banks, merchants, educators, and others, are set up to provide financial counseling to anyone, but offer special help to overextended families and individuals in an effort to find ways to get them out of trouble.

Check the nearest Family Service Agency. Hundreds of Family Service Agencies across the nation offer either financial counseling or can refer you to some agency offering such counseling. If you don't know which agency offers such help in your area, write the Family Service Association of America, 44 East Twenty-third Street, New York, N.Y. 10010.

Another good source of help could be your church. Other sources from which you may get some form of debt counseling include:

legal aid societies;

your labor union's community services counselors;

your employer's personnel department.

The Army and Navy also maintain debt counseling services to assist servicemen and their families.

Above all, heed this warning: If you find your payments, when added to your necessary living expenses, are more than your pay check, don't try to hide out from your creditors! Instead ask for help!

How to Go Bankrupt

But let's say all efforts and plans to bail you out have failed. The debt counseling service hasn't been able to come up with a plan your creditors will accept. No consolidation loan is available. The only option left seems to be bankruptcy.

If so, here are your final two "outs":

(1) "Chapter XIII." This method of debt reorganization is provided for under Chapter XIII of the Federal Bankruptcy Law. Under Chapter XIII, debtor, creditors, and a referee—all supervised by a federal judge—get together to work out a way for the debtor to pay his debts on an installment basis.

This is known as the wage earner plan, because it protects the wages and essential property of a debtor who wants to stay away from straight bankruptcy by repaying his or her debts from future earnings.

Whether rooted in puritanism, pride, or ego, the general attitude toward bankruptcy is negative and you well may find it difficult to live with. But there are other than social aspects to be considered. Co-signed loans become the debts of the co-signers; the cost of going into bankruptcy may reach $300 to $500 or more; bankruptcy almost invariably is the blackest possible mark on a credit rating.

Here's how the wage earner plan works.

Either you, the debtor, get a written extension of your debts, with more time to pay them off in full; or, less commonly, you arrange a "composition" in which you pay off only a certain percentage of the amount you owe each creditor.

One half of your creditors must approve your filing of the Chapter XIII petition, at which time all interest charges usually stop. Your wages, personal property, your home and furniture, secured loans, particularly mortgages on real estate, usually are not included in the plan for distribution of your assets to creditors.

In addition to legal fees, which a Chapter XIII petitioner must pay to the lawyer who files the petition, there are filing fees of about $15 and a trustee's fee of up to 5 per cent of the debts, plus expenses.

You, the debtor, make your required payments, spread over three years, to the trustee, who then pays your creditors—thus making the federal government, in effect, a collection agency. An employer may agree to deduct the payment from a debtor's salary and forward it to the trustee.

There is no uniformity of application of Chapter XIII, and top legal experts deplore the fact that it is not more widely used.

Important Note: If you successfully complete this plan, it will be considered a "plus" on your credit rating.

(2) Voluntary bankruptcy. Finally, there is the voluntary petition for straight bankruptcy. To do this you must put together a list of all your assets and liabilities and pay a $50 filing fee. Ordinarily, the rest is routine. Except for clothing, tools, a selected list of household goods, and other items depending on the exemption laws of your state, all your assets will be collected by the court and liquidated—and the proceeds will then be distributed among your creditors. Once you, the debtor, have been discharged by the court, your financial slate is clean—except for the bankruptcy record, which, no matter what you are told, will dog your footsteps for years.

THE BAFFLEGAB OF BORROWING

Many of the most crucially important terms to you in the sphere of credit already have been exhaustively explained in the immediately preceding pages. But many other words which you'll hear or read have not yet been put into simple language. You'll come across them frequently enough, though, and they are of sufficient meaning to you to demand that they be as clearly explained as possible.

ACCELERATION CLAUSE: See page 145.

ADD-ON RATE: See page 127.

ADD-ON CLAUSE: See page 145.

ANNUAL PERCENTAGE RATE: See page 126.

ASSETS: Everything you own which has monetary worth.

BALANCE: The amount you owe on an account or loan at any given time.

BALLOON CONTRACT: See page 145.

BORROWER: The person who borrows cash or who buys something on time.

CARRYING CHARGE: The charge you pay a store or any other lender for the privilege of having a period of time in which to pay for the goods or services you have already bought and which you may use in advance of payment.

CHARGE ACCOUNT: See pages 123–24.

CHARGE OFF: To declare a loss and remove a loan from the assets of a lender because the loan cannot be collected from the debtor.

CHATTEL MORTGAGE: A legal document in which your personal property (chattels) is put up as security for payment of your debt but generally is left in your hands so long as you keep up the payments as contracted.

CHECK CREDIT PLANS: Consumer loan programs similar to credit lines businesses have under which the loans are approved in advance and funds are available when needed. The consumer who has been approved for check credit may borrow up to a stated amount at any time simply by writing a check. As the loan is repaid, the credit limit returns to the stated maximum. See "How to Use Ready Credit," pages 108–9.

CLOSING DATE: The day of the month on which credit accounts and monthly bills are calculated. Payments made after the closing date—or new charges or returns of merchandise—will not show on the bill you receive until the following month, when the next closing date will show subsequent payments, charges, and returns.

COLLATERAL: Anything of value which you have against which you may borrow money—for example, equity in an automobile, real estate, stocks and bonds, savings account passbooks, the cash-surrender value of life insurance policies. If you fail to repay your loan, the lender can take possession of whatever you have put up as collateral. Note: Not all loans must be secured by collateral.

CO-MAKER OR CO-SIGNER: The other signer of a note when two people jointly guarantee to pay a loan. Parents often co-sign loans taken out by their minor children. Minors may not legally execute contracts.

CONDITIONAL SALES CONTRACT: Form of installment contract under which you do not legally own the product—say a car—until you've made the final payment. And you must make your payments even if you are not satisfied with the purchase. You cannot cancel your obligation by just giving back the product (car). Term no longer in common use in many areas.

CONSOLIDATE: To bring together several financial obligations under one agreement, contract, or note.

CONSUMER: Any person who uses goods and/or services for personal, household, or family purposes.

CONSUMER CREDIT: Credit offered or extended to a person primarily for personal or family purposes, for which a finance charge is imposed and which is repayable in installments. All consumer credit transactions divide into two types (1) *open-end credit,* which includes *revolving charge accounts* and transactions through *credit cards;* and (2) *installment credit,* which is used by consumers to buy big-ticket items such as automobiles and appliances.

The one fact that consumer credit is used by *individuals* for *personal* and *family* needs distinguishes it from credit used for business, agricultural, or government purposes. Consumer credit usually refers to short-term and intermediate-term debt, thus excluding long-term home mortgage debt.

CONSUMER FINANCE COMPANIES: State-licensed companies which make installment cash loans to consumers.

CONSUMER LOANS: Loans to individuals or families, the proceeds to be used for personal consumption, as contrasted to loans for business or investment purposes.

CREDIT APPLICATION: A form which you must fill out when you want to use consumer credit. It usually contains questions concerning your present and previous places of residence, work history, present earnings, other credit transactions, and loans outstanding.

CREDIT CARD: See pages 124–25; 131–37; 138–46.

CREDIT CHARGE: See Finance Charge.

CREDIT CONTRACT: Usually a written agreement that says how, when, and how much you will pay.

CREDIT INVESTIGATION: An inquiry undertaken by a prospective lender or creditor to verify information you give in your credit application or to investigate other aspects about you which the creditor considers relevant to your credit-worthiness.

CREDIT LIFE INSURANCE: A type of term life insurance policy, required by some lenders, which pays off a loan in the event of the borrower's death.

CREDIT LINES (See Check Credit Plans): Pre-approved loan privileges made available by banks to big businesses which qualify and maintain specified minimum checking account balances.

CREDITOR OR LENDER: The person, store, company, bank, dealer, credit union, or other organization that lends money or sells things or services on time. Creditors are those to whom you owe money.

CREDIT RATE: The ratio—expressed as a percentage—between credit charges and the average principal amount.

CREDIT RATING (also Credit Standing): An evaluation of your qualifications to receive credit based, in large measure, on your past record of meeting credit payments.

CREDIT RISK: The chance of loss through non-payment of debt.

CREDIT SALE: Any sale in which you are given time to pay for the goods you buy. There's usually an extra charge for the privilege of buying on time, and you usually pay for the goods in a series of installment payments which come due at regular intervals.

CREDIT SALE DISCLOSURE STATEMENT: The form a dealer must fill out giving you the essential details of your financing costs when you buy any product or service on the installment plan. This is required under the Consumer Credit Protection (Truth in Lending) Act.

CREDIT-WORTHY: Given a favorable credit rating and therefore entitled to use credit facilities.

DECLINING BALANCE: The decreasing amount which you owe on a debt as you make your monthly payments.

DEFAULT: Failure to pay a debt when due or to meet other terms of the contract.

DEFERRED PAYMENT: Future payment or series of future payments on a contract entered into sometime before the payment or payments are made.

DELINQUENT: A credit account which is past due and for which the debtor has made no satisfactory arrangement with the lender.

DISCOUNT (OR CASH CREDIT DISCOUNT): Deduction of finance charges from the total amount of your loan before you, the borrower, receive the balance in cash.

DISCOUNT RATE: See page 128.

DOLLAR COST: A way of stating the cost of credit. It is the difference between what you receive as a loan or in merchandise and what you must pay back.

DOWN PAYMENT: Cash required at the outset of an installment sales credit transaction. Sometimes a used car, piece of furniture, or other durable goods will be accepted in place of part or all of the down payment.

DURABLE GOODS: Usually big-ticket things which are useful to you, the consumer, over an extended period of time, such as automobiles, furniture, appliances.

FACE AMOUNT: Total amount of your loan before deduction of finance charges.

FINANCE CHARGE: See pages 126–31.

FINANCIAL COUNSELING: Expert advice on money and credit management.

FORFEIT: Lose or let go—as giving up to a creditor some security when you, the borrower, have failed to meet a contractual obligation.

HIDDEN CLAUSE: Any obscure provision in your credit contract which may stipulate requirements that may be against your interests—for instance, purchase of extra items you do not want.

HOLDER IN DUE COURSE: See pages 144–45.

INSTALLMENT: One of a series of payments to pay off a debt.

INSTALLMENT CASH CREDIT: Cash loaned directly to an individual and repaid in periodic payments (usually monthly) within a specified period of time.

INSTALLMENT SALES CREDIT: Credit through which an item of durable goods (a car, appliance) is bought and paid for in installment payments within a specified period of time.

INTERMEDIATE-TERM CREDIT: Credit which is extended for a period ranging from three to ten years.

LENDING INSTITUTION: A bank, loan company, or other organization which lends money and which makes money by advancing funds to others.

LICENSED LENDER: A lending organization authorized by license to conduct business in the state in which it is located.

LOAN RATE: The rate you are charged for borrowing money at a specific date for a specified period of time.

LOAN SHARK: See pages 121–22.

LONG-TERM CREDIT: Credit which is extended for a period of ten years or more.

MARKET PLACE: Any place where a transaction is made or prices are quoted on goods or services.

MATURED: Fully paid up, fully carried out as to terms, completed as to time or as to contract.

MATURITY DATE (also DUE DATE): Date on which final payment on cash loan or installment purchase is due.

MORTGAGE: A written pledge of valuable property to assure payment of a debt, providing automatic transfer of the item (e.g., a house) pledged the creditor in case of default.

MORTGAGE CREDIT: Money owed for those borrowing for the acquisition of land and/or buildings (frequently, homes) and which is paid back over an extended period of time.

NON-INSTALLMENT CREDIT: A financial obligation which is repaid in a single lump sum.

NOTE: A written, signed promise to pay which lists details of the repayment agreement: where, when, and in what size installments, etc. A note can be transferred to a third party.

OBLIGATION: An amount of money one is morally or legally bound to pay.

OPEN-END CREDIT OR REVOLVING CREDIT: See pages 123–24.

OUTSTANDING: The still unpaid part of a loan.

PAPER: Nickname for a loan contract.

PERSONAL INSTALLMENT LOAN: Money borrowed by an individual for personal needs which is repaid in regular monthly installments over a period of time.

PREPAYMENT PRIVILEGE: The privilege, stated in loan contract, of repaying part or all of a loan in advance of date or dates stated in contract—with or without interest penalty for the prepayment.

PRINCIPAL: The amount of money you borrow or the amount of credit you receive.

PROCEEDS: The actual amount of money handed to a borrower—after deductions for interest charges, fees, etc.

PROMISSORY NOTE: A paper you sign promising to repay the total sum you owe on specified terms.

REBATE: Return of a portion of a payment. For instance, you receive a rebate when you pay off your debt in advance instead of in the monthly installments you agreed upon. It then costs you less to borrow your money, because you are paying off in a shorter period.

REFINANCE: Revision of a payment timetable and, often, revision of the interest charges on the debt also.

REPOSSESSION: The reclaiming or taking back of goods which you have purchased on an installment sales contract and for which you have fallen behind in your payments.

REVOLVING CHARGE ACCOUNT: See page 124.

RIGHT OF RESCISSION: Your right, guaranteed by the Consumer Credit Protection Act or various state statutes, to cancel a contract under certain circumstances (including cases in which you have put up an interest in your home as security) within three business days—without penalty and with full refund of any deposits you may have paid. The right to a "cooling-off period" is most frequently used in home improvement contracts and the home improvement contractor must provide you with written notice of this right. It also applies, under a Federal Trade Commission rule, to sales made by door-to-door salespeople.

SHORT-TERM CREDIT: Credit extended for a period up to one year.

SOLVENT: Ability of the individual or group or organization to pay all of the debts owed. What the debtor owns is more than the total of the debts.

TERM: The prescribed time you have in which to make installment or other payments, under your loan or credit contract.

TERMS: Details and conditions of a loan (or other) contract: cash price, payment schedule, due date, etc.

THIRD-PARTY TRANSACTION: A three-way business transaction involving a buyer, a seller, and a source of consumer credit.

TITLE: Legal ownership.

TOP CREDIT: Ready credit. See Check Credit Plans.

TRADE IN: Practice of trading in an old product for a new one. Trade-in allowance is the amount of money allowed for the article traded in as against the total purchase price of the article being bought.

TRUTH IN LENDING: Popular name for the historic Consumer Credit Protection Act of 1969. The law applies to virtually all consumer borrowing transactions to individuals which involve amounts up to $25,000.

UNPAID BALANCE: On a credit purchase, difference between purchase price and down payment or trade-in allowance. On cash loan, difference between total loan made and amount still owed (with charges included, of course).

UNSECURED LOAN: Loan extended solely on basis of borrower's ability and pledge to repay.

WAGE ASSIGNMENT: Clause in installment contract under which an employer may be requested to collect part of an employee's wages to pay off the employee's debt to the wage assignment holder.

WAGE EARNER PLAN: See pages 150–51.

WAGE GARNISHMENT: Classic legal procedure which creditors have used for generations to collect debts. Under "income execution" (its other name) a creditor gets a court order instructing the employer of the debtor to withhold a specified portion of his employee's wages until his debt is repaid.

4

HOW TO SHOP
AND SAVE ON EVERYTHING

THE REAL REASONS YOU FIND IT SO HARD TO MAKE
  ENDS MEET   161
YOUR KEY WEAPONS AGAINST RISING COSTS   164
A DOZEN WISE RULES FOR SHOPPING FOR EVERYTHING   165
QUIZ YOURSELF INTO BUYING WISELY   167
CALENDAR FOR BARGAINS   168
"SCRAPING BY" ON $40,000 A YEAR   172

THE REAL REASONS YOU FIND IT SO HARD
TO MAKE ENDS MEET

You know how fast prices have been rising for everything. You also know that never have you earned so much money as now, never have you had such good prospects.

You feel confident that you are an excellent money manager. You also feel poorer than a year ago, more pinched than ever.

Why?

I am sure this question is echoed in tens of millions of homes in every area of the land and in every income bracket. I am sure too that most of you are not prepared for the complexities of an honest answer. Thus, as an introduction to this chapter on how to shop and save on everything, here are the *real* reasons you find it so hard to make ends meet on the biggest income of your life.

REAL REASON NO. 1

At every level of government, taxes have been rising along with the cost of living and therefore you mislead yourself into thinking you are richer than you actually are when you say your income is what you gross.

Your income is not your gross: it is your net after taxes and after allowing for a continuing high rate of inflation, even though price increases may be only modest in some years.

Say you're the sole support of a family of four who earned $10,000 just a few years ago and say you've had increases of 30 per cent since. Do you have $13,000 to spend? *No.* Your new high pay is actually worth *less* in the market place than your $10,000 was worth because of the erosion in your dollar's value due to inflation and to the bite of soaring Social Security taxes as well as higher income tax rate on your rising earnings.

Or let's say you are the breadwinner who earned $30,000 and now earns $39,000. Do you have $9,000 more to spend? *No*. Your new pay buys *less* than your former pay. And so it goes through all income categories.

Look at Chapter 19, "Planning for Your Financial and Personal Security," and you'll find more starkly dramatic illustrations of the extent to which your dollar's value has been eroded by increases in the cost of living and by climbing taxes in recent times. And I have not included by any means the entire bite in your dollar taken by all types of taxes. If this total "gobble" were included, you would have to be running even faster just to stand still.

If you had put $100 of your wedding present cash in your jewel box in 1967 to have handy "just in case" and you took it out in 1975, this sum would buy you less than $67 worth of food, shelter, clothing, and other necessities and non-necessities of life. If your parents had put the $100 away back in 1939 and you took it out in 1975, you could buy only about $28 worth of the essentials that $100 would have bought in '39.

What I am trying to smash home to you via these figures are the realities of taxes and inflation, for only when you face these realities will you stop kidding yourselves and start adopting the money management policies which will help protect your family.

REAL REASON NO. 2

You are using far more services than ever before and all services cost far more than ever before. You have, in short, chosen to live in a "service society" and you must pay the price demanded by that society.

Let me illustrate this with a list of my own activities on two long work-play days in the country one recent fall day. I took an early morning golf lesson; called the typewriter repairman to fix my new electric portable; paid the piano tuner for his regular quarterly visit; phoned our broker to confirm a decision on our stock account; arranged to have my teeth cleaned and to get my annual physical checkup; had lunch in a nearby restaurant with two economics professors; had my hair and nails done, and dropped off the laundry and dry cleaning on the way; had a lengthy talk with my housekeeper about the need to call the plumber, the electrician, and the exterminator to check the house; took my car to the local garage for its New York State inspection; made notes about what I was doing as I went along.

What was the characteristic which linked each of my activities? Each was or each involved a *service*. Each was a service clearly reflecting our affluent society. And each was a service costing more than ever before. My family's use of so many services to this unprecedented degree is a fundamental reason our cost of living is climbing so fast—and it's a fundamental reason for your pocketbook pinch too.

If you will just stop to think right now about your own activities, you will realize that never have you used so broad a variety of services to such an extent in your own daily life. The rise in your demand for services has far outpaced the rise in your demand for goods. You also will realize that never have virtually all services cost so much. In recent years the upsurge in the cost of services has dwarfed the rise in all consumer prices—with the most severe pinches in the huge areas of education, hospital fees, and interest rates.

Putting it even more succinctly, the average cost of sending your soiled clothes to a laundry has jumped much faster than the cost of a washing machine, while the cost of having a daily household worker do your laundry has zoomed. Again, the rise in the cost of buying a new car is modest compared to the rise in the cost of taking a city bus or subway. The cost of going out to a movie has jumped, but the cost of buying a TV set on which to see a movie at home has hardly moved.

What's more, there is no doubt about the uptrend of service costs in general. The only question—the *only* one—is the degree of rise.

And though you may resent the upward pressures, you are not in a good position to resist them, for when you need most services you need them at once. All I have to think of when I would like to make a peep of protest is that I can't cure an illness or fix an electric typewriter or tune a piano or repair a car, etc.

Even economists who are confident that over the long span the over-all rise in consumer prices will go back into the 4-per-cent-a-year range expect that the rise in service costs will beat that average.

REAL REASON NO. 3

For years you have been continually upgrading your demands—turning the luxuries of yesterday into the necessities of today. You have come to feel entitled to fairly sharp year-to-year increases in your living standards and have become accustomed to boosting your spending budget to new records each year, even though there may be a year now and then when the boosts are unwarranted. Because of this attitude, you are inclined almost routinely to overspend and then to feel pinched when you wake up to the fact that you have spent more than the amount of your raise.

To be even more specific, in your new homes you have been buying more built-in major appliances, more carpeted or linoleum-covered floors, more easy-care counter tops, more recreation rooms, sewing rooms, central air conditioning. The appliances themselves are being steadily upgraded—to self-defrosting refrigerators, eye-level ovens, etc. New homes bought with FHA insured mortgages in 1974 had an average 5.8 rooms; nearly 63 per cent had two or more bathrooms; nearly 54 per cent had garages; 30 per cent had carports.

In the great majority of your new cars you're paying for automatic transmissions and for air conditioning. Moreover, the auto insurance liability limits you're buying are increasingly likely to be in the $100,000 to $300,000 range against the previous $10,000 to $20,000 range of coverage. In your food baskets, the upgrading is unmistakable, as Chapter 6, "The Everyday Necessity of Food," dramatically illustrates.

You have been indeed translating the pipe dreams of the 1950s into the tangible possessions of the 1970s—and translating pipe dreams costs money.

You well may feel you're going broke on the highest income of your lives, but if you will look honestly at how you live, you might ruefully conclude that you're at least going broke in style.

Your Key Weapons Against Rising Costs

It could be that you are an extraordinarily perceptive shopper. Even so, I'll wager that I can show you how to become a far more perceptive shopper. In fact, I'll go further and wager that in the following pages—and despite my preceding analysis—you'll find ways to shave your costs from a minimum of 5 per cent to as much as 50 per cent or more in *every area* of your family budget.

Behind the over-all increases in your living costs each year, there always will be sharp variations of which you can take advantage. There always will be moves you can make to cushion the impact of inflation on your own budget. Your fundamental safeguards are awareness of the trends and understanding of the ways to protect yourself against the trends. Now here are your four key weapons:

(1) *Substituting* for these items, wherever and whenever you can, others of a similar nature on which prices are holding the line.

(2) *Switching* to less expensive versions of increasingly costly goods and services.

(3) *Shopping* harder than ever for the best possible deal on items you must have and on which prices are soaring.

(4) *Eliminating* items which are of no real value and even are of harm to you.

For instance, contributing tremendously to the increases in food prices have been climbing costs of meat. But within this food category, you can make many delicious substitutions. You also can choose a vegetable in season for one that isn't. And you have great control over how often you eat out, even greater control over what you eat when you are out.

Again, to illustrate, over-all transportation costs have been climbing steadily—but among the real "villains" behind this inflation have been soaring parking charges and public transportation costs. You can't do much but you can do some things to save on public transportation costs —and you can do plenty to curb your parking charges.

You can switch forms of entertainment for activities which are going out of sight. You certainly can save on cigarettes simply by quitting smoking. You have a wide variety of choices in clothing. I could go on and on but there is no need.

With the basic guidance in these pages, you can use your own imagination and carry on superbly from here.

A Dozen Wise Rules for Shopping for Everything

(1) Shop around. Prices do vary even from day to day on items ranging from food to furniture, from cars to cosmetics. Comparison-shop at stores in your area. Keep an eye on the ads. Know which stores have built their reputations by offering values on certain types of merchandise.

(2) Watch for genuine sales and specials and study the "calendar for bargains" which is provided in this chapter. Not everything adver-

tised is at a better price today than it will be tomorrow. Hunt out the real bargains. There always are some around. Stock up on things you need when prices are seasonally reduced, as at semi-annual clothing sales or inventory clearance sales. Watch and learn which stores put what things on sale and when—particularly on big-ticket major things.

(3) Watch for differences in quality. It well may be that the extra luxury or utility of the higher-priced items is really worth the extra cost. But don't spend unnecessarily for quality; buy only the grade of the item you need. Grades A and B tomatoes, for instance, look best—but Grade C, the lowest in price, will be just as good in stews and casseroles.

(4) Hold periodic family councils to discuss money matters. You can cut back on costs better in an atmosphere of co-operation and understanding.

(5) Keep control of your credit purchases, make sure your monthly charge account balances are at a reasonable minimum, and shop for credit with utmost care (see Chapter 3, "How to Borrow Cash and Use Credit Wisely.")

(6) Be careful about impulse buying. Supermarket shoppers consistently buy more than they put down on their shopping lists. Don't permit impulse to trick you into buying things you don't need or even want.

(7) Buy what's right for *you*. In clothing, for example, classic styles may be more appropriate for you (and last longer) than the latest fashion craze. And many combinations of the same basic garment may be a far sounder purchase than any spectacular outfit. Let your own experience guide you.

(8) Buy in bulk but only when you'll use it *all*. All things are not necessarily "cheaper by the dozen." Spoilage and discards can eat up your apparent savings on quite a variety of bulk and "economy" purchases. Check whether the bulk price really is more attractive than what you would pay for a smaller size or amount before you stock up on things you buy regularly.

(9) Investigate the private brands in food, clothing, and appliance lines which may be priced more favorably than national brands. Test the quality, learn which private labels you can rely upon. On major purchases, be sure service facilities are available.

(10) Read the label information. Clothing labels will tell you essential facts about materials used and proper cleaning methods. Even the fanciest packages often carry important data that you will neglect to your sorrow.

(11) Give a plus to low maintenance. Many product improvements in recent years have concentrated on easy care—ranging from permanent-press fabrics and stain repellents to extra-durable furniture. They're worth the slightly higher price tags that may be attached. But don't pay more for convenience than it is worth to you—the other side of "easy care."

(12) Consider service and "returns." Deal with retailers and manufacturers who stand solidly behind what they sell and who never balk at servicing or replacing a product. If they go out of their way to serve you, they want your business, and they deserve it.

QUIZ YOURSELF INTO BUYING WISELY

When you're wondering whether you should or should not buy, give yourself this quiz, prepared by the Council for Family Financial Education, and find out.

1. Do you really need this item?	Yes	No
2. Is the price reasonable?	Yes	No
3. Is this the best time to buy the item?	Yes	No
4. If this is a bargain, is it a current model (if that matters to you)?	Yes	No
5. If "on sale," is the price a true sale price?	Yes	No
6. Are you sure no less expensive item can be substituted?	Yes	No
7. Are you sure there are no major disadvantages? ...	Yes	No
8. If excessive in price, will it truly satisfy an inner need? (If not excessive, just check "yes.")	Yes	No
9. Have you checked and researched the item?	Yes	No
10. Do you know the retailer's reputation?	Yes	No
11. Does this retailer offer any special services with the item?	Yes	No

Score your answers as follows:

9–11 yeses—buy the product:
6–8 yeses—think again:
Fewer than 6 yeses—forget it.

CALENDAR FOR BARGAINS

February is an excellent month in which to buy air conditioners, used cars, rugs, and lamps. Do so—and you can save 10 to 30 per cent or even more on each item's cost.

August is a fine month in which to buy furs, fans, gardening equipment and men's coats. Do so—and you also can easily save 10 to 30 per cent or more.

Buy refrigerators in January . . . Buy millinery in July . . . Buy toys during the post-Christmas clearances . . . And bathing suits during the post-July 4 markdowns . . .

These are the seasonal savings—and they are and will continue to be available throughout the years. Merely by planning your spending to take advantage of the seasonal sales the year round, you can easily slash your spending by hundreds of dollars! Just by ignoring the seasonal "bargain calendar" I submit below, you can "waste" hundreds of dollars.

There are three major periods for store-wide clearance sales: after Easter, after July 4th, and after Christmas. These are excellent times to pick up clothes, linens, dozens of other items, although you may run into shortages of styles, sizes, and colors if you don't shop early in the sales. There also are the well-publicized August white sales; specials for George Washington's birthday, for Columbus Day, Veterans' Day, similar holidays.

And this applies just as strongly to foods. Again to illustrate: If you can manage to resist buying fresh strawberries until June or July—when prices drop sharply from their peaks at the beginning of the strawberry season in April—you will save money on this delicacy. On the other hand, if you are unable to resist buying watermelons as they begin to appear on supermarket shelves in June—instead of waiting until August when watermelon prices will have dropped sharply—your indulgence will cost you plenty.

Do not let the simplicity of the following calendars for foods and non-foods mislead you into downgrading their importance to your pocketbook! These bargain guides alone can put you well on the way to beating any foreseeable price spiral in the future. This *strategy of timing your buying* alone can more than offset any apparent annual rise in the cost of living.

If You Want to Buy	Good Months to Buy Are
Air conditioners	February, July, August
Appliances	January
Art supplies	January, February
Bathing suits	After July Fourth, August
Batteries and mufflers	September
Bedding	February, August
Bicycles	January, February, September, October, November
Blankets	January, May, November, December
Books	January
Building materials, lumber	June
Camping equipment	August
Carriages	January, August
Cars (new)	August, September
(used)	February, November, December
Car seat covers	February, November
Children's clothing	July, September, November, December
China	January, February, September, October
Christmas gifts	Any time but Christmas
Clothes dryers	January, February, March, April
Clothing (spring)	March
Coats (women's, children's)	April, August, November, December
(men's)	January, August
(winter)	March
Costume jewelry	January

If You Want to Buy	Good Months to Buy Are
Curtains	February
Dishes	January, February, September
Drapes and curtains	February, August
Dresses	January, April, June, November
Fans	August
Fishing equipment	October
Frozen foods	June
Fuel oil	July
Furniture	January, February, June, August, September
Furs	January, August
Gardening equipment	August, September
Glassware	January, February, September, October
Handbags	January, May, July
Hardware	August, September
Hats (children's)	July, December
(men's)	January, July
(women's)	February, April, July
Home appliances	July
Home furnishings	January, February, August
Hosiery	March, October
Housecoats	April, May, June, October, November
Housewares	January, February, August, September
Infants' wear	January, March, April, July
Lamps	February, August, September

IF YOU WANT TO BUY	GOOD MONTHS TO BUY ARE
Laundry appliances	March
Linens	January, May
Lingerie	January, May, July
Luggage	March
Men's clothing	August, December
Men's shirts	January, February, July
Paints	August, September
Party items	December
Piece goods	June, September, November
Quilts	January, November, December
Radios, phonographs	January, February, July
Ranges	April, November
Refrigerators and freezers	January, July
Rugs and carpets	January, February, July, August, May, September
School clothes	August, October
School supplies	August, October
Shoes (boys' and girls')	January, March, July
(men's and women's)	January, July, November, December
Silverware	February, October
Skates	March
Ski equipment	March
Sportswear	January, February, May, July
Stereo equipment	January, February, July
Storm windows	January, February, March

If You Want to Buy	Good Months to Buy Are
Suits (men's and boys')	April, November, December
Summer clothes and fabrics	June, July
Summer sports equipment	July
Tablecloths	January, May
Television sets	May, June
Tires	May, end of August
Toiletries	January, July
Toilet water and colognes	July
Towels	January, May, August
Toys	January, February
Water heaters	January, November

"SCRAPING BY" ON $40,000 A YEAR

Billy, a bright young executive with three teen-age children, boasted in 1974 that his family had adopted these moneysaving measures:

• adjusted the engine on their fancy foreign car to run on regular gasoline;

• instructed the local druggist to cut by 20 per cent the number of pills in all prescriptions filled for the family;

• found a factory outlet store where the family can buy underwear at a saving of 20 to 25 per cent;

• switched to trains for all relatively short hops and pledged to use trains instead of planes for other trips whenever possible;

• stopped home milk deliveries (at premium prices);

• started using cold-water detergents in laundering to save on hot water;

• vowed to buy all ski equipment at bargain prices at season's end;

• pledged also to buy all swimming pool-purifying chemicals in bulk to save $20 a year.

What's fascinating is not the variety of angles for saving. What's fascinating is the family, for the executive is a $40,000-a-year man—an income bracket inhabited by a tiny per cent of U.S. households.

The plain fact is that the wealthier among us are feeling the pinch of climbing living costs and soaring taxes just as the less affluent are. Admittedly, the wealthier live on a more luxurious scale and are cutting *their* costs on skiing, pools, and high-test gas, but that doesn't make their pinch any less real to them. Here's a rough breakdown of Bill's $40,000 budget:

ITEM	YEARLY COST
Food, incidentals	$ 9,700
Car depreciation and upkeep	1,440
School tuition, transportation	5,472
Home mortgage; improvement loan	4,800
All insurance	1,788
Medical and dental bills	1,500
Social Security and pension contribution	1,500
Property taxes	1,440
Federal and state income taxes	12,360

Immediately, three points jump out of this breakdown:

First, "school"—for three youngsters in private day school—is one of this family's biggest expenses. Reason: "The public schools in our area simply don't offer quality education." This family, like millions of others, pays increasingly steep school taxes—*plus* steep private tuitions. Private schooling has become a necessity rather than a luxury to many parents across the U.S.

Second, all types of taxes, totaling $13,800 a year, amount to a fat 35 per cent of the budget. The importance of taxes in today's middle-upper income squeeze cannot be exaggerated.

Third, the budget makes *no* special provision for the costs of vacations (this family has simply stopped taking them), restaurant eating, gifts, clothes. And the omission of any savings is appallingly dangerous.

In addition to finding "exotic" cost-cutting devices, what are other upper-income families doing to ease the squeeze? They're taking on more and more moonlighting jobs—in anything from teaching to consulting; demanding bigger and bigger raises from their employers; urging their wives to go back to work. Many, too, are simply using for day-to-day living the capital they had accumulated toward college costs or retirement.

And of course they are seeking and welcoming every moneysaving hint they can find. Which explains why I tell this tale of the $40,000-a-year family. Like them, search out every cost-cutting suggestion in every section of this book. Use each and all in the confidence that no matter what your income bracket—how high or how low—countless others are using them too.

5

THE EXTRA COST
OF BEING BROKE

As I've emphasized as hard as I could in this section, a superb way to save money on your food budget is through shopping the specials at the supermarkets and loading up on bargain-priced foods which you can store in your home freezer.

But let's say you're a young man and woman just starting out together and you're already straining your pay check or checks to finance your day-to-day purchases of food. Where will you get the extra cash implicit in use of this moneysaving hint? Even assuming you have a freezer in good working condition—quite an assumption—how can you afford to take advantage of this indisputably sound advice?

As I've also stressed as hard as I could, a top-notch way to save money on your clothing budget is through buying staple, basic items at out-of-season sales and always being on the lookout for things you know you'll have to buy during the year. November is a traditional month for sales on women's and children's coats; December is a traditional month for sales on men's and boys' suits; January is the prime month for sales on a wide variety of clothing ranging from lingerie to shoes.

But how can you—already limiting yourself, let's say, to a minimum of new clothes so you will have the money to finance your education—take advantage of this moneysaving hint? Just my suggestion that you shop these traditional sales has more than a touch of arrogance about it.

Again, a major way to save money on items ranging from big-ticket appliances to minor cosmetics is through shopping a discount store in the area. Savings can easily range 25 to 30 per cent.

But to repeat the refrain once more, how will you get to a discount store located many miles away? The bus or train fare will be an obstacle by itself—and I surely can't take for granted that you have a car at your disposal and can afford the gas and oil—as well as the ready cash to finance major purchases at the discount stores.

It is obvious when I put it this way, isn't it? And I could continue to place virtually every one of my major moneysaving guides in this context. In blunt and honest summary, my sound pocketbook advice is cruelly unrealistic to those of you who are broke.

And that goes whether you are living on an exceedingly limited budget while you are in school . . . or are just married and living to the hilt of your income . . . or are single, spending all you can earn on non-things and things more important to you now than the goods and services I've discussed in these pages . . . or whatever. . . .

In an excellent analysis entitled "The Extra Cost of Being Poor," Trienah Meyers of the Department of Agriculture zeroed in on these points at a Washington conference a while ago:

"While the buying habits of the more affluent members of the buying public are determined at least partially by convenience," she said, "those of the poor are dictated almost exclusively by an existing need. 'Poor' is buying when you can. . . . 'Poor' is buying in the neighborhood, at whatever the prices happen to be. . . . 'Poor' is buying in amounts you can afford, usually one at a time. . . . 'Poor' is buying whatever quality of brand or item you can manage on your time payments. . . ."

Enough. Surely the points are painfully apparent. The poor not only have less money, they also have less economic freedom on all purchasing fronts: time, place, amount, type, quality.

BUT!

You are not *doomed* to poverty: *you* are just in a transition stage.

You are not among the unskilled, the underprivileged, the ignorant: *you* are in the process of becoming skilled, of earning your right to privileges, of gaining the knowledge that you need to move into a more satisfying and rewarding world.

So! Learn and remember the guides in these pages for your maximum benefit when you have enough money to use them. These rules have been tested by time. They will always help you when you can take advantage of them.

6

THE EVERYDAY NECESSITY OF FOOD

FOOD PRICES IN PERSPECTIVE   179
HOW MUCH DOES YOUR FAMILY COST TO FEED?   179
DO SMALL FAMILIES PAY MORE?   179
NON-FOODS IN FOOD STORES   180
THE HIGH COST OF CONVENIENCE FOODS   183
OTHER "HIDDEN" FORCES PUSHING UP FOOD PRICES   184
YOUR CHANGING EATING HABITS   184
BASIC RULES FOR SAVING ON FOOD   186
TWENTY KEYS   187
STILL MORE SAVINGS VIA "TRADING DOWN"   191
SHOPPING THE DISCOUNT STORES   194
START YOUR OWN FOOD BUYING CLUB   194
HOW THE CLUBS WORK   195
WHOLESALE UNITS   196
WHERE TO GET INFORMATION   197
HOW TO READ FOOD LABELS   197
LABEL STANDARDS FOR WELL-KNOWN FOODS   198
"TRUTH IN MEAT" LABELING   202
"OPEN DATING"   202
HOW TO COMPARE UNIT COSTS PER POUND OF FOOD   203
WHICH IS THE BIGGER BARGAIN?   203
HOW TO USE UNIT PRICING   204
UNIT COST TABLE   205
HOW TO SAVE ON MEAT   208
CLASSIC DEMAND-PULL INFLATION   208

How to Save on Meat (*cont'd*)

    General Moneysaving Hints   209

    The True Cost of a Serving of Meat   211

    Protein Bargains   212

    How to Use Beef "Grades"   215

    But Number 1: Shop the Meat Specials!   216

    Savings by Buying Beef in Bulk   216

How to Use Your Home Freezer for Top Savings   221

    The Rules   221

    How Much Will You Use One?   223

    How to Buy   224

    Beware: The Dishonest "Freezer Food Plan"   225

    Beware: "Bait and Switch" in Bulk Beef
        Buying   226

How to Spot Bargains in Poultry   229

    A Key Is Form in Which You Buy   229

    Ways to Save on Buying Turkeys   230

Organic Foods   230

    The Boom Takes Off   230

    What Is "Organic" Food?   232

    Ten Rules for Buying Organic Foods   234

    Beware! Organic Food Traps   235

Whiskey and Wine   237

    How to Cut Your Liquor Bills   237

    How to Cut Your Wine Bills   239

How to Save on Parties   240

The High Cost of Eating Out   242

    Trend: Up, Up, Up   242

    Rules for Curbing Costs   242

Food Prices in Perspective

HOW MUCH DOES YOUR FAMILY COST TO FEED?

The amount *your* family spends on food depends on:

• the size of your family pay check (the lower your income bracket, the higher the proportion of your budget goes for food);

• the age of each family member (teen-agers are the most expensive to feed);

• the amount of entertaining your family does;

• the types of foods you eat—and don't eat;

• the importance of food as compared to your other needs and wants;

• food price levels at a given time and in a given place;

• how much time and effort various members of your family are able and willing to spend on food preparation;

• the area of the country in which you live;

• how much you eat out in restaurants, fast food places, etc.;

• whether or not you have a family vegetable garden or raise other foods, and whether your family preserves or freezes significant amounts of home-grown foods.

DO SMALL FAMILIES PAY MORE?

And what if yours is a smaller- or larger-sized family—how much does yours cost to feed? Here are key guides:

For each $1.00 a six-person family spends on food, a four-person household spends $1.03, a two-person household spends $1.07, and a single individual living alone spends $1.11.

On a per-person basis, the large family always pays less than the small family—a point which is becoming increasingly important as food prices continue spiraling ever upward. In fact, the one-person household in the United States pays fully 11 per cent more for the same list of foods than the family consisting of two parents and four children, according to a study by the U. S. Agriculture Department.

NON-FOODS IN FOOD STORES

How complex is the story of your rising food budget? Merely to suggest the ramifications:

• Part of your higher grocery-supermarket bills can be traced to your ever rising preference for gourmet foods and relatively expensive condiments.

• Part can be traced to your ever rising fondness for snacks, which have become a kind of "fourth meal" in the American home.

• Part of the bigger bills can be traced, as you all admit, to your ever rising preference for convenience foods and to the huge wave of big-eating teen-agers moving through our population.

What's more, the tremendous strides we have made in food distribution have made possible nationwide availability of foods grown thousands of miles away.

The modern distribution system also is providing year-round availability of most seasonal foods. This, too, adds to costs. Clearly, anyone who buys fresh corn on the cob in Maine in February is going to pay a lot more for the corn than in Kansas in August.

A huge volume of the food we eat is imported from nations as distant as Brazil and Ghana. So weather and other factors affecting the whole food supply-demand picture in other nations also bear on the prices we pay in our supermarkets for such items as coffee, tea, cocoa, bananas, spices. And all of us, all consumers, pay for the cost to the manufacturer of developing an estimated 5,000 new food items each year—of which only 1,500 reach food store shelves and only 500 last as long as one year.

But the big surge in spending has been in *non-foods*—and these now represent about one fourth of our total store bills.

Item: Among the fastest sale gainers in the nation's supermarkets and grocery stores in recent years have been non-foods ranging from paper towels and greeting cards to dishwasher compounds, furniture polish, and deodorant soaps. Also among the fastest gainers have been cat food, canned soft drinks, and dietetic soft drinks.

Item: More than half of all the toothpaste we buy in the United States is from supermarkets and grocery stores, not drugstores. We now buy more than half of all our aspirin in food stores, and nearly half of our shampoo and shaving products. In addition, we get one third of our first aid equipment in supermarkets plus an astounding one in ten of our phonograph records and more than one in ten of our comic books and magazines.

One less obvious force propelling the non-food upswing in food stores is the domestic do-it-yourself trend in our land. You are spending sharply increased amounts in supermarkets for such things as home spot cleaning fluids, self-polishing floor waxes, shoe polishes, housewares.

Another force is the steady upgrading in our health and sanitary standards. This explains the huge increases in supermarket sales of aerosol household deodorizers and disinfectants, plastic film wraps for food storage, garbage can liners, drain cleaners, deodorant soaps, personal deodorants, all types of first aid equipment.

Here is how you divided up a $20 bill in the supermarket-grocery in 1973. The relationships have not changed and this breakdown will clinch the tale of your spending for non-foods as well as foods in the supermarket in the mid-1970s.

CLASSIFICATION	TOTAL
Perishables	
Baked goods, snacks	$ 1.14
Dairy products (including eggs and margarine)	1.29
Frozen foods	1.06
Meat, fish, poultry	4.69
Produce	2.19
TOTAL FOR PERISHABLES	$10.37
Dry Groceries	
Beer	$ .91
Wine and distilled spirits	.13
Baby foods (excluding cereals)	.09
Cereals and rice	.27

CLASSIFICATION	TOTAL
Dry Groceries (cont'd)	
Candy and chewing gum	$ .20
Canned foods	
Fruits	.18
Juices and drinks	.18
Meat and poultry	.22
Milk	.05
Seafood	.13
Soups	.12
Vegetables	.28
Coffee and tea (including instants)	.52
Dried fruits, vegetables, milk	.22
Jams, jellies, preserves	.07
Macaroni, spaghetti, noodles	.09
Puddings (packaged gelatin and instant desserts)	.03
Soft drinks	.45
Sugar	.15
All other foods	1.07
TOTAL FOR DRY GROCERIES	$ 5.36
Other Groceries	
Paper goods	$ .42
Soaps, detergents, laundry	.43
Other household products	.37
Pet foods	.27
Tobacco products	.75
Miscellaneous	.14
TOTAL FOR OTHER GROCERIES	$ 2.38
General Merchandise	
Health and beauty aids	$ .76
Prescriptions	.08
Housewares	.19
All other general merchandise	.86
TOTAL FOR GENERAL MERCHANDISE	$ 1.89
GRAND TOTAL	$20.00

THE HIGH COST OF CONVENIENCE FOODS

If you serve your family a store-bought pizza pie, it will cost you about 60 per cent more than if you put the ingredients together yourself. Or if you serve prepared hashed brown potatoes, it'll cost nearly twice the amount per serving it would cost if you had hashed them at home. And the cost of one slice of store-bought apple pie also may be double the cost of a home-baked pie.

Your willingness to pay extra for expensive maid service built into the foods you buy is a well-known force behind rising food prices, but you persist in underestimating how much your own demands for convenience foods are adding to your own food budgets. You don't *have* to buy the ready-made pizza at almost twice the price of making the pie at home—but you do.

As you wheel your cart through today's fantastic selection of supermarket foods, you are increasingly apt to choose the package of frozen beans with butter already added, the box of breakfast cereal coated with sugar or mixed with freeze-dried fruit over the box of plain cereal, the just-add-milk pancake mix over the half dozen separate ingredients which go into pancakes.

The Department of Agriculture calculates that your per capita consumption of fresh fruits and vegetables has been dropping steadily and your consumption of canned fruit has remained fairly stable. But your consumption of canned and frozen vegetables has been climbing steeply. Most dramatically, your purchases of frozen potato products and processed items like instant mashed potatoes have skyrocketed while consumption of fresh potatoes has declined.

A full 10 per cent of the eggs you now consume are pre-emptied and preprocessed, and by the end of this decade, says the Agriculture Department, the proportion of eggs in forms ranging from cake mixes to "instant" scrambled eggs will soar to one third of your total egg consumption.

• Today, about half of all supermarkets have a delicatessen department, and almost every new supermarket has one. Many also have their own kitchens in which 60 to 100 different items are prepared—most of them higher-priced convenience foods.

There's absolutely no basis for expecting any of these trends to slow, much less reverse. And now you are moving to the convenience of the *whole take-home meal*—the carton of chicken or fish and chips or whatever, bought at the fast food, limited-menu store—and this meal certainly costs more than the made-from-scratch version.

OTHER "HIDDEN" FORCES PUSHING UP FOOD PRICES

What I have described so far are only the obvious factors. There also are many other "hidden" forces which may not appear of significance when considered separately but which do add up to real pressure on your food budget when considered as a group. To illustrate with a sampling:

Pollution controls: The steps that farmers, food processors, and others take to reduce runoff of chemical fertilizers into water supplies, to curtail use of dangerous pesticides, to dispose of by-products in ways that won't pollute the air and water.

Tightened food inspection rules: Regulations which have raised the food standards in this country to the highest in the history of man and made our current food supply the safest ever—despite admitted gaps still remaining.

Rising skepticism about food additives, colorings, etc.: Our questioning the safety of these substances—including preservatives—is forcing food processors to stiffen their standards for using the substances, to increase their spending on research, to risk higher losses from spoilage.

Better labeling: This improvement for us has added to the costs of some foods.

Import quotas: These restrictions cost us literally billions of dollars each year.

Then there's the weather (droughts, killing frosts), always a factor. There are periodic, costly dock strikes. There are numerous labor practices which limit productivity and raise labor costs. And there is the organic farming boom which may swell food budgets by hundreds of millions of dollars.

YOUR CHANGING EATING HABITS

"My daughter, fourteen, loves all food. My son, sixteen, likes oriental, kosher, and Italian. He is a gourmet. He likes chocolate-covered ants and grasshoppers. My son, nineteen, will eat anything that won't eat him first."

This was a Los Angeles housewife speaking in a recent survey of U.S. homemakers. Her colorful words illustrate today's complete breakdown in the traditional patterns of which foods go together with which other foods. They highlight the development of one new trend, what might be called a new "ethnic" jumbling together of foods: Italian, kosher, Chinese, soul food, etc., and suggest our billion-dollar-a-year stampede to exotic, gourmet foods.

In addition to this development, here are other key trends and changes in your eating habits:

(1) From a nutritional viewpoint, you are eating less well than in the mid-fifties. Only half of all American households are eating a good diet today, according to a massive and alarming Agriculture Department study. Nearly one family in ten in the $10,000-and-up income bracket has a diet rated as poor, and over all, one in five families has a diet rated as poor. Our per capita national consumption of such nutritional cornerstones as milk, fresh fruits, and vegetables has been declining steadily—replaced to a considerable extent by sweet snacks, sweet soft drinks, etc.

In the past two generations the proportion of calories we as a nation eat in the form of starches has dropped from 68 to 48 per cent, while the proportion in the form of sugar and other sweeteners has soared from 32 to 52 per cent. The old-fashioned fresh potato, one of the richest sources of key vitamins and minerals if you eat it in its skin, is being shunned, although potatoes actually contain fewer calories on an ounce-for-ounce basis than lima beans, prunes, rice, bran flakes, and most fruits canned in heavy syrup. Our per capita consumption of fresh potatoes in 1973 was 82 pounds a year, versus 97 pounds in 1960.

(2) "Isolated eating" is in a strong uptrend. Breakfast, for millions of Americans, has become nothing more than a foraging expedition through the refrigerator and food cupboards, with each family member gulping down whatever foods are at hand and then hurrying off to work or school. Or it's "instant" breakfast made up of hopefully nutritious imitations.

Lunch also, for millions of children and jobholders, has become an institutional meal, served in school cafeterias or company restaurants. Only the homebound mother and her preschool children may eat lunch together. In fact, for a startling number of families, even sitting down to dinner is now strictly a weekend affair. The kids eat when they come home from school; if the father hasn't eaten downtown, he eats when he comes home hours later; the mother eats whenever.

This haphazard eating is blurring the old demarcation lines between meals. An increasing part of what is eaten is in the form of snacks.

(3) You are often skipping meals altogether, in most cases in your efforts to lose weight. According to a recent study, about one in five Americans in the nineteen- to twenty-four-age bracket regularly skips lunch; 16 per cent skip breakfast; one in ten forgoes the evening meal.

(4) Eating out is on the increase—in restaurants, snack bars, fast food stores and stands. The proportion of our food dollar going for eating out (as contrasted with eating at home) is now 20 per cent.

(5) There has been a steady expansion of the office and factory coffee break. With orange juice or some similar food, pastries or rolls, and coffee now included, the coffee break has become a substitute for breakfast at home for workers at every level across the land.

This is not nearly as farfetched as it may appear, for as today's housewife finds she is little more than a short-order cook for her family, she will channel her culinary efforts into special meals for special occasions. She will do her short-order cooking as efficiently and quickly as possible, simultaneously investing ever larger amounts of her time and money in cooking schools, gourmet food guides, chafing dishes, barbecue pits, hibachis, etc. And, incidentally, the evidence is that she is teaching her daughter to cook this way too—to prepare foods on a piecemeal basis rather than systematically as a full meal.

BASIC RULES FOR SAVING ON FOOD

If you make an error in buying furniture, you're almost surely stuck. It may take you years to correct your mistake and you'll probably come out with a painful loss. But *if* you make an error in buying fruit, you can quickly learn from your mistake and only days later come out ahead when you again go shopping for food.

Food is among the biggest items in our cost of living and it is among the most expensive items in the budgets of low- and low-middle-income families. Yet, in contrast to the big-ticket items you buy only from time to time—furniture, automobiles, appliances—you buy food at least once or twice a week. Food is virtually the only major cash-and-carry item left in the typical budget. Thus, food is the one area where you can correct costly errors easily and start saving substantially from the day you determine to concentrate on so doing.

TWENTY KEYS

To be specific, here are twenty keys to saving:

(1) To begin with, plan before you go shopping. Always have a pad handy so you can note food items you need as your supplies run low. Group together the same kinds of foods and supplies to simplify your shopping in any store. Inspect your refrigerator, freezer, and cabinet or pantry shelves to see what you have on hand and what you need. Consult the store ads as you make up your shopping list and group the items on your list into the following categories:

> Groceries and canned foods
> Bakery products and cereals
> Dairy products
> Fresh fruits and vegetables
> Frozen foods
> Meat, fish, and poultry
> Non-foods (cleaning products, paper, etc.)
> Other

When your shopping list is ready, go over it to be sure you have chosen foods on the basis of their nutritional value—the amounts and proportions of protein, vitamins, minerals they contain—rather than strictly on the basis of their "taste appeal." Spend your money first for those items, then go on to other foods that you merely want.

Use your list as you shop, and also take along whatever throwaway shopper ads might lead you to the bargains. Glance too at the price specials advertised in store windows—for clues to items you might want to add.

(2) Avoid snacks—among the most expensive food extras you can buy. They easily can add 10 per cent to your weekly food bill but will be among the least valuable nutritionally. Or, as an alternative, stick to snacks and beverages which have some nutritionally redeeming value—i.e., orange juice versus orange pop, fresh fruit versus candy, and whole-

grain crackers, oatmeal-raisin-peanut-butter cookies versus chocolate or cream-filled ones.

(3) Keep in mind—as you make out your food lists and as you actually shop for food—what you'll do with inevitable leftovers. If you plan to make split pea soup using a hambone, for example, buy the split peas when you buy the ham. Also use the little leftovers in your refrigerator—bits of cheese, a dab of tuna fish or chicken, a slice or two of salami or ham—to make a smorgasbord that can serve as a complete lunch or supper. Or use the leftovers in a soup. Or make them the basis for a delicious platter of hors d'oeuvre. That's how hors d'oeuvre came into being, you know—out of bits of leftovers.

(4) If you possibly can, shop in person in the store: this will *always* give you the best value for your money and there is no real or comparably inexpensive substitute for this practice. You select the foods, you pay cash, you carry your purchases home. If you shop by telephone, have food delivered to your home, and charge these food purchases, you will pay for these conveniences—and the costs over a year will add up to whopping totals.

Do not—if you are a wife and can avoid it—let your husband come along on the weekly supermarket shopping trip (unless your husband routinely does the shopping). Husbands are notorious impulse buyers and almost inevitably overload the shopping cart with non-essentials and badly chosen brands and varieties of needed items.

Do not go shopping for food on an empty stomach, if you can help it. Shopping hungry is another way to boost your impulse buying. Surveys reveal those who shop after meals spend up to 17 per cent *less* than those who shop when hungry.

(5) Keep records of prices you're paying—particularly for such big items as meat—and shift your menus as prices dictate.

(6) Shop the specials and stock your freezer and pantry with foods you need or want when they are marked down.

(7) Consider quality in relation to your use of the food. If corn on the cob is the heart of your meal, of course you will buy the best quality you can afford. But if you're using corn as part of another dish, you'll do just as well with a much less expensive form of corn.

(8) Check the prices of private versus nationally advertised brands of foods you use frequently. Every food chain and many independent stores sell private-label foods, at savings running to as much as 20 per cent. The reasons: no advertising expenses are built into the private

brands; no salesmen or promotion campaigns are pushing up the costs; and in many cases transportation is a smaller expense on private than on nationally advertised brands. The quality of many private-label products compares favorably with that of nationally advertised brands. And many brands are of identical quality because they're packed for retailers by the processors of the nationally advertised brands. Buy the brand you like best but try the less expensive private-label product at least once.

(9) Check the containers with care when you buy frozen foods and never buy an item that is covered with frost. Select only food that is stored below the freezer line at 0° or below. Under *no* circumstances buy a can of food that is bulging—and if you uncover such a can in your own pantry, toss it out.

(10) Buy such foods as meat by cost per portion rather than by over-all price. To find this cost, divide the price of the amount you purchase by the number of portions the amount will supply. More on this later.

(11) Buy such foods as bread or cereals by cost per ounce or pound. There is no waste involved here, so see which package offers the most weight for the identical price. More on this later, too.

Buy bulk items such as flour and sugar in bags rather than in boxes. By so doing, you're likely to save an average of nearly 20 per cent.

(12) Compare package sizes in relation to how quickly you will consume the contents. The "family economy size" is no bargain to you if you end up throwing out a lot of leftovers.

(13) Analyze the real cost of cooking from scratch versus buying "built-in maid service." It's not usual, but the cost of ingredients to prepare something at home may sometimes be *more* than the prepackaged convenience equivalent—especially if staples are left over.

(14) Compare different forms of food. More and more foods are sold in today's market in different forms—fresh, canned, frozen, chilled, and dried. Save money by comparing costs between different forms. As just one illustration of possible savings, per-serving costs of condensed soup run as little as one third the cost of water-added varieties. Before buying a particular item, check to see whether it's cheaper *to buy it fresh, canned, or frozen*. Relative costs change with seasonal patterns. Taste well may be your deciding factor; the difference in nutrition may be insignificant.

When you shop for low-calorie foods, stick to ordinary foods as much as possible—fresh celery, carrots, and radishes, plain beef consommé or chicken broth, fresh fruits and vegetables, regular canned tuna fish, low-fat milk—and avoid higher-priced items on the special diet shelf.

(15) Always remember the seasonal specials. Many of the fruits and vegetables which come to market in abundance in summer, cost 50 per cent less than in winter. But don't buy the *first* of a crop; prices will go down as the supply increases. Also time buying of canned and frozen fruits and vegetables to take advantage of the end-of-summer surpluses after new packs come in. And when these specials are advertised, stock up.

(16) Weigh the cost of gasoline—and time—in choosing a supermarket. The least expensive supermarket in your area almost surely won't be the cheapest for you if you have to drive twice the distance to reach it.

As a general rule, small convenience stores which stay open long hours seven days a week charge the highest prices. Next come small neighborhood "Mom and Pop" stores. Then supermarkets and the food discount stores.

(17) Substitute among protein foods as prices dictate. Try beef or pork liver instead of calf's liver; poultry instead of red meats; bean, cheese, and egg dishes instead of meat dishes. Among today's best protein bargains: chicken, hamburger, eggs, cottage cheese, peanut butter, dry beans, American process cheese.

(18) Use the recipes and food-buying tips offered to you by the Department of Agriculture, your local consumer organizations, and your local newspaper's food editor.

(19) Also use the Agriculture Department's publications, which are designed to help you. The department is loaded with booklets and pamphlets on how to buy, raise, store, cook, and combine food of all kinds—available from the Superintendent of Documents, Washington, D.C. 20402.

Among the key titles:

Your Money's Worth in Foods (Home and Garden Bulletin No. 183)
Family Fare: A Guide to Good Nutrition (Home and Garden Bulletin No. 1)
Beef and Veal in Family Meals (Home and Garden Bulletin No. 118)
Family Food Buying, A Guide for Calculating Amounts to Buy and Comparing Costs (Home Economics Research Report No. 37)

Toward the New, A Report on Better Foods and Nutrition from Agricultural Research (Agriculture Information Bulletin No. 341)

The Food We Eat (Miscellaneous Publication No. 870)

Conserving the Nutritive Values in Foods (Home and Garden Booklet No. 90)

Composition of Foods, Raw, Processed, Prepared (Agriculture Handbook No. 8)

(20) Hunt for the nutrition bargains and *don't* overbuy meat. Use the following guides, developed by the U. S. Department of Agriculture on the minimum amounts of each major type of food we at various ages should consume daily for proper nutrition:

Milk: children under 9 years, 2 to 3 cups; 9 to 12 years, 3 or more cups; teen-agers, 4 or more cups; adults, 2 or more cups; pregnant women, 3 or more cups; nursing mothers, 4 or more cups. (Note: Cheese, ice cream, and milk used in cooking count as part of the day's milk.)

Meat: 2 or more servings of either beef or veal, pork, lamb, poultry, fish, shellfish, eggs—with dry beans, peas, nuts as alternates.

Vegetables and fruits: 4 or more servings with a dark green or deep yellow vegetable at least every other day; a citrus fruit or other fruit or vegetable rich in vitamin C daily; other vegetables and fruits, including potatoes.

Bread and cereal: 4 or more servings—whole grain, enriched, or restored—of breads, bakery foods, cereals, crackers, grits, macaroni, spaghetti, noodles, rice.

STILL MORE SAVINGS VIA "TRADING DOWN"

Do you realize how much you could reduce your food bill by "trading down" in the supermarket today—by choosing the least expensive version available of each item on your grocery list? You're surely generally aware that you could achieve big savings simply by doing this instead of trading up to the highest-quality, most convenient, fanciest-label foods. But would you have guessed that the savings I recorded in a recent shopping experiment of my own amounted to 88 per cent?

For the experiment, I asked an eagle-eyed young housewife-friend to wheel two shopping carts through a huge supermarket in my area of the country; first she would load cart number 1 with the most expensive possible items and then load cart number 2 with the least expensive.

In the milk category, it was regular fresh milk in cart number 1 and powdered milk in cart number 2. And "potatoes" meant fancy Idahos for cart number 1 but plain old Maine spuds for cart number 2. And so on down the line. . . .

When she checked the two carts for me, the bargain cart came to $22.54 less than the most expensive assortment. I won't give you the complete breakdown on the carts, because prices for specific items vary so widely from time to time and area to area. But the total is representative—and if you multiplied it by fifty-two weeks, you would have savings amounting to $1,172.08 a year!

Here is my full shopping list, with the dollar difference *and* the percentage savings between high- and low-priced items:

Item	$ Difference	% Saving
Frankfurters (2 lbs.)	$ .49	22%
Hamburger (3 lbs.)	1.62	39
Liver (2 lbs.)	1.80	64
Bacon (2 lbs.)	1.00	42
Steak (3 lbs.)	5.40	69
Eggs (2 doz.)	.12	8
Butter (2 lbs.)	.06	3
Milk (8 qts.)	1.57	61
Coffee (2 lbs.)	.08	5
White bread (2 loaves)	.48	49
Frozen peas (6 pkgs.)	1.41	52
Pears (2 large cans)	.20	17
Mayonnaise (large jar)	.06	9
Vegetable soup (4 cans)	.44	44
Cat food (3 cans)	.24	41
Frozen orange juice (4 6-oz. cans)	.39	33
Tomatoes (2 large cans)	.19	22
Salad oil (1 qt.)	1.26	62
Beer (6-pack)	2.60	72
Cookies (1 box)	.70	71
Onions (3 lbs.)	.49	42

ITEM	$ DIFFERENCE	% SAVING
Spaghetti (2 boxes)	.10	18
Potatoes (10 lbs.)	.89	41
Liquid detergent (1 qt.)	.50	56
Flour (5 lbs.)	.45	49

The rundown speaks for itself. In some cases, splurge items cost twice to three times as much as non-splurge items. In some cases, too, the shopper has obviously sacrificed quality (although probably not much nutritional value). In other cases, though, there's no significant difference between the cart number 1 item and the cart number 2 item.

Convenience, too, was ignored in cart number 2—e.g., no pre-peeled vegetables, no butter added to frozen foods, no pre-pattied hamburgers, no individual servings of this or that. But, of course, convenience is part of the sacrifice a careful shopper must pay to reap the maximum savings from trading down.

I'm not suggesting you stick strictly to the cheapest available foods or other items. Most of you don't want to nor do you need to. But even though you can afford to splurge and trade up, not down, is it not fascinating to see how much you could save if you tried to trade down? And you need not go this far. All you really need to do is to buy essentially the same foods in less expensive form.

Here, for instance, are two menus which reveal that you can almost double the cost of your meal by choosing the more expensive variety of meat, fruit, or vegetable or, conversely, you can cut it nearly in half by choosing the less expensive variety.

LESS EXPENSIVE	MORE EXPENSIVE
Grapefruit half	Cantaloupe
Chuck steak	Sirloin steak
Baked potato with sour cream	Frozen creamed potato with chives
Frozen peas buttered at home	Frozen peas in butter sauce
Tossed salad	Salad with tomatoes, avocados
Rye bread	Garlic bread
Chocolate pudding	Frozen éclairs

These two menus were priced in 1974. For four persons, the less expensive menu came to $3.80; the more expensive totaled $6.60.

SHOPPING THE DISCOUNT STORES

Discounting has become the biggest, hottest trend in food retailing today. And you are shouting your preference for this no-frills, big-scale, moneysaving method of food buying.

How much do you save by shopping in discount food stores? According to a major study by A&P, weekly savings run around 11 per cent. Other studies indicate over-all savings generally at from 5 to 15 per cent.

There are two key types of discount operations: general merchandise discount stores which include a food department, and separate stores devoted solely to food.

If you shop in discount stores you'll probably have to travel some distance—and in view of fuel costs, have to space your shopping trips more widely to reap in full the bargains they offer. You'll probably forfeit many of the usual supermarket amenities—ranging from carry-out service to Muzak. You probably won't find trading stamps in these places. You may even have to pick some of your foods out of cut cases instead of neat shelf displays—and in some cases you may have to make do with a smaller variety of products.

But if none of these aspects bothers you and if you have the gas, oil, and use of a car at least once a week, try out the local discount stores. Ask friends about their experience with these stores. Read newspaper ads and compare prices. Then see how much money *you* can save.

Start Your Own Food Buying Club

If food co-operatives, food warehouses, and other wholesale outlets are operating in your area, by all means use them too. You'll buy staples such as rice, sugar, flour in 25- or 50-pound bags; you'll bag your own purchases and you'll pick the produce you want to buy straight out of packing cases.

You'll also achieve savings ranging from 20 per cent up.

Or you can join with other families to start your own food buying club.

HOW THE CLUBS WORK

Here are tips from New York City's Department of Consumer Affairs on how these clubs work and on how to make a success out of this type of arrangement:

• A buying club may consist of as few as ten to twelve families. Clubs often sell items to members practically at cost. Their small size eliminates the need for the usual supermarket overhead—such as trucks, large distribution centers, hired helpers.

• Members must be compatible—both in personality and in food tastes. Each member must be willing to do his or her share of the work load, to avoid having to hire the outside help which raises costs and defeats the purpose of small-group buying.

• There must be several people for each job: driving, simple book-keeping, distributing, and buying. This system permits rotation of tasks and prevents any one member from being too heavily burdened.

• Members must be willing to do as much shopping as possible through the club.

• Buying is usually done by two or more buyers going once a week to wholesale markets, which are generally listed in the Yellow Pages. Each week, one buyer who has gone the week before accompanies a novice, to lend his or her previous experience (for example; a and b, then b and c, then c and d). The general shopping list for produce is: two types of fruit, one cooking vegetable, salad vegetables, potatoes, and onions. Meat is often ordered in advance from a distributor or a reliable local butcher who will give discounts.

• After the food is purchased, it is taken to a prearranged point for distribution, often a member's house or apartment. The food is sold at a price to cover the purchase price plus gasoline, oil, other incidentals.

• Buying clubs do *not* compete with each other. In fact, small clubs find it beneficial to co-operate in exchanging names of stores, recipes, and new ideas. Several buying clubs may co-operate on large-scale purchases for which an individual club would not receive a discount.

• A key problem for the clubs may be losses resulting from spoilage of unsold goods. This leftover food might be sold to outsiders via a "leftover list" of names of people who may be called after members have shopped.

• Another problem might arise when members feel that small children prevent them from participating. Some buying clubs have successfully added a baby-sitting system to their operation on buying days.

• Members should pay for their food not later than the day before the next week's buying. Members who regularly fail to pay on time, refuse to help, or do little buying harm the club. It is often best for the club to drop such members.

There must be open discussion of disagreements in order to reach constructive answers to the club's problems, whatever they turn out to be.

• Buying clubs of this type report big savings. The clubs find, moreover, that the quality of their food improves as well. And they have more bargaining power since wholesalers try to please large purchasers.

WHOLESALE UNITS

Here are the wholesale units in which food is boxed or weighed for wholesale:

Dairy and Produce

1. American cheese—5 lbs.
2. Eggs—30 doz.
3. Rice—25, 50, 100 lbs. (bags)
4. Lettuce—24 (box)
5. Tomatoes—20 lbs. (box)
6. Potatoes—50 lbs. (bag)
7. Onions—50 lbs. (bag)
8. Apples—36 or 40 lbs. (box)
9. Oranges—48, 56, 64, 72, 80 (box)
10. Bananas—40 lbs. (box)

Meats (may vary from place to place)

1. Chicken—per head
2. Ground chuck—10 lbs. or more
3. Bacon—12 lbs. (box)
4. Frankfurters—12 lbs. (box)
5. Flank steak—15 lbs.
6. Stew beef—10 lbs.
7. Pork chops—16–20 lbs.
8. Spare ribs—30 lbs.
9. Liver—8–11 lbs.

WHERE TO GET INFORMATION

An excellent source of further information on food buying clubs and co-ops and on shopping for wholesale foods is: The Cooperative League of the U.S.A., Suite 1100, 1828 L Street, N.W., Washington, D.C. 20036.

How to Read Food Labels

Q. *What is the difference between chicken "patties" and chicken "burgers"—in terms of the amount of chicken each contains?*

A. Chicken burgers must consist of 100 per cent chicken. If cereals or other fillers are used, they must be labeled patties.

Q. *How much meat must spaghetti with meatballs contain?*

A. Twelve per cent or more meat.

Q. *What's the difference between "beef and gravy" and "gravy and beef"?*

A. In beef and gravy, the primary ingredient is beef. With gravy and beef, it's the other way around.

These and other vital details, which are at least implied by the labels of hundreds of food products you buy regularly—or which may be stated among our many federal food standards—are key clues to how much of a bargain you are getting for your food dollar. Many labels tell you, too, how much of major nutrients, especially protein, are contained in each can or package.

The true value of what you are buying lies in what amounts of basic ingredients you are getting—not simply in the net weight of the food. Thus, by knowing something about food standards and some of the rules for reading food labels, you can consistently stretch your food dollar.

Here is a valuable rundown on labels and standards* to use to compare products and prices in the supermarket:

• Under federal law as of 1974, every package of food, drugs, or cosmetics must contain the following information on its label in plain English: name of the product; name and address of manufacturer,

* 1974.

packer, or distributor; net amount of contents or weight in pounds and ounces and in the total number of ounces; details of dietary characteristics, if appropriate; note of whether the product contains artificial coloring, flavoring, or chemical preservatives; a list of the ingredients, except for certain products (e.g., mayonnaise, macaroni, bread, jams, ketchup, canned fruits and vegetables) for which federal "standards of identity" defining basic ingredients have been established.

• Next, certain descriptive details are required for certain products, primarily canned fruits and vegetables: the variety (white or yellow corn, for instance); style of pack (whole, diced); material in which packaged (sugar, syrup, water).

• Ingredients must be listed in *descending* order of their volume (if a beef stew list shows beef way down and potatoes way up on the list, this is your clue that you are buying mostly potatoes).

• If the food is an imitation, this fact must be stated, and if there is a picture of the product within, it must be accurate.

• Baby food labels must state the nutritional elements they contain—proteins, vitamins, minerals—plus, in the case of strained baby foods, a list of the ingredients.

• Meats and other foods to which special vitamins and minerals have been added or which are claimed to have special nutritional properties ("enriched") must carry labels telling their calorie content, amounts of proteins, and amounts of key vitamins and minerals.

• On the major cuts of the carcasses, meats may carry the U. S. Department of Agriculture's inspection stamp. Federally inspected poultry —fresh or frozen—carries a stamp "inspected for wholesomeness."

• Then there are federal standards covering a host of prepared and convenience foods, especially those containing meat or poultry, that are not stated on the label.

• In addition, you may or may not find on a food package a brand name; directions for storage or suggestions for cooking; a food quality grade set by the Department of Agriculture.

LABEL STANDARDS FOR WELL-KNOWN FOODS

Many labels will undergo marked improvements as the Agriculture Department and Food and Drug Administration continue to revise their labeling rules and its standards. But you can use the following list of standards right now to help you shop for a variety of well-known products and to stretch your food dollar at least a bit more:

Baby Food (High Meat Dinner)—At least 30 per cent meat.

Baby Food (Vegetable and Meat)—At least 8 per cent meat.

Barbecue Sauce with Meat—At least 35 per cent meat.

Beans with Frankfurters in Sauce—At least 20 per cent franks.

Beef Burgundy—At least 50 per cent beef.

Beef Sausage (raw)—No more than 30 per cent fat.

Beef Stroganoff—At least 45 per cent fresh uncooked or 30 per cent cooked beef.

Beef with Gravy—At least 50 per cent beef.

Gravy with Beef—At least 35 per cent beef.

Breaded Steaks, Chops, etc.—Breading can't exceed 30 per cent of finished product weight.

Breakfast (frozen product containing meat)—At least 15 per cent meat.

Breakfast Sausage—No more than 50 per cent fat.

Cannelloni with Meat and Sauce—At least 10 per cent meat.

Chili con Carne—At least 40 per cent meat.

Chili con Carne with Beans—At least 25 per cent meat.

Chop Suey (American Style) *with Macaroni and Meat*—At least 25 per cent meat.

Chow Mein Vegetables with Meat—At least 12 per cent meat.

Deviled Ham—No more than 35 per cent fat.

Dinners (frozen with meat)—At least 25 per cent meat.

Egg Rolls with Meat—At least 10 per cent meat.

Enchiladas with Meat—At least 15 per cent meat.

Frankfurters, Bologna, Other Cooked Sausage—"Beef" hot dogs may contain beef only. Hot dogs made of other animals must be so labeled. Foods labeled "frankfurter," "bologna," and the like may contain only skeletal meat (the muscle part of beef). Up to 15 per cent poultry meat, water, sweeteners, and curing agents are allowed too. Any binders such as cereals, non-fat dry milk, or soy protein must be clearly listed on the labels—for instance, "franks, non-fat dry milk added." The maximum for binders is 3½ per cent. Non-skeletal meat, such as tongues and internal organs, may be included if the term "with variety meats" or "with by-products" appears on the label.

Gravies—At least 25 per cent stock or broth, or at least 6 per cent meat.

Ham (*canned*)—Limited to 8 per cent total weight gain via juices after processing.

Ham (*not canned*)—Must not weigh more after processing than the fresh ham weighs before curing and smoking; if contains up to 10 per cent added weight, must be labeled "Ham—Water Added"; if more than 10 per cent, must be labeled "Imitation Ham."

Hamburger or Ground Beef—No more than 30 per cent fat; no extenders.

Ham Spread—At least 50 per cent ham.

Hash—At least 35 per cent meat.

Lasagna with Meat and Sauce—At least 12 per cent meat.

Liver Sausage, Liver Paste, and similar liver products—At least 30 per cent liver.

Meatballs—No more than 12 per cent extenders (cereal, etc.).

Meatballs in Sauce—At least 50 per cent meatballs.

Meat Pies—At least 25 per cent meat.

Meat Ravioli—At least 10 per cent meat in ravioli filling.

Meat Ravioli in Sauce—At least 10 per cent meat.

Meat Soups (*ready to eat*)—At least 5 per cent meat.

Meat Soups (*condensed*)—At least 10 per cent meat.

Meat Spreads—At least 50 per cent meat.

Pâté de Foie—At least 30 per cent liver.

Pizza with Meat—At least 15 per cent meat.

Pizza with Sausage—At least 12 per cent sausage (cooked basis) or 10 per cent dry sausage.

Pork Sausage—Not more than 50 per cent fat.

Sauce with Meat or Meat Sauce—At least 6 per cent meat.

Scrapple—At least 40 per cent meat and/or meat by-products.

Shepherd's Pie—At least 25 per cent meat; no more than 50 per cent mashed potatoes.

Stews (Beef, Lamb, and the like)—At least 25 per cent meat.

Stuffed Cabbage with Meat in Sauce—At least 12 per cent meat.

Swiss Steak with Gravy—At least 50 per cent meat.

Gravy and Swiss Steak—At least 35 per cent meat.

Tamales—At least 25 per cent meat.

Veal Parmigiana—At least 40 per cent breaded meat product in sauce.

Breaded Poultry—No more than 30 per cent breading.

Canned Boned Poultry—At least 90 per cent poultry meat, skin, and fat.

Poultry à la King—At least 20 per cent poultry meat.

Poultry Chow Mein, without Noodles—At least 4 per cent poultry meat.

Poultry Dinners—At least 18 per cent poultry meat.

Poultry Fricassee—At least 20 per cent poultry meat.

Poultry Pies—At least 14 per cent poultry meat.

Poultry Salad—At least 25 per cent poultry meat.

Poultry Soup—At least 2 per cent poultry meat.

Poultry Tetrazzini—At least 15 per cent poultry meat.

Corned Beef Hash—At least 35 per cent beef; also must contain potatoes, curing agents, and seasonings; no more than 15 per cent fat. Nor more than 72 per cent moisture.

Chopped Ham—Must contain fresh, cured, or smoked ham, along with certain specified kinds of curing agents and seasonings.

Oleomargarine or Margarine—Fat in finished product may not exceed 80 per cent; label must indicate whether product is from animal or vegetable origin or both.

These standards signify progress. Far more meaningful disclosures will come when we also have information in the following areas:

Nutrition: Information on just how much of each vitamin and mineral a package contains surely would be a boon to all of us.

Calorie counts: I cannot exaggerate the frustration I feel when I buy a food labeled "diet" and then cannot find how many calories there are in a slice or cup or tablespoon. This should be mandatory on at least the diet foods. We also should be able to tell how much lower in fats the so-called lower-fat foods are.

Drained weight: If we knew the net weight of soups, minus water, for instance, we could compare the volume of real food—meat, vegetables, etc.—in various soups. In many cases, we would find a concentrated, thick meaty soup is a much greater value at 45¢ a can than a watered-down equivalent at 30¢.

Key ingredients: Labels should tell us much more clearly what proportion of "beef stew" actually is beef, what proportion of fruit is in a fruit drink.

Recommended food storage conditions: Labels should specify how long a package of frozen beans may be kept in the freezer, for instance.

A universal simple "ABC" grading system: Such a system for foods would eliminate our confusion because of the variety of federal food grading systems (especially important in meat).

"TRUTH IN MEAT" LABELING

Look carefully in your supermarket meat counter. Has the piece of beef you've known as "California roast" been transformed into a "Beef Chuck—Under Blade Roast"? Has the old-time "London broil" been renamed a "Beef Flank Steak"? Or the traditional "Delmonico steak" reappeared as "Beef Rib—Eye Steak"?

Starting in late 1973, a whole new system of meat labeling was introduced in supermarkets, meat markets and grocery stores from coast to coast. The "Truth in Meat" program is voluntary but it is the meat industry's big push to let you know not only what you're getting for your money but also how to cook it.

Thus, here's what to look for in the stores where you do your meat buying:

• Each package of meat labeled with the name of the animal species (beef, veal, pork, lamb); the "primal cut"—breast or brisket, shoulder (chuck) arm, shoulder (chuck) blade; rib, loin, sirloin (hip), and leg (round); and one of its more than 300 common, standardized retail names. (In addition, if it wants to, a store may add its own fanciful name—such as "his and her" steaks or "Paradise roast." Hamburger, though, is "ground beef" or "ground sirloin" or "ground chuck." T-bone steak is beef loin T-bone.

• The lean meat ratio of ground meat labeled, with the maximum percentage of fat set at 25 per cent.

• A variety of booklets and meat identification charts available next to meat counters—giveaways detailing both the "what you're getting" and "how to cook it" angles.

The system has been hailed by the meat industry as "the most significant meat-counter improvement since the introduction of self-service nearly four decades ago." But it is just one step toward real consumer information protection at the meat counter. There's a long way to go.

"OPEN DATING"

"Open dating" means the clear marking on all packages or containers of perishable or semiperishable foods with a date "pull" after which they should be removed from sale to you. These products are guaranteed to have a normal period of use in the home after the date.

As a result of this form of labeling, disappearing from store shelves are the cryptic grocery codes that tell store managers the condition of the foods on sale but make a secret of the same information to us.

To get the maximum benefit:

(1) Learn the basic fact that the date on a package or container of perishable foods is frequently the "pull" date—the last permissible day of sale for that item from its normal shelf position in the store. After that day the product must be removed from regular sale.

(2) If you see an item on sale after that date, it should be in an off-shelf special display position and be offered at a greatly reduced price. It also must still be safe for consumption, of course.

(3) If you find cryptic codes on some items, ask the store for an explanation or for a free explanatory booklet and be sure you understand.

(4) If you do discover that you have bought an out-of-date item that was not on special sale as such, take it back at once and demand a refund.

(5) Use your own head about the proper storage and refrigeration of perishables. According to a Rutgers University study, temperature is seven times as important as time in maintaining freshness—and that applies whether you have the food in hand or whether it is still in the store. Don't buy perishables and then stop on the way home to have lunch or pick up your children or whatever.

How to Compare Unit Costs Per Pound of Food

WHICH IS THE BIGGER BARGAIN?

Q. *Which is the bigger bargain: $4.77 for a box of powder to make 20 quarts of non-fat dry milk or $3.27 for a box to make 12 quarts of the same brand of dry milk?*

A. The 20-quart package works out to 24¢ a quart and is therefore a bigger bargain than the 12-quart package, which works out to 27¢ a quart.

Q. *Which is cheaper: a 1-lb. 2-oz. jar of peanut butter costing 53¢ or a 12-oz. jar of the same brand costing 35¢?*

A. Neither. In both cases, the per pound cost is 47¢.

Q. *Which is more economical: a 1-lb. 14-oz. can of sliced pineapple costing 47¢ or an 8½-oz. can costing 21¢?*

A. The larger can—by far. The pineapple costs 25¢ a pound in the larger can, but 40¢ a pound in the small can.

These illustrations underline the extent to which you, the manager of the family pocketbook, can make errors in your purchases if you do not know the price per measure as well as the total dollar price.

At the same time, the comparisons indicate the enormous savings which you can achieve by buying large versus small packages. You don't have to be a mathematical genius to figure out, just from these few examples, that you could save hundreds of dollars per year—without necessarily sacrificing any quality in any item—just by buying the large package sizes instead of the small.

But there are infuriating exceptions. In one study of one major dry detergent, the per ounce cost of the *largest* available size (more than 16 pounds) was significantly *greater* than the cost of either of the next two smaller sizes.

The trend across the land is relentlessly toward new laws requiring retailers to provide shelf labels under each item with a price per ounce, quart, pound, or other unit as well as with the total retail price for the package. Most of the major retail food chains now use some kind of unit pricing system. In almost every major city the pricing system has become available. Increasing numbers of states have laws requiring unit pricing on a state-wide basis.

In this era of record and rising food prices, unit pricing could be the U.S. food shopper's biggest moneysaving weapon. For it is virtually your sole means of comparing the true unit cost of what you buy in the supermarket.

HOW TO USE UNIT PRICING

Next time you go to the food store, look on the edge of the shelf under the article you are considering buying. If the store uses unit pricing, you will find a label which tells the cost per measure (pound, pint, number, etc.) of the item. That's the unit price. This breaks down the total cost of the particular package or can into a simple standard so that you can now choose between brands and sizes on the basis of price.

You'll find other numbers on most labels, but they'll be inventory numbers which you need not bother about.

For instance, say you are buying tomato juice.

A 46-ounce can of a store brand is priced 2 for 65¢, the unit price is 23¢ a quart; a 1-quart bottle of brand A sells for 35¢, the unit price is 35¢ a quart; an 18-ounce of brand B sells at 2 for 35¢, the unit price is 31¢ a quart; a 6-pack of 5½-ounce cans of brand B sells at 51¢, the unit price is 49¢ a quart.

If you look at the unit prices, it will be easy to find the best buy. And surely it's worth while to discover that you can buy more than two quarts of the first for the price of one quart of the fourth. With prices given per quart, all you need do is look and compare.

Or to give you another illustration—how "pretty" do you like your olives?

A 2-ounce jar of "thrown" olives (those put in the jar at random) costs seven cents less than a jar of "placed" olives (those put in the jar in a pattern with the pimentos nicely facing out and lined up). On this week's grocery bill the difference may seem small, but on a cents-per-pound basis the gap really grows.

Of course, you will shop for quality and in terms of your personal preferences too—but why not use unit pricing to save money when quality is not of prime importance and when you have no special preferences? *Why not use the weapon now that you have it?*

UNIT COST TABLE

Unit pricing is not yet universal—not by far.

And, a recent survey revealed, shoppers make the "wrong" choices a shocking 40 per cent of the time on which can or bottle or package is cheapest—on a per-ounce or per-pound basis—*when the packages are not unit-priced.* These errors translate into an average cost of 10¢ on every $1.00 spent in the grocery store. Thus, on a food bill of $100, $10 may be going down the drain simply because you are not choosing the most economical food.

So until unit pricing is in every store, here's a "Cost Weight Table" which you can translate on your own into extraordinary savings. Copy it and put it into your purse to refer to when you shop from now on.

To calculate the unit cost of a product, no matter what size or shape package it comes in, first locate the net weight of the food package in the left-hand column. Then locate the total price of the package along the top of the table. These reference points will lead you directly to the price per pound in the appropriate middle column. By comparing the unit cost of one package with another size, you can discover which is the better bargain.

PACKAGE WEIGHT (IN OUNCES)	COST PER POUND IF THE COST PER PACKAGE IS:				
	5¢	10¢	15¢	20¢	25¢
1	$ .80	$1.60	$2.40	$3.20	$4.00
2	.40	.80	1.20	1.60	2.00
3	.27	.53	.80	1.07	1.33
4	.20	.40	.60	.80	1.00
5	.16	.32	.48	.64	.80
6	.13	.27	.40	.53	.67
7	.11	.23	.34	.46	.57
8	.10	.20	.30	.40	.50
9	.09	.18	.27	.36	.44
10	.08	.16	.24	.32	.40
11	.07	.15	.22	.29	.36
12	.07	.13	.20	.27	.33
13	.06	.12	.18	.25	.31
14	.06	.11	.17	.23	.29
15	.05	.11	.16	.21	.27
16	.05	.10	.15	.20	.25
17	.05	.09	.14	.19	.24
18	.04	.09	.13	.18	.22
19	.04	.08	.13	.17	.21
20	.04	.08	.12	.16	.20
21	.04	.08	.11	.15	.19
22	.04	.07	.11	.15	.18
23	.03	.07	.10	.14	.17
24	.03	.07	.10	.13	.17
25	.03	.06	.10	.13	.16
26	.03	.06	.09	.12	.15
27	.03	.06	.09	.12	.15
28	.03	.06	.09	.11	.14
29	.03	.06	.08	.11	.14
30	.03	.05	.08	.11	.13
31	.03	.05	.08	.11	.13
32	.03	.05	.08	.10	.13
33	.02	.05	.07	.10	.12
34	.02	.05	.07	.09	.12
35	.02	.05	.07	.09	.11
36	.02	.04	.07	.09	.11

PACKAGE WEIGHT (IN OUNCES)	COST PER POUND IF THE COST PER PACKAGE IS:				
	5¢	10¢	15¢	20¢	25¢
37	$ .02	$ .04	$ .06	$ .09	$ .11
38	.02	.04	.06	.08	.11
39	.02	.04	.06	.08	.10
40	.02	.04	.06	.08	.10

PACKAGE WEIGHT (IN OUNCES)	COST PER POUND IF THE COST PER PACKAGE IS:				
	30¢	35¢	40¢	45¢	50¢
1	$4.80	$5.60	$6.40	$7.20	$8.00
2	2.40	2.80	3.20	3.60	4.00
3	1.60	1.87	2.13	2.40	2.67
4	1.20	1.40	1.60	1.80	2.00
5	.96	1.12	1.28	1.44	1.60
6	.80	.93	1.07	1.20	1.33
7	.69	.80	.91	1.03	1.14
8	.60	.70	.80	.90	1.00
9	.53	.62	.71	.80	.89
10	.48	.56	.64	.72	.80
11	.44	.51	.58	.65	.73
12	.40	.47	.53	.60	.67
13	.37	.43	.49	.55	.62
14	.34	.40	.46	.51	.57
15	.32	.37	.43	.48	.53
16	.30	.35	.40	.45	.50
17	.28	.33	.38	.42	.47
18	.27	.31	.36	.40	.44
19	.25	.29	.34	.38	.42
20	.24	.28	.32	.36	.40
21	.23	.27	.30	.34	.38
22	.22	.25	.29	.33	.36
23	.21	.24	.28	.31	.35
24	.20	.23	.27	.30	.33
25	.19	.22	.26	.29	.32
26	.18	.22	.25	.28	.31
27	.18	.21	.24	.27	.30
28	.17	.20	.23	.26	.29

PACKAGE WEIGHT (IN OUNCES)	COST PER POUND IF THE COST PER PACKAGE IS:				
	30¢	35¢	40¢	45¢	50¢
29	$ .17	$ .19	$ .22	$ .25	$ .28
30	.16	.19	.21	.24	.27
31	.15	.18	.21	.23	.26
32	.15	.18	.20	.23	.25
33	.15	.17	.19	.22	.24
34	.14	.16	.19	.21	.24
35	.14	.16	.18	.21	.23
36	.13	.16	.18	.20	.22
37	.13	.15	.17	.19	.22
38	.13	.15	.17	.19	.21
39	.12	.14	.16	.18	.21
40	.12	.14	.16	.18	.20

NOTES: *Change the weight on a package to ounces if necessary:*

1 pound=16 ounces
1 pint=16 fluid ounces

This will help you figure out weights which are in between a single pound or pint. For instance, 1 pound 10 ounces or 1 pint 10 ounces may be translated into 16 ounces plus 10 ounces, or 26 ounces. Thus, if a product weighs 26 ounces and is priced at 35¢, the price per pound is 22¢.

You can use this table if a package weighs more than 40 ounces or more than 50 cents. Just divide the weight and price of any package weighing more than 40 ounces by 2 and, with the resulting figures, use the table above. Or just divide the price and weight of any package priced at more than 50¢ by 2 and also use the table above.

How to Save on Meat

CLASSIC DEMAND-PULL INFLATION

In food prices—and especially in meat prices—we saw in the post-World War II period a classic illustration of demand-pull inflation.

When *you demand* more and more meat, when you steadily increase your purchases of higher-quality meats across the board, when you stand in line at the supermarket counters, your relentless buying *pulls* up the prices of all the meats in your market basket. This is what economists call *demand-pull* inflation.

Although the blow-off in meat prices generally and in beef prices in particular in 1973–74 interrupted the long-term upsurge in our consumption of meat, the fundamental remains: as our family incomes rise, so do the proportions of our budgets allocated to meats. In three days out of five, we eat red meat and that meat usually is beef. Between one fourth and one third of your annual food bill is spent on meat, poultry, and fish—making these the biggest items in your food budget.

GENERAL MONEYSAVING HINTS

The retail price you pay for meat is not necessarily a reliable guide to its quality, nutritive value, *or* tenderness. Meat prices, instead, depend on such factors as the popularity of a given meat cut or brand or grade; the season of the year; the type of store in which the meat is sold; the type and amount of handling and processing.

As a general rule, beef prices are lower in winter and higher in late summer. Steak prices tend to be highest during the summer "cookout" months and roasts cost more in the late fall and early winter "oven-cooking" months. In contrast, veal prices tend to be lowest in the spring and summer and highest in the winter.

Now here are vitally important general hints for saving money on meat—including "old" ones which a surprising number of Americans have been pulling out of their memories and "new" ones recently put together by consumer economists:

• Shift your family to less expensive cuts of each type of meat. Since nearly four fifths of the beef we buy is *not* naturally tender enough to broil, barbecue, or roast, in this area you will find your biggest meat bargains. With a little special handling, the less expensive cuts can be made virtually as tender and tasteful as the costlier cuts.

Important note: The nutrient content of these cuts is at least as great as that of the more expensive cuts while the fat content in most cases is significantly lower. (See Protein Bargains chart, p. 213, for details on this point.) For example, you can buy good chuck steaks and roasts at bargain prices. Short ribs are another delicious cut of beef which you can barbecue indoors or out. So are beef shank, brisket, and short loin. Lamb chops cut from the shoulder often cost 20 to 40¢ less per pound than rib or loin chops.

Among the other less expensive cuts and types of meat are: ground beef, stew meat, pot roast, beef shank, brisket, short loin, heel of round roast, pork shoulder and rump, lamb shanks, ground lamb.

Among steaks, some of the least expensive cuts are blade and arm chuck steaks, flank steak, sirloin tip, and bottom round. The "broiling steaks"—sirloin, porterhouse, etc.—rarely are bargains except as occasional sales features.

• Experiment with the help of your gourmet cookbook, preparing such "variety" meats as liver, heart, sweetbreads, tripe, kidneys, tongue, brains. Most of these rank high in nutrition. They also are among the "great" foods in Europe and are served in the finest French restaurants everywhere.

• Save simply by learning the cooking rules in your cookbook. You will save an impressive amount on meats, for instance, if you roast them at no more than 300° to 325°F. They will shrink less; be tenderer; be easier to carve. Remember, the higher the temperature of your oven, the more your meats will shrink.

• Check what "family packs" are available—such as bulk hamburger, chops, chicken. Meat in larger quantities is almost invariably offered at lower prices than in smaller packages. You can always do a bit of home butchering—e.g., cutting your own rib steaks from an extra-thick roast beef or cutting a whole pork loin three ways. (An inexpensive hack saw with a good blade will substitute for a butcher's saw when you have to cut through bone.) You can then use the center section as chops, which will cost you considerably less than if you buy the chops in a package by themselves. Or, if you buy bologna, buy it in a chunk. By slicing it at home, you may cut as much as 10¢ a pound from the piece.

• Try buying 2- or 3-pound boxes of bacon "ends and pieces." It may be slightly less lean than regularly packaged bacon and it's not cut uniformly. But it comes from the same animal and may cost only one third or one half what regular bacon costs. Also, consider bacon a condiment rather than meat in view of its high cost per serving and try to serve only two pieces per person instead of three or four. Typically, a pound of bacon dwindles to 3 to 5 ounces and some brands yield as little as 18 to 20 per cent of their original volume.

• Study and compare prices of canned meats—ham, beef roast, corned beef, chopped beef, luncheon loaves, meat in barbecue sauce, turkey, and chicken, to name just a few. Every ounce of these is edible. Canned-meat meals tend to be even greater money- and timesavers for small families.

• Don't overfeed your family with meat, a definitely concentrated source of calories. Overweight is one of our country's leading health problems, and the top cause for overweight is overeating. Meat also tends to be high in cholesterol. There is no reason to feed any family member more than 6 to 8 ounces of meat in one meal. Or try experimenting with even smaller servings (e.g., 3 ounces per meal) for a week—and see who, if anybody, screams.

• When you buy ground beef, try the least expensive forms first and "work your way up" if these don't satisfy your tastes. In a major study of hamburger, Consumers Union found that the price difference from hamburger grade to grade—e.g., from ground beef to ground chuck to ground round—was as much as 40¢ a pound in the same store, although analysis showed that the differences in amounts of fat, water, and protein were "indistinguishable."

• Try buying meat at local discount stores, where you frequently can achieve significant savings over supermarkets (though they may not offer the convenience of the supermarket).

• Shop for meat in terms of meals—and consider, as you buy, what you'll do with the leftovers. Plan to use all the meat you buy. Melt down fat trimmings for drippings; simmer bones and lean cuttings for soup stock and gravy.

• If scales are available for you to use in the supermarket in which you shop, *use them* to reweigh prepriced meat packages. And if you find any discrepancy, point this out immediately to the store manager.

• Read labels with care. Also remember that 3½ pounds is not 3 pounds 5 ounces but 3 pounds 8 ounces.

• Check and compare prices of prefrozen and imported meat. For example, you'll almost surely save by buying frozen lamb which has been imported from Australia or New Zealand.

THE TRUE COST OF A SERVING OF MEAT

Buy according to the true value of any type or cut of meat—as measured in terms of the true cost of a given portion of the final cooked product.

As a rule of thumb, you get two to three cooked servings from each pound of roast beef, pork, lamb, or veal, whole ham, chicken or turkey, trimmed fish, certain types of steaks and chops. And you get only one or two servings from each pound of meat loaded with fat, bone, and gristle—such as rib chops, spareribs, short ribs, plate and breast of veal, lamb shank, chicken wings and backs, T-bone or porterhouse steaks.

Here is a rundown of servings per pound of various meats. Fill in the current cost of each item in your area. Then figure the cost per serving by dividing the per-pound price by the number of servings. This is your key guide to where the bargains are.

Meat	Approximate Servings per Pound	Retail Price per Pound	Cost per Serving
Beef			
Hamburger	4	——	——
Sirloin steak	3	——	——
Round steak	3	——	——
Rump roast, boneless	3	——	——
Chuck roast	3	——	——
Rib roast, with bone	2	——	——
Pork, fresh			
Pork chops	2½	——	——
Loin roast	2½	——	——
Pork smoked			
Canned ham, boneless	4	——	——
Cooked ham, with bone	3½	——	——
Picnic shoulder, with bone	2½	——	——
Poultry			
Turkey	2	——	——
Frying chicken	2	——	——

PROTEIN BARGAINS

Compare meat prices by finding out how much of a "protein bargain" you are getting.

To illustrate: here is a rundown on three key price categories of beef you can buy today—showing the relative amounts of protein, fat, and calories in one lean 3½-ounce cooked serving of each cut:

	PROTEIN (GRAMS)	FAT (GRAMS)	TOTAL CALORIES
Most Tender Cuts			
Standing rib roast	22	21	285
Tenderloin	26	13	224
Porterhouse steak	25	15	242
T-bone steak	25	15	247
Club steak	26	19	280
Rib steak	25	17	262
Top sirloin steak	26	11	208
Medium Tender Cuts			
Standing rump roast or rolled rump roast	32	11	235
Sirloin tip roast	30	4	168
Sirloin tip steak	27	6	166
Heel of round	33	5	189
Full cut round steak	38	8	229
Top round steak	39	7	229
Bottom round steak or roast	36	10	238
Eye of round steak or roast	38	6	219
Stew meat—round	33	13	260
Flank steak	34	7	209
Less Tender Cuts			
Short ribs or cross ribs	32	15	272
English cut or boston cut	33	14	263
Blade chuck pot roast, blade chuck steak, or boneless shoulder steak	35	17	298
Arm chuck pot roast, arm chuck or boneless shoulder steak	35	8	219
Rolled shoulder roast	33	14	263

Just divide the prevailing price by the number of calories or amount of protein in any of these cuts. The resulting figure will tell you how much of a calorie bargain or protein bargain each cut is.

An even more direct route to the best protein bargains is knowing the cost of various forms of protein—meats, fishes, and meat alternatives. To calculate the price per gram of protein, divide the current price per pound (or quart or dozen) being charged in your area for the foods listed in the table below by the number of grams listed.

FOOD	GRAMS OF PROTEIN PER POUND	FOOD	GRAMS OF PROTEIN PER POUND
Lima beans	78.9	Fish sticks	78.7
Peanut butter	72.0	Chili con carne	39.3
Pork and beans	27.5	Whole ham	58.2
Beef liver	88.9	Frankfurters	56.0
Chicken	72.3	Beef chuck steak	43.0
Eggs	71.0 (per dozen)	Round steak	79.6
Cottage cheese	64.0	Pizza	41.7
American cheese	107.0	Bologna	48.7
Tuna fish	118.5	Bacon	42.8
Hamburger	86.4	Rib roast	47.4
Milk	33.8 (per quart)	Sirloin steak	63.6
Ocean perch	69.9		

For example: if peanut butter costs 48 cents per pound, divide 48 cents by 72 grams per pound and you get a total of two-thirds cent per gram of protein. At 71 cents per dozen, eggs would cost one cent per gram of protein and thus, would not be as good a buy as peanut butter.

Of course, protein is by no means the only key nutrient. It's vitally important to know that pork is rich in thiamin, that cheese is rich in calcium, that beans contain large amounts of vitamin B_6 and magnesium. Probably your best source of nutritional details is the U. S. Department of Agriculture's Handbook No. 8, entitled *Composition of Foods, Raw, Processed, Prepared.*

HOW TO USE BEEF "GRADES"

• Learn the U. S. Department of Agriculture grades of meat and use them not only to compare price and quality (tenderness, juiciness, and flavor) but also as a guide to the best meat for a particular type of meal.

The five top USDA beef grades are: prime, normally available only in restaurants, fancy meat stores, and from specialty mail-order houses; choice and good, the two grades most commonly found in supermarkets and butcher shops; standard and commercial, definitely inferior as far as your palate is concerned.

The top veal grades are: prime, choice, good, standard, and utility.

The top lamb grades are: prime, choice, and good. Spring lamb should bear the U. S. Government certification "Genuine Spring Lamb."

Choose lower meat grades. For instance, with beef, good versus choice; with lamb, choice versus prime. They may be less tender, but they are also leaner and equally nourishing. Using anything above U.S. good for chopped beef or stew meat is a waste of money, because in these cuts you do not need to worry, for example, about how tender the meat is.

Lower grades should cost even less. However, the taste may be equal if you cook them right—e.g., as pot roast—or if you apply such tenderizing techniques as grinding, pounding, marinating, pot-roasting, using commercial tenderizers, and cubing.

• As another guide to quality, study meat color and texture.

For general freshness, beef should be somewhere between light and dark red. Roasts and most steaks should be at least lightly "marbled" with fat.

Veal should be very pale grayish pink in color; the flesh should be firm and smooth. It should have almost no fat—just a thin coat outside.

Pork, too, should be pale pink and should have only a thin layer of fat.

Lamb should be a dull pink. Spring lamb should be colored somewhere between pink and red—not too dark—and it should have a velvety

texture. The bone should be pinkish and there should be a slight amount
of marbling.

BUT NUMBER 1: SHOP THE MEAT SPECIALS!

Your number 1 way to save on meat is to shop regularly and seriously for meat specials and stock your home freezer with your purchases.
You can save as much as one third on your meat bills simply by buying
meat at special rather than regular prices. See preceding pages for table
dramatizing the point.

Thursday, Friday, and Saturday remain the big days for meat specials, but also watch for specials on such off days as Monday, Tuesday,
and even Sunday. (Try to shop as early in the day as possible.)

When you shop for advertised meat specials, make sure the price
marked on the package reflects the advertised special. And if you can't
find any packages left at the special price, remind the supermarket manager that a Federal Trade Commission rule requires that advertised specials be adequately stocked *at* or below the advertised special prices.
At the very least, you should get a rain check.

Watch closely to see whether more fat has been left on the meat
that's on sale—particularly on beef and pork chops.

Important note: On any given day you'll probably find only a limited number of items on special, and you'll also find that many if not most
stores in your area will offer a very similar set of specials—particularly
on weekends.

SAVINGS BY BUYING BEEF IN BULK

How about saving money by buying beef in bulk? Okay. No matter how casual a shopper you are, it's increasingly likely that you will
try to curb your meat costs by buying beef in bulk and storing it in your
home freezer.

But it's a good way to go—only *if* you are on guard against the estimated hundreds of "bait and switch" beef swindlers in the United
States today . . . *if* you instead patronize one of thousands of entirely
ethical freezer meat operators situated all over the country . . . and *if*

you know and scrupulously obey the rules when you buy beef or other types of meat via the wholesale route.

Below you will find 11 specific rules for this type of buying:

(1) Do not buy a side of beef in hasty response to a tempting ad. If you really want and need as much beef as this and if you can arrange to store it properly, plan your purchase ahead, then shop intelligently for the meat.

(2) Before you buy, decide whether you will want a large quantity of steaks or whether your family will be happy with less fancy cuts or whether you would prefer to have a wide variety of cuts, including lots of stew meat and hamburger.

(3) To help yourself reach these decisions, study the beef-cut charts posted in your butcher shop or available from the U. S. Department of Agriculture in Washington.

(4) Use the following guide to tell you what proportion of what cuts you are likely to find in bulk beef.

In general, if you want more steaks and roasts, you'll probably want a hindquarter. A typical, trimmed beef hindquarter originally weighing about 200 pounds consists of 58 per cent steaks and oven roasts.

Here's the breakdown:

HINDQUARTER

Round steak	20.6%
Boneless rump roast	6.0
Sirloin steak	13.0
T-bone, porterhouse club steak	10.1
Flank steak	.9
Total lean trim	17.1.
Fat, bone, and shrinkage	32.3
TOTAL	100.0%

If you want a lot of stew beef and hamburger, you'll probably be best off with a forequarter. A typical, trimmed forequarter, originally weighing 215 to 220 pounds, breaks down into 37 per cent stew and ground meat.

Here's the breakdown on this:

FOREQUARTER

Rib roast	13.5%
Short ribs	6.4
Blade chuck	20.9
Arm chuck	12.5
Boneless brisket	4.1
Total lean trim	23.9
Fat, bone, and shrinkage	18.7
TOTAL	100.0%

If you want a wide variety of cuts, a half carcass will probably be the purchase for you. The usable meat from a whole beef carcass breaks down into approximately 25 per cent steaks, 25 per cent roasts, 25 per cent ground beef or stew, 25 per cent waste.

More specifically, a typical U.S. choice beef carcass weighing 300 pounds is likely to break down this way:

RETAIL CUTS	PER CENT OF CARCASS	POUNDS
Round steak	11.0%	33.0 lbs.
Rump roast (boneless)	3.3	9.9
Porterhouse, T-bone, club steak	5.1	15.3
Sirloin steak	8.3	24.9
Rib roast	6.1	18.3
Chuck blade roast	8.9	26.7
Chuck arm roast (boneless)	5.8	17.4
Ground beef	11.1	33.3
Stew meat	10.3	30.9
Brisket	2.1	6.3
Flank steak	.5	1.5
Kidney	.3	.9
Total usable retail cuts	72.8	218.4
Waste (fat, bone, shrinkage)	27.2	81.6
TOTAL	100.0%	300.0 lbs.

And here are a few more important guides on other meats:

A lamb with a carcass weight of 50 pounds trims out to about 75 per cent legs, chops, and shoulders, 15 per cent breast and stew, 10 per cent bones and waste.

The breakdown for a typical lamb is:

RETAIL CUTS	PER CENT OF CARCASS	POUNDS
Loin and sirloin chops	16.5%	8.25 lbs.
Rib chops	8.2	4.10
Legs (short cut)	20.5	10.25
Shoulder roast	22.3	11.15
Foreshanks	3.1	1.55
Breast	7.9	3.95
Flank	2.9	1.45
Stew meat	1.9	.95
Kidney	.5	.25
Total usable retail cuts	83.8	41.90
Waste (fat, bone, shrinkage)	16.2	8.10
TOTAL	100.0%	50.00 lbs.

A hog carcass weighing 175 pounds or so divides up into about 50 per cent hams, shoulders, and bacon, 20 per cent loins, ribs and sausage, and most of the rest lard.

(5) Don't overlook the importance of "yield grades" in helping you avoid waste! In addition to the basic guides given you above, do you know that typical amounts of waste vary from beef side to beef side—from a minimum of about 20 per cent to as much as 34 per cent—a fact which greatly influences the real-life price you might pay for and the value you get from this beef?

For example, if a quarter of beef weighing 125 pounds ("carcass weight") is advertised at 69¢ a pound and if this quarter trims out to a typical 87 pounds, the effect of this "shrinkage" is to push the price back *up* to 99¢ a pound.

And this is merely the *average* price—which hides the fact that you have bought a hefty percentage of such cheaper meats as stew and hamburger.

The "yield grade," I repeat, is among your best yardsticks of value if you are trying to save money by buying beef in bulk—for it gives you the vital clues on the percentages of the various boneless retail cuts you'll get after fat and bone have been trimmed away.

There are five yield grades, numbered 1 through 5, with 1 the highest, 5 the lowest.

The typical difference in amount of meat yields is 4.6 per cent between grades.

Here are the percentage yields of each grade level for a 600-pound beef carcass:

GRADE	FAT TRIM	BONE	EDIBLE MEAT
1	7.5%	10.5%	82.0%
2	12.6	10.0	77.4
3	17.7	9.5	72.8
4	22.8	9.0	68.2
5	27.9	8.5	63.6

And here is a more detailed comparison of the percentages of beef carcass weight of USDA yield grades 2 and 4. It's assumed that the meat is trimmed to ½ inch of fat.

CUT	YIELD GRADE 2	YIELD GRADE 4
Rump, boneless	3.5%	3.1%
Inside round	4.5	3.7
Outside round	4.6	4.2
Round tip	2.6	2.4
Sirloin	8.7	7.9
Short loin	5.2	5.0
Rib, short cut (7″)	6.2	6.0
Blade chuck	9.4	8.4
Chuck, arm, boneless	6.1	5.5
Brisket, boneless	2.3	1.9
Flank steak	.5	.5
Lean trim	11.3	9.3
Ground beef	12.2	10.0
Fat	12.7	22.9
Bone	9.9	8.9
Kidney	.3	.3
TOTAL	100.0%	100.0%

With these statistics in mind when you are shopping for a side or a quarter of beef, you can get a good idea of the amounts of meat various grades will yield you after cutting and trimming. This will permit you to make sound comparisons with prices charged on beef cuts during the supermarket specials in your area.

And this in turn will tell you how much of a bargain—or non-bargain—each side of wholesale beef really is to you.

(6) When buying in bulk, figure not only what you are paying per pound for the actual meat minus fat, bones, etc., but also what price you are paying for cutting, packaging, and quick freezing. These procedures can easily add 8 to 10 cents a pound to the net cost of your meat if they are not included in the basic price.

(7) If the ads include such terms as "beef order," "steak package," or "steak bundle," find out precisely what these terms mean and cover.

(8) If unbelievably low-priced extras or "bonuses" are thrown in to sweeten the deal—say, 10 pounds of frying chickens for 50¢ or five pounds of hot dogs for $1.00 or 30 pork chops for free—use your head. No butcher could afford giveaways such as these.

(9) And never forget for a minute that the bait-and-switch racketeers use this sort of lure—for instance, ads for sides or quarters of beef at fantastically low prices—in order to bait you and then switch you to a much higher-priced carcass.

(10) If the deal involves payments by you on time, check whether the terms are spelled out as required under the Truth in Lending law—the total finance charge, the yearly percentage interest rate, the number and schedule of payments. Also, which bank or finance company will actually hold the paper you sign?

(11) Learn well the key signs of fresh, good-quality beef and other meats. For example, with beef, the bone should be ivory white, the sign of a young steer, not yellowed; the fat should be white as against yellow and there shouldn't be an excessive amount of fat; the tenderest beef is well marbled, meaning it has streaks of fat throughout the meat, but marbling also means calories and saturated fat.

How to Use Your Home Freezer for Top Savings

THE RULES

To take the maximum advantage of meat and other specials, and to have the convenience of a "supermarket" in your own home, you must have a home freezer.

To illustrate the savings in just one purchase:

If you could buy 100 pounds of meat on sale at $1.79 per pound against the "regular" price of $2.01, your savings on this purchase alone would be $22.

These savings must, however, be compared to the costs of owning a home freezer—including depreciation, repairs, and electricity.

And there are disadvantages—in addition to annual costs summarized in the preceding paragraph. They include: the possibility of spoilage due to a power failure; the certainty of electricity rate rises in the years ahead; the nuisance of defrosting; the need to plan meals well in advance because the frozen food must be brought to room temperature or will need longer cooking time; the need to have space in which to keep the freezer; other minor annoyances.

But to millions, the advantages seem to win—which leads to the rules for getting the utmost benefits from your freezer:

• Package the meats to be frozen in sizes your family is likely to use and make sure each is tightly wrapped before freezing.

• Set your freezer at the lowest possible temperature the day before you intend to put in any large amount of meat to be frozen and, once frozen, hold the temperature at below 0°F.

• Don't add too much "warm" meat at a time—not more than two pounds per cubic feet of storage space. This means that large purchases, like the 100 pounds of meat, should be prefrozen by the meat packer in his large, high-powered freezer.

• Date and label with its contents each package of food you put in the freezer and consume your frozen food on a "first in, first out" basis.

• Stock your freezer as full as feasible for you: use the food frequently and restock; the higher the turnover of food, the lower the per pound cost to you.

• Keep all foods covered. Clean interiors regularly, including the defrost drainage tubes. Vacuum and wipe down coils and other mechanisms; dirt accumulation makes for inefficient operating.

• Open doors as little as possible to cut down frost. Defrost as often as necessary to keep no more than a fourth to a half inch of frost from accumulating. Don't place unit in a warm area—such as near the furnace. Check the gasket frequently to make certain it seals the door tightly.

• If you live in an area where your electricity goes off for as long as a day or so, set your freezer thermostat at 10° to 20° below zero or as low as it will go. If the power stays off longer, either take your frozen food to a freeze locker or put blocks of dry ice in your freezer. A 25 pound block should be enough to keep the contents of your freezer below zero for two to three days.

• Make sure your frozen food packages are firm, clean, and well sealed.

• Buy frozen foods at the last stop on your shopping trip.

• Keep foods in your freezer only for the recommended periods of time.

• And once you buy a freezer, USE it.

FREEZERS

HOW MUCH WILL YOU USE ONE?

Whether a freezer will be a money saver for you will depend on how much you use it, but the odds are it will *not* save you money—unless you live on a farm, or must drive a long distance to shop.

In 1974, it cost $123 a year to own a 480-pound capacity manual defrost freezer (about 16 cubic feet), including depreciation, electricity, and average repairs. If you stored and used only 480 pounds of food in your freezer during the year, costs worked out to an average of 26¢ per pound. If you stored 540 pounds, the cost dropped to 23¢ a pound and if you stored and used 900 pounds of food, down to 14¢. With a 480-pound capacity freezer, you would have to use more than 900 pounds of frozen food a year and save more than 14¢ a pound on the food you buy for the freezer before it would begin to break even. Your bargains would have to average at least 22¢ a pound less than prices at the time you eat the food to come out ahead with a frost-free freezer.

Here are a few more clues to the key costs of operating a home freezer today:

Depreciation. Figure this annual cost as one-fifteenth of the initial purchase price, including any finance charge.

Electricity. If your local electric rates are, say, 4¢ per kilowatt hour, costs are about $54 a year to keep a 450 to 500 pound freezer 80 per cent full.

Repairs. Freezers are among the least troublesome appliances and repair costs normally average well under $5.00 a year.

Packaging. Typical costs of materials run 3¢ to 4¢ per pound of food you package and freeze yourself.

Lost Interest. On the purchase price of the freezer and also on your outlay for the food you buy to fill it.

HOW TO BUY

Now here are the basic points to ponder when you are considering the purchase of a home freezer:

• Decide in advance whether an upright or chest model is best for you. The chest type requires more floor space, and it is less convenient because much unloading and rearranging are required to get food in and out on a proper rotation plan designed to eliminate spoilage. However, this type gives you extra counter space on which to work, accumulates less frost, maintains more even temperatures for longer storage times, and uses about half as much electricity as an upright freezer. The upright takes less floor space and is easier to defrost, but may cost $10 to $30 more than a chest-type freezer.

• Decide also what size freezer is adequate and appropriate for your family. Today's freezers come with capacities ranging from three to thirty-one cubic feet, but the most popular models have twelve to seventeen cubic feet of storage space. The general rule is you'll want three to four cubic feet for each member of the family and five or six per person if you have a vegetable garden and thus do a lot of home freezing or if you shop only every ten days or two weeks.

• Be sure to have adequate space for—and a sturdy floor under—your freezer. When full, this appliance can weigh as much as half a ton.

• Set a budget for your freezer: In the mid-1970s, price tags ranged from about $175 for a no-frills 12-cubic-foot freezer to $250 to $270 for a 16- to 17-cubic-foot model, and $300 to $400 for a luxury 17- to 18-cubic-foot, frost-free model.

• Decide which "extras" you really want and need. Frost-free (self-defrosting) freezers are considerably more convenient than models you must defrost yourself. But you'll pay $50 to $60 more for this feature. A self-defrosting freezer also costs substantially more to operate than a standard upright model, and nearly three times as much as a manual defrost chest. Similarly, a "flash defroster" feature may cut defrosting time to 15 minutes but you'll pay $30 or so extra for this time saving.

Among the other extras you can get—at a price—when you buy a freezer today are:

an interior light;

a special fast-freezing compartment;

a warning signal showing a dangerous temperature rise or power cutoff;

special baskets, trays, and racks for storage;

a built-in door lock.

• Finally, find out—*before* you buy a freezer—whether there is a warranty and exactly what it covers. Does it cover just repairs for the freezer? Or your losses in food spoilage as well if and when the freezer breaks down? And who will honor the warranty?

• Take special care to investigate the reliability of the dealer before you buy—for if and when a freezer breaks down, it must be repaired within twenty-four hours if you are to avoid losing your entire investment in its contents. Your dealer is of critical importance at that time.

BEWARE: THE DISHONEST "FREEZER FOOD PLAN"

There are two major traps associated with buying and owning a home freezer: the dishonest "freezer food plan" and the "bait and switch" in bulk beef buying.

Under the freezer food plan, you buy a freezer and also sign up for regular purchases of bargain-priced foods to put in it. The savings on the food, the ads say, actually will pay for the freezer itself. In effect, you'll get the freezer "free."

But if you commit yourself to such a deal and it turns out to be a come-on, you well may discover that you are obligated to pay a grossly inflated price for the freezer as well as grossly expensive finance charges on the installment loan you use to make the purchase.

The freezer you get may be much larger (and more expensive to operate) than your family really needs.

The seller may fail to deliver the promised food on the promised timetable. Or he may substitute inferior varieties of meats and other items for which you've signed up. Or he may welch on providing the "bonuses" or "free gifts" he used to lure you into the deal.

The guarantee may turn out to be worthless.

What the freezer plan salesman has done is to dazzle you with a promise of whopping savings on future food purchases—to the point where you fail to notice that he has jacked up the price of the freezer part of the deal as much as $200 to $300 over the price of a regular freezer.

Then, after you have signed a contract for the deal, he, in turn, sells it to a finance company and simply fades out of the picture—leaving you quite possibly badly stuck.

Your obvious ways to avoid the freezer plan trap are:

• Compare prices of the freezer you'd buy through regular retailers with those charged by the freezer plan salespeople.

• Also compare costs of the food offered through these plans with the costs of food you buy on special at the local supermarket.

• Be suspicious of any deal in which the food to be provided is advertised vaguely as "enough food for a family of four."

And once you have decided that you want to buy a certain food freezer plan, check the following points in the contract before you sign:

(1) Does the contract state clearly that you have to pay for the freezer?

(2) Does it state the price of the freezer, the total price of the food you are buying, the finance or carrying charges, and any other additional charges?

(3) Does it state the model, year of manufacture, and cubic capacity of the freezer?

(4) Does it state that food prices change and thus the price offer in the present plan will not remain the same?

(5) Does it state the quantity and types of food you will receive, their exact weights, and the grades of the food?

(6) Does it state that the food, should it spoil, is covered by insurance but that you have to pay for this insurance?

(7) Does it state the minimum and maximum quantities of food you must buy?

(8) If the salesman tells you he is making an introductory offer, is this specified in the contract?

(9) Is there a guarantee on the freezer? If so, does it clearly state what is guaranteed and for how long? (Don't believe unreasonable statements like "lifetime" or "unconditional" guarantees.)

BEWARE: "BAIT AND SWITCH" IN BULK BEEF BUYING

A while ago an inspector for the Virginia Department of Agriculture and Commerce visited a bulk-meat retail plant in northern Virginia which had advertised a side of beef at less than half the price the beef, in suitable cuts, was quoted in the supermarkets. On making a test purchase, the inspector (who didn't identify himself as a VDAC agent) was told that the bargain-priced beef was old, tough, and wouldn't be satisfactory for general cooking. He was also advised that the cutting and trimming loss on the meat would be high, as much as 70 per cent of the gross weight. He was then guided to a more expensive meat—USDA choice—and told this beef would be much better and the cutting loss would be less than 20 per cent.

After indicating that he would take a quantity of the higher-priced meat, the inspector began bargaining with the meat dealer. He finally bought 188 pounds of choice beef at a "reduced" price.

Back at the VDAC laboratory in Richmond, the inspector weighed the beef and found he had received a little over 120 pounds—a 36 per cent cutting loss against the guarantee of less than 20 per cent.

Thus, the 120 pounds of meat actually cost much more than the original quoted price for the hanging, uncut beef. And on top of this, more than half of the 120 pounds delivered represented hamburger!

This test purchase of bulk beef also revealed that close to $100 could have been saved on the same quantities of the same grade and cuts at a simultaneous local supermarket sale. The bulk dealer was charged and convicted of "advertising without intent to sell" and "delivering less than the quantity represented." He was fined $1,000 and costs on each count.

In meat, the dangers are very real that you'll be caught in a "bait and switch" racket. Your warning signals of deception will include:

• The ads will fail to disclose that as much as half of the weight will be lost in cutting, dressing, and trimming—in effect, doubling the price per pound. Or the operator's "estimated" trimming loss will turn out to be a "mistake"—costing you, the consumer, a painful sum.

• The low advertised prices will not be honest offers to sell beef but instead will be lures to bring you into the stores. Here, salesmen will downgrade the advertised meat in order to sell you higher-priced beef.

• The advertised "sale" or "special" prices will be the regular prices, not temporary bargains. The ads will place heavy emphasis on the scary aspects of soaring prices and potential food shortages.

• Credit disclosures required under the Truth in Lending law on installment purchases will be omitted altogether from the ad.

• Even if you agree to buy the better meat at a higher price, the seller may still deliver inferior meat—and you have no way of knowing exactly what has been delivered to you. (In one case reported by the Federal Trade Commission, a "bait and switch" operator sold a single "model" carcass of beef ten times during a single day!)

• Although there may be a money-back guarantee if you're dissatisfied, you may have a hard time actually getting either a replacement of the meat or a refund of your money—because of fine-print conditions and limitations which didn't appear in the advertised guarantee.

• You may discover, when your order of beef is delivered to you, that the stated maximum of ground beef (e.g., 12 per cent) is exceeded.

• The operator's definition of a "half of beef" may turn out to be the two forequarters or front half of the beef—where the steaks and other choice cuts *aren't,* but where much of the waste and bone *are.*

• The advertised "Heavy Western Beef" may turn out to be *cow* meat which is just as laden with yellow fat as beef under some other label.

Here are guidelines that will protect you:

• To find an honest freezer meat provisioner who may be able to lead you to a real meat-in-bulk bargain, ask about dealers who are well-established in your community and whose services your friends can recommend personally. The honest dealer will *not* advertise sides of beef at prices you know are unrealistically low. He will not try to lure you into a deal in which you're persuaded to buy beef at sky-high prices.

• Do not sign up for any bulk meat deal until you have exhaustively checked the reputation of the dealer. Do not permit any meat dealer to use high-pressure sales tactics on you. Give yourself plenty of time to think and to figure out what you are getting for your money.

• Find out whether the meat has been graded and what grade it is. If it is graded utility, it is likely to be tough and stringy and the net yield after cutting also may be low. Meats sold in most supermarkets are usually USDA choice.

• Have the dealer tell you how much trimming loss there will be and what net amount of meat you will receive. Then you can calculate exactly what you will be paying per pound for the meat.

• Once you have calculated the real net costs of the meat *after* trimming and cutting, compare these costs with prices of meats sold on specials.

• Know what cuts of meat—and how much—you will get in your delivered package. It is ridiculous for you to pay for a lot of stew meat when you really want steak, or vice versa.

• If you think you have been gypped, complain and complain loudly to the dealer. If you are not satisfied, do not hesitate to complain to local or state authorities.

The "bait and switch" racket is old and tenacious. It is particularly widespread and particularly vicious in meats because most of us are so ignorant about the rules for judging what is or is not a bargain. Heed these warnings well.

How to Spot Bargains in Poultry

A KEY IS FORM IN WHICH YOU BUY

Although poultry is among the least costly and most popular of main-dish foods, the form in which you buy it often will determine how big a bargain it is.

For example, chicken sold whole generally will be a few cents cheaper per pound than chicken cut up. Whole chicken also will usually be a better buy than chicken breasts and legs.

You also can achieve dramatic savings by buying specials on 5-pound boxes of chicken legs or breasts. Compared to the same quantity in smaller packages, you can save as much as $1.00 on this single purchase.

Here's a table showing the price per pound of a fryer, ready-to-cook, and of several chicken parts that would give you equal amounts of edible chicken for the money:

If the price per pound of whole fryers, ready-to-cook is:	BREAST HALF	DRUMSTICK AND THIGH	DRUMSTICK	THIGH	WING
33¢	44¢	35¢	34¢	37¢	27¢
35	46	38	36	39	28
37	49	40	38	41	30
39	52	42	40	43	31
41	54	44	42	46	33
43	57	46	44	48	35
45	59	48	46	50	36
47	62	50	48	52	38
49	65	53	50	55	39
51	67	55	53	57	41
53	70	57	55	59	43
55	73	59	57	61	44

Chicken parts are an equally good buy if price per pound is —

A chicken should be neither too white nor too yellow but rather a creamy color. Figure about one pound per person for whole chicken.

WAYS TO SAVE ON BUYING TURKEYS

Turkeys are inexpensive, too, and now come in quarters, in the form of legs only, breast slices, rolled roasts, etc. Turkey can be barbecued as easily and as quickly as chicken.

You'll get more meat for your money from whole ready-to-cook turkey than from boned, rolled turkey roast. The bigger the bird, the more meat it will have in proportion to bone. A turkey weighing less than 12 pounds is one half waste. Thus, half of a 20-pound bird may cost less than a whole 10-pound one. Look for a plump, squarish turkey for maximum meat yield. And check the label for a note of "parts missing."

Buy prepared turkey roasts or rolls on the basis of cost per serving.

Other Guides:

• If you invest in the convenience of a self-basting turkey which has had oil, water, flavors, fats, phosphates, and other materials injected into it to make it tenderer and more flavorful, you are paying the same price per pound for these ingredients as you're paying for the gobbler.

• "Turkey loaf" may, by law, contain as little as 35 per cent turkey.

• In other products, such as turkey and gravy, the proportion of turkey also is 35 per cent if *"turkey"* is the first word mentioned on the label. However, if the label says, for example, "giblet gravy and sliced turkey," the proportion of turkey may be as small as 15 per cent.

• The turkey label may or may not tell you what grade the bird is (A, B, or C) since grading is not legally required. There probably will be an indication of the turkey's "class," though—for instance, "young hen," "mature," "broiler," etc.

ORGANIC FOODS

THE BOOM TAKES OFF

In 1972 a volunteer shopper for New York's Department of Consumer Affairs found these gaps between prices of regular goods and their "organically produced" counterparts:

ITEM	REGULAR	ORGANIC
Apple juice, qt.	$ .37	$ .80
Grape juice, qt.	.37	.80
Peanut butter, lb.	.99	2.05
Honey, lb.	.53	.90
Eggs, doz.	.53	1.15
Dried prunes, lb.	.49	1.00
Cider vinegar, qt.	.33	1.00
Wheat bread, lb. loaf	.43	.95

The same shopper found these gaps between prices of regular vitamins and their "natural" counterparts:

VITAMIN	REGULAR	NATURAL
C 500 Mg., 100 tabs.	$1.98	$3.50
B-complex, 100 tabs.	1.79	2.60
E 100 I.U., 100 caps.	2.55	3.30
Multivitamins, 100 tabs.	3.45	9.95

• "Organic living"—at markups ranging to 30, 40, even 50 per cent! —has taken off. Our purchases of organic foods are skyrocketing. The organic foods list has ballooned far, far beyond wheat germ, Tiger's Milk, and blackstrap molasses. It now includes fresh fruits and vegetables, seaweed, organic bakery products, herb teas and coffees, spaghetti and macaroni, milled grains and whole grains of many types, seeds, oils, peanut butter and jelly, breakfast cereals, meats, a dizzying range of snacks.

Thousands of organic food stores from coast to coast also are selling organic food cookbooks and gardening guides, biodegradable soaps and cleaning compounds, home yogurt makers, untreated organic seeds for planting. Among the newer organic food customers are colleges, universities, communes, religious organizations, bakeries.

• Supermarkets are setting up special sections for organic foods. Newspapers are printing organic food columns. Some schools and colleges are offering courses on "organic living." Some towns are launching community organic gardens—for commercial as well as conservation purposes.

Countless thousands of you are now regularly gulping the vitamins and foods. Organic gardening clubs are multiplying and *Organic Gardening and Farming* magazine, published in Emmaus, Pennsylvania, had in 1974 more than 750,000 subscribers—a number which certainly brings this once far-out publication into the big leagues.

• One of the nation's biggest organic food wholesalers, Erewhon Trading Co. in Boston, has farms with more than 25,000 acres under contract and tight quality controls to produce seeds, grains, fruits, and other foods. Erewhon's product list includes more than 150 items and new ones are being added each month.

Theoretically, at least, there could be an organic equivalent of virtually every food product you now find on supermarket shelves.

WHAT IS "ORGANIC" FOOD?

Exactly what constitutes "organic" food? According to the National Farmers Organization in Iowa, it is "food grown without pesticides; grown without artificial fertilizers; grown in soil whose humus content is increased by the addition of organic matter" and "food which has not been treated with preservatives, hormones, antibiotics, etc."

Organically grown beef and other meats are raised on organically managed land; are fed with foods which are free from pesticides and herbicides, antibiotics, feed additives, growth and other medicinal hormones; and tend toward grass grazing over grain feeding.

How do organic foods differ from "natural" foods and "health" foods?

There are no legal definitions, but here are guidelines which are widely agreed upon:

• Natural foods contain no preservatives, emulsifiers, or artificial ingredients. They are sold to provide consumers with an alternative to conventional foods which may contain such additives and preservatives.

• Organic foods are more or less the same as natural foods, except that "organic" implies greater care of soils and plant environment to exclude pesticides and artificial fertilizers.

• Health foods are different from the other two categories. They include dietetic, vegetarian, and other products not necessarily free of chemical additives.

But what could possibly be the advantage of chewing on desiccated liver when you can buy—and probably eat with pleasure—regular fresh liver at far lower cost? Are such products as dulse and kelp, soybean flour, rose hips, sesame seeds, and safflower oil really necessary for *your* good health? Is it honestly worth it to pay 30, 40, even 50 per cent more for specially grown "organic" foods—in terms of their purity and nutritional value to you, the consumer?

You well may be among the millions of us who feel caught between the cross fire of claims and counterclaims by organic food buffs, food faddists, the Food and Drug Administration in Washington, nutritionists on both sides of the organic food argument today.

On one side are the organic food supporters who are (1) issuing dire warnings that we are being poisoned en masse by additives, preservatives, emulsifiers, pesticides, chemical fertilizers, other foreign substances which are routinely added to so many foods we eat, and who (2) point out quite persuasively, that many food manufacturers and processors first remove most or all key nutrients and perhaps put back only a few of them in certain "fortified" foods.

On the other side are many of the world's top nutritionists who (1) insist that most foods on today's supermarket shelves are just as safe, healthy, and nutritious as their more expensive organic counterparts and (2) argue that the only difference between "natural" and synthetic vitamins is that the natural ones cost more.

The FDA lists some 600 different food additives—artificial colors and flavors, monosodium glutamate, synthetic sugar and salt substitutes and preservatives, emulsifiers, and other chemicals—as GRAS (Generally Recognized as Safe). However, the FDA admits that few of these additives have been extensively tested. In the past, the FDA's over-all approach has been to consider an additive safe unless and until it is proven to be otherwise. However, adamant consumer advocates have been increasingly challenging that attitude—and the rules have been steadily tightened.

Somewhere in between are the majority of us who are legitimately worried about the questions raised in recent years concerning pesticides and additives and about our national case of malnutrition. And there's no doubt, as one New York City expert remarked, some labels "read like a qualitative analysis of the East River."

In sum, the dilemma is that most of us just don't know whether we're being ripped off by organic food stores or whether organic foods are really better for us and are worth paying twice the price for them.

And a final touch: we simply have no way of knowing whether the "organic" foods we do buy actually were produced without chemicals or were processed without either removing important nutrients or adding forbidden substances.

TEN RULES FOR BUYING ORGANIC FOODS

If *you* are sold or even partially sold on the idea of organic foods, here are ten basic guidelines on how to buy them and how to get the most for your money:

(1) Start by patronizing the biggest and best established organic food store in your area, then explore others and compare products and prices as you go. Check knowledgeable friends for hints. Stick to stores that appear neat and clean. Stay away from the ill-kept ones with open flour, grain, and seed bins into which all of you are invited to dip your hands to get what you want. Also avoid stores which offer an obviously kooky line of products along with the organic foods: vibrators, fountain-of-youth products, hair restorers, etc.

(2) Interview the proprietor and listen with care. How much control does he keep over the product he sells? What proof (such as certification from known food growers) can he offer you that the foods he sells actually are organically grown? Does he personally know his major suppliers and the farmers? Since there are relatively few large-scale growers of organic foods, it's no great chore to be acquainted with them all. Or if he doesn't know his suppliers and growers personally, does he at least require them to provide affidavits on the authenticity of their organic foods? Can you see these affidavits?

(3) Study organic food labels for details on: ingredients; where, who, and by whom grown (you can easily get to know the names of reputable growers, processors, and distributors); conditions under which the foods were grown and processed, including types of soil, water, and fertilizers used; appropriate disclaimers on pesticides, additives, herbicides, commercial fertilizers; recipes.

(4) Check with care the contents of breakfast cereal products—consisting of rolled oats, soybean oil, brown sugar, perhaps a few other items. Many varieties on the market are neither organically grown nor particularly nutritious. Note whether the contents of other products—

such as juices—are not precisely the same as the contents of their regular supermarket counterparts.

(5) On vitamins, study the source of their "natural" components, as well as the proportions of each substance. Be sure the amounts of ingredients listed are for one tablet or capsule (not five or six).

(6) Comparison-shop, especially on high-priced items. An excellent way to do this is to compare prices of staple items.

(7) Ask yourself: will your family eat the foods? You won't improve your health—and certainly not your budget—by buying foods which end up in the garbage pail (or even the compost heap). Also will you really invest the necessary time to prepare meals from organic "raw materials"?

(8) Be skeptical of exorbitantly priced "organic" toothpastes, shampoos, facial creams, raw sugar (chemically identical to refined sugar), similar products. Certainly be wary if salesclerks tout any of those wares as "wonder foods."

(9) Buy such items as whole grains, wheat germ, cereals, soy beans, lentils, and other beans in bulk.

(10) Write, if you have any questions about various foods and how they're grown, to their producers or suppliers. The top producers and suppliers will respond to your legitimate inquiries. Be wary of any firm which gives you a runaround or no reply at all.

BEWARE! ORGANIC FOOD TRAPS

As you might suspect, the deceivers and gypsters have been crowding into this exploding field and making a mockery of the very definition of organic food. All kinds of packagers have been buying up ordinary foods, labeling them "organic," and passing them off on naïve retailers and an innocent public.

Says the president of one of the nation's largest organic food wholesalers: "Ninety per cent of the 'organic' apple juice now being sold in California is not made from organically grown apples. At least half of the organically grown rice now being sold on the East Coast, isn't."

How, then, can you, a food shopper who buys this type of product, protect yourself against the profiteering charlatans? By using this rundown of current traps in the field:

Deceptive labeling: Probably the biggest trap is using an "organic," "natural," "nature's own," etc., label when this is not the case. In the most flagrant cases, unscrupulous retailers simply paste an "organic" label over the brand name of a non-organic product or its package. Or the "organically grown" food may be merely food which hasn't been sprayed with pesticides—but which fails to meet other generally accepted criteria for organic foods.

Many unscrupulous suppliers, for instance, sell "natural organic" honey (a major health food product), although they have had no control over the antibiotics which may have been used in bee feed or over what types of sprays are used around the bees' base.

Non-organic foods: Often mixed in with organic products in organic food stores, leading you to believe they're somehow special and worth paying extra for.

Small type: Frequently dried fruits which are labeled "natural organic" have preservatives listed in tiny type in an inconspicuous section of the label.

Exaggerated claims: Some protein supplements are being sold with the promise that they'll improve not only your physical fitness but even your appearance.

Sheer misinformation: This is often aimed at innocent older people who are constantly worried about their health. Some health food store operators, once they've sold a customer one bottle of vitamins or minerals, will then try to sell another to "balance" the first one.

Overpricing: The 50 per cent markups on vitamin pills and protein supplements are common. Moreover, most of the vitamin C now being sold as "natural" consists almost entirely of ascorbic acid—the same stuff you find in "unnatural" vitamin C.

Nutrition nonsense: Almost everybody is trying to climb on the health food bandwagon and make a healthy profit in the process. Of questionable nutritional value surely are "organic" variations in toothpaste, refined oils, refined sea salt, syrup.

Low calorie fruits and vegetables: These may be labeled as "natural organic" but actually they're the same as all diet foods.

Your best—and most obvious—safeguards are to know the proprietor of the store you patronize and study carefully the labels of each product you buy. And if you feel you've been deceived or cheated, report the details to your local Better Business Bureau and your Consumer Protection Agency.

WHISKEY AND WINE

HOW TO CUT YOUR LIQUOR BILLS

When did you last add up your liquor bills and face up to how much this one item contributes to your pocketbook pinch?

If you're merely moderate drinkers, spend only $10 a week on liquor, and throw only three cocktail parties a year involving liquor bills of only $50 each, your annual liquor bill amounts to $670. If you're heavier drinkers and entertain lots of friends and neighbors, your annual bill easily may be in the $1,000 to $2,000 range.

Okay. How can you save on liquor without going on the wagon?

• Sample "house brands" of liquor sold locally—especially at delicatessen-type stores (whose house brands often are made by the nation's top distillers). If the house brands taste at least as good to you as the more expensive names you have been buying, adopt them for regular use or at least for large cocktail parties.

• When you throw a cocktail party, offer some "house special," building interestingly on one of the less expensive liquors—gin, vodka, rum. Of course, if you use fruit juices and mixers extensively, it's less important to have expensive, top-quality brands than if you're serving martinis or scotch on the rocks, or Bourbon and branch water. Or try something like a May wine punch with fresh strawberries; you might find that many of your guests actually would prefer this lighter and less costly drink.

• Shop for bargains in cocktail mixers as well as in the cocktails themselves. To me, many of the large-size, lower-cost mixers taste as good as the well-known brands costing 20 to 25 per cent more. But in any event, stick to the larger-size bottles when you're shopping for a party.

• Consider the premixed bottled cocktails (martinis, manhattans, etc.)—*if* they will eliminate your need to hire a bartender. Otherwise they're no bargain since you pay a premium of 25 per cent or so for the convenience. (A homemade 1½-ounce martini costs about 30¢ versus 35¢ to 40¢ for the premixed equivalent.)

• Consider less expensive Virgin Island rum as an alternative to Puerto Rican rum.

• Try out imported whiskey which has been bottled in the U.S. rather than abroad.

• If you happen to be fans of "B & B," save 20 per cent on this liqueur by buying a bottle of Benedictine and another of inexpensive French cognac and mixing your own B & B.

• Unless higher proof (e.g., 100 proof) liquor is far more expensive than its lower proof counterpart (e.g., 86 proof), the higher proof is probably the better deal. You simply dilute it yourself.

• Look for liquor sales. Although liquor prices often tend to be controlled in any given area by state laws and other factors, sales *do* happen in some places, and bargains can be found. The best time to find liquor sales—and to stock up—is after a big holiday.

• Finally, consider the liquor cost on a *per ounce* basis. If a quart of Brand X costs $3.20, the cost per ounce is 10¢, and a fifth of the identical liquor would have to cost less than $2.56 to be a better value (which it almost never is). If a fifth costs $6.40, a quart of the identical liquor would have to cost less than $8.00 to be a bargain.

There are 32 ounces in a quart and 25⅗ ounces in a fifth (four fifths of a quart). Here's a chart to give you *per ounce* equivalents in the typical price range for hard liquors.

QUART	FIFTH	COST PER OZ.
$3.20	$2.56	$.10
3.84	3.07	.12
4.48	3.58	.14
4.80	3.84	.15
5.12	4.10	.16
5.44	4.35	.17
5.76	4.61	.18
6.08	4.86	.19
6.40	5.12	.20
6.72	5.38	.21
7.04	5.63	.22
7.36	5.89	.23
7.68	6.14	.24
8.00	6.40	.25

HOW TO CUT YOUR WINE BILLS

It's scarcely a secret that drinking of wine is in a great boom all over the world—very definitely, even spectacularly, including millions of us in the United States. As it has been with meat, so it has been with wine: this is another classic case of "demand-pull" inflation. To translate, the demand for wine is outrunning the supply of wine and, as a result, prices are being "pulled" relentlessly upward.

Meanwhile, wine collecting and wine "talk" have become among the most "in" of hobbies. "Wine" has joined the great leisure activities.

What should and can you—an amateur wine drinker and collector —do to hold down your costs in this area?

• Become adventuresome and seek out wines that please you at prices that please you. In this process, you must abandon the big names "just as," say the wine experts, "The art collector must stop buying Picasso and Chagall if he wants to pay a reasonable price."

• Develop a relationship of trust with a knowledgeable, established wine merchant and seek sound advice on labels to buy, what wines to store and not to store, etc. You will discover personal favorites at a fraction of the prices of well-known, best-selling trade names that have priced you out of the market. And you'll have fun as well on your odyssey in wines.

• Consider joining an established wine-buying club which buys its wine in large batches and also is backed by professional advisers who are trying to help you save money.

• Buy wine by the case for savings of up to 10 per cent.

• Buy wine on sale for savings of another 10 to 20 per cent.

Before you make a major commitment in wine, try to taste a single bottle of the exact type and vintage; in many cases, small "splits" are available to buyers.

Learn and stick to the great wine years for the bordeaux and burgundies.

If you have no storage area, see if you can arrange storage with a wine dealer (usually at a monthly charge of 50¢ a case).

• As for table wines, try out a variety of the type which sells by the half gallon or gallon—starting with the least expensive you can find. Be your own "wine taster" and trust your own judgments. Remember, in most European families, this is the category of wine consumed day in and day out—at a per-liter cost which is about the same as the cost of milk. Of course, the better domestic U.S. wines are more expensive—but there are less expensive ones, too, which are well worth a try.

Sample, also, wines now being imported from regions and countries other than the famed wine-producing ones—e.g., Chile, Switzerland, Greece, Portugal, the Eastern European countries, and, within France, the Loire and Rhone valleys, the Alps, Alsace.

How to Save on Parties

If you have given parties you must be aware that costs easily can run double or even triple the amount you have budgeted. Yet there are many ways to save substantial sums on your party without compromising its gaiety or quality. Here are the fundamental rules.

• Whatever type of party it is—whether it's a cocktail or a dinner party—set a per-person budget and stay with it. Liquor, hors d'oeuvre, and other trimmings probably will cost between $2.00 and $6.00 a head; a dinner party can cost from $3.00 to $5.00 up, but it's possible to put on a fairly elegant spread for around $10 a person. How much can you *really* afford to spend? How many people do you *really* want to invite?

• Consider one big party—which would undoubtedly be cheaper (and easier)—rather than a smattering of medium-sized parties throughout the year. But if your home cannot take a large number of guests, try parties on successive days—or a brunch and a cocktail party on the same day. By so doing, you can take maximum advantage of mass cooking, flowers, whatever party equipment you've rented, other extras you're paying for.

• As suggested earlier, buy the larger sizes of liquor—quarts over fifths, and half gallons over any of the smaller sizes. A case almost always is cheaper than the purchase of individual bottles, of course. A quart serves 16 two-ounce drinks, so if everybody drinks an average of three drinks, one quart will serve about five people. Ask your liquor dealer if he will take back unused bottles; many will.

• When mixing drinks, use a measure and follow a recipe if the drink requires this. Don't overpour.

• Don't overprepare. It's false economy to prepare a pitcher of some drink and then find you'll serve only a couple of drinks during the entire party. Plan your ingredients, have them ready, then prepare your drinks as you are asked for them.

• Buy the largest available bottles of mixers and the least expensive varieties of soda, mix, tomato juice, etc. Have ginger ale and other non-alcoholic beverages available; some people do prefer these.

• Serve wine and punches at a fraction of what cocktails would cost. You'll be delighted to discover how many of your guests will be grateful. Also try Irish coffee, Café Diable, such non-alcoholic drinks as espresso and cappuccino. These are far less expensive than liqueurs. And if yours is a dinner party, try the European custom of serving a predinner apéritif—such as a glass of champagne or a white wine or vermouth.

• Instead of hiring a bartender, have your husband mix the first drink for everybody and then suggest that everybody mix his own after that. People tend to drink less, incidentally, if an overgracious host doesn't plunge for empty glasses the instant they are drained. Or hire a college student to tend bar with the help of a few notes and advance lessons on how to mix what. If it's a dinner party try to hire a reliable, mature teen-ager in your area (or your own daughter) to help with preparations and cleaning up afterward.

• Place the bar where people aren't apt to congregate, and set the food in another corner. This will help distribute your guests and, incidentally, draw them away from the bar and toward your food.

• Even if you're the type who insists on flowers for every table in the house, consider buying just a dozen or so well-chosen ones, plus a bundle of pretty greenery. One or two flowers in the right-size vase can look just as good as a profusion, if you arrange them right.

• In summer, take everything you can from your garden, and from friends and neighbors. Don't order florist flowers over the telephone. Find out if any neighborhood florists offer a special of the week. Take advantage of these.

• Save on hors d'oeuvre by serving only made-in-U.S. items. Don't feel you must offer a full-scale delicatessen. One beautifully presented wheel of good domestic cheese or a platter of well-chosen cold cuts surrounded by a variety of crackers will be economical and will avoid the inevitable waste of a big variety.

Save on more elaborate food by making your foods from scratch and substituting your time for more expensive packaged convenience foods.

• Also save by serving cold foods. Buckets of ice for cold snacks are far less costly than renting or buying the necessary equipment for hot foods.

• And give a break to the millions of us who are struggling to keep trim figures. All we want is the simplest, lowest-cal crackers and rabbit food.

You probably can dwarf my list. The point is that real savings *are* possible. All *you* need do is plan.

THE HIGH COST OF EATING OUT

TREND: UP, UP, UP

If you are among the tens of millions of us who must or want to eat out regularly, you are acutely aware that the cost of restaurant meals has been skyrocketing. Just between 1967 and 1975 the cost of eating out jumped more than 65 per cent nationally.

And no relief appears in sight. The long-range outlook for restaurant meal prices is up, up, up—with the estimate that as of 1975, we are spending $2.00 out of every $10 of food dollars for food outside our homes.

RULES FOR CURBING COSTS

But you *can* hold down your eating-out costs and not sacrifice the quality of the food you get. Here are the rules which will slash your restaurant bills 10 to 25 per cent.

(1) Avoid restaurants where you must give individual tips to a large staff: headwaiter, maître d'hotel, doorman, hat check girl, restroom attendant—as well as your own waiter. These tips alone can add up to $10 to $15.

(2) Have a couple of drinks at home before you go and restrict yourself to one (or no) drinks at the restaurant. Today, three drinks each for a couple typically costs $9.00 to $12 in a good restaurant—plus the 15 per cent or more you tip on this total.

(3) Look for good new restaurants which do not yet have their liquor licenses but which may permit you to bring your own bottle of wine—with savings depending on the amount of wine and liquor you normally drink.

(4) Keep in mind that the typical markup on wine in restaurants is around 100 per cent; so do your fancy wine drinking when you have dinner at home.

(5) Favor restaurants which have relatively short, simple menus. You save because food is not wasted in the kitchen and you can get a far more elegant meal for your money if the chef and his staff can concentrate on a few menu items.

(6) Steer clear of purely snob appeal restaurants—unless it's really worth cash to you to sit across the room from a celebrity or a tycoon.

(7) Patronize restaurants in neighborhoods where you can benefit from the fact that rents and other overhead costs may be 30 to 50 per cent lower than in midtown. If you're trying to save money, this alone can do it for you.

And a final note: don't be mesmerized by exotic, fanciful adjectives or the writing on a menu. You're not eating the menu.

The trend of prices for food at restaurants will still be up, but with these guides you can maneuver nicely within that trend to eat out and actually save.

7

THE NOW-AND-THEN
NECESSITY OF CLOTHES

FINDING YOUR WAY AROUND THE CLOTHING
   "SUPERMARKET"   245
THE FUNDAMENTALS   246
   SHOP FOR WHAT'S RIGHT FOR YOU   246
   BUY ONLY CLOTHES THAT FIT YOU PROPERLY   246
   STUDY CLOTHES LABELS   248
   PLAN YOUR WARDROBE WITH MORE THAN ONE
      PURPOSE IN MIND   250
   LOOK FOR GOOD WORKMANSHIP   250
   AVOID IMPULSE BUYING   251
   MAKE A CLOTHING BUDGET—AND STICK TO IT   251
TEN WAYS TO SLASH YOUR CLOTHING BUDGET   252
SIX RULES ON DRESSING FOR THE OFFICE   256
SAVE MORE CLOTHING DOLLARS BY SEWING   257
   THE BOOM THAT KNOWS NO BOUNDARIES   257
   HOW TO BUY A SEWING MACHINE   258
   BEWARE: SEWING MACHINE TRAPS   262
CUTTING YOUR CLOTHES CARE COSTS   263
   THE TIME-TESTED TIPS   263
   HOW TO USE CLOTHES CARE LABELS   264
TWELVE WAYS TO REDUCE YOUR SHOE BILLS   264

Finding Your Way Around the Clothing "Supermarket"

Most clothing stores in this era are something like supermarkets. It's up to *you* to plan what you want in your wardrobe yourself, to search the shelves and racks for sizes and styles to suit you and your budget, to determine the quality of everything you buy from socks to suits. Salespeople (if you can find them) are frequently untrained and inexperienced, and far more concerned with making a sale than with helping you to dress properly and attractively.

Modern fabrics and finishes are also a maze in which you can find your way only if you know the hieroglyphics of acrylics and modacrylics, wovens and non-wovens, furs and fake furs, polyesters and foam-bonded materials, and on and on. Today, there are *more than 700* trade names for various manufactured fibers. A clothes label, as one wag put it, often looks "like an inventory list of a chemical factory."

On the minus side is the blunt fact that, if you choose wrong or misjudge quality and a dress or suit falls apart after a few wearings, you almost surely will not be able to get your money back. And you well may not be able to get the item repaired or get a replacement for it.

But on the plus side are the far more important facts that:

A greater variety of clothes styles, fabrics, finishes, is available to you today than ever before in our history.

The price range also is the broadest ever.

Federal laws protecting you against mislabeling never have been so numerous or strict.

And you can draw on an unprecedented wealth of information sources to help you shop for the very best and most suitable wardrobe for you and your family.

In the following pages you'll find this "wealth" broken down into the most valuable nuggets that *you* can use to plan your wardrobe and shop for clothes to fill it.

THE FUNDAMENTALS

SHOP FOR WHAT'S RIGHT FOR YOU

Simple, classic clothing styles may be more suitable for you (and also may last longer) than the latest, most alluring fashion craze. Basic clothes, which never go out of style, are real bargains. And the chance to wear many combinations may be a better addition to your wardrobe than a wild, utterly unforgettable outfit.

If you must buy or cannot resist a way-out style (and this includes shoes), buy the least expensive you can find. Try to establish a simple color theme—perhaps building on one or two basic colors which can be mixed and matched as you choose.

BUY ONLY CLOTHES THAT FIT YOU PROPERLY

This will add to the life of your suit, dress, or coat as well as to your comfort and good appearance.

Don't make the common error of buying sizes that are *too small* for you on the assumption that you are about to lose ten or fifteen pounds! If you cannot get a really good fit, buy a size which is slightly *too large* rather than one that is slightly too small. It's usually possible to alter a dress or a coat from a large size to a smaller size, but often impossible to do the opposite.

Use the following table, prepared by the Money Management Institute of Household Finance Corporation, Chicago, Illinois, and included in the Institute's booklet "Your Clothing Dollar," as a guide to size ranges used by most clothing manufacturers for women's clothes. Note that, in addition to regular sizes, some type of clothing may be marked "tall," "medium" or "average," and "short" or "petite."

Size Classification	Size Range	Figure Type
Junior Petite	3–15	For figures 5'1" or shorter. The neckline and armholes are smaller and length from shoulder to waist and from waist to hemline is shorter than a Junior.
Junior	3–17	For figures 5'1½" to 5'5½" with a higher, smaller bust, narrower shoulders, and a shorter waistline than the Misses.
Misses Petite	8–18	For figures 4'11½" to 5'2" with a longer waist and a fuller bust than a Junior Petite. Smaller neckline and armholes than a Misses.
Misses	6–22	For the well-proportioned figure 5'2½" to 5'6½". Hips moderately larger than bust and normal to low waist.
Misses Tall	10–22	For the well-proportioned figure over 5'7½".
Half Sizes	12½–26½	A mature Junior. Fuller throughout the bust, back, and shoulders and shorter waisted than the Junior.
Women's Sizes	34–52	The mature, more developed Misses figure. Fuller in the back and shoulders and longer waisted than the Misses.

And use the following chart, also published in "Your Clothing Dollar,"* as your guide to standard children's sizes, corresponding to body weight, height, and other measurements:

	Size	Weight	Height	Chest	Waist	Hip
Infants' and Babies'	(mos.)					
	3	13	24	17		
	6	18	26½	18		
	12	22	29	19		
	18	26	31½	20		
	24	29	34	21		
	36	32	36½	22		
Toddlers'	(Years)					
	1	25	31	20	20	
	2	29	34	21	20½	
	3	34	37	22	21	
	4	38	40	23	21½	
Children's	2	29	34	21	20½	21½
	3	34	37	22	21	22½
	4	38	40	23	21½	23½
	5	44	43	24	22	24½
	6	49	46	25	22½	25½
	6X	54	48	25½	23	26½

STUDY CLOTHES LABELS

You are protected in the United States by the Federal Textile Fiber Products Identification Act. Under this law, clothes and other textile products must contain the following information on their labels:

• the *generic name* of the fibers (cotton, polyester, etc.), listed in order of the weight of each fiber;

• the percentage weight of each fiber weighing 5 per cent or more of the total;

• the *name* or registered number of the manufacturer or seller;

• the *country* from which an imported item comes.

* Money Management Institute, Household Finance Corporation, Chicago, Illinois, Copyright 1972.

In addition, wool products must be labeled, under the Wool Products Labeling Act, with the percentage of wool contained, the type of wool (e.g., wool, reprocessed wool, etc.), the percentage of non-wool fibers included, and the identity of the manufacturer.

This information can be more important—and a better clue to quality—than a brand name on natural fibers. For example, the satisfaction you get from a properly made shirt of preshrunk combed cotton can be the same—whether the shirt is a national brand, carries the store's name, or bears no brand at all.

Save the tags from any new garments which do not have permanent care labels, and mark them for identification so you'll know how the clothes should be cleaned. Index and file them in a box you can keep in the laundry area.

Learn at least the basics on the major fabrics and finishes in clothes today—and what each type implies in upkeep, durability, cleaning, laundering, and looks.

The International Fabricare Institute has put together 78 "Facts About Fabrics" leaflets. You can get any of the 78 from member cleaners or by writing the Institute, Doris and Chicago Avenue, Joliet, Illinois 60434, enclosing a postage-paid, self-addressed envelope. Be as specific as you can about the type of fabric (fiber content, woven, knitted, etc.) on which you need information.

Here are some of the key clothing finishes now available. Most of them will boost the price of an item of clothing but will increase its convenience too:

Wash and wear (needs little or no ironing after washing).

Permanent press (can certainly be a savings if you're in the habit of sending your shirts to a hand laundry or your slacks to a dry cleaner, and material stays unwrinkled and fresh-looking all day long, too; bed linens continue to look newly laundered from one bed change to another).

Sanforized (fabric will not shrink more than 1 per cent in either direction; there are other similar finishes).

Water repellent (fabric sheds water but allows air to go through; won't work in a downpour without an umbrella, however).

Stain and spot resistant (fabric resists water and oily stains easily).

Look for clues to these finishes on the label—along with clues to the proper care of the particular item.

Look also for details on:

• Whether or not the fabric is "vat-dyed" or "sun-fast"—assurances (though not guarantees) that the fabrics will not fade in sunlight or with normal laundering. Man-made fibers are almost always totally color-fast. But, as with natural fibers, check the labels for a non-fade statement before you buy.

• Whether or not it is a stretch fabric. (Comfort stretch for every-day use, action stretch for ski wear, etc.) Labels won't tell you how much stretch to expect in a stretch fabric. A test at the store is some help, but it can't guarantee that changes won't occur later. Your best safeguard is to buy from a reputable retailer and clothing manufacturer, both of whom will heed your complaints and, if justified, will make re-funds or exchanges.

PLAN YOUR WARDROBE WITH MORE THAN ONE PURPOSE IN MIND

For instance, in men's clothes, a top-notch buy is a raincoat with a detachable lining. Without lining, it can double as a topcoat in mild weather. With lining, it can get you through the coldest weather. Women's raincoats with detachable linings can be equally good buys.

Another bargain is a tweed suit with a coat which can double as a good-looking jacket to wear with slacks.

And either a man or a woman can buy a flannel suit with pants that can be worn with other jackets or jackets that can be worn with other pants.

LOOK FOR GOOD WORKMANSHIP

Consumers Union, the most prestigious consumer testing labora-tory in the field, publishes in its monthly *Consumer Reports* and its an-nual Buying Guide issue excellent reports of controlled tests on standard clothing brands—from diapers to dinner jackets. You'll benefit from these reports on durability, color-fastness, appearance, laundering ease, quality of workmanship, etc., and learn exactly what to look for when you shop.

Specifically:

Seams should be smooth (no "puckering"), wide enough to let out if necessary, properly finished to prevent fraying.

Hems should be even, properly bound with tape, securely fastened, invisibly stitched, deep enough to permit lengthening.

Stitching should be even and close together.

Buttonholes should be sewn through on both sides of the cloth.

Linings—of the fabric and pockets—should be firm, closely woven, and made of a material which will not stretch or shrink.

Zippers, snaps, and decorative trim should be firmly attached and properly placed.

AVOID IMPULSE BUYING

If you need a spring raincoat, don't stop off at the section reserved for bathing suits and buy a bikini at top price. (And don't laugh, I've done this sort of thing plenty of times and I'll bet you have too!) The same goes for "bargains" which have no place at all in your wardrobe. They are *not* bargains to you if you don't need or really want the items.

And this applies equally to a variety of clothing accessories which you may find tempting in the store but which you didn't even dream of wanting until you spotted them.

MAKE A CLOTHING BUDGET—AND STICK TO IT

Clothes are among the most flexible of all your budget items but, as a general guide, below are a few national "averages" from the Bureau of Labor Statistics in Washington:

• On average, out of each $1.00 a U.S. family spends on everything, about 9¢ goes for clothes and shoes. The share rises to more than 10½¢ when the cost of clothes upkeep is included.

• Our annual national clothes-and-shoes bill now runs about $333 a year for each man, woman, and child.

• Typically, clothing costs triple to quadruple between the ages of one and eighteen.

• On average, women spend $3.00 out of every $5.00 of the family's clothing dollars.

• The average adult American woman owns four to five dresses, two to three suits, two to three coats, five skirts and five sweaters, three to four pairs of pants, two knit dresses, and two knit suits.

• The average teen-age American girl owns similar numbers of each item of clothing, plus a couple of extra skirts and sweaters, but fewer knit dresses and suits.

But these are merely averages and almost certainly they do *not* apply to you.

Only *you* can set your own clothing budgets, priorities, and preferences.

In *your* clothing budget:

Make room for luxuries as well as for necessities.

List all the items you *must* have and then the luxury items you'd *like* to have. Ask yourself what kind of clothing you need: for the office; for sports and leisure-time activities; for social occasions. Just the listing will help you pinpoint the necessities you can appropriately buy at minimum prices and you then can apply whatever amounts you have saved to your luxury purchases.

TEN WAYS TO SLASH YOUR CLOTHING BUDGET

You can truly slash your clothing costs—and be better dressed than ever!—by learning and following these ten specific guides:

(1) *Buy clothes off season*—and achieve savings running to a sensational 30 to 50 per cent. March is the best time to buy ski outfits, for instance. January and August are good months to buy furs.

There are three major periods for store-wide clearance sales: after Easter, after July 4, and after Christmas. These are excellent times to pick up clothes as well as a long list of other items—although you may run into shortages of styles, sizes, and colors if you don't shop as early as you possibly can in the sale (if possible, the day it begins).

List the clothing items of standard styles which you know you will need during the next six to twelve months. Study and use the clothing bargain calendar which follows.

Budget your cash and your credit so you have the funds to buy the items you need and want during the clothes-buying bargain seasons.

Your Calendar

Back-to-school clothes—August, October
Bathing suits—after Fourth of July in July and August
Children's clothing—July, September, November, December
Coats (women's, children's)—April, August, November, December

Coats (men's)—January, August
Costume jewelry—January
Dresses—January, April, June, November
Furs—January, August
Handbags—January, May, July
Hats (children's)—July, December
Hats (men's)—January, July
Hosiery—March, October
Housecoats—April, May, June, October, November
Infants' wear—January, March, April, July
Lingerie—January, May, July
Millinery—February, April, July
Men's shirts—January, February, July
Men's and boys' suits—April, November, December
Piece goods—June, September, November
Shoes (boys' and girls')—January, March, July
Shoes (men's and women's)—January, July, November, December
Sportswear—January, February, May, July
Toiletries—January, July

Of course, bargains also turn up at odd times through the year because of special circumstances—a store going out of business or into business or moving, an anniversary celebration, an unusual holiday, etc. You can always use these opportunities to buy items you know you'll need later.

A warning is necessary at this point, though: Watch out for those "going-out-of-business" sales on clothes. They can be phonies—and you can spot one if the sale has been going on for months or even years.

(2) *Buy certain items in quantity*—and save 10 to 30 per cent.

If, say, you buy one pair of stockings or panty hose or one pair of socks, a single run or hole can mean a total loss. But if you buy six pairs of the same type and color, you can match what is left and prolong the useful life of each item. (You can cut one leg out of a pair of panty hose when it runs, then one leg out of another pair, and wear both "good legs.") Buying in quantity is particularly practical if yours is a large family. Much clothing is sold on a "three for X dollars" basis.

(3) *Buy standard sizes*. If you're buying a man's sport shirt you will save by buying a small, medium, or large size. The price goes up when you buy shirts in more detailed neck and sleeve sizes. This prin-

ciple holds for socks, gloves, and many other types of clothing—men's and women's.

(4) *Find and patronize economical clothing stores.* Chain stores and mail-order houses are excellent for such "staples" as jeans, underwear, shirts, athletic socks, sneakers, boots, pajamas and nightgowns, scarves, belts, and work clothes.

Discount stores vary and stocks within individual discount stores also vary but they are worth a very serious check—particularly Army-Navy stores and "factory discount stores" which are outlets for slightly irregular items or oversupplies at drastic markdowns. Savings run approximately 25 per cent at the typical self-service, cash-only discount store, and often more.

Your key questions in shopping at a discount store should be: How does quality compare with other stores? How does each store handle customer complaints on defective or unsafe merchandise?

Look carefully, too, into local thrift and consignment shops, where you may buy next-to-new well-made and high-fashion secondhand clothes at very low prices.

And before you splurge on a high-fashion, high-priced dress or coat or suit, find out if the city in which you live (or a city nearby) has a high-fashion discount store. Two of the best-known stores of this type are Loehmann's in New York (and several other cities), and Filene's Automatic Bargain Basement in Boston. Typical reductions at this type of store: a minimum of 25 per cent and often 40 to 60 per cent.

(5) *Learn the various departments of your stores.* Within a given department store, check into the different departments and what type and price merchandise each carries. The bargain basement *may* carry designer clothes as well as bottom-of-the-line seconds, but this department usually specializes in high-volume, low-overhead, low-markup business. Durability is stressed more than style.

Although low-priced irregulars and seconds are often available in bargain basements, don't assume that prices are always lower in the basement than upstairs. Check the prices as well as the quality carefully.

Upstairs, you'll find a wide price range as well. If you can find a dress you like in the department store's sportswear department, it may cost less than one of comparable quality in the dress department. If clothes from the teen-age department are appropriate for and fit you, they'll probably be less expensive, too.

(6) *Look without prejudice at clothing seconds.* As a general rule, the bigger the flaws in clothing seconds, the greater will be the price cut. The key point you must consider before buying seconds is whether the flaw is "basic" or simply on the surface. Will the blemish significantly reduce the item's usefulness, attractiveness, or durability? Can the defect be easily and inexpensively repaired? If the answers are favorable to the purchase, it could be an extraordinarily good one for you.

(7) *Steer away from frills,* especially on utility items. As an illustration, a sweater with a lavish belt or fur collar will be far more costly than the same sweater without the extras. The simple sweater also will be more useful, for the simpler it is the more occasions you'll be able to wear it (and the more you'll be able to dress it up or down on your own).

(8) *Match prices against utility.* For instance, if you have young children, the mortality rate on play clothes will be exceedingly high. Thus it's smart to get them at rock-bottom prices. You can extend this rule to a wide range of clothing purchases for every member of your family, particularly in sports clothes. And, incidentally, remember this rule when you're shopping for your husband. Don't push him into the latest "peacock revolution"—wild frills, rainbow-colored shirts, new-fangled shaped suits—if that's not where he's at.

(9) *Buy children's clothes by size, not age.* Buy according to *your* child's height and weight. Buy clothes which have room for growth as your child grows (i.e., deep hems and pants cuffs, adjustable straps on overalls and jumpers, elastic waistbands, raglan sleeves). Buy clothes which are durable and don't show wrinkles and dirt too readily. And don't impose *your* adult tastes on your child.

(10) *Use credit plans with caution.* You can easily overspend with easy charge plans. You also may miss sales opportunities in other stores because you're still paying off old bills to the store in which you have the revolving charge account. But if you have charge accounts at various stores you'll often get *advance* notice of special customer clearances—and you can use those clearances to get bargains.

Many department stores and clothing shops hold private "courtesy days" sales for charge-account customers a week or so before advertising them widely to the public. If you have charge accounts, you'll be on the stores' mailing lists and you'll have first pick of the sale items.

When you are fully aware of the advantages as well as the pitfalls of store credit plans you can use them for your own benefit. See Chapter 3, "How to Borrow Cash and Use Credit Wisely," pages 123–24, for details on department store charge accounts.

SIX RULES ON DRESSING FOR THE OFFICE

During the attempt of the dress industry to force us into the midi at the start of the 1970s, mini skirts remained very much in evidence. Most young office workers simply would not junk their wardrobes— and they didn't. Pants became far more acceptable attire for the office as women turned some of their minis into tunics, combined them with pants, and created instant "suits." For millions of us, wardrobes became multiple-length collections from which we chose whatever we liked to fit an occasion. No dress length appeared truly out of place at any social occasion. This was a rebellion. It is now an accepted way of life.

Do not underestimate its dollars-and-cents importance to you this very day, though, for what this phenomenon of fashion underlined was one of the most basic rules on dressing for work.

(1) It is: *avoid* imprisoning yourself in the latest fashions or even being in the advance guard of any new clothing trend.

Here are other rules on clothes for the office:

(2) Never buy a new wardrobe all at once.

(3) Wait until a new fashion trend has caught on before you make any significant investment in it (for the office or elsewhere).

(4) Test the wearability of any garment you choose for a full day's wear in the office by crinkling part of it in your hand to see if it returns to its original shape. If it doesn't, pass it up.

For the office, the most practical fibers and fabrics are alpaca, camel's hair, cashmere, crepe, flannel, foulard, piqué, sharkskin, tweed, wool, jersey, and any of the man-made, stay-press fabrics.

Almost all fibers can be suitable for office wear, though—depending on the fabric construction. Silk and linen are the least practical because they wrinkle. Air conditioning and central heating have sharply expanded the usefulness of the widest variety of fibers and fabrics.

(5) Be sure any garment you intend to wear in the office all day long is comfortable. Thus, when you try on clothes, sit down, raise your arms, bend over in front of a mirror.

(6) And when you find two dresses equally becoming, one costing, say, $100 and the other $50, buy the better-quality dress for economy every time.

SAVE MORE CLOTHING DOLLARS BY SEWING

THE BOOM THAT KNOWS NO BOUNDARIES

For Ann-Marie's seventeenth birthday, her wealthy mother offered her a present of a new wardrobe: daytime dress, dinner dress, pants suit, skirt, shirt, sweater, all to be selected by her at the store of her choice. I was tucked into a corner chair in my friend's living room when she announced the lavish present and I turned eagerly to see her daughter's response.

"Thanks, Mom," said she, "but do me a favor, huh? Outside of the sweater, use all the money you expect to spend on the clothes to buy me the materials instead. I'll make what I want. You buy the fabrics because you always spend more than I would. Thanks."

"But, Ann-Marie, it's your birthday," protested my friend. "I want you to use your time studying, not sewing for your present."

"Mom, please do like I say," was the answer. "I'll come out with much better clothes than I would buy in any store and I'll end up with a lot more to wear too."

• Some 52 million American women and girls are now involved in making apparel at home. Over 8 million of them are teen-age girls. More than half of the women who sew learned to sew in home economics classes in junior and senior high schools. About 6 million girls a year study home sewing in school. Among teen-age girls, the vast majority know how to sew.

• Literally hundreds of millions of pieces of apparel are sewn at home each year. And the number of garments sewn at home continues to soar year after year.

• Retail fabric sales—a direct reflection of home sewing, of course —are now running to more than $2 billion a year. In addition, the sale of sewing notions such as thread, buttons, zippers, and pins runs into the hundreds of millions of dollars. Thousands of outlets now sell fabrics.

Enough. The centuries-old home sewing story has been completely rewritten in our land in recent years. The boom knows no boundaries—crosses all income levels, all age categories, all regions, all color and ethnic groups.

Why? This has to be much more than another do-it-yourself offshoot, and it is. A key point, which Ann-Marie hit herself, is that you can save as much as 50¢ out of every $1.00 spent on clothes by making them yourself. A second major point is that, if you are at all competent, you can get far superior workmanship.

Another factor is that home sewing has turned from a "square" to an "in" activity. Many are sewing in order to reproduce at acceptable cost some creation of a high-style designer. Moreover, the pattern companies are aggressively educating millions of youngsters in home sewing.

And men are learning how to sew—and becoming sewing enthusiasts—in ever mounting numbers too.

HOW TO BUY A SEWING MACHINE

With roughly 44 million home sewing machines already in use and with millions being added in our homes each year, let's assume *you* are now in the market for a sewing machine—either a new one or one to replace your aging model. How should you shop? What type of machine should you buy?

• Make up your mind how you will use your machine before you buy. If you'll be doing only utilitarian sewing, then you'll need only a basic, inexpensive machine, without many frills. If you love to create fancy things with a lot of embroidery, you may want a machine with all today's built-in features, which can cost hundreds of dollars.

• Decide what you want your new machine to be able to do. Take a sewing course first if you do not know and rent a machine while you do it.

• If you are a beginner, you might start with a basic portable machine that has straight, reverse, and zigzag stitching capabilities and which may be available for less than $100. These are neither heavy-duty machines nor do they have a long anticipated life span. They are basic models, so try several before deciding which machine suits your needs.

As an alternative, you might buy a secondhand or reconditioned machine from a dealer you are sure you can trust and learn on that one. (You may even decide to keep it indefinitely.)

Most sewing machine dealers will give basic operating instructions for your new machine even if it is a less expensive brand. Both the manufacturers and authorized dealers of the European machines are especially eager that you learn to take advantage of every feature on your new machine. One manufacturer even has a learn-by-doing instruction book. The new owner, under the supervision of the dealer, makes her own samples of each sewing technique and puts them in the instruction book for future reference. The fabric for the samples, also provided by the manufacturer, comes with the machine.

• Stick to a well-known brand sold by a company which has an extensive network of sales and service dealerships throughout the country. If properly used and cared for, even a medium-priced sewing machine will last your lifetime.

Off brands, or "private labels," are a particular problem in the sewing machine business. If you buy an off brand in Los Angeles, and later move to New York, you probably will find that you are unable to locate a dealer who handles that brand; therefore, service and parts are for all practical purposes unattainable. A dealer in New York may handle exactly the same sewing machine you have but sell it under his own name. He is reluctant to accept your machine for service because he cannot tell from the outside whether he has the parts or can get them. The simplest way out, and the usual answer, is "This cannot be repaired," even though in reality the parts are often interchangeable.

• The two most wanted features in more sophisticated sewing machines are the zigzag and stretch stitches. There are zigzag attachments available for less expensive machines: these attachments, though, move the fabric back and forth (as opposed to the built-in zigzag where the needle moves back and forth), they cannot handle all fabrics, and they are inconvenient and inefficient. The zigzag feature is invaluable for mending, sewing with elastic, making buttonholes, overcasting, and reinforcing that might otherwise have to be done by hand. It also permits some basic embroidery.

Don't be pushed into a decision beyond your needs and budget. Buy a machine with a zigzag or stretch stitch only *if you really intend to use them*. Start basic and trade up as your needs and skills increase.

• A portable sewing machine will save you $30 or more over a cabinet model, assuming you have a permanent surface—possibly an old desk or kitchen table—so the machine will always be easily available. The salesman may tell you a cabinet is a must so that dust won't get into the machine. But the dust argument is nonsense, because if the portable doesn't come with a cover, all you need do to solve the dust problem is to whip up a simple dust cover as your first project—something like the covers used for office typewriters or your toaster. It's a lot less expensive than purchase of a bulky cabinet.

• However, though a sewing machine cabinet does add to the original investment, it can save money in the long run.

First, by making the set-up task easier, you well may sew more often—especially mending and maintenance sewing. Or may use an available hour rather than wait for a full evening or day for sewing.

Second, a cabinet will add to your comfort—less eye strain, tension, aggravation—and thus tend to produce better results.

Third, a cabinet is safer—less danger of dropping, knocking over—and thus protects your machine.

• With either a portable or a cabinet model, be certain:

> It is a comfortable height for you to work on.
> You sit with center of your body in front of the needle.
> Leg room is adequate for you.
> Controller comfortably positioned.
> Table leaf is well supported.
> Cutout holds machine level.

• Most sewing machine manufacturers suggest to their dealers a demonstration technique—and the better ones include the demonstrations of how the machines work on various commonly used fabrics. By all means, take advantage of the demonstrations; ask for them.

Be suspicious if your sewing machine dealer demonstrates a machine *only* on the very stiff cotton fabric that all dealers use. This fabric cannot show the shortcomings or the advantages of the various machines you may be considering. Remember that you will probably be sewing on many different fabrics from soft nylon tricots (many dress fabrics are nylon tricot) to bulky wools, corduroys, or fake furs.

The most convincing sales demonstrations are those that show the performance of a machine on many different types of fabric, such as sweater knits, double knits, lycra, nylon tricot, bulky wool or corduroy, leather, various stretch fabrics, and also problem fabrics. You may think you won't use all these, but how can you be certain now what fabric you will wish to sew on next year or the year after?

• If your sewing machine dealer does not have any "real fabric" bring some of your own (bring some anyway!) and try the machine yourself. First, stitch on three or four layers of closely constructed synthetic knit. If the machine skips stitches, you may have a problem when you want to top-stitch a synthetic knit fabric.

Now work with medium heavy fabric, fold to create at least four layers, and stitch across the folds in a perpendicular direction. If you need to push the fabric, or the stitch length varies from very short to very long, you can count on the same trouble almost every time you stitch a seam where two seams meet (such as neck facing). Next, take two pieces of almost any fabric (say, cotton), that are of *exactly* equal length. Stitch a seam about 12 inches long. If the top piece comes out longer at the end, this is what will happen when you try to match plaids on this machine. One more test requires two layers of soft fabric. Cut them in a curve, like a neckline curve, then stitch a ⅝-inch seam around the curve. How easy is it to guide your stitching accurately around the curve? There are vast differences between the way various machines can handle this. *Tests such as these are especially important when purchasing any relatively inexpensive machine.*

• If you're planning to buy a medium- or high-quality brand, look for these features:

> automatic tension adjustment for any weight of fabric
> clip-on presser feet (no screws!)
> one-motion threading
> wide comfortable foot control
> two-speed motor
> built-in cams (nothing to insert)
> built-in buttonholer
> streamlined free arm (for tubular sewing) with slide on table
> rich, full-looking embroidery patterns
> pattern indicator for matching embroidery
> knee lever to raise presser foot (a true convenience!)
> feed-dog lowering at the touch of a knob
> tailor tacking, basting, and various stretch stitches

When your sewing machine is delivered, make sure it is the same model—and sews as well—as the one demonstrated to you. If it isn't—

or doesn't—go right back and demand that the dealer make the proper exchange or adjustments.

• After each use clean away thread and lint, and clean and oil the machine regularly as directed by the manufacturer. Always keep your dust cover on your machine when it's not being used.

• Once you buy, use the machine. Your complaints will be handled more equitably early in your ownership than later. Don't grumble to yourself or your friends for a year before you tell the dealer of your dissatisfaction.

BEWARE: SEWING MACHINE TRAPS

Be particularly wary of the gypsters who operate on a grand scale in the area of sewing machines. A dealer, for example, may pass off inexpensive foreign-made machines as American-made by stenciling the names of well-known American machines on them, or by obliterating foreign-origin markings. Others may misrepresent old, well-known machines as being rebuilt by the manufacturer when actually they've only been given a once-over-lightly cleaning by some back-room mechanic. Some imply in their ads that a sewing machine is zig-zag equipped—but not, as you later discover, at the advertised price.

Some insist that their fabulous sewing machine offer is "good for today only"—to keep you from going out and comparing prices. Some give you (or send you) a discount in the form of a "check" for, say, $150—made payable to you but as yet unsigned. However, the price of the sewing machine well may have been jacked up so that it more than covers the discount. Or you may be a second prize winner in a contest—entitling you to receive a sewing machine *only* if you buy an overpriced cabinet. Or you may be given the "opportunity" for a "free" sewing machine—and pay *"only"* $79.50 for a 10-year service contract. But the catch here is that most machines don't need much—if any—servicing within the first five years and you are still paying $79.50 for the machine, no matter what the disguise is.

Or it may be a "repossessed" sewing machine which has not actually been repossessed. Or the claim may be that the price charged is only the very low amount of the "unpaid balance"—which, by no coincidence, turns out to be just about what the machine is worth.

Beware these traps. And if you unluckily fall into any one, check your nearest consumer protection agency at once to find out your rights under federal and/or state law or regulation.

CUTTING YOUR CLOTHES CARE COSTS

Buying (or making) clothes is only part of your investment in your wardrobe. Over the long run, an even larger chunk of your money may go to the cleaning, washing, storing, and repairing of many items in your wardrobe.

How do you keep *these* costs to a minimum—and at the same time make your clothes last as long and look as good as possible?

THE TIME-TESTED TIPS

When you buy clothes, check the manufacturers' tags carefully for details on fabrics and finishes. Try to buy clothing made of fabrics that can without danger of damage be laundered at home or cleaned in self-service machines.

Keep your clothes in a dry, airy, cool place.

Brush your clothes frequently. Once dirt is permitted to set in the material, it gets harder to remove and increases the need for frequent dry cleaning or washing. Dirt also may attract moths and insects.

Mend small rips before they become large ones.

Use proper spot-cleaning solution. Nail polish remover, perfume, or cologne applied directly may seriously damage certain fabrics.

Use shoe trees for your best shoes and keep others in shoe bags.

Wear waterproof shoe covers when it rains to protect your shoes (or wear boots and carry your shoes).

Hang up your clothes on a suitably shaped hanger immediately after each wearing. Don't hang clothes in a closet when they're wet.

Always clean or launder seasonal garments before putting them away in the off season (although it may be a good idea to wait to iron summer clothes until summer arrives). Don't store dirty clothing.

In home washing and drying permanent-press fabrics and clothes with stain-resistant finishes, load your washer only to about 80 per cent capacity and remove the clothes from the dryer just as soon as they are dry.

Slash your dry cleaning bills by using self-service dry cleaning machines for the appropriate garments. These machines are especially valuable for children's winter jackets, woolen sweaters, and most of a long and varied list of items for which delicate hand pressing and steaming aren't necessary.

Follow clothes care labels when you iron. And remember that letting clothes simply steam awhile in the bathroom while you take a shower often will do the ironing for you.

Also study the care labels on washing stretch fabrics. While most of these fabrics can be washed, the kind of fiber, the weave or knit, the color, and the finish may dictate the method and temperature to be used —and this will be indicated on the labels. (Be particularly careful with your stretch ski wear, which often can't even be washed, much less machine-dried.) Dry your stretch fabrics in a tumbler dryer, set at the correct temperature for the fabric. If you don't have a dryer, lay the garment flat and block it if necessary to insure that, when dry, the garment comes back to the correct size. Never hang a garment to dry if it has lengthwise stretch. Never wear a damp stretch garment; it will lose its shape. Don't hang stretch garments for long periods even if dry. Store the garments flat in a drawer or on a shelf.

HOW TO USE CLOTHES CARE LABELS

You are protected by a 1972 Federal Trade Commission ruling requiring permanent clothes care labels or tags to be affixed to most types of clothes you now buy.

Specifically, the labels on clothes must now (1) fully inform the purchaser about regular care and maintenance procedures, (2) warn the purchaser of care methods that should not be used, (3) remain legible for the useful life of the article, and (4) be made readily visible to the user. Key exceptions: gloves, shoes, hats, furs, stockings.

Here are illustrations of the phraseology suggested by the FTC:

"Machine wash in sudsy water at medium temperature."

"Machine wash warm. Gentle cycle. Do not use chlorine bleach."

"Hand wash cold. Do not twist or wring. Reshape. Dry flat. Do not dry clean."

"Dry clean only."

Twelve Ways to Reduce Your Shoe Bills

Each year we buy an *average* of three to four pairs of shoes per person. Sneakers, slippers, galoshes, other footwear push the total to more than one billion pairs of shoes a year. Our annual footwear bill averages about $175 per family.

With the guides that follow, though, you can spectacularly reduce your shoe bills—and you'll also find you're enjoying your shoes far more.

(1) Obey the rules for a proper fit: make sure that your big toe doesn't reach the tip of the shoe when you're standing, that your little toe lies flat in the shoe, that the heel fits snugly, and that the sides don't yawn. (Poorly fitting shoes can impose the "hidden" extra cost of podiatrists' bills.)

(2) Don't buy shoes by size alone. A size 8 may fit perfectly in one style but not in another. Have each pair fitted.

(3) Shop for shoes in the middle of the day. Typically, the human foot swells 5 per cent with exercise and this swelling can obviously make a big difference in how a shoe fits.

(4) Economize on shoes you won't wear frequently, such as women's shoes dyed to match an outfit. Don't economize on work shoes or hiking shoes: the savings won't be savings if the shoes aren't comfortable or if they wear out quickly.

(5) Save money in men's shoes by buying those with rubber-type soles, usually less expensive and more serviceable than leather.

(6) Choose simple, traditional styles. A simply styled shoe may cost one third less than its high-style counterpart. And stick to darker colors which look better for a longer time than lighter colors.

(7) Buy children's shoes at least a half size larger than is indicated by the measurement. But sturdy, well-fitting shoes are vital for children, so economize only on style. Use the following chart to guide you on how rapidly children's shoe sizes change as they grow up.

Rate of Change: Children's Shoe Sizes

AGE OF CHILD	SIZE CHANGES EVERY:
1–6 years	1–2 months
6–10 years	2–3 months
10–12 years	3–4 months
12–15 years	4–5 months
15 years and older	6 months or more

(8) Don't misuse shoes by, say, wearing them out in the rain. Polish shoes regularly to protect them against dirt and bad weather. And note: few shoes can survive a washing machine.

(9) If your shoes become wet, stuff them with paper, dry them away from direct heat with a soft cloth, and rub them with a light film of mineral oil.

(10) Change your shoes at least once a day to give them a chance to "rest" and dry out from foot moisture. If you do this, two pairs of shoes will outlast three which are not alternated during a day.

(11) When buying, look for: smooth, soft linings and smooth inside seams; stitching which is not too close to the edge of the shoe sole; flexible "uppers" and evenly trimmed edges; good material; reputable brand from a reputable retailer.

(12) Buy shoes for yourselves and children during the seasonal sales—using both the winter and summer sales for maximum savings.

8

THE HIGH COST
OF GOOD HEALTH

WHAT YOU CAN EXPECT YOUR HEALTH BILL TO BE   270
     FASTEST-RISING OF ALL PERSONAL EXPENSES   270
     HEALTH INSURANCE: CAN YOU AFFORD NOT TO
       HAVE IT?   270
     FIVE KEY TYPES OF COVERAGE   271
HOW TO SHOP FOR HEALTH INSURANCE   272
     HOW MUCH COVERAGE DO YOU NEED?   272
     THE MEDICAL CATASTROPHE: DO'S AND DON'TS   274
MONEYSAVING TIPS ON HEALTH INSURANCE   275
     ELEVEN BASIC GUIDES   275
HEALTH INSURANCE BAFFLEGAB GUIDE   277
YOUR MEDICARE BENEFITS   279
     YOUR BASIC BENEFITS   279
     MEDICARE BENEFITS FOR YOUNGER AMERICANS   280
     OTHER MEDICARE BENEFITS   282
     HOW MUCH YOU MUST PAY   283
WHAT TO WATCH OUT FOR IN MAIL ORDER HEALTH
INSURANCE   284
     NOT THE BEST HEALTH CARE INSURANCE   284
     KEY GUIDES   284
     CHECK LIST FOR READING MAIL ORDER ADS   286
WHAT IF YOU'RE DISABLED?   288
     SOURCES OF HELP   288
WHAT YOU SHOULD KNOW ABOUT SOCIAL SECURITY
DISABILITY BENEFITS   289

WHAT YOU SHOULD KNOW ABOUT SOCIAL SECURITY (*cont'd*)
    HUGE NUMBERS COLLECTING BENEFITS EACH YEAR   289
    FACTS ABOUT BENEFITS   290
WHAT'S YOUR WORKERS' COMPENSATION WORTH?   292
    THE HIGH COST OF WORK ACCIDENTS   292
    QUESTIONS AND ANSWERS ON BENEFITS   293
PRIVATE DISABILITY INSURANCE COVERAGE   295
    WHAT WOULD IT COST YOU?   295
    CHECK LIST FOR COVERAGES   295
    MAKING DEDUCTIBLES WORK FOR YOU   296
HOW TO SLASH YOUR MEDICAL BILLS   297
    SHOP FOR A HOSPITAL   297
    HAVE A FAMILY PHYSICIAN   299
    DON'T WAIT TO SEE YOUR PHYSICIAN UNTIL
        YOU'RE ILL   299
    HAVE REGULAR CHECKUPS   300
    ALWAYS DISCUSS YOUR PHYSICIAN'S FEES WITH
        HIM   300
    GO TO THE DOCTOR'S OFFICE   300
    USE THE TELEPHONE   301
    FOLLOW YOUR DOCTOR'S ORDERS   301
YOUR COMMUNITY HEALTH RESOURCES   301
    DON'T OVERLOOK THEM!   301
    SAMPLING OF SERVICES   302
HOW TO SLASH YOUR DRUG BILLS   302
    NINE BASIC HINTS   302
HOW TO SHOP FOR DENTAL SERVICES   304
    FUNDAMENTAL APPROACHES   304
    TELLTALE SIGNS   305
    HOW CAN YOU TELL IF THE FEE IS FAIR?   306
IF YOU NEED A PSYCHIATRIST   306
    HOW DO YOU GO ABOUT FINDING ONE?   307
    HOW MUCH MONEY AND TIME ARE INVOLVED IN
        TREATMENT?   307
    WILL HEALTH INSURANCE HANDLE PART OF THE
        TREATMENT?   307
    IS IT POSSIBLE TO SHOP FOR THESE SERVICES?   308
HOW TO BEAT OUR $15 BILLION HANGOVER   308
    THE STAGGERING BURDEN   308
    WHERE DO YOU FIND HELP?   309

CARING FOR OUR ELDERLY   310
  WHAT WOULD YOU DO?   310
  THE ALTERNATIVES AVAILABLE TO YOU   311
  SHOPPING FOR NURSING HOMES   312
  MEDICARE'S YARDSTICKS   313
  WHERE TO COMPLAIN   313
HEALTH MAINTENANCE ORGANIZATIONS   314
  PREVIEW OF THE FUTURE   314
  AN HMO FOR YOUR COMMUNITY?   315
  HEALTH BAFFLEGAB GUIDE   315
  KEY QUESTIONS TO CONSIDER   318
  SHOULD YOU JOIN AN HMO?   318
  CHECK LIST FOR HMO SERVICES   319
TEST YOUR CHANCES OF STAYING ALIVE   320
  REVEALING QUESTIONS   320
YOUR BLOOD BANK ACCOUNT   321
  HOW TO PROTECT YOURSELF   322
  QUESTIONS AND ANSWERS   323
HEALTH HOAXES   324
  DIET COME-ONS   324
  "STOP SMOKING"   326
  QUACK MEDICAL DEVICES   327
  CANCER QUACKERY   329
  THE PSYCHOQUACK   330
  ARTHRITIS "CURES"   332

WHAT YOU CAN EXPECT YOUR HEALTH BILL TO BE

FASTEST-RISING OF ALL PERSONAL EXPENSES

The high cost of personal health in the United States had become a major economic factor in the lives of most American families by the mid-seventies.

• Our spending on health care goods and services ranging from Band-aids to open-heart surgery and cancer research was passing $100 billion a year. For each of us, this represented an average health bill of close to $450 or nearly $1,800 for a family of four.

• The cost of health care services had increased in the late sixties and early seventies faster than any other type of personal expense—one and one half times the rate of rise for our over-all cost of living.

• Hospital bills accounted for the lion's share of our total national health spending. By the mid-seventies it cost an average of more than $105 to spend a day in a community hospital and at a growing number of hospitals the cost was $150 to $200 per day. Some luxury private room costs went even higher.

• Physicians' and dentists' bills, nursing home costs and drug costs —all were soaring.

HEALTH INSURANCE: CAN YOU AFFORD NOT TO HAVE IT?

A widow in Missouri is hospitalized with pneumonia. She needs round-the-clock nursing care for four days until she is out of danger. There are no complications and no surgery is required. She remains in the hospital for three weeks. Total cost: $2,400.

A New York executive has a moderately severe heart attack. The result is three weeks in the hospital, including one week in the intensive care unit. Total cost: $4,700.

A fifteen-year-old Pennsylvania boy is severely injured in an automobile accident requiring more than four months' hospitalization, plus extensive skin grafts and cosmetic surgery. Total cost: $19,880.

How many, even in affluent America, can afford medical bills as astronomical as these?

Just because medical care today is so overpoweringly expensive and because we do not yet have a system of national health insurance, you must regard some form of health insurance as absolutely imperative. What form you choose will depend on the organization from which you buy, the size and age of your family, where you live, where you work, a variety of other factors.

As a general rule, the simplest way to plan the best insurance package for your family is to decide which hazards are the greatest threat to you and to cover these with insurance. Then, to the extent you can afford it, begin to cover the less likely risks.

For instance, if you are a couple beyond childbearing age it would be silly to buy a health insurance policy with maternity benefits. On the other hand, young people would be wise to include in their health insurance package a major medical policy to guard against the big medical bills which could result from automobile accidents that constitute a major hazard for this age group.

FIVE KEY TYPES OF COVERAGE

Here is a rundown on five key types of coverages available today whether you are covered under a group plan where you work or by an individual or single-family policy:

(1) *Hospital Expense Insurance.* This is the best-known and most widely held form. It provides benefits for varying periods of time, usually ranging from 21 days to 365 days or longer. It is offered by Blue Cross plans and by commercial insurance companies.

Benefits under these policies are used to pay for in-hospital services such as room and board, routine nursing care, and minor medical supplies.

In recent years, many Blue Cross plans have been offering coverage for such outpatient and out-of-hospital services as home care, pre-admission testing, nursing home care, dental and vision care, prescription drugs, and a variety of diagnostic and preventive services.

(2) *Surgical Expense Insurance*. This coverage, offered by Blue Shield plans and commercial policies, is used to defray the cost of operations. Policies contain listings of surgical operations and the maximum benefit they will pay for each.

(3) *Physicians' Expense Insurance*. This coverage is almost always combined with hospital and surgical expense insurance, and the three form what is referred to as the "basic" coverage. Physicians' expense benefits usually cover a specific number of in-hospital visits to you by your doctor. Some policies provide benefits for home and office visits as well.

(4) *Major Medical Insurance*. This type picks up where basic coverage leaves off. It pays for most types of care in or out of hospital, with benefit maximums ranging to $250,000 and up. Blue Cross plans offer this coverage too. These policies use a deductible, which is the amount you must pay before benefits start, and a co-insurance factor, which is a percentage of the total bill you also must pay.

(5) *Disability Insurance*. This type is used to replace earnings lost because of disability. Maximum benefits during disability can go up to $1,000 or more a month, although the maximum is usually about 60 per cent of your gross earnings.

How to Shop for Health Insurance

HOW MUCH COVERAGE DO YOU NEED?

The most economical way to buy health insurance is to insure yourself and your family against the most serious and financially disastrous losses that can result from an illness or an accident. Your minor medical expenses should be met as part of your family's over-all financial plan.

A general rule of thumb is that your basic benefit package should cover at least 75 per cent of your anticipated expenses from any illness or injury.

Other guidelines when you're shopping for health insurance are:
• If you are buying health insurance for the first time, look into the

possibility of getting the coverage through a group—a union, an employer-employee plan, a fraternal organization. Group insurance costs 15 to 40 per cent *less* than the same coverage bought on an individual basis. Other advantages of group coverage: Your coverage can't be canceled—unless and until you leave the group. You don't have to take a physical examination to qualify for coverage. And a pre-existing illness does not disqualify you, although it may mean a waiting period to qualify for maternity benefits.

• Find out how many days in the hospital each policy you are considering buying will cover. This is one of the most frequent selling points used by insurers and prepayment plans—and one of the most *misleading*. All basic hospital policies, whether issued by Blue Cross plans or commercial insurers, express benefits in terms of days, with benefit periods of from 21 days to 365 days. But is it really necessary to buy 365 days of basic coverage? Government statistics show that the average length of stay in a hospital is just under 8 days, and that only 3 per cent of all hospital confinements in the country last beyond 31 days.

• Also find out how much each policy pays per day and how the benefits are paid. Basic benefits are paid in two ways: Blue Cross makes payments directly to the hospital for services rendered to you; commercial insurers pay a specified dollar amount either to you *or* to the hospital. The Blue Cross arrangement is generally regarded as preferable to you as a policyholder because Blue Cross plans have direct contractual arrangements with hospitals which grant them (as bulk purchasers) discounts which are passed along to you. The service benefits offered by Blue Cross cover virtually all costs, whereas the specified dollar amount in the indemnity policies offered by the commercial insurers generally represent only a fraction of the costs incurred. There are, though, many exceptions in which both plans offer comparable benefits at comparable costs.

• If you already are covered by health insurance, be sure to keep this coverage updated. If your basic benefits are paid on an indemnity basis (i.e., the commercial insurers' approach), check *frequently* on the current medical and hospital costs in *your own area*. The rates for a hospital in, say, Mississippi, will be substantially less than for one in New York or California. If you have a policy which will pay $40 a day and you live in an area where the average hospital cost is $100, you'll pay the difference. Another point: in recent years hospital charges have been increasing sharply. Thus, if you had an indemnity plan that paid 80 per cent of the hospital charges in the year in which you bought it, chances are there has been steady "slippage" ever since. A mere two years later, your policy will probably cover only 50 per cent of the hospital charges.

THE MEDICAL CATASTROPHE: DO'S AND DON'TS

At today's medical prices, most of you would be plunged deeply into debt in the event of a really serious accident or illness. Every day throughout the country, newspapers carry horror stories telling of the enormous costs faced by families who have suffered this type of misfortune.

The insurance designed for this contingency is called the major medical plan, and if you are about thirty years old and if your family can afford the $175 or so per year it costs in premiums, it can certainly add to your peace of mind.

This type of insurance, like the others, is complex. In the thicket of terminology are such unfamiliar phrases as "inside limits," "co-insurance," "deductibles." Here are do's and don'ts which will make it easier to hack through this jungle.

Don't be dazzled by big benefit maximums such as $250,000 and the like. Even with today's soaring medical costs, it's highly improbable that you'll ever have expenses at this level for a single illness or injury. Keep benefits such as these in perspective, just as you would if someone tried to sell you a policy covering undulant fever or being run down by a herd of buffalo at noon on Main Street. A more realistic ceiling for major medical benefits would be somewhere between $20,000 and $50,000.

Do look into the possibility of getting this coverage through a group. As with your basic coverage, you can achieve big savings by insuring this way.

Do study the deductible and co-insurance features. For example, the usual co-insurance ratio is 75-25 or 80-20, with the 25 or 20 per cent being your share of the medical expenses. If you're willing to take the higher co-insurance percentage offered by one company over another, you may find your premiums proportionately lower.

Do study with care, too, what benefits you get from the way you set up your major medical coverage. You can do this in one of two ways:

either as a supplement to your basic coverage or as a single-plan or "comprehensive" major medical plan.

As a general rule, the supplementary type of major medical insurance starts paying at the point where your basic hospital-surgical coverage stops. The "single-plan major medical" covers both basic and catastrophic expenses. Sometimes your deductible is absorbed by your basic coverage in one policy.

Other types of major medical insurance utilize what is known as a "corridor" deductible. That is the amount you must pay above your basic coverage before your major medical takes over. This is available on group health insurance only.

The deductible *applies separately to each family member* (in most cases, up to an annual maximum) for each illness covered by the policy.

Do choose the highest deductible your budget can take. Deductibles usually range from $100 to $1,000. If you feel you can afford to pay the first $1,000 toward medical bills out of your own pocket, the premiums will be lower than if you want to cover everything but the first $100.

And, by hiking your deductible, you can apply the savings you get through lower premiums to building up extra coverage in other areas that will give you an added dimension of protection.

MONEYSAVING TIPS ON HEALTH INSURANCE

ELEVEN BASIC GUIDES

The following tips on health insurance could save you great aggravation *and* money:

(1) Hold onto any old disability policy you might have if your health is impaired. If you want to expand your disability insurance, keep your old policy and supplement it. Why not replace it? Simply because your present policy undoubtedly carries a lower premium, reflecting your younger age when you bought it. If your health is good, you may be able to get cheaper coverage, even though you are now older.

(2) Check whether a group or family policy has a conversion privilege, so that you can, if necessary, transfer your coverage to an individual

basis—if, say, you leave an employee group for a new job, or you marry —without having restrictive waiting periods reimposed on you.

(3) At the same time, be sure you check whether any refund is owed to you on your previous policy.

(4) Investigate carefully how maternity benefits are paid, if you are a single woman and plan to remain so. Important changes are being made in response to changing attitudes about morals and sex discrimination. Some insurers are altering their hospital and medical coverages to keep up with the new attitudes: more plans, for instance, are providing payments for unmarried women, including maternity benefits for babies born out of wedlock.

(5) Don't waste your money carrying duplicate coverage. It's possible you'll be able to collect on both policies—and maybe even make a profit on an illness—but many insurers are co-ordinating their payments to prevent this. Usually one policy, the first or primary one, is given preference by the company and the second policy will pay only that part of the medical bill not covered by the first. You'll find it increasingly difficult to beat the computers on this.

(6) Health insurance coverage for mental illness is becoming more readily available. Much of the time this condition is covered by major medical policies on a full-payment basis while the patient is hospitalized and with limited payments outside the hospital. But if you have a disability policy you may be able to collect under it. You're entitled to full payment of these expenses under many policies if you are totally disabled as the result of a mental condition—say, a nervous breakdown. If your disability is only partial, your payments will normally cover up to half of the out-of-hospital costs. Another approach to this type of benefit is a sort of "share-the-cost" plan for psychiatric treatment, either through a stated number of visits you make to the psychiatrist or psychologist or through a stated benefit ceiling for psychiatric treatments.

Many Blue Cross policyholders have some mental illness coverage, but in most cases it is sharply limited.

(7) Look into a little-known benefit now available in some disability insurance policies called "income insurance for the breadwinner's wife." This covers the cost of household help if she becomes ill or disabled.

(8) Although this may not be your problem, alcoholism is sufficiently widespread for you to become aware that many insurance policies cover alcoholics and will provide personal medical and social aid, often

sending the alcoholic to a specialized rehabilitation center. And even those insurers which do not pay for such specialized treatment almost always cover treatment for alcoholism in their hospital and disability policies.

(9) Note at what age your policy covers your children. Children should be covered from birth and *not,* as some policies state, from the age of two weeks. It's the first two weeks in the life of your baby that are very often his or her most expensive medically.

(10) If you pay your own premiums directly, try to arrange to pay on an annual or quarterly rather than monthly basis. You'll save money by so doing.

(11) And one final reminder. Although it's important to know just what is covered under your health insurance policy, it's even more important to know what is *excluded* from coverage. Frequently excluded services include psychiatric care, extensive periodontal surgery, foot surgery by podiatrists, cosmetic surgery, care for pre-existing conditions. Knowing what's excluded won't help you pay for the condition if it arises, but at least you won't be in line for an unexpected shock at the worst possible time—when you're flat on your back.

HEALTH INSURANCE BAFFLEGAB GUIDE

ACCIDENTAL DEATH AND DISMEMBERMENT BENEFIT: Payment to a beneficiary, usually through a disability income policy, when an insured person is killed or loses his sight or a limb in an accident.

BENEFICIARY: Person who is designated in an insurance policy to receive a specified cash payment if the policyholder is killed by accident.

CLAIM: Demand by a person covered by health or other insurance for financial benefits provided in his or her policy.

CO-INSURANCE: Special condition, usually found in major medical insurance, in which you and your insurance company share costs. Typically, the insurer pays 50 to 80 per cent of hospital and medical expenses, and you pay the rest.

DEDUCTIBLE: Share of the hospital and medical expenses which you, the insured person, must pay before your insurance policy starts paying.

DISABILITY (OR "INSURED SALARY CONTINUANCE") INSURANCE: Coverage (often group) providing regular weekly or monthly cash benefits to help replace earnings you have lost if you become disabled from just about any cause. In some cases, payment is made for only a limited number of years, and in others, for life.

ELIMINATION PERIOD: Waiting period before benefits (e.g., disability benefits) begin.

FAMILY EXPENSE POLICY: Type of health insurance policy covering you, your wife, and your children.

HOSPITAL EXPENSE INSURANCE: Insurance providing reimbursement of hospital care costs—usually including room and board charges, routine nursing care, anesthesia, surgical facilities, special diets, the like—for illness or injury.

INDIVIDUAL (OR "PERSONAL") INSURANCE: Protection of individual policyholders and their families, as distinct from lower-cost group insurance which may be offered by employers, labor unions, or professional associations.

MAJOR MEDICAL EXPENSE INSURANCE: Protection against the huge expenses implied by a catastrophic injury or illness. This type of insurance usually pays 75 to 80 per cent of physicians' and hospital bills, after a deductible paid by the insured, up to a maximum from $10,000 to $100,000 or more, and $250,000 for Blue Cross coverage. "Supplementary" major medical insurance builds on top of basic protection through an ordinary hospital and medical expense policy. A "comprehensive" policy provides both basic and major medical insurance coverage, usually has a low deductible amount.

MEDICAL EXPENSE INSURANCE: Payment, usually partial, of doctors' fees for non-surgical care in the hospital, but sometimes also at home or at the office. Medical expense benefits are sometimes included in hospital expense policies.

SUBSTANDARD HEALTH INSURANCE: Policies issued to those who cannot meet normal health requirements of standard health insurance policies, usually involving a higher premium.

SURGICAL EXPENSE INSURANCE: Benefits to help pay surgeons' fees and other costs of surgical procedures.

Your Medicare Benefits

In the mid-seventies, tens of millions of older Americans—most of them age sixty-five or over—were getting billions of dollars in annual Medicare insurance benefits.

Tens of millions were participating in Medicare's voluntary Part B insurance which covered doctor bills—representing all but a tiny fraction of the elderly. For millions of elderly Americans—plus younger disabled people—Medicare spelled the difference between economic peace of mind when illness struck and instant destitution.

YOUR BASIC BENEFITS

What are your Medicare benefits today under the two separate categories of insurance? Here, first, were the basic Medicare benefits as of 1976:

Medicare Hospital Insurance (Part A) covers, after the deductible, completely or in part, when medically necessary:

• The first 90 days in a hospital or skilled nursing facility for each "benefit period." A "benefit period" begins when you enter a hospital and ends when you have been out of a hospital or any facility providing mainly skilled nursing or rehabilitation care for 60 consecutive days—after which a new benefit period begins if you must go into a hospital again.

• Up to 60 more days of a "lifetime reserve" of extra hospital days.

• Up to 100 days of care in a skilled nursing facility in each benefit period, after you have been hospitalized for at least 3 days in a row.

• Up to 100 home health visits from a participating home health agency within the one-year period after you have been in a hospital for at least 3 days in a row or have received covered care in a skilled nursing facility. Home health services include part-time skilled nursing care, physical or speech therapy, services by home health aides, occupational therapy, and medical supplies and appliances furnished by the agency.

Medicare Medical Insurance (Part B) pays, after the deductible, completely or in part:

• Physicians' services, no matter where you receive them in the United States—in the doctor's office, the hospital, your home, or elsewhere—including medical supplies usually furnished by a doctor in his office, services of his office nurse, and drugs he administers as part of his treatment and which you cannot administer yourself.

• Outpatient hospital services for diagnosis and treatment in an emergency room or an outpatient clinic of a hospital.

• Up to 100 home health visits in each calendar year from a participating home health agency, when prescribed by your physician because you need part-time skilled nursing care or physical or speech therapy and are confined to your home. (These visits are in addition to the post-hospital visits covered under hospital insurance.)

• Outpatient physical therapy and speech pathology services— whether or not you are homebound—furnished under supervision of participating hospitals, skilled nursing facilities, home health agencies, or approved clinics, rehabilitation agencies, or public health agencies under a plan established and periodically reviewed by a doctor.

• Other medical and health services prescribed by your doctor such as diagnostic services; X-ray or other radiation treatments; surgical dressings, colostomy supplies, splints, casts, braces; artificial limbs and eyes; and rental or purchase of durable medical equipment such as a wheel chair or oxygen equipment for use in your home.

• Certain ambulance services.

MEDICARE BENEFITS FOR YOUNGER AMERICANS

Full Medicare health insurance benefits also are available to Americans under age sixty-five who suffer from chronic kidney disease which requires them to undergo regular kidney dialysis or a kidney transplant. Moreover, some 2.3 million disabled Americans under the age of sixty-five are now eligible for *full* Medicare hospital and doctor bill benefits.

What are the rules covering these two key categories of benefits? What must you do to be sure you'll receive the benefits due you (or your parent or relative or friend who might be eligible)?

Q. Who are the disabled persons eligible for medicare benefits?

A. People who are (or have been) entitled to at least twenty-four consecutive months of Social Security disability benefits because they are disabled. Included are:

disabled workers at any age;

disabled widows;

disabled dependent widowers between the ages of fifty and sixty-four;

women aged fifty or older who are entitled to mother's benefits who, for twenty-four months prior to the first month they would have been entitled to Medicare protection, met all the requirements for disability benefits except for actual filing of a disability claim;

people aged eighteen and over who receive Social Security benefits because they became disabled before reaching age twenty-two.

Medicare for the disabled provides precisely the same protection as Medicare offers others when they reach age sixty-five.

Q. When does this protection begin?

A. In the twenty-fifth consecutive month after you originally became entitled to Social Security disability benefits.

Q. What do you have to do to be sure your new Medicare disability insurance goes into effect?

A. You will be automatically notified by the Social Security Administration prior to the first time you are entitled to this coverage. You will also be automatically signed up for the special Part B doctor bill insurance *unless* you specifically inform the Social Security Administration that you do not want this coverage.

This premium will be automatically deducted from your Social Security or Railroad Retirement disability check—starting with the check you receive in the month in which you first become eligible for Medicare coverage.

Caution: If you *don't* accept this Part B coverage (for which the federal government pays at least half the cost) now, but later change your mind, your monthly premium will be hiked 10 per cent for each one-year period you let go by without signing up.

Of course, if your disability ceases before you reach age sixty-five (when you become eligible for regular Medicare benefits), your eligibility for Medicare also ceases.

To be eligible for kidney disease coverage you must be fully insured *or* be receiving Social Security benefits (e.g., as a widow or as a disabled person) or be the spouse or dependent child of a person who meets the above criteria.

Not only hospital services in the treatment of kidney disease will be paid for, but also treatment in approved special kidney treatment centers or "limited care centers," and also the costs of home dialysis equipment and supplies. In addition, persons covered under this provision are eligible for all other Medicare benefits.

Actual Medicare coverage begins on the first day of the third month after the month in which dialysis begins or, if earlier, the month you are hospitalized for a kidney transplant. To illustrate: If your dialysis begins on June 15, Medicare coverage starts on September 1.

Coverage continues a full year after the month you have a kidney transplant or your dialysis treatment ends—and resumes in the third month after treatment begins again.

These are extraordinarily valuable benefits for younger Americans who are suffering from grave disabilities.

OTHER MEDICARE BENEFITS

Here, next, is a rundown on other Medicare benefits which went into effect in 1973:

limited services by chiropractors;

services by physical therapists in an office *or* at your home;

payment by Medicare of your capitation premium for covered services if you join a Health Maintenance Organization (see later, this chapter) or a prepaid group medical practice or a medical foundation or a neighborhood health center;

elimination of co-insurance for home health benefits under Part B;

non-emergency and emergency services in a foreign hospital (e.g., in Canada or Mexico) *if* it happens to be closer to your home or more easily accessible than the nearest suitable U.S. hospital and emergency services for beneficiaries traveling between Alaska and another state.

Also, elderly Americans who before mid-1973 failed to qualify for Medicare hospital coverage (e.g., because they hadn't worked long enough under Social Security to qualify) can now buy into the system at a moderate monthly cost. But they also *must* buy the "voluntary" Part B medical insurance, also at a moderate cost.

HOW MUCH YOU MUST PAY

Here are costs you, the Medicare beneficiary (or your parent or relative or friend who is a beneficiary), must pay under the law as of January 1, 1976:

• the first $104 of your hospital bill for each "benefit period";

• $26 a day in "co-insurance" for *each* day you have to stay in a hospital from your sixty-first day through the ninetieth day you are in the hospital;

• the first $52 a day in costs for each day you use of your additional 60-day "lifetime reserve" of hospital coverage;

• $13 a day between the twenty-first and hundredth day you spend in a skilled nursing facility or up to a total of 100 days covered by Medicare in such a facility;

• costs of the first three pints of blood you may need during each "benefit period" under hospital insurance, or the first three pints in a calendar year under medical insurance;

• costs of any private-duty nurses you may need, and costs of any "personal comfort" items for which you sign up in the hospital—e.g., telephone, radio, TV;

• the per month cost of Part B Medicare insurance covering doctor bills—a premium which is being hiked periodically as costs of medical services rise;

• the first $60 of your doctor bills (or other expenses covered by your Part B insurance each year), except for hospital inpatient lab and radiology services performed by doctors for which Medicare pays 100 per cent of the "reasonable charges";

• 20 per cent of your remaining medical bills after you have paid this .$60 deductible—plus any charges above and beyond the amounts approved, unless an assignment has been taken by the doctor;

• expenses of physical therapy services in your home or the therapist's office over $100 a year.

Among the key items which were *not* covered at all by Medicare as of 1976's law were: routine physical exams and immunizations; out-of-hospital prescription drugs; routine eye exams for eyeglasses; hearing aids; dentures; routine dental care; orthopedic shoes; custodial nursing home care; most cosmetic surgery; services furnished free or payable under government programs; services furnished by the members of the patient's household or immediate relatives; and, of course, any services not considered reasonable and necessary for the diagnosis and treatment of an illness or injury.

WHAT TO WATCH OUT FOR IN MAIL ORDER HEALTH INSURANCE

NOT THE BEST HEALTH CARE INSURANCE

Americans are now investing hundreds of millions of dollars each year in mail order health insurance—lured by aggressive advertising, no-strings-attached benefits, low monthly premiums.

Most experts, however, do not regard this type of insurance as the best way to finance your basic health care.

As just one illustration, one survey disclosed that companies which sell this insurance return only 40¢ of each premium dollar in the form of benefits—compared with an average of close to 92¢ on group Blue Cross policies. Even the better state lotteries return more: about 45¢ on the dollar.

KEY GUIDES

If, therefore, you are thinking of buying a mail order policy, obey the following guides:

Consider this coverage as strictly *supplementary*. Most of these companies advertise benefits of $100 to $125 a week. But if you don't have an adequate basic health insurance plan, $100 a week will provide picayune protection in an era when your hospital costs alone can come to more than $100 *a day*. Also, though they may offer benefits for as long as 100 weeks, and this may unduly impress you, remember the average hospital stay is only around eight days.

Study the advertisements carefully. Sometimes enthusiastic copy writing implies that the policy can deliver more dollars than it actually will. For instance, one major company in the mail order health insurance field has an ad which contains this paragraph near the beginning of the text:

"How long could you stay in the hospital without worrying about the pile-up of daily expenses? Who will pay for the expenses of costly X-rays, doctor bills, drugs and medicines? And how about the expenses at home—rent, food, telephone and others that just go on and on? With expenses like these could you avoid having your savings wiped out and your family life upset?"

Then the following paragraph makes the statement (italics added): "Wouldn't it be comforting to know *these problems* could be solved by your Extra Cash Income Plan . . . the plan that gives you $100 a week IN CASH. . . ."

The implication is that this plan, which offers approximately $14.29 per day, will solve the problems of X-rays, drugs, medicines, doctor bills, rent, food, telephone, and all the rest when, in actuality, such an amount would not even pay for more than a fraction of the hospital bill itself, let alone all the other bills.

Be wary of direct-mail pieces which contain approaches such as: "Dear Friend: I know that YOU DON'T DRINK. Because of this I can offer you the Blue Chip (Green Comet; Silver Bullet) brand new hospitalization plan that will pay you $100 a week EXTRA CASH. . . . As a non-drinker, why should you be forced to pay as much for health insurance as people who drink? Our actuaries say that non-drinkers take better care of themselves, so doesn't a non-drinker like you deserve a lower rate? . . ."

A mail order piece such as this is a mass-merchandised catchall unrelated to actuarial realities, for there is no way for the company issuing the piece to know whether you, the addressee, are in fact a non-drinker. In addition, there has been no study by the nationally known Society of Actuaries to support the contention that non-drinkers are better health insurance risks. In many instances the premium charged may even be higher than for a policy from a company which does not use this type of gimmickry.

Buy whatever insurance you do decide to take only from a company licensed to do business in your own state. This is a fundamental rule.

Because the mails and mass-circulation advertising cross state lines, the ads you see easily may be those of a company which is unlicensed in your particular state. This can increase your difficulty of collecting in the event of claims. By purchasing this insurance you not only deprive yourself of the protection of your own state laws but also, if a dispute arises over a claim, you may have to go to the state where the company is based to bring suit. You can find out whether or not a company is licensed in your state simply by phoning or writing to your state insurance department.

Since premiums are usually paid monthly, take the trouble to learn how much leeway you have should you inadvertently permit a lapse in payment. The usual grace period is ten days, or, if you pay the premium weekly, seven days. Remember: Since companies usually do not issue reminder notices, you are obligated to keep track of your payments yourself. If a policy lapses because of non-payment, a new round of waiting periods may be reinstalled.

Analyze the exclusions and waiting periods. Many policies, for example, exclude coverage if the hospitalization results from mental illness. Some policies use large type to state NO WAITING PERIODS, but in the smaller type use a phrase which restricts this significantly.

Another key point: there's nothing special about the advertised tax-free benefits of the payouts. Most health insurance payments are tax-free. And, unlike regular health insurance policies, *premiums* on this type of policy may not be tax-deductible.

CHECK LIST FOR READING MAIL ORDER ADS

There are no direct federal controls over mail order health insurers and until recently most state regulatory insurance departments have been grossly understaffed and reluctant or unable to crack down on misleading ads that could conceal loopholes or exaggerate benefits. Use this check list to your own advantage when you read an ad:

What's covered: Are illnesses as well as accidents covered? What illnesses are excluded? Many policies exclude payments for treating such conditions as alcoholism, pregnancy, miscarriage, mental disorders, and some policies exclude cancer, tuberculosis, or heart disease. Most will cover you only if you are actually confined to a hospital, but not if you are being treated in the hospital's outpatient department.

Waiting periods: When do you begin to receive benefits? If you've had an accident, you can probably collect from the first day you're in the hospital. In the case of illness, however, the waiting period may be from three to eight days, with an average wait of six days. Moreover, eligibility for sickness benefits often does not begin until the policy has been in force for thirty days. And there is usually also a six-month waiting period for coverage of certain specific diseases such as tuberculosis, diabetes, hernia, cancer, or heart disease.

"Pre-existing" conditions: Among the most agonizing loopholes in many of these contracts are the provisions covering "pre-existing" conditions. In one policy, this small-print clause reads:

"No claim or loss incurred after two years from the date of this policy shall be reduced or denied on the ground that a disease or physical condition not excluded from coverage by name or specific description effective on the date of loss had existed prior to the effective date of coverage of this policy."

At first glance, this may look like a helpful provision aimed at protecting *you,* the insured. But what it really says is that for the first two years your policy is in force you can't collect for any condition you had when you first took out the policy—even if you weren't aware of the condition at the time. Incidentally, one factor helping to hold down the cost of these policies is the high number of claims rejected because of pre-existing conditions. Some companies routinely reject from one half to four fifths of policyholders' claims for this reason.

Benefits paid: Don't be dazzled by the advertised lump-sum figures of $100 a week or $600 a month: Instead, figure what the policy would pay you *per day*. A payment of $100 a week comes to $14.29 a day; $600 a month works out to $20 a day.

And what would be your chances of collecting the sums advertised? Say an illness keeps you in the hospital for the eight days and your policy has a six-day waiting period before you can begin collecting benefits. You collect for only two days or, in the case of the $600-a-month policy, a total of $40 for your eight-day hospital stay.

And to collect the maximum $39,000 over a five-year period some ads promise, you would have to be virtually a basket case.

Premiums: A 25¢ or $1.00 "introductory premium" may look inviting but that's just for the first month and typical premiums are $5.00 or so a month thereafter. Rates also may be sharply hiked later or the contract may call for higher premiums at age sixty-five. So, if you're in doubt, write the insurance company and ask for a complete schedule of premium payments.

Enrollment period: Is there a deadline for applying? Often a "limited enrollment period" is advertised and this may create a sense of false urgency. The deadline also may serve to prevent you from making inquiries, since it may leave you only two or three days to enroll. (One company's ads, published on January 3, specified an enrollment period ending midnight, January 6. The company advertised again on February 22, again specifying a three-day enrollment period.)

Renewability: How long will the policy stay in force? Under what conditions can it be renewed—or canceled? You well may get the impression that policies may be renewed indefinitely. But the catch here is that rate changes or policy cancellations may occur as long as they are made state-wide or apply to all policyholders of your "classification." This is subject to wide interpretation: it could for example, mean people of your age group. Raising premiums state-wide is by no means uncommon. If the rates are raised to prohibitive levels, that alone could in effect force many to drop their policies.

This is merely a brief sampling but surely it warns you to read a health insurance ad with healthy skepticism and to check with your state insurance department, if you have any doubts or questions.

And I emphasize again the first guide: *Never* buy this type of policy as a substitute for the broader types of hospital policies which pay virtually your entire bill and which can be supplemented by extra coverage available at moderate additional cost.

What If You're Disabled?

SOURCES OF HELP

What would you do if you became, through some tragic accident, permanently and totally disabled? Could *your* family survive on the average Social Security disability benefit?

Long-term disability insurance, like major medical coverage, also is being overlooked by the vast majority of Americans. Only about one in three of us has any private disability insurance protection. And even in the cases of those who have the insurance, the monthly benefit is often inadequate and the term that benefits are paid is too short to be meaningful. (The average disability lasts five years.)

Disability insurance (often called loss-of-income insurance) pays cash benefits designed to help replace earnings you have lost because of disability up to a maximum of about 60 per cent of your gross earnings. The policies begin paying benefits anywhere from a week following the start of the disability to six months later. They pay benefits from as few as thirteen weeks to as long as a lifetime.

There's little point in trying to insure yourself privately against the loss of your entire gross income because you will have other sources of disability income which will make up much of the difference.

For example, your employer well may have some form of wage-continuation policy which will keep income flowing in for a number of weeks or months after you have become disabled.

Or your union contract may include certain sick-leave benefits.

There also are state workers' compensation payments for job-connected disability.

There's Social Security: you're eligible for benefits in the sixth month of disability, so long as the disability is expected to last at least twelve months.

Look into all these sources plus any veterans' benefits for which you think you might be eligible.

What You Should Know About Social Security Disability Benefits

HUGE NUMBERS COLLECTING BENEFITS EACH YEAR

"How bad must my husband's blindness be to qualify him for Social Security disability benefits?" the letter began in a handwriting which wiggled with emotional distress. "My husband has been laid off because of his failing eyesight. He isn't even trying to get another job and he says he can't get disability benefits." Then the letter continued with an urgent plea for guidance.

The answer to this question of the understandably distraught wife is this:

Blindness is defined in the Social Security law as either central visual acuity of 20/200 or less in the better eye with the use of corrective lenses, or visual field reduction to 20 degrees or less.*

In 1974 more than 2 million disabled Americans plus more than

* If a worker's visual impairment falls short of this test, consideration may be given to his age, education, training, and work experience to determine whether or not he is disabled.

1.6 million of their dependent wives and children were collecting about $5 billion in Social Security disability benefits each year. A full four out of five men and women in the age brackets from twenty-one to sixty-four are "insured"; that is, they are covered under Social Security.

In all likelihood, *you* can count on monthly cash benefits in the event that a severe and prolonged disability keeps you from working. And, in addition, disabled workers who have been collecting Social Security benefits for at least twenty-four months also are eligible for Medicare hospital and doctor bill benefits (see preceding section, "Medicare Benefits for Younger Americans," for details on this coverage).

FACTS ABOUT BENEFITS

Because so many of you do not understand the requirements that may qualify or disqualify you, the need for greater knowledge is enormous. Here, therefore, are key facts about these benefits:

Q. *How do you qualify for disability benefits?*

A. In addition to qualifying as "disabled," you must have earned twenty quarters (five years) of coverage during the ten years before you were disabled and be fully insured. If you become disabled before age thirty-one, you will need less work credit—only half the quarters between the age of twenty-one and the time you are disabled, with a minimum of six quarters. Payments begin with the sixth full month of your disability. You must provide the names and addresses of doctors and hospitals involved with your medical treatment and you must accept rehabilitation.

Q. *At what age can you start collecting benefits?*

A. At *any* age under sixty-five if you qualify as disabled. A disability can be mental or physical, but it must be "medically determinable" and it must be expected either to result in death or expected to last (or have lasted) at least twelve months. Also, with few exceptions, it must make you unable to do any substantial gainful work anywhere in our economy.

Q. *What about wives and children of disabled workers?*

A. While you are receiving benefits as a disabled worker, payments to your dependents can be made as follows:

Each unmarried child can get a monthly benefit if he or she is under eighteen; (this is in addition to your benefit); if he or she is a full-time student age eighteen through twenty-one or suffering from a disability which began before age twenty-two. Stepchildren and adopted children similarly qualify.

Your wife can get up to 50 per cent of your full benefit too if she's caring for a child eligible for benefits (except that she can't collect if the child is a full-time student between eighteen and twenty-two). Or she can collect, if she is sixty-two, a reduced benefit, even if there are no children entitled to benefits. At sixty-five, she can collect 50 per cent.

A dependent husband sixty-two or older also can qualify for benefits—50 per cent benefit at age sixty-five, less if benefits begin earlier.

Q. *How much of a benefit would you get?*

A. Disability benefits are based on your average monthly wages and are the same as the full retirement benefits you would get if you had reached sixty-five at the time you became disabled. If you are under sixty-two, though, the total benefits paid to you and your dependents may be reduced if you are receiving workmen's compensation.

Q. *What if a disabled worker with an impairment not expected to improve wants to try going back to work? Does he continue getting benefits for a transition period?*

A. If you return to work, your benefit may continue to be paid during a trial work period of up to nine months—although these need not be consecutive months. If, after these nine months of testing your ability to work, it is decided that you are able to hold a substantial job, your benefit will be paid for an "adjustment period" of three more months. After that, you're on your own.

Q. *Why is there a waiting period of five full months before a disabled worker can begin to receive benefits after applying?*

A. Because usually there are payments made by the employer, a group insurance plan, a private health insurance policy—or, if the injury occurred on the job, by workers' compensation.

Q. *What are the key types of disability for which workers are now receiving benefits?*

A. In the mid-seventies, diseases of the circulatory system (heart disease) ranked first. Emphysema was next and schizophrenia was third.

Check any questions with your nearest Social Security office. You'll find the address under "Social Security Administration" in the phone book. If you can't leave the house, a Social Security representative will come to you. Telephone or write or have a friend do this for you. These are your rights.

WHAT'S YOUR WORKERS' COMPENSATION WORTH?

THE HIGH COST OF WORK ACCIDENTS

When a coal mine disaster hits the front pages, as one does with heartbreaking frequency, our attention is riveted on the tragedy of fatal on-the-job accidents. Yet headlines such as these touch only the tip of the accident iceberg.

Each year, about 14,000 Americans lose their lives in on-the-job accidents. Each year, workers suffer a startling 10 million injuries on the job.

Merely in economic terms, the cost of work accidents and injuries was approximately $10 billion a year in the mid-seventies, double the total for 1962. This included lost wages, medical costs, damages to equipment and materials, delays in production, insurance, etc.

Injuries are a daily fact of life in today's most hazardous industries: coal mining, longshoring, roofing and sheet metal work, meat and meat products (especially cutting and handling), mobile home manufacturing, lumber and wood products, construction.

Workers' compensation, formerly known as workmen's compensation, for job-related accidents, illnesses, and injuries is the oldest form of social insurance in the United States—dating back to 1908 when Congress set up a program under the Federal Employees Compensation Act to cover certain federal employees in hazardous occupations. State after state followed with its own workmen's compensation law until, today, all fifty states have programs of their own, with the coverage paid for completely by the employer and employees getting these free benefits through private insurance, self-insurance, and state insurance funds.

Today the yearly dollar outlay of workers' compensation benefits is in a neck-and-neck race with the massive Social Security disability program.

However, the rules vary widely from state to state and there also is a wide variation in the proportion of lost wages which are replaced.

The states are, therefore, now facing a federal take-over of their workers' compensation systems if they are not brought up to much higher standards. As a result there is a solid trend toward liberalization of the laws across the land.

Among the significant liberalizations:

Employees of smaller and smaller firms are being brought under the workers' compensation umbrella. The number of states with compulsory coverage is rising and the trend in more and more states is toward including at least some farm and domestic workers. More states are providing benefit limits which increase along with the state-wide wage scale.

Limitations on the amount of reimbursable medical, surgical, and hospital expenses are being eliminated. Compensation periods for permanent disabilities—such as loss of limb—are being stretched out. More states are providing complete coverage for occupational diseases. Injured employees are often being given a free choice from a panel of recognized physicians and specialists. There has been a steady succession of hikes in benefits. Every state now has a retroactive pay provision covering the waiting period before normal workers' compensation benefits begin.

The potential importance to you of this coverage must not be downgraded: glance back at those figures on how many workers are injured and killed in on-the-job accidents.

QUESTIONS AND ANSWERS ON BENEFITS

But do *you* know what your workers' compensation coverage is worth to you? Are you aware of how much this insurance would pay if a serious accident befell you while you were working?

Q. *How many of us are covered?*

A. Between eight and nine out of ten workers.

Q. *Who's eligible?*

A. Covered workers who are partially or totally disabled as a result of an accident or injury on the job—regardless of blame. The interpretation of "on the job" varies, but in California the state Supreme Court recently ruled that the widow of a worker killed in an auto accident at night after attending a job-related class was still eligible for workers' compensation benefits.

Q. *Who isn't covered?*

A. It varies from state to state but among the occupations with large numbers of non-covered workers are agricultural work, domestic work, work for religious, charitable, and non-profit organizations, "casual" labor, self-employed, workers in small firms.

Q. *How much do benefits run?*

A. Normally, maximum benefits are between 60 and 80 per cent of the pre-disability wage and often there's a dollar ceiling on benefits. In several states there's an extra allowance for workers who have dependents, which brings typical benefits to 60 to 65 per cent of the amount of take-home pay.

Q. *What types of benefits does the program pay?*

A. Three types. The biggest chunk goes to make up for income loss due to disability incurred on the job. The next biggest chunk goes for medical costs. The rest goes for death benefits paid to the worker's survivors. Included in the program are hundreds of millions of dollars in "black lung" benefits paid by the federal government to coal miners suffering from pneumoconiosis—a serious lung disease which comes from inhaling coal dust—and to their dependents.

Q. *How long are benefits paid?*

A. Most state programs pay benefits as long as the disability lasts. Note: More than one in six of our civilian working-age population has some kind of limitation on his or her ability to work because of a chronic disability or health condition.

Q. *Who pays for the workers' compensation program?*

A. In most cases, employers pay insurance premiums either to state insurance programs or to private health insurance carriers or they insure employees themselves. The average cost to employers in covered employment is about 1 per cent of payroll, although costs range in some states up to nearly 3 per cent. Generally, the costs of administering workers' compensation come out of the state's general revenues instead of from employers.

Q. *Can you collect both Social Security benefits and workers' compensation benefits at the same time?*

A. Yes, if the combination does not exceed 80 per cent of your pre-disability monthly earnings. Beyond that, Social Security payments are trimmed to keep the total at the 80 per cent mark.

Q. *What about private health insurance benefits?*

A. There's usually a provision that private health insurance won't pay for any medical conditions covered by the compensation law. But if your employer has "long-term" disability insurance for employees this will make up the difference if workers' compensation provides a smaller amount.

Use the above guidelines to help you find out whether the *total* amount of benefits you and your family would get if you, the bread-winner, became disabled would or wouldn't be adequate to meet your family's needs. Also include company insurance, Social Security, your savings and investments.

PRIVATE DISABILITY INSURANCE COVERAGE

WHAT WOULD IT COST YOU?

Let's say you use the guidelines in the preceding section, check your various benefits, and come to the firm conclusion that your benefits would be seriously inadequate in case of need.

How much would it cost you to buy supplementary private dis-ability insurance—to add to your protection from Social Security, work-ers' compensation, and other sources?

If you get a private individual policy providing $100 a week for up to two years, it'll probably cost you $76 to $115 a year. If the cov-erage lasts up to five years, your annual premiums probably would be between $128 and $180—with office workers generally paying less. And there is usually a thirty-day waiting period before any private disability insurance benefits may begin.

With this as a yardstick, you can compute what the coverage you need will cost, keeping in mind that the longer the waiting period the less your premium cost will be. Also, the longer the benefit continues, the more your cost will be.

CHECK LIST FOR COVERAGES

Check with care these points about private disability coverages:

(1) How is "disability" defined in your policy or the policy you are considering buying? Generally, these policies state that you must be "totally" disabled before benefits are paid.

Your policy may have a variation of this definition:

"Unable to engage in any gainful occupation for which the policy-holder is suited by education, training, or experience."

(2) What is the difference in benefit periods for an accident and for an illness? For instance, the same policy might provide benefits for two years for sickness and five years for an accident.

(3) What waiting period is appropriate for you? Take into account the length of time your regular earnings would continue, as well as all the other sources of income, then decide whether you should accept a seven-, fourteen-, thirty-, ninety-day waiting period—or longer.

MAKING DEDUCTIBLES WORK FOR YOU

As in major medical insurance, the best way to save money in your disability coverage is to select the highest deductible your budget can stand. In this type of insurance, the deductible amount is expressed in terms of the waiting period. By extending the waiting—or, as it is called, the "elimination"—period before benefits start, you can cut your costs and either save the money or use it to build up your protection. Since you're less likely to have major medical and disability coverage than you are to have basic protection, it's probable that you'll work out some combination of these.

Here's how you can juggle the deductible to your advantage:

One major medical policy offered by a large insurer would provide a twenty-eight-year-old man with $10,000 maximum coverage for himself, his wife, and two children, with a $250 deductible, at a cost of about $225 per year.

If he raised this deductible to $750 he could get a policy which would cut his annual premium to about $182. Then, with the money saved, he could buy a short-term disability policy which would pay him $200 a month for two years after a thirty-day waiting period. Both policies would have a waiting period before benefits are payable—three months for a disability and six months for illness.

Now, to dramatize for you the effect of lengthening the disability policy waiting period, consider this typical policy from another insurer. His policy provides benefits of $200 a month for sixty months and costs $66.40 per year if the waiting period is only fourteen days. But the cost of the same policy providing the same monthly benefit to age sixty-five —roughly thirty-two years more than the first policy for a twenty-eight-year-old man—is only $44.80 a year if the waiting period is upped to ninety days.

How to Slash Your Medical Bills

There's no hope for anything more than a slowing of the pace of rise in medical expenses in the decade of the 1970s.

But there are many ways you can cut your own costs. Below you will find fundamental rules that you could translate into big savings for yourself and family—without in any way jeopardizing your health.

SHOP FOR A HOSPITAL

In shopping for health services, perhaps the most difficult area is the hospital. You can't merely pick out one and walk in. Invariably, unless you're an emergency case, you must be admitted by a physician who is affiliated with the hospital.

Few of the one out of every seven Americans admitted to a hospital each year, I'm sure, ever even think about "shopping" for a hospital. But it can be done.

The easiest way would be to telephone each hospital in your city or nearby area until you found the one with the lowest daily rate. But the trouble with this approach is that the hospital you pick in this manner may not be on your doctor's affiliation list, so you'll have to get another doctor. And chances are the institution with the lowest rate is a municipal or "city" hospital. You may not regard municipal institutions with the same esteem you have for private voluntary community hospitals. Private health insurance usually does not cover any tax-supported hospital where no charge is made for service.

You'll find that your physician is probably affiliated with more than one hospital. If he doesn't have strong feelings about admitting you to a particular institution for a particular reason (if the hospital to which your physician wants to send you is the only one in town with a cobalt radiation unit and you need cobalt radiation treatment, you have little choice in the matter), then bear these points in mind:

• *Do* select the hospital on your physician's list that is a teaching institution and also has a strong research program. If a hospital has affiliations such as these, it has sources of revenue and talent not normally open to other community hospitals which are supported almost exclusively by taxes and patient charges. This is also the facility that will give you the greatest range of diagnostic and treatment resources.

• *Don't* confuse bigness with best. Depending on your condition and the type of treatment you need, maybe a smaller hospital would provide you with less hurried and more personal tender loving care—a difficult item to put a price tag on.

• *Do* check whether your state regulatory agencies can help steer you toward a lower-cost hospital. For instance, in Pennsylvania a few years ago, the state's insurance department published a "Shopper's Guide to Hospitals." This guide compared costs charged by the 101 hospitals in the Philadelphia area—and found that the *daily* charges varied by as much as $50.

• *Don't,* unless it means a big sacrifice to you, go into the hospital on a Friday. A large-scale study a while ago showed that the day of the week you go into the hospital is the single largest factor in determining how long you'll stay there. Admissions on Friday, the study disclosed, resulted in longer stays than admissions on any other day. The reason: the hospital is not fully staffed on weekends and if you go in on a Friday you'll have to wait until Monday before all the necessary laboratory and other diagnostic tests can be performed. Meanwhile, you well may be paying $100 or more a day for your "hotel room."

The study also revealed that the *shortest* average length of stay was found for patients admitted on a Tuesday.

If you have an indemnity-type health insurance policy which leaves you with part of the hospital bill to pay out of pocket, getting out just a day or two earlier can be a considerable relief to your budget. In fact, it has been estimated that, if we could cut the average hospital stay by just one day from its 7.9 days in the mid-seventies, the nation could save $1 billion annually.

• *Do* ask your doctor if it's possible to have some of your routine lab tests done *before* you're admitted to the hospital. An increasing number of hospitals participate in pre-admission testing programs of this type. More than one out of every three Blue Cross plans will pay benefits for this type of visit to the outpatient department, and many insurers also pay through diagnostic riders to their contracts.

• And finally, *do,* unless you feel you absolutely must have complete privacy, take a semi-private room, for it is far less expensive than a private room. Many hospitals will charge less for a four-bed semi-private room than for a two-bed room and it's becoming easier to get exactly what you want. Also, semi-private accommodations are usually paid for in full by Blue Cross and also by commercial insurance company indemnity policies.

HAVE A FAMILY PHYSICIAN

Choose him (or her) carefully—for his reputation in the community, the type of practice he has developed, and his availability. If you are a newcomer in the area, the local county medical society will supply you with the names of physicians from whom you can make a choice. You may want to become acquainted with several before deciding.

But don't make your selection solely on the recommendation of a local medical society. Membership in these organizations tells you only that a doctor is licensed to practice and has paid his dues. Also don't assume that because a doctor is well known in his community he is good. He may be prominent for reasons other than medical skill.

One clue to his competence will be his membership on the medical staff of a good hospital, especially a hospital affiliated with a medical school. If so, you can be well assured that he's above average.

Your doctor may practice medicine alone, in a group, or in a large clinic, but he should be a person who knows you and your family and is interested in your *health,* not just your illnesses.

He will keep a permanent record of your medical history.

He will know your background and be better able to tell promptly if anything is wrong.

He will control a key portion of your medical spending, simply because he will determine what drugs you will buy, whether or when you must go to a hospital, whether or when you must see a specialist. And when you must consult a specialist or go to a hospital, he will save you money by making sure you do not repeat costly, time-consuming tests. He also may save you money by referring you to a nurse practitioner for routine health problems.

DON'T WAIT TO SEE YOUR PHYSICIAN UNTIL YOU'RE ILL

If you try to save money on medical bills by not seeing the doctor until you are seriously ill you will defeat the purpose of preventive medicine—the *only sound way* to preserve your health. And it will be more expensive in the long run, for once a disease process has started, it often lasts longer, costs more to cure.

Emergencies are always more expensive, whether the crisis involves the family car, the household plumbing, or your health. And if you are rushed to a hospital emergency room, you really may compound your misfortune—financial as well as physical.

HAVE REGULAR CHECKUPS

A complete physical examination each year is really a must. Try to schedule your exam during your birthday week if possible. Early detection of a disease obviously gives you a better chance to control and cure it. By one estimate, it costs nine times more to cure a disease than to prevent it in the first place. Moreover, your past medical record in your physician's hands will help you should you be hit by a severe accident or illness. Typical cost range in the mid-seventies for a comprehensive physical, including lab fees: $40 to $180. And part of this cost well might be covered by your health insurance or offered as a special employee benefit.

ALWAYS DISCUSS YOUR PHYSICIAN'S FEES WITH HIM

Fees are not inflexible, and physicians frequently adjust their charges to meet your financial situation. Be sure, though, to discuss fees at your first meeting; do *not* wait until after you receive the bill. If you decide a medical fee is unreasonable after a service has been provided, the first step is to negotiate directly with the doctor.

Be particularly careful to discuss fees at the start with a specialist, who may be very expensive but who also may reduce and stretch out payment for his charges to fit your budget.

GO TO THE DOCTOR'S OFFICE

House calls are not only more expensive but also less efficient. Without office equipment and a trained staff, your physician cannot perform a complete examination. (Of course, chronically ill, confined patients can be seen only at home.)

What's more, a house call may not be adequate for the doctor and he'll ask you to come to his office for further consultation. Result: two fees instead of one.

Reserve house calls for real emergencies.

USE THE TELEPHONE

This saves money and also makes good medical sense. A family doctor who has examined you regularly is familiar with your health history. Consequently, he often can advise you over the phone about minor health problems. For anything that seems to be serious, he will ask you to come to his office to be examined.

But call the doctor only when you have adequate reasons—and confine discussions of your appointments and other routine matters to his nurse.

FOLLOW YOUR DOCTOR'S ORDERS

Just as a commonplace illustration, have you ever been told to take off ten pounds and get more exercise? Did you do it? If you refuse to follow the expert advise you solicit and pay for, you are throwing your money away.

YOUR COMMUNITY HEALTH RESOURCES

DON'T OVERLOOK THEM!

All around you are a great number and variety of community health services. They are available to you, and they could mean considerable savings to you over the long term. Don't overlook them!

These resources range from your public hospitals and clinics to volunteer ambulance services, local blood banks, visiting nurse service, rehabilitation and mental health counseling, vocational rehabilitation and retraining programs. In addition, there are special services, such as free screening and immunization programs, especially if you live in a highly populated area. The list of these services is almost endless, combating health problems ranging from deafness to drug abuse, and fighting illnesses ranging from alcoholism to venereal disease.

On top of your community resources are other facilities backed by labor groups, private foundations, business organizations, and social service agencies. And don't forget government programs. As one illustration, the Veterans Administration conducts a large-scale national program of medical care and rehabilitation services.

Your Department of Health is the place to go to start finding out just what services you might use. Every state has one, and so do many cities and counties, although in some areas you may find this function is fulfilled by a health officer instead of a department. In any event, the Department of Health or the health officer will be able to refer you to the health services that are available through the department or through private agencies.

SAMPLING OF SERVICES

Here are some of the areas of special services you might need or want which are there for your asking:

Abortion	Drugs
Adoption	Family Planning
Aging	Food Stamps
Alcoholism	Handicapped children
Ambulance service	Heart disease
Arthritis	Hemophilia
Birth defects	Kidney disease
Blindness	Leukemia
Blood banks	Maternity care
Cancer	Medicare and Medicaid
Cerebral palsy	Mental retardation
Child placement	Nursing and homemaker services
Chronic illness	Prescription emergency services
Convalescent care	Rehabilitation
Day care	Speech handicaps
Deafness	Unmarried parents
Dental services	Venereal disease
Diabetes	Welfare services

How to Slash Your Drug Bills

NINE BASIC HINTS

(1) Take only the drugs and medications prescribed or recommended by your doctor.

(2) Urge the pharmacist filling a prescription to follow your doctor's instructions at the lowest possible cost. But *do not* decide on your own to substitute a generic equivalent for a trade-name drug—assuming you are now taking one of these drugs or one is prescribed for you. Let your physician make the decision.

(3) Ask your physician to steer you to drugstores in your area which offer quality drugs at the lowest cost. The American Medical Association is now urging physicians to do this as a matter of course.

(4) Shop the drugstores recommended to you, for the variations can be astounding. As a general guide, discount drugstores will fill prescriptions at lower cost to you than regular drugstores. Co-op pharmacies are scarce, but if you can find a co-op, it will be an excellent place to patronize.

(5) Don't buy non-prescription drugs in large quantities unless they are really needed. A 1,000-tablet aspirin bottle may seem more economical than a small size, but aspirin—and many other medicines—deteriorate with time. On the other hand, if you suffer from a chronic illness that calls for the use of prescription drugs over a long period, your doctor may prescribe in relatively large quantities and this may result in some savings.

(6) Get "starter" supplies of drugs from your physician. Most doctors are deluged with samples from drug firms and here you save in two ways: you get your initial supply free and you can try out the medication for its effectiveness before you buy a larger supply.

(7) Make sure you're not paying a professional charge for a nonprescription over-the-counter drug. Sometimes physicians recommend drugs which can be sold without prescriptions. But if the drugs are handled as regular prescriptions, the pharmacist will charge his usual fee. Ask your physician if the drug is a prescription item at the time he gives you the slip from his pad. If there's any doubt in your mind, look for the legend on the label. Any drug that does not have this legend: "Caution: Federal law prohibits dispensing without prescription" on the label can probably be sold without a prescription.

(8) Buy the cheapest brand of aspirin, as it is a specific chemical compound. (Aspirin tablets are required by law to meet the standards of strength, quality, and purity set forth in *Pharmacopoeia,* a book of drug standards recognized by the Federal Food, Drug and Cosmetic Act as an official compendium. Aspirin must be packaged and labeled in the manner prescribed in this book.)

(9) If you are over age fifty-five, join the American Association of Retired Persons (1909 K Street, N.W., Washington, D.C. 20049) and save through this association's non-profit mail order pharmacy service.

How to Shop for Dental Services

FUNDAMENTAL APPROACHES

Despite the enormous sums we spend for dental services alone, only 20 per cent of us are estimated as receiving proper preventive dental care.

Are you getting this care? Most likely you can't tell. In fact, it is virtually impossible for the average person, lacking professional training, to distinguish between good, adequate, and poor dental service.

There are some basic guides, though, and here goes.

The key to proper dental care is to find a good dentist. One widely used obvious route is through the recommendations of your friends or relatives. Odds are that if a dentist has proved satisfactory to someone whose opinion you value he or she probably will prove satisfactory to you as well.

A second, if you move, is to ask your previous dentist to recommend a practitioner in your new home town. Or call the local dental society, which will usually recommend three names of dentists in the area and supply such information as their schools, graduation dates, and specialties. Keep in mind that about 10 per cent of all dentists are specialists. Among the specialties:

orthodontics, concerned with aligning teeth;

periodontics, treatment of gums;

prosthodontics, denture work;

endodontics, a new and growing specialty of root canal treatment, saving teeth that fifteen years ago might have been extracted;

pedodontics, also a relatively new specialty devoted entirely to the treatment of children's dental problems;

oral surgery;

oral pathology;

public health dentistry.

• Try to find a dentist in a group practice. Such a dentist is under the direct and constant scrutiny of other dentists in the group. This tends to keep all of them on their toes, since their reputations rest on the excellence of one another's work.

• Call the nearest university dental school; ask for the name of a dentist for your family who maintains a private practice near the school and who is interested in preventive dentistry. Or ask the name of a professor who maintains a private practice near the school. Being a professor doesn't necessarily make him a good dentist, but chances are better than even that he's a top-notch practitioner.

TELLTALE SIGNS

Despite the difficulties of distinguishing between good, adequate, and poor care, there are telltale signs to look for that can alert you to the bad dentist, to the one who overcharges, or to the one who does overly fast work and uses too many short cuts.

• Expect a moderate amount of discomfort, particularly if you have neglected your teeth. If nothing ever hurts, you may not be getting quality work. Beware of the dentist who zips you in and out of the chair with a quick drill and fill. It may indicate a perfunctory job.

• Be on guard if he seems to emphasize extractions. Pulling a tooth is one of the easiest jobs in dentistry, but often is not necessary. No replacement is ever as good as your own tooth. A good dentist will extract only as a last resort.

• At your first meeting, note whether the dentist takes time to discuss fully your dental problems; whether he asks if you are seeking emergency care or are looking for a family dentist. And most important, find out if he is willing to discuss fees frankly and determine in advance a method of payment. Don't patronize a dentist who is not willing to discuss his fees at your request.

• Finally, seriously consider these factors before deciding whether this is or is not the right dentist for you:

Is the general appearance of the office and the dentist and his staff neat, clean, and orderly?

How available is he, both in location and appointment schedule?

Is he prevention-oriented?

Does he use X-rays in his diagnosis? Dental X-rays are one of the most valuable diagnostic tools in modern dentistry. A good dentist will probably have a full-mouth set of X-rays taken, unless suitable X-rays are available from your previous dentist.

HOW CAN YOU TELL IF THE FEE IS FAIR?

This isn't easy, since charges vary from dentist to dentist and depend on such factors as location and complications involved in a specific case. However, it is becoming somewhat easier to get information on dental fees.

One way to check the fee for a particular service is through the local dental society.

A good dollars-and-cents guide on dental fees is included in "A Shopper's Guide to Dentistry" published by the Pennsylvania Department of Insurance. Pennsylvania residents can get a copy by sending a self-addressed 9- by 12-inch envelope with 16¢ postage to "Shopper's Guide," Pennsylvania Insurance Department, Harrisburg, Pa. 17120. Out-of-staters can get a copy by sending $1.00 plus a self-addressed 9- by 12-inch envelope with 16¢ postage to "Consumer Insurance," 813 National Press Building, Washington, D.C. 20045. (See Part IV, "Your Rights and How to Get Them," page 1119, for details on other shoppers' guides published by the Pennsylvania Insurance Department.)

IF YOU NEED A PSYCHIATRIST

According to the National Association for Mental Health, about one in ten persons in the United States will at some time develop a form of mental or emotional disorder requiring psychiatric care. On any given day of the year, nearly 400,000 persons are in state, county, and private mental hospitals.

The American public spends literally billions of dollars each year on the treatment and prevention of mental illness; the economy loses many more billions because of the decreased productivity of mental patients. Over all, it's a problem costing more than $20 billion a year in our country alone.

HOW DO YOU GO ABOUT FINDING ONE?

First, if you believe you need such help, consult your primary personal physician. He knows what kind of person you are and which psychiatrist might be of most benefit to you. He probably also will know which particular psychiatrists are highly regarded by his own medical colleagues.

Or you might turn to your county medical society or your local mental health association for the name of a qualified psychiatrist in your area. Or if you have a local community mental health clinic or center, you might find these a source of service—no matter what your ability to pay.

HOW MUCH MONEY AND TIME ARE INVOLVED IN TREATMENT?

How much you can expect to pay and how long your treatment will last will depend on your condition and the treatment chosen for you. The most typical charge for a psychiatrist's time in 1974, according to the American Psychiatric Association's Hospital and Community Psychiatry Service, was about $40 an hour. The fee for your initial psychiatric consultation would depend on the time involved and might be slightly more than the hourly therapy charge. A majority of patients will be treated for less than 20 sessions. For some, longer-term psychotherapy will be needed. For a few in psychoanalysis the number of sessions may range from 300 to 500 although this depends on the patient and the progress, and the span for you could vary considerably from these totals.

WILL HEALTH INSURANCE HANDLE PART OF THE TREATMENT?

The daily costs of psychiatric hospitalization are often less than the cost of hospitalization for any other reason. Most health insurance plans today will cover the cost of treatment of mental conditions while the person is confined to the hospital, although there is a wide variation as to the extent of the coverage. Many will pay for treatment as an outpatient, but the per cent of the bill covered is usually less than in the case of other illnesses. Outpatient benefits are being written into an increasing number of group policies, including those of Blue Cross and Blue Shield plans.

IS IT POSSIBLE TO SHOP FOR THESE SERVICES?

Yes, it *is* possible to shop for psychiatric services.

By checking with your local health and welfare departments, religious leaders and others, by the simple expedient of checking in the telephone directory, you will discover the range of low-cost psychiatric services available in your community. And they may be of great money-saving value to you.

How to Beat Our $15 Billion Hangover

THE STAGGERING BURDEN

The United States today is suffering from a national alcoholic hangover which claims thousands of lives and is costing a staggering $15 billion a year.

Of this, the National Institute on Alcohol Abuse and Alcoholism estimated in a special report to Congress, $10 billion is the price our economy pays for lost work time and $5 billion the cost of welfare payments and of the damage to the alcoholic's health and to property.

More than 9 million Americans (one in fifteen of us over the age of eighteen) are alcoholics and alcohol abusers. The yearly cost of the estimated 4 million on-the-job alcoholics, according to the National Council on Alcoholism, is at least $8 billion, translating into a drain of $32 million on business and industry *each working day*.

Absenteeism is two and a half to three times as great for alcoholics as for non-alcoholic workers. Alcoholics average three times as much sick pay as others, and their accident rates also are much higher. Many alcoholic workers lose a full month of working days each year.

Even more devastating is the towering problem of "on-the-job absenteeism"—where an alcoholic employee may fritter away hours each morning recovering from a hangover or sleep off a multi-martini lunch in the local movie house.

Moreover, alcoholism is everywhere and does not respect corporate names or job descriptions. An estimated 45 per cent of the alcoholics in this country are professional or managerial workers; the typical alcoholic has been at his job twelve years; he is between the ages of thirty-five and fifty-four, the key productive years; his alcoholism has been present but unrecognized for years.

If you are the typical alcoholic, you are almost surely spending tremendous time and effort trying to disguise your problem so cleverly that neither you nor your company will become aware of its seriousness. Yet the cost of your illness to you *and* your company (and, of course, also your family) may be enormous—in terms of loss of time, mismanaged business deals, bad decisions, missed promotions, etc. And continued drinking not only can get you fired from your present job but also can become a towering barrier in your search for another.

Whether or not *you* admit you are an alcoholic, you have at least one enormous incentive to seek help—and that incentive is your desire to hold your job.

WHERE DO YOU FIND HELP?

A first step is to inquire whether your employer offers counseling and/or rehabilitative services to employees. Hundreds of companies do, although most of these programs reach only a small number of alcoholics.

Your best single source of help is Alcoholics Anonymous, which for years has been carrying the alcoholism problem almost single-handedly—and, incidentally, very successfully. Today AA is available to virtually all who wish to use its services, with 16,500 local groups in 92 countries. AA's key resource is an army of 500,000 recovered alcoholics who stand ready, around the clock, to give free help to anyone with a drinking problem. AA meetings are now being held not only in churches and regular meeting halls but also in such places as airplane hangars and at state reformatories.

Other sources of help have been proliferating too. To be specific:
• Since the National Institute on Alcohol Abuse and Alcoholism was set up in 1970, dozens of community action programs and neighborhood health centers have, for the first time, allocated funds to treat alcoholics.

• More and more general hospitals are now treating alcoholics. A few have set up special alcoholism services.

• City after city has been setting up a variety of alcoholism programs.

• Blue Cross and other insurers have begun to add hospitalization benefits for alcoholics.

• The military services, too, are beefing up their programs for alcoholic servicemen.

CARING FOR OUR ELDERLY

WHAT WOULD YOU DO?

What would you do if this problem came before you—or a member of your family?

You, one of your parents, a grandparent or other close relative or friend is over sixty-five;

faces increasingly severe medical, nutritional, living, and other problems;

knows that something has to be done—but is uncertain as to just what;

and is worried about the costs as well as terrified about the unspoken agony of change.

Even today, a full 10 per cent in the United States are over sixty-five and that number may double in less than a decade from now. *Even as early as 1974, 24 cents out of every $1.00 of federal spending was going for Social Security, Medicare, federal retirement, and other benefits.*

"Once, it was conventional wisdom that elderly persons no longer able to live alone or with families should enter a safe, decent place to live where medical care was available," explains William I. Riegelman, president of the board of trustees of the Jewish Home and Hospital for the Aged, a non-profit member of the Federation of Jewish Philanthropies of New York. "That wisdom is no longer enough and one reason is that the cost of nursing home care now runs into five figures annually per person."

"Parents and children are caught in the struggle of the elderly for independence and survival," adds the Rev. Richard Thomas of the Division of Aging of the Federation of Protestant Welfare Agencies in New York. "The greatest thrust now is in independent and congregate living with assistance."

"A planned program of medical, social, and environmental care supports a relatively independent way of life," emphasizes a recent report from Manhattan's Mary Manning Walsh Home, operated by the Carmelite Sisters for the Aged and Infirm. The home offers a "total package" under one roof.

Throughout the United States an increasing range of services is being made available for elderly people—and an urgent search is on for better services at less expense.

The shocking estimate is that perhaps 10 per cent of the elderly are institutionalized too soon because of lack of knowledge of available alternative facilities.

What, then, are the alternatives available if you are facing the problem?

THE ALTERNATIVES AVAILABLE TO YOU

Home care program: An elderly person remains at home, receiving homemaker assistance, outpatient medical care—and, if and when needed on a temporary basis, emergency admission to a full-care institution. Sponsoring organizations may allocate $250 and more a month for each individual served.

Day hospital and treatment centers: a new concept, which enables older people to remain at home with all the advantages of geriatric and general medical facilities. The trend is growing. Cost, as of 1974, around $250 a month per person.

Apartment residences: There are several throughout the United States. JHHA operates Kittay House in the New York area, a pioneering experiment in independent living with a service package including two daily meals, weekly maid service, other assistance. Efficiency apartments plus the service package at institutions such as this ranged in the mid-seventies from $375 for an individual to $650 a month for a couple.

Proprietary or profit-making residences: These provide similar services to apartment residences operated by institutions—rooms, meals, programs. Such homes usually do not provide medical services. As a result, their costs often are less.

Homes and hospitals for the aged: These are run by voluntary, non-profit agencies, with the largest institutions offering the broadest range of services. All residents share the high overhead, in part, but not every resident needs all the services available. Costs in the mid-seventies ran from $8,700 to $17,000 annually.

Even though Medicaid and Medicare pay the bills for a majority of nursing home residents, it is essential that you become aware of your alternatives. For instance, in recent experiments, this thought-provoking pattern has emerged:

First, the elderly person uses the home care program; then the apartment residence; then, as required, he or she moves to intermediate or extended nursing care. Ask yourself:

Can this person truly benefit from institutional living; Is he or she capable of adjusting to special requirements?

SHOPPING FOR NURSING HOMES

Good nursing home care isn't cheap. As a rule you can expect to pay about one third of the cost of maintaining a patient in a nearby hospital—with basic monthly charges in the mid-seventies $500 or so for a semi-private and $800 to $1,000 for a private room. Find out what services are included in the basic fees and what extra charges are. Most homes charge extra for patients requiring feeding and incontinence care. Find out how drug costs are handled and whether you can bring in medicine. Routine services—haircuts, shampoos, personal laundry, linen charges, room TV rental, etc.—may be listed as extras. Charges of your personal physician are never included.

By all means, visit a nursing home before selecting it. Spend at least a couple of hours inspecting the staff; standards; physical, recreational, and occupational therapy facilities; safety devices. Ask about special diets, meal schedules. Spot-check for cleanliness, odor, maintenance, the general atmosphere.

Check what recreational facilities there are and whether the home is a member of professional organizations devoted to professional care.

Look for a nursing home offering rehabilitation services and periodical re-examination of patients to determine whether their needs have changed, for better or worse.

Discuss what financial help you may get with the home's administrator, your Social Security and/or welfare office.

MEDICARE'S YARDSTICKS

Here are the yardsticks Medicare uses in deciding whether or not a skilled nursing care facility is eligible for Medicare payments.

Each skilled nursing facility must:

• have physicians admit patients and supervise their care;

• maintain an organized nursing service, directed by a full-time professional registered nurse, with at least one licensed practical nurse on duty at all times and with enough attendants and nurses' aides to assure each patient adequate care;

• keep a current, separate medical record and patient care plan for each patient;

• assure that each patient is visited by a doctor at least once every thirty days;

• have an active program of restorative nursing care;

• assure that drugs and medications are properly administered;

• provide for promptly obtaining needed X-ray and lab services;

• be able to identify medically related social and emotional needs;

• have a dietary service that meets the institutional needs of patients, including special diets;

• provide for adequate medical attention to patients during medical emergencies, including possible transfer to an accredited hospital;

• assure compliance with state and local fire protection codes, availability of fire extinguishers on each floor, and unobstructed doorways, passageways, and stairwells;

• maintain hygienic conditions, proper lighting levels and ventilation, heating and air conditioning facilities, a hot water supply, and laundry services;

• carry out utilization review of services provided, at least to inpatients.

WHERE TO COMPLAIN

If you have a complaint about a nursing home, for whatever reason, you can tell it to:

(1) The nursing home administrator.

(2) Your local Social Security district office. It functions as a clearinghouse for complaints about all nursing homes, whether or not they receive government funds.

(3) The patient's case worker or the county welfare office if the patient is covered by Medicaid.

(4) The state Medicaid Agency if the home is certified for that program.

(5) The state Health Department and state licensing authority.

(6) The nursing home ombudsman if such an office has been established in your community.

(7) The state board responsible for licensing nursing home administrators. (Get address information from the welfare department.)

(8) Your congressmen and senators. (Address congressmen at House of Representatives, Washington, D.C. 20515; senators at United States Senate, Washington, D.C. 20510.)

(9) Your state and local elected representatives.

(10) The Joint Commission on Accreditation of Hospitals (875 North Michigan Avenue, Suite 2201, Chicago, Ill. 60611) if the home has a JCAH certificate.

(11) The American Nursing Home Association (1200 15th St., N.W., Washington, D.C. 20036) if the home is a member.

(12) The American Association of Homes for the Aging (529 14th Street, N.W., Washington, D.C. 20004) if the home is a member.

(13) The American College of Nursing Home Administrators (8641 Colesville Road, Silver Spring, Md. 20910) if the administrator is a member.

(14) Your local Better Business Bureau and Chamber of Commerce.

(15) Your local hospital association and medical society.

(16) A reputable lawyer or legal aid society.

HEALTH MAINTENANCE ORGANIZATIONS:

PREVIEW OF THE FUTURE

The Blue Cross Association defines a Health Maintenance Organization as "an organized health care delivery system which promotes early detection and continuity of care through an arrangement holding a single organization responsible for assuring delivery of an agreed set of institutional and physician services to an enrolled population for a stipulated period of time in exchange for a fixed and periodic payment."

Mounting millions of Americans are now getting the opportunity to join these Health Maintenance Organizations—which, to put it in plain English, are organizations of doctors, hospitals, and others offering enrolling members a wide range of health services in exchange for a flat fee paid in advance, usually monthly or quarterly.

AN HMO FOR YOUR COMMUNITY?

The federal government is now actively pushing the development of HMOs via the 1973 Health Maintenance Act. Federally supported family health centers also are being transformed into HMOs, providing prepaid health care to people in areas where adequate health care is unavailable. The hope is that these centers will develop into self-supporting comprehensive-care HMOs. On the private front, many Blue Cross plans and private insurance companies are promoting HMOs or tying in their coverage with existing organizations.

What might you expect?

Services. Virtually all you might need—with such exceptions as dental care, long-term psychiatric care, rare and expensive types of care for the few at the expense of the many. Or you might be asked to pay nominal fees for each visit to the doctor or for outpatient prescription drugs. Also excluded are medical services covered or provided by others—such as workers' compensation (see earlier, this chapter), employment physicals, and accident insurance.

Fees. If you're a family of four, a monthly payment ranging between $40 and $80. If you're an individual, a monthly cost ranging between $15 and $30.

HEALTH BAFFLEGAB GUIDE

Do you know the difference between a Health Maintenance Organization, a Health Co-op, and a Health Maintenance Plan? What "capitation" payments are as opposed to "fees for services"? The meaning of a "prepayment plan" for health services? This is the jargon of our unfolding system of health care—soon to become a language you must be able to understand.

CAPITATION FEES: Payments to anyone providing health care of a certain amount of money per month, for each patient for whom the practitioner provides a certain specified range of services.

CATASTROPHIC COVERAGE: Health insurance with a high deductible—payable by you—but also a high ceiling ($50,000 to $250,000) so catastrophically costly care would be paid by the plan.

COMPREHENSIVE HEALTH CARE: Generally includes, both in and out of hospital, the whole works. Specifically:

>*preventive care*—e.g., periodic physical checkups, immunizations, various diagnostic tests at appropriate intervals; counseling, e.g., diet, exercise, etc.;

>*primary care*—or medical care by a family doctor or general physician, aimed at maintaining or restoring good health, up to the limits of the physician's capabilities;

>*specialty care*—by board-certified specialists for complicated illnesses;

>*rehabilitation*—for patients who have suffered from disabling accidents, strokes, mental breakdowns (plans usually exclude illnesses and injuries which require permanent medical maintenance);

>*extended care*—in nursing homes and other facilities—for nonpermanent chronic conditions needing medical attention, geriatric problems and adjustment.

DUAL CHOICE: Setup in company offered plans in which you are allowed to choose between two alternative plans (typically, fee for service or a prepaid group practice plan).

FEE FOR SERVICE: A sum of money paid by the patient for each individual service performed by a practitioner.

GROUP PRACTICE: Organized delivery of health care, by a group of two or more physicians with a prearranged system for sharing income. Some groups are highly specialized (representing a single specialty); others cover a variety of specialties. Most groups charge a fee for each service rendered.

HEALTH CARE PROVIDER: A physician-hospital or other institution, such as an HMO or prepaid group practice plan, providing health care services.

HEALTH CO-OPERATIVE: A health plan involving ownership and board participation in the plan by the members of the plan.

HEALTH MAINTENANCE ORGANIZATIONS: Typically prepaid group practice with dual goals of comprehensive continuous health care and more health care per dollar and with stress on early disease detection and prevention. More than 5 million Americans now enrolled, getting high-quality care at a cost as much as one third lower than traditional forms.

MEDICAL INDIGENT: Person not legally poor but likely to become poor instantly if hit by expensive illness.

MULTIPHASIC SCREENING: Battery of tests and exams to determine person's state of health and detect signs of illness. Tests usually performed by specialists in lab work, with interpretation by doctors.

PEER REVIEW: Ideally, formal review of medical decisions or procedures by an outside doctor or group of doctors with equivalent training and experience *and* in possession of essential data in each case. Typically, peer review covers quality and appropriateness of care, and charges for medical service.

PREPAYMENT: Health plan concept pioneered by unions—via Blue Cross—in which the subscriber pays a given sum in advance in the event that insured health benefits are needed. Payment is made in advance and limits the individual's liability as against paying for each separate service after it has been performed with unlimited liability.

Millions of Americans belong to some type of prepaid group practice plan. The cost of health care in these organizations has been less because doctors and hospitals maximize the use of facilities, personnel, etc. There are built-in incentives for preventive health care (immunizations, physical checkups) and against overuse of costly hospital facilities. Many problems are handled on an outpatient basis rather than by admission to a hospital where care is extremely expensive. The frequency of elective (non-obligatory) surgery tends to be far less in prepaid group plans since surgeons do not have any financial incentive to perform operations.

KEY QUESTIONS TO CONSIDER

Let's say a group in your community is considering setting up an HMO. What basics should the plan include? Here are key questions you—and everybody else involved in launching an HMO—should ask:

• Is there strong emphasis on such aspects as primary preventive care and health education?

• Are you, a consumer, involved along with health practitioners in determining the planning and delivery of services?

• Is the HMO co-operating with state and local planning agencies to avoid duplicate facilities and services and, thus, unnecessary costs?

• What mechanisms are there to permit continual assessment of the system as a whole, to tell how well it is working?

• What review-evaluation techniques are there to maintain a high quality of service—e.g., peer review by doctors and others? The new problem oriented patient record system? One of the key requirements under the 1973 HMO Act is an "ongoing quality assurance program."

• Are there open enrollment periods at least once a year—also required under the 1973 HMO Act?

• Are there provisions for hospital and doctor emergency services both inside and outside the area? Is there referral to specialists and super-specialists? Who pays how much for the costs of these services?

• Are there incentives to cut health care costs to patients?

SHOULD YOU JOIN AN HMO?

Let's say that a local medical group, hospital, university, or other organization is setting up an HMO. Or the Blue Cross plan to which you subscribe is offering an HMO-type plan as an alternative to your regular coverage.

Costs and coverages vary all over the place—but costs easily can run $500 to $1,000 or more a year for a family. Should *you* join an HMO under these circumstances? How can you tell whether or not it is a bargain for you? Here's your guide:

• Read with utmost care all the literature on the plan, what's covered and what's excluded, how long the coverage lasts.

• Check the monthly premiums and the extra costs you'll be required to pay for non-included items, deductibles, etc.

• Compare these totals with the amounts you've been paying in health insurance premiums, doctor bills, out-of-pocket cash, costs of services not covered or only partially covered in your present insurance, including that provided by your employer.

• Find out the arrangements for choosing and keeping a physician.

• Investigate the provisions for prescription drugs outside the hospital. Does the plan cover these or offer a way you can save when you buy? (Some HMOs have their own pharmacies.) And what about prosthetics and appliances?

• Check other subscribers' opinions. If they are already in a plan, are they satisfied with the medical attention?

• Find out what hours full HMO services are available and what the procedure is for care in evenings and over weekends.

• Ask whether the outpatient services and facilities you use most—physicians' offices, lab facilities, pharmacy—are under a single roof. Is this roof located conveniently for your family?

• Make sure preventive care services are stressed—early disease detection via diagnostic screening, periodic physical checkups, appropriate immunization.

• Investigate what hospital accommodations are provided—private, semi-private? Are such extras as special-duty nursing and private room included if your physician thinks they are essential?

• Are there age limits in the plan—such as when a son or daughter reaches age nineteen? Or marries?

• What medical facilities are included in the hospital to which you would go—such as coronary care, radiation therapy? What exclusions, if any, are there for health handicaps?

CHECK LIST FOR HMO SERVICES

Here is a check list of "basic" services, most of which an HMO is required to offer under the 1973 HMO Act. Use it to judge the comprehensiveness of any HMO, but also weigh it against your own list of health priorities:

physician services (including consultant and referral services by a physician);

inpatient and outpatient hospital services;

medically necessary emergency health services;

short-term (not to exceed twenty visits), outpatient evaluative and crisis intervention mental health services;

medical treatment and referral services (including referral services to appropriate ancillary services) for the abuse of or addiction to alcohol and drugs;

diagnostic laboratory and diagnostic and therapeutic radiology services; home health services; and

preventive health services (including family planning services, infertility services, preventive dental care for children and children's eye examinations conducted to determine the need for vision correction).

TEST YOUR CHANCES OF STAYING ALIVE

REVEALING QUESTIONS

How often do you exercise? Daily, three times a week, weekends only, rarely or never?

How much do you smoke? Not at all, five cigarettes a day, one half to a pack, two packs or more?

What's your weight as against your height and age?

What are your cholesterol and triglyceride levels? Your blood pressure?

Do you drink an average of more than three ounces of alcohol daily?

Have such between-meal snacks as potato chips, peanuts?

When was your last physical checkup?

The medical bill for circulatory diseases in our country is now an almost unbelievable 10 per cent of our national bill for all illnesses. At the top of all killers in the United States are diseases of the heart and blood vessels.

The loss to the nation in terms of income and productivity from deaths caused by heart attacks tops $1 billion a year, with half of it lost in the top-productive age group of forty-five to sixty-four. The bulk of the loss to the nation in terms of income and productivity from persons becoming ill of heart conditions and unable to work also is in the most productive age group of forty-five to sixty-four. The convalescence period can stretch to many months.

The economic costs involved in heart and blood vessel diseases alone—not to mention the emotional and other costs—are vast. What's more, our costs are jumping instead of sinking. We are actually falling behind other nations in keeping our men alive longer.

You surely are aware of the danger of a high cholesterol level, although this is not the terrible bugaboo it has been pictured. New discoveries in another blood fat—triglycerides—have added a second warning device, with the two comprising what are called blood lipids. In some patients, cholesterol is found to be relatively normal, while blood triglyceride count is dangerously high. (Question to you: Has your physician ever had your triglyceride count checked? Interpreted it with your cholesterol level?)

During the German occupation of Scandinavian countries, when butter, milk, and cream became scarce, the incidence of coronary artery diseases went way down. But the disease rate went way back up after World War II when these foods again became abundant—"pretty good proof on a large scale," say physicians, "that there is something to dietary control."

Stress aggravates high blood pressure and circulating blood fats—high-risk factors in heart diseases—but exercise lowers them.

And sex is also a very good exercise.

We can't do anything about any adverse family histories we may have, but we can do a great deal about every life-shortening activity or life-lengthening hint. Just by honestly answering the few revealing questions in the quiz alone, you're helping yourself to stay alive.

Your Blood Bank Account

If you are unfortunate enough to have a serious accident or illness requiring extensive blood transfusions, your total needs could amount to 50 to 100 pints of blood. If you must pay (as some do) $25 to $50 per pint, your cost of blood alone could come to $2,500 to $5,000. If you must use a heart-lung machine in the course of surgery, it may take between 12 and 15 pints of blood just to prime the machine for you. And if you happen to have a very rare blood type, you could pay astronomical sums.

Even if you are able to find donors to replace the blood you use, you'll probably have to pay the cost of processing this blood—and this can run $20 a pint or more. To date, the typical blood transfusion involves three pints of blood.

Each year our need for blood rises relentlessly. To meet our civilian needs alone, we needed to collect more than 8 million pints a year in the mid-seventies.

HOW TO PROTECT YOURSELF

How can you protect yourself and your family against the prospect of crippling high costs should you need a large amount of blood for a transfusion?

• Contribute blood periodically through a union, your employer, fraternal club, church, or other organized group which has an agreement with a community blood bank or the Red Cross. Merely by being a member of a group which meets a prescribed quota you will become eligible to receive blood—and there is no limit on the amount of blood which you or members of your family may receive if and when necessary.

• Or set up your own individual blood plan simply by giving blood to the Red Cross, to your local hospital blood banks, or to community blood centers. By donating once a year, you too may achieve the same eligibility status.

To give blood, you must be at least seventeen and not past your sixty-sixth birthday; must weigh at least 110 pounds, be reasonably healthy and free of conditions and diseases such as high blood pressure, jaundice, anemia, malaria, diabetes, and syphilis. You may give up to a maximum of five times a year and at intervals of at least eight weeks. In some blood banks, you may withdraw only the blood you donate, and it must have been donated within a period specified by the blood bank —typically, one to two years. A member of your family elsewhere can withdraw from your account with your permission—through the American Association of Blood Banks' National Clearinghouse Program, run in collaboration with the Red Cross.

QUESTIONS AND ANSWERS

Q. *What about getting blood via your health insurance?*

A. Coverage varies from company to company and plan to plan. But many plans cover processing fees only—and many hospitals require a "replacement fee" to encourage volunteer replacement.

Q. *What about commercial "blood insurance" plans?*

A. One such plan charges $5.00 a year for an individual and $7.50 a year for a family. This may seem welcome protection but most plans draw exclusively on blood from paid donors who may fail to report serious diseases to the collector—an obvious risk to you. You also may find important exclusions, and commercial blood plans unfortunately reduce the incentive for voluntary donations.

Q. *Is blood covered under Medicare for older people?*

A. Yes, under Part A—Medicare's hospital coverage—the full cost is covered after the first three pints used in each "benefit period" (spell of illness). Under Part B, which covers doctor bills, 80 per cent of blood costs subject to the yearly $60 deductible are covered after the first three pints.

Q. *How else can you save on costs of blood?*

A. If you are scheduled for elective surgery involving transfusions, ask friends and relatives to donate blood in advance to the bank with which your hospital is associated. If this hospital has a policy requiring blood replacement, find out in advance just what the terms are. Ask whether friends and relatives in other areas may help you replace blood you use via the Clearinghouse Program.

If you are among the one in 100 of us with a rare blood type, register with the rare donor registries operated by the AABB and ARC. In the Red Cross rare donor registry, for instance, there are now more than 7,000 donors whose names and blood types have been computerized: these rare donors include only those whose blood types are found less than once in 200 persons. The extremely rare types are collected regularly, frozen, and made available to anyone. Extremely rare types are frequently sent to hospitals for use without charge by specific patients.

HEALTH HOAXES

Down through the ages mankind has been plagued by the charlatan with his claim of being able to heal the sick, rejuvenate the aged, to make that which is drab a thing of beauty forever. In fact, health hoaxes extend so far back into history that they appear on the first known written medical record, the Ebers Papyrus (circa 1500 B.C.), which contained a prescription for preventing baldness. This ancient Egyptian remedy included, among other things, fats of the lion, hippopotamus, crocodile, goose, serpent, and ibex.

It didn't work—and not because anything was left out.

Things have not changed so much in the 3,475 years since this old Egyptian gyp. Today, we are still under a constant bombardment of come-ons, exaggerated advertising, gimmicks of dubious value, and pure-and-simple fraudulent claims, ranging over a wide area of products which affect your health.

Following is merely a sampling of what to watch out for. If it serves only to put you on guard against a hoax in the health sphere, I will have accomplished my aim.

DIET COME-ONS

You are young, you are in normal health, you want to look attractive—and you are overweight. It is to you that ads such as these are directed:

"I lost 54 pounds of ugly, dangerous fat!! . . . in only THREE short months!! without a doctor, a diet or calorie counting."

"A definite weight loss of 10–20–50 pounds, even 100 pounds or more may be accomplished in a short time."

The ads go on to claim that you, the overweight person in normal health, may continue to enjoy such foods as cream of mushroom soup, malted milks, spaghetti, pizza, and french toast—and still lose significant amounts of weight in "a short time." A key to these amazing achievements is a "miraculous formulation" involving pills for which you pay "only" $20 for a 120-day supply.

Then comes the fine print, along with the pills for which you have already paid a substantial sum. As it turns out, the spaghetti isn't really spaghetti, the pizza contains no pastry, and the malted milk must be made with skim milk or buttermilk.

Thus it is to you that this warning must also be directed:

Any claim of a cure for overweight which does not even mention dieting is fraudulent. No type of diet pill or program available today can achieve significant, permanent weight loss within a specified period unless the user takes strict dieting measures as well.

Tens of millions of overweight Americans are spending hundreds of millions of dollars a year on an unprecedented array of gadgets, gimmicks, pills, and potions to help them lose weight. Thousands of U.S. physicians are now devoting part or all of their practices to the problem of obesity. No one knows just how much money is being wasted on useless weight reduction schemes or how many of the obesity doctors actually manage to achieve major long-term weight reduction for their patients.

But it is known that the Food and Drug Administration in Washington has year after year seized millions of doses of multicolored "rainbow pills" used in weight reduction schemes on the grounds that they are either useless or dangerous. And the FDA and the American Medical Association have declared over and over that many of today's so-called diet pills may cause serious side effects.

You cannot lose weight on a diet of whiskey and whipped cream.

You cannot expect reducing pills to have any long-term effect—without the usual dietary restrictions and change in your eating habits.

You cannot "melt away fatty tissue" by wearing special tight-fitting plastic belts, blouses, and slacks.

To be blunt: there is no such thing as "effortless" reducing. Loss of pounds is directly dependent on using up more calories by exercise than you consume in food and drink.

Calories *do* count. For any major weight reduction program, you should enlist the help of a physician.

If you are among the millions with a problem of overweight, here are four fundamental rules for facing your problem and avoiding the many useless weight reduction programs now available:

(1) Avoid all "miraculous" formulas and high-powered pills recommended by *anybody*.

(2) Stay away from all gimmicks such as "slimming underwear" and vibrating machines if they are advertised as capable of achieving

a permanent loss of X number of pounds in X number of days, weeks, or months.

(3) Be suspicious of any weight reduction schemes involving special pills, "diet cocktails," or self-hypnosis if they do not also involve a lowering of your calorie consumption.

(4) In sum, if you have an overweight problem, consult your physician or your psychiatrist and follow your doctor's advice—which easily might include the suggestion that you join a respected local weight-reduction club or organization operating under medical supervision.

"STOP SMOKING"

A three-day supply of a new product which is supposed to help you stop smoking costs close to $3.00 a package at any local drugstore. If you complete the entire four-week program recommended in the directions, your total investment might add up to $20 or more.

This is a big bargain if you manage to quit smoking, of course. If you are a three-pack-a-day addict, you will spend many hundreds of dollars a year to support your habit—and you can add hundreds of dollars more to this if your spouse chain-smokes too. Also, today's non-smoker may be eligible for non-smoker life insurance at considerable savings in premiums.

But the estimate is that, of the millions of adult U.S. smokers who try to stop smoking each year, only a fraction succeeds. Would-be non-smokers are now spending tens of millions of dollars to buy the products of today's "Stop Smoking Industry"—ranging from pills to gum, lozenges, "pacifiers," stop-smoking books, etc.

Are you among the majority of U.S. smokers who, according to the U. S. Public Health Service, have made at least one serious attempt to quit smoking? How much money have *you* spent on the stop-smoking products—or on losing bets with other would-be non-smokers?

If you are gulping sugar pills and concoctions of ordinary spice such as ginger, licorice, clove, coriander—as well as pharmaceutical preparations—to stamp out your cigarette craving . . .

If you are taking up fake cigarettes—dubbed "smokes" or "adult pacifiers" which contain such non-nicotinic ingredients as menthol crystals, cabbage, lettuce, or just flavored cigarette paper—to keep your nervous hands busy and permit you to "smoke without fear" . . .

If you are falling for suggestive stop-smoking phonograph records . . .

If you are devouring no-smoke tablets and how-to-stop-smoking pamphlets . . .

Here are a few straight guides for you:

Despite the welter of new labels, there are no really "new" substances on the market to help you stop smoking. Old ones simply have been dressed up or combined to appear new.

The three standard types of anti-smoking medications now available are the nicotine substitute (e.g., lobeline sulfate), which alleviates cigarette craving; substances which make smoking taste unpleasant (e.g., silver nitrate); and local anesthetics (e.g., benzocaine), which numb the mouth and reduce desire for the puffing part of the smoking ritual.

Many of these products do, in fact, help you quit smoking temporarily. But none does the job permanently without a generous dose of will power on your part. Most are harmless, but a few cases of nausea, stomach pain, and loss of appetite have been reported as side effects.

A far more effective and more economical approach could be the Stop Smoking clinic. The programs at the better clinics are drawn up by physicians and psychologists. Most conduct regular meetings and seminars, some patterned on the highly successful Alcoholics Anonymous concept. You may or may not pay a small fee to attend the meetings.

QUACK MEDICAL DEVICES

If you have a naggingly painful disease or if you become seriously ill, you could well join the millions of Americans who each year spend billions of dollars for all forms of medical quackery—most of it for worthless and possibly dangerous gadgets and machines.

To illustrate with one horror story, tens of thousands have fallen for a contraption claimed capable of diagnosing and treating conditions ranging from cancer to chicken pox and jealousy—on the basis of a single drop of blood from the patient. When federal officials ran their own test, the machine failed to detect the fact that it was being fed blood samples from a turkey, a pig, and a sheep rather than from three children. Nevertheless, once a "diagnosis" had been made, the practitioner arrived at a special "vibration rate" for each patient and treated the patient's disease by radioing back into the patient the supposedly "normal" vibration rate. For those unable to visit the practitioner's office it was said that healing vibrations could be broadcast to reach anywhere on earth.

To illustrate with another equally shocking tale, suffering Americans have paid as much as $475 for an elaborate machine claimed to be able to cure cancer, diabetes, heart disease, and a wide variety of other serious conditions by "attuned color waves" shined on parts of the body. The primary medical qualification of the machine's inventor was an "honorary M.D."

To illustrate with still another, desperate Americans have paid important sums to another practitioner who claimed he could diagnose and cure anything from double vision to a "bone" in the colon—simply by using an elaborate-looking radio device.

Then there are devices—for which trusting (or despairing) souls among us have actually spent money—which "charge" your body with electrical energy and determine the "wave length" of your cells so that the wave length can be rearranged to restore your health and magnetize or demagnetize you depending on your needs.

There's even a machine which can, in the words of its inventor, "straighten out people who walk lopsided." Most quack devices are fitted with impressive-looking dials, switches, buttons, flashing lights, other space-age trimmings.

Why do countless thousands of Americans, including the intelligent and well educated, fall every year for this unbelievable array of quack gadgets and machines?

The victim of a devastatingly painful, progressive, or fatal disease often will find a quack cut-and-dried diagnosis and sure "cure" completely irresistible—and the very fact that we are living in an era of such medical "miracles" as laser surgery, heart transplants, cardiac pacemakers, nylon arteries, and artificial kidneys has made the machines of the quacks believable. What's more, federal regulation of medical devices has not kept pace with the proliferation of the devices—even legitimate ones.

Thus, basically, it comes down to this: you must protect yourself and your friends and relatives (particularly if they are aged) from the medical quacks.

And your basic protections are:

Stick with a legitimate, trained, medically qualified physician.

Avoid any quick, easy "secret" machine.

Be acutely skeptical of any electronic wonder or formula advertised by a practitioner who claims that the medical establishment is afraid of the "competition" of his sure cure.

CANCER QUACKERY

Today, more than half of all cancers can be cured if they are diagnosed in time and treated properly by surgery, radiation, chemotherapy, or a combination of these. In many types of cancers, such as skin or cervical cancer, the odds are even better: the vast majority of cases can be cured if they are detected early and correctly treated.

Yet thousands of cancer victims continue to refuse or postpone to a fatal degree legitimate treatment and to seek instead the services or elixirs of the cancer quack. Too frequently huge sums are spent by frightened elderly citizens who are already on the brink of bankruptcy and who may not have the disease to begin with.

Why? The key reasons, says the American Cancer Society, are the cancer victim's fear of incurability, fear of the high cost of treatment, fear of the prospect of radical surgery, fear of radiation treatment. In view of the number who develop cancer in our country and the odds on survival, many people are quite understandably quick to suspect its dread presence.

The cancer quack can be a devastatingly expensive economic drain as well as a devastatingly dangerous physical threat. Thus, here are the key guides to spotting the quack.

First, you must know that any qualified specialist will invariably conduct standard tests for any cancer at a recognized hospital or clinic and he will plan a course of therapy according to the results of these tests.

But the quack will:

• Neither perform recognized tests nor be associated with a recognized hospital or clinic—although the tests he does perform will invariably produce a diagnosis of cancer. He very well may advise against biopsy to verify cancer, using the excuse that "it will only spread the cancer."

• Boast that he has many well-known patients, including politicians, lawyers, movie actors, writers, etc. (This, incidentally, may be perfectly true.)

• Produce testimonials from former patients who claim he has cured their cancer. No reputable doctor advertises accomplishments or boasts in print about his famous patients. And, if you look behind the testimonials carefully, you may find those quoted died shortly after they authored the glowing accounts of their cures.

• Claim, when challenged to put his treatment to a scientific test, that he "won't get a fair trial" because the medical establishment is prejudiced against his method. Or he may challenge the medical establishment to test his product—then either fail to deliver a sample or insist on designing the test conditions himself.

• Insist, perhaps to help justify the high cost, that his cancer cure is "secret"—something no reputable member of the medical community would do for obvious reasons.

Until a universal cure or cures for cancer are found, our most potent—and also least expensive—weapons against this dread disease are regular medical checkups and awareness of the seven widely published cancer warning signals.

THE PSYCHOQUACK

If you are a relative or friend of one of the nation's 5 million mentally retarded citizens, you are acutely aware of the heartbreaking, frustrating search for effective treatment of this most widespread and debilitating of all medical problems. You also must be aware of the extent to which parents of the retarded are tempted by the mental health quack, both here and abroad.

There are no hard figures on how many tens of millions of dollars Americans are spending each year to line the pockets of quacks, unqualified psychotherapists, and untrained marriage counselors. But in the past, parents of retarded children have been reported to be laying out $1,000 apiece to have their children injected with worthless serum. In other forms of pseudoprofessional treatments by fringe practitioners, ex-mental patients have been recruited as "adjunctive therapists" to treat other patients, "nude psychotherapy" has been practiced by borderline psychotherapists, and any number of quacks have managed to persuade parents that their retarded child's problem actually was an allergy, a vitamin deficiency, a low blood sugar level, or some other condition which could be treated relatively easily.

The mental health quack today is often difficult to detect by an average citizen, who probably doesn't know the difference between a psychologist, psychiatrist, psychoanalyst, and psychotherapist. Many of the fringe practitioners are forming quasi-medical organizations, adopting scientific jargon, and using a smattering of accepted therapeutic techniques.

Why the upsurge in this form of quackery? How can you tell a quack from a non-quack in this field?

A first reason why mental health quackery (and particularly quackery aimed at the retarded) is thriving now is the simple fact that there is a growing market for the treatment of retardation. Every year in our country an estimated 3 per cent of all babies born are retarded babies.

Another is that the rate of spontaneous "cures" ranges up to two thirds for some types of mental disturbances. Thus, even the quack can claim a high percentage of successes which would have occurred anyway.

Still another reason is the severe shortage of qualified mental health professionals in the nation. Waiting lists at mental health facilities are frequently long; treatments are often stretched out over months or years and seldom result in what could be termed complete "cures." This frustration alone may easily translate into an open invitation to the fringe practitioner to move in.

Finally, state laws today are grossly inadequate in the regulation of practitioners in this field. There are still many areas of the United States in which an utterly unqualified person can legally hang up a shingle designating himself a psychologist, psychotherapist, or marriage counselor.

To protect yourself against the psychoquack, *beware of anybody who:*

• offers services for which his or her training is obviously inadequate;

• makes exaggerated claims, not backed up by the medical literature, about their treatments;

• uses articles in the popular press, frequently written by the person himself, as advertisements for his treatments;

• touts his treatments as more "natural" than other kinds of treatment;

• turns directly to threats and lawsuits rather than debate in professional circles as an answer to criticism;

• offers to administer various treatments outside the United States because the "cures" are banned in this country.

In sum, always deal only with qualified physicians and other trained mental health personnel.

ARTHRITIS "CURES"

Would you pay $200 or more to sit in a "uranium tunnel" at an arthritis "clinic" in the Midwest (actually an abandoned uranium mine)?

Or would you buy a "magic spike" containing less than a penny's worth of barium chloride for over $300 and wear it as an arthritis cure?

Or attempt to treat your painful joints by bathing them in colored light with a $50 gadget consisting of a light bulb and a plastic lampshade? Or try to help your arthritis simply by attaching a metal disk to a joint, then placing a cylinder, connected by a cord to the disk, into cold water? Or would you risk taking a powerful drug developed in another country and banned in the United States because its side effects include internal hemorrhaging and mental derangement?

Perhaps you would, if you were suffering enough from this often excruciatingly painful disease. For the fact is that today's extraordinary array of nostrums and devices promoted as capable of curing or relieving arthritis seems to be as tempting as ever to the victims, who include the well educated and well to do as well as the ignorant and poor.

Unproved "bootleg" drugs and devices are coming into this country via a thriving underground network of quackery, dispensed sometimes by the patients themselves. Americans are traveling, by the planeload, to other countries for arthritis "cures" banned here.

In some cases, potentially useful and legitimate treatment is delayed because the arthritic sufferer is so involved with quacks. Also the quacks are aided by the fact that in rheumatoid arthritis, the most serious form of the disease, pain comes and goes intermittently, so over the years the quack can frequently claim success.

The copper "arthritis bracelet" has staged a spectacular comeback —with countless hundreds of thousands of Americans spending from $1.00 to $10 to $100 for this form of copper jewelry on the claim that it will help prevent and/or cure this disease. Although precise statistics are unavailable, this single slice of the "anti-arthritis business" now accounts for tens of millions of dollars in annual sales and covers copper jewelry ranging from tie clips to cuff links, from bracelets to anklets.

And this is occurring in the face of the fact that the Post Office Department, the Federal Trade Commission, and the Food and Drug Administration have repeatedly condemned as fraudulent any claims that copper bracelets would cure arthritis (although admittedly, in most cases, no written claims are actually made). Also utterly phony are any claims that two copper bracelets, one worn on each wrist or each inner sole, create a special therapeutic "circuit."

Nevertheless, just because arthritis now affects one out of every twelve Americans and the number of sufferers is growing by 250,000 a year, any suggestion of relief is immediately seized upon by millions and immediately mounts into big-time money.

The total economic cost of arthritis is approaching a record $10 billion a year, estimates the Arthritis Foundation of New York—in the form of medical care costs and wage losses, lost homemaking services, and premature deaths. On top of this, the "hidden" costs—in the form of spending on worthless arthritis "clinics" and treatments—are approaching $500 million, almost double yearly costs in the 1960s.

As you would expect, financial outlays for fake cures and phony treatments swell with the number of arthritis sufferers. Worthless cures tagged by the Arthritis Foundation now cover white metal and plastic "electrogalvanic" bracelets; expandable "magnetic" bracelets; special electrical vibrators; hyper-immune milk; high-priced "magic spikes" containing a few pennies' worth of various vitamins, laxatives, and ointments; bootleg drugs illegally imported here from Mexico and Canada.

I will not downgrade one tiny bit the anxiety of a person suffering from great pain or a terminal illness to try anything at any cost in the hope of relief or cure. But the tragedy is that you might delay legitimate diagnosis and treatment, you might waste the most precious time as well as money in your commitment to quacks.

The bright fact is that we are at a moment in medical history when nearly three out of four cases of crippling arthritis can be headed off by early detection and proper treatment. The merciful prospect is that we are near major breakthroughs in drugs to treat arthritis.

Thus, if you are among the 17 million sufferers or close to an individual who is, heed these warnings:

• Be wary of any person who uses "testimonials" from former patients as a lure and avoid "home cures" not prescribed or at least approved by your own physician.

• Don't postpone conventional treatment or abandon an ongoing program to patronize an unconventional course of therapy.

9

YOUR TRANSPORTATION—
BY WHEELS, WINGS, AND WATER

How to Buy a New Car	338
WHAT TO DO FIRST	339
SHOPPING FOR A DEALER	342
THE TRADE-IN	345
How to Buy a Used Car	347
CONSTRUCTIVE RULES FOR BUYING	347
CHECK LIST FOR BUYING A USED CAR	351
AUTOMOBILE BUYING TRAPS—AND HOW TO	
AVOID THEM	358
How to Shop for Auto Options	360
YOU CAN EASILY OVERLOAD	360
RUNDOWN ON KEY OPTIONS	361
SIX WAYS TO SAVE ON OPTIONS	364
Auto Warranties—and How to Compare Them	364
WHAT IS—AND WHAT ISN'T—A WARRANTY?	365
HOW TO SHOP FOR A WARRANTY	367
HOW TO GET YOUR CAR WARRANTY HONORED	367
How to Finance Your Car	368
THE BEST WAYS TO SHOP FOR AN AUTO LOAN	368
CHECK LIST FOR COMPARING CAR FINANCING COSTS	370
The Real Cost of Car Ownership	371
YOUR CAR'S COSTS TO YOU	371
AUTOMOBILE COSTS BROKEN DOWN BY SIZE OF CAR	372
HOW TO SLASH YOUR CAR COSTS	373
HOW TO INCREASE YOUR GAS MILEAGE	374

THE REAL COST OF CAR OWNERSHIP (*cont'd*)
   WHEN SHOULD YOU TRADE IN?   376
   CHECK LIST FOR ESTIMATING YOUR CAR
      EXPENSES   378
HOW TO STRETCH YOUR TIRE DOLLAR   378
   TIRE BUYING RULES   379
   TIRE TRAPS—AND HOW TO AVOID THEM   380
   RUNDOWN ON TIRE TYPES   382
   WHICH IS LEAST EXPENSIVE FOR YOU?   382
   SNOW TIRES   383
   FINAL HINTS   384
HOW TO INSURE YOUR CAR   385
   NO-FAULT AUTO INSURANCE IS HERE   385
   HOW YOU CAN SLASH YOUR INSURANCE COSTS   386
   IF YOUR INSURANCE IS CANCELED   389
   IF YOU'RE A BAD RISK   390
THE BAFFLEGAB OF AUTO INSURANCE   391
HOW TO INSURE YOUR MOTORCYCLE   395
   FATAL FACTS   395
   HOW COSTS COMPARE   396
HOW TO CURB YOUR AUTO REPAIR BILLS   397
   A MONSTROUS DRAIN   397
   HOW TO SHOP FOR AN AUTO MECHANIC   398
   HOW AND WHERE TO SHOP FOR BIG-TICKET
      REPAIRS   401
   MOTOR REPAIR MYTHS   403
   THE QUICK AND DIRTY TRICKS AWAY FROM HOME   404
   HOW TO AVOID THE TRICKS ON A TRIP   405
HOW TO CUT THE HIGH COST OF ACCIDENTS   406
   THE DRIVE FOR SAFETY   406
   HOW TO REDUCE YOUR ODDS ON AN AUTO
      ACCIDENT   407
WHAT TO DO IF YOU ARE IN AN ACCIDENT   407
   HOW INFORMED ARE YOU?   407
   KEY RULES   408
   ACCIDENT REPORT FORM   411
HOW TO FOIL CAR THIEVES   413
   BASIC WAYS TO PROTECT YOUR CAR   413
   IF YOUR CAR IS STOLEN   415

How to Save on Your Parking Charges 416
    parking: can be huge cost 416
    ten ways to save on parking charges 417
What About Renting a Car? 418
    how to tell which is the best deal 418
    rules for comparison shopping 420
By Air—"It's the Only Way to Go" 421
    bargain air fares 421
    charter flight bargains 422
    rules for buying charter flights 423
"Leave the Driving to Them" 423
    travel tips 424
Amtrak: Railroads into the Twentieth Century 425
Recreational Vehicles 426
    which type for you? 426
    shopping guides 427
Boats and Bikes 428
    boats for fun 428
    buying a used boat 428
    tips for buying bicycles 430
Enough! 433

Americans of all ages today are carrying on a love affair with mobility. And our love affair goes way beyond the obvious automobile. It also embraces airplanes, buses and trains, motorcycles, campers and snowmobiles, boats and bikes, even horses!

In the mid-1970s we owned at least 112 million cars, trucks, and other vehicles—more than one vehicle for every other man, woman, and child in the United States. More than two out of five families owned two or more cars. Fewer than one in five American families today are without a car.

Every year Americans drive more than *1 trillion* miles, the equivalent of more than 5,000 round trips between the earth and sun. For many, a car is almost a "second home."

Moreover, transportation—notably cars—is the second biggest item in today's American family budget. In fact, if you match merely the *average* moderate-income U.S. family right now, you are earmarking a fantastic 14¢ to 15¢ out of every spending dollar just to buy transportation —primarily by auto and plane. You are spending more than $70 billion a year just to buy fuel, insure, park, and care for your automobile.

I'm taking for granted, therefore, that you know something about buying and insuring a car.

But no matter what the extent of your car dealing has been, I'll also wager you are not fully aware of the great savings you can achieve in your car buying, insuring—and repairing.

How to Buy a New Car

You are in the market for a new car. How do you choose a reliable car dealer? When is the best time of the year to buy? Which accessories are worth the extra cost? How can you tell whether or not you are getting a fair deal if you're trading in your old car?

WHAT TO DO FIRST

(1) In advance, set a maximum price you are willing and able to pay for the car—everything included.

If you are a family with average income and expenses, plan to hold your monthly payments on a car you are buying over a period of three years to one half or less of your monthly housing costs (mortgage and taxes *or* rent). The average amount paid for a new car in the mid-1970s was more than $4,400, and after deducting trade-in allowances, the average dropped to $3,000.

Here was the general price range of most models in various car sizes:

Subcompact (or mini-compacts): between $2,800 and $3,200 (subcompact station wagons cost $150 to $300 more than sedans).

Compacts: between $3,200 and $3,600.

Intermediates: between $3,400 and $4,100, an average of $400 to $500 more than compact cars.

Big four-door sedans: between $4,400 and $6,500.

Station wagons: between $3,600 and $6,000, or $400 to $700 more than a comparable four-door sedan.

Specialty cars, primarily "sporty" cars: between $3,500 and $8,500, with some of the super muscle cars now up to $9,000 to $10,000.

(2) Also in advance, decide in some detail what kind of car you want.

This includes make, size, body type, engine, transmission. Will the size you choose meet your actual family needs, including those of growing children? Is the price within your automobile budget? Are you looking for an all-purpose family first car? Or one mainly for your job? Or mainly for long trips? Or just to go back and forth from the railroad station? What kind of weather will you be driving in? In what kind of traffic conditions? How much cargo room do you regularly need—honestly? (Roof racks or rented trailers are more economical for very occasional cargo hauling than an investment in a station wagon.)

(3) Do your homework before you buy.

Among your best sources are: the "Annual Roundup for New Car Buyers" issue of *Consumer Reports,* which includes frequency-of-repair records for popular makes and models, published in April and available at newsstands; the yearly "Buying Guide" issue of *Consumer Reports,* published in December and available at newsstands or from Consumers Union of U.S., Inc., 256 Washington Street, Mount Vernon, N.Y. 10550; *Edmund's New Car Prices* (American makes) or *Foreign Car Prices,* from Edmund Publications Corp., 295 Northern Boulevard, Great Neck, N.Y. 11021; Car/Puter's *Auto Facts—New Car Prices,* from Davis Publications, Inc., 229 Park Avenue South, New York, N.Y. 10003; such auto and motor journals as *Car and Driver, Road and Track, Motor Trend, Road Test,* which compare performance and other aspects of each new model; the results of the Union 76 Performance Trials held early each year. Ford Motor Company publishes "Car Buying Made Easier," which is full of easily understandable information on car buying. For a free copy, write: Ford Motor Company Listens, P. O. Box 1975, The American Road, Dearborn, Mich. 48121. (The box number usually is the year in which you write.)

(4) Use the following abbreviated chart to rate various new cars you are considering buying, and to compare costs:

	CAR 1	CAR 2	CAR 3
Net cash price:	_____	_____	_____
Taxes:	_____	_____	_____
Preparation costs:	_____	_____	_____
Cost of other extras:	_____	_____	_____
Cost of options you want:	_____	_____	_____
Key warranty coverage:			
Miles	_____	_____	_____
Years	_____	_____	_____
Parts	_____	_____	_____
Labor	_____	_____	_____
Other	_____	_____	_____
Expected gas mileage:	_____	_____	_____
Safety features:	_____	_____	_____
Convenience of seat belts	_____	_____	_____
Passing ability	_____	_____	_____
Stopping distance	_____	_____	_____
Tire reserve load	_____	_____	_____
Space:	_____	_____	_____
Ride:	_____	_____	_____

	CAR 1	CAR 2	CAR 3
Frequency-of-repair record:			
Handling:			
Luggage space:			
Passenger space:			
Ease of getting in and out:			
Looks:			
Dealer's reputation:			
Availability of parts, service:			
Efficiency of service:			

(5) Be honest with yourself about how important status is to you, as expressed by an automobile.

If you had to make a trade-off, would you prefer a more expensive model with almost no extras? Or the best of the lower-priced models, with budget room for the extras you want?

(6) Ask yourself how long you intend to keep the car you buy.

If you plan to trade it in after only a couple of years, the traditional summer-fall car bargains (available just before the new models are introduced in the autumn) are probably not a good deal. A car you buy in September will be considered a year old in only a month or so, and its market value will depreciate by one fourth in just a few weeks.

However, if you plan to drive the car into the ground, August and September are definitely the best months to find a bargain. You'll often be offered 5 to 35 per cent below regular prices. Also, if you are hunting for discounts, look at the year's less popular models which the dealer may have had a hard time selling. These may sell 20 to 40 per cent below regular prices. Of course, an ugly duckling may be more difficult to trade in, but if you intend to keep your car for several years that won't be a problem.

(7) Make up your mind what "extras" you really want.

A radio (FM or regular?), air conditioner, white-wall tires, an adjustable steering wheel, power seats and windows, automatic transmission, speed regulator, vinyl-covered roof, remote control outside mirrors, rear window defogger? If the dealer does not have a car with precisely the options you want, he might be willing to give you a good buy on another car with only the options most important to you. Many accessories are simply frills on which you will get no return when you sell or trade.

(8) Consider not only the purchase price of various makes and models but also your probable future gas and maintenance costs. Starting with the 1977 models, new cars must carry stickers listing their gasoline mileage and comparing their costs of fuel per mile with costs of other cars in the same class.

The range of gas mileage on popular cars in the mid-1970s ran all the way from 8 to 30 miles per gallon. A weekly savings of only $5.00 on gas would add up to an average saving of $260 every year you own the car. Check the sticker in the window of the car you may buy, or a sticker like it, for an estimate of the gas mileage you will get. As a general rule, the fewer the number of cylinders, the lower the fuel and upkeep costs—as well as the lower the original price tag.

(9) Time your shopping to get the best deal.

No matter who or where the dealer, there are certain prime times for getting a car bargain. Among them:

Three to four months after the announcement date for brand-new models (generally late September). By this time, winter sluggishness has set in and car buying is at a low ebb, but cars are still rolling off the assembly lines and inventories start to bulge all along the line.

On the last business day of a month, when there is a special promotion (such as "Spring Cleaning Days") which may involve a sales contest among dealers. Cars sold during promotions often produce for a dealer an extra bonus of $100 or even $200, and he may be willing to share part of this bonus with you in the form of a discount to make the sale.

During a blizzard, or after a spell of rotten weather which has reduced traffic in the showroom. Often, dealers find they are short of working cash at these times (business falls off in the service department, too) and will offer big discounts to boost sales.

Of course the very best time to shop would combine *all* of these characteristics. At such a time you might be able to get a car practically at wholesale cost.

SHOPPING FOR A DEALER

Now you have done a reasonable amount of homework. You are ready to start shopping for a dealer.

• Ask your neighbors and friends for guidance on local automobile dealers. Find out not only whether a dealer has a reputation for offering a fair deal but also whether he follows through by delivering the car when he promises to, by reliable servicing, by honoring warranties. How long must his customers wait for routine servicing and for emergency repairs both in and out of warranty? What days—and hours—does the repair shop operate? Saturdays? Any evenings? Will the dealer pick up and/or return your car if you need this type of convenience? Is his advertising honest or does he claim "fantastic savings"?

• Stick to dealers in your own neighborhood. You can reach them easily and they can't duck you easily. If, though, you choose to buy a new car from a dealer some distance from your home, try to estimate what it would cost in fuel alone to go back and forth for repairs, servicing, warranty work. Don't ignore the cost of time lost from work.

• Also, stick to members of the National Automobile Dealers Association and dealers who are franchised by the major automobile manufacturers (the auto manufacturers will give you the names and addresses of such dealers in your area if you ask for them). The key advantage of dealing with a franchise dealer is that you can ask the manufacturer to put the screws on him if he fails to honor the warranty he gives you, fails to make repairs he has promised, etc.

• Read and compare the warranties offered by each dealer. What does each cover and not cover? Parts? Labor costs? And how long does each warranty last? Warning: If problems crop up after you have bought a car, you'll need your warranty to back up your demands to your dealer for repairs. So have the warranty *in hand* before you close any deal.

• Explore with care how much of a discount from the car's suggested list price the dealer offers. Cars rarely sell at or even near their "sticker" prices, although the law requires that stickers be affixed to every new car which itemize the manufacturer's suggested list price, special preparation charges, sales taxes, transportation costs from the factory as well as the costs of already installed extras.

This sticker is not to be removed or altered in any way until the car has actually been delivered to you. Insist on seeing the sticker. It's the major point of price reference you have.

As one guideline on discounts, the dealer's typical markup is $300 to $800 from the wholesale cost of a medium-priced car (to which he already has added taxes, shipping costs, a "preparation" charge, and sometimes a "clerical" or "documentation" charge of questionable legitimacy). This is the "band" within which he'll bargain with you.

A way you can decipher a dealer's discount offer is by figuring out how much the new car actually cost the dealer. Here's a rough guide to the dealer's cost:

Find the total cost (including transportation) from the price sticker on the car window. Subtract the transportation charge. Then take either: 80 per cent of the balance (for a full-sized car); 81 per cent (for an intermediate-sized car); or 85 per cent (for a compact-sized car). Add back the transportation costs. The result comes very close to the dealer's actual cost.

• Inquire about a computerized auto buying service. One called Car/Puter (1603 Bushwick Avenue, Brooklyn, N.Y. 11207) can provide you with either:

(1) An itemized computer rundown on what any given car you are considering buying cost your local dealer, along with basic costs of the options in which you are interested and the "fixed" cost for transportation, taxes, preparation, etc. This analysis could well be worth its minor cost as you negotiate retail prices from dealer to dealer.

(2) Or the particular car you want to buy at a fixed cost of a modest $125 above the dealer's cost, delivered through a participating local dealer.

Among other computerized services are: United Buying Service (1855 Broadway, New York, N.Y. 10023); Masterson Fleet Auto, Inc. (1957 Chestnut Street, San Francisco, Calif. 94123); Nationwide Purchasing, Inc. (14411 W. Eight Mile Road, Detroit, Mich.).

A most important point in going this car-buying route is to nail down firmly—both by direct discussions with the dealer and by inquiries among other people who have bought their cars this way—how the dealer will handle warranty work which he is obligated to perform and future repairs.

• Be sure the dealer gives you a pamphlet containing full details on safety aspects of the car you are buying, now required by federal law. Among the facts you should receive: the car's acceleration and passing ability, measured in the number of feet and seconds it takes the car to pass a 55-foot truck; stopping distance in feet, from 60 miles per hour, both with a light load and with a maximum load; tire reserve load or safety margin (the capacity of tires, expressed as a percentage, to carry excess weight safely, beyond the maximum number of pounds suggested by the manufacturer).

• When you have made your decision to buy, get a written sales agreement which has been approved by the sales manager, and read it with utmost care before you sign. Have all blank spaces crossed out or marked *void* by the dealer. On extra charges for such services as "preparation" or "undercoating" of the car, keep in mind that preparation (an item usually costing between $35 and $150) is included in the advertised retail price of all U.S. cars and undercoating should not cost much more than $30.

And make sure any oral promises the salesman has made to you regarding special servicing or adjustments to the car are included in the sales contract before you sign it.

THE TRADE-IN

If you want to sell your used car on your own, you'll save the cut of $100 or more a car dealer would tack on as his profit. But you'll have to do your own advertising and selling. And you'll have to find out, too, what is a fair price for the car—considering its make, model, warranty status, age, looks, and mechanical condition.

Consider the fact that you may have to pay a higher finance charge on your new car if you sell your old car on your own. If, for instance, you keep your $1,200 used car for a time-consuming sale to a private individual, you'll raise the amount of the new car loan by $1,200. This could boost the finance charge by more than $200 over a three-year period.

Also, if you live in a state where trading an old car for a new one reduces the sales tax on the new one (you pay sales tax only on the cash amount you pay the dealer), recognize that you'll have to get a higher price from an individual to make up the loss of this saving. For instance, the sales tax saving from trading a $1,200 car in a 6 per cent sales tax state would be $72; you would have to get $1,272 for the car on the open market to get a deal equal to a trade-in.

Do not depend on one dealer or two, or the man at your local service station, to quote you an accurate asking price for your car.

Do not regard a dealer's proposed trade-in allowance toward the new car he wants to sell you as necessarily a reliable guide to the market value of your old car.

Use the information sources listed in the following section, "How to Buy a Used Car," to help you arrive at an objective evaluation of the car you want to trade.

Before you even discuss a trade-in, follow this procedure: first check the approximate market value of your old car; next, ask the new car dealer how much the car you want would cost if you paid cash; *then* ask him what it would cost with a trade-in of your old car. Get both quotations in writing.

If the *trade-in is less* than you would get from a used car dealer, you probably will want to sell the old car on your own and take the cash deal. What's important is *not the "allowance" off the new car's list price that the dealer will give you* for your old car, but the *balance* you have to pay. Repeat the process with other nearby dealers and compare the total package offered by each for *total* charges on the same (or similar) car, the same options, and the same warranty.

If you do decide to trade your car or sell it on your own, these do's and don'ts will help you get a better price.

Do:

wash the car;
polish it;
touch up paint and chrome;
clean stains from upholstery;
vacuum the interior;
wash floor mats;
clean out trunk, glove compartment, and other storage areas;
check all fluid levels (gas, water, oil, transmission and brake fluid) to insure proper operation during a test drive;
check tires and adjust pressures;
replace any burned-out light bulbs.

Take off equipment that might arouse the suspicion that you have used the car for racing or have abused it in other ways: special hubcaps, decals, fender skirts. These racy accessories may tend to drive away instead of bring in buyers.

In addition to using the obvious classified ads in local or regional newspapers or shopping throw-aways, try all free or inexpensive methods of advertising when you put your car on the market: word of mouth, notices on bulletin boards, classified ads in company newspapers, a prominent sign on the car, a "trading post" announcement on your local radio station. Be sure to include times and telephone numbers at which you can be reached by prospective buyers.

When you arrange meetings with possible buyers, try to accommodate their preferences for times. Be honest, but not apologetic, about your car. Do not permit a demonstration drive if your car is not insured for other drivers or if the prospective buyer cannot show you his driver's license.

Be firm about the price, assuming it is in the "book value" range. You may come down to a lower price if the buyer looks right, but don't begin by indicating the price is flexible.

If a buyer needs time to arrange financing, insist on a binder payment of 5 to 10 per cent of your asking price before you agree to hold it for him. And accept payment only in the form of cash or a cashier's check.

Don't:

invest in a new paint job—it will only cost money and raise suspicions in a potential buyer's mind of what you may be trying to hide;

invest in major repairs—it's too late for them, and you will be able to recover only a small fraction of their cost;

spend money on little details a potential buyer well may shrug off: a clock that doesn't run, a window that sticks, that sort of thing.

How to Buy a Used Car

CONSTRUCTIVE RULES FOR BUYING

The used car business in this country is loaded with frauds and misrepresentations—as well as with a wondrous array of entirely legal ways to inspire you to spend a lot more money than you had planned or can afford in order to put yourself on wheels. Just how loaded and how wondrous you'll glimpse in the following section on used car traps and guides for side-stepping them.

To begin with, though, here are the constructive rules for buying a used car:

• Choose a used car dealer only after thorough investigation. Look for one who is a member of a local, state, or national car dealers' association. Query friends on their experience with local dealers and follow their recommendations. Don't go too far from home, or servicing problems could become a real nuisance. Study dealers' ads in your local newspapers and on local TV programs. Are the ads *reasonable* and *believable* to you? If not, don't deal. Also, check with your local Better Business Bureau, which is likely to have a bulging file of complaints on certain local used car gypsters and deceivers.

• Check your local new car dealers to see whether they also have their better trade-in cars for sale—frequently backed by warranties they are prepared to honor in their service shops (they usually sell their lemons to used car dealers).

• Avoid, if possible, shopping for a used car during the peak summer season when millions of other Americans are competing against you to buy a used car for vacation travel.

• Consider as *part* of the purchase price the total finance charges, immediate repairs for which you know you must pay, optional equipment, sales and other taxes, insurance. But *don't,* when you approach a dealer, announce that you have, say $750 and want to know what he has in that price range.

• Choose—if you are trying to find the best bargain in strictly dollars-and-cents terms—a relatively recent compact or other lower-priced model with comparatively few complicated extras over an older, higher-priced model with a lot of extras. The latter well may mean stiff repair costs later.

• Consult the National Automobile Dealers Association's *Official Used Car Guide* or, on the West Coast, *The Kelly Auto Market Report* (*Blue Book*), listing current average retail car values for most U.S. and foreign models, makes, and years. These guides, which your dealer or the loan department of your local bank should be willing to show you, dramatize the fact that prices for a given car can vary as much as $500, depending on whether its condition is "extra clean," "clean," "fair," or "rough."

• Consult, also, *Consumer Reports,* which regularly rates used cars as well as new ones and can serve as a valuable guide to used car bargains. Get a copy both of Consumers Union's pamphlet entitled "How to Buy a Used Car," which gives details on 20 tests you should run on any used car you are considering buying and of *Edmund's Used Car Prices,* available from Edmund Publications Corp., 295 Northern Boulevard, Great Neck, N.Y. 11021. Also get Car/Puter's *Auto Facts—Used Car Prices,* available from Davis Publications, Inc., 229 Park Avenue South, New York, N.Y. 10003. And look over *Motor Trend* magazine's yearly issue devoted exclusively to used car buying.

• Don't fall for the salesman's well-worn come-on, "I'm losing money on the deal." How could the dealer stay in business if he does that?

• Take into consideration the fact that a new car's value drops about 50 per cent during the first two years of its life owing to depreciation—although on certain imported cars the rate of depreciation tends to be lower because of less drastic year-to-year style changes. This suggests that a well-cared-for two- to three-year-old car may be a good buy.

• Test-drive any car which seems to meet your needs—or get a trusted mechanic to test-drive it for you. Try it out in a variety of traffic conditions; on a dirt road as well as a paved superhighway; on a hill as well as on the level.

• Hire a mechanic or diagnostic clinic to check the motor, brakes, clutch, transmission, other vital parts, and expect to pay $15 to $25 for this service—well worth it, even if the check results in your *not* buying the car.

• Ignore the odometer reading—despite the fact that turning the odometer back to zero or otherwise tampering with it is against the law. *A better gauge* of how many miles a used car has been driven is to multiply its age by 10,000 to 15,000 (miles per year). Check the driver's seat for wear. Does the mileage on the odometer equal interior wear? If not, be suspicious of the odometer.

• Heed these guidelines and clues to how much a used car has been used:

The original tires on a car which has been driven 15,000 miles or less will still have good tread. But by 25,000 miles the tread will probably be well worn. As a clue to whether or not the tires are the originals, check to see if all four are of the same brand and similar serial numbers.

At 25,000 miles, the battery may have been replaced. Look for a sticker with a guarantee date.

At 30,000 miles you'll see considerable wear on the brake pedal, and if this or the floor mat has been replaced the car probably has gone more than 40,000 miles. Also at 40,000 miles you may be able to detect a brake pedal wobble.

Another clue to a car's age is its most recent service stickers, giving the mileage at the latest lubrication and oil change. If these have been torn off, that alone should beg the question: "Why?"

• Although most used cars are sold "as is," try to get a guarantee that the dealer will pay in full for all necessary repairs within thirty days of the time you purchase the car. Or perhaps you can get a written guarantee that will protect you against major repairs, or a pledge that the car will pass state inspection. If you do settle for the more typical fifty-fifty deal in which the buyer and seller share the repair costs for the first thirty days, keep in mind that a wheeler-dealer might try to double the repair charges so that you would end up paying the full cost instead of half.

• Ask a dealer if he will give you the name and address of a car's previous owner (some will)—and query this person on possible problems, defects, or advantages of the car. If the former owner turns out to be a traveling salesman, this could serve as a warning to you that the car may have been driven an unusually large number of miles. Or it could turn out to be the proverbial "little old lady."

Important note: In some areas, a contract to buy a used car is not binding if you are unable to move it off the lot—even if you have bought a car "as is."

• Do not assume that because a used car bears an inspection sticker it's in good mechanical fettle. Normally, state inspection laws cover breaks, steering, tires, horn, windshield wipers, headlights, brake lights, etc.—but the laws do *not* cover in any sense the condition of the engine or transmission. And in many states it is easy for a dealer to get a sticker from a friendly mechanic who has made only a cursory inspection. The dealer himself may even have an inspection license in states where private mechanics hold state inspection licenses.

• If you buy a used car from a private individual, try to pay no more than $100 over the wholesale price. And try to get a money-back guarantee to cover you if the car fails to live up to the way in which it was represented to you.

• See if you, as a buyer of a recent-model used car, can have the warranty transferred to you. You can *if* there is documentation of the date of delivery to the car's original owner.

• Make notes on each car which interests you—including the year, make, model, and vehicle identification number—so you can identify it if you return to the dealer. Take a notebook along when you inspect cars on each lot and when you test-drive.

• Compare the deals offered on a comparable car by several local dealers and choose the best for you.

• Then shop among local lenders for the best financing terms as carefully as you shopped for the car itself. The rules on financing follow later in this chapter.

CHECK LIST FOR BUYING A USED CAR

The following check list for buying a used car is exhaustive. With it at hand, it would be difficult for you to go wrong! The guide is adapted from *Family Financial Education for Adults* and was prepared by L. W. Erickson of the Graduate School of Education, University of California.

I. Preliminary Check on the Lot (Exterior)

    A. Paint
        1. Is it faded, scratched, pitted, or peeling? Does it need repainting?
        2. Pry up rubber on door edges; look for difference in paint. Check for accidental paint spray on moldings. If car has been repainted, look for other signs of overhaul.

    B. Body
        1. Look to see if sheet metal is dented or scratched in several places.
        2. Probe door bottoms and fender joints for signs of rust. A "rusted-out" car has little value.
        3. Look for paint overspray or damaged metal on underside of trunk lid. (Lid may have been wrecked.)
        4. Open and close all doors to see if they are sprung or sagging.
        5. Check fit of hood and trunk lid to see if they latch easily.
        6. Check door handles for looseness, indicating hard use.

    C. Glass
        1. Is windshield cracked or scratched by wiper blades? A damaged one may fail state inspection.
        2. Work windows. Note whether excessively loose or stiff.
        3. Check vents and windows for cracks.

    D. Chrome
        1. Are bumpers and molding rusted or pitted?
        2. Molding missing or loose?

3. Bumper bent, crooked, or loose?

4. Grille badly damaged or rusted?

E. Tires

1. If car's mileage is said to be less than 20,000 all tires should be of the same make, similar serial numbers—and evenly worn. If they are not, mileage is probably over 20,000.

2. Measure tread depth. New tires have 9/16 inch, worn-out tires, less than 1/16 inch.

3. Note chafes, tears, and bulges: all indicate replacement is needed.

4. Look for front tires showing uneven wear: means front end is out of alignment.

5. Heavy wear on rear tires could mean "rubber burning" by dragster.

F. Suspension

1. Does car sag on level ground? Could mean one or more weak or broken springs.

2. Bounce front of car. If it continues to bounce when you release it, shocks are worn.

3. Stoop directly in front of car about 20 feet away. If front wheels lean inward at top, they need alignment.

4. Grasp the top of a front tire and vigorously push it in and out. Clunking sound means worn parts in the front-end assembly.

G. Leaks

1. Look under the car near the engine and transmission. Oily spots on the ground indicate leaks that may be costly to repair.

2. See if ground or frame beneath radiator is wet with water.

3. Inspect the inner side of all wheels. Dark areas indicate leaking brake cylinders or grease seals.

H. Chassis

1. Look at the frame for weld marks or heated areas—indicating repairs made after an accident.

II. Preliminary Check on the Lot (Interior)

A. Upholstery
1. Generally dirty?
2. Seats or back rests torn or frayed?
3. Springs in seats sagging?
4. Armrests missing or frayed?
5. Door panels torn or frayed?
6. Overhead lining torn or frayed?
7. Sun visors missing or frayed?

B. Dash
1. Paint scratched or pitted? Car had hard use.
2. Dash freshly repainted? Car may have been a taxi or police car. Reject such cars.
3. Glove compartment door loose, sprung, or won't latch?
4. How is oil pressure gauge? It should read high on starting, then drop to middle of dial at a fast idle as engine warms. If indicator type, light should go out on starting. If gauge isn't normal, engine bearings may be worn.
5. Does fuel gauge register?
6. Check ammeter. It should show charge at fast idle or, if indicator type, light should go out on starting. If not operating there may be trouble in generator or regulator.
7. Is water temperature gauge working?
8. Are light switches broken? Check dome and backup lights.
9. Does ignition switch stick?
10. Are heater and vent controls stiff or inoperative?
11. Is windshield wiper control stiff or inoperative?
12. Check radio, if any. Working?
13. Check clock, if any. Working?
14. Are knobs missing on any dash controls?

C. General
1. Is horn working?
2. Are directional signals working?
3. Is steering wheel safe? Gently rotate it. More than two inches of play before the wheels respond is unsafe.
4. Is seat adjustment stuck or broken?

5. Are floor mats torn or worn?
6. Are pedals worn more than mileage indicates? Or are they new pedals?
7. Is foot switch for dimming headlights working?
8. Does brake pedal sink slowly under steady foot pressure? This indicates a leak in the hydraulic system or worn master cylinder. Check leaks again as previously suggested. Spongy feeling means air in system, needs attention.
9. Open door and look to rear of car while you race the engine. Blue smoke from exhaust means a ring job is needed.

III. Preliminary Check on the Lot (Engine)

A. Engine idling
1. Examine engine for oil leaks or rust on block. Look closer for cracks in such areas. Be wary of a "steam-cleaned" engine. A dirty one will at least show you what might be leaking.
2. Is head cracked or welded? If so, new one is probably needed.
3. Are manifolds cracked or warped? Repairs needed.
4. Is engine idling too fast? Have idle speed reduced, as fast idle can cover irregular engine operation or tendency to stall.
5. Is throttle linkage bent or worn, keeping engine from returning to normal idle after being raced? (Can be dangerous.)
6. Is there sputtering sound when engine is raced? Often indicates clogged jets or worn accelerator pump in carburetor.
7. Is air cleaner missing or damaged?
8. Are there sounds of knocking, grinding, squealing, or hissing? All are potentially expensive.
9. Are there regular clicking noises in engine with hydraulic valve lifters? Could be tip-off that lifters may have to be removed, cleaned, or replaced.
10. Is generator noisy? Signals worn bearings.
11. Are there traces of gas or oil on fuel pump? Diaphragm may be worn.

12. Is water pump leaking or noisy?
13. Is radiator hose leaking?
14. Are there rusted areas on radiator? Or is it leaking?
15. Do you see oil or bubbles in coolant? Could be internal crack in block.
16. When you kneel beside car, do you hear sputtering sounds? Could indicate dangerous pinholes in muffler or loose connection to exhaust pipe.
17. Is tail pipe rusted or kinked?

B. Engine off
1. Is oil level very low? Car may be an oil burner or a leaker. Recheck for blue smoke in exhaust and oil drippings under car.
2. Are there water droplets on oil dipstick? May indicate internally cracked block.
3. Is oil pan dented? Look carefully under recent-model low cars.
4. Is fan belt worn or frayed? On a low-mileage car, a worn belt suggests the mileage has been set back.
5. Is distributor cap or case loose or cracked? If so, replacement is needed.
6. Are ignition wires brittle or cracked?
7. Look for bulging battery case or cell tops, loose or cracked terminals and cell connectors that mean battery is about finished.
8. Remove wire from center of coil and crank engine for ten or fifteen seconds. Starter should turn engine over quietly and smoothly.
9. Listen for clanking sounds or broken teeth on flywheel gear while cranking engine as above. Entire flywheel may have to be replaced.
10. With coil wire still removed as above, crank engine. Uneven cranking may indicate unequal compression caused by a burned or sticking valve.

IV. Road-testing the Car

A. Brakes
1. Is pedal low? Brakes need relining or adjustment.
2. Do brakes pull car to one side when applied?

3. Do brakes grab or chatter, squeal or scrape?
4. Does hand brake hold on hill?

B. Steering
   1. Does car wander or drift from side to side on straight, flat road?
   2. Is there a loose, uncertain feel of steering wheel?
   3. Make a series of "S" turns on a quiet road. Is it hard to steer on quick turns or when parking? Could be a defective pump or merely a slipping drive belt.
   4. Does steering wheel bind on tight turns?
   5. Do front wheels shimmy above 40 mph on smooth roads? Wheels need balancing.
   6. Do front wheels shimmy on rough roads at low speeds? Front end needs work.

C. Standard Transmission
   1. With hand brake set and transmission in second gear, slowly release clutch pedal and depress accelerator. Engine should stall, or clutch is slipping.
   2. Check clutch pedal free play. Pedal should move 1 to 1½ inches before it begins to disengage clutch. If it doesn't clutch, facing may be worn.
   3. Drive a block or more in each speed range and listen for sounds of chipped gears.
   4. Depress the clutch pedal. Lever should move easily into all ranges and there should be no clashing of gears.
   5. Check for slipping out of gear while driving. This means transmission is worn.
   6. Check on noisy transmission. This means bearings are worn.
   7. Check overdrive (if equipped) for operation per owner's manual.

D. Automatic transmission
   1. Is transmission jerky when engaged in low or reverse?
   2. Do shifts take place smoothly?
   3. Does transmission squeal, whistle, or whine? Trouble may be imminent.
   4. Can you hold a park position on a hill?

5. Does selector lever move easily? If not, linkage may be bent or out of adjustment.

E. Rear axle

1. Run car at 20 mph and listen for metallic clanking or grinding noises that indicate wear or damage. You will hear these noises better down a narrow street lined with buildings.

2. Alternately depress and release the gas pedal to jerk the car while in motion. Clicks or thumping sounds mean too much play in power train parts.

F. Engine

1. Reduce speed to about 15 mph in high gear or drive range, then accelerate moderately—not hard enough to downshift automatic transmission. Sputtering, hesitation, or backfiring indicate poor carburetion, valves, or ignition.

G. Wheels

1. Open door slightly on your side and listen for crunching sound of chewed-up wheel bearings. Don't confuse the sound with sound of clicking wheel covers. Remove covers if you are uncertain of origin.

2. Check for bent wheels by watching them while friend or dealer drives car.

H. Frame

Watch car from behind as it is driven; wheels should track.

I. Speedometer

1. Is speedometer working as it should? As measure of speed and mileage?

2. Does needle flutter or vibrate?

3. Is there a ticking or grating sound, indicating a kinked or very dry speedometer cable? If so, it needs oiling or replacement.

V. Final Inspection Back on the Lot

A. Last checks

1. Recheck the engine to see that nothing has opened while on road.

2. Hubcaps missing?
3. Wiper blades missing or deteriorated?
4. Cigarette lighter missing or inoperative?
5. License plate brackets missing or damaged?
6. Spare tire useless, flat, or missing?
7. Jack and lug wrench the correct ones for car?
8. Wheel lugs missing or threads stripped?
9. Radio antenna missing or bent?
10. Keys work in all locks? Check inside door locks.
11. Courtesy lights and switches on door pillars working?
12. Serial numbers agree with dealer's papers? Have dealer rectify any error and prove title before you buy, or you might drive out with a hot car. At a minimum, you will have trouble at state inspection stations.

AUTOMOBILE BUYING TRAPS—AND HOW TO AVOID THEM

Whenever you enter the market for a used car you become a target for one of the slickest groups of high-pressure promoters in our land. And you well may turn into a victim unless you are aware of the pitfalls.

To warn you and guide you, here is a short "dictionary" of today's most widespread car traps, come-ons, and gyps. Read and remember!

Doping. You are told that the used car you want has been completely "reconditioned" and your test drive seems to confirm this claim. But within a few days it develops a host of mechanical problems, for the dealer has used a variety of methods which temporarily—but only temporarily—disguise the car's faults.

The "almost new" car. This may be a bargain late-model "leftover" car which may have been used as a demonstrator. Or it may be a last year's model advertised by mail at the unbelievably low price of, say, $799. The catch with mail order cars is that they often turn out to be repainted taxis, rental, or police cars, etc., which may have been driven 100,000 miles or more. You would not be able to tell this from the odometer reading.

Bushing. Here the new car dealer hikes the price after you have made a deposit—or he lowers the generous trade-in allowance he has offered to keep you from shopping around. You can avoid bushing by insisting on a signed statement promising a refund if the car is not delivered on the specified terms and at a specified time.

Packing. This means heaping extra charges—special fees, exorbitant finance-insurance charges, the like—on top of the purchase price. In some cases the dealer gets a rebate from the finance company. Make sure there is no packing *before* you sign any deal.

The bumper or balloon note. In this deal, you pay relatively low installments at the start and a fat lump sum at the end. Although the only deception here is if the dealer fails to tell you about the "balloon" at the end, you are caught if you cannot meet the final payment.

Bait and switch. Cars are advertised in such tempting terms as "below cost," "below wholesale," etc. *But*—and this will be your warning—when you arrive at the lot you find that the advertised car is not available. The ad has been used as bait to get you to the lot, then switch you to another, costlier deal.

Macing. In this racket, you are the victim of a used car dealer to whom you have sold, on your own, your used car, at a favorable price to you. The dealer pays you a small amount of cash and the rest of your purchase price in notes or a postdated check. At its due date, the check turns out worthless. Or, by the time the notes mature, the fly-by-night operator has flown and the notes also turn out to be worthless paper.

Odometer tampering. Although many states and the federal government have laws against turning back odometers, enforcement is difficult. To the expert, it's no problem to crank an odometer back tens of thousands of miles. Use the rules on page 349 to figure out on your own how many miles a car has been driven, and see Part IV, "Your Rights and How to Get Them," or remedies available to you if you have been taken by a dishonest operator.

The highball. This is part of the bushing racket—in which a new car dealer makes a fantastically attractive-sounding trade-in offer and thereby halts your efforts to comparison-shop. However, when it comes time to deliver your new car, the dealer suddenly starts uncovering flaws in your old car—all of which diminish the sum he's actually willing to allow you on it for the trade-in.

The lowball. This is the opposite side of the above trap in which a dealer quotes an unrealistically low price for a new car as "insurance" that a prospective customer will return to his showroom after he has made the rounds of other local dealers. When you return, though, the quote inevitably expands to a more realistic level.

"Would you take . . ." You park your car on a street, go away, and then return to find a card under your windshield wiper which says,

"I have a buyer for your car. Would you take $1,500 in trade for a brand-new ——? Call or bring in your car today." If you follow up, you will discover that the price of the new car has been jacked up so it more than makes up for the overgenerous trade-in offer; or the promised trade-in allowance has been somehow diminished to a realistic sum. This one is pure misrepresentation.

The basic rules for avoiding all of these traps are:

1. Deal only with a respected, reliable dealer.

2. Or shop newspaper ads by private owners for low mileage, one-owner cars, other pluses pinpointed in the preceding pages.

3. Resist the temptation of questionable "bargains."

4. Have a qualified mechanic or automotive clinic inspect any used car you are considering buying.

5. Read and understand any contract before you sign it.

6. Shop among several sources of used cars to find the best deal for you.

7. Try to get at least a 30-day warranty with the dealer responsible for paying in full for all needed repairs.

8. Be sure, if reconditioning has been done, that the warranty spells out the details—and whether the car is guaranteed to pass state inspection.

How to Shop for Auto Options

YOU CAN EASILY OVERLOAD

If you load the new car you buy with optional equipment, you can nearly double the car's cost to you. In fact, if you buy just a relatively few "basic" but expensive options, you can raise the price of your car by one third or more.

Do you really understand what options can cost you? Here's a run-down showing you how fast and how far the basic price you pay for a car can rise under two conditions: (1) you add only today's most commonplace options, such as an automatic transmission, air conditioning, tinted glass on all windows, an AM radio, special interior trim, white-wall tires, a remote-control outside mirror, and power brakes; (2) you load the car with every possible extra.

MODEL	BASE PRICE*	WITH TYPICAL OPTIONS*	"LOADED"*
AMC Gremlin	$ 2,889	$ 3,834	$ 5,932
Ford Pinto	2,976	4,048	6,499
Chevrolet Vega	2,984	4,004	7,804
Plymouth Duster	3,216	4,398	6,648
AMC Matador	3,627	4,824	6,467
Plymouth Fury	3,629	4,669	8,346
Ford Granada	3,797	4,871	9,872
Chevrolet Impala	4,507	5,182	8,080
Chrysler New Yorker	6,641	7,397	10,185
Lincoln Continental	9,277	9,497	17,687
Cadillac Fleetwood	10,586	10,821	17,992

* 1976.

Which options you choose will depend on the relative importance of each improvement to you, of course—but the vast assortment of alternatives is in itself a major buying hazard. How do you find your way around? Which options are the best buys? In the rundown below, note particularly the high costs of operating and repairing air conditioners.

RUNDOWN ON KEY OPTIONS

Larger engine, costing $70 to $500: Move your car around with much more pep and can improve safety when passing or in other situations where you must accelerate rapidly. But they often make a car more difficult to handle on wet or snowy pavement, they use more gas, and an eight-cylinder engine almost always will cost more to maintain and repair than a six-cylinder.

Note: Although most dealers and manufacturers recommend an eight-cylinder engine for any car equipped with an air conditioner and although most buyers go along with this advice, an eight-cylinder engine is *not* necessary to operate an air conditioner properly. Many four-cylinder cars have air conditioners and get along fine. The engine's *horsepower rating,* not the number of cylinders, is the key here; as a general guideline you'll need 15 to 30 extra horsepower to run an air conditioner on a small car, and 30 more horsepower on a larger car.

Automatic transmission, $250 to $350: Makes driving a lot easier, particularly for non-mechanically minded people and in heavy, stop-and-go city traffic. An automatic can often pay for itself by preventing wear which an indifferent driver might put on the engine, clutch, and gears of a car equipped with a manual transmission. Moreover, part of its cost will be returned at trade-in time. On the negative side: the owner of a car with an automatic transmission will probably pay more in repair bills and slightly more for gas than a skilled driver with a manual transmission. Still, for the majority of car owners, a good buy.

Air conditioner, $425 to $640: Considered virtually a necessity in the South, and also popular in many Northern cities where summertime can be sweltering. "Hang-on" units (not factory-installed) and air conditioners installed in foreign cars are currently considered less satisfactory by buyers, according to Consumers Union surveys of car owners. Many models also offer fully automatic, year-round temperature control (for about $75), but such systems tend to be unreliable. Comfort is the primary advantage of air conditioning, but this option also can help find a buyer at resale time.

On the debit side, air conditioners use a significant amount of extra gasoline and need repairs fairly often—more than one in five within a year. This is by far the single most expensive option most people buy and it tends to beget other options too—such as a bigger engine, power steering, power brakes, heavy-duty suspension, oversize tires, tinted glass. Thus, eliminating it could be a major way to save money—if you can manage without it. With or without air conditioning, consider the newly available synthetic fiber cloth-upholstered seats. They are durable and stain-resistant and more comfortable than vinyl.

Power steering, $120 to $140: Makes handling an intermediate- or full-sized car easier, and safer under some circumstances. Most modern power steering gives good road feel, makes parking nearly effortless, and provides quicker steering response on the highway than non-power steering.

Power brakes, $55 to $100: Probably worthwhile on any large car. They don't make a car stop more quickly but they considerably reduce pedal effort.

Tinted windows, $45 to $70: Make an air conditioner's job easier and improve comfort. However, they do reduce the margin of safety of a driver with poor night vision and should be avoided by this type of driver. Some critics claim tinted glass doesn't even help drivers with good vision.

Remote-control outside mirrors, $10 to $20: Nice, but prone to failure. May become non-adjustable by any means when they fail, and repairs can cost more than the option's price in the first place.

AM radio, $70 to $100: Useful for breaking the monotony of long trips, for listening to music, news, traffic congestion warnings, weather reports. Also of some value when you resell. But fancier sound setups (AM/FM radio, tape deck, stereo) return only a small part of their cost at trade-in and are good buys only if *you* get your money's worth while you own the car. Also, the FM part of an AM/FM radio will do you very little good if you live more than twenty-five miles from a major metropolitan area.

Limited slip differential, $50 to $65: Transfers power to the other wheel when one slips. Will be a great help if you do much driving on back roads in winter or spring, but may be a mixed blessing if you are primarily a highway driver. A more expensive ($105) anti-wheel spin option is available on some luxury cars.

Rear window defoggers, $40 to $100: Most don't work as well as windshield defrosters, but in areas with much cold or damp weather any help at all improves safety considerably. Thus the best rear window defogger you can get is probably a good buy.

A vinyl roof, $75 to $170: May have beauty in the eyes of some beholders, but its practical advantages are nil. A black one makes a car hotter, just about offsetting the effect of tinted windows and increasing the gasoline consumption of an air-conditioned car; may delaminate from the underlying metal; is expensive to repair.

Power windows, $95 to $170: Pleasant luxuries. All are failure-prone and expensive to repair. Power windows also can be a safety hazard with children.

Most "heavy duty" optional components such as springs ($20), shock absorbers ($5.00), battery ($15), alternator ($10), radiator ($15), cost relatively little and more than repay their cost if you own a car more than a year or two. The major exception to this might be a heavy-duty suspension, if the ride is stable enough without it and you generally drive with your car lightly loaded. Test-driving cars with both types of suspension will help you determine this.

SIX WAYS TO SAVE ON OPTIONS

Now here are six general tips on how to save money on options when you buy your car:

(1) Have firmly in mind the use to which you expect to put your car and try in your mind to rate the options according to how much each will add to the capacity of *your* car to perform adequately for *you*.

(2) Put together a personal shopping list of options before you go to the showroom. Do not permit yourself to be dazzled by the overwhelming array of improvements available. *Edmund's New Car Prices,* which lists all the options offered on the new cars in the market and roughly what amount you can expect to pay for each, is one good place to do this homework.

(3) When choosing engines, at least specify one that will run on regular fuel. All but a very few models—small or large—offer regular fuel engines. The performance advantage made possible by engines requiring premium fuel is so slight that it is important only in racing; premium gas, though, costs about 10 per cent more than regular.

(4) Choose options which contribute to durability; avoid those which add to complexity.

(5) Be willing to wait until exactly the car you want can be shipped to your dealer—even though the wait may be as long as several months. Don't waste money on taking some overequipped car he may have in stock. Caution: This may be difficult to do in late summer, early fall, when all the emphasis is on the next model year. But by sticking to your own shopping list and buying only the options you need and you choose to buy for your car, you'll slash the automobile's cost to you.

(6) Be sure to have all options installed by the factory when you buy the car. Later installation can be costly. For instance, say you later decide to install an electric clock, which would have cost $14 at the time of purchase. A dealer might charge you well over $30 for this same clock if he had to install it.

Auto Warranties—and How to Compare Them

Do you, the buyer of a new car, know how long the warranty on the car will last? And whether it covers parts, labor, or both?

Do you know how often you must have the oil changed in order to keep the warranty valid?

Do you know whether or not you must use a certain grade of oil and/or type of oil filter to fulfill your part of the warranty?

You may know the general terms of your warranty, but it's highly probable you know little or nothing about the details, the disclaimers, the exceptions.

Yet the warranty, a promise of quality and safety of a car, can be critically important to you—for better or for worse. It can be worth cash in your pocket: car manufacturers estimate that they spend about $120 per car on warranty work over the life of the warranty. You, the car owner, would spend considerably more than this if you had no warranty protection at all: auto manufacturers pay dealers less for repair work than dealers charge their customers for non-warranty work. And when the time comes to sell or trade your car, you may get an extra $50 to $200 for it if the warranty is still in force: the amount will depend on the make, model, and age of the car.

WHAT IS—AND WHAT ISN'T—A WARRANTY?

Just what *is* an automobile warranty—and, even more important, what *isn't* it?

A *warranty is* a pledge made by a seller of an automobile to a buyer. Legally it is part of the sales contract and if the promise of the warranty turns out to be false this invalidates the entire sale.

A *written warranty,* such as the one you get with a new car, is called an *express warranty.* Usually it describes what the seller is obligated to do for you, in terms of repairs, etc., and also what you, the buyer, must do to keep the warranty valid.

An *implied warranty* is an unwritten (but legally binding) promise the seller makes to a buyer simply by the act of selling. It guarantees "merchantability" and "fitness for purpose." Merchantability simply means that the product being sold is what the seller says it is: what everyone considers a car to be. If, for example, a dealer from whom you agreed to buy a Ford sedan instead delivered a tractor to you, that would be a breach of the "merchantability" aspect of the warranty. Fitness for purpose promises that the merchandise will perform the function that it ordinarily would be expected to perform, or that the buyer and seller have agreed it will perform. A car which just won't go more than ten miles an hour would flunk the "fitness" test.

Many warranties specifically disclaim the implied warranty—with a statement such as "This warranty is expressly in lieu of any other express or implied warranty, condition or guarantee on the vehicle or any part thereof, including any implied warranty of merchantability or fitness, and of any other obligation on the part of the manufacturer or dealer."

A *typical auto warranty* in 1975 covered all parts of the car—except tires and batteries—against defects of materials and manufacturing for 12,000 miles or twelve months, whichever comes first. Some warranties covered, in addition, the engine and drive train (the collection of parts which transmits motion from a car's engine to its wheels). Specifically, this type of warranty includes the engine block, head, internal engine parts, oil pan and gaskets, water pump, intake manifold, transmission, torque converter, drive shaft, universal joints, rear axle, and internal parts—for 24,000 miles or twenty-four months, whichever comes first.

Some cars equipped with premium batteries carry a battery guarantee for 12,000 miles or twelve months.

Tires are warrantied separately by their manufacturers. The terms of tire warranties vary widely, and you may not even be able to obtain a copy of the warranty on the tires which come with your new car.

Although major improvements are being considered and may be on the way, virtually no warranties cover:

repairs beyond the stated period;

repairs if you have not taken certain specified maintenance measures;

your loss of time while your car is laid up;

additional damage caused by a defective part;

defects which a dealer finds he *cannot* fix (almost certainly he will also refuse to replace your car);

"adjustments";

"normal maintenance items" such as installing spark plugs, points, condenser, fan belt;

your satisfaction: no automobile warranty guarantees that *you* will be satisfied.

Used car warranties, if they exist at all, are even more limited than warranties on new cars. Ordinarily the term of a used car warranty is only thirty to sixty days, and often the buyer must pay 50 per cent of the cost of any warranty repairs.

Watch out for extravagant mileage claims often made in used car warranties. The 10,000-mile part of a warranty advertised as good for 10,000 miles, or thirty days, whichever comes first, is obviously just about meaningless—unless you're planning to crisscross the continent several times just after you buy the car.

However, getting the most out of your warranty protection is primarily up to you. Specifically:

HOW TO SHOP FOR A WARRANTY

Shop for warranties just as you shop for other important features of a car. Most warranties have the same time and mileage limitations, on cars manufactured in any one year, although there may be significant differences if you are shopping among used cars with valid warranties issued in different years.

The majority of manufacturing defects will show up well before the expiration of even the shortest new car warranty, dealers agree. Thus the *exceptions* to the warranty coverage (such as batteries, tires, and "normal maintenance items") and restrictions (such as requirements that you have certain maintenance operations performed at scheduled times in a manufacturer-authorized service shop) are more important than the duration of the warranty.

• Before you buy, find out the dealer's reputation for honoring warranties. This is one of the most crucial "preventive measures" you can take.

• Also before you buy, take a good look at the dealer's service facilities. You may not be able to judge a service shop, but if it is messier or dirtier than others you have seen, this may be a clue that repair work will be sloppy as well. Be prepared for trouble, too, if service facilities comprise less than 60 per cent of the dealer's establishment. Try to see the service manager, even if you don't feel qualified to judge his competence. If he is hard to find now, he will be equally hard to find later.

HOW TO GET YOUR CAR WARRANTY HONORED

If you have a warranty problem, take the steps outlined for you in Chapter 26, "Your Rights as a Consumer," pages 1142–43. These steps

will help you get the proper treatment from the car dealer and manufacturer.

How to Finance Your Car

You have located the car you want to buy and arrived at a fair price.
Now you are shopping for the best possible deal in financing the car—
for I'm assuming that you, like two out of three new car buyers and half
of used car buyers, plan to buy on time. On top of today's steep interest
rates on automobile loans, financing costs also are being hoisted by the
trends toward longer and longer repayment periods (typically, two years
on a used car, three to four years on a new car); lower and lower down
payments (often only 20 per cent); and larger and larger loans (the
other 80 per cent). In the mid-1970s the *average* new car loan was for
more than $3,500. The *average* monthly car payment was more than
$100.

THE BEST WAYS TO SHOP FOR AN AUTO LOAN

Here, therefore, are your best ways to shop for the best deal in financing your car:

• Ask the dealer from whom you intend to buy the car exactly what
financing terms he'll offer. Don't consider *any* deal unless the total financing charges, over the full life of the loan, are spelled out clearly in
writing—including the amount of the cash down payment, the unpaid
balance to be financed, and the true annual percentage cost. This detailed disclosure is required by the Truth in Lending law: be warned if
it isn't made.

• Ignore such slogans as "easy payment terms" until you know exactly what these terms actually mean in dollars and cents.

• Plan to make the biggest down payment you can—if possible, at
least one fourth to one third of the purchase price—and try to repay in
the shortest period you can manage. Of course, your monthly payments
will be larger this way than if you stretched out the loan, but you may
save hundreds of dollars in interest.

Study this stark table showing what you pay in finance charges on a $1,000 loan extended for twelve, twenty-four, or thirty-six months at various rates.

$1,000 Loan

RATE	12 MONTHS	24 MONTHS	36 MONTHS
8%	$ 43.90	$ 85.50	$128.10
9%	49.40	96.40	144.80
10%	55.00	107.50	161.60
11%	60.60	118.60	178.60
12%	66.20	129.80	195.70
14%	77.40	152.30	230.40
16%	88.80	175.10	265.70
18%	100.20	198.20	301.50
20%	111.60	221.50	337.90
24%	134.70	268.90	412.40
28%	158.10	317.30	489.10
32%	181.70	366.70	568.00
36%	205.50	417.10	648.90
40%	229.70	468.50	732.00

• Once you have the facts on financing a car through your car dealer, visit your local bank or, if you belong to one, your credit union. Ask the loan department what terms the bank or credit union will offer. Make sure such variables as the down payment you intend to make and the period (in months or years) during which you will repay the loan are the same when you compare each lender's terms.

In general, the most expensive sources of automobile credit are new and used car dealers, the automobile finance companies which often work with them, and small loan companies. The least expensive sources are credit unions, which usually charge the lowest rate of true annual interest and which tend to lend relatively large amounts toward purchase of new or used cars; commercial banks, which charge auto loan interest rates generally comparable to those of credit unions; and your life insurance company, if you have a policy with a cash value against which you can borrow at the lowest rate of all.

By all means, put up collateral—securities you own or other assets or a savings passbook—if this will reduce the net cost of your loan to you.

• Find out what provisions are offered by each lender for prepayment of the loan. Will you get a full or nearly full refund of finance charges if you are able to repay the loan more rapidly than you have planned? Is there a penalty for late payments? What are your rights in the event of repossession—such as fair warning before this takes place? Does the contract include an "acceleration clause," making all payments due immediately if you fail to make a payment on time?

• Shop for automobile insurance separately. Don't merely accept the package offered by an automobile dealer, for very possibly you will find that your regular insurance agent will offer the same coverage at a lower cost. Avoid being pushed into a costly credit life insurance provision. This would pay off the car loan in the event of your death, but the cost of credit life insurance tends to be relatively far greater than that of your regular life insurance—which should be sufficient to pay off your smaller debts.

CHECK LIST FOR COMPARING CAR FINANCING COSTS

Here's a check list which will show you how to figure and compare the dollar cost of financing your car:

	Lender A	Lender B	Lender C
Price of the car, including taxes, options, and all other extras			
Minus down payment			
Minus trade-in allowance			
Amount to be financed			
Amount of monthly payment			
Number of monthly payments			
Total amount of monthly payments			
Total dollar cost of auto loan			

THE REAL COST OF CAR OWNERSHIP

YOUR CAR'S COSTS TO YOU

How much does *your* car cost *you* to own and operate?

Here are facts and guidelines to use in making your own personal calculations:

Car ownership costs are basically of two kinds: *Fixed costs,* which are independent of the amount of driving you do; and flexible, *variable costs*—or operating costs—which depend on the number of miles you drive your car. Both depend on the type of car (and trimmings) you buy in the first place. You can figure the real cost, per mile, of running your car by dividing your *total* fixed and flexible costs by the *total* number of miles you drive over any period of time you choose.

Here are your *fixed costs:*

• *Depreciation,* or the amount of value a car loses as it becomes older: As a rough guide, a car depreciates by 30 per cent of its value during the first year you own it; 18 per cent the second; 14 per cent the third; 11 per cent the fourth; 8 per cent the fifth; 6 per cent the sixth; 5 per cent the seventh; and about 2 per cent each year thereafter. Some small imports, though, depreciate only 25 per cent in their first two years.

For non-mathematicians probably the easiest way to find out how much your car actually has depreciated is to look up its wholesale value in the National Automobile Dealers Association's *Used Car Guide.* Simply subtract the figure you find in this guide from the price you paid for your car.

• *Insurance:* These costs may range from less than $100 a year for a good driver of an inexpensive car to $600 or more a year for a young, high-risk driver of an expensive muscle car in a big city.

• *Other fixed costs:*

    Registration
    Purchase taxes (including sales taxes)
    Property taxes
    Financing costs
    Garaging costs

Your *variable costs* include:

> Gas and oil
> Maintenance
> Repairs
> Accessories and parts
> Tires
> Tolls and parking expenses

If you attach a dollars-and-cents figure to each of these categories of car ownership costs, I'll wager that the total will astound you.

AUTOMOBILE COSTS BROKEN DOWN BY SIZE OF CAR

Let's say you are deliberating over what size car to buy. You really need a standard-size car for your size family but don't know how much more it would cost in terms of gas, oil, etc. than a compact or subcompact.

Here is a rundown on the various costs of each size car over a 10-year life of the car by the Federal Highway Administration. The comparisons are for the 1975 models.

EXPENSE	STANDARD	COMPACT	SUBCOMPACT
Depreciation	$ 4,864.00	$ 3,830.00	$ 3,189.00
Repairs, maintenance	3,664.13	2,961.00	2,659.97
Replacement tires	448.00	387.20	350.00
Accessories added after purchase	91.50	86.00	89.00
Gasoline	3,193.32	2,280.94	1,651.72
Oil	169.60	169.60	154.23
Insurance	1,678.00	1,594.00	1,511.00
Garaging, parking, tolls, etc.	2,208.80	2,108.80	2,108.80
Federal and state taxes and fees	1,561.61	1,143.92	924.63
10-year Total	$17,878.96	$14,561.46	$12,638.35

The standard-size car will cost you 17.88¢ a mile over its 10-year life; the compact will cost you 14.56¢ a mile; the subcompact will cost you 12.64¢ a mile.

HOW TO SLASH YOUR CAR COSTS

How can you slash these costs?

• When you *buy,* choose the smallest car available which will still meet your needs. The annual cost of operating a car is estimated at 35¢ a pound—one good indication of your potential savings.

• Postpone owning a second car as long as possible. Owning two cars can nearly double your over-all automotive expenses.

Although keeping the car you already own for a second car instead of trading it in hardly seems a wild waste of money—you already own it so it's "free," isn't it?—this can, in actuality, be a real extravagance.

Your insurance costs will be considerably higher no matter how you handle it; your maintenance, gas, and repair costs will be way up if only because you just naturally drive two cars more than one; you'll spend more for license fees and other trivial but still real costs, of course. And since you'll not have the old car to trade in, you'll have to use money to purchase a new car that otherwise could be invested to be earning interest or dividends for you.

• Give your new car a gentle breaking-in period. While many manufacturers will tell you it doesn't need it, what they may mean is that today's cars don't need as much breaking-in care as they did in the past. But by avoiding fast starts, holding your speed down to 55 or 50 mph, and frequently varying the speed at which you drive for the first few thousand miles, you can prolong the life of your engine.

• Read the owner's manual carefully the first time, and reread it occasionally. Particularly important is the list of recommended maintenance measures to improve efficiency in operating your car. Among the moneysaving tips you may find in your owner's manual is how to avoid "overmaintenance."

• Learn the warranty terms well.

• Equip your car properly for trailer towing or carrying heavy loads if you intend to use it this way—including heavy-duty tires, springs, shock absorbers, radiator, and transmission cooler. By thus equipping your car, you'll avoid premature damage to its suspension system and engine.

• Have tune-ups done at regular, appropriate intervals, as suggested in your manual.

At the time of your tune-up, also have your brakes and parking brake checked and/or adjusted or fixed; get a lubrication or oil change; have your automatic transmission fluid checked; have your clutch checked and adjusted; take whatever winterizing or summerizing measures are in order; have your tires rotated; check the list in your owner's manual and warranty for other maintenance moves.

Tune-ups cost from $10 to $50, but since they save you money on fuel consumption and engine wear, they just about pay for themselves. A further payoff is the increased dependability your well-tuned car will provide. The total cost of a good preventive maintenance program usually is less than $75 a year. You can save money by doing tune-ups yourself if you are so inclined. Many of the modern compact cars are designed with this specifically in mind, and their manufacturers offer detailed instructions and inexpensive tune-up parts kits.

HOW TO INCREASE YOUR GAS MILEAGE

You need not be an expert to increase your gas mileage about 30 per cent above the average.

To measure your gas consumption, have your tank filled so you can see gasoline in the filler pipe, record the odometer reading, and drive until the tank is nearly empty. Then refill the tank and again note the mileage reading. Divide the miles you have driven by the number of gallons in the second fillup; this gives you your mileage per gallon. Repeat this process several times to give an accurate result, since variable factors such as head winds can substantially change the mileage you get from a single tankful of gas.

Now:

• Make a habit of driving smoothly and steadily. Jack-rabbit starts gulp gasoline as do high speeds and quick speed changes. The U. S. Department of Transportation measured gas mileage for a typical 4,000-pound car and found that it traveled 11.08 miles per gallon at 70 miles per hour, 13.67 mpg at 60 mph, 16.98 mpg at 50 mph, and 14.89 mpg at 40 mph.

• Keep your tires inflated to two or three pounds above the lowest recommended pressures listed in the owner's manual.

• Don't buy premium gas unless your engine requires it: even some of the fanciest cars today run on regular gas. In fact, except for automobiles with the most powerful engines, all cars will run well on *sub-regular* gas. The average motorist pays $50 to $75 a year on unnecessarily high octane gas. High-test gas costs about 10 per cent more than regular, but it's entirely wasted if the car runs properly on regular. Moreover, using a higher grade than necessary needlessly increases air pollution by lead particles. Your owner's manual tells you what octane rating your car needs.

• In winter, keep your gas tank as full as possible to reduce condensation of water vapor in the tank and the risk of a subsequent freeze-up of the fuel line.

• Instead of wasting gas on prolonged warm-ups in winter, start off slowly and increase your speed as the engine warms up.

• In winter or summer, turn off the engine whenever it is not needed to move the car. A minute of idling uses more gas than it takes to restart. Idling usually uses nearly a gallon of gas an hour, increases pollution, and may clog your engine.

• Don't fall for what one expert calls "additive madness"—the slew of "new," "scientific" products which you simply pour into your gas tank or oil supply or clip onto your motor and which are advertised in glowing phrases ranging from "Run your car half on gas, half on air!" to "Drive up to 700 Miles on a Single Tank of Gas!"

To illustrate, the promoters claimed one typical "mileage booster," costing $3.98, would convert plain air into "high-powered fuel" and save you up to 1,000 gallons of gas a year. The ingenious promotion pointed out that 70 per cent of the gas you put in your car is "wasted" and, to prove it, the ad suggested a simple test: place a wad of cotton on your exhaust pipe and notice how quickly it becomes soaking wet.

But the fact is the moisture coming out of the exhaust pipe is not gas. It's water condensation. The fact also is that, in some cases, independent laboratory tests show the "miracle" additives and gimmicks actually *decrease* the efficiency of gas in your tank. On "gas-saving" products, your best source of advice is your responsible local station service mechanic.

• Aren't there, then, any "aftermarket" items which can really help us get more miles per gallon? Yes:

A first item is a comprehensive shop manual. This will make it possible for you, if you're at all handy, to keep your car in proper tune. Another item is a "vacuum gauge," an accessory which will tell you when you are applying more gas pedal pressure than you need to, consistent with the most economical operation of your car. And one gasoline additive which does have merit in cold, wet winter climates is gas line anti-freeze, which prevents water condensed in your gas tank from freezing and blocking the fuel line.

• Under no circumstances, try to extend your weekend cruising range by having accessory fuel tanks installed in the trunk of your car. A car's trunk is among its most vulnerable areas, and in a rear-end collision a trunk-mounted gas tank might rupture and cause a fire. In addition, Federal Environmental Protection Agency rules make it illegal for an automobile dealer to install an accessory gasoline tank that does not meet present evaporation control standards. The fine could be up to $10,000.

Also, if an auto dealer is found tampering with any of the emission control devices on new cars, the same fine could be the punishment. And if you, the motorist, either remove the devices yourself or have them removed by an independent mechanic you're possibly liable too.

On top of the possible fine, you face a stiff complete engine rebuild bill if you are to gain anything. The reason is that present emission systems are functional parts of the engines and the simple removal of one or two components might actually result in a decrease in mileage or not improve it at all.

WHEN SHOULD YOU TRADE IN?

When is the most economical moment to trade in a car today? This is a crucial but exceedingly difficult question to answer precisely because each of your situations is different. However, if you keep detailed records, here is a way to calculate the answer for yourself:

Each month, total all the automobile expenses you have paid up to that point, including an allowance for depreciation. Divide this total by the total number of miles you have driven. This will give you your average cost per mile to date. Over the life of most cars this average drops steeply at first, then levels off, and finally starts to rise again. The economically "ideal" time to trade in your car is just before your per-mile cost begins to rise.

Normally this point comes between three and six years after manufacture and your purchase of a new car. Other factors, though—such as your car's declining reliability (which can cost you money, too), its appearance and comfort—will enter into your final decision.

Don't make the mistake of trading in your car far too early. As underlined in the section "How to Curb Your Auto Repair Bills," pages 397–406, you probably will not need major repairs until your car has passed the 50,000 milestone—and even then you can slash your repair bills by following the basic rules.

Typically, your heaviest repair bills will come when you have driven 60,000 to 70,000 miles. In the earlier years, your bills mount up to those peaks and in the later years they decline. Because of this decline, it is slightly more economical to keep a car as long as possible—although dependability, comfort, and appearance are important non-economic factors which might lead you to trade in early.

Here are estimates by the U. S. Department of Transportation on annual depreciation, repairs, and maintenance for a car purchased at $4,379 (excluding taxes) and owned over a ten-year period.

YEAR	ESTIMATED ANNUAL DEPRECIATION	ESTIMATED ANNUAL REPAIRS AND MAINTENANCE	DEPRECIATION, REPAIRS, MAINTENANCE COMBINED
One	$1,215	$ 157.05	$1,372.05
Two	748	199.95	947.95
Three	627	414.67	1,041.67
Four	466	548.03	1,014.03
Five	340	406.52	746.52
Six	306	471.46	777.46
Seven	292	704.82	996.82
Eight	292	280.80	572.80
Nine	291	431.20	722.20
Ten	277	49.63	326.63
TOTAL	$4,854	$3,664.13	$8,518.13

Notice that over the ten-year period the depreciation is close to $4,864—the cost of the car. But also notice that your annual depreciation varies, is highest in the early years of your ownership and lowest in the later years. If you traded in this car each year, your depreciation alone would cost you $12,150 over ten years of automobile purchases or ten times the first year's ($1,215) depreciation. If you traded in this model of car every two years, your depreciation would come to five times the depreciation of the first two years ($9,815).

But while your depreciation costs are declining as your car ages, you will note that your maintenance and repair costs are climbing too.

CHECK LIST FOR ESTIMATING YOUR CAR EXPENSES

Here, finally, is a check list you can use in estimating your annual and per-mile automobile expenses: To get the per-mile total, simply divide your annual expense totals by your annual mileage.

FIXED EXPENSES (ANNUAL)   ANNUAL MILEAGE:_____

Depreciation   _____
Insurance   _____
License and registration_____
State property tax   _____
Finance charges   _____
Garage or parking fees _____
Auto club dues, misc.   _____
         TOTAL   _____   Per Mile: _____

VARIABLE OPERATING EXPENSES
(ANNUAL)

Gasoline   _____(Annual mileage divided
                              by miles per gal. times
                              avg. price per gal.)

Oil   _____(No. qts. used times price
                              per qt.)

Tires   _____(Generally 0.4¢ to 0.6¢ a
                              mile)

Maintenance   _____(Generally 0.70¢ to 0.75¢
                              a mile)

         TOTAL   _____ Per mile:_____

HOW TO STRETCH YOUR TIRE DOLLAR

Our annual bill for tires in this country had reached the $6 billion range by the mid-1970s. We are buying replacement tires for our cars at an annual rate of about 150 million. And this is on top of the 55 million tires with which the new cars we buy already are fitted.

If you drive a not untypical 20,000 miles a year—as many of you who live in the suburbs, exurbs, and rural areas do—your annual tire bill for *each* car in the family easily can amount to $100. If you live in an area in which you go through snow tires at a relatively rapid rate during the winter, your bill easily can be even more.

Your tires, and the air inside them, are your most important single item of armor between you and the road—or the telephone pole, or the pedestrian, or the onroaring trailer truck. Ask any professional racing car driver and he'll confirm that the amount of performance *and* protection you get from your car depend to a very considerable extent on the way in which you choose and care for your tires.

Thus, if you fail to shop carefully and if you fail to take proper care of your tires, you will greatly increase your tire costs, year in and year out—not to mention the risks to your life implied by defective, ill-chosen, or abused tires. And if yours is a two-, three-, four-, or more car family, you can multiply your extra costs—and your risks—by this figure.

Do not take your tires for granted.

Do not assume that your tires are safe unless and until you have taken all the steps and precautions reasonably in your power to make sure that they are safe.

Do not assume that the tires which happen to be attached to the new car you are about to buy are really suitable for *your* personal driving habits and needs. These may be fine for the "average" driver but they may not be fine for *you*. And in many ways greater safety translates into greater economy in the long range.

How do you judge a tire which is on sale for $12 against one carrying a $65 price tag?

How can you, the amateur tire buyer, plow your way through the complex language of tire sizes and plies, cords and studs, belts and biases, treads and retreads—to find the best deal? How can *you* cut *your* tire bill without sacrificing any vital aspect of safety?

TIRE BUYING RULES

• No matter whether you are buying tires as an option on a new car or as a replacement for tires already on your car, your *best* guide to the *best* deal is a reputable and conscientious dealer.

This is a fundamental rule in every area of purchasing—as this book surely has underlined by now. A conscientious dealer will make an honest effort to sell you the type of tires best suited to your driving needs. He will make no bones about the cost difference between, say, white-wall tires and plain black ones. He will not try to sell you super-duper (and super-costly) sports car tires if "sporty" just isn't your automotive style. He will honor his tire warranty, which also will save you money in the long run.

In general, the most reliable dealers are franchised dealers of nationally known and advertised brands of tires, large mail order retailers, and established automobile service stations. Probably your best guide to a satisfactory dealer is a satisfied customer; query your car-owning friends about their experiences with tire dealers in your area.

• Shop locally among reputable dealers, service stations, etc., and compare prices. Look for legitimate tire sales they may be having.

• Compare prices *and* warranties. Is mounting included? Sales tax? Balancing? How many miles—or months—does the warranty cover? Is there a lifetime guarantee against road hazards? Today, some manufacturers will pay part of the price of a new tire, if you accidentally run over an old muffler or a beer bottle and their tire does not survive intact.

TIRE TRAPS—AND HOW TO AVOID THEM

• Do not, if it's at all possible, buy tires when you're in a hurry. An unscrupulous tire salesman operating along some desolate stretch of the interstate highway system may ask any price he wants to replace your blown-out tire.

• Steer clear of vague, extravagant performance claims which some tire salesmen continue to make. For example, "Stops 25 per cent quicker." (Quicker than what—a train?)

Or "50 per cent more traction." (Again, than what—ice skates?)

Or "Safety tested at 130 mph." (Just what does that *prove?*)

Such claims are utterly meaningless.

• Look out also for the unscrupulous tire dealer who advertises huge but misleading discounts. As with many other types of merchandise sold through this lure, the "original" prices may be pure fiction. Moreover, with tires, warranties are based on list—not sale—prices.

Thus, when you get a discount from the advertised list price you must discount the guarantee by a like amount.

• Do not permit yourself to be pulled in by such come-ons as "Buy three tires and get the fourth free!" Real tire bargains do exist, and you may be able to find them by shopping carefully. But use your common sense: no profit-minded businessman is going to give anybody a free tire.

The extravagant claims, the misleading bargains, the fictitious price cuts—the above are the main tire traps in which you easily could lose money. But there are other pitfalls.

• When you buy new tires, insist that the dealer register your name and address and the identification numbers of every tire. This is required by federal law to enable tire companies to recall tires in the event a safety defect is discovered. Many dealers, though, continue to violate this law and, as of now, riding herd on the dealer is your *only* way of being warned if you have a potentially dangerous tire.

Tires which are cosmetically "blemished"—have smudged white sidewalls, for example—are *not* safety rejects if they have the initials "DOT" (for Department of Transportation) on the sidewall. Often, they are a bargain for you too if you can find them. But they may be sold with a reduced warranty or without any warranty at all.

Tire designations such as "first line," "one hundred level," "premium," are strictly subjective claims of tire quality. New national tire quality standards now rate tires according to high-speed performance, traction, and tread wear. The best high-speed tires are rated A, while those of minimum acceptable quality are rated C. Traction and tread wear are rated as a percentage of the values attained by a "control tire" built to DOT specifications. These ratings are molded into the tire and appear on a tag which explains the ratings.

Additional objective information is molded into the sidewall of the tire: size; maximum permissible inflation pressure; brand name and manufacturer's code number; composition of the cord; number of plies (sidewall and tread); tubeless or tube type; the word "radial" if the tire is a radial type; and "DOT" when the tire conforms to federal Motor Vehicle Safety Standards enforced by the U. S. Department of Transportation. Information helpful in choosing tires must be displayed on the glove compartment door of your car or in some other easily accessible place. This includes the vehicle weight, seating capacity, recommended cold tire inflation pressure for the vehicle's maximum loaded weight, and its recommended tire size.

A final point: *do not,* once you have decided which tires you want to buy, automatically permit the dealer from whom you are buying to put the tires on your car—*until* you know what he will charge (if anything) for this service. Exorbitant tire mounting fees can wipe out any savings you may have achieved in the tire purchase—and then some. If the charge is more than a couple of dollars per wheel, simply take the job to another service station.

RUNDOWN ON TIRE TYPES

Now, how do you find the best type of tire for *your* budget and *your* driving habits and *your* car? To help guide you through today's maze of jargon and baffling labels, here is a brief rundown on the major types of tires available today:

Bias ply tires: generally the least expensive available, have cords which wrap around the tire at an angle, tend to ride the most smoothly, and handle well at moderate speeds. Their disadvantage is they may wear out more rapidly than other types of tires.

Belted bias ply tires: cost somewhat more than plain bias ply but, to offset this price disadvantage, they wear longer; have a reinforcing belt of glass fiber or some other material running around the tire beneath the tread, which helps to reduce tread scuffing, and thus permits longer wear but at a cost of a somewhat harsher ride.

Radial ply tires: the highest-quality tire available today; have special plies running straight across the treads, tire-chain style, and a stiff belt (sometimes made of steel) beneath the tread; wear long, handle very well, are capable of improving gas mileage by 3 to 10 per cent. Although one of the most costly categories of tires, their quality, safety features, and the "hidden" gas economy they allow make them the top premium tire.

WHICH IS LEAST EXPENSIVE FOR YOU?

Use this rough guide to make your own price comparisons as you shop:

A radial ply tire will last about 40,000 miles.

A belted bias ply tire will last about 25,000 miles.
A good bias ply tire will last 15,000 to 20,000 miles.

You can figure out the tire cost per mile in each category depending on the going prices in your area but you may be surprised to discover that the "premium" radial ply tires are the least expensive—particularly when you include your gasoline savings over a distance of 40,000 miles.

If you do not intend to drive your car this long, though, you may not want to make such a large, long-term investment in expensive tires. Or, if you do not drive a great deal or at very high speeds or with heavy loads, less expensive tires may be the most economical type for you.

The major factors to consider in choosing your tires are: the type of car you drive, the amount of 60 mph (or over) driving you do, the type of roads you ride on, the type of loads you carry in your car, the number of miles you cover during the year, and how you handle your car—in terms of starting, stopping, and cornering.

If yours is a heavier car, if you do most of your driving on superhighways or rough country roads and if you put at least 15,000 miles on your car each year, radial or belted bias tires are probably the most economical choice for you.

If you drive 10,000 miles or less each year and do less than 30 per cent of your driving at high speeds, your best bet probably is a belted bias or a good conventional bias ply tire.

If you are a sports car buff and want optimum performance from your tires, the radial or belted bias types also will be best for you.

If you are driving over rough or rocky roads or carrying heavy loads, you need heavy-duty tires built to take hard treatment. Ask your dealer—and if he cannot or will not answer your questions satisfactorily, go to another dealer who will.

SNOW TIRES

Snow tires are available in all major tire types, and usually cost more than summer tires of comparable quality. In snowy climates, snow tires more than pay for themselves through reduced accident risks and towing charges.

Usually, the open, heavier treads have better traction in snow and mud but build heat and wear poorly on dry pavement, so be guided in your choice of tread style by the prevalence of snow where you drive most.

Most snow tires can be bought with steel-jacketed tungsten carbide studs, usually for $5.00 to $10 extra per tire. Studs significantly improve traction on hard-packed snow or ice but they decrease traction slightly on wet or clear roads or on ice at subzero temperatures. Thus they are *not* a good buy if you do most of your driving in the city or on main roads in a climate where snow does not stay on roads long. Also studs are much more effective on radial ply tires than on any other kind.

FINAL HINTS

You have now decided what general type of tire you want. Your next questions: Should they be tube or tubeless? What size? How many plies? What type cord material?

Buy the size recommended in your car owner's manual or, in the case of snow tires, at most one size larger.

For the majority of uses, two plies of modern cord materials are sufficient. Federal tire standards rate tires according to their load-carrying ability, a far more useful yardstick than a statement of the number of plies. The total load capacity of four tires should be equal to the weight of your car, fully loaded.

Caution: Do *not* combine radial tires with bias ply or belted bias tires on the same axle. If you buy radial tires (or wide tires) buy four if you can; otherwise put a pair on the drive wheels first, and a pair on the rolling wheels later.

Retreaded tires now cost somewhat more than half the prices of comparable new tires. An undamaged casing, properly retreaded, is no more likely to fail than a new tire. And warranties now being offered on retreads are similar to those available on new tires.

How can you buy retreads most safely?

Again, the most fundamental of fundamental rules comes first: *buy from a good dealer, who gets his retreads from a shop which does quality work and inspects used tires carefully before retreading them.*

Have your own used tires retreaded, since you know how they have been used (or abused) to date. Having your own casings recapped costs less than $20 per tire. If you go this route, shop for a good recapping firm. An excellent way to avoid the risks of poor-quality work is to deal with firms which also do fleet work—e.g., for taxi companies or government agencies.

If you deal with a reputable recapper, and *if* the quality of his work is indisputable, you can consider retreads as good as new tires and thus save a substantial amount on your tire bill. Caution: Tires for passenger cars should *never* be retreaded more than once, and a reputable firm will refuse to do so.

Finally, *avoid* the false economy of riding around on near-bald tires—to get the last sixteenth of an inch of wear from them. If you are one of these "economizers," note this warning by the Tire Industry Safety Council: A bald or near-bald tire is far more likely to skid on a wet road than one with adequate amount of tread; *and* a tire with less than 1/16 inch of tread is eighteen times more likely to blow out or be punctured than one with more than this amount of tread. Among the new federal safety regulations covering tires is a requirement that manufacturers include wear indicators which show as smooth, narrow bands across the tread so you can tell when only 1/16 inch of tread remains. Look for this indicator as your tires wear down. After it appears *you are risking your life.*

How to Insure Your Car

NO-FAULT AUTO INSURANCE IS HERE

At last, our monstrous system of automobile insurance is in the process of a complete overhaul. Many of the inequities—e.g., in the insurance rates *good* drivers pay to make up for the sins of bad drivers—are disappearing. What is emerging is a brand-new system in which every insured accident victim is being paid for lost wages, medical expenses, and other direct economic losses—*whether the accident was his fault or not.* The traditional huge payoff for "pain and suffering," often negotiated in costly liability court proceedings, is being scrapped. Taking its place is a nationwide system of no-fault auto insurance, starting with individual state laws and going on to the clear prospect that these laws will become subject to federal no-fault standards. In essence, our automobile insurance companies are relinquishing their roles as punishers of reckless drivers.

HOW YOU CAN SLASH YOUR INSURANCE COSTS

Go over the following analysis with your insurance agent if you have any reason to believe you are not now getting the full advantage of discounts and reductions available to you.

• Decide first what types and amounts of coverage you need; then check the costs of the coverage you want offered through auto dealers and from reputable insurance agents and firms. One good approach is to solicit bids for your business from several reputable insurers. Reason: rates for liability coverage alone can vary by as much as 50 per cent from one insurer to the next in a given area.

Use this chart to make cost comparisons:

COVERAGE	AMT. OF LIMITS	Rates Quoted		
		Co. A	Co. B	Co. C
Liability	.../.../...	___	___	___
Medical payments		___	___	___
Personal injury protection		___	___	___
Uninsured motorist		___	___	___
Collision	...deductible	___	___	___
Comprehensive	...deductible	___	___	___

• Find out if such "extras" as towing and temporary car rental costs are included in each package.

• Check the reputations of dealers for financial soundness in *Best's Insurance Reports* and try to stick to dealers with a *Best's* rating of A or A+. This is only a guideline; many reputable dealers have lesser ratings.

• If you are a student, enroll in a recognized driver training course to qualify for a 5 to 10 per cent premium cut. Nearly 14,000 schools in the United States now offer these courses. In addition, the National Safety Council has launched a "Defensive Driving Course" whose graduates in some states are being offered substantial premium reductions.

• If you are a student age sixteen or over with a high (B or better) scholastic average, you'll be eligible for a "good student" discount of up to 25 per cent. You also may get a substantial discount if you attend a school more than a hundred road miles from home or wherever the family car is kept.

• Explore, if you are a young driver, the possibility of getting a "restricted" policy, using your family's coattails as a form of financial security.

• If you change your commuting habits—switch from a car to a train or bus—notify your insurer at once so he can reduce your premium rate accordingly.

• If you are an older person, ask about special policies and discounts offered by most companies based on your age bracket's good driving record. In many states, the typical discount for drivers over age sixty-five is 5 per cent.

• If you drive your car fewer than 6,500 miles a year, check whether you're eligible for as much as a 10 per cent rate cut.

• If you quit smoking or drinking, find out whether your company offers reductions for non-smokers or teetotalers.

• If you work for a large company or are a member of a union, social, or professional group, check whether you can get low-cost group auto insurance. If not, find out whether a local insurance company will develop this low-cost insurance for your group. This *alone* can cut your own premiums 15 per cent or more.

• Check carefully what's offered by a reputable mail order insurer; savings could run to 15 per cent.

• If the dealer from whom you are buying a car offers you collision or comprehensive insurance as part of the deal (to protect himself or the firm which is financing your purchase), find out whether your local insurance company or agent will offer you a lower-cost deal.

• If you already have health insurance, make sure you are not taking on medical payments coverage which duplicates the coverage in your group or individual health insurance policy. Today, more than four out of five Americans are covered by medical insurance, and some auto insurance policies rule out duplicate payment if your health insurance policy already fully covers you. (On the other hand, you might want to *increase* your medical payments coverage if you regularly drive a group of children to school or fellow commuters to work.)

• If you move from one state to another, inquire immediately about auto insurance rates, for these rates vary widely in the United States today. For example, the cost of $50/$100,000 bodily injury liability insurance on a recent-model Chevrolet Impala four-door sedan driven by a thirty-year-old married man with a clean driving record was $34 in Bismarck, North Dakota, against $126 in New York City. Comprehensive coverage for this same man and vehicle was $50 in Bismarck in contrast to $122 in New York.

• If you're a farmer or rancher and use your car or pickup truck only on and around your farm or range, check on your eligibility for a farmer's auto insurance discount.

• If you're buying a new car, keep in mind that rates on a "muscle" or high-performance car may run 20 to 50 per cent higher than average. If you buy an inexpensive or low-powered car, though, you will be charged a lower-than-average premium.

• If you are unmarried and you insure your car in your family's name, stating that you are the principal driver, you are likely to pay a lower insurance premium than if the car is registered in your name and you are listed as the sole driver.

• If you are a family head, insure all the family cars under the same policy: a second family car generally can be insured at a discount of about 20 per cent on the grounds that two cars in one family are likely to be exposed to less risk than two single cars would be.

• And save by paying your premiums annually.

• Inquire about any less well known discounts which your insurance company might offer—for instance, discounts of up to 20 per cent for models with bumpers that meet certain damage-resistance standards.

• Don't file collision claims which are just over your deductible or you may lose your "good driver" discount.

• Leave your car outside the city limits; your rates won't be as high if you can show you don't bring your car into a city. If you park your car in a garage, tell your agent; this could qualify you for lower rates than regular onstreet parking.

• *But* over and above all the preceding moneysaving hints is this single best way you, the average automobile owner, can slash your auto insurance premiums on your own: *up all* your present auto insurance deductibles.

Typically, the deductible on collision coverage is $100, but considerably higher deductibles are available—and if you sign up for higher deductibles, you'll save substantially on premiums. To illustrate, if $100 deductible collision coverage costs you $50, your cost with a $250 deductible will be only $30 and with a $500 deductible only $23.

Similarly, if full comprehensive coverage now costs you $50, the cost will drop to $28 if you tack on a $50 deductible and to $21 if you up the deductible to $100.

If your car is more than three years old, or a jalopy worth less than $1,000, you may find it's not worth it to carry collision insurance at all.

You also might simply make your coverage a little less comprehensive. Normally, comprehensive insurance protects you not only against fire and theft but also, if you wish, against a whole list of other perils including flying or falling objects, explosions, vandalism, earthquakes, windstorms, hail, water, floods, civil commotions, riots, and collision with a bird or animal. To illustrate the possible savings, if you are now paying a $30 annual premium for full comprehensive coverage, you might pay only $9.00 a year for insurance against fire and theft only.

The important point to remember about automobile insurance is that it is intended to protect you against a financial catastrophe, especially if you do not have other means of protecting yourself against such a catastrophe.

Automobile insurance (and this also goes for other types of insurance) was *never* intended to help you budget. It was never designed to pay for small repair bills for which you ought to be able to budget routinely. Common sense should urge you to trade off a higher deductible for a higher upper range of liability coverage.

A typical car owner carries at least a minimum "10/20/5" (see "Liability Limits," page 394) auto liability insurance policy—the minimum required under state "financial responsibility" laws. (Some states require 15/30/5 or even 20/40/10.) But if you should be found responsible for a fatal accident, the jury verdict against you easily could amount to $50,000, $100,000 or even $1 million and up.

Here, then, is a table showing you the typical—minor—cost of raising your present bodily injury liability coverage to meaningful levels.

COVERAGE	TYPICAL YEARLY PREMIUM COST
$ 10– 20,000	$50.00
25– 50,000	59.50
50–100,000	65.00
100–300,000	70.50

IF YOUR INSURANCE IS CANCELED

You have not had an auto accident and your driving performance generally has been good—but suddenly your auto insurance policy is not renewed. Or suppose you do have a rotten driving record and you're having trouble getting any insurance coverage at all. What should you do?

Countless millions of you have been exposed to the frustrations of these typical auto insurance problems. If this includes you now or in the future, here's what you should do:

If your policy is not renewed, first contact the agent or salesman who sold you the policy and find out why. In many instances the non-renewal may have nothing to do with your driving record. For instance, the agent may no longer be doing business with that company or the company may have withdrawn from your area. You then may find the agent already has switched your policy and you have no problem at all.

If you learn that the non-renewal was for cause and feel this is unwarranted, write the company. In most states an auto insurer is required to provide an explanation if you, the policyholder, ask for it. If the non-renewal is related to a change in your credit standing, you have the right to know the name and address of the credit rating bureau so you can check your credit file and correct any misinformation that may have crept into it.

If you find erroneous information about you or your driving record in the insurer's files, it is essential for your own benefit that you correct it. If, on the other hand, the non-renewal had nothing to do with your personal characteristics, this information will be helpful when you seek coverage from another company.

IF YOU'RE A BAD RISK

Among the strikes against you when you go to buy auto insurance today in addition to your accident or conviction record—if it's a bad one:

> your age—if you're under thirty;
>
> your race—if you're non-white;
>
> your residence—if it's in a city ghetto.

If you're an American under twenty-five years old, and particularly a single American male, you may be paying a penalty of as much as four times the automobile insurance rates being paid by other drivers.

You pay so much more for automobile insurance simply because your age bracket has the highest accident rate in the nation. Traffic accidents, in fact, are responsible for one half of all deaths of Americans between age fifteen and twenty-five.

If you have trouble getting any auto insurance, shop around. Many insurers have companion companies that specialize in insuring those with a higher-than-average risk exposure. If your insurance agent is unable to get coverage for you, apply to the Automobile Insurance Plan. Every state, except Maryland, has an AIP and any licensed agent can handle your application. (In Maryland, the AIP was replaced in 1973 by a state-run agency called the Maryland Auto Insurance Fund.) States usually require companies in the plan to keep bad risks at least three years. Most drivers can get regular insurance after a three-year good driving record.

The rates charged for insurance in the AIPs are the same as those charged in the regular market in some states and are slightly higher— typically, 5 to 15 per cent higher—in others. Drivers with poor records, though, always pay higher rates whether they are in or out of an AIP.

In shopping for high-risk insurance coverage, watch out for the gypsters. Beware of advertised rates which are suspiciously below those charged by other insurers in your area for your risk category.

If you question the legitimacy of *any* high-risk mail order insurer (and note: *most* are legitimate and do offer insurance below rates charged by insurers with elaborate offices and sales organizations), inquire about the insurer's reputation at your State Insurance Department or State Commissioner of Insurance. And check *Best's Insurance Guide* for the record of financial soundness of any high-risk mail order company with which you're considering doing business.

If all else fails, and if your previous policy has been canceled for reasons you consider to be unfair—send a written complaint to your State Insurance Commissioner, with copies to your local Better Business Bureau and also your congressman. And find out what limitations (if any) your state may put on auto insurance cancellations.

The Bafflegab of Auto Insurance

ADJUSTER: Employee or agent of an insurance company whose job it is to help settle auto insurance claims by deciding the extent of financial loss in an accident, and also the extent of the insurance company's liability.

APPRAISAL: Estimate of the amount of loss sustained by a car in an accident—which becomes the basis for a settlement by the insurance company.

ASSIGNED-RISK PLANS (or *Automobile Insurance Plans*): Plans in operation in all fifty states, the District of Columbia, and Puerto Rico, which sell bare-bones protection to drivers who cannot otherwise get liability coverage.

BAD RISKS: Individuals whom the auto insurance industry labels such bad drivers, with such bad accident records or such poor statistical odds of keeping out of an accident, that they are required to pay extra-high insurance premiums—even assuming they can be insured at all through regular channels.

BODILY INJURY LIABILITY INSURANCE: Pays damages and legal costs if your car kills or injures people in an accident and only if the driver of your car is at fault.

CANCELLATION: Termination—by you or by your insurance company—of your auto insurance policy before it actually expires. Rules for cancellation of auto insurance by the company should be spelled out in the insurance contract.

CLAIM: Demand by an insured individual for the amount of his or her loss insured and covered by the insurance policy. A *claimant* is the person making a claim.

CLASSIFICATION: Categorization of insured individuals according to the extent of risk they represent—statistically—to the company. Taken into account are the individual's occupation, age, similar factors.

COLLISION INSURANCE: Insurance which pays for damage to *your car* if you collide with another car or object, or turn your car over. If an accident is clearly the other fellow's fault and if he has liability insurance, his policy probably would pay to have your car repaired or replaced. However, if there's no way to prove whose fault the accident was, or if the other person involved isn't insured, collision insurance helps cover losses.

COMMISSIONER OF INSURANCE (or *Superintendent of Insurance* or *Director of Insurance*): Key official in your state whose job it is to oversee and enforce the state's auto insurance laws.

COMPREHENSIVE INSURANCE: Insurance which pays for damage to your car from a variety of mishaps other than collision, including not only fire and theft, but also damage from missiles, falling objects, larceny, explosion, earthquake, lightning, windstorm, hail, water, broken glass, flood, malicious mischief or vandalism, riot or civil commotion, and collision with a bird or animal. Comprehensive insurance also covers the cost of renting a car if yours is stolen.

CREAM: The best drivers—statistically speaking—and, therefore, also the best auto insurance risks. These pay the lowest premiums and include Americans over age sixty-five, women over age twenty-five, and middle-aged family men.

DEDUCTIBLE INSURANCE: Coverage under which a policyholder agrees to pay up to a specified sum in each claim or accident toward the total amount of the insured loss. The higher the deductible, the lower your premium.

DOC (Drive Other Cars) INSURANCE: Coverage which protects you, the driver, against liability or bodily injury or property damage while you are driving a borrowed car or a company car.

FINANCIAL RESPONSIBILITY LAWS: State laws under which car owners are required to prove they are financially responsible—a requirement most people meet by owning a certain minimum dollar amount of auto insurance. Such proof is required either to register a car or to preserve your right to return to the road after you have had an accident.

FULL COVERAGE: Coverage for the full amount of covered losses, without any deductibles.

GUARANTEED RENEWABLE: Insurance policy which the covered individual may renew up to a certain age (e.g., sixty or sixty-five) or over a certain specified number of years.

LIABILITY INSURANCE: Protection against claims in the event you injure or kill someone else—or damage his property. This insurance covers legal expenses and also protects others driving your car with your permission, and it protects you and members of your family when you drive someone else's car with their permission.

LIABILITY LIMITS: Maximum amount for which you are covered by a given policy—frequently expressed by a succession of three numbers separated by slashes, designating maximum coverage for bodily injury and for property damage. For example, "10/20/5" means insurance protection of up to $10,000 payable to any one accident victim in an accident caused by you; up to $20,000 in protection for *all* victims in such an accident; and up to $5,000 in insurance protection against property damage caused by your car to other cars, other people's garages, etc.

MEDICAL PAYMENTS: Coverage of a wide range of "reasonable" medical or funeral expenses within a year of an accident not only for the car owner but also for reasonable expenses of any other people who are injured or killed in his car. Medical payments coverage also applies to the policyholder and members of his family while riding in or being struck by any other car. Payment is made no matter who caused the accident.

NO-FAULT: Type of automobile insurance under which an accident victim is automatically compensated for part or all of his medical costs, wage losses, and other expenses associated with the accident by his own insurance company, without regard to who caused the accident.

NON-OWNERSHIP AUTOMOBILE LIABILITY: Liability coverage for loss or damage caused by you while you are driving a car not owned by you.

PAIN AND SUFFERING: Vague, albeit very real, category of claim in auto liability lawsuits for financial compensation to cover intangible losses such as fright, mental anguish, emotional shock, etc.

PROPERTY DAMAGE LIABILITY INSURANCE: Insurance which protects you if your car damages another person's property, and if driver of your car is at fault. This usually means the other person's car, but it also can mean Japanese gardens, garages, lampposts, telephone poles, and buildings.

RISK: Insured person or thing. In the case of your automobile insurance coverage, you and your car are the principal "risks."

SAFE DRIVER PLAN: Widely used system under which insurance rates are adjusted up or down according to your own driving record.

SCRAP VALUE: Estimated value of a car which has been involved in an accident if it were sold as junk.

TOTAL LOSS: Car which has been so badly damaged that it is not considered to be worth repairing.

UNINSURED MOTORIST INSURANCE: Insurance, sometimes called family protection, which covers you, all members of your family, and any guests in your car for bodily injury losses when an uninsured or flagrant hit-and-run driver causes the accident. This type of insurance also pays medical bills and income loss due to bodily injury if the insurance company of the other driver, who caused the accident, goes bankrupt. And it covers you and all members of your family who are injured by uninsured or hit-and-run drivers, while you are walking or riding on bicycles. Payments are limited to the required liability minimums in your state. In some states, this insurance does *not* pay for bodily injuries.

UNSATISFIED JUDGMENT FUND: An alternative, in a few states, to uninsured motorist coverage, for this is a fund against which you may file a claim if you are hit by an uninsured motorist.

How to Insure Your Motorcycle

FATAL FACTS

If you're among the nation's 3.5 million-plus motorcyclists—or if you are planning to join this expanding army soon—you'll have to face these facts: You are just about the most unloved driver there is. You will be forced to pay big premiums by insurance companies in order to get liability coverage and you will find it is far less comprehensive than similar coverage for an automobile. You will simply be unable to get certain coverages which are typical for cars—at any price.

The reason motorcyclists are getting so cold a shoulder from the insurers is that the danger of a fatal motorcycle accident is four times as great as the chance of this accident in a car. In the mid-1970s, says the National Safety Council, more than 325,000 motorcycles, motor scooters and motorbikes were involved in accidents each year and thousands of them were fatal.

So far as the insurers are concerned, the under-thirty age group is the worst—simply because the highest rate of motorcycle deaths are found in this group. Nearly seven out of ten motorcycle drivers involved in accidents are between the ages of sixteen and twenty-four.

Motorcycle insurance rates, like car insurance rates, vary from state to state and from area to area within the state, and from company to company too. If you can't get this insurance from your regular auto insurance company, you'll probably have to seek out a company in your area which specializes in this type of insurance.

Insurance coverage for a motorcycle may differ radically from ordinary car insurance. Many liability insurance policies for motorcycles, for example, do not cover passengers on the cycle. Under many motorcycle liability insurance policies, coverage is limited to the owner-driver himself—and doesn't cover any other operators. Also, liability coverage may become invalid if a driver is speeding or racing. In addition, many motorcycle policies exclude coverage for medical payments for injuries to the operator.

It is vitally important to check with your insurance agent to make sure you know just what is and what is not covered.

HOW COSTS COMPARE

Just how much more expensive is motorcycle insurance than car insurance? It depends on where you live, how old you are, what your own driving record has been, and on a number of other factors. But here are a few general hints on how costs compare and how possible savings stack up:

If your cycle has an engine size under 200 c.c., it will cost relatively less to insure than one with a larger-sized engine.

If your cycle weighs 300 pounds or less, the premium for liability insurance coverage in most states will be about 60 per cent of the basic auto insurance rate. (In a few cases it will be only one half the car rate.)

But, if you are an unmarried man under thirty years of age your cost of insuring this motorcycle will be about 150 per cent of the basic auto insurance rate—about the same rate an unmarried man in his mid-twenties would pay for insurance on his automobile.

If your cycle weighs more than 300 pounds you will have to pay double the rate for the smaller bikes—or about 220 per cent of the basic automobile insurance rate.

If you are an unmarried male under age thirty and you are riding a 300-pound-plus cycle, you will have to pay 300 per cent of the basic auto premium rate in order to insure it. This is approximately what an unmarried teen-age boy would pay for insurance on a car.

And what if you can't find motorcycle insurance through normal sources of auto insurance? As with cars, the insurers operate assigned-risk pools in every state for high-risk motorcyclists as well as high-risk car drivers.

How to Curb Your Auto Repair Bills

A MONSTROUS DRAIN

By one estimate, a monstrous $8 to $10 billion of our $25 to $30 billion annual bill for auto repairs and maintenance goes down the drain—in the form of repairs improperly done, repairs unnecessarily performed, or repairs promised and not done at all.

If you are lucky, you won't need any major auto repairs until your car has gone 20,000 miles or more. And many repair bills will be paid for through your warranty. After that mark, though, you well may face a parade of minor repairs: brake relining; reconditioning of brake drums; possibly an alternator overhaul; replacement of cylinders, hoses, shock absorbers, muffler and/or other parts of the exhaust system, battery and numerous smaller parts of the electrical system ranging from headlights to the voltage regulator and ignition coil. You're also likely to be confronted with a variety of problems involving the various pumps —water, oil, and fuel—that help keep your car running.

If you keep your car past the 50,000 milestone, you almost surely will need some major repairs—a transmission overhaul or even a whole new transmission, a "valve job," involving extensive repair or replacement of your engine's valves and related parts. At this point, too, the likelihood also becomes all too real that you'll have to have your car's engine overhauled or even replaced at a cost of hundreds of dollars. Some of your car's complex options—air conditioning, power windows —also may start to fail.

Or if you are in a costly collision at any stage of your auto's life, you may face big-ticket repairs running into hundreds of dollars.

Larger, more expensive cars tend to cost more to repair than small ones. On the other side of the repair cost coin, though, is the fact that larger cars usually provide more "people protection" in the event of a higher-speed collision.

Now in effect are federal standards requiring certain "safety related" automobile components—such as lights, brakes, and suspensions —to operate "normally" after a car hits a test barrier at specified speeds an hour both head on and going backward. However, the federal standards do not cover damage to such key items as windshields and side and rear windows.

HOW TO SHOP FOR AN AUTO MECHANIC

• Start shopping for repairs *before* you need them. It's too late when your car conks out and you need service at once. Make a plan of action now; have a list of places you would take your car should you need minor repairs, major repairs, simple maintenance, etc.

• Check with your friends and acquaintances on their experiences with local auto repair shops.

• In states which license auto repair facilities, stick to the licensed establishments.

• Make a deliberate choice between your new car dealer, repair boys in local gas stations, independent general mechanics who do not sell gas, and shops in specialties such as brake relining, muffler replacement, or wheel alignment—and recognize you do have these four alternatives.

For instance, if you like the dealer from whom you bought the car and have come to trust him, his shop is probably your best bet. He is apt to give you good, fairly priced service in the hope that you will also buy your next car from him. And he probably will be familiar with your car's quirks and will have an ample stock of the parts the car is most likely to need. But if the dealer from whom you bought seems not interested in servicing, go elsewhere.

Convenience is the key advantage of a local service station—and you easily can establish a valuable relationship with a station if you buy your gas there and take your car to the station for regular servicing. Here too, look for the proprietor who considers his service area a major part of his gas station operation. Many gas stations are not equipped for complex repairs, though, and—as a result—generate customer complaints.

Your third alternative is the independent mechanic whose earnings depend primarily on repairs and servicing, his ability and reputation. The independent, though, may not be as conveniently located as a gas station, may not be able to do repairs on as short notice as an automobile dealer—and may not have as complex a line of special tools and parts as the dealer.

For some types of work—such as muffler replacement or brake relining—you may be able to save money by patronizing a specialty shop which does a large volume of repairs in these areas and which has accumulated all the special equipment, parts, and expertise needed to perform them. But carefully check out the reputation of any outside specialty shop before you turn your back on your regular mechanic. And remember that these shops are sometimes highly skilled at selling you repairs you don't need.

• Whatever type of establishment you choose to patronize for repairs, note whether the mechanic and/or owner solicits your repeat business. The competent, honest shop will want you back. Its mechanics will schedule work with as much regard for your convenience as possible; will explain as much about the repairs your car needs as you seem capable of absorbing. They will take the time to make a careful diagnosis of your car's problem instead of casually informing you, "That sounds like your 'whatzit' and will cost $20 to fix." They even may tell you the work you thought you needed isn't necessary until later—or isn't needed at all.

• Look for a membership certificate for the Better Business Bureau or the Independent Garage Owners of America.

• Try to find a place where you can talk face to face with the man who will actually work on your car. In many shops, the customer sees only a person who writes work orders for the mechanics to follow. This fellow is primarily a salesman, rather than a mechanic. He well may be working on a commission basis, so that the more repairs and parts he sells you the more he earns. If you speak directly with the mechanic, you're less likely to be talked into unnecessary or inappropriate service. Also, two-way communication is much clearer than a few words scrawled on a service order. And the mechanic is likely to feel more responsibility toward the job if he has discussed it with you personally.

If an establishment won't let you speak directly to the mechanic, even when you indicate you're willing to pay for the time he spends talking to you, go elsewhere.

• Consider taking a course on auto mechanics at a local extension college, night school, or similar place. Even if you never work on a car, it will help you to evaluate the mechanical competence of others.

• Be your own mechanic whenever possible, if you're capable and so inclined. First you'll save money—most obviously on simple repairs, for which you pay a skilled mechanic the same hourly rate as for complicated ones. With a little practice, you'll also be assured that what you do is done right. Most important, you'll become better acquainted with your car's workings and will be less easily baffled or intimidated by a serviceman if a breakdown occurs on the road.

In some areas, do-it-yourself auto service centers, which rent repair bays and tools (at $3.00 to $4.00 or so an hour, depending on the equipment you use), make it easier to do at least some of your own work. They may even provide free advice if you run into problems. If there is no such facility in your area, there may be one soon: the idea is catching on fast. Savings, even after rental fees, can run to 75 per cent on some jobs.   .

• Look for reasonably detailed estimates on repairs which also indicate what work may be optional. A good repair shop will itemize parts on its bill and the parts which mechanics have taken from your car will be available for you to inspect and keep (if you wish). And although labor probably will not be itemized among repairs—very difficult to do and would cost more than it is worth—the mechanic can estimate the proportion of his time devoted to each job.

• Give preference to shops willing to warrant their work. For instance, many dealers will now guarantee repair work for 4,000 miles or 90 days.

• If you suspect you have been overcharged for any parts, demand to see the suppliers' parts price list—giving both wholesale and estimated retail prices on parts of every description. To this you must add labor costs, of course. If a mechanic refuses to show you his copy of this book, be warned. You may have been gypped this time. Start looking at once for another shop to patronize the next time you need service.

• Once you have found a mechanic or service repair station you feel confident will give you honest, skilled, and reliable service, stay put. Many service stations automatically separate their customers into either regular, bread-and-butter business or once-in-a-while customers. And, understandably enough, they tend to provide better treatment for the regulars—a great help when your car won't start on a bitter sub-zero morning.

• Whenever possible, make an appointment in advance for work you want done. This makes your mechanic's job easier, more profitable, and ultimately more economical for you.

• Try to avoid scheduling work on Mondays or Fridays, the busiest times in any repair shop.

• When you ask for a tune-up, or any other collection of procedures customarily lumped under one term, be sure you and your mechanic know exactly what you mean. There are nearly as many definitions of a tune-up as there are mechanics.

• When you discuss your problems with a mechanic, describe symptoms rather than giving your opinion on what needs fixing. Your view will tend to prejudice even a good mechanic and can lead to a wrong diagnosis.

• If you cannot wait to see the mechanic, leave a note on your windshield, describing what you want done if you have particular services in mind, and problem symptoms if a diagnosis is necessary. Leave your name and phone number, and leave instructions such as: "Call me before making additional repairs."

• Whenever you deal with the service writer in a large shop, make your own list of what you want done, date it, and sign it. The service writer can staple your list to his to have your signature. This will protect you from having additions made to the service order after you leave and will permit you to refuse to pay for work you did not request.

HOW AND WHERE TO SHOP FOR BIG-TICKET REPAIRS

How can you tell if, say, a new transmission or an engine overhaul is really needed?

A transmission overhaul is among the first big, costly repair jobs your car is likely to need—and it's a job that easily could pit you against some of the biggest swindlers in the auto repair business today. This is a reconditioning of the unit which transmits the power that moves your car from the car's engine to its wheels. Among the key symptoms of trouble are: puddles of fluid on your driveway; erratic gear shifting or refusal to shift at all; engine racing between shifts.

But these symptoms do not necessarily mean you need a complete transmission overhaul costing from $100 to $250. Erratic shifting can often be corrected by adding fluid or by quick and inexpensive repairs; leakage of transmission fluid frequently can be corrected for less than $65.

To find out just what kind of transmission work is required, a mechanic *must,* at a minimum, road-test the car and make a close inspection. In some instances, he must disassemble the transmission to determine exactly what is needed. For this diagnosis, you must expect to pay a reasonable fee. Beware, though, of the repair shop that will refuse to reassemble your transmission without being paid a whopping amount. Check into this with care *before* the shop takes apart your whole transmission.

Steer clear of any outfit which advertises a transmission overhaul at a flat rate—especially a ridiculously low rate of, say, less than $75. Don't be misled by claims that your transmission needs only an "adjustment." Most modern automatic transmissions cannot be adjusted at all, and even in older ones little adjustment is possible. Don't be taken in by a mechanic who shows you metal filings in the bottom of your automatic transmission case and says you need a complete overhaul—some metal filings are a normal result of using the transmission.

Also be just as cautious about a "valve job"—another category of big-ticket auto repairs which can cost up to $150 or more. Although a rough-running engine, lack of power, and declining gas mileage are symptoms of poor valves, here too they may be signs of other problems as well. A properly performed compression test is a *must* for a correct diagnosis of sick valves. Be suspicious of any repairman who says you need a valve job without doing this test.

Now, what about an engine overhaul? If your car's performance falls off drastically, a complete engine overhaul may become necessary at a cost of $150 to $800. But as an alternative to an overhaul, you might buy a rebuilt engine. Assuming the engine has been properly rebuilt by a qualified factory, it is virtually the equivalent of a new engine, and factory-rebuilt engines are commonly referred to as "new." The costs of the engine overhaul and the rebuilt engine will be about the same, but the rebuilt engine usually can be installed a lot faster than the repair shop can perform an overhaul. Your old engine will normally be taken in trade, rebuilt, and later sold to someone else—which certainly should warn you to be sure the engine you are buying is actually *rebuilt* and not simply used.

"Motor exchangers" deal in rebuilt engines and some of these offer a worth-while service at fair prices. But the motor exchange business is loaded with unscrupulous fringe operators who resort to just about any lure you can name to get your patronage and your money. Here is a sampling of the myths they use to trap you:

MOTOR REPAIR MYTHS

Myth No. 1: "Your motor can be replaced for a low flat rate." You, the customer, are told over the phone that the cost of a motor for your car will be $129.80, exchange." The conversation quickly switches to where and when the operator can pick up your car. What he does *not* tell you is that there will be an additional charge of $40 for such items as installation, gaskets, oil, perhaps a "federal tax." Nor are you told of the $30 to $35 charge to be made if your engine block turns out to be damaged "beyond repair." Nor does the dealer mention that the $129.80 price omits a lot more parts you need just to make your car run. Upshot: after the old motor has been removed, you discover you must pay $208 for other parts and accessories, for a new total of $337.80.

Myth No. 2: "Make no down payment; take 18 months to pay." Few motor exchanges extend their own credit. In most cases, you must pay cash for your repairs and arrange your own loan with a financial institution.

Myth No. 3: "We can give you one-day service." Under ideal circumstances, an engine can be installed in one day, but it doesn't happen very often. You must be prepared to wait several days until space becomes available in the shop or while your loan application is being approved.

Myth No. 4: "You get a 10,000-mile guarantee in writing." But nothing is said about the time limit on this guarantee—which may be as short as 30 days.

Avoid repair shops which give you bargain basement estimates on accident repairs; they also may do low-quality work and your insurance company is almost surely willing to pay the cost of a decent job.

Be warned: Once your car is in the shop and is being dismantled, you're over the barrel.

THE QUICK AND DIRTY TRICKS AWAY FROM HOME

What if your car unexpectedly grinds to a halt on a trip, hundreds or even thousands of miles from your home where you know nothing about the local service stations and there's no Better Business Bureau to call?

Although most service stations on the road are no more anxious to swindle you than those near home, some "last chance" stations actually specialize in "skinning the dude"—especially along lonely stretches of the nation's 42,500-mile interstate highway system. They may try to sell you an oil change or a new oil filter by flashing a dipstick covered with "dirty" oil (all oil in a car looks "dirty" after a few minutes of circulation in the engine). Or some swindlers will actually slash your tires ("honking") while you aren't looking in order to sell you new ones. Or they will refuse to remount tires they have removed until you agree to buy a new set (at an exorbitant price, of course).

Or they will tell you your tires have dangerous "flaws" and must be replaced. The gullible itinerant may not only get talked into buying an expensive set of new tires, she or he also will leave the "old" still good tires behind. While your car is jacked up for new tires, they may wobble the front wheels as "proof" you need new ball joints too—but all suspension systems are designed to have some looseness when the weight is off the wheels.

Among their other quick and dirty tricks:

draining the acid out of a battery cell, replacing it with plain water, then "proving" the battery is dead by a hydrometer check;

bending windshield wiper blades and pointing out you need new ones;

"boiling batteries"—putting an alkali such as baking soda or Alka-Seltzer in a battery to make it foam and appear damaged or dead or pouring soapy water on the top to produce the same appearance;

"short sticking"—pouring "oil" from an empty can;

"short thumbing"—or not pushing the dipstick all the way in;

"the liquid smoke trick"—inducing smoke from an engine by spraying it with chemicals;

puncturing radiator hoses;

slashing the fan belt;

switching ignition wires around to make the engine run roughly or not at all;

bending wires on the alternator to make the red warning light glow;

squirting oil on the engine to simulate a leaking fuel pump or oil pump;

filling the gas tank from one pump and charging the higher amount registered on an adjacent pump;

altering amounts or adding sums to the credit card slip after you leave—or imprinting blank bills with your card to be filled in after you have gone.

Then there are "freeway runners"—advance men who hang around exits shouting friendly warnings of wobbly wheels to terrified travelers and thereby forcing them to head for the nearest service station where, of course, collaborating con artists are waiting.

HOW TO AVOID THE TRICKS ON A TRIP

To avoid these fast-buck maneuvers, stand by and carefully watch all operations performed at any service station whose reputation is unknown to you.

If you suspect your oil has been incorrectly checked, ask to have the check repeated.

Watch the gas tank filling operations.

Don't leave your car unattended, and if you must, even for a few minutes, lock your doors.

If you want to use the rest room, lock your car and do so *before* you even talk to the service people about your car's problems.

Check the credit card slip for the correct amount before you sign and save your copies to check your bill at home before paying. Never let your credit card out of your sight.

Have your car checked regularly for possible trouble spots: e.g., tire tread, fan belt, battery, ignition and other electrical equipment, radiator hoses, spark plugs, brake fluid. Without fail, have this checkup done *before* you leave home for a long automobile trip.

Experts, in fact, say that if you're going to put on the miles—6,000 or more round trip—install a complete new or almost new set of tires before you go and take along a spare with as much tread as your regular tires. When you're pulling a camper, another two good spares are a must for the camper, if they're an odd, hard-to-get size.

If all precautions fail and you begin to suspect you are in trouble on a trip, heed the warning signals your car is putting out. *Stop early*. You will save the cost and nuisance of having to be towed off the highway. You'll also have a chance to shop around, rather than being forced to accept the services of whatever shop the tow truck delivers you to.

Make sure your travel budget earmarks at least $150 for automobile emergencies far from home.

Generally, the rules for finding reliable service on the road are the same as the ones you would use at home, but you'll have to substitute advice from the local Better Business Bureau and chapters of automobile clubs for the advice of friends. An additional tip: try to find a repair shop which is a member of the Independent Garage Owners of America. Members subscribe to a nationwide guarantee plan which provides that any member garage will make good on work done improperly by another.

How to Cut the High Cost of Accidents

THE DRIVE FOR SAFETY

Obviously spurring today's extraordinary auto safety drive are our persistently costly accident rates.

The annual death toll from auto accidents was more than 55,000 in the early years of this decade—plus another 5 million injured. The annual economic loss has been running to $20 billion, including car repairs, medical bills, lost wages, other losses related to accidents.

Today, the typical driver on American roads has about one chance in three of having an accident within a year.

HOW TO REDUCE YOUR ODDS ON AN AUTO ACCIDENT

What can *you* do to reduce the odds that you'll have an auto accident?

• At the very beginning, when you are looking for a new or used car, *comparison-shop for safety features*—just as you comparison-shop for options, comforts, economies. Ask car dealers you visit to give you the federally required free rundown on the safety aspects of each car you are considering—ranging from acceleration and passing ability to tire reserve loads and stopping distance.

• Before you buy a car, new or used, check whether the model and make you want has been the subject of a federal safety recall—and if so, for what reason.

• If you receive a recall notice on the car you already own, don't ignore it. Take in your car *immediately* for the suggested repairs and/or adjustments.

• Don't try to side-step your state's motor vehicle inspection laws —e.g., by sweet-talking an inspection station into overlooking such hazardous problems as too worn tires or a burned-out headlight or brakes on the blink. Have the recommended (and, remember, legally *required*) repairs performed promptly—and be grateful the problems have been spotted before they can kill you.

• *Drinking* may account for as many as half of all fatal car crashes today. Although the ideal rule is "If you drink, don't drive," this may be unrealistic for many. Thus, an alternative rule, offered by the National Safety Council, is: take no more than one normal drink per hour —and do not drive until at least one hour after the last drink.

• *Don't* drive when you're overly fatigued or in an angry or depressed mood. These conditions frequently lead to *fatal* accidents.

• At night don't try to guess what may be beyond the reach of your headlights: most cars going at 60 mph cannot stop within this range.

WHAT TO DO IF YOU ARE IN AN ACCIDENT

HOW INFORMED ARE YOU?

If you become involved in *any* auto accident, report the facts at once to your insurance agent—even if the other driver involved is completely at fault, admits it, and promises to have his insurance company pay for any damage. Do this simply because the other driver's oral promises are worthless to you. He (or she) could change his mind any time—or even turn around and claim it was *you* who caused the accident.

Follow up this call with a registered letter to the company writing your insurance, stating that you have been in an accident and giving your policy number as well as the name of your auto insurance agent.

This rule holds true even in cases in which visible damages are minimal and in which reporting the accident may end up costing you more in hiked premium rates than the expense of just having the car fixed yourself. Reason: should the accident turn out to be more serious than it first appeared (i.e., if the other driver later develops signs of whiplash injury), you may lose the benefit of your insurance coverage because you did not report the accident within the prescribed number of days.

Also in order to *collect full benefits* due you on your automobile insurance, you may be required by the company writing your policy to report any accident in which you become involved within a certain limited period of time. If you don't report, the insurance company may be able to disclaim any and all legal responsibility in the affair.

KEY RULES

Do you know what moves you must make in order to be confident you'll collect the full amount of insurance actually due you? If you're among the majority who don't, here are the key rules to guide you:

• After you have stopped your cars, checked to see if there are any injuries needing medical attention, set up some kind of system to route other vehicles around the accident area, and called the police, exchange drivers' license and registration numbers. Take down the other person's name and address plus the make, model, and year of the other car. Exchange telephone numbers and the names and addresses of your respective insurance companies and/or agents.

• Get names and addresses of:

all other drivers involved in the accident;

the insurance companies of these drivers;

two or three witnesses (if you fail to get their names, at least get their license plate numbers so you can track them down later if you need to).

• Write down the name, badge number, station number, and jurisdiction of the policeman who arrives at the scene of the accident.

• Make accurate notes on the following circumstances surrounding the accident:

The date, place, and time.

Weather conditions—Rain? Snow? Fog? Sleet? Clear?

Road conditions—Icy? Dry? Wet? Slushy?

Any evidence of physical injury to either party.

Whether either or both cars were under—or out of—control.

The car seats in which passengers in the other car were sitting.

How fast you—and the other car—were going at the time of the accident.

Where on the road each car was (e.g., on his own side of the road?).

Whether there is evidence of either driver being drunk (encourage a breath test for *both* of you when the police officer arrives if there's any question about this aspect).

Whether the other person's driver's license lists any relevant restrictions—such as a requirement that he or she wear glasses while driving (obviously particularly important if you noticed that the other driver was *not* wearing glasses when the accident occurred).

• Make your own notes even though the policeman or state trooper also is taking lengthy notes on the same topics.

• Make a sketch of the cars and placement of people and cars involved in the accident in relation to each other as well as to the road. If you have to move your car from the place it was hit, make marks on the road indicating the original position.

• If you should have a camera with you, snap a few pictures of the accident, the people involved, details of the damage.

• *Do not* disclose the extent of your insurance coverage.

• *Do not* confess guilt, even at the scene of an accident you have caused, and do not pledge to "have everything taken care of by your insurance company."

• *Do not* sign any waivers of liability or any assurances that you have not been physically injured. Such injury might not become evident for days or even weeks.

• *Do not* attempt to answer by yourself letters or telephone queries from the other party involved in an accident. Send all along to your insurance agent to handle.

• If the accident is a serious one—particularly one involving injury to others—consult a lawyer. But avoid the services of any lawyer who claims he can win an unusually large settlement, the proceeds of which he might offer to split with you. And if it's a serious or complicated accident resign yourself to staying in the area awhile—even if it's far from home. It'll be cheaper than trying to resolve difficult problems by long-distance phone.

• Go to two or three reputable auto body shops and compare estimates for properly repairing your car. Steer clear of any repair shop which offers to jack up its estimate—and later its bill—to cover the cost of your deductible. The shop which goes in for this type of cheating may not stop short of compromising the quality of its work on your car.

• Keep a record of your substitute transportation costs while your car is being fixed: the costs to you of renting a car, or taking taxis, or whatever.

• Make a copy of these rules and keep the guide in the glove compartment of your car. Otherwise you'll more than likely forget most of the important ones when and as you do get involved in an accident.

• Also keep in your glove compartment the insurance identification card your insurance agent may have given you—listing his office phone number and also the name of the company insuring you. This card may include the addresses and phone numbers of branch offices—most useful information if you smash your car up a few hundred miles from home.

• As a practical alternative, ask your insurance agent and/or state police to give you copies of the accident report form they would require you to fill out in the event of an accident, and keep these forms in your glove compartment to remind you which details to get when you have an accident.

• Or copy the following "composite" form I have put together from several different insurance companies and keep this guide in your glove compartment.

Whichever alternative you choose, just be sure you choose one!

ACCIDENT REPORT FORM

Policyholder and Driver

Name of policyholder_____Policy number_____
If married, name of husband or wife_____
Home address_____Phone_____
Business address_____Phone_____
Occupation_____Employed by_____
Driver's name_____Address_____Phone_____
Driver's license number_____Years driving experience_____
Driver's age_____
Relation to policyholder_____
Who authorized him to drive?_____
_____
Names of occupants of policyholder's car_____
_____

Policyholder's Automobile

Make_____Year_____Body type_____Model_____
State license number_____Motor number_____Serial number_____
Name of holder of auto loan, if any_____
Name of owner if other than policyholder_____
Address_____Telephone_____
Car garaged at_____

Details of Accident

Date of accident_____Time_____
Where accident occurred_____
City_____State_____
Purpose for which car was being used_____
Was driver on errand for owner?_____
Where may car be seen during day?_____
Name of claim representative handling claim_____
Name of insurance firm_____
Direction my automobile was going_____
What side of street?_____How fast?_____Speed limit_____
Were headlights on?_____Signals?_____Condition of street_____

If object collided with was moving, in what direction?_____
How fast?_____Which side of street?_____
Any signals given?_____
If an automobile, were lights on?_____
Was either driver violating traffic regulations?_____
Was accident investigated by police?_____
What department and precinct?_____
Were any charges brought?_____Against whom?_____
Give full account of accident, including direction of all vehicles involved and traffic controls present (draw a diagram):_____
_____
_____

Personal Injuries

Name of injured person(s)	Address	Age	Occupation
_____	_____	___	___
_____	_____	___	___

Situation of Each Injured Person

Driver_____Pedestrian_____Rider in your car_____
Rider in other car_____
Describe injuries_____
_____
Name, address, and phone number of physician called_____
_____
Where was injured person taken?_____
Were there seat belts in your car?_____
If so, were they in use?_____

Damage to Property of Others

Name and address of owner of damaged automobile or other property
_____
Home phone number_____Business phone number_____
Name of other party's insurance company_____
Policy number_____
Make of auto_____Year_____Body type_____Model_____
Describe damage_____
Estimated repair cost_____
Name of driver of other car_____Age_____
Address_____
Driver's license number_____State registration number_____

Occupants of other car   Address

_____   _____

_____   _____

Where can other car be seen?_____

What was said between you and other driver?_____

_____

Is claim being made against you?_____

Are you making claim against other party?_____

Damage to Your Automobile

Date of damage_____

Description and damage—itemize parts damaged_____

_____

Estimated cost of repairs (attach estimate)_____

If car was stolen, were police notified?_____

Officer's name and number_____

Give make, size, and mileage of tires stolen or damaged_____

_____

Age of convertible top_____

Purchase date and warranty of battery_____

Witnesses to Accident

Name   Address   Telephone number

_____   _____   _____

_____   _____   _____

Date of report_____Policyholder's signature_____

How to Foil Car Thieves

BASIC WAYS TO PROTECT YOUR CAR

• Be wary of super-bargains in Johnny-come-lately car lots. Be leery of any sale being made in the street. If you innocently buy a stolen car, you will have little chance of recovering your investment: if such a car is traced to you, you'll have to give it up, of course, so it can be returned to its rightful owner.

• *Do not* tempt a car "window-shopper" by leaving suitcases, gift boxes, obvious valuables within sight inside the car. At a minimum, keep your tapes in the glove compartment or elsewhere out of sight.

You might also "mark" your stereo player and tapes—and record these "fingerprints" to help you establish your ownership if they're stolen later and traced.

• Mark your engine, transmission, and other valuable accessories not bearing identification numbers with your initials—to help police recover the items if they're stolen and to identify them as yours.

• Identify your car by dropping your business card in the slot between the door and window or by scratching your initials in some hidden place. This will help you particularly if the engine numbers and other identification have been tampered with.

• Park in lighted, well-trafficked areas—preferably near a street lamp or lighted store window. Most thieves won't risk working on a locked car in the light. At home, lock your car in the garage if you have one; many cars are stolen right in their owners' driveways. If you lack garage space for all your cars, put the most desirable ones inside and block the driveway with the others.

• If you leave your car in a public garage or parking lot, do not be definite about when you will pick it up. Dishonest attendants can easily steal new equipment from your car and replace it with the old parts when they know how much time you will be away. Double-check your mileage to make sure it's the same as when you parked the car. This will reveal whether thieves have driven your car while you were away to a spot in which they could switch equipment.

Assuming your state laws do not force you to keep the car's title and registration certificate in the glove compartment, leave them home or carry them on your person. Pro auto thieves steal these documents, then forge them for their own use.

• *Keep your car locked*—both doors and windows. If you're afraid of locking yourself out—with your keys accidentally left inside—carry a second set of car keys with you. Do not "hide" extra keys, though, in what you consider safe places but to which thieves turn at once: under a seat, fender, floor mat, the hood, the like.

• *Always* take the keys out of your ignition. Even when you're on a brief errand, remove your keys. Never leave your engine running. By always removing your keys you'll not only slash the chances of having your car stolen but also eliminate the possible hazard of being faced with liability charges if your stolen car later becomes involved in an accident.

• If your car breaks down or runs out of gas, continue to follow the rules on locking your car and taking out the keys. Just because you can't start your car doesn't mean a thief can't.

IF YOUR CAR IS STOLEN

But let's say that, despite all your defenses, your car is stolen. If or when this happens, you will find out at once that the police, your insurance company, and possibly the National Automobile Theft Bureau will ask you to supply critical information necessary to trace your car.

Will you at that moment have the essential data at hand—some twenty items including detailed information on your car, license, insurance, bank or finance company?

To help you be prepared, here is a form developed by the American Mutual Insurance Alliance which you should fill out *now* so that you will have all the facts on file for ready reference. You might carry a card in your wallet which gives all this information—to speed the search for your car if it is stolen.

Vehicle Information

Make_____Year_____
Model_____Body style_____
Vehicle identification number_____Color (upper/lower)_____
Type and size of engine_____Type of transmission_____
Ignition key number_____Trunk compartment key number_____
Repair work, dents, secret marks, or other peculiarities which would help identify vehicle

_____

_____

License Information

License number (and state)_____Year license expires_____
City registration number_____

Additional Information

Insurance company_____Policy number_____
Agent_____
Bank or finance company holding title_____
_____Account number_____
Purchased (new/used) from_____
Address_____Date_____

Optional equipment or other items usually kept with auto (list serial numbers)

_____

_____

Now here is another form, also developed by the AMIA, for your use immediately after the theft. This information will provide a permanent record of the facts surrounding your case and will be helpful in co-ordinating efforts to find your car.

If Your Car Is Stolen
> Date of theft_____Place of theft_____
> Time of theft_____Speedometer reading_____
> Personal items in auto when stolen_____
> _____
> _____
> Law enforcement agency contacted_____
>   Date_____Complaint number_____
>   Officer investigating theft_____
> Insurance company contacted (date)_____Claim number_____
>   Claims representative_____
> Auto recovered at_____Date_____
>   By (law enforcement agency)_____
> Condition of car (list damage)_____
> _____
> _____

How to Save on Your Parking Charges

PARKING: CAN BE HUGE COST

In New York City, *daily* parking charges at downtown garages in the mid-1970s ran as much as $5.00 to $7.50. For a commuting businessman, this could mean a monthly cost of parking his car in Manhattan as high as $165. Even at less expensive garages, typical monthly parking charges in New York ran from $80 to $100.

Although you probably think of your car primarily as "wheels in motion," the fact is it is *parked,* on average, more than 95 per cent of the time. If you are a regular automobile commuter in a major U.S. city today, your yearly parking costs probably run between $300 and $1,000, your daily charges between $1.50 and $3.00. Parking, in sum, can be a huge part of the cost of owning a car for millions of city and suburban families.

If today's parking costs seem exorbitant to you, tomorrow's charges will be even more so. The reasons are a cinch:

• In virtually every big U.S. city, land costs are soaring—along with demand for space to build offices, stores, apartment buildings, hospitals. City parking lots are being erased by these more lucrative uses of land.

• Parking also has become a major burden at suburban shopping centers, hotels, airports, hospitals, universities. What was once free parking is being replaced by monthly charges to growing numbers of students, doctors, others. As high a proportion as 75 per cent of leading U.S. colleges and universities are now slapping parking charges on students: the argument is that a car takes up the same amount of space as a seminar room for twenty students.

"Free" parking downtown surely is doomed to disappear altogether —along with all on-street parking in densely populated areas. Even in suburban towns, street parking is being banned—and in some cases monthly charges are being assessed for street parking.

TEN WAYS TO SAVE ON PARKING CHARGES

(1) Form a car pool and arrange a monthly contract with a downtown garage under which it won't matter whose car is parked each day. Quite a few garages will do this for you and some will provide movable plastic stickers so car-poolers can take turns during the month. In some cases, a car pool can be less expensive than public transportation.

(2) Shop for a garage a short distance from the central business district. A daily walk of as little as five or six blocks can mean as much as a 50 per cent cut in your parking charges.

(3) When you drive downtown for shopping, find out which of your favorite stores offers free or reduced-rate parking. Merchants of all types across the country have arrangements with parking companies to provide free or reduced-rate parking for customers.

(4) If you're commuting alone, do so, if you can, with a compact

car: these often qualify you for preferential garage rates because they can be slipped into spaces which are too small for the larger cars.

(5) If you are renting a car from a company which also owns parking facilities, check what parking benefits you might get as part of your rental agreement.

(6) Be careful about adding steep charges to your bill by taking your car in and out of a long-term parking garage; taxis might be cheaper.

(7) Compare monthly and daily parking costs. Monthly rates might come out cheaper even if you don't use the garage every day.

(8) Seriously consider parking your car at a low-cost facility at the edge of the city and taking a bus, subway, or train from there to the office. Such facilities are being expanded and made more convenient in response to gasoline shortages.

(9) Avoid all extra charges by obeying the rules of the garage. For instance, if the garage requests you leave your key in the car, do so, and thereby avoid possible penalty charges.

(10) Be sure your brakes are in top-notch condition to avoid damage due to an accident in the garage.

What About Renting a Car?

HOW TO TELL WHICH IS THE BEST DEAL

You get off a plane in a strange city and start shopping for a car to rent. At one rental counter the use of a car will cost you $18 a day, plus 18¢ a mile, plus the cost of gas. At the next booth you can get the same car for $20 a day and 20¢ a mile, but the gas is furnished by the car rental company. And you also read in an ad that just a block from the airport there's an economy car rental outfit offering subcompacts for about half the price charged at the airport offices.

How can you tell which is the best deal in a car rental? What is the most important thing to look for?

Take the example of the $18-a-day versus the $20-a-day car. Your total costs for driving the first car 300 miles are $90, including $18 you must pay for gas. However, the second car would actually cost you $10 *less*—or $80. This example points up how important it is for you to figure total car rental costs on a *daily* basis.

Car rental costs vary widely from company to company. To illustrate, the daily rental rate of a Ford Pinto in one major U.S. city in the mid-1970s ranged from $7.00, plus 10¢ a mile, to $14, plus 14¢ a mile. Thus, if you drive Pinto A 200 miles a day, the daily cost was $27 against $42 a day for Pinto B from another company. Over a five-day period this difference amounts to $75.

From coast to coast, the daily rental rate for various types and sizes of cars in the mid-seventies ranged from $1.00 to $90. Weekly rates typically ranged from $35 to $100. And on a monthly basis the spread is similarly wide. In some cases you get a certain number of miles free; in others you get unlimited mileage; in still others there is a mileage charge of 5¢ to 25¢ depending on the car and the company.

Why pay up to twice the car rental rate and mileage charge from a big-car, big-name company when far less expensive deals might be made around the corner?

Item: Frequently, the biggest companies offer newer cars with newer tires than do the smaller companies. But this does not necessarily mean that the cars rented out by big-name companies are always safer or significantly more trouble-free.

Item: The bigger companies have hundreds or even thousands of offices across the United States—usually in the most convenient places such as airports, downtown hotel lobbies, etc. And you can make car reservations over toll-free telephone lines from anywhere in the country.

But the budget car rental companies usually will deliver a rental car to you quickly if you call them, often on a direct-line telephone from an airport or hotel lobby—or, in some cases, also on a toll-free line from wherever you are. They also are frequently willing to let you drop off a car wherever you want when you are ready to return it, for a small charge or no charge at all.

Item: The bigger companies tend to keep their offices open for longer hours than do the smaller companies, and to offer you a long list of travel assistance. But smaller companies often will make special arrangements for off-hour needs or returns and also will provide you with maps, directions, etc.

Item: The bigger companies will let you drop off a rented car at another U.S. city—either at a small drop-off charge or at no charge. In this case, the smaller companies may not have an office at your destination.

Item: Both small and large companies probably will let you charge a car rental on any major credit card.

Enough. What *is* the most important thing to look for when you rent a car—a low, flat daily charge or a low mileage charge?

Should you pay that "nominal" $1.50 to $2.00 a day charge to waive the first $100 in damage to the car you rent?

At what point does it become more economical to rent on a weekly versus a daily basis?

RULES FOR COMPARISON SHOPPING

Here are your major rules for comparison shopping. If you follow just these, the likelihood is that you'll save hundreds of dollars in the next few times you rent a car.

• Estimate, in advance, how many miles you *realistically* think you'll drive during the rental period. You're typical if you usually underestimate the mileage, so don't just count the number of miles between where you are and your destination. Add at least one third as many more miles to make up for getting lost, making unexpected detours and side trips, etc. If you plan to travel any significant distance, shop for the car with the lowest per-mile charge.

• Figure out, in advance, just how many days you'll need the car. If you'll need it five days or less, the daily rate probably is the best deal. But if you'll need it longer, the weekly (or even monthly) rate is probably better.

• Make up your mind how important are the comforts of big, fancy limousines versus relatively spartan small cars. To show you the differences in costs, a Cadillac costing $23 a day and 23¢ a mile, which you rent for five days and drive an average of 200 miles a day, will cost you a total of $345—an average of $69 a day. But an economy car costing $10 a day and 10¢ a mile over the same period will cost you a total of $150—an average of $30 a day.

Note: If you decide on an economy car, reserve it well ahead of time.

• Ask about the special deals—such as the low-cost "weekend specials" which are usually available from Friday noon to Monday noon, X number of "free" miles, "businessman's specials." See if you "fit" one of them.

• Find out, if you intend to leave the car in another city, whether there is a drop-off charge. Between major cities you usually can find a deal in which you pay only a minimum or no drop-off charge at all.

• Although the ads say there is only a "nominal" charge for waiving the renter's responsibility for damage up to $100, this charge usually is at least $1.50 a day—which amounts to an annual rate of at least $547.50. And this is not for full collision coverage. It usually covers *only* the $100 deductible which most of you could afford to pay if necessary. I suggest rejecting this extra coverage on the basis of its cost. Just be sure to inspect the car you rent and point out any obvious dents or scratches to the agent so they can be noted on the rental contract before you initial the waiver and inspect the rental contract carefully to be sure it is *only* the first $100 of coverage you are waiving.

• Whatever deal you choose, if you don't have any recognized credit cards, expect to make a cash deposit on a rented car of an amount roughly equivalent to your expected total rental charge.

But don't *count* on being permitted to pay for a rented car with cash—especially during evenings and weekends. Some firms *require* you to show them credit cards, no matter how much cash you have in your pocket. Reason: thefts of rental cars are a major problem for car rental firms and some are understandably hesitant to lend you, say, $5,000 worth of property without first checking whether you have sound credit credentials.

By Air—"It's the Only Way to Go"

If your time is limited and you're traveling a fairly long distance, a plane is the only way to go. If your funds also are limited and you're traveling a long way, a plane can be an economical form of transportation too. But how economical it will be will depend on your knowledge of and ability to take advantage of what has become a fantastic web of air fare bargains, low-cost package deals, and travel discounts.

BARGAIN AIR FARES

The basic fare the majority of travelers pay today is the *"Y"*— for coach. Every $1.00 on this fare costs $1.37 to $1.63 first class. There are also many special stopover and "circle" deals offered by most airlines. There are lots of angles—such as scheduling your flight at meal-time to save on restaurants, traveling light to save porter's tips.

Be on the alert, though, for major changes in all arrangements under which you now fly. The Civil Aeronautics Board, which regulates the U.S. air travel industry, is making and will continue to make fundamental alterations in the criteria governing all fares in coming years.

Consult a knowledgeable travel agent or inquire at various airlines about the best bargain deals and the rules for taking advantage of them.

Avoid being overcharged by checking the fare for the flight you want with more than one airline or more than one ticket agent.

CHARTER FLIGHT BARGAINS

"Travel abroad" has a lot in common with any familiar consumer product. You can buy it in a wide range of brands, grades, quality, types, and guarantees. You can buy it at list price. Or you can buy it marked down for sale. Or you can buy it "hot" from a fence.

To illustrate: There are the individual fares available on the scheduled airlines which offer you the greatest flexibility in schedules and the highest guarantees of service and responsibility. These are at the very top of the price range.

Then there are the package tours, and special group fares offered by the scheduled airlines and their agents which are subject to limitations that do not apply to normal fares but which still have built-in service guarantees and negotiability (meaning the tickets may be exchanged for other dates and airlines).

Finally, there are the charters which can be bought from a variety of sources in a variety of forms and are the least expensive of all. You can take a three-stop inclusive tour charter (ITC) or a travel group charter (TGC). A recent variation is the One-stop tour charter (OTC) designed for the unaffiliated individual traveler. You must sign up at least 15–30 days in advance, depending on whether your destination is domestic or international, pay for air transportation and ground accommodations, agree to stay a minimum of four–seven days. You need not remain with the group as long as you leave and return on the same plane and pay for the ground package.

Most charter flights are safe, well managed, and compare quite favorably with regular scheduled airline flights.

RULES FOR BUYING CHARTER FLIGHTS

If you buy a bargain charter flight for transportation only, make sure it *is* a bargain. Compare the charter price with the lowest fare on a scheduled flight; consider how much side trips might boost your costs. New York to London on a charter may be a bargain. But short trips elsewhere and back to London could hike your cost above a group fare package on a scheduled flight which usually permits some stopovers at no extra charge.

If you're sharing costs with other passengers, check the costs for accuracy. Ask the tour operator or group that arranged the flight for the facts; they must give them. Beware of last-minute surcharges, dues, or fees which can raise your costs. Exception: the entirely legal price hikes necessitated by rising fuel costs, about which you are warned in tour descriptions.

If you are traveling with children under twelve, check the rules on lower fare rates.

Consider the negotiability or refund value of your ticket if your charter doesn't make the return trip or you can't go back on schedule. You do not get your money back if you change your mind about the return date.

Read all the literature on a tour package to satisfy yourself the trip is well planned. Check prices item by item.

If you have valid complaints, report to an appropriate law enforcement agency, the Better Business Bureau and/or the Civil Aeronautics Board, 1825 Connecticut Avenue, N.W., Washington, D.C. 20428.

And best guide of all: find and use *a good travel agent*. See Chapter 12, "How to Save on Vacations," for details.

"LEAVE THE DRIVING TO THEM"

More than 30,000 towns still depend on the bus for their sole means of scheduled transportation. In countless instances, people can't operate a car or can't afford one—because, say, of youth or old age, location or income level. And even if you have a car, on a short trip you might want someone else to do the driving. Moreover, many buses are now equipped with reclining seats, individual reading lights, and lavatories.

What is a "short" trip? Up to 500 miles is an accepted rule of thumb. Generally speaking, cost aside, a plane might be more comfortable and convenient over a longer trip. But the point is the very turnpikes which have made the automobile so popular also are a boon to the bus. The flexibility of the bus hasn't been approached by the trains or planes because the buses follow the highways and the highways follow the people.

TRAVEL TIPS

Q. *What about valuables and breakables?*

A. Carry them with you. Most companies will insure items up to $50 in value, free of charge, with added coverage available.

Q. *What about reservations and luggage on intercity trips?*

A. A reservation is not vital. During peak periods back-up buses are ready. To avoid crowds, travel in midweek or midday. If you're in a hurry, check on express buses. Check luggage you can't carry on at the terminal about a half hour in advance. Be sure you have your identification tags on all luggage.

Q. *How do I find the right company for a charter?*

A. Ask your local college or athletic team: they use dozens of charters and know the good firms.

Q. *What are guidelines for prices on chartered buses?*

A. Prices are generally quoted in either of two ways, depending on the trip's distance. For local work of up to fifty miles in one direction, the price is quoted on a per-hour basis.

For trips of more than fifty miles in one direction, prices are usually quoted on a per-mile basis. In addition, there is usually an hourly charge if the trip goes over a specified number of hours because the driver must be paid, no matter whether the bus is moving or standing still.

Q. *What are hidden cost pitfalls to look out for?*

A. Does the quoted price include tolls, parking charges, permits? Is the cost of the driver's lodging and/or food included if yours is an overnight trip? Check each of these items in advance.

Prices are usually higher on weekends, so consider scheduling your event during the week.

Order the bus to report as late as possible to reduce unproductive waiting time for the inevitable last-minute arrivals.

Use box lunches and save money.

Also, for your own comfort, make sure the bus you charter has sufficient baggage capacity for your luggage—particularly ski gear—and that the seating capacity of the bus itself is adequate.

AMTRAK: RAILROADS INTO THE TWENTIETH CENTURY

Trains, like buses, are among the least expensive ways for people to travel today—and they also leave the driving to someone else, permitting you, the passenger, to relax, read, look out the window.

Trains also are a far more efficient means of transportation than cars and highways, and therefore are far easier on our fuel supplies: one railroad train can accommodate as many people as fifty cars. One track can replace twenty lanes of superhighway. A train gets twice as many passenger miles from a gallon of fuel as a fully loaded economy car.

The National Railroad Passenger Corporation, Amtrak—created by Congress as a quasi-public corporation early in this decade to help passenger trains stage a comeback—has been making giant strides toward bringing this nearly moribund system of travel into the twentieth century.

Among other moves, Amtrak has:

Placed experimental high-speed turbo trains in service and has ordered more;

Ordered many brand-new cars, including dozens of new Metroliner cars and a whole series of new-style, bi-level long-distance coaches, diners, lounges, and sleepers;

Greatly upgraded the general quality of passenger trains, by picking the best 2,000 passenger cars out of the more than 3,000 formerly on the tracks, then completely refurbishing a considerable number of these;

Installed a nationwide, centralized ticket-and-reservation system;

Begun building a string of "satellite" train stations for suburban travelers;

Started the acquisition and refurbishing of hundreds of old passenger stations;

Reintroduced long-haul sleeper routes throughout the United States—and started a complete redesign of the cars to make them more efficient and comfortable;

Improved connections on long hauls to eliminate many long waits for trains;

Made noticeable improvements on many trains in dining cars and other food service facilities;

Cleaned up the train rest rooms so that, as one official notes, "the whole train no longer smells like a bathroom";

Made moves to ease buying of train tickets. You can pay for your ticket with American Express, a Master Charge, Diners Club, Carte Blanche, BankAmericard, or a Rail Travel card. Thousands of travel agents can help you make arrangements for travel on the Amtrak system. You can order tickets by phone to be mailed to you and billed to your credit card;

Introduced a uniform ticket format across the country.

You can get reservations and information on Amtrak schedules by calling this toll-free number: (800) 523-5720.

RECREATIONAL VEHICLES

WHICH TYPE FOR YOU?

If you are in the market for a recreational vehicle and if you are starting your hunt from scratch, here are the five basic types—a list you can use as a preliminary shopping guide:

Camping trailers: compact folding "cottages on wheels" which you tow with your own car. Typical campers sleep four to six; are equipped with bunks, kitchenette, and portable toilet; cost $500 to $2,500, average $1,500.

Truck-mounted campers: in two variations—the slide-in truck camper which fits into the back of a pickup; the chassis-mount truck camper which is *permanently* mounted on a truck's chassis (with the truck bed and sides removed). "Truck-mounts" have bunks, kitchenette, plumbing; are 6 to 11½ feet long; cost $1,500 to $5,000 for slide-ins, and $4,000 to $10,000 for chassis-mount units.

Pickup covers: simple structures with few, if any, built-in conveniences; attach to a pickup to create a sheltered space; cost $300 to $1,000, average $350.

Travel trailers: up to 35 feet long and 8 feet wide; pulled by your car; come with baths, kitchens, bedrooms; cost $700 to $18,000 or more, average $3,800. Newest and largest travel trailer is the "fifth wheel" unit which is towed by a pickup truck by means of a special swivel hitch located directly above the truck's rear axle, making the huge unit easy to tow. Prices range from $4,500 to $10,000 or more.

Motor homes: most luxurious, are comfortable carhouses in one unit; 20 to 35 feet long; cost $5,000 to $35,000, average less than $10,000.

Then there's a whole new family of "fun" cars and specialty vehicles ranging from jeeps to snowmobiles.

SHOPPING GUIDES

Whatever type you choose, look for one which is convincingly described by the manufacturer as sturdy and stable in winds. If at all possible, test-drive on a windy day before buying. Many, if not most, recreational vehicles are very unstable in winds and so flimsy they splinter in a rollover (frames are often wooden). Consumer advocates are pressing for government safety standards for recreational vehicles but, as of the mid-seventies, they had made little progress.

Don't spend a penny on buying until you have rented the equipment you think you would like best. You might properly rent more than one type before you settle on anything.

Buy a good, *used* unit when you begin: since many campers trade up to bigger units or different types as they go along, lots of good used equipment is for sale. Be sure, though, that an experienced mechanic checks the equipment—particularly the engine and transmission—before you buy. Don't buy a used lemon.

Finally, don't fail to count costs of owning and running a recreational vehicle. These include registration and insurance (which often run more than the costs of registering and insuring an ordinary car); increased fuel costs of towing a trailer or driving a large motor home over costs of fueling a car by itself; extra garaging costs; extra maintenance and repair costs; financing charges and/or the interest you lose on your initial cash investment.

BOATS AND BIKES

The fundamental rules of buying stressed over and over—and over—in this book can easily be translated from area to area, and thus you can without difficulty translate them for yourself into the spheres of boats or bikes or even horses.

BOATS FOR FUN

In our country in the mid-seventies, boats numbered 8 to 10 million—more than double the number of only two decades ago, and boating is now a multibillion-dollar industry with about one in five Americans now counted as a boater. Each spring, literally millions of boats change hands. Outboard motorboats cost from $200 to $5,000, new, are far and away the most popular type, and are familiar sights in every part of our country. Many of today's boats run into thousands of dollars. And with maintenance, repairs, insurance, and a trailer to haul the boat, plus the frequently high cost of winter storage in or out of the water, a boat can become among the most costly possessions of an unwary family.

BUYING A USED BOAT

Buying a used boat can be a particularly tricky thing—and for this purchase, therefore, there are several special rules.

Under a typical cycle, a buyer's interest might first be grabbed by the fanciest styles; his attention would then be heightened by the flashiest accessories; finally, a transfer might be clinched by nothing more than the most colorful "cosmetics" added by an earlier owner (owners).

But this is not the way to buy a used boat. Instead what you, a potential buyer, should do is "kick the tires." What should govern your decisions is the same degree of caution that would be in order when you buy a used car—and that's caution! Specifically:

• Grasp from the start that used boats do *not* depreciate, as automobiles do, by a rule-of-thumb annual percentage and that some late-model boats, in fact, grow in value. So comparison shopping is absolutely essential—after you have listed the basics you really want. Are you looking for a specific construction or type? Do you want the craft for day sailing or fishing? Inshore or offshore? What do you need in accommodations, speed, and size? How much do you want to spend —and no more?

As one general rule, the more experienced a boatsman you are, the less elaborate accommodations you will want.

As another, a boat used inshore may be less sturdy than a boat used offshore or in the Great Lakes—*even once*. The latter must—literally—be strong enough to withstand being dropped into the water from ten or more feet up *without any damage*.

• Check the hull once you have narrowed your choice to a couple of boats, for hulls determine the real value of a boat and you must inspect their safety. On wooden hulls, check that all butts, seams, and joints are tight. Also look carefully for rot—especially in corners where soft spots tend to "hide." With fiberglass boats, check the gel coat for cracking. Also check around the hull for any accumulation of slight cracks, for although this is primarily a cosmetic problem, a concentration of small cracks might indicate an impact area.

• When the boat is out of water, examine the keel and bottom for damage. Small gouges can be repaired easily but a badly mauled keel may have to be replaced. Inside the boat, check that hull fittings are sound, that hoses don't have cracks, that hose clamps fit tightly. Study the fuel connections, for a faulty hookup can cause a fire or even a major explosion. Check, too, the wiring and fuse systems for short circuits and improper insulation.

• Make a list of the approved equipment the Coast Guard requires, under federal and state laws, for the area in which you intend to do your boating. This equipment usually includes fire extinguishers, life preservers, horns, proper lights, and sufficient ventilation. Be sure this equipment is still installed on the boat and is in top condition. Don't try to cut any corners on it.

• Be sure the boat is fitted with whatever anti-pollution devices (e.g., toilet holding tanks) are required locally, or wherever you intend to use your boat.

• Check the installation and ventilation of the engine and fuel tank areas. Look for tank corrosion and leaks. You can get information on current ventilation requirements from your local Coast Guard offices.

• Have the engine checked by a marine mechanic. When the salesman says the boat has "very little running time," does he mean the engine has given the previous owner trouble?

• Check the steering controls by rotating the helm from one limit to the other. Make sure the rudder or outboard motor moves without binding or requiring undue force. Then take a trial run. Does everything work? Does the boat perform as you expected? Is your "crew" satisfied?

• If you're in the market for a sailboat, inspect every inch of sails, spars, masts, and rigging. Check for abnormal wear, evidence of strain and compression cracks in the mast.

• And your personal inspection of these areas may well not be nearly enough. It may be more than worth your time and money to get the advice of a professional marine surveyor—particularly if you are spending more than $5,000 for the boat.

• In fact, if your purchase is into these high dollar ranges, the advice of a professional surveyor whose interest is your interest would seem to me to be mere common sense.

TIPS FOR BUYING BICYCLES

Do you remember (I do) when $20 to $30 was a standard price for a bicycle and $50 meant you were buying "all the extras"? Do you realize that a bike has now become one of the costlier pieces of equipment you can buy and that your spending for bikes is now reaching for the landmark of $1 billion a year?

We are now buying more than 15 million bicycles a year and our bicyclist population by the mid-1970s had crossed the believe-it-or-not peak of 83 million (two in five of us).

Against this background, tips on how to shop for and save on a bicycle seem singularly appropriate for you—and you—and you. Here goes:

• Decide in advance how much a bike is worth to you and what kind is right for you. Your choices are:

Middleweights: weighing 50 to 60 pounds, costing $30 to $40 and rugged. They're one speed only and hard work to pedal.

Touring bicycles: miscalled "English racers," weighing 35 to 40 pounds, costing $50 to $100. Most have three speeds, are good for normal use, are your best buy if you're a casual cyclist.

Lightweights: racing bicycles, weighing less than 30 pounds, costing $80 to $500. Have from 5 to 15 speeds, with 10 typical. Need fairly frequent maintenance, are tops in efficient pedaling for the serious cyclist.

Stores also carry a variety of children's bikes, "high risers" which look like motorcycles, folding bikes, three-wheelers for adults with poor balance, tandems, even unicycles.

• Test-ride any bike you're considering to see how it feels and "fits." A lightweight's turned-down handlebars will feel awkward at first, but it will be most comfortable for long jaunts. A way to test-ride is to rent one or more bikes before you buy.

• Get the correct frame size (distance from pedal crank to point where seat mounts) for you. The range is 17 to 24 inches. To get your size, subtract 9 or 10 inches from the length of your inseam, measured to the floor.

• Be sure your child's bike fits. Do *not* buy a big—but unsafe—bike that he'll "grow into." Just allow a reasonable range of seat and handlebar adjustment for some growth.

• Check the brakes before you test-ride. The bike may have a coaster brake on the rear wheel activated by back-pedaling, or caliper brakes activated by hand levers on the handlebars. A coaster brake takes longer to apply than calipers and is more difficult to service, but it rarely needs service and works better in wet weather. Dual caliper brakes will give you a quicker stop in dry weather, but they will be poor or worse when wet. Self-adjusting caliper brakes are a strong plus. Note: Don't buy a child's bike with caliper brakes unless the child has a big enough hand to use them easily. Even some adults do not have strong enough hands for some caliper brakes.

• Also, while testing, find out how springy the frame is. A more rigid frame means less pedaling wasted. Guard against raw, sharp, or rough edges on any parts, even parts protected by guards and grips. On children's bikes, be wary of gearshift levers placed far back on the horizontal bar, "sissy bars" (high back on seat), small front wheels. The Bicycle Manufacturers Association thumbs-downed all these features some time ago as hazardous. Beware too of elongated "banana seats" (unless you prohibit riding double on them). Look for a red, white, and blue "BMA/6" seal of certification on the post just under the seat of an American children's bike. This indicates that the bicycle meets the most recent standards of this organization. Note: No imported bicycles (even the best) can get this seal, and some excellent American bikes lack it too—so use it primarily as a guide to children's bicycles.

• Bikes, like cars, have options, or accessories. Although the cost of bike accessories is much less than car options, you'll still want to be discriminating in what you buy, for all add complexity and weight. Here are the most popular and useful:

Bell or horn: a bell is more reliable than a horn and doesn't consume batteries. Both will warn pedestrians of your presence, but neither will help you in your interactions with cars, unless you invest in a marine-type freon-powered air horn.

Chain and lock: these are your first line of defense against bicycle thieves, who steal hundreds of thousands of bikes each year. The chain should be long enough to go through both wheels, the frame, and around a fixed object. It also should be hard enough to resist cutting by ordinary instruments. Your lock should be of equal quality.

Light: generator types eliminate the battery hassle but significantly increase pedaling effort when they're on—and go out when you stop. A small battery light which clips to your left leg is also a good idea, since it quickly identifies you as a cyclist by its motion. A taillight is as important for safety as a headlight.

Luggage rack or basket: either makes a bike more useful for small errands and larger outings.

The list of possible accessories you can load onto a bike is long. It includes an odometer or speedometer (some types make a bicycle pedal harder; see a good dealer for recommendations); a tool kit; a tire patch kit; an extra inner tube; a water bottle for long trips; a kiddie seat for taking a small child along; an aerosol can of bike-chasing dog repellent; special cycling clothes; and a protective helmet for areas with dangerous traffic.

• To save money, buy a used bike—but if it's in good condition, expect to pay 75 per cent of the price of a new one. A low price for a good used bicycle is a warning that it may have been stolen. Inspect any used bike with care—or pay a qualified mechanic a few dollars to go over the bike for you.

• Assemble a new bike yourself—a job which will also save money by teaching you how to repair it. Have a competent repairman check your work to be sure you did it right.

• Be prepared to wait until the type of bicycle you want can be shipped to you; do not be talked into a more expensive model on hand. Few bicycle shops have any used ones, and bikes generally are in such demand that your choice may be very limited if you are not prepared to wait. You can, of course, widen your choice considerably by shopping around.

• If yours is a big family, you may be able to save literally hundreds of dollars over the years by letting your children earn the money for their own bikes, rather than providing them as gifts. An earned bike will probably last two or three times as long as a gift bike.

• After you have bought your bike, register it with the local police. Many communities impound unregistered bicycles, and, in any event, registration sharply increases your chance of recovering your bike if it is stolen.

• Check your homeowners insurance to see if it covers a bicycle. If not, you can get a special policy at about $10.50 a year for a $125 bicycle.

• And two final points: Don't set your heart on one bike as an absolute must. Until you get way up in the $200 price range, there is not that much difference between them. And in inexpensive bikes, a good dealer is your key to value, for he, rather than any manufacturer's guarantee, will stand behind your machine.

ENOUGH!

This chapter by no means covers all forms of locomotion. In addition, there are roller skates and pogo sticks, horses, snowshoes and parachutes.

But this is just a book, not an encyclopedia.

10

A COLLEGE EDUCATION
AND HOW TO FINANCE IT

COLLEGE EDUCATION COSTS SOARING	435
SHOPPING FOR COLLEGE	435
BARGAIN EDUCATION	439
HOW TO COMPARE COLLEGE COSTS	440
WHERE WILL THE MONEY COME FROM?	442
SCHOLARSHIPS	443
THE SCHOLARSHIP SQUEEZE	443
SCHOLARSHIP SHOPPING LIST	444
WHAT DOES IT TAKE TO GET A SCHOLARSHIP?	446
"HIDDEN" SCHOLARSHIPS	448
HOW TO GET A GRADUATE FELLOWSHIP	450
EARN YOUR WAY: IT'S "IN"	451
COLLEGE CO-OP PROGRAMS	451
THE FEDERAL WORK-STUDY PROGRAM	453
LOANS	454
HOW TO SHOP FOR A COLLEGE LOAN	454
THE LOANS AVAILABLE TO YOU: A LIST	455
COLLEGE LOANS FROM COLLEGES THEMSELVES	456
FEDERALLY ASSISTED STUDENT LOAN PROGRAMS	456
LOANS FROM CIVIC ORGANIZATIONS	465
LOANS FROM PRIVATE FINANCIAL INSTITUTIONS	466
POSTPONING TUITION—OR "PAYE"	467
"NEW" IDEA FOR FINANCING HIGHER EDUCATION	467
WHERE TO GET ADDITIONAL HELPFUL INFORMATION	469
BEWARE: HOME STUDY GYPS	469

College Education Costs Soaring

A college education has become close to essential in today's workplace—in fact, a *must* if you are to qualify for many jobs in industry, business, government, education, in the health professions, in hundreds of other occupational areas. But in recent years the cost of college education has soared far beyond even the middle-income family's ability to pay. The scramble for the limited number of scholarships, loans, and on-campus jobs is becoming ever more furious each year. For millions, the dream of college has become a nightmare.

A few revealing points:

The average cost of tuition and room and board at a public college rose 45 per cent in the one decade of the 1960s.

The increase at private institutions was even greater—a whopping 65 per cent.

On average, these costs are mounting 8 to 10 per cent a year, year after year.

The cost of going to a good, private American college for four years, as the mid-1970s approached could run to as much as $30,000.

If you have a brother or sister or two who also are at college age, your family's total expense could be an astronomical $60,000 to $90,000. And this assumes—unrealistically—that college costs will stay at today's levels. Obviously, they won't.

Shopping for College

Let's say you are not poor enough to qualify for a scholarship or grant. What *can* you do to cut the costs of going to college?

A prime way to cut your costs at the very start is through your own selection of a college or university. Your basic guidelines are:

• The least expensive way to get a college education is to live at home and go to a free or low-tuition college or two or four year college, or live at home and participate in an external degree program (see section "Bargain Education" in this chapter).

• Next is the state college in your own state.

• After that is a state college out of your home state.

• The most expensive is the private university—even if you live at home.

Tuition, fees, room and board charges vary widely from college to college, both public and private. A public college will usually charge much less than a private school and, taking other factors into consideration, your savings could amount to as much as $2,000 to $3,000 *per year*.

To illustrate, let's take two well-known universities in one state: the University of Pennsylvania, a private institution in Philadelphia, and Pennsylvania State University, in University Park in the western part of the state. Both are major coeducational institutions; both are highly respected for their faculties and programs.

For the 1976–77 school year, the University of Pennsylvania charged about $4,100 in tuition and fees and $2,200 for room and board—for a total of $6,300 per year.

For the same year, if you were a resident of the state and chose Pennsylvania State University, you would have been charged $1,095 in tuition and fees, and $1,389 in room and board charges—for a total of $2,484.

If you found that two institutions both offered you comparable programs for the purposes of your studies, and you chose the state university, *your annual savings would have been $3,816*.

Here is a sampling of resident charges made around the country in private and public four-year colleges, large and small. It is excerpted from "Student Expenses at Postsecondary Institutions, 1976–77," available for $2.50 from the CSS, College Entrance Examination Board, Box 2815, Princeton, N.J. 08540. This is one of the best guides of its kind; it includes average costs at about 930 two-year institutions and 1,568 four-year institutions.

Private colleges

NAME AND LOCATION	TUITION, FEES	ROOM, BOARD	OTHER EXPENSES	TOTAL EXPENSES
Beloit College, Beloit, Wis.	$3,540	$1,280	$ 500	$5,320
Bennington College, Bennington, Vt.	5,150	1,400	400	6,950
Boston College, Chestnut Hill, Mass.	$3,350	$1,525	$ 925	$5,800
*Brandeis University, Waltham, Mass.	3,550	1,750	650	5,950
*University of Chicago, Chicago, Ill.	3,225	1,775	670	5,670
Colgate University, Hamilton, N.Y.	3,800	1,640	660	6,100
Dartmouth College, Hanover, N.H.	4,230	1,975	1,755	7,960
Duke University, Durham, N.C.	3,300	1,600	650	5,550
Emory University, Atlanta, Ga.	3,150	1,551	1,074	5,775
Fairleigh Dickinson University, Rutherford, N.J.	2,550	1,550	700	4,800
George Washington University, Washington, D.C.	2,750	1,900	850	5,500
Howard University, Washington, D.C.	1,518	1,186	1,150	3,854
Johns Hopkins University, Baltimore, Md.	3,600	2,050	950	6,600
Knox College, Galesburg, Ill.	3,530	1,270	750	5,550

* Indicates data for the 1975–76 academic year.

Name and Location	Tuition, Fees	Room, Board	Other Expenses	Total Expenses
**Loyola University, New Orleans, La.	1,750	1,100	800	3,650
Massachusetts Institute of Technology, Cambridge, Ma.	4,150	2,750	750	7,650
Northwestern University, Evanston, Ill.	3,840	1,570	700	6,110
Oberlin College, Oberlin, Ohio	3,838	1,540	450	5,828
University of Richmond, Richmond, Va.	2,600	1,350	800	4,750
Sarah Lawrence College, Bronxville, N.Y.	4,190	2,100	1,100	7,390
Tulane University, New Orleans, La.	3,330	1,695	575	5,600
Vassar College, Poughkeepsie, N.Y.	3,410	1,500	800	5,710
Wilkes College, Wilkes-Barre, Pa.	2,500	1,300	650	4,450
Xavier University, Cincinnati, O.	2,100	1,460	765	4,325
Public colleges				
** University of Alabama, Huntsville, Ala.	$ 525	$1,180	$ 820	$2,525
Arizona State University, Tempe, Ariz.	450	1,750	950	3,150
University of Florida, Gainesville, Fla.	660	1,665	780	3,105
*Indiana State University, Terre Haute, Ind.	744	1,139	617	2,500
University of Maryland, College Park, Md.	778	1,600	775	3,153

* Data for 1975–76 year; ** Data for 1973–74 year.

Name and Location	Tuition, Fees	Room, Board	Other Expenses	Total Expenses
**University of Michigan, Ann Arbor, Mich.	$ 696	$1,236	$ 768	$2,700
Ohio State University, Columbus, O.	810	1,500	665	2,975
University of Texas, Arlington, Tex.	370	1,585	890	2,845
University of Virginia, Charlottesville, Va.	750	1,400	650	2,800

** Indicates data for the 1973–74 academic year.

BARGAIN EDUCATION

Other ways to slash your college costs are through a telescoped, three-year degree program; through credit by examination programs, such as the College Level Examination Program (CLEP), or through an "external degree program."

Three-year degree options are offered by an increasing number of colleges. They are ordinarily open only to the ablest students, because you must not only take on a heavier load of courses but you must also, normally, attend classes during the summer. This obviously reduces your ability to earn money to meet college expenses. Nevertheless, the possibility of paying only three years of tuition and living expenses for a college degree, combined with the time saving, make three-year degree programs a very attractive deal financially.

The College Level Examination Program permits you to cut college costs by demonstrating knowledge of a subject in an examination. CLEP exams are given monthly at 650 different locations throughout the United States—and more than 2,000 colleges and universities grant credit toward degrees to those who score high enough on the tests.

For details, write to CLEP, College Entrance Examination Board, Box 2815, Princeton, N.J. 08540, or Box 1025, Berkeley, Calif. 94701. Home study courses which might not by themselves qualify for college credit can help you toward a college degree if they enable you to get a passing score on the appropriate CLEP test.

(Caution: If you are in the market for this type of study, heed the warnings later in the section "Beware: Home Study Gyps.")

In an *external degree program* you do your regular college studies off campus. It's a unique form of low-cost education with particular appeal if you must maintain a job while you study. It also opens up many new opportunities for millions of you—housewives and others—who might never have a chance otherwise to get a degree.

If you, a student, live and study at home, your education may cost only about half as much as the cost of an on-campus education. One large experiment of this kind is New York State's new Empire State College, where costs for New York residents ran only $1,067 for a recent twelve-month year. Another is the New York Regents External Degree Program, which is unique in its willingness to grant a degree to an applicant who has not followed any prescribed program of study—if he can demonstrate his ability in his field.

The degree you get through one of these external degree programs is *not* a cut-rate mail order diploma in any sense. It is the same high-quality, specialized degree granted the normal way by a given institution. Despite the fact that these programs still are experimental, they do offer you great potential—if you are capable of studying independently.

How to Compare College Costs

You have made the basic choice of what type of college you want to go to and in what state. Now write the three or four institutions you would like to attend. Ask each for its catalogues and whatever material it has available on local living costs, financial-aid programs, and the like.

Then, using this material and your own estimates of other costs, make out financial work sheets to give yourself an idea of what a year's total expenses will be. If you're careful, you'll come very close to the actual amount.

Two tips: *Add* 7 per cent a year for the second year, 15 per cent for the third year, and 23 per cent for the fourth year to take inflation and other price-boosting factors into account. *Don't* underestimate, and thus invite a rude shock later on.

Use the following college-expense work sheet to estimate and compare college costs:

ANNUAL EXPENSE ITEM*	COLLEGE A	COLLEGE B	COLLEGE C
Tuition			
All fees (student activity, library, application, breakage, etc.)			
Room and board			
Books			
Equipment and supplies			
Laboratory charges			
Travel to and from school			
All other travel			
Recreation and entertainment			
Clothing			
Laundry, dry cleaning, etc.			
Dues for fraternity or sorority			
Grooming (cosmetics, haircuts, etc.)			
Health expenditure (incl. insurance premiums)			
Snacks, cigarettes, etc.			
Church and charity contributions			
Your capital expenditures, prorated annually (car, bicycle, record player and records, musical instruments, sports equipment, etc.)			
Miscellaneous current expenses			
Total annual estimate			

* If you are a married couple, see Chapter 1, "Your Personal Money Manager," pages 24–26.

WHERE WILL THE MONEY COME FROM?

The essential element in getting a college education is the motivation of you and your family. Despite the enormous price tag, if you *really* want an education, you'll get the funds for it somehow.

Obviously, the first answer to the question "Where will the money come from?" is from family savings built up over many years for precisely this purpose. This is where the motivation of parents comes in, for the savings must be accumulated through long-term planning, periodic investment, discipline, and dedication.

If your children are young enough, it may be possible for you to put away enough in savings to get a head start on college costs. However, unless you're most unusual your savings will not be enough.

A second answer, therefore, must be deductions from current income. This is where the working mother enters the picture in brilliant light—for it is her earnings which have become, are, and will be among the biggest sources for college education funds. Without the contributions of their mothers to their education funds, millions of students simply could not make it.

But neither of these answers is anywhere near adequate.

So we come to the fundamental point that most families trying to get one or more children through school must have help. Here are the other key sources of college education money:

• A student's own savings and earnings, part time and during vacations.

• Loans. These can range from federal and state loans to those arranged through civic organizations, social clubs, churches, and commercial lending institutions.

• Scholarships. Perhaps the most sought-after single source of aid, scholarships are awarded by the colleges and universities themselves, by corporations, veterans' groups, civic groups, cities, states, private philanthropies and foundations, a host of others.

• Grants. Much of this money goes to the low-income student, and most of the funds come from the federal government—although corporations and foundations offer substantial amounts of grant money as well. For most grant money, academic achievement is not a factor.

You probably will find that you will wind up with some combination of all of these.

SCHOLARSHIPS

THE SCHOLARSHIP SQUEEZE

Every few months a headline in newpapers across the country proclaims "Millions in Scholarships Go Begging." The story usually is released by firms that use computers to search for scholarships, which match the needs, interests, and qualifications of students against huge banks of details on the scholarships actually available to them today.

And there are a lot of specialized scholarships knocking around, for would-be organic vegetable growers, future rodeo ropers, pottery majors, prospective missionaries, direct descendants of Union soldiers who served in the Civil War, etc.

I would never downgrade *any* effective scholarship matching service—computerized or otherwise. I certainly won't claim that every penny of available scholarship money is actually being used, particularly those "funny funds" for students with special interests or special backgrounds. But I *will* quarrel with the cruel implication that huge sums of scholarship money are being wasted because students and parents simply don't know where to find such funds. It just isn't true. The students who are in college now are up against the biggest scholarship squeeze in our history.

Among the facts on scholarships today:

• At a growing number of colleges more than half of the student body is getting some type of financial assistance.

• Federal funds of all kinds to assist college students, which were counted in the millions only a decade or so ago, now are counted in the billions. *But* most federal funds are going today into low-cost publicly subsidized loans and work-study grants, rather than into straight scholarships.

• Scholarships are, as always, by far the most eagerly fought-over source of financial aid, whether the giver is government, colleges, corporations, foundations, cities, states, or civic organizations. If *you* let yourself count on getting one, chances are you'll be bitterly disappointed, for only a fraction of those who apply ever get one. Furthermore, the individual amounts involved often are $500 or less—a sum which barely touches real-life financial needs.

SCHOLARSHIP SHOPPING LIST

Here's a rundown on some scholarships now available.

• *The National Merit Scholarship Corporation,* which hands out millions in scholarships each year, is the largest, best-known, and most widely sought private scholarship source in the United States today. More than a million students take the combined PSAT/NMSQT three-hour test every fall in high schools across the country both for guidance purposes and in competition for one of these scholarships. But only about 3,000 ever get one. The scholarships range in value from $100 to $1,500 a year for four years, with financial need being the yardstick to determine who gets the $1,500. Some winners simply get one-shot stipends of $1,000. Just about every high school in the country takes part, so you might as well try. See your guidance counselor.

There is one added dividend here. Even if you're not one of the lucky finalists, you could be one of the 50,000 who receive special commendations and citations because of your test scores. *These can help you when you look for financial help elsewhere.*

• *State scholarships* number in the thousands, vary all over the lot in size, terms, etc. For information, check with your school guidance counselor or state Department of Education. If you are a handicapped student, check with your state Department of Vocational Rehabilitation.

• *Labor unions* also now award large numbers of scholarships. Check with either your union or the union your parents belong to. Or write for the "Student Aid Bulletin—Scholarships Offered by Labor Unions" ($2.00 prepaid; Chronicle Guidance Publications, Moravia, New York, 13118).

• *Corporation scholarships* are a worth-while source of funds, so don't overlook them. Many businesses now offer scholarships for children of employees. Some companies award scholarships to students who have no connection with the company.

• *Trade associations* often have their own scholarships for children of members.

• *Civic and fraternal organizations* sponsoring scholarships range from the American Legion posts or auxiliary units to the Elks, Lions, Masons, Parent-Teacher Associations, and Daughters of the American Revolution. In most instances scholarships are for young men and women living in the community in which the organization is located.

• *Other sponsors include* the Boy Scouts, 4-H Clubs, Chamber of Commerce, Jaycees, Junior Achievement, a wide range of religious organizations.

• Black students are aided by the National Scholarship Service and Fund for Negro Students (1776 Broadway, New York, N.Y. 10019).

• *Professional associations* are worth following up, and if you already have plans to enter a specialty after you finish college, check with the professional associations in your future specialty for what financial aid they offer. Many try to stimulate young students to enter their fields through scholarships and fellowships.

• *The Supplemental Educational Opportunity Grant Program* is the federal government's key scholarship source. This is not a scholarship program in the usual sense, for the primary criterion is not academic excellence but rather *exceptional* financial need. Still, some 400,000 low-income students (family income less than $9,000) got a total of $240 million in grants in fiscal 1975.

Eligible students received grants for up to four years of undergraduate work and the amounts ranged from $200 to $1,500 per year, up to $4,000 for four years of college, $5,000 for a five-year program. The total may not exceed one half of a student's estimated financial needs. To qualify, students must be exceptionally needy, but need not be academic stars. These grants are matched by the institutions with other forms of aid such as loans and jobs. Nearly 3,400 colleges and universities participated in this program during the 1975–76 academic year, making awards directly to the students. Check with the director of student financial aid at the institution you want to attend for more details.

• *Basic Educational Opportunity Grants,* authorized by the Education Amendments of 1972, are available to half- or full-time undergraduate college, vocational, and technical school students.

The grants are designed to add up to half the total costs of attending a school. Theoretically, the amounts go up to $1,400 a year—but the average in 1975 was about $800 per student. To apply, get an "application for determination of expected financial contribution" from your high school guidance counselor, public library, college financial aid officer, or the U. S. Office of Education. Fill out the form and send it to the address indicated. A computer will estimate what your family should be able to contribute toward your education.

When this data is returned to you, report the amount to the financial aid officer at your chosen school.

• *ROTC scholarships* are being awarded to students at hundreds of colleges in most states of the United States. ROTC scholarships gained in popularity after the end of the Vietnam war and during the economic slump of 1975–76.

These scholarships are aimed at students wanting to pursue careers as officers in the military services. In most programs, full costs of tuition, books, and fees—plus a monthly allowance for living expenses—are covered. In return, you, the participant, must commit yourself to a military career. In the Army, though, you can retire after only twenty years of service at one half your base pay. To apply, contact the appropriate military service or the ROTC office at the participating college of your choice. Application deadlines in most cases are in November and December.

• The federal government also has substantial sums available to students going into special fields—particularly health. Scholarships range up to $3,500 per year. To get details, write to the Bureau of Health Resources Development, National Institutes of Health, 9000 Rockville Pike, Bethesda, Md. 20014.

This is only a sampling. Any complete listing of scholarships available in this country today would be so extensive that it would make a book of its own.

WHAT DOES IT TAKE TO GET A SCHOLARSHIP?

How needy must you—or your family—be? What factors, in addition to academic standing, boost a student's chances for a scholarship today?

Generally speaking, a high school student today must graduate with at least a B average and rank in the top half of his class to get into a good four-year college. The requirements are understandably tougher for scholarships.

But high grades are not the sole yardstick for winning a scholarship. Even without a superior academic record these other factors can help tremendously toward a scholarship: a student's outstanding personality, a demonstrated capacity for leadership, an unusual or special talent (say in music, art, sports, foreign languages).

Special consideration is now often given, too, to students from minority groups or candidates who have overcome a severe handicap or misfortune during their lives.

How needy must your family be?

Whether you are merely a better-than-average student or one with a straight A record, your key to getting a scholarship will be *proving need*. You cannot just *plead* poverty; you must *prove* it.

The gifted child of the very needy has the best chances for most scholarships. But some help is also available to students whose families have other burdensome expenses. Or help may be available if college costs are especially high at the institution the child wishes to attend.

For instance, even the $20,000-a-year family may be considered "needy"—if there are three children to support and if the college charges $3,000 to $4,000 or more a year.

Although less needy students and their families are expected to contribute substantial shares of their earnings, savings, and assets toward college costs, a family's total financial picture is taken into account —and the amount the family is expected to pay is measured by what it can "reasonably afford." Today's student financial aid is designed to fill the gap between that sum and total college costs.

How are "total" costs and family "need" figured today?

Here are the basic guidelines of the College Scholarship Service, part of the non-profit service of the College Entrance Examination Board in New York City, which helps major U.S. colleges determine eligibility of students for financial aid.

In calculating total college costs, the CSS includes not only tuition and fees but also room, board, transportation, clothing, books, spending money.

In calculating family need, it takes into account these major factors: family income, number of other children to support, the breadwinner's age and retirement plans, unusual financial burdens such as other children in college at the same time, an expensive illness, whether the spouse works, size of debts.

The CSS also weighs total family assets—cash savings, equity in the home, securities owned, etc.—and applies a share of this total to the amount a family can afford to contribute. This share, though, is comparatively small—12 per cent—and assets up to $10,000 are usually not counted. If the family head is more than fifty-five years old, even higher asset totals are disregarded.

You, the scholarship seeker, are expected to contribute part of your total college costs. Typically, your expected contribution would include 30 per cent of your current savings for each year that you are in college. Also about $500 in summer earnings must be contributed for the first year (before you enter college), and increasing amounts for the following years.

Here is what the CSS believes families should be able to contribute in the 1977–78 academic year toward college costs for one child—at various income levels and with varying numbers of dependent children.

INCOME BEFORE TAXES	ONE CHILD	TWO CHILDREN	THREE CHILDREN
$ 8,000	$ 97	$ 0	$ 0
10,000	410	124	0
12,000	707	419	164
14,000	1,013	724	473
16,000	1,386	1,042	779
18,000	1,832	1,418	1,109
20,000	2,368	1,856	1,484

These are just "suggested" contributions. By no means do they bind any college to provide the balance of the costs. They do give you a general indication of what financial efforts are expected in the mid-1970s from the student and his family. They also indicate what financial help many colleges are trying to provide you or your child via scholarships, loans, and student jobs.

"HIDDEN" SCHOLARSHIPS

Are you aware that Social Security benefits are a major source of income for many students? Could it be that you're among the many qualifying for such benefits today but you don't know it?

All of you who are unmarried full-time students qualify for this Social Security program, which can be a major income supplement to help you meet college costs—*if you are children of deceased, disabled, or retired workers.* Check at once at your nearest Social Security office.

And do you realize that veterans' educational benefits are now being paid to hundreds of thousands of college students—and tens of thousands of veterans' wives, widows, and children are also receiving college benefits? These benefits represent more help to students than all scholarships at all U.S. colleges and universities put together.

Under the Veterans Readjustment Benefits Act of 1966 (the "Cold War GI Bill"), single veterans who have been at some time on active duty since January 31, 1955, were being paid $270 a month in 1974 if they attended an accredited college or other educational institution. Married veterans were getting as much as $321 a month. Married veterans with one child were getting up to $366 a month—and $22 for each additional child. Stipends were reduced for veterans studying less than full time. For example, the monthly benefit for a single half-time student was $135 ($160 for a married student).

You, as a veteran, can get these "scholarships" not only to attend college but also to complete high school if you have not already done so; or to attend business school; or to enroll in a wide variety of vocational training programs. There are provisions for farm co-operative training and 90 per cent reimbursement programs for correspondence school and flight training. If you have difficulty with your studies, the VA will pay for tutoring (up to $60 a month). Veterans in apprenticeship or on-the-job training programs in 1974 were eligible for stipends of $196 per month if single, or $220 per month if married and more if there were children.

In addition, under the so-called "Junior GI Bill," if you are a wife, widow, widower, or child of a veteran who died or became permanently and totally disabled as a result of his military service, you can get similar monthly stipends to attend college.

And if you're already enrolled in a VA educational program, you can get extra allowances if you agree to work up to 250 hours for the VA (up to $625 per semester in 1975).

HOW TO GET A GRADUATE FELLOWSHIP

A single year of graduate study now costs a staggering $4,500 to $8,000. A Ph.D. may cost $25,000 to $30,000 or more, on top of as much as $30,000 for undergraduate schooling.

Obviously the vast majority of you cannot afford such sums, even though you may be acutely aware of the potential long-range return on the investment. You must have financial help. Fellowships, which have jumped to an average of about $3,000 a year today, are a major solution.

However, the number of fellowships is diminishing and competition for graduate fellowships is fierce, particularly in the sciences and particularly for the fattest fellowships. There are only a limited number of fellowships available to the non-genius with a serious interest in higher education. For him or her, the emphasis is on loans and jobs.

So, if you are considering graduate study and need a fellowship to help support it, here are five basic rules for finding and applying for one:

(1) Consult your graduate study adviser and professors in your major department on kinds and sources of fellowships and on institutions you might want to attend. Write the graduate school of each university to which you intend to apply and ask what financial assistance is available. The universities administer not only their own fellowship funds but also many of the government and private foundation funds as well.

(2) Find out all the financial details of each fellowship for which you think you might qualify. Exactly what does it cover: Tuition? Travel? The full year? Or only the academic year? Will the funds be tax-free? Are there special allowances for dependents?

(3) Focus on three or four fellowship sources, and confine your efforts to those for which you think you really qualify.

(4) Fill out application forms neatly, concisely, thoughtfully, and correctly. Pay special attention to your statement on why you want a fellowship and how you intend to use it. Include with your application *all* supporting documents which may be required, letters of recommendation, special tests, academic records, financial information, etc.

(5) Get your application in on time. Deadlines for some fellowships are as early as the fall of your senior year in college. Preparation

of your applications can easily take as long as six months before the deadline.

EARN YOUR WAY: IT'S "IN"

COLLEGE CO-OP PROGRAMS

You should be able to earn $5,000 to $13,000 or more during your college years without endangering your college standing. With other financial assistance you can get, you should be able to boost your income to $18,000 over the college period, a major portion of the cost of education at even the more expensive private universities.

It is actually easier to work your way through college than it has ever been. It also is "in" as never before. Even at such institutions as Massachusetts Institute of Technology and Harvard, half or more of all undergraduates hold jobs during the school year. Today literally millions of U.S. students are earning more than half of their total instructional costs at private colleges and one third of these costs at public colleges.

The typical part-time job at college now pays $400 to $800 during the academic year.

Here is a typical four-year income program:

$2,100 for four summers or $525 a year, including a pre-freshman summer;

$240 each year for the Christmas, mid-season, and spring vacations;

$450 each year for part-time work while school is in session.

This approximates $5,000 for the four years.

Meanwhile, co-operative education programs—under which students alternate periods of study with periods of work, frequently in their field of interest—are multiplying. Some 125,000 college students at more than 500 colleges the nation over are now using these work-study programs to earn an estimated $300 million during the school year. Another 400 are considering establishing these programs on an optional basis or in certain departments. At some schools, including Antioch, Wilberforce, and Boston's huge Northeastern University (one of the pioneers in the co-operative education movement), participation in this kind of plan is *mandatory*.

Although the programs differ from place to place, the basic aim is the same: to spread the financial burden so that the student shares part of the loan with parents and/or the college. Most plans also spread tuition costs as well, simply by requiring five years to earn a degree instead of the usual four.

At Northeastern, more than 15,000 full-time students were enrolled in some 46 different degree programs in a recent year and also worked for more than 2,000 employers across the nation. Here's how the five-year Northeastern study schedule works:

As in most plans of this type, the freshman year is spent in regular, full-time, on-campus study. During the next four years the student alternates between three months of school and three months working on a paying job. He is paired with another student so that the job is covered full time throughout the year without a break. At the end of five years the graduate has his degree, plus about two years of relevant job experience—and that's a *priceless* plus these days.

The college usually will find the job for you and, ideally, the position will be related in some way to your field of study. When the job market is tight, you may not be able to count on getting just the kind of job you had in mind and business cutbacks may also temporarily cut down on your choice of jobs. But these cycles run their course in time. Employers also are showing increasing sympathy to the needs of students and willingness to employ them on a temporary, part-time basis.

How much can you earn in a work-study program of this type? The *average* annual earnings of the co-op student in the mid-1970s were approaching $3,000. This was about $1,500 higher than the earnings of the student in the more traditional type of school.

Most students can earn between $60 and $200 per week during work assignments—with the average about $113 a week. Thus, if you live at home during the work periods, you should be able to earn and save about half your tuition.

For example, at Philadelphia's Drexel University the tuition, fees, and room and board in the 1972–73 academic year were $14,288 for the traditional four-year course, and $15,295 for the five-year co-op plan also offered by the school.

A four-year student, working summers and vacations, can earn perhaps $5,000. This leaves a tab of $9,288 to be paid. On the other hand, a co-op student can earn about $12,850 in engineering and about $14,690 in business. This leaves only another $2,445 for the engineer or $605 for the business student to pay over a period of five years.

And don't discount the *intangibles* of co-op education: many students, for instance, find the work experience gives them a heightened sense of responsibility, more confidence in their decisions, and greater maturity.

For a list of colleges offering co-op programs write: National Commission for Cooperative Education, 360 Huntington Avenue, Boston, Mass. 02115.

THE FEDERAL WORK-STUDY PROGRAM

Since 1965 more than a million college students from low-income families have been helped by the federal government's work-study program.

This program, which should not be confused with co-operative education, is strictly aimed at promoting summer and part-time employment of students with great financial need in order to help them get through school. The jobs are *not* necessarily related to the anticipated careers for which the students are studying but in some cases they are career-geared.

Here's how it works: the government provides up to 80 per cent of the salaries of those students who qualify for jobs on campus or by nearby employers; the latter must be non-profit, non-religious, and non-political. Students are paid at least the basic national minimum wage.

You may qualify if you can demonstrate need. You'll probably average about fifteen hours of work while you're attending classes, and work about forty hours a week between semesters and during the summer.

More than half a million students and about 3,000 institutions were participating in 1974. So it's more than likely that the college you prefer participates in this program.

Many governmental agencies are also taking part in the work-study program as employers. There's a whole range of them you should look into. For instance:

• The Civil Service Commission hires students during summer periods in a variety of specialties, including such esoteric fields as ocean-ography.

• The U. S. Weather Bureau hires students to train in meteorology.

• The Army, Navy, and Coast Guard all have co-operative pro-grams and hire undergraduate technical students in engineering, mathe-matics, science, and accounting.

Other agencies involved include the Federal Aviation Agency, the Federal Communications Commission, the National Aeronautics and Space Administration, and the Departments of Commerce, Agriculture, and Interior.

The federal "academic apprentice" program is operated very much like other co-operative-education programs in that students alternate study and work periods. It will give you a chance to earn while you learn, and may give you a clue as to whether you would enjoy govern-ment work later on.

For information, contact the Civil Service Commission or those government agencies which have departments in your specialty. If you have *any* questions, check with your college placement office.

LOANS

HOW TO SHOP FOR A COLLEGE LOAN

For you, the students with high grades and great financial need, there will be an unprecedented number of scholarships and low-cost student loans to help you through college.

But what about the millions of you who are students with marks which are less than excellent? What about the millions of students who aren't considered needy enough by federal, state, or university stand-ards to qualify for a scholarship or a loan at little or no interest? What about parents in the middle to higher income brackets who suddenly face the staggering drain of a college education for two or more chil-dren?

Confronted by the steep and rising costs of college education, mounting numbers of families are turning to commercial banks, sav-ings and loan associations, insurance companies, credit unions, and other lending institutions for college loans. Thousands of private lending institutions are now offering an increasing variety of college loan plans with a wide variety of repayment terms and interest costs.

How can you—a student or a parent—find your way through the maze of college loan plans? This point is as vital in this sphere as in all others: You must shop. You must shop for a college loan as you would for a mortgage or any major personal purchase.

Here, then, are basic rules for finding the best deal—assuming you do not qualify for scholarship assistance or a loan at little or no interest:

• As I urged you at the start of this chapter, first draw up a total budget for all anticipated college costs—including tuition, board, room, books, clothes, transportation, spending money. Divide this amount by the total number of semesters of school attendance.

• Decide how big a debt you can handle and don't exceed your limit.

• Decide how long you will need to repay the loan.

• Present these figures to at least two or three different lenders and ask what monthly payments would be required—including any charges for insurance.

• Compare the bids. The lowest monthly charge will be the most favorable to you—assuming equal repayment periods, equal loan amounts, and equal insurance charges.

THE LOANS AVAILABLE TO YOU: A LIST

Here are the kinds of loans available to you as a student, starting with the least expensive. Look into them in this order:

(1) A college loan involving low interest on the loan, which is repayable starting sometime after graduation.

(2) A federal government loan which is administered by a college.

(3) A loan that is guaranteed by a state and/or the federal government.

(4) A low-interest loan through a civic or religious group.

(5) A deferred-tuition plan offered by a number of schools.

(6) A loan from a credit union, if you're a member.

(7) A bank or insurance company loan.

(8) As a last resort, a finance company loan.

Now, the details . . .

COLLEGE LOANS FROM COLLEGES THEMSELVES

What to Do

Hundreds of colleges and universities are now offering long-term loan programs of their own to you, the student. Almost all of these are bargains in terms of low interest rates and tolerable repayment schedules.

You'll find that the amount of money available through these loans does not begin to compare with the huge sums available from other sources. But if you're lucky enough to borrow through a school's own program, most of your financial worries will be minimized from the very beginning.

Loans made to:	Students
Loans made by:	College itself. May be short-term emergency loan. Or may be in co-operation with federal government for long-term. Or may be a long-term loan under a postponed tuition plan.
Amount of loans:	Varies widely. Can be small if short-term emergency loan or can run into thousands of dollars.
Interest rates:	Also vary widely, no fixed rate, but almost always compare *very favorably* with rates charged by others.
Repayment:	Starts at graduation or a year thereafter if ordinary college loan; can be stretched out over a very long period. Repayment is likely to be deferred for as long as the student is in graduate school.
How to apply:	Go directly to the financial aid officer at your college.

FEDERALLY ASSISTED STUDENT LOAN PROGRAMS

National Direct Student Loans

The 1958 National Defense Education Act established an unprecedented program of low-interest, long-term loans to students with financial need. This legislation literally multiplied the volume of loan funds for higher education. More recently, the National Defense Education Act was superseded by the Educational Amendments of 1972, and the revised program was renamed the National Direct Student Loans. Key facts of this program:

Loans made to: Students who are citizens or permanent residents of the United States and plan to study at a college in this country.

Loans approved by: Colleges on the basis of student's needs. College student aid officers on campus determine which students are eligible and the amount of money to be loaned.

This is a vital point, for you must demonstrate that you are *in financial need* to get one of these loans if your income is above $15,000. The student financial aid officer may expect you to accept some part-time work to minimize your loan needs and to give the college making the loan an opportunity to spread available funds among a larger number of students.

Some colleges also require parents to complete a detailed account of the family's *entire* financial picture as a way of determining how much the parents can be expected to contribute to the student's educational costs.

Who puts up money: For each NDS loan, the federal government puts up 90 per cent of the money and the college itself puts up 10 per cent.

Amount of loans: Up to $10,000 for graduate or professional students; up to $5,000 for students who have finished two years of a program leading to a bachelor's degree; and up to $2,500 for all other students.

The size of the loan for you will probably *not be these maximums,* though. The amount you get will depend on *your* individual financial

Amount of loans: *(cont'd)*	need as well as on the funds available at the college you will attend.
Interest rates:	3 per cent a year, paid by the student beginning with the start of the repayment period.
Repayment starts:	Nine months after the student ceases at least half-time study.
Repayment period:	Can be stretched out over a ten-year period.
How to apply:	Go directly to the student financial aid officer on your campus.
Other points:	No repayment is required and no interest is charged for any period up to three years during which you are serving in the armed forces, Peace Corps, or Vista.
	Up to half your loan may be canceled at the rate of 12.5 per cent for each complete year of armed forces service in a combat zone.
	Also, if you, the student, become a teacher for the handicapped, or Head Start, or in a school in an unusually low-income area, all of your loan may be canceled at the rate of 15 per cent a year.
	As part of the application procedure, you must sign, and have notarized, an affidavit affirming that the loan will be used for educational purposes only.
	There are several other direct loan programs for students in special fields, notably health professions and law enforcement. For information on these programs, see your guidance counselor or financial aid officer.

Government Guaranteed Student Loan Programs

Before 1965 a number of states financed programs guaranteeing repayment of college loans to protect private lenders against default by students, in order to make such loans more attractive to the lenders.

Since then, the Higher Education Act of 1965, the National Vocational Student Loan Insurance Act of 1965, and the Educational Amendments of 1972 have made federal loan repayment guarantees available in states without programs of their own. The key facts:

Loans made to: Students who are enrolled and in good standing, or accepted for enrollment, at an eligible school. Some states require full-time attendance, but the federal government and most states accept half-time students for their programs.

Borrowers must be citizens or permanent residents of the United States.

Eligible schools: Most public and private institutions of higher education. Also eligible: many vocational, business, trade, correspondence, and technical schools, and some schools located in 55 countries abroad—a vital point you should not miss. In the mid-seventies more than 8,000 institutions were eligible. The Accreditation and Eligibility Staff of the Office of Education, Washington, D.C. 20202, can tell you whether or not a particular school is eligible.

Loans made by: Nearly 20,000 participating lenders—commercial banks, savings and loan associations, credit unions, mutual savings banks, some colleges, insurance companies, and pension plans.

Amount of loans: You normally may borrow as much as $2,500 per year toward your education, depending on your educational costs. However, some state programs may place a lower ceiling on borrowing than this. And, of course, a lender may be unwilling to lend you the maximum for his own reasons. Your total loan may not exceed $7,500 if you are an undergraduate or vocational student, or $10,000 if you are borrowing for graduate study.

Interest rates: A maximum rate to you of 7 per cent per year, in simple annual interest. In addition, the federal government pays a "special allowance" of up to 3 per cent, readjusted quarterly, to lenders to make the loans more attractive to them.

Loans may be available at lower rates at times of very low general interest rates, but you ordinarily should expect to pay the 7 per cent maximum. In addition, there may be a charge for an insurance premium up to ½ per cent a year on the unpaid principal balance (this is limited to ¼ per cent on federally insured loans).

If your adjusted family income is less than $15,000 a year, you will not face a needs analysis test and the federal government will pay your interest until the start of your repayment period. You may still qualify for these federal interest benefits if your gross adjusted income is above $15,000, but then you must pass a needs test.

Repayment starts: Nine to twelve months after you leave school.

Repayment period: May extend to ten years after you leave school —subject to a maximum of fifteen years from the date the loan was made. The minimum yearly payment is $360.

If you join the Peace Corps or Vista after graduation, or if you go into military service, payments may be deferred for up to three years. Repayment also may be deferred for any time you spend in further full-time study at an eligible school.

Your federal interest subsidy resumes during the payment-deferral period if you were eligible before.

Prepayment: Allowed without penalty.

How to apply: Go to the financial aid officer of the college you

How to apply:
(cont'd)

plan to attend and fill out the appropriate forms. Then go to one or more lenders in your own town or city where you or your parents have accounts or other established business relationships, and find out whether they participate in the Guaranteed Student Loan Program. Visit banks and savings institutions, of course, but do not forget credit unions.

If you do not find a participating lender, write or go immediately to the financial aid officer of your college, or the nearest regional office of the U. S. Office of Education or state guarantee agency (see pages 462–65 for appropriate addresses), and ask for the names and locations of financial institutions near your home which do participate.

Ask the appropriate officer at the lending institution to help you complete the necessary forms. Your college's financial aid office may help you with the forms (and it should analyze your finances to determine your loan needs) to be submitted as a recommendation to the lender. You also will have to sign an affidavit declaring that your loan will be used only for educational purposes. The affidavit must be notarized.

The lender will evaluate your application and the school's recommendation and decide how large a loan will qualify for federal interest benefits and how much it will lend you.

You might find it difficult to locate a lender when money is tight, though the history of the program suggests that if you keep trying you will find one.

By all means, when you apply, check on what restrictions the lender makes on loan recipients. This could save you a lot of time and work as well as the disappointment of getting needlessly involved in the elaborate application process at a balky financial institution.

United Student Aid Funds

The largest private guarantor of student loans today is the non-profit United Student Aid Funds (845 Third Avenue, New York, N.Y. 10022), supported primarily by foundations and private business contributions. The USAF is not only a major participant in the Government Guaranteed Student Loan Programs, in its role as the administrator of a number of state programs; it also has a separate guaranteed student loan program with many hundreds of colleges and universities participating in all fifty states. The key characteristics of these loans are exactly the same as previously described for government guaranteed student loan programs.

Where can you get detailed information on the Government Guaranteed Student Loan Program operating in your state?

Here are the addresses:

ALABAMA
Director of Higher Education
Office of Education, Region IV
50 Seventh Street, N.E.
Atlanta, Ga. 30323

ALASKA
Student Aid Officer
State Education Office
Pouch F, AOB
Juneau, Alas. 99801

ARIZONA
Director of Higher Education
Office of Education, Region IX
50 Fulton Street
San Francisco, Calif. 94102

ARKANSAS
Student Loan Guarantee
    Foundation of Arkansas
Suite 515, 1515 West 7th Street
Little Rock, Ark. 72202

CALIFORNIA (*see* Arizona)

COLORADO
Director of Higher Education
Office of Education, Region VIII
9017 Federal Office Building
19th & Stout Streets
Denver, Colo. 80202

CONNECTICUT
Connecticut Student Loan
    Foundation
251 Asylum Street
Hartford, Conn. 06103

DELAWARE
Delaware Higher Education Loan
    Program
c/o Brandywine College
P. O. Box 7139
Wilmington, Del. 19803

DISTRICT OF COLUMBIA
D.C. Student Loan Insurance
    Program
1329 E Street, N.W.
Washington, D.C. 20004

FLORIDA (*see* Alabama)

GEORGIA
Georgia Higher Education
    Assistance Corporation
9 LaVista Perimeter Park
2187 Worthlake Parkway
Atlanta, Ga. 30084

HAWAII (*see* Arizona)

IDAHO
Director of Higher Education
Office of Education, Region X
1321 Second Avenue
Seattle, Wash. 98101

ILLINOIS
Illinois Guaranteed Loan Program
102 Wilmot Road, P. O. Box 33
Deerfield, Ill. 60015

INDIANA
Director of Higher Education
Office of Education, Region V
300 South Wacker Drive
Chicago, Ill. 60606

IOWA
Director of Higher Education
Office of Education, Region VII
601 East 12th Street
Kansas City, Mo. 64106

KANSAS (*see* Iowa)

KENTUCKY (*see* Alabama)

LOUISIANA
Louisiana Higher Education
    Assistance Commission
P. O. Box 44095
Capitol Station
Baton Rouge, La. 70804

MAINE
Maine State Department of
    Education and Cultural
    Services
Augusta, Me. 04330

MARYLAND
Maryland Higher Education Loan
    Corporation
2100 Guilford Avenue
Baltimore, Md. 21218

MASSACHUSETTS
Massachusetts Higher Education
    Assistance Corporation
511 Statler Building
Boston, Mass. 02116

MICHIGAN
Michigan Higher Education
    Assistance Authority
309 North Washington Avenue
Lansing, Mich. 48902

MINNESOTA (*see* Indiana)

MISSISSIPPI (*see* Alabama)

MISSOURI (*see* Iowa)

MONTANA (*see* Colorado)

NEBRASKA (*see* Iowa)

NEVADA
State Department of Education
Carson City, Nev. 89701

NEW HAMPSHIRE
New Hampshire Higher Education
    Assistance Foundation
3 Capitol Street
Concord, N.H. 03301

NEW JERSEY
New Jersey Higher Education
    Assistance Authority
65 Prospect Street
P. O. Box 1293
Trenton, N.J. 08625

NEW MEXICO
Director of Higher Education
Office of Education, Region VI
1114 Commerce Street
Dallas, Tex. 75202

NEW YORK
New York Higher Education
    Assistance Corporation
50 Wolf Road
Albany, N.Y. 12205

NORTH CAROLINA
State Education Assistance
    Authority
P. O. Box 2688
Chapel Hill, N.C. 27514

NORTH DAKOTA (see Colorado)

OHIO
Ohio Student Loan Commission
33 North High Street
Columbus, O. 43215

OKLAHOMA
Oklahoma State Regents for
    Higher Education
118 Capitol Building
Oklahoma City, Okla. 73105

OREGON
Oregon State Scholarship
    Commission
1445 Willamette Street
Eugene, Ore. 97401

PENNSYLVANIA
Pennsylvania Higher Education
    Assistance Agency
Towne House, 660 Boas Street
Harrisburg, Pa. 17102

PUERTO RICO
Director of Higher Education
Office of Education, Region II
26 Federal Plaza
New York, N.Y. 10007

RHODE ISLAND
Rhode Island Higher Education
    Assistance Corporation
Room 414, 187 Westminster Mall
P. O. Box 579
Providence, R.I. 02901

SOUTH CAROLINA (see Alaska)

SOUTH DAKOTA (see Colorado)

TENNESSEE
Tennessee Education Loan
    Corporation
Cordell Hull Building
Fl. C-3, Rm. 301
Nashville, Tenn. 37219

TEXAS (see New Mexico)

UTAH (see Colorado)

VERMONT
Vermont Student Assistance
    Corporation
191 College Street
Burlington, Vt. 05401

VIRGINIA
Virginia State Education Assist-
    ance Authority
501 East Franklin Street
Suite 311
Professional Building
Richmond, Va. 23219

WASHINGTON (see Idaho)

WEST VIRGINIA
Director of Higher Education
Office of Education, Region III
P. O. Box 12900
Philadelphia, Pa. 19108

WISCONSIN
Wisconsin Higher Education
    Corporation
State Office Building
115 West Wilson Street
Madison, Wis. 53902

WYOMING (see Colorado)

AMERICAN SAMOA (see Arizona)

GUAM (see Arizona)

TRUST TERRITORY (see Arizona)

VIRGIN ISLANDS
United Student Aid Funds, Inc.
845 Third Avenue
New York, N.Y. 10022

LOANS FROM CIVIC ORGANIZATIONS

What to Do

Sources of college loans which are frequently overlooked but which might be ideal for you are local civic groups. Or perhaps your best bet would be a labor union or a church group.

Whatever the group, before you turn to a commercial lender, check into organizations such as these in your town. You well might find that one or more of them have substantial low-interest loans available to students.

Loans made to:	Students
Loans made by:	Organizations sponsoring the loan program: Rotary, Lions, Kiwanis, PTA, labor unions, churches, employers, etc.
Amounts:	Vary, depending on the financial resources of the organization and the student's need.
Interest rates:	Comparatively low against the money market at the time of loan.

Repayment:	Generally deferred for a while after graduation but also varies, according to the agreement between lender and borrower.
How to apply:	Consult your high school guidance counselor, your community center, your church, similar likely sources for information on what loans are available and your eligibility.

LOANS FROM PRIVATE FINANCIAL INSTITUTIONS

What to Do

If you can't develop other alternatives to finance your college education and must go the commercial loan route, do not hesitate to do so.

If a loan—even a long-term debt of thousands of dollars—is the difference between going to college and not going, consider it among the best investments you ever made.

Loans made to:	Parents, guardians, or students—usually the adults and students of legal majority age.
Loans made by:	Commercial banks, savings institutions, finance companies, credit unions, other financial sources.
Amount of loans:	Not specifically limited, if the borrower has demonstrable ability to repay or satisfactory collateral. This is, in short, an ordinary personal loan for education purposes. Maximum, though, is usually $8,000 to $10,000. Funds usually given to borrower in lump sums at start of each semester.
Interest rates:	Vary, depending on state of money market, area of country, caliber of borrower, term of loan.
	Generally rates are relatively high against levels of the money markets at the time—and a minimum "service charge" may be added.
Repayment:	Terms vary and depend on deal agreed upon but a period of six to eight years is fairly typical and repayments often start at the end of the first month of the loan's life.

"Special" College Loan Sources Then there are private lending companies which specialize in education loans. Some offer special arrangements—"budget" plans, revolving credit accounts under which borrowers may repay loans in installments and prepay whenever possible, etc. The plans might involve a fee for joining, monthly service charge, insurance premium, possibly a cancellation charge, possibly other fees too.

The costs of each and all of these plans should be carefully compared—a chore which you will find made easier by the Truth in Lending law which requires the lenders to disclose all important details of the charges to you.

A major company specializing in education loans is: The Tuition Plan, Inc., 575 Madison Avenue, New York, N.Y. 10022.

Questions to Ask Each Lender

What is the simple interest rate on your loan? Remember, by law, this rate must be disclosed.

What extra charges are involved?

How much may your family borrow for each child?

Can the lender terminate the plan? Under what conditions? Does it have to give you notice before cancellation?

Can you, the borrower, terminate the loan before the expiration of the contract? How much notice are you required to give? Are there any prepayment penalties involved?

Is there an age limit above which a parent will no longer qualify for the loan?

What other restrictions are there?

POSTPONING TUITION—OR "PAYE"

"NEW" IDEA FOR FINANCING HIGHER EDUCATION

When my brother John was going to medical school in the depression years of the 1930s there was only one way he could finance it: through high-interest education loans, co-signed by the most financially respectable friends we had. Those loans were renewed . . . renewed . . . renewed . . . until many years later, when John had graduated from med school, returned from World War II, and was earning money as a physician, he was able to repay the debt out of his current income.

It was a clumsy, monstrously expensive way to meet the costs of his education but it was the best we could do. John got his education and became a physician and surgeon. His loans, although stretched out over a long period, were finally and honorably repaid. Both goals were achieved and that's all any of us cared about.

Now in the 1970s, a "new" idea for financing a college or graduate school education is a revolutionary refined version of John's makeshift plan. The idea has various names: "the Yale plan"; "deferred tuition"; "tuition postponement"; "pay as you earn" (or "PAYE"). But fundamentally the student does in the 1970s what John did in the 1930s; he or she postpones paying at least part of the tuition until the years after graduation, when he is earning money and can manage it out of his own income.

Yale was the pioneer in the experiment and other colleges have developed their own variations. A national tuition postponement option plan, patterned after Yale's program, is very much a possibility, if not a probability, in coming years. But a national tuition postponement plan remains in the future. Here, meanwhile, are the key features you'll find in most of today's plans:

• The schools borrow the funds from private sources such as banks. Because of the caliber of the borrower and because the loan is a single large transaction, rather than a lot of little ones, the interest charges are comparatively favorable. These charges are certainly much lower than you would be charged for a conventional loan at the same institution.

• The student defers tuition by getting a loan from this fund. Then, after graduation, he repays what he has deferred.

• Repayment is geared to the graduate's income. Some will pay back more than the cost of their respective loans; others a bit less, depending on their income level. Essentially, this means that those fortunate enough to earn more money in later life will help pay toward the education of those who earn less. Students can borrow to meet the cost of their education without losing the opportunity to take low-paying but possibly challenging jobs after graduation.

WHERE TO GET ADDITIONAL HELPFUL INFORMATION

Here is a sampling of free or inexpensive publications which should be of extraordinary help to you as you pursue this subject by yourself.

"Meeting College Costs: A Guide for Parents and Students." College Entrance Examination Board, Publications Order Office, Box 2815, Princeton, N.J. 08540. (Free. Updated annually.)

"College Costs Today," Promotion Services, Room 1108, New York Life Insurance Company, Career Information Service, 51 Madison Avenue, New York, N.Y. 10010. (Single copies free with self-addressed, stamped envelope.)

"Information for Students," U. S. Office of Education, Washington, D.C. 20202. (Free.)

"Need a Lift?" American Legion, Attention: Need a Lift, P. O. Box 1055, Indianapolis, Ind. 56206. (50¢.)

"How About College Financing," American Personnel and Guidance Association, 1607 New Hampshire Avenue N.W., Washington, D.C. 20009. (30¢.)

BEWARE: HOME STUDY GYPS

Today more home study courses are available by mail than you could possibly pursue in any single geographic region, or even at any of the nation's largest universities. Home study has truly "come of age" in the United States—a great force in upgrading the educational-economic status of millions, and a potent weapon in our nation's struggle to overcome skill shortages.

But as legitimate, worth-while home study courses have gone into a record boom, the racketeering fringe has expanded too. At last count, nearly one in twenty correspondence schools was granting unearned degrees. Among the many areas in which the gypsters have been "specializing": civil service training, electronics, operation of heavy equipment, real estate appraisal, nursing, and jet airplane mechanics.

For instance, not long ago a trio of gypsters peddled correspondence courses in such subjects as jet engine mechanics and missile design drafting at costs up to $660 with guarantees of jobs with leading U.S. corporations. The "school" failed to place a single student in any paying job. Total loss by the public: $2 million.

In another case, worthless correspondence courses in practical nursing were sold to women high school dropouts. Total take by this team over a ten-year period: about $3 million.

In a third scheme, the exact same "training course," supposedly for the U. S. Civil Service, was sold to different individuals wanting to become a law enforcement officer, a government meat inspector, and a park ranger.

How can you tell the worth-while home study program from the worthless and often exorbitantly priced one? Here are your guidelines:

• *No* legitimate correspondence school will or can guarantee a job after completion of its course.

• *Nobody* can qualify as a practical nurse through correspondence study alone.

• Be suspicious if a correspondence school uses a high-paying job opportunity as a come-on in an advertisement and this is followed by a high-pressure salesman who comes to your door to inform you that further training is needed to fulfill the job requirements (through the course he is peddling, naturally).

• If you have any doubt whatsoever about the value of any home study school or course you have seen advertised, check its reputation with the local Better Business Bureau, Chamber of Commerce, or state Department of Education.

• To find out what legitimate courses are available to you in the field you wish to pursue, consult a high school, college, or guidance counselor.

• Finally, get a free list of accredited, reputable home study schools from the National Home Study Council, 1601 Eighteenth Street N.W., Washington, D.C. 20009.

In the case of correspondence courses offered by *accredited* colleges and universities, a similar list entitled "Guide to Independent Study Through Correspondence Instruction" is available from National University Extension Association, Suite 360, 1 Dupont Circle N.W., Washington, D.C. 20036. ($1.00.)

You'll also find useful information on choosing a correspondence school in "Tips on Home Study Schools," a pamphlet available from the Council of Better Business Bureaus, Inc., 1150 Seventeenth Street N.W., Washington, D.C. 20036. (Single copies free.)

For a second useful barsdination on choosing a correspondence
school in [fig] on Home Study Courses, a pamphlet available from
the Consumer Product Information [fig], [figr.] 15000 Scottsdale Street,
Washington, D.C. 20209. (Free or nominal fee.)

11

YOUR JOB, CAREER, OR BUSINESS

BASIC ASSUMPTIONS   476
WHERE WILL THE JOBS BE?   476
   TRUE OR FALSE?   476
   REVOLUTION IN THE U.S. WORKPLACE   478
   KEY TRENDS IN JOBS AND CAREERS   479
   CHANGES COMING IN YOUR WORK WEEK   480
   WHERE WILL THE JOB OPPORTUNITIES GROW
     FASTEST?   481
CHOOSING A CAREER   485
   KEY GUIDES FOR YOU   485
   GUIDES FOR PARENTS   486
YOUR EDUCATION AND YOUR JOB   487
GOOD CAREERS FOR COLLEGE GRADUATES   489
GOOD JOBS FOR HIGH SCHOOL GRADUATES   493
   COLLEGE GRADUATE STILL IN MINORITY   493
   SAMPLING OF OCCUPATIONS   493
GOOD JOBS FOR HIGH SCHOOL DROPOUTS   497
   THE BRIGHTER BACKGROUND   497
   WHERE THESE JOBS ARE   498
AND CAREERS FOR OPT-OUTS   500
   THE IMPORTANCE OF AN "OCCUPATION"   500
HOW TO LOOK FOR—AND GET—A JOB   501
   AN INVENTORY OF YOURSELF   501
   YOUR RÉSUMÉ   503
   SOURCES OF HELP FOR JOB HUNTERS   504

How to Look for—and Get—a Job (cont'd)

    HOW TO USE A PRIVATE EMPLOYMENT AGENCY 505

    YOUR LETTER OF APPLICATION 507

    HOW TO HANDLE A JOB INTERVIEW 509

Where to Get Job Training 510

    CONSIDER AN APPRENTICESHIP 511

    SOME OTHER WAYS TO ACQUIRE WORK SKILLS 512

    FEDERAL JOB TRAINING PROGRAMS 513

    BUSINESS, TECHNICAL, TRADE SCHOOLS 513

Why Join a Union? 514

Your Sources of Career Information 515

    A LISTING 515

    HOW TO LOOK 528

How to Get a Good Summer Job 528

    HOW TO SHOP 528

    SOURCES OF JOB LEADS 530

    HOW ABOUT A NON-JOB? 531

What About Working Abroad This Summer? 532

    BEST SOURCES OF JOBS 532

    BEST SOURCES OF INFORMATION 533

    KEY QUESTIONS TO ASK 534

"Tailored Pay Checks" 534

    KEY TRENDS IN COMPENSATION 534

    COMPENSATION GEARED TO YOUR AGE 535

    AND "PERKS" 536

Shop for Fringe Benefits, Too! 536

    ROUTINE DEDUCTIONS 536

    PAID VACATIONS AND HOLIDAYS 538

    GROUP INSURANCE 538

    EDUCATIONAL BENEFITS 538

    MOVING BENEFITS 539

    TIME OFF TO VOTE 539

    SPECIAL INVESTMENT PLANS 539

    DIVIDEND REINVESTMENT PLANS 539

    PROFIT-SHARING PLANS 539

    NEW "EXTRAS" 540

    EXOTIC BENEFITS 541

If You Are a Woman 541

    YOU PROBABLY WORK 541

IF YOU ARE A WOMAN (cont'd)
 WOMEN WORKERS AND FAMILY INCOME 542
 GET READY NOW FOR THE "EMPTY NEST" 543
 BASIC CAREER GUIDES 545
 MYTHS ABOUT WOMEN WORKERS 546
 WHAT'S A HOUSEWIFE WORTH? 548
 HOW TO FIND A DAY CARE CENTER 550
 DAY CARE CENTER QUIZ TO GUIDE YOU 551
 IS IT REALLY WORTH IT? 552
HOW TO PLAY "SUCCESS CHESS" 554
 YOUR LIFETIME JOB GUIDE 554
 WHAT MOVES TO MAKE 556
 FIVE CLUES ON PROMOTIONS 557
SHOULD YOU QUIT YOUR JOB? 558
 DO'S AND DON'TS ON QUITTING 559
WHAT IF YOU LOSE YOUR JOB? 560
 INTERVIEW YOURSELF 561
 "HIDDEN" RESERVE 562
 WHY? 562
 MERGER! 563
 A QUIZ TO PROTECT YOURSELF 563
GUIDE FOR EXECUTIVE JOB HUNTERS 564
 WHO DOES WHAT IN EXECUTIVE SEARCH 565
 WHO PAYS—AND HOW MUCH 566
 BEWARE: JOB-FINDING TRAPS 566
 TEN QUESTIONS TO ASK 568
JOB-HUNTING TIPS FOR THE OVER-FORTY-FIVE 568
SHOULD YOU GO INTO BUSINESS FOR YOURSELF? 570
 WHY BUSINESSES FAIL 570
 A QUIZ TO SUCCESS 570
 FUNDAMENTAL RULES 572
IS FRANCHISING FOR YOU? 573
 ANOTHER WAY TO GO INTO BUSINESS 573
 QUESTION AND ANSWER GUIDE FOR POTENTIAL
  INVESTORS 574
 FRANCHISING CHECK LISTS 576
 SOURCES FOR ADVICE ON JUDGING A FRANCHISE 578
CRIME INSURANCE FOR SMALL BUSINESSMEN 579
 A PROGRAM TO INVESTIGATE 579

BEWARE: "BUSINESS OPPORTUNITIES" SWINDLES 580
    RACK ROUTES 580
    TRAVEL 582
    PYRAMID SELLING 584
    VENDING MACHINES 585
    DISTRIBUTORSHIPS 587
WHAT ABOUT WORKING AT HOME? 588
    A POWERFUL TREND 588
    SAMPLING OF "AT HOME" CAREERS 589
    BEWARE: "EARN MONEY AT HOME" SWINDLES! 590
    OBVIOUS EARMARKS OF A FRAUDULENT SCHEME 592
    KEY QUESTIONS ABOUT ADS 592
NEEDED: VOLUNTEERS 593
    THE GREAT NON-PAID PRODUCER 593
    WHERE THE VOLUNTEER JOBS ARE 594
    "MOST WANTED" 597
    HOW DO YOU VOLUNTEER? 597

BASIC ASSUMPTIONS

The U. S. Bureau of Labor Statistics is the source of the ten-year projections quoted in this chapter. The Bureau of Labor Statistics, in turn, based them on the following major assumptions:

that we will maintain today's system of government and institutions;

that we will have a relatively low, although fluctuating rate of unemployment in this decade;

that the international climate will improve and our armed forces will be reduced and held at approximately 2 million men and women or below.

Given these basic assumptions . . .

WHERE WILL THE JOBS BE?

TRUE OR FALSE?

• The fastest growth in government jobs in the years ahead will be jobs in federal agencies.

• Most workers in the United States work for companies producing goods.

• In view of the U.S. population explosion, the biggest expansion in jobs for teachers will be in elementary and secondary schools.

• Increasing automation in the office will slash the number of jobs for office workers.

• Good jobs for high school graduates will shrink dramatically as more and more employers demand that workers have college degrees.

• Jobs in agriculture also will dwindle near to zero because of mechanization of farm work along with the virtual disappearance of the small farm.

• Our work force is growing older as our population generally lives longer, and thus more and more key positions are being filled by middle-aged and older employees.

If you answered "true" to *any* of these questions, you were wrong. If you answered "true" to most, you flunked.

Taking the questions one by one:

• There will be considerable growth in the number of government jobs. But the growth will be *much greater at the state and local levels* than at the federal level.

• More than half of the U.S. work force today is producing *services* —medical, teaching, banking, insurance, painting, writing, advising, planning, etc.—making us the first service-dominated economy in all world history. The vast majority of the new jobs now opening up are in the services. By contrast, manufacturing jobs are increasing an average of only a little more than 1 per cent a year during the 1970s.

• The fastest expansion in teaching jobs will be in adult education and at the two-year college level. During this decade the number of elementary schoolteachers is expected to increase only slightly. Our population not only isn't "exploding"; our growth rate has come to a virtual standstill.

• Automation in the office has reduced opportunities for certain types of workers but sharply increased demand for other important categories ranging from business machine operators and copying machine repair people to computer programers, tape librarians, and tape perforator typists.

• Despite the stress on college education in the 1970s, three out of four jobs will still be open to people who have *not* completed four years of college—including high school dropouts as well as high school graduates. More and more training is being required of young people, but it is not necessarily college training.

• The decline of the small farm has been going on for more than a century and by 1980 our entire food supply probably will be grown by a minuscule 3 per cent of the labor force. However, many new agricultural occupations are opening up in big "agribusinesses" which employ large numbers in fields ranging from stenography to surgery. And more and more farmers are going to college to learn biology, soil science, engineering, agronomy.

• Finally, instead of growing older, our work force actually has been growing steadily *younger,* with a majority of new jobs being filled during this decade by Americans in their twenties and thirties. A key force behind this trend is today's relative scarcity of middle-aged workers. (Not many babies were being born in the depression 1930s.) As a result, corporations and other employers are being compelled to reach into the younger age brackets to find executive and other talent—and this is creating major opportunities for many American men and women now in their late twenties and thirties.

REVOLUTION IN THE U.S. WORKPLACE

Can you define the following occupational fields?

Cryogenics
Fiber-optics
Geomagnetics
Pattern recognition

These are some of the job categories and occupational specialties which have just begun to appear on the U.S. job landscape.

Here are brief definitions of each:

Cryogenics: Study and use of super-cold temperatures, ranging from 110° F. below zero (the temperature of dry ice) to nearly 460° below zero ("absolute zero"). Cryogenic temperatures are used today for making liquid air, liquid natural gas, and for fast-freezing certain foods.

Fiber-optics: Use of transparent fibers made of glass or other materials to transmit light along curves and around corners. The technique is now being used to light otherwise inaccessible places such as inside the human body.

Geomagnetics: Study of the earth's composition (geology) through the measurement of irregularities or disturbances in its magnetic field.

Pattern recognition: Study of how to recognize patterns, especially when the patterns are hidden, incomplete, or partially obscured (e.g., in images, facts, concepts, information, etc.).

Just the strange sound of the above job titles underscores the extent to which whole new occupations are emerging under our eyes, while old occupations—ranging from the elevator operator to the railroad foreman—disappear.

KEY TRENDS IN JOBS AND CAREERS

Here are other key U.S. employment trends to watch for in the years directly ahead. Let them guide you not only in your initial career choice (if indeed you make such a "choice") but also in any of your deliberations over a *second* career.

• Demand for *professional and technical workers* will increase twice as fast as demand for all workers.

• Increasingly, *scientists and engineers* will become the heads of U.S. corporations.

• And hopefully, manufacturers, under pressure from consumers and government regulatory agencies, will be hiring workers to attend to *social and environmental* as well as strictly technical considerations—e.g., pollution controls, accident proofing of cars, factories, toys, and homes.

• Physicians also will be moving toward outpatient care and comprehensive, continuous health care for groups of people for whom this care has not previously been available, such as the urban poor and those living in isolated rural areas. (And for the "haves" as well.)

• Today's *"minorities"*—especially women and blacks—will find many new and better jobs as companies vie with each other to eliminate discrimination.

• *Part-time* jobs will open in many fields, creating new work opportunities for students, young mothers, older workers.

• Expanded *vocational rehabilitation* programs will boost job chances for the handicapped, the retarded, and ex-criminal offenders.

What message does this sampling of employment trends shout to you? This above all:

Before you settle on a final career choice you should at least scan the literally hundreds of different occupations which will be open to you in the years ahead. Find out which occupations within each career field seem to interest you. Then check the most promising job opportunities in each occupation. Then, and only then, zero in on the career you want.

CHANGES COMING IN YOUR WORK WEEK

One further vitally important trend in the U.S. workplace is a re-shuffling of your workday, work week, and work year.

Thousands of Americans are now moving to a four-day, forty-hour week, and unions are pushing for a four-day, thirty-two-hour week. Thousands of companies already are on some kind of rearranged week and this is a trend virtually sure to prevail in the years directly ahead.

The average full-time worker now puts in about 2,000 hours a year. Well within the career span of today's young college graduate—thirty years—trade unions hope the average American will be working as few as 1,600 hours a year, 20 per cent fewer than today.

The variations of work patterns are endless. Workers and employers may come around to "negotiating" their schedules and thus getting far more out of each other than they do now. One trend may be toward the "gliding" workday, with workers arriving and departing when they choose within a twelve-hour day; their only obligation would be to work a certain number of hours a week.

As for the advantages of extended time off, it can be a real antidote to on-the-job boredom—by permitting a worker to recharge his physical and mental abilities periodically. Moreover, many people find they can do things with extended periods of leisure that they cannot manage otherwise.

Experiments in a rearranged work week are, in fact, part of a broader trend toward greater employment flexibility which could well emerge in future years as a major cure for many of today's major sources of on-the-job discontent—particularly, enforced retirement. A shorter work week could meet the need of many older Americans to remain active—and also leave people more time to devote to community affairs and volunteer work.

Since the trend seems relentless, though, it is only common sense to start preparing now for the time when "5-40" gives way to "4-40" and then swings into "4-32." (How have you handled yourself on previous three-day holidays?) Look into the fascinating choices in volunteer work, the absorbing possibilities of second careers in services starving for you, the many deeply satisfying alternatives in the vast expanse of non-work.

Killing time is suicide on the installment plan.

WHERE WILL THE JOB OPPORTUNITIES GROW FASTEST?

First, here are the U. S. Labor Department's projections for growth in major occupational categories during the decade of the 1970s:

FIELD	PER CENT CHANGE 1970–80
Professional and technical workers	+39%
Service workers (except private household), e.g., hospital attendants, policemen, waitresses	+35
Clerical workers	+26
Sales workers	+24
Craftsmen and foremen	+20
Managers, officials, proprietors	+15
Operatives (assemblers, truck drivers, bus drivers)	+11
Non-farm laborers	− 6
Farm workers	−17
All occupations	+21

Here, even more specifically, is a list of occupations with job requirements projected to 1985:

OCCUPATION	ESTIMATED EMPLOYMENT 1972	PROJECTED REQUIREMENTS TO 1985
Business administration and related professions		
Accountants	714,000	935,000
Clergy		
Ministers (Protestant)	325,000	360,000

Occupation	Estimated Employment 1972	Projected Requirements to 1985
Engineers		
Electrical	231,000	330,000
Mechanical	209,000	280,000
Civil	177,000	235,000
Industrial	125,000	190,000
Health service occupations		
Registered nurses	748,000	1,050,000
Licensed practical nurses	425,000	835,000
Physicians, M.D.s and D.O.s	330,000	485,000
Medical assistants	200,000	320,000
Pharmacists	131,000	163,000
Medical laboratory workers	165,000	210,000
Dentists	105,000	140,000
X-ray technologists	55,000	87,000
Dental assistants	115,000	155,000
Teachers		
Kindergarten and elementary schoolteachers	1,274,000	1,590,000
Secondary schoolteachers	1,023,000	1,045,000
College and university teachers	525,000	630,000
Technicians		
Engineering and science technicians	707,000	1,050,000
Draftsmen	327,000	485,000
Other professional and related occupations		
Lawyers	303,000	380,000
Programers	186,000	290,000
Social workers	185,000	275,000
Librarians	120,000	162,000
Home economists	120,000	140,000
Systems analysts	103,000	185,000

Occupation	Estimated Employment 1972	Projected Requirements to 1985
Managerial occupations		
Managers and assistants (hotel)	110,000	160,000
Bank officers	219,000	308,000
Clerical and related occupations		
Stenographers and secretaries	3,074,000	4,950,000
Bookkeeping workers	1,584,000	1,900,000
Cashiers	998,000	1,360,000
Typists	1,021,000	1,400,000
Bank clerks	473,000	665,000
Stock clerks	511,000	750,000
Telephone operators	230,000	232,000
Shipping and receiving clerks	451,000	490,000
Office machine operators	195,000	230,000
Receptionists	436,000	650,000
Electronic computer operating personnel	480,000	531,000
File clerks	272,000	318,000
Bank tellers	248,000	350,000
Sales occupations		
Retail trade sales workers	2,778,000	3,330,000
Wholesale trade sales workers	688,000	860,000
Manufacturers' sales workers	423,000	545,000
Insurance brokers and agents	385,000	450,000
Real estate sales workers and brokers	349,000	435,000
Securities sales workers	220,000	290,000
Service occupations		
Private household workers	1,437,000	1,000,000
Building custodians	1,885,000	2,430,000
Waiters and waitresses	1,124,000	1,300,000
Hospital attendants	900,000	1,360,000
Cosmetologists	500,000	670,000
Police officers (municipal)	370,000	490,000

Occupation	Estimated Employment 1972	Projected Requirements to 1985
Service occupations (cont'd)		
Guards and watchmen	250,000	320,000
Meat cutters	200,000	198,000
Firefighters	200,000	315,000
Barbers	157,000	147,000
Bartenders	200,000	235,000
Building trades		
Carpenters	1,000,000	1,200,000
Painters and paperhangers	420,000	460,000
Plumbers and pipe fitters	400,000	500,000
Operating engineers (construction machinery operators)	435,000	570,000
Electricians (construction)	240,000	325,000
Bricklayers	180,000	225,000
Elevator constructors	17,000	25,000
Mechanics and Repairmen		
Automobile mechanics	727,000	860,000
Maintenance electricians	260,000	325,000
Appliance service workers	130,000	175,000
Industrial machinery repairers	430,000	850,000
Aircraft mechanics	123,000	190,000
Air conditioning, refrigeration, and heating mechanics	135,000	265,000
Truck and bus mechanics	130,000	165,000
Telephone and PBX installers and repairers	108,000	120,000
Instrument repairers	100,000	140,000
Business machine service workers	69,000	97,000
Other craft occupations		
Blue collar worker supervisors	1,400,000	1,700,000
Driving occupations		
Truck drivers, local	1,600,000	1,800,000
Truck drivers, over-the-road	570,000	670,000
Power truck operators	300,000	370,000

OCCUPATION	ESTIMATED EMPLOYMENT 1972	PROJECTED REQUIREMENTS TO 1985
Other operative occupations		
Assemblers	1,017,000	1,100,000
Inspectors (manufacturing)	725,000	940,000
Welders and oxygen and arc cutters	554,000	770,000
Machine tool operators	546,000	670,000
Gasoline service station attendants	435,000	545,000
Other		
Construction laborers and hod carriers	876,000	1,000,000
All-round machinists	320,000	400,000
Musicians and music teachers	85,000	111,000
Life scientists	180,000	235,000
Chemists	134,000	184,000

CHOOSING A CAREER

Next to choosing a mate, the choice of a career may be the most important one you make in your entire life.

Where do you begin? How do you protect yourself against the ever increasing fickleness of today's job market?

KEY GUIDES FOR YOU

• First and most obviously, study the full range of options and combinations open to you—and the range is vast indeed.

If you were asked to list, in a reasonable period of time, all the occupations you could think of, I'll wager you would name fewer than fifty. Yet the U. S. Labor Department's *Occupational Outlook Handbook* describes more than 800 occupations—many of them not even in existence a few years back. And the U. S. Government's *Dictionary of Occupations Titles* lists approximately 40,000 different job titles!

• *Don't,* though, make the mistake of abandoning a career goal you genuinely want just because your choice isn't among the fastest-growing occupations. Simply accept the likelihood that you will have to face stiff competition—and possibly a certain amount of job insecurity too. Explore the new careers, for you may find there an unsuspected offshoot of your dream career.

• Think of your career as a "black box" *inside you. Your* career is *not* in the minds of your parents or the files of your school counselor or anywhere else. It's *yours* to unwrap and unlock and pursue.

• Understand thoroughly the extent of education and training which may be required—and available—for any given occupation. Today's machinist, for instance, must have a solid foundation in mathematics and numerical controls. Today's top-notch secretary must know how to operate a range of new office machinery, possibly must know a foreign language or have a secretarial specialty (such as law or medicine). Today's plumber needs at least a high school diploma to qualify for a job or for additional on-the-job training. For a majority of occupations, some post-high school education or training has become a minimum.

• Recognize that, whatever occupation you choose, broad general knowledge ranks in importance with the specific education directly related to the occupation. In this era's rapidly changing job market, flexibility is crucial.

• Keep open your chances to change careers throughout your whole working life. The choice of an occupation is *not* a single decision. Rather, it is at least a ten-year process, says manpower expert Dr. Eli Ginzberg, involving a long-term strategy which could include several different careers.

If you are now entering the labor market, you can expect to change jobs at least a half dozen times over your working lifetime. You well may change your entire career at some point; in fact, two or three careers in a lifetime are becoming increasingly commonplace. This holds for the physicist as it holds for the pipe fitter: both can anticipate a continuous process of training and re-education throughout their working lives.

GUIDES FOR PARENTS

As for you, the parents of a young person beginning his or her career hunt, here are five "Do's and Don'ts" to guide you on counseling your children:

Don't force your own occupational choice on your child. The idea that your son must be a doctor because you are or wanted to be is ridiculous. A career choice involves much more than intelligence. It involves the child's values, attitudes toward work and life, emotional maturity.

Do be understanding if your child is in no hurry to choose a career. Even if he or she drops out of college in the second year, it could be a sign of wisdom. Be supportive as your child explores the occupational options open to him or her.

Don't try to drive your child to "get ahead." The young generation has watched their parents become great "career successes"—at the cost of discontent, divorce, alcoholism, absentee fathers. Relax. You've had your chances to make your choices. Let your kids have the same.

Do understand that your home is the single best source of values and that your attitudes toward work generally can be a real and important influence. Stress the values you cherish.

Don't plague a child who does not have the required intellectual equipment to become a professional or even to complete college. You'll only create impossible conflicts for him or her.

Your Education and Your Job

Today's relentless trend is toward more and more education to qualify for most jobs, higher and higher degrees to aspire to the very top in many fields, lower and lower esteem for the less-than-college-educated individual.

Do these ever rising educational requirements reflect *real* job requirements—or merely "creeping credentialism"?

Some of both. Specifically:

The U. S. Bureau of Labor Statistics estimates that in the 1972–85 period demand for professionals will increase at twice the rate of rise in demand for all other workers. But it also estimates that about 50,000 more college graduates will be entering the job market between 1972 and 1980 than there will be jobs for them; in the 1980–85 period, the "surplus" is due to expand to 700,000. This means that large numbers of college graduates may have to downgrade their expectations. In fact, an increasing number of college graduates even now are entering management and sales rather than the field for which they trained. Moreover, as the demand for paraprofessionals has soared, particularly in the health, education, law, and environmental fields, so has the number of two-year colleges and/or job-training opportunities—points not to be overlooked or underrated.

Meanwhile, the oversupply of Ph.D.s as of the mid-1970s is balanced by real shortages of skilled craftsmen and technical supportive personnel in many areas. As we have pushed back the limits of scientific and academic knowledge, we have tended to undervalue craftsmanship. Dropouts who took up carpentry or pottery were among the first to rediscover that working with one's hands could be deeply satisfying. Now educators and economists realize the urgent need to give status to those who have manual talents. (In pay, many craftsmen, such as electricians, carpenters, plumbers, already more than compete with high-paying white-collar jobs. It's how society views the craftsmen that is different.)

Does this mean guidance counselors will stop encouraging students to go to college? No. But it does mean counselors will increasingly endeavor to persuade overanxious parents of something many young people have long suspected: college isn't for everyone and this is nothing to be ashamed of.

It also means that the educational systems of the future must be designed to turn out fewer specialists and more generalists in both the "humanities" and the sciences so that young people will be able to shift among a number of different professions. For example, a young man or woman interested in children might train simultaneously for child care, recreation, mental health, and education, in order to be able to step into whichever field most needs his or her talents at a given time.

And it means that training programs, apprenticeships—in fact all forms of vocational training—will come in for more serious consideration than ever before. Says a noted educator: "We are going to have to make the same resources available for the would-be hairdresser as we are doing for the Ivy League collegian."

What then will be the new status of education? More than ever, education for its own sake will be a prime concern in this country. Colleges will make their educational facilities available to the community at large, enabling professionals (and paraprofessionals) to keep abreast of change and to enrich all those leisure hours which are coming, as the work week shifts from five to four and eventually three days.

Yes, the pay will remain somewhat higher for the college graduate who can find work, and it will still take a degree to get to the very top.

But a college degree is no longer a guarantee of employment, whereas certain crafts, paratechnical and paraprofessional areas are crying for help. Already graduates of two-year colleges who cost less and do a perfectly adequate job are being preferred in many areas where the B.A. had become a bloated requirement.

In essence, what all this says to you is:

Read the projections in this chapter with two points always in mind. First, our society is changing faster than ever before, reacting to technological breakthroughs with unpredictable impacts on the job market. And second, where evidence is unmistakable that work exists to be done, such as in the rebuilding of our cities, the key factor in determining how many jobs will be available for the trained worker will depend on the future reordering of our national priorities.

Against this background, it is no more than common sense to try to start with as broad and sound an education as you can get; to choose your general field of work as late as you can to give yourself as much and as varied a training in that field as possible. Then you will enter the job market supported by the widest range of capabilities from which you can only benefit.

GOOD CAREERS FOR COLLEGE GRADUATES

You will find most of the details on which jobs require which levels of education or training in the current edition of the U. S. Labor Department's *Occupational Outlook Handbook* or in another guide, *Occupational Outlook for College Graduates*. Both of these are well worth the few dollars the government charges for them. Look for them in your school guidance office or library.

Here is a synopsis of some of the careers for those of you who have had at least some higher education—including junior and community colleges, business schools, vocational or technical institutes—in terms of the numbers of jobs opening each year and also in terms of job requirements:

Accountant: College degree required for higher-paying jobs; junior college, business school, or correspondence school courses acceptable for others.

Advertising: Keen competition for beginners. Employers increasingly prefer college training although some jobs go to those without degrees who have other extraordinary qualifications.

Architect: License required. Usually earned by a five-year course leading to a bachelor of architecture degree, followed by three years' experience.

Bank officer: Thousands of openings each year. Management trainee should have a major in business administration. Courses in accounting, economics, commercial law, political science, and statistics also are valuable.

Chemist: Favorable employment prospects. Bachelor's degree with major in chemistry is minimum; graduate training usually necessary for research or teaching.

Clergy: Wide education range. Some religions have no formal requirements but an increasing number require several years of theology after college graduation.

Commercial artist: Usually two or three years of art school required. Training in vocational high school or home study courses helpful. Artistic talent essential.

Counselor (school): Favorable employment opportunities. Most states require both a teaching and a counseling certificate—involving graduate work in guidance plus, usually, one to five years' teaching experience.

Dentist: Four years in dental college preceded by two or three years of predental college work. License is required in all states.

Draftsman: Best prospects for those with post-high school training. Junior college, technical institute, vocational school training usually required. Also good preparation is a three- or four-year apprenticeship.

Engineering or science technician: Demand will be strongest for graduates of post-high school technical training programs. However, some train on the job.

Engineers, all specialties: A bachelor's degree in engineering is minimum basic requirement.

Home economist: Very good employment opportunities, especially for teachers in secondary schools and colleges. Bachelor's degree in home economics necessary. Graduate degree required for college teaching and research work.

Lawyer: Moderate rise in employment. Keen competition for salaried positions. Usually four years of college followed by three years of law school. Must be admitted to the state bar for court practice.

Librarian: Bright employment prospects, particularly in public and special libraries. Required in most cases are four years of college followed by one year of specialized study in library science.

Library technical assistants: Good prospects, especially for graduates of academic programs. Best opportunities in large public and college university libraries.

Life scientist: Severe competition since number of graduates expected to exceed number of openings. Those with advanced degrees will experience the least competition. Best opportunities for medical scientists.

Mathematician: Best opportunities for those with Ph.D. degree. Increasing competition for entry positions as the number of new entrants may exceed openings. Graduate degree required for teaching and research and valuable for advancement in all specialties.

Manufacturer's sales worker: Best opportunities for those trained to sell technical products. College graduates generally preferred, though many successful sales workers have less education.

Medical lab technologists: Usually must have completed three years of college plus a training program in medical technology.

Musician: Stiff competition for performers. Prospects brightest for teachers. For teachers in public schools, a four-year course in a college or conservatory usually required; also a state certificate.

Personnel: Opportunities best for college graduates majoring in this field.

Pharmacist: Usually required are three to four years of professional study in a college of pharmacy following two years of pre-pharmacy college education. License necessary.

Physician: Excellent employment opportunities despite limited capacity of medical schools. Four years in medical school preceded usually by four years of college. At least one year of internship generally required plus a license to practice.

Physicist: Favorable employment opportunities, particularly for holders of advanced degrees. Holders of bachelor's degree will have limited opportunities, but may find openings in other occupations that utilize their training.

Psychologist: Outlook good for clinical and counseling psychologists. Ph.D. degree increasingly vital for advancement.

Public relations: Moderate opportunities. College education best preparation.

Purchasing agent: Moderate employment growth. Greatest demand for business administration graduates who have had courses in purchasing.

Recreation workers: Excellent job opportunities. Bachelor's degree, with major in recreation, social science, or physical education generally preferred.

Registered nurse: Three types of training available: diploma programs (three years), mainly in hospitals; associate degree programs (two years) in junior and community colleges; and baccalaureate degree programs (four to five years) in colleges or universities. License required.

Securities sales worker: Good employment opportunities. College education increasingly important and degree in business administration or economics good preparation. Most states require securities sales workers to be licensed.

Social worker: Excellent employment opportunities for those with master's degree in social work. Bachelor's degree generally the minimum.

Systems analyst: Excellent employment opportunities in this very rapidly expanding occupation. Most employers prefer a college background and experience in computer programing.

Teacher (college or university): Entrants may face keen competition. New doctoral and masters' degree holders, the main source of teacher supply, may exceed the demand for these teachers.

Teacher (kindergarten, elementary and high school): In competitive environment, greater emphasis will be placed on quality of applicant's training and academic achievement. Teaching certificate necessary in public schools and some parochial and other private schools. Certification usually requires a bachelor's degree and certain education courses, sometimes a master's degree.

Technical writer: Beginners with good writing ability and appropriate education should find opportunities. Usually four years of college, including technical and/or writing courses necessary.

Veterinarian: A license, based on four years of professional study in a college of veterinary medicine, necessary—following two years of pre-veterinary college work.

GOOD JOBS FOR HIGH SCHOOL GRADUATES

COLLEGE GRADUATE STILL IN MINORITY

The first fact is that *half* of the young Americans who are now receiving their high school diplomas will *not* be going on to college. The second fact is that only one in five young Americans graduates from college today. The clincher is that millions of young people will be going from high school directly to shopping for permanent careers or looking for extra training in trade schools.

If you (or your son or daughter) are not college bound, you will find hundreds of thousands of good jobs with bright futures and substantial pay checks looking for people to fill them. Growing numbers of employers now are offering extensive on-the-job training and paying trainees substantial wages while they learn. In some cases the high school graduate can expect to be earning $15,000 or more a year within just a few years of entering the job market.

SAMPLING OF OCCUPATIONS

Here is a sampling of occupations in which opportunity is relatively great—all now open to the high school graduate—with a few details on how much education training is needed for each.

Air conditioning, refrigeration, or heating mechanic: Most job openings will be for air conditioning and refrigeration mechanics. Most begin as helpers and learn on the job.

Aircraft mechanic: Most airlines train apprentices in three- or four-year programs. Some train in federal government-approved schools. Mechanics must be licensed to practice. Prospect is for rapid growth through 1980.

Airline pilot or copilot: Must be licensed and meet flight-training requirements. Written and physical exams required. Some airlines require two or more years of college. Training is rugged but pay is excellent.

Animal health technician: "Assistant veterinarians" (both male and female) can now take two years of post-high school training at certain colleges and junior colleges.

Blue collar worker supervisors: Usually must be about forty-five years of age and have spent several years learning skills on the job. Ability to motivate employees, command respect, and get along with people especially helpful.

Bookkeeper: Post-high school education sometimes needed. Courses in business arithmetic and bookkeeping are helpful. Large number of openings anticipated.

Business machine service worker: Outlook bright for work with electronic business machines. Usually trained on the job or in manufacturers' training schools. Basic knowledge of electricity and electronics very helpful.

Composing-room occupations: Technological changes will cause slow employment decline. Most compositors learn trade through six-year apprenticeship. Some learn on the job. Tape-perforating machine operators usually learn typing in high school or business school.

Computer programers and other computer workers: Demand for computer programers is expected to continue growing. Candidates needn't be mathematicians; basics can be learned in high school. Many companies train beginning computer workers themselves.

Cooks, chefs: Shortages of trained chefs in the nation's restaurants and hotels translate into major opportunities and high pay for those interested in this field.

Electrician (*construction*): A four-year apprenticeship recommended, but possible to learn this trade through job experience.

Electronic computer operating personnel: Very rapid employment increase on way. On-the-job training usually provided. To become a console operator, some college training may be required.

Firefighter: Competition keen because of large number of applicants. Must be at least twenty-one and in good physical condition; also pass a written intelligence test.

Health service workers: Less obvious occupations calling for applicants are medical record technician, laboratory assistant, dental technician, occupational therapy aide, child care attendant for retarded children—in addition to the obvious categories of hospital attendant and licensed practical nurse.

Hotel front office clerk: Clerical skills, including typing and bookkeeping, helpful.

Hotel manager: Increasing emphasis on college education, though successful hotel experience is generally chief requirement.

Instrument repairman: Training may be acquired on the job, in an apprenticeship (usually four years), in a technical institute or junior college, or at armed forces technical school. High school courses in math and science, including electronics, useful.

Insurance agent or broker: A competitive field. Courses in accounting, economics, and insurance useful. All agents and most brokers must obtain state licenses.

Lithographic craftsman: A four- or five-year apprenticeship usually required after high school.

Machine tool setup man: Must be all-round machinist or skilled machine tool specialist.

Machinist, all-round: A four-year apprenticeship best way to learn trade, but many learn on the job.

Medical laboratory workers: There are three different levels, with differences in educational requirements and pay. Assistants usually need only a high school education plus on-the-job training. Technicians usually need one or more years of post-high school training. Technologists usually must have completed three years of college plus a training program in medical technology.

Model: Employment to increase moderately through the 1970s. Most openings, however, will be for replacement, since the work life span of most models is relatively short. Modeling school training usually preferred. Courses in art, speech, drama, fashion design, dancing, and salesmanship also useful.

Office machine operator: Some on-the-job training usually provided. Business school training helpful. Specialized training needed for some jobs.

Operating engineer (construction): Many learn through informal training and experience, but three years' apprenticeship recommended.

Photographer: Employment opportunities relatively limited, but best for industrial photographers. Many train on the job or in three-year apprenticeship programs. For some specialties, post-high school training is needed.

Police officer: Tendency toward specialized assignments. Generally must be twenty-one and a U.S. citizen. Local civil service regulations usually govern appointment. College training often required for women because of their specialized duties.

Printing pressman or assistant: Usually a two- to five-year apprenticeship. Some learn through on-the-job and technical school training.

Radiologic (X-ray) technician: Very good prospects for both full-time and part-time employment. Usually a twenty-four-month, post-high school training program.

Real estate salesperson or broker: Increasing opportunities for women. License necessary; requirements include passing a written test on regulations affecting real estate transactions.

Receptionist: Business courses as well as some college training useful.

Sheet-metal worker: A four-year apprenticeship recommended, though many learn through on-the-job experience. Trade or correspondence school courses helpful.

Stationary engineer: Many learn on the job, but four-year apprenticeship recommended. Large numbers of states and cities require licenses.

Stenographer and secretary: High school courses in typing and shorthand or post-high school course in business subjects helpful.

Surveyor: Usually special training following high school plus training on the job. For some specialties, a college degree is required.

Telephone operator: Courses in English and business arithmetic important. Training in typing and other commercial subjects helpful for PBX operators.

Telephone installers and repairers: Telephone companies provide their own training courses.

Television and radio service technician: Skills acquired through technical or vocational school training, correspondence courses, training on the job, or military service courses. Some learn entirely through experience on the job.

Tool and diemaker: Either a four- or five-year apprenticeship or long-term training on the job needed.

Typist: Must meet fairly high standards of accuracy and speed (generally 40 to 50 words a minute).

Waste water treatment plant operators: Candidates for these jobs are now being offered paid college-level, on-the-job training under the GI bill and under several other programs too.

Welfare aides, outreach workers, and recreation aides: These workers are often designated "human service workers." Work may be part time. Many jobs are supported by federal and state governments—including the employment service, welfare and social service agencies, and the public school system.

Wholesale trade sales worker: Specialties involving sale of scientific or technical equipment; training beyond a high school education often required.

In addition, the job outlook for high school graduates is bright for appliance servicemen, retail salesmen and -women, truck drivers, welders, and many others.

So if you, the high school graduate, or you, his or her parents, are now discussing a career, study the full range of opportunities. Look beyond a big beginning pay check for a job offering training in a field which interests you. Choose a job which leads in the direction you think you might really want to go.

Good Jobs for High School Dropouts

THE BRIGHTER BACKGROUND

You've heard the figures: the unemployment rate for high school dropouts is always way above that for the labor force as a whole in this country; dropouts almost always land—and almost always remain—at the bottom rung of the occupational-wage ladder; when there's a layoff, the typical dropout is usually the first to go, and when the rehiring begins, the typical dropout is usually the last to be rehired.

Of course, there is some truth to this grim blueprint. But the truth also is that the vast majority of high school dropouts either have decent jobs today or could have—if they would seek a relatively small amount of training and preparation. In literally *hundreds* of occupational categories—which pay good salaries—workers are desperately needed and a high school diploma, although it may be preferred, is not necessarily required to move into this work.

In many cases the training is available under a variety of government programs.

And where are the jobs for dropouts today? Here is a sampling of the many opportunities for dropouts:

Appliance service worker: Rapid increase in employment is on the way. Mechanical ability necessary. Skills learned on the job. Courses in electricity, mathematics, and physics helpful.

Assembler: Must have aptitude for mechanical work and be in good physical condition. Most learn skills on the job.

Automobile body repairer: Three- to four-year apprenticeship recommended, but not necessarily a requirement.

Automobile mechanic: Good outlook. Most learn skills on the job, though a three- or four-year apprenticeship is recommended. Requirements are similar for auto body repairman.

Barber: Practically all states require licensing, for which applicants usually must be sixteen to eighteen years old and be graduates of a state-approved barber school.

Building custodian: Most learn skills on the job. High school shop courses helpful.

Bus driver, local transit: Applicant should be at least twenty-one and must be in good physical condition. Chauffeur's license required in most states.

Carpenter: Many openings each year in this very large occupation. Applicant usually must be at least seventeen. Some learn skills informally on the job, but a four-year apprenticeship is recommended.

Cashier: Numerous opportunities for part-time work. Applicants who have taken distributive education or business subjects preferred.

Construction laborer: Little formal training required. Applicant usually must be at least eighteen years old and in good physical condition.

Cook and chef: Excellent employment opportunities. Skills usually learned on the job. Courses in cooking schools an advantage for work in large hotels and restaurants. Some train as apprentices.

Cosmetologist: Job opportunities to be very good for full- or part-time work. License required. Applicant usually must be at least sixteen and have completed a state-approved cosmetology course. Some states require an apprenticeship.

Gasoline service station attendant: Most learn on the job. Must have driver's license and know simple arithmetic.

Hospital attendant: Generally trained on the job, sometimes combined with classroom instruction.

Licensed practical nurse: Candidates must be seventeen or eighteen years old, must have completed at least two years of high school, and must have a state-approved practical nursing course as well as pass a licensing examination.

Machine tool operator: Usually skills learned on the job. Courses in mathematics and blueprint reading useful.

Mail carrier: Slow employment rise expected. Must be citizen, eighteen years of age, and pass civil service and physical examinations.

Painter or paperhanger: Applicants usually must be at least sixteen. Many acquire skill informally through on-the-job experience, but three-year apprenticeship recommended.

Plumber or pipe fitter: Applicants usually must be at least sixteen. A five-year apprenticeship recommended, but many learn on the job. Trade or correspondence courses can be helpful.

Private household worker: General housework, cooking, and care for children are expected. Skills usually learned at home.

Sales worker (retail trade): Many opportunities for full- or part-time work. Distributive education courses useful.

Shipping or receiving clerk: Business courses useful.

Taxi driver: Many employment opportunities, though number of cab drivers is declining. In general, must be over twenty-one, have chauffeur's license and special taxicab operator's license.

Truck driver: Generally, must be at least twenty-one. Some employers prefer two to four years of high school. Must be in good physical condition and have a chauffeur's license.

Waiter and waitress: Majority of jobs for women. Men preferred, however, for jobs in formal dining establishments. Many employers prefer two or three years of high school. On-the-job training common. Ability to do simple calculations needed.

Welder or oxygen and arc cutter: Sharp increase on way in employment. Generally, several years of training on job required. Some less skilled jobs can be learned after a few months of training.

AND CAREERS FOR OPT-OUTS

But what if your goal is a career in farming? Organic gardening? Leather working? Running an organic food store? Weaving or wool spinning? Or a job as a waiter in a Greenwich Village coffee shop? Or driving a taxi in San Francisco? Or delivering newspapers in Denver?

THE IMPORTANCE OF AN "OCCUPATION"

Mounting numbers—maybe millions—of you are rejecting America's long-standing occupational values of money, security, success, challenge, position. You are turning your backs on the standard careers which I have listed in previous pages. You are trading well-paying jobs you could perform excellently for non-paying jobs in conservation, political campaigns, consumer organizations.

Confirming this is a recent study of college students which reveals a startling downgrading of the importance of an "occupation" among life's satisfactions:

SOURCE OF SATISFACTION	1ST CHOICE	2ND CHOICE
Family	55%	35%
Leisure	23%	20%
Occupation	14%	37%
Other	8%	8%

It is conceivable that within twenty-five years working solely to earn a pay check won't even appear on a list of reasons young Americans choose a trade, skill, profession.

If you are a college dropout and especially one who hates competition, computers, machines, executive authority, the profit motive, you well may already have become a revolutionary or an emigrant to the backwoods where the preferred occupations are homesteading and manual crafts.

But there are other alternatives for you, the young humanist, in blending such fields as engineering with social consciousness, technology with ethics.

Perhaps you have seen the old vocational aptitude tests on which you found such questions as "Would you rather read novels to a blind old lady or repair a broken garbage disposal unit?" If you checked the former, you were classed as preferring the social service type occupations; the latter, as a budding scientist. It could be that one of the choices on tomorrow's tests will turn out to be "scientific social service" (that is, repairing a garbage disposal unit for a blind old lady). The tests already are being rewritten to include that sort of option.

How to Look for—and Get—a Job

You have just graduated from high school or college. You are now ready to look for your first full-time, year-round job.

Or you are currently stuck in a dreary, dead-end position. You are yearning to escape to another, more challenging and interesting job.

Or you are a woman with skills which the market place needs but you have been out of the job world for years while you raised your children to school age. You are determined now to return to an outside job.

How do you begin your job hunt? How do you apply? How do you get ready for job interviews? How should you handle yourself during this "ordeal"? How do you write a résumé—and what information should it include? How, in sum, do you sell yourself to prospective employers?

AN INVENTORY OF YOURSELF

Before you even begin to pursue specific job openings, take a good look at yourself—personally and occupationally. Sit down in a quiet corner and, with deliberation, make an honest inventory of your interests, experience, and skills. Write it all down. (This inventory, incidentally, will be a valuable fund of information for you when you later prepare your résumé.)

Here are the key areas to explore and the key questions to think about:

Your Skills, Talents, and Abilities

What are you really good at? Have you special personal qualities which you could bring to a job? Such as an ability to lead? To analyze difficult problems? To organize? To work with children, old people, sick people—or other workers? To be patient with details? Imagination? What type of education, job training, and general experience do you have which might apply to a new job?

Your Actual Work History

List *all* the jobs—including summer jobs, campus jobs, and volunteer jobs—you have had, along with the nature of your duties at each. What aspects did you like and dislike about each? Why did you take and why did you quit each? Or if you were fired, why, honestly why?

Your Education

Which schools, colleges, and technical training courses have you attended? When and for how long? What were your key courses? What subjects did you most enjoy (and least enjoy) and why? What degrees, scholarships, and special honors did you earn? What were your extracurricular activities? How might these count as job skills?

Your "Outside" Activities

What serious hobbies do you have which might relate in any way to a job? What volunteer jobs have you held? These cannot only serve as a form of work experience and training but also be a key clue to your real interests.

Are you, for example, good at drawing? Painting? Cooking? Caring for children? Can you play a musical instrument? Or sing well? Do you speak a foreign language? Have you traveled widely—within or outside the United States?

Your Physical Condition

Are you in good physical shape or handicapped in any way which might limit your ability to work? If you do happen to have a major handicap, there are many special schools, courses, and rehabilitation programs to help you—and the employment service or the Vocational Rehabilitation Administration can steer you to them.

Your Financial Position

Do you have an adequate financial cushion to fall back on if you are entering or considering a job or career field involving high risks of layoffs, cutbacks, etc.? Can you afford to take the time now to find a job which is really suitable to *you?* Can you manage a period of relatively low, entry-level wages in a new occupation?

Your Career Goal

What types of jobs, activities would you like to be doing now? What type of work do you think you would like to be doing a year or five years from now? Does this long-range goal suggest added training you should consider getting now? Is your present career field truly one in which you want to remain indefinitely? Or is now the time to consider a Big Switch to another field?

Your Interests

What do you really want out of the work you choose to do, the job you choose to take, the career you choose to follow? Money? Security? Status? Power? Challenge? Fun? Usefulness? Adventure? Social contact? A chance to change the world in some meaningful way? Recognition for your achievement?

Your goals and values may differ greatly from the norms and averages—but whatever they may be, think about them, sort them out, decide what's really important to *you.*

Now *study* your personal inventory. What kinds of jobs can you list which would use *your* talents and skills to their best advantage?

With your completion of your inventory of yourself, you have begun an intelligent job hunt.

YOUR RÉSUMÉ

Your next step in this vital "how to" section is to write your résumé—your key means to get your foot in your prospective employer's door.

From the inventory of yourself you have prepared, select and organize with utmost care the facts which will help most to sell *you.* Keep the résumé concise and uncluttered—no more than two pages long and, of course, have it neatly typed. Include all of the following items of information about yourself, more or less in this order:

> your name, address, and phone number;
>
> the date of your birth, your marital status, and number of your dependents, if any;

your physical limitations, if any;

your education—giving data on your highest degree first, and then working backward;

name and location of each school;

major (and minor) courses of study (omit if you are well along in your career);

scholastic standing (if now in school);

honors and activities (include honorary and professional societies, awards, extracurricular activities, college jobs and amount of college expenses earned);

your work experience—listing your last employer first: employer, length of service, type of work performed (including non-paid volunteer work);

other relevant experience such as your special skills and hobbies, a few details on your travels (including ambitious hitchhiking and bicycling trips, community activities);

three or four references whose names or positions or achievements might reflect favorably on you (get the permission of your references to use their names, and give their addresses).

For samples of effective résumés and more pointers on how to write one, get a copy of "Merchandising Your Job Talents," free from the U. S. Department of Labor, Manpower Administration, Washington, D.C. 20210.

SOURCES OF HELP FOR JOB HUNTERS

With your inventory of yourself clearly in your mind and your résumé typed, you are ready to start looking for the best possible jobs in your chosen career field.

Among your sources of jobs and job leads:

Friends and relatives, obviously. If a friend or relative helps you find a job, he or she is automatically giving you a valuable reference. (If you get the job this way, you also take on something of a moral obligation to the friend or relative and employer.)

Help Wanted advertisements in newspapers, professional journals, trade magazines.

The Yellow Pages of your telephone directory (assuming you want a specific occupational category).

Your high school guidance counselor or college job placement officer.

Unions in your field.

Nearby army bases.

The YMCA, YWCA, and other local civic organizations.

Job referral services of professional and trade associations.

The U. S. Civil Service Commission—for U. S. Government jobs of all types both in the United States and abroad.

Professional associations.

A Situation Wanted ad you place in the local paper.

And the U. S. Employment Service—among free job placement facilities, undoubtedly the biggest and best with more job listings in more different occupations than any other single job source in the United States today. The USES has more than 2,000 offices throughout the country offering many new and/or specialized services for job hunters.

If you are a professional, use the many branches of the employment service which have national registers for professional occupations ranging from anthropology to economics and library science.

If you are a young American in a low-income bracket, investigate the USES offices' special programs for high school dropouts, including counseling as well as referral to training and job opportunities.

If you are a worker who is willing to take a job in some other city or state, use the USES' nationwide computerized job bank, which has details on job openings throughout the United States.

If you are interested in training programs, ask the USES to pinpoint programs appropriate for you.

HOW TO USE A PRIVATE EMPLOYMENT AGENCY

In a category by itself goes the private employment agency. There are thousands of licensed employment agencies operating in the United States today—many of them specializing in particular career fields, but most attempting to match almost any type of job hunter with the type of job he's seeking. Some offer you extensive job counseling—ranging from tips on job interviews to guidance on locating the really appropriate career field for you. Others offer no such services.

Employment agencies must be licensed in almost all states. Many states fix legal ceilings on the fees employment agencies may charge, and many regulate their practices. But, typically, fees charged by non-executive employment agencies run about one half of the first month's salary in the $400-a-month range, or 5 to 10 per cent of the first year's salary. Frequently, too, *you* must pay the fee—normally over a period of several months. And the fee is figured as a percentage of your base salary—*not* your take-home pay.

Note: Some employment agencies charge *all* applicants a "registration fee." Reputable employment agencies consider these fees unethical, though they are common for unskilled applicants. State regulations normally require the fee to be refundable on demand if employment is not obtained and specify that the fee must be credited against the total fee if a job is found.

Here are the basic rules to help you get the most benefit from *any* private employment agency:

• *In advance,* find out precisely how much the fees will be and by whom and how they will be paid. Find out *in advance* what the agency's policy is in the event the job falls far short of your expectations within days after you begin working. If the policy is to refund your money if the job goes sour, find out what the time limit is for your eligibility for a refund. *These details should be in writing*.

• No matter how "ideal" the job is portrayed to you, take the time to look it over with the utmost care. Since the typical employment agency earns its fee only if it places you in a job, there's a real "incentive" to sell you on any opening which happens to be available—whether or not it suits *your* career objectives.

• Don't be swayed by scare tactics such as warning you how tight the job market is or implying that, with *your* limited skills and talents, you're lucky to get *any* job.

• Make sure you read and understand any contract before you sign it—and make sure you get your copy of it.

• Be direct and straightforward, and don't attempt to hide adverse aspects of your records (a recent firing, a previous serious physical or mental illness); these facts easily could come out when your references are checked and do you a lot more damage than if you had stated them matter-of-factly in the beginning.

• Communicate and co-operate with the agency as your job hunt proceeds. Let the agency know how each interview went, whether or not you got the job.

• Do not return to any agency which refers you to a company which, it turns out, is not seeking employees.

• Make sure, if yours is a state which requires employment agencies to be licensed, that the agency with which you wish to deal actually is licensed.

• If in any doubt, assure yourself on the credentials of an employment agency with which you're considering doing business by checking whether it's a member of the National Employment Association, the industry's self-policing organization (2000 K Street, N.W., Washington, D.C. 20006).

YOUR LETTER OF APPLICATION

Next, here are the rules on how to write a covering letter of application to a prospective employer:

• Apply for a specific job—not just for "anything that is available."

• Keep your letter to one page; let your résumé (which should be attached to this letter of application) give the details.

• State *what you have to offer* your employer clearly, concisely, neatly—not just what you *want* from the employer. Avoid jargon, gimmicky or flowery language.

• Address your letter to a specific individual—the head of the personnel department, the camp director, the person in charge of the department, or *whomever;* double-check the spelling of his or her name before you make a final copy.

• After you have written a draft and edited it to cut out unnecessary verbiage and to correct any spelling mistakes, etc., retype it neatly on 8½ by 11-inch bond paper. Or, if you can't type, get someone who can to do this for you.

• Do *not* send a duplicated letter to several employers. This is insulting because it suggests an "assembly line."

• Do *not* give details on the former salaries you may have earned.

• Be sure to include a proper return address for yourself—including your telephone number and zip code.

• Make—and keep—a carbon of each letter you write, for reference in the event an employer responds positively to your application.

• Enclose a business-size stamped self-addressed envelope.

• Enclose a passport-size photograph of yourself.

• If you are looking for a summer job, apply early. Christmas vacation isn't too soon.

• Keep in mind that your letter of application is your prospective employer's first impression of you; it's his *sole* initial guide to your sense of neatness, your personality, your capacity for organization of thoughts, plans, etc.

• If the employer sends you an application form in response to your letter, fill it out neatly and completely—and follow all directions on extra documents requested, references, deadlines, etc.

You might use the following as a "model" for your letter of application:

150 W. Ask Street

Anywhere U.S.A.12345

Anytime, 1975

Dr. Timothy Street

Neighborhood Health Center

55 Wentworth Avenue

Seattle, Washington 98107

Dear Dr. Street:

This is my application for a job as a health aide, which I learned about through the employment service office.

My goal is a career in the field of medicine and I am seeking experience in community work—the aspect of medicine which interests me most. I have worked with disadvantaged people in volunteer jobs during the past three summers, both in the city and on an Indian reservation.

My résumé, a picture of myself, and return envelope are enclosed. I am prepared to come for a personal interview at any time. If you wish to know more about my qualifications, please tell me what additional information to submit.

Thank you for your consideration.

Sincerely yours,

Jane Doe

HOW TO HANDLE A JOB INTERVIEW

Your first face-to-face confrontation with your prospective employer—the job interview—will be your best single chance to get (or lose) the job you are seeking. It also will be an excellent opportunity to get real-life impressions of what it might be like to work for his or her company. Heed, then, these guidelines on job interviews:

Before the interview, find out as much as you can about the company—e.g., the goods and services it sells, its business philosophy, its size and financial standing, its markets, its problems, its competition.

Clearly organize in your mind what skills or talents you want to stress, and what you think you can contribute to the company.

Be able to tell the interviewer *why* you want to work for this particular company.

Take along extra copies of your résumé—just in case the copy you have already sent has been mislaid. Also take, if you are, say, an artist or a writer, examples of your work. And take copies of any letters of recommendation you may have.

Pay attention to such amenities as neat appearance, civilized grooming, and punctuality. Whatever generation you belong to, the odds are strong that your would-be employer belongs to an older and more conservative era. At the same time, do not overdress for the interview. *Do not* permit your girl friend, boy friend, relative—*or anybody,* for that matter—to come along on the interview. Your interviewer is interested solely in how *you* act and react *on your own.*

Avoid being vague, overaggressive, or wordy. Understate rather than oversell your qualifications. Listen carefully to the interviewer and follow the conversational directions he or she sets. Answer questions briefly and naturally.

Have a fairly good idea of what salary you expect to earn. But *let the interviewer bring up the subject of money.* And be as flexible as you can when you discuss salary—particularly if you find that your expectations are significantly above prevailing rates in the area or at the interviewer's particular company.

When the subject of pay does come up, be sure you give proper value to fringe benefits such as company-paid health insurance, pension plans, vacation time, year-end bonuses, etc. These easily could add up to an extra 25¢ in pay for every $1.00 you receive.

Do not hesitate to ask the interviewer questions about the company or about the job for which you are applying. Asking good questions not only may get you interesting answers but also will give the interviewer further clues to your enthusiasm for and knowledge of the company and your prospective job.

Don't criticize former employers, discuss your domestic or financial problems (unless specifically asked about them), make promises you can't keep, talk in monosyllables, stare at the ceiling, drag out the interview. And *don't panic*. Your world won't come to an end if you flunk the interview and miss out on this particular job.

Find out, if you can, whether you will be expected to take any intelligence, ability, aptitude, personality, or other tests at the time of your job interview and approximately how long they will take. Leave plenty of time for this procedure. When you are actually taking the tests, carefully listen to (or carefully read) whatever instructions you are given —especially the rules covering time limits. And again, don't panic. The worst you can do is flunk and that, also, is not the end of your world.

Finally, study the following key reasons given by employers for rejecting job applicants—in descending order of importance. Learn from these reasons what to do to help yourself. The list is based on a study by Northwestern University's director of placement, Dr. Frank C. Endicott:

Poor personal appearance.
Inability to express oneself clearly—poor voice, diction, grammar.
Lack of planning for career—no purposes or goals.
Lack of interest and enthusiasm—passive, indifferent.
Failure to participate in activities.
Overemphasis on money.
Poor scholastic record—just got by.
Unwilling to start at the bottom—expects too much too soon.

WHERE TO GET JOB TRAINING

The range of job training opportunities in the United States today is broad and attractive—and in many cases the training is accompanied by very respectable pay checks.

Where will you find these opportunities?

CONSIDER AN APPRENTICESHIP

Consider one of the oldest (at least four thousand years)—but once again rapidly growing—ways to acquire important job skills: apprenticeship. This type of training is open to women as well as men; hundreds of women, in fact, are now being trained in fields ranging from plumbing to aircraft mechanics, auto mechanics, fire fighting, machining, sheet-metal work, carpentry, pipe fitting, shoe repair, jet engine assembly, cheese making, embalming, computer repair, and even as purser-pharmacist mates on oceangoing vessels. In the mid-seventies, hundreds of thousands of apprentices were being trained each year in more than 350 trades ranging from stained-glass window making to musical-instrument repair, photography, and leather working.

As a general rule, apprentice training programs run two to five years. You, the apprentice, learn on the job, under the guidance of an experienced craftsman who probably was an apprentice himself some years ago. You also may spend a few hours a week in a classroom: technical instruction will be an important part of your apprenticeship.

Apprenticeship programs are generally a joint labor-management effort and generally are registered with the U. S. Department of Labor's Bureau of Apprenticeship and Training, or with your state's apprenticeship agency. Such programs are open to you if you are a man or woman of legal working age.

Your best local sources of information on apprenticeship programs available in your area are:

the local AFL-CIO building and construction trades council;

the Urban League;

the Recruitment Training Program, Inc.;

the Apprenticeship Information Center at the local state employment service office;

your state's apprenticeship agency;

a corporation employing workers in your field of interest;

the union which represents the trade in which you are interested.

In addition there are pre-apprenticeship programs, backed by the

federal government and geared to meet the needs of those whose qualifications are insufficient to get them into formal apprenticeship programs. These consist of a combination of work training, tutoring, and
classroom instruction.

Normally, starting apprentices earn 40 to 50 per cent of the going
pay to journeymen (journeymen are those who have satisfactorily completed apprenticeship training). Apprentices also normally are granted
pay raises every six months until the end of the training period when
the pay scales reach 90 per cent of the current rate paid to journeymen.
In addition, there may be valuable fringe benefits—including paid vacations and holidays, health insurance, pension plans.

Here was a typical pay ladder in the mid-seventies for an apprentice
who had chosen a trade in which the going rate for skilled workers was
$5.00 an hour—after four years of apprenticeship:

Training Period	Hourly Pay
First 6 months	$2.50
Second 6 months	2.80
Third 6 months	3.10
Fourth 6 months	3.40
Fifth 6 months	3.70
Sixth 6 months	4.00
Seventh 6 months	4.30
Eighth 6 months	4.50

Moreover, if you are a veteran who is eligible for benefits under
the Veterans Pension and Readjustment Assistance Act of 1966 and
amendments, you will receive from the VA starting monthly training
allowances, the size of which will depend on your number of dependents. This allowance decreases as the apprenticeship period pro-
gresses—but the sums you receive are *over and above* the amounts you
receive from your employer.

SOME OTHER WAYS TO ACQUIRE WORK SKILLS

Apprenticeship is only one of many different forms of job training
available today. Another is on-the-job "vestibule" training. You work
at the employer's place of business, under the guidance of experienced

workers, foremen, or instructors. In some cases you may get classroom instruction in math, reading, or other subjects. In many instances such programs are federally subsidized, but traditionally they are strictly a private industry effort.

Normally, your training period will range from one month to two years. Normally, also, you will receive an allowance which is below going pay scales for skilled workers in your field but still adequate to support you until you have completed the training period. For information on training programs available to you in your field, ask major employers in your area and also the local office of the U. S. Employment Service.

Still another way to get job training is through a *co-operative education program*—a system in which you, a student, attend high school or college for a semester (or other period of time), then work a semester at a paying job in a field related to your study program. The result is a degree *plus* valuable on-the-job experience *plus* a significant amount of pay during the year. Many schools offer this type of program. See "College Co-op Programs," Chapter 10, for more details.

FEDERAL JOB TRAINING PROGRAMS

You also will find a wide range of government job training and assistance programs are now in operation. Most are open only to low- and medium-income applicants. The biggest and best-known federal programs are the packages of job training retraining, and upgrading offered under various federal laws.

For information on federally administered programs, your key source is the local office of your state employment service.

BUSINESS, TECHNICAL, TRADE SCHOOLS

In addition, of course, hundreds of business, technical, and trade schools throughout the United States offer you an unprecedented variety of job training opportunities in an unprecedented number of different fields.

Among the typical courses you can get at junior and community colleges today: accounting, dental hygiene, fashion design, food-service administration, nursing, scientific technology, secretarial specialties— e.g., legal, medical, technical.

Among the typical courses you can get at business, trade, and technical schools: beauty culture, bookkeeping, drafting, medical laboratory work, nursing, office machine work, photography, salesmanship, secretarial skills, technical skills.

Your high school vocational counselor and the state employment service are among the best sources of information on which schools are best for your needs and wants.

A free guide intended to help you avoid wasting time and money on the wrong vocational school is "Pocket Guide to Choosing a Vocational School," available from Consumer Information, Pueblo, Colo. 81009. More extensive and detailed is the New York *Times*'s *Guide to Continuing Education in America* (Quadrangle Books, $4.95). Compiled by the College Entrance Examination Board, it describes more than 2,000 schools in fifty states especially suited to continuing education. Look also at the "Directory of Post-secondary Schools with Occupational Programs," an excellent listing from the U. S. Government Printing Office, Washington, D.C. 20402.

WHY JOIN A UNION?

What are the pros *and* cons of joining a union today? What could a union do for you and not do for you if you joined?

First, a few obvious disadvantages:

• There is the cost: union dues in 1974 ran between $3.00 and $7.00 a month in most cases, but reached to $10 to $12. There is usually also a one-shot initiation fee which ranges from $5.00 to $15 but sometimes is as high as $100. And there may be special assessments to pay for union activities and obligations which aren't covered by the regular monthly dues.

• There is the cost of strikes. Although the overwhelming majority of union workers do not become involved in strikes, huge numbers of workers do go out on strike each year, they usually lose at least some pay, and for some types of workers (teachers or government workers) strikes are getting longer.

But despite these and other disadvantages, there seems no doubt that the pros far outweigh the cons. Specifically:

• Pay scales for union workers are far above those for non-union workers—as much as 40 to 50 per cent above in heavily unionized industries and trades.

• Along with job training, joining a union is one of the surest and fastest routes to higher pay in the U.S. workplace today. The *average* earnings of a full-time worker who belonged to a union in the early 1970s, reports the U. S. Labor Department, were 14 to 16 per cent more than the average earnings of the non-union worker. Union membership has become synonymous with superior pension coverage and with the fatter fringe benefits which now make up 25 to 30 per cent of the wage-fringe cost to the union worker's employer.

• Job training programs tend to be more widely accessible to union members than to non-union workers.

• Grievance mechanisms are another key benefit to union members. If you are summarily fired, laid off, or even treated unfairly, your union contract provides for some procedure you can use to appeal. The typical collective bargaining agreement also provides for some form of impartial arbitration if the problem can't be worked out using regular grievance mechanisms. Non-union employers may not offer these mechanisms.

YOUR SOURCES OF CAREER INFORMATION

A LISTING

Even the preceding smattering of clues to a random sampling of career fields must dramatize the importance of getting a broad background and detailed facts about any area that intrigues you before you even begin to commit yourself.

But where do you get this information?

The U. S. Labor Department's *Occupational Outlook Handbook* heads the list. I repeat, though it is probably available in your school or local library, or high school counseling office, or employment service office, buy a copy from the Superintendent of Documents, U. S. Department of Labor, Washington, D.C. 20402, for $6.25. Also check the two-volume *Encyclopedia of Careers and Vocational Guidance* (J. G. Ferguson—Doubleday).

Here, next, is a listing of trade associations, government agencies, and individual companies which can provide you with career information in specific fields:

ACCOUNTANT
American Institute of Certified
   Public Accountants
666 Fifth Avenue
New York, N.Y. 10019

ADVERTISER
American Association of
   Advertising Agencies
200 Park Avenue
New York, N.Y. 10017

AEROSPACE ENGINEER
American Institute of Aeronautics
   and Astronautics
1290 Avenue of the Americas
New York, N.Y. 10010

National Aeronautics and Space
   Administration
Washington, D.C. 20546

AGRICULTURE AND AGRICULTURAL
   RESEARCH
Office of Personnel
U. S. Department of Agriculture
Washington, D.C. 20250

AIR CONDITIONING AND
   REFRIGERATION MECHANIC
Refrigeration Engineers and
   Technicians
435 North Michigan Avenue
Chicago, Ill. 60611

AIRPLANE MECHANIC
Air Transport Association of
   America
1000 Connecticut Avenue, N.W.
Washington, D.C. 20036

Federal Aviation Agency
Department of Transportation
Washington, D.C. 20553

ANTHROPOLOGIST
American Anthropological
   Association
1703 New Hampshire Avenue,
   N.W.
Washington, D.C. 20009

APPAREL DESIGNER
Fashion Institute of Technology
227 West 27th Street
New York, N.Y. 10001

APPLIANCE SERVICEMAN
National Appliance Service
   Association
1525 Broadway
Kansas City, Mo. 64108

National Appliance & Radio-TV
   Dealers Association
318 West Randolph Street
Chicago, Ill. 60606

National Association of Service
   Managers
6650 Northwest Highway
Chicago, Ill. 60631

Appliance Service News
5841 West Montrose Avenue
Chicago, Ill. 60634

ARCHITECT
The American Institute of
   Architects
1735 New York Avenue, N.W.
Washington, D.C. 20036

ASTRONOMER
American Astronomical Society
211 FitzRandolph Road
Princeton, N.J. 08540

AUTO MECHANIC AND BODY REPAIR
U. S. Trade Schools
500 East Ninth Street
Kansas City, Mo. 64106

Automotive Services Industry
   Association
230 North Michigan Avenue
Chicago, Ill. 60601

National Automobile Dealers
   Association
2000 K Street, N.W.
Washington, D.C. 20006

AUTOMOTIVE ENGINEER
The Society of Automotive
   Engineers, Inc.
Two Pennsylvania Plaza
New York, N.Y. 10001

BANKER, BANK TELLER
American Bankers Association
1120 Connecticut Avenue, N.W.
Washington, D.C. 20036

BIOLOGIST
American Institute of Biological
   Sciences
3900 Wisconsin Avenue, N.W.
Washington, D.C. 20016

BOTANIST
Botanical Society of America
Department of Botany
Indiana University
Bloomington, Ind. 47401

BRICKLAYER
Bricklayers, Masons and Plasterers
   International Union
815 15th Street, N.W.
Washington, D.C. 20005

BUSINESS MANAGEMENT
The American Management
   Association
135 West 50th Street
New York, N.Y. 10015

CARPENTER
United Brotherhood of Carpenters
   and Joiners of America
101 Constitution Avenue, N.W.
Washington, D.C. 20001

CHEMICAL ENGINEER
American Institute of Chemical
   Engineers
345 East 47th Street
New York, N.Y. 10017

CHEMIST
American Chemical Society
1155 16th Street, N.W.
Washington, D.C. 20036

Manufacturing Chemists
Association
1825 Connecticut Avenue, N.W.
Washington, D.C. 20009

CHILD WELFARE WORKER
Division of Family and Child
Welfare Services
Community Service Administration
Social and Rehabilitation Service
U. S. Department of Health,
Education and Welfare
330 C Street, S.W.
Washington, D.C. 20201

CITY PLANNING
American Institute of Planners
1776 Massachusetts Avenue,
N.W.
Washington, D.C. 20036

American Society of Planning
Officials
1313 East 60th Street
Chicago, Ill. 60637

CLERICAL WORKER
United Business Schools
Association
1730 M Street, N.W.
Washington, D.C. 20036

COMMUNITY ACTION WORKER
National Association for
Community Development
Room 106
1424 16th Street, N.W.
Washington, D.C. 20036

Office of Economic Opportunity
Community Action Program
1200 19th Street, N.W.
Washington, D.C. 20506

COMPUTER OPERATOR,
PROGRAMER, SYSTEMS
ANALYST
American Federation of
Information Processing
Societies
210 Summit Avenue
Montvale, N.J. 07645

Data Processing Management
Association
505 Busse Highway
Park Ridge, Ill. 60068

Association for Computing
Machinery
1133 Avenue of the Americas
New York, N.Y. 10036

CONSERVATIONIST
The Conservation Foundation
1717 Massachusetts Avenue, N.W.
Washington, D.C. 20036

The Wildlife Society
3900 Wisconsin Avenue, N.W.
Washington, D.C. 20016

The Nature Conservancy
1800 North Kent Street
Arlington, Va. 22209

The Wilderness Society
1901 Pennsylvania Avenue, N.W.
Washington, D.C. 20006

Office of Personnel
Environmental Protection Agency
401 M Street, S.W.
Washington, D.C. 20460

National Wildlife Federation
8925 Leesburg Pike
Vienna, Va. 22180

Scientists Institute for Public
Information
30 East 68 Street
New York, N.Y. 10021

Natural Resources Council
1025 Connecticut Avenue, N.W.
Washington, D.C. 20036

National Parks & Conservation
Association
1701 18th Street, N.W.
Washington, D.C. 20009

American Public Works Association
1313 East 60 Street
Chicago, Ill. 60637

National Audubon Society
950 Third Avenue
New York, N.Y. 10022

COOK, CHEF
Educational Director
National Restaurant Association
One IBM Plaza, Suite 2600
Chicago, Ill. 60611

DATA PROCESSOR
American Federation of
Information Processing
Societies
201 Summit Avenue
Montvale, N.J. 07645

DAY CARE WORKER
Day Care and Child Development
Council of America, Inc.
1401 K Street, N.W.
Washington, D.C. 20005

DENTAL HYGIENIST
Division of Education Service
American Dental Hygienists
Association
211 East Chicago Avenue
Chicago, Ill. 60611

Division of Dental Health
Public Health Service
U. S. Department of Health,
Education and Welfare
Washington, D.C. 20201

DENTIST AND DENTAL ASSISTANT
Division of Career Guidance
Council on Dental Education
American Dental Association
211 East Chicago Avenue
Chicago, Ill. 60611

American Dental Assistants
Association
211 East Chicago Avenue
Chicago, Ill. 60611

DIESEL MECHANIC
International Association of
Machinists & Aerospace
Workers
1300 Connecticut Avenue, N.W.
Washington, D.C. 20036

DIETITIAN
The American Dietetic Association
620 North Michigan Avenue
Chicago, Ill. 60611

DIRECT SELLING
Direct Selling Association
1730 M Street, N.W.
Washington, D.C. 20036

ECONOMIST
American Economic Association
1313 21st Avenue, South
Nashville, Tenn. 37212

EDUCATION
American Association of School
    Administrators
1801 North Moore Street
Arlington, Va. 22209

National Education Association
1201 16th Street, N.W.
Washington, D.C. 20036

ELECTRICAL CONTRACTING
National Electrical Contractors
    Association
7315 Wisconsin Avenue
Bethesda, Md. 20014

ELECTRICAL-ELECTRONIC
    TECHNICIAN (RADIO AND TV)
Electronic Industries Association
2001 Eye Street, N.W.
Washington, D.C. 20006

ELECTRICIAN
International Brotherhood of
    Electrical Workers
1125 15th Street, N.W.
Washington, D.C. 20005

National Joint Apprenticeship and
    Training Committee for the
    Electrical Industry
1730 Rhode Island Avenue, N.W.
Washington, D.C. 20036

ENGINEER
National Society of Professional
    Engineers
2029 K Street, N.W.
Washington, D.C. 20006

Engineers Council for Professional
    Development
345 East 47th Street
New York, N.Y. 10017

FAMILY AND HOME ECONOMICS,
    NUTRITIONIST
American Home Economics
    Association
2010 Massachusetts Avenue, N.W.
Washington, D.C. 20036

FARMER, AGRICULTURAL
    RESEARCH WORKER
Public Information Office
U. S. Department of Agriculture
Washington, D.C. 20250

FLIGHT ATTENDANTS
Air Transport Association of
    America
1000 Connecticut Avenue, N.W.
Washington, D.C. 20036

FOOD INDUSTRY WORKER
National Association of Food
    Chains Educational Council
1725 Eye Street, N.W.
Washington, D.C. 20006

FOOD SCIENTIST
Institute of Food Technologists
Suite 2120
221 North LaSalle Street
Chicago, Ill. 60601

FOREIGN SERVICE
Director, Foreign Service
    Recruitment
Board of Examiners
Department of State
Washington, D.C. 20520

FORESTER
Society of American Foresters
1010 16th Street, N.W.
Washington, D.C. 20036

U. S. Forest Service
U. S. Department of Agriculture
Washington, D.C. 20250

American Forestry Association
1319 18th Street, N.W.
Washington, D.C. 20036

GEOGRAPHER
Association of American
    Geographers
1710 16th Street, N.W.
Washington, D.C. 20009

GEOLOGIST
American Geological Institute
2201 M Street, N.W.
Washington, D.C. 20037

GEOPHYSICIST
American Geophysical Union
1707 L Street, N.W.
Washington, D.C. 20036

Society of Exploration
    Geophysicists
P. O. Box 3098
Tulsa, Okla. 74101

GOVERNMENT JOBS
U. S. Civil Service Commission
Bureau of Recruiting and
    Examining
Room 1416A
1900 E Street, N.W.
Washington, D.C. 20415

HEALTH
Division of Careers and
    Recruitment
American Hospital Association
840 North Lake Shore Drive
Chicago, Ill. 60611

National Health Council
Health Careers Program
1740 Broadway
New York, N.Y. 10019

Health Resources Administration
Bethesda, Md. 20014

Program Services Department
American Medical Association
535 North Dearborn Street
Chicago, Ill. 60610

HOSPITAL ADMINISTRATOR
American College of Hospital
    Administrators
840 North Lake Shore Drive
Chicago, Ill. 60611

HOTEL-MOTEL WORKER
American Hotel and Motel
    Association
888 Seventh Avenue
New York, N.Y. 10019

The Council on Hotel, Restaurant
    and Institutional Education
Suite 534
1522 K Street, N.W.
Washington, D.C. 20005

INSTRUMENT REPAIRMAN
Instrument Society of America
400 Stanwix Street
Pittsburgh, Pa. 15222

INSURANCE UNDERWRITER OR
    CLAIM EXAMINER
Institute of Life Insurance
277 Park Avenue
New York, N.Y. 10017

Insurance Information Institute
110 William Street
New York, N.Y. 10038

American Mutual Insurance
    Alliance
20 North Wacker Drive
Chicago, Ill. 60606

JOURNALISM
Sigma Delta Chi
35 East Wacker Drive
Chicago, Ill. 60601

American Newspaper Publishers
    Association Foundation
Box 17407
Dulles International Airport
Washington, D.C. 20041

Journalism schools at major
    universities (e.g.,
    University of Missouri,
    Columbia, New York City;
    Columbia).

LAWYER AND LEGAL ASSISTANT
    (PARALEGAL)
Association of American Law
    Schools
Suite 370
1 Dupont Circle, N.W.
Washington, D.C. 20036

Pre-Law Handbook
c/o Educational Testing Service
Box 944
Princeton, N.J. 08540

American Civil Liberties Union
22 East 40th Street
New York, N.Y. 10016

Law Students Civil Rights
    Research Council, Inc.
22 East 40th Street
New York, N.Y. 10016

National Lawyers Guild
23 Cornelia Street
New York, N.Y. 10014

LIBRARIAN
Office for Library Manpower
American Library Association
50 East Huron Street
Chicago, Ill. 60603

LICENSED PRACTICAL NURSE
National Federation of Licensed
    Practical Nurses, Inc.
250 West 57th Street
New York, N.Y. 10019

National League for Nursing, Inc.
10 Columbus Circle
New York, N.Y. 10019

LIFE INSURANCE SALES WORKERS
Institute of Life Insurance
277 Park Avenue
New York, N.Y. 10017

MACHINIST
The National Machine Tool
    Builders Association
7901 West Park Drive
McLean, Va. 22101

MASON
Bricklayers, Masons and Plasterers
International Union
815 15th Street, N.W.
Washington, D.C. 20005

MEDICAL ASSISTANTS
American Association of Medical
Assistants
1 East Wacker Drive
Chicago, Ill. 60601

American Medical Association
Department of Allied Medical
Professions
535 North Dearborn Street
Chicago, Ill. 60610

MEDICAL LABORATORY ASSISTANT
National Committee for Careers in
the Medical Laboratory
9650 Rockville Pike
Bethesda, Md. 20014

MEDICAL RECORD LIBRARIAN
American Medical Record
Association
Suite 1850
875 North Michigan Avenue
Chicago, Ill. 60611

MEDICAL TECHNOLOGIST AND
MEDICAL TECHNICIAN
American Medical Association
Department of Allied Medical
Professions
535 North Dearborn Street
Chicago, Ill. 60610

American Society for Medical
Technology
Suite 200
5555 West Loop
Houston, Tex. 77401

METEOROLOGIST
American Meteorological Society
45 Beacon Street
Boston, Mass. 02108

MINERAL INDUSTRY WORKER
Chief, Division of Personnel
Bureau of Mines
U. S. Department of the Interior
18th and C Streets, N.W.
Washington, D.C. 20240

MUSEUM WORKER
American Association of Museums
2233 Wisconsin Avenue, N.W.
Washington, D.C. 20007

MUSIC TEACHER
Music Educators National
Conference
1201 16th Street, N.W.
Washington, D.C. 20036

NATIONAL PARK SERVICE WORKER
Department of the Interior
Division of Personnel
National Park Service
18th and C Streets, N.W.
Washington, D.C. 20240

NURSE AIDE
American Hospital Association
840 Lake Shore Drive
Chicago, Ill. 60611

NURSING
Nursing Information Service
National League for Nursing, Inc.
10 Columbus Circle
New York, N.Y. 10019

American Nursing Association
1200 15th Street, N.W.
Washington, D.C. 20036

OCCUPATIONAL THERAPIST
American Occupational Therapy
    Association
6000 Executive Boulevard
Suite 200
Rockville, Md. 20852

OCEANOGRAPHER
International Oceanographic
    Foundation
1 Rickenbacker Causeway
Virginia Key
Miami, Fla. 33149

American Society for
    Oceanography
Marine Technology Society
1730 M Street, N.W.
Washington, D.C. 20036

National Oceanic and Atmospheric
    Administration
Office of Public Affairs
6001 Executive Boulevard
Rockville, Md. 20852

Scripps Institution of
    Oceanography
La Jolla, Calif. 92037

Woods Hole Oceanographic
    Institution
Woods Hole, Mass. 02543

OIL INDUSTRY
American Petroleum Institute
1801 K Street, N.W.
Washington, D.C. 20006

OPTOMETRIST
American Optometric Association
7000 Chippewa Street
St. Louis, Mo. 63119

PAINTER
Painting and Decorating
    Contractors of America
7223 Lee Highway
Falls Church, Va. 22046

PAPER INDUSTRY
American Paper Institute
260 Madison Avenue
New York, N.Y. 10016

PATHOLOGIST
American Society of Clinical
    Pathologists
2100 West Harrison Street
Chicago, Ill. 60612

American Medical Association
Department of Allied Medical
    Professions
535 North Dearborn Street
Chicago, Ill. 60610

PHARMACIST
American Pharmaceutical
    Association
2215 Constitution Avenue, N.W.
Washington, D.C. 20037

American Association of Colleges
    of Pharmacy
8121 Georgia Avenue
Silver Spring, Md. 20910

PHOTOGRAPHY
Eastman Kodak Co.
Rochester, N.Y. 14650

PHYSICIAN
Association of American Medical
    Colleges
1 Dupont Circle, N.W.
Washington, D.C. 20036

American Medical Association
535 North Dearborn Street
Chicago, Ill. 60610

PHYSICIAN'S ASSISTANT
Health Resources Administration
Bethesda, Md. 20014

American Medical Association
Dept., Allied Medical Association
535 North Dearborn Street
Chicago, Ill. 60610

PHYSICIST
American Institute of Physics
335 East 45th Street
New York, N.Y. 10017

PHYSIOLOGIST
American Physiological Society
9650 Rockville Pike
Bethesda, Md. 20014

PLASTERER
Bricklayers, Masons and Plasterers
International Union
815 15th Street, N.W.
Washington, D.C. 20005

PLUMBER, PIPE FITTER
National Associations of
Plumbing-Heating-Cooling
Contractors
1016 20th Street, N.W.
Washington, D.C. 20036

POLICEMAN
International Association of Chiefs
of Police
11 Firstfield Road
Gaithersburg, Md. 20760

POLLUTION CONTROL
Water Pollution Control
Federation
3900 Wisconsin Avenue, N.W.
Washington, D.C. 20016

Air Pollution Control Association
4400 5th Avenue
Pittsburgh, Pa. 15213

Office of Personnel
Environmental Protection Agency
Washington, D.C. 20460

PSYCHIATRIC SOCIAL WORKER
National Association of Social
Workers
600 Southern Bldg.
15th and H Streets, N.W.
Washington, D.C. 20005

PSYCHIATRIST
American Psychiatric Association
1700 18th Street, N.W.
Washington, D.C. 20009

National Association for Mental
Health
1800 North Kent Street
Rosslyn Station
Arlington, Va. 22209

National Institute of Mental Health
5600 Fishers Lane
Rockville, Md. 20852

PSYCHOLOGIST
American Psychological
Association
1200 17th Street, N.W.
Washington, D.C. 20036

PUBLIC HEALTH WORKER
American Public Health
    Association, Inc.
1015 18th Street, N.W.
Washington, D.C. 20036

National Health Council
1740 Broadway
New York, N.Y. 10019

Health Resources Administration
Bethesda, Md. 20014

PUBLIC RELATIONS WORKER
Career Information Service
Public Relations Society of
    America
845 Third Avenue
New York, N.Y. 10022

RADIO AND TELEVISION
National Association of
    Broadcasters
1771 N Street, N.W.
Washington, D.C. 20006

RADIOLOGIST
American Medical Association
535 North Dearborn Street
Chicago, Ill. 60610

RECREATION THERAPIST
National Recreation and Park
    Association
1600 Kent Street
Arlington, Va. 22209

RECREATION WORKER
National Recreation and Park
    Association
1601 Kent Street
Arlington, Va. 22209

REFRIGERATION AND AIR
    CONDITIONING MECHANIC
Refrigeration Engineers and
    Technicians
435 North Michigan Avenue
Chicago, Ill. 60611

RESPIRATORY THERAPIST
American Association for
    Respiratory Therapy
7411 Hines Place
Dallas, Tex. 75235

SANITARY ENGINEER
National Environmental Health
    Association
1600 Pennsylvania Street
Denver, Colo. 80203

SCIENTIST
Scientific Manpower Commission
1776 Massachusetts Avenue,
    N.W.
6th Floor
Washington, D.C. 20036

Occupational Outlook Service
Bureau of Labor Statistics
Department of Labor
Washington, D.C. 20210

SECRETARY
United Business Schools
    Association
1730 M Street, N.W.
Suite 401
Washington, D.C. 20036

National Secretary's Association
240 Pershing Road
Kansas City, Mo. 64108

SOCIAL WORKER
The National Association of Social
Workers
600 Southern Bldg.
15th and H Streets, N.W.
Washington, D.C. 20005

SOCIOLOGIST
The American Sociological
Association
1722 N Street, N.W.
Washington, D.C. 20002

SOIL CONSERVATIONIST
Soil Conservation Society of
America
7515 Northeast Ankeny Road
Ankeny, Ia. 50021

SOIL SCIENTIST
The American Society of
Agronomy
677 South Segoe Road
Madison, Wisc. 53711

Office of Personnel
U. S. Department of Agriculture
Washington, D.C. 20250

SPEECH PATHOLOGIST
American Speech and Hearing
Association
9030 Old Georgetown Road
Washington, D.C. 20014

STATISTICS
American Statistical Association
806 15th Street, N.W.
Washington, D.C. 20005

TAX WORK
Chief, Recruitment Section
Internal Revenue Service
Washington, D.C. 20224

TEACHING
National Commission on Teacher
Education and Professional
Standards
National Education Association
1201 16th Street, N.W.
Washington, D.C. 20036

TECHNICIAN
National Association of Trade and
Technical Schools
2021 L Street, N.W.
Washington, D.C. 20036

Engineer's Council for
Professional Development
345 East 47th Street
New York, N.Y. 10017

TELEVISION-RADIO SERVICEMAN
National Alliance of Television
and Electronic Service
Associations
5908 South Troy Street
Chicago, Ill. 60629

TILE SETTER
Bricklayers, Masons and Plasterers
International Union
815 15th Street, N.W.
Washington, D.C. 20005

TOOL AND DIEMAKER
International Association of
Machinists and Aerospace
Workers
1300 Connecticut Avenue, N.W.
Washington, D.C. 20036

Skilled Trades Department, United
Automobile Workers of
America
8000 East Jefferson Avenue
Detroit, Mich. 48214

VETERINARIAN

American Veterinary Medical
    Association
600 South Michigan Avenue
Chicago, Ill. 60605

VOCATIONAL REHABILITATION

Social and Rehabilitation Service
U. S. Department of Health,
    Education and Welfare
330 C Street, S.W.
Washington, D.C. 20201

WELDER

The American Welding Society
2501 Northwest 7th Street
Miami, Fla. 33125

X-RAY TECHNICIAN

The American Society of
    Radiologic Technologists
645 North Michigan Avenue
Chicago, Ill. 60611

HOW TO LOOK

The above list is as important in showing you how to look for information as it is in guiding you to specific sources.

Note that, in most cases, a trade association will exist for members of the occupation. Note also that its name will almost always include the identification of the career—so that a check of the telephone books of major headquarters cities (Washington, New York, Chicago, Los Angeles, San Francisco) will probably lead you to a key source. Note, too, that colleges, universities, and big corporations are excellent places at which to seek guidance.

How to Get a Good Summer Job

Competition for summer jobs can be brutal, for this is the time of year when millions of high school and college graduates also are flooding into the labor market.

Thus, the earlier in the year you start your summer job hunt, the better are your chances of landing a good one. And the more you familiarize yourself with the basic rules on summer job hunting, the better off you'll be.

HOW TO SHOP

Here is how to shop for the summer job best suited to *you*.

If your biggest need is to earn and save money to finance your education, concentrate on the lucrative "summer industries." For example: resort hotels and motels; country clubs; drive-in movies; swimming pools and beaches; restaurants on highways; playgrounds; road and other types of construction; air conditioning and boat rental businesses; marinas; landscaping and home maintenance; ice cream parlors and distribution services; parks and playgrounds; moving companies; dude ranches and riding stables; gas stations and car washers; baseball parks; community recreation centers.

If you are looking for a summer camp job, an excellent source of information is the yearly *Directory of Accredited Camps for Boys and Girls,* available either in your library or, for a few dollars, from the Publications Service, American Camping Association, Bradford Woods, Martinsville, Ind. 46151.

Among the jobs open to students and teachers at summer camps: counselors, business managers, nurses, caretakers, dietitians, cooks, recreation specialists.

If you are interested in an office job, you may find work as a spare-time typist, file clerk, or secretary, or you might get temporary work in a library.

If you're a college student with some travel experience, you may get a job as a tour guide. Travel bureaus will give you the names of tour companies.

If you are willing to accept the challenge, try setting up your own enterprise. For instance: washing and waxing cars; baby sitting; operating a typing service; performing lawn or garden chores; arranging parties for small children. Door-to-door selling is worth trying, too.

For the past several years the Youth Conservation Corps has been putting young people to work on important conservation projects in camps across the country, paying them a modest salary, and giving them environmental instruction. For details, contact the Division of Manpower and Youth Conservation Programs, Forest Service, U. S. Department of Agriculture, Washington, D.C. 20250.

The Canadian government recently backed a program entitled Federal Opportunities for Youth Program (OYP), under which young people who came up with worth-while ecological projects were given grants to organize them. Perhaps you can persuade your state or town to do something similar.

A surprising number of students manage to earn $1,000, $1,500, or even $2,000 in the course of a summer.

However, if you have the choice of a job paying $2.50 an hour and one paying $3.00 an hour, don't automatically grab the higher-paying job if the $2.50-an-hour one offers more challenging work, more responsibility, better job training. Your loss in pay would be compensated by these other benefits.

If economic considerations are *not* top priority for you, use your summer job as a "career proving ground." If you have not decided on a career, use the summer to find out more about your own interests and abilities. Each summer, take jobs in different fields in which you have some interest to get an idea what goes on in each.

If you have already decided on a career, use the summer to explore different aspects of that field. For instance, if you plan to become a social worker, you might take jobs (especially volunteer jobs) that would expose you to the different problems of city slum children, adult illiterates, etc. If you are interested in medicine, consider successive jobs that might acquaint you with allied fields ranging from public health to occupational therapy. If you are interested in archaeology, consider joining a "dig," either in the United States or abroad.

If you think you might be interested in business as a career, find out *now* about "summer intern" programs offered by a growing number of corporations. In these, you are not only well paid but also receive valuable training and, most important, a firsthand view of the business world. Many corporations are now actively trying to attract students—via scholarships and summer job training programs. Their aim, of course, is to line up future employees—but a summer internship by no means commits you to work later for any corporation.

If you are a girl, don't restrict yourself to "women's jobs." You will have more and more opportunity in almost any job field for which you may later qualify.

In sum, give your summer job the same attention as you would a permanent job. Plan enough ahead to give yourself the best possible chance for the best job. Use the summer to broaden your experience, sharpen your skills, and sift your interests.

SOURCES OF JOB LEADS

Here are some of the best sources of job leads, and of guidance generally, to help steer you to a suitable summer job:

• Classified ads in your local newspapers.

• Friends, relatives, and neighbors; local businessmen.

• The state employment service with its more than 2,000 offices throughout the United States, many of them equipped with computerized job banks. In many cases, also the employment service offices have guidance counseling specialists in summer job-finding.

• The YMCA, YWCA, YMHA, and other community service organizations—not only for sources of information and leads on paying summer jobs but also for volunteer positions.

HOW ABOUT A NON-JOB?

What if you just can't find a summer job of any kind? What if you aren't poor enough to qualify for special help and are not eligible for a publicly subsidized job? What should you do?

First answer this question with utter honesty: Can you possibly afford to invest twelve weeks in a project which doesn't pay you a salary? If your answer is "yes," here are just a few of the many valuable possibilities:

• Go to summer school and take courses which will put you ahead during the coming fall semester, help you in a future job, or simply appeal to you. Community colleges, state universities, high schools, and many other institutions offer, at remarkably low or no cost, courses in subjects ranging from remedial reading to typing, foreign languages, art history, and investments.

• Travel in the United States or abroad. Many bargains are available to students. For example: a student identity card, available from American Youth Hostels, Inc., in New York will get you big discounts at student unions, restaurants, museums, etc., throughout Europe. See Chapter 12, "How to Save on Vacations," for more suggestions.

• Get into a political campaign. You may not yet have a vote but your volunteer time and talents could be even more important to a political candidate of your choice than a vote.

• Try your hand at farm work, as an educational switch from whatever you have been doing. The pay is low, but probably not as low as you think. And you might use your creativity to help alleviate the plight of the migrant harvester during the summer months.

• Take a trip within the United States—camping, biking, driving, flying. And if you have the courage, try working your way to your destination.

• Use this summer to cultivate a hobby. Check with your school on tutoring programs in which you may enroll to tutor students who need your skills. Learning to use your leisure time will be almost as important in the future as learning a profession or marketable skill.

If you must earn money, many volunteer jobs will pay you at least a pittance. (See section "Needed: Volunteers," at end of this chapter.)

Volunteer work will not only keep you busy. It also will be experience which can assist you in choosing a future career or getting into college. Admissions officials are showing a growing interest in the extracurricular activities listed by college applicants.

What About Working Abroad This Summer?

What about spending the summer abroad—either working as a volunteer or in a paying job? The key drawbacks to working abroad are: competition is keen; pay is low; many countries have restrictions on employment of foreigners; work permits often are required and these can be difficult to get; language can be a barrier.

Nevertheless, overseas jobs do exist—and your best bet in finding a good one is to work through an established, reputable job-finding organization.

BEST SOURCES OF JOBS

Among the best sources of summer jobs abroad are:

(1) The Association for the International Exchange of Students in Economics and Commerce (AIESEC), Room 1110, 52 Vanderbilt Avenue, New York, N.Y. 10017, which has an internship exchange program in more than 53 countries for undergraduate and graduate business students.

(2) The International Association for the Exchange of Students for Technical Experience (IAESTE), American City Building, Suite 217, Columbia, Md. 21044, which specifically seeks engineering, science, architecture, and agriculture majors who want to work abroad during the summer.

(3) Summer Jobs in Britain and Australia, run by the Council on

International Educational Exchange (CIEE), which is qualified to help you find a job in Great Britain and Australia (see below for address).

BEST SOURCES OF INFORMATION

• The CIEE issues low-cost student identity cards and publishes a yearly study-work-travel directory entitled, *Whole World Handbook* ($2.95). Write to the Council at 777 United Nations Plaza, New York, N.Y. 10017, for details.

• The National Student Travel Bureau will refer students to reputable agencies that arrange transportation and jobs overseas. Address: 2115 S Street, N.W., Washington, D.C. 20008.

Excellent publications, too, covering overseas student study and travel programs are:

• "Working Abroad." Free from CIEE.

• "A Word of Caution." Free from the Director of Public Information and Reports Staff, Bureau of Educational and Cultural Affairs, Department of State, Washington, D.C. 20520.

• "Summer Study Abroad." Published yearly by the Institute of International Education, 809 United Nations Plaza, New York, N.Y. 10017 ($2.00).

• *Study Abroad.* Available from the UNESCO Publications Center, P. O. Box 433, New York, N.Y. 10016 ($6.00).

• "Invest Yourself." Available from the Commission on Voluntary Service and Action, 475 Riverside Drive, Room 830, New York, N.Y. 10027 ($1.00).

• "Summer Jobs in Europe." Available from Vacation Work, 266 Ludlow Avenue, Cincinnati, O. 45220.

• *The Directory of Overseas Summer Jobs.* Available from National Directory Service, 266 Ludlow Avenue, Cincinnati, O. 45220 ($4.95).

You also will find the following good sources of information on summer jobs, study, and travel programs abroad:

Experiment in International Living American Institute for Foreign
Kipling Road   Study
Brattleboro, Vt. 05301   102 Greenwich Avenue
                                                          Greenwich, Conn. 06830

Finally, here are key questions to ask about any private agency whose services you might enlist to help locate a summer job abroad and about any specific programs offered:

Can the organization tell you of and refer you to someone from your campus who has used its services?

What does the organization charge for its services compared with other agencies?

Is the total cost to you, the participant, clearly spelled out?

Does the literature specify what is covered and, more importantly, what is not covered?

What percentage of the total cost goes for administration? Commissions?

Will the fee be refunded should you have to cancel?

Does the organization have an official base in the United States which would be legally responsible in the event of complications?

Does the organization secure low-cost passage and living arrangements for you?

Are special student identification and discount cards offered?

In work-abroad programs, does the organization specify exactly which types of jobs are available to you? The hours? The pay? Whether meals and lodging are included?

"TAILORED PAY CHECKS"

KEY TRENDS IN COMPENSATION

The "tailor-made pay check" is becoming ever more widespread—permitting you, an individual employee, to shape your own pay checks (so much cash, such and such a pension deal, this or that type savings or stock purchase plan) according to your own individual wants and needs. For example:

If you're in your late twenties, at the start of your career, married, with young children and a load of debts, what you need from your employer is all the current cash income and protection against death or disability you can get. What you don't need is a retirement income plan to which you are required to make fat contributions.

But if you're in your late fifties, around the peak of your taxable earnings and free of many of your family burdens, what you need is assurance of a lifetime retirement income for you and your wife. What you don't need is more current cash income on which you'll pay more taxes.

COMPENSATION GEARED TO YOUR AGE

Let's take a more detailed specific example of a middle-income manager called John Jones.

In his late twenties, Jones holds an accountant's position in an industrial corporation which pays him $15,000. Married and with three children, he finds it hard to keep up with his mounting family obligations despite several raises. Though his life insurance program is barely adequate, he complains of being "insurance poor." His requirements at this stage are easily defined.

He needs all the cash income he can command plus protection for his family. Thus, salary compensation, medical coverage, life insurance, and disability income protection are key elements in his pay package, with a minimum of employee contribution requirements.

Consider Jones fifteen years later, in his mid-forties, holding a higher job paying $25,000. Now one son is in college, another is a year away, his teen-age daughter is having expensive orthodontal work, his debts and tax obligations are higher, and his auto insurance bill is painful. He still needs all the cash he can command.

But he needs to be able to count on the cash regularly. Thus, bonus dollars in lieu of salary dollars offer little attraction because of their uncertainty. And though various forms of protection continue important, he must start building toward a retirement income in the years he has left at work.

Now consider Jones at fifty-seven, earning $40,000 in a job he'll almost certainly keep until retirement. His expenses have declined but his peak earnings have been cut by peak taxes and he still is far from achieving his retirement fund goal. Social Security (an increasingly important source of retirement income) will help but his most urgent need now is additional retirement income from his company's program.

The idea of "tailored pay checks" (or "cafeteria compensation") is becoming ever more widespread. But as company management explores their use as a powerful and sensible motivating force, you, the middle manager, will increasingly reap the benefits of a personalized pay package custom-designed for you.

AND "PERKS"

On top of all the cash compensation, the fringe benefits, and the tailoring of pay checks to meet the individual's changing circumstances comes a long and lengthening list of "perks"—perquisites—for executives: use of company hotel rooms and resort facilities; use of company planes; company autos; medical care; personal money management, etc.

In many cases the perks are old-fashioned, tax-loophole frivolities. In others they are highly imaginative incentives to executives.

(P.S. One "extra" which virtually no executive enjoys is overtime pay. No matter what the rules for premium pay for overtime work under the federal wage-hour law, these men and women work sixty, seventy, eighty hours a week or more for no extra pay at all. Why? They love what they do, they want to work, that's why!)

SHOP FOR FRINGE BENEFITS, TOO!

ROUTINE DEDUCTIONS

You're not at all untypical today if as much as one third of your pay is "missing" by the time you receive your check. And you're not at all untypical if, aside from the large chunk you pay for taxes, your deductions cover a dozen or more different items, offered by your employer as a fringe benefit at lower-than-usual cost or as a convenience to you.

Here is a partial list of goods and services for which deductions from pay checks are now routinely being made: federal and state income taxes; Social Security ("FICA") and Medicare taxes; life insurance premiums; health and disability insurance premiums; contributions toward company profit-sharing plans, and stock purchase plans; purchase of U. S. Savings Bonds; homeowners insurance premiums; personal catastrophe liability insurance premiums; repayments to credit unions for many types of loans.

A key attraction of fringe benefits rests on our income tax structure. If your employer simply increased your pay so that you could buy your own life insurance, health insurance, etc., you would have to pay income taxes on your fatter pay check. But if he offers these as fringe benefits you get the coverage *without* paying increased taxes. Moreover, your employer can get a better buy on many fringes (such as group health insurance) than you could get as an individual for yourself.

The extent to which increases in fringe benefits have entered and are continuing to enter crucial wage negotiations involving millions of workers dramatizes this fundamental and yet still startlingly understated point: in a mounting number of cases, improvements in fringe benefits are becoming as important as—or even more important than—cash pay hikes themselves.

For the majority of U.S. workers in the economic mainstream fringe benefits are a real blessing. But for the have-nots in our society they are a potent source of discontent. Reason: the "fringe binge" perpetuates the gap between those who are eligible for valuable fringes and those who are ineligible—because they are unemployed, employed part time, or work for marginal employers who cannot finance the extras.

Nevertheless, focusing strictly on the "haves":

• Today, if you're an average U.S. worker, for every $1.00 you are earning in regular pay, you are getting another 25¢ to 30¢ in fringe benefits. That translates into an extra $2,500 to $3,000 in fringes for every $10,000 of yearly pay.

• In the mid-1970s, if you were typical, you were receiving about $1.00 an hour in the form of "hidden" pay which didn't appear on your regular dollars-and-cents pay check, against only 25¢ of "hidden" benefits in the late 1940s.

• Fringe benefits have been increasing in recent years at two to three times the rate of increase in cash wages and salaries; in recent years the growth has been a hefty 10 to 12 per cent a year.

To help you compare your benefits with what others are receiving and to help you shop for benefits as you compare one prospective new job with another, here is a brief rundown on key benefits and trends today:

PAID VACATIONS AND HOLIDAYS

Typical today is a two-week vacation plus at least six to eight paid holidays. But this norm is rapidly becoming three weeks and ten to twelve paid holidays after just a few years of service.

Also the typical employer grants employees the equivalent of another two weeks' "vacation" in the form of a couple of coffee breaks each day.

The trend is toward ever lengthening vacations as well as vacation-splitting—permitting you to divide your vacation into chunks. Moreover, a growing number of companies are switching to the four-day (but still forty-hour) work week—giving you no fewer than fifty-two long weekends during the year. See Chapter 12, "How to Save on Vacations," for more details on how your vacations compare with those other workers get.

GROUP INSURANCE

Nearly all U.S. companies now make at least some contribution toward some type of insurance for their employees. Health and life insurance are the most common but the trend is toward group automobile insurance, and even group homeowners insurance. The typical company-paid policy is canceled when you move to another job, but often you can convert your group coverage to a low-cost individual policy if you do so within a stated period of time.

The new trends in health insurance are toward increasing amounts of major medical coverage for catastrophic illness, outpatient psychiatric care as well as in-hospital care, dental bills and eye care, yearly physical exams. A few employers provide coverage for totally disabled dependents and make prescription drugs available at bargain prices. For more details on health insurance coverage and costs, see Chapter 8, "The High Cost of Good Health."

In life insurance, the trend is toward substantial group coverage not only for workers themselves but also for their wives and children.

EDUCATIONAL BENEFITS

Many employers today will pay the full costs of further education and training—even programs lasting as long as a year. In a few cases employers also are offering college scholarships for workers' children.

MOVING BENEFITS

A growing minority of top U.S. corporations will pay at least part of your mortgage interest costs when you are reassigned to a new post in a new location. Many also will extend a low-cost loan to you to help you with the down payment on this new house. Virtually all companies will pay at least some of your direct moving expenses. For other fringes now being offered to employees on the move, see Chapter 13, "A Roof Over Your Head."

TIME OFF TO VOTE

The overwhelming majority of firms make some time-off arrangements for employees—both hourly and salaried—to vote. The usual thing is to give workers whatever time is needed "within reason." Only a dwindling minority says "no time off," on the basis that their employees have ample opportunity to get to the polls on their own time. Incidentally, most states now have laws providing for time off to vote, and many require that time off with pay be provided.

SPECIAL INVESTMENT PLANS

Under these plans, which vary widely from employer to employer, employees may invest regularly in company stock, in government bonds, in securities of outside companies, or in mutual funds. See Chapter 20, "How to Invest in Stocks," for more details.

DIVIDEND REINVESTMENT PLANS

See Chapter 20, "How to Invest in Stocks," for full analysis.

PROFIT-SHARING PLANS

Today, millions of workers—both white- and blue-collar—participate in private corporation profit-sharing plans often as an alternative to private pension plans, and thousands of new plans are being set up annually. In some, profits are distributed as periodic bonuses to employees. But in the vast majority of plans funds are held in trust until you, the employee, quit or retire. A key advantage of the typical "deferred" profit-sharing plan is that you pay no federal income taxes on your cut until you actually withdraw it from the profit pool. These plans are being set up by smaller and smaller companies. Employees are becoming eligible to participate in them and to withdraw their full funds after fewer and fewer years of service.

To suggest how significant such plans can be, Chicago's Continental Bank has calculated that if an employer of a thirty-year-old, $10,000-a-year man contributed an average of 10 per cent of these earnings to a profit-sharing account each year, if the worker matched this amount, and if the investment grew at 7 per cent compounded annually, the worker would have accumulated $228,000 by the time he retired at age sixty-five.

NEW "EXTRAS"

After reporting its findings in a recent every-other-year survey of fringe benefits in private industry, the U. S. Chamber of Commerce suggested that we stop labeling them "fringe" benefits. The Chamber has a point. For here is a sampling of extras already offered by *some* corporations:

• Free or reduced-price meals in company cafeterias.
• Paid membership in clubs, professional, and trade associations.
• Medical help for alcoholic and drug-abusing employees.
• Discounts on company products and services.
• Free or low-cost day care services for preschool children of employed working mothers.
• Free or nominal-cost use of company vacation and recreation facilities.
• Free retirement counseling to middle-aged workers in such areas as financial planning, Medicare benefits, how to turn a hobby into a part-time job.
• Financial aid for adoption expenses—to parallel maternity benefits.
• Fat bonuses for valuable employee suggestions.
• And free flying lessons . . . paternity leave for expectant fathers . . . time off for working mothers to consult with schoolteachers . . . company-paid legal services . . . taxis to and from work . . . free park-

ing . . . employer-paid funerals (about the last word in paternalism!) . . .

And this is not all.

EXOTIC BENEFITS

Here's an abbreviated list of some of the exotic fringe benefits which knowledgeable students of this type of "pay" are predicting for the decade of the seventies and beyond:

• Free concert and theater tickets at regular intervals.

• Use of company computer facilities for your own purposes.

• Loans via employer credit cards which you'll repay by deductions from your pay check.

• Company-run private schools for your children—particularly if you live in an area where public schools are below average.

• Free financial advice from experts paid by the company for which you work.

Before 1985, many experts think, fringe benefits might include coverage of more than 50 per cent of the costs of home nursing care for employees, maternity benefits for the unwed as well as the wed, and subsidized homes in company-owned retirement communities.

They see sharply expanded protection against increases in our cost of living through escalator clauses in retirement pensions and more and more leeway for you to choose which hours of the day and which days of the week you want to work.

But, of course, towering above all other fringe benefits is the private pension plan—next to your salary, quite likely your most important single point of comparison between Job A and Job B.

It's so important, in fact, that it demands a key place in Chapter 19 on "Planning for Your Future Financial and Personal Security." And that's where you will find full details on pensions.

IF YOU ARE A WOMAN

YOU PROBABLY WORK

If you are a woman between the ages of eighteen and sixty-five, the odds are better than fifty-fifty that you are now holding a job. The chances are nine out of ten that you will work or have worked at some time during your life.

Even if you are married, you are almost as likely to be holding a job as not; more than four out of ten of all married American women are now in the U.S. labor force.

And even if you have children, the chances are good that you're working too. Nearly half of the millions of working wives have children under age eighteen. Even the mothers of very young children work; 4.8 million working mothers in the mid-seventies had children under the age of six.

Of course, if you're not married, it's even more likely that you are working. More than half of all single women are in the labor force—as are two out of three divorcees and one in four widows (many of whom are old and unable to work).

As a general rule, the more education a woman has and the older her children, the bigger the odds she is in the labor force. More than half of the wives who have completed four years of college are in the labor force.

If you're typical, you'll marry in your early twenties, raise your children, and then go back to work. On average, the birth of one child reduces your work-like expectancy by ten years. And the birth of each additional child reduces your work-life expectancy another two to three years.

Children or not, though, you'll probably work in a paying job a total of twenty-five years during your lifetime.

WOMEN WORKERS AND FAMILY INCOME

Like men, women work primarily because they need to earn money. For most working women, the question of working purely for personal fulfillment simply is not the issue. Almost all of the 7 million-plus single working women and the more than 6 million women workers who were widowed, divorced, or separated in the mid-seventies were working to support themselves and—in the latter cases—often their children too. These are all women who must work because they do not have husbands to support them.

But wives and mothers work too; and for a great many of these women, financial need also is the compelling force keeping them in the labor market. These wives—many of them with young children—need to work to keep their families afloat; because their husbands are unemployed; to raise the family's standard of living. On average, wives' earnings contribute 27.5 per cent to family incomes, with the wives' contribution to family income ranging from 39 per cent for those who work full time all year down to 12 per cent for those who work less.

And they need to work because they are what the Labor Department calls "female heads of families"—women with young children to support and no husband to help. There are more than 6 million families in the United States headed by women.

Moreover survey after survey has shown that a very large percentage of the women who are not in the labor force would like to work if they thought they had a chance at a job. These women don't actively look for work (and are therefore not counted as being "in the labor force") because they think racial or sex discrimination would bar them, or they lack skills, or they have family responsibilities that keep them at home. Many would go to work if decent day care facilities were available.

The income level for families with children under age eighteen and headed by women, however, is low. When we talk about the low incomes of families headed by a woman, we are talking about one of the root causes of poverty in our society. Until we can improve the situation of these women—by upgrading their skills, expanding their job opportunities, abolishing sex discrimination in pay levels, and providing adequate child care—our welfare problem will continue to plague us and millions of our children will continue to grow up on a hopeless treadmill of poverty.

For information on how to fight job discrimination on account of sex see Part IV, "Your Rights and How to Get Them."

GET READY NOW FOR THE "EMPTY NEST"

But what if you're among the many, many mothers who *want* to stay at home with your young children, and who are financially able to do so? Fine—but, at the very least, realize now that your children, too, will grow up and leave home. And when they do, you, the full-time mother, will be a still young, vigorous woman. What will you do then?

For the last several years my husband and I have been what economists call an "empty nest"—an economic unit which has become enormously significant in our society, the family in which both parents are alive and the last child has left home. A full one in seven families in the United States are empty nests—families with no children under eighteen living at home.

And now that I have lived this story and learned its true dimensions, I cannot urge you too strongly to start preparing for your empty nest early in your life! Start before you are married and even have a nest of your own.

The empty nest is very much a phenomenon of modern times. At the turn of the century the average American family never knew an empty nest; typically, the father died before the last child left home. A half century ago, if an empty nest did develop, it lasted only a year or so, until one spouse died. But now, as a result of trends toward longer life spans, smaller families, and concentration of childbearing before the age of twenty-six, an empty nest in the United States will last an average fourteen years. Some couples will spend thirty or forty years together between the time when the last child leaves home and the death of either spouse.

The number of empty-nesters is impressive enough and growing rapidly—but the reasons they are so important stretch far beyond numbers alone. Specifically, this unit includes:

• The most affluent of all age groups. When the typical empty nest occurs, the husband is at the peak of his earning years. Although this group represents one tenth of our total population, it gets one fifth of our annual personal income.

• The least debt-burdened of all age groups. By the time the nest empties, most parents have slashed their debts and the overwhelming majority own their own homes. They are financially "free" to an unprecedented degree.

• Consumers who are eager buyers of leisure-time and luxury items of all types. Here are the big spenders for foreign travel, eating out, costly clothes and cars—all the goods and services they had to forgo while bringing up the children.

• Devoted buyers of small packages of almost everything. There are still tremendous gaps in goods and services designed for the small adult family unit.

• And most important, a towering percentage of working wives. Among women in their middle years (in their forties and over) the non-working wife is becoming the *exception!* Of those holding a college degree, more than two out of three are in the labor force, and of those with graduate training it's four out of five.

The economic implications of all these points are clear—and equally unmistakable should be the message to you, as a girl in school, a young bride, a mother of babies or teen-agers. If you are still in school, remain there until you have achieved the education to get and hold a job which interests you. If you are a young bride or young mother who chooses not to work temporarily, keep your education up to date. If you are a mother of teen-agers, actively refresh your training to be ready to go to work part or full time.

Abysmally lost is the wife who does not have something to occupy herself when the nest empties. Don't wait to find out for yourself how true this is; prepare now to avoid the experience.

BASIC CAREER GUIDES

Let's say you are a young woman planning for a career in today's challenging era. What basic guides could I give you to help you fulfill yourself as well as to make a significant contribution to your family and to the national economy?

• Before you decide on your career, study the enormous range of occupations now open to you. You'll find the guides in the previous pages of this chapter.

• Set your career goals as high as you dare, or think about how you might upgrade your goals within a given field you've already picked. For example, if you're thinking about becoming a nurse, ask yourself whether you might qualify for training as a nursing teacher or a psychologist. If you want to become a secretary, consider upgrading to a high-paying specialty such as medical, legal, or bilingual secretarial work.

• Make a long-range plan to meet the requirements for the occupation you choose. Your immediate goal probably will be to complete college; the statistical likelihood is that you'll then get married and raise a family. But you can go on to specialized education-training later, or pick it up on a part-time basis while you're an active housewife. Today hundreds of organizations, and colleges and universities, including community colleges and university extensions, offer "continuing education programs" for adult women. In some cases, class schedules are geared to the hours you're likely to be free from domestic duties. See Chapter 10, "A College Education and How to Finance It."

• If you received professional training or graduate education before you married and left the labor force, do everything possible to keep that training up to date while you're at home. Maintain your membership in professional associations. Subscribe to, and read, technical journals in your field. Attend any seminars or lectures in your field which you can. Keep in touch with other members of your profession. Use your education and practice your skills through part-time jobs or volunteer work in your field.

• Explore the possibility of studying at home—via correspondence courses, adult education programs, educational television, independent study—then taking examinations leading to a high school diploma or giving college credit toward a degree. Ask your local board of education, community college, or state employment service for details on high school equivalency examinations. You'll find information on home study approaches to a college education in Chapter 10, "A College Education and How to Finance It."

An excellent source of information on continuing education programs for women is the Women's Bureau, Employment Standards Administration, U. S. Department of Labor, Washington, D.C. 20210. You can buy a copy for a modest price of the Women's Bureau's publication, "Continuing Education Programs and Services for Women" from the Superintendent of Documents, Washington, D.C. 20402. Also useful are: "Directory of Post-secondary Schools with Occupational Programs," (Superintendent of Documents) and the New York *Times*'s *Guide to Continuing Education in America* (Quadrangle Books, $4.95).

• When you're free to take a full-time job, don't just "take a job." Look for work in the field in which you were originally educated or trained. If it requires more training or retraining, get it. Or if you want to start over on a new career, do that.

MYTHS ABOUT WOMEN WORKERS

Not long ago a young acquaintance who works in a private employment service and who is compensated according to the number of jobs he is actually able to fill received from an employer a request for mechanical engineer specializing in fluid control devices—e.g., heat exchangers, centrifugal pumps, valves; substantial salary for the qualified person. But there was a catch. The employee had to be a *woman*. Although sure that a search would be fruitless, the young man nevertheless called his firm's Chicago office. Within minutes this office produced the names of six eligible candidates and one was promptly hired for this job.

You're in the majority if you never would have considered an engineering specialty in "fluid control devices" a woman's job. You also are in the majority if you continue to indulge in unfair, illegal "job labeling" which arbitrarily insists that one occupation is for men only and another for women only.

Aptitude tests have repeatedly shown that women can perform just about any job as well as men can. Women are now represented in virtually every one of the 400-plus occupations listed in the 1970 census. Yet, in defiance of all equal opportunity laws, job labeling persists—and it continues to bar women from the higher-level, higher-paying jobs.

In defiance of the 1964 Civil Rights Act—prohibiting job discrimination on the grounds of sex as well as race—employers continue to indulge in such flagrant examples of discrimination as: automatic firing of women within sixty days of marriage; refusal to allow women to work overtime, even though state laws permit the overtime; banning women even from training for managerial jobs. And unions, too, continue to engage in such grossly unfair practices as clinging to collective bargaining agreement clauses which reserve certain jobs for men and others, usually at lower pay, for women.

Here, in addition to the "women's jobs" myth are other myths which mock this era of equal job rights.

Myth: Women are absent from their jobs because of illness more than men are, thus cost the employer more money.

Reality: The absenteeism rate due to illness or injury currently averages 5.2 days a year for women, 5.1 days for men. Moreover, these figures ignore the fact that relatively few women work in high managerial positions, which always have been associated with lower absenteeism rates, and thus they may be distorted.

Myth: Women switch jobs much more frequently than men do.

Reality: Labor Department studies show that women's job-changing rates are slightly lower than rates for men if proper allowance is made for the fact that low-paid workers of either sex switch jobs often.

Myth: In any high-unemployment period, women take jobs away from men, the traditional breadwinners.

Reality: There are millions more married women in the labor force than there are unemployed men! Thus, if all married women quit and if all the unemployed men moved into their empty jobs, there would remain tens of millions of unfilled jobs—causing one of the most horrendous economic disasters imaginable. What's more: few of today's unemployed men have the education, skills, or other qualifications to fill jobs held by women as secretaries, nurses, schoolteachers.

Myth: Women work only for "pin money."

Reality: That has been answered. Of all women now in the labor force, nearly half are working because they are single, widowed, divorced, separated, or have very low-income husbands.

Myth: Training women is a waste of money since they quit when they marry or have children.

Reality: The separations are only temporary. Even taking into account her child-rearing, non-working years, the average woman worker has a work-life expectancy of twenty-five years. For a single woman, the average is forty-five years versus an over-all average of forty-three years for men, married or single.

Myth: Men don't like to work for women.

Reality: Notes the Department of Labor's Women's Bureau: "Most men who complain about women supervisors have never worked for a woman."

And an examination of attitudes entitled "Are Women Executives People?" first printed in the *Harvard Business Review,* found that only one man in seventeen was "strongly unfavorable" to the idea of women managers. In contrast, one in ten was "strongly favorable" and the other attitudes ranged from "mildly favorable" to "mildly unfavorable."

WHAT'S A HOUSEWIFE WORTH?

If you are a typical "non-jobholding" U.S housewife, you fill at least 12 well-defined occupations valued in the open market at a minimum of $300 a week for an actual pay in dollars of $000.

If you are among the tens of millions of American women classified as "married, not in the labor force," you put in 100 or more hours per week working at these occupations—and frequently many, many more—again, for the dollar pay of $000.

You have no set hours and it's normal for you to start early and stop late. You have no specified schedule for rest. You have no assurance of any vacation worth the name at any time for any duration. You get little, if any, recognition for your job performance as such. It's taken for granted that you'll be good.

As a "card-carrying" pioneer in the world of women's lib, I have understandably concentrated on the working women—and our right to equal pay for equal work, equal recognition, equal opportunity, all the rest. But I have also studied the "non-jobholding" housewives among my friends in the exurb where we have a country home. Without their being aware of my scrutiny, I have checked their performance without any help as cook, chauffeur, seamstress, housekeeper, laundress, etc.

I've watched most of them go to work at 6 A.M. to feed their families before sending them off to the commuting trains or school. And I've watched most of them start another cycle of several hours of work involving dinner and cleanup at 6 P.M., a mere twelve hours later.

What's more, a housewife's work is not only non-paid, it's not even counted in our output as a nation. When I turn out something, I'm paid for my production and my pay is included in our nation's Gross National Product. But when a housewife sews a magnificent dinner skirt, all that counts toward GNP is what she spent for the material, the thread, whatever else she bought. Her labor, without which the skirt would not have come into existence, doesn't count one whit. (If she had hired someone to sew the skirt for her, though, and had paid her, what the seamstress earned from her would count.)

Imagine what our GNP would swell to if we counted in just the $300 a week being earned by tens of millions of women!

Use the following chart to figure *your* worth as a housewife in *your* area, at current wage rates:

JOB	HOURS PER WEEK	LOCAL RATE PER HOUR	YOUR "VALUE" PER WEEK
Nursemaid			
Housekeeper			
Cook			
Dishwasher			
Laundress			
Food buyer			
Chauffeur			
Gardener			
Maintenance man			
Seamstress			
Dietitian			
Practical nurse			
TOTAL			

HOW TO FIND A DAY CARE CENTER

If you are a typical young family with small children, an absolute *must* before you, the mother, can take even a part-time paying job is a good nursery school, baby-sitting service, or day care facility at a cost you can afford.

If you could find a top-notch day care center, it could be a boon not only to you but also to your child—for if it's top-notch it will be well staffed, well equipped, well populated with other children, and well supplied with a variety of cultural-educational stimuli.

Where and how do you find good child care arrangements? What are the costs likely to be?

• Start by checking your would-be employer's day care facilities. Many, many companies—ranging from hospitals to factories, baby food companies, and government agencies—have set up day care facilities. In most cases you pay a modest sum each week, for your child.

If you are considering taking a job in a hospital, weigh the presence or absence of day care facilities before you choose a particular institution. Hundreds of hospitals have day care centers today—as a way to attract nurses and other health service workers who otherwise might be housebound. And hundreds more are in the process of setting up day care facilities. Almost all have opened their doors just within the past few years.

• If you work for the federal government, check with the several agencies which now have day care centers—including the Department of Labor, the Department of Agriculture, and the U. S. Office of Education.

• Make inquiries at local civic and religious organizations about available day care facilities run by these organizations or by other agencies.

• Certainly canvass with care the wide variety of private day care combinations—including nursery schools, baby-sitting services, communal care, informal child care agreements among neighbors.

• Investigate—if you're a college student—whether the college you're attending (or plan to attend) has some type of low-cost day care facility.

• Check, if you're a member of a labor union, whether your union runs a day care center.

• Look among available publicly supported preschool programs—

particularly any federally financed programs aimed primarily at preschool-age children from lower-income families, but not always segregated along economic lines.

• Use these sources of guidance and information on child care services for you and in your community: The Day Care and Child Development Council of America, 1025 14th Street, N.W., Washington, D.C. 20005; the federal Department of Health, Education and Welfare's Office of Child Development, Washington, D.C. 20201; also regional offices of this agency; the local chapter of the National Organization for Women.

• Ask your library to help you get a copy of *The Early Childhood Education Directory* (New York, R. R. Bowker Co.)—a descriptive compendium of more than 2,000 nursery schools, federally financed centers, and day care centers throughout the country.

• Order the Office of Child Development publication, *Finding the Best Day Care for Your Children,* from Consumer Information, Pueblo, Colorado 81009.

• If you can't find decent day care facilities at a cost you can manage in your home community, try pooling your own ideas, children, time, skills, with those of other neighbors and friends who are working mothers. Share out-of-pocket costs—and rotate responsibilities among you. Or try to hire, at least part time, someone who has been trained in this field.

• Another alternative is to try to find a conscientious college student willing to trade bed and board, say, for looking after your small children part time. You might even be able to track down an *au pair* foreign student through an agent specializing in making arrangements for such young people to live in your home—for a small sum per week plus room and board.

DAY CARE CENTER QUIZ TO GUIDE YOU

Here are the key questions to ask about any day care center to which you are considering entrusting your child and to which you may be committing yourself to pay substantial fees, charges, or tuitions:

• Is the center a professionally staffed, decently equipped place in which your child is likely to learn something? Or is it merely a baby-sitting service?

• What are the center's hours—and does it operate five, six, or seven days a week? Is this schedule convenient for *you*?

• Will your child be permitted to "try out" the center for, say, a couple of weeks before he or she is committed to sign up for a longer period?

• Do toys, equipment, and the layout of the center itself appear to add up to a safe place to be and play and learn?

• Is a doctor and/or nurse on call—especially if the center is a relatively large one?

• Is the center licensed by the state or some other public agency (most licensed centers are listed in the Yellow Pages of your telephone book)?

• What meals and/or snacks are offered and is their content of real nutritional value?

• Who and how many are on the staff—and what kind of training (if any) have they had in early childhood education?

• What is the child-to-teacher ratio? An adequate ratio would be around 10 to 1.

• How varied are the activities and experiences to which your child will be exposed?

• What are daily or weekly charges? Are there special rates for half days and for second or third children from a single family? Is there a special charge for lunch? If fees are based on your family's ability to pay, just what would that mean?

IS IT REALLY WORTH IT?

Every word in this section surely must shout to you my own profound conviction that "it" is worth it indeed.

Every line in this discussion surely must disclose how intellectually and emotionally I am committed to the *right* of a girl and a woman to have her own career and the importance of this to her own sense of values and dignity. And surely my own life underlines how I have translated my beliefs into reality.

But *you* may want to calculate the advantages strictly in financial terms.

Okay. Let's say your before-tax salary was $150 a week and that deductions for various federal, state, and Social Security taxes and for group health insurance amounted to $35.88. That would leave you $114.12.

Then deduct $1.00 a day for transportation to and from work, $1.50 a day for lunch, and $5.00 a day for the baby sitter or day care services.

Next figure that the extra clothes, personal-care costs, and other personal items will cost you about $5.00 a week.

Then try to estimate the higher household expenses you're likely to have, such as more expensive convenience foods to save you cooking time. Say these come to $15 a week.

The total comes to $57.50 a week, meaning $93.38 will be deducted from your $150 pay check. This leaves you $56.62 a week, or less than half of your before-tax pay. And your husband may argue with even that figure for income tax reasons.

But I cannot say it too strongly: the amount left is *not* the key point! What *is* the key is that, if you want to work, you should. If you want to take extra training to upgrade your job and your pay, you should.

To estimate *your* own costs, fill in this chart—and weigh the total against your own pay check.

Gross Weekly Salary $_____

Deductions:
    Federal income tax _____
    State income tax _____
    State disability _____
    Social Security _____
    Group life insurance _____
    Group health insurance _____
    Pension plan _____

Total deductions _____
Amount of take-home pay $_____

Weekly Expenses:
    Transportation $_____
    Lunches _____
    Child care _____
    Personal grooming (including extra
      cleaning and laundry) _____

Weekly Expenses (cont'd)

Extra clothes _____

Dues (professional, union, etc.) _____

Household help _____

Added household expenses
(convenience foods, paying for
things you might have done
yourself, etc.) _____

Office contributions, etc. _____

Other _____

Total Weekly Expenses $_____

Take-home pay $_____

Minus weekly expenses $_____

Your real pay net $_____

How to Play "Success Chess"

YOUR LIFETIME JOB GUIDE

"At what ages," asked Terry, a twenty-nine-year-old investment banker obviously destined to climb the success ladder, "is it entirely okay for you to change jobs frequently in order to test yourself on what you want to be and do?"

In what age range, both of us then debated, should you be finding the industry in which you want to spend your future years and should you be moving from job to job within that industry in order to build up your skills and experience?

By what age should you have definitely located your own industry, be set to move vertically toward the job goals you have concluded are right for you?

Spurred by Terry's penetrating questions, I went to one of the top executive recruiting and management training firms in the world—charging, for counseling on a single job, fees ranging up to $3,000 for an individual, $30,000 for a corporation.

Since it's highly unlikely you'll have the opportunity—not to mention the fee—to ask such a firm in person for specific advice about jobs, I did the asking for you.

Important note: The advice that follows applies as much to "Theresa" as to "Terry." In fact, the experts at this firm went out of their way to emphasize that the guides are for young women as well as for men.

Now here are six practical guides to job success this firm developed over years of helping to mold the careers of famous industrialists.

(1) In the first five years of your job career—say from age twenty-two to twenty-eight—try to find out what you want to *do,* what you want to *be.* Don't hesitate to make several job changes, for you are testing yourself. As a young man or woman, ask yourself: "What do I want out of life? What do I want to do?"

In these years young men or women who are unmarried are generally more successful than married individuals, because they can more easily move around on their own or more easily be moved by their firms.

(2) Also, in the twenty-two to twenty-eight age range, concentrate on finding the industry in which you want to stay.

The future top leaders are to an impressive extent the ones who were set in their own industry in their twenties and who then moved within it to gain know-how.

(3) At the age of thirty, stop and think hard. Take the time to sit down quietly and write out some answers to yourself on such questions as these: Where do you want to live? Where would you and your spouse be happiest? How much annual pay will you need to earn ten or fifteen years from now to meet the standard of living you want? You'll have a much clearer concept of your goals after you've honestly made this effort to "know thyself"—which well may be among the hardest tasks you'll ever undertake.

(4) For the next ten years—say to age forty—prepare yourself deliberately for what you want to be. Grade yourself on these qualities for success: drive, responsibility, health, good character, ability to communicate, ability to think, ability to get along with people, ability to keep your perspectives (i.e., recognize your responsibilities to society even while you're watching your competitors in business).

(5) In the forty to forty-two age bracket you'll hit a treacherous

phase of "cyclical restlessness" when you may mistakenly change jobs because you're looking for the "greener grass." Be on guard: again, quietly check up on your goals.

(6) After age forty-five, start consolidating—use the years to broaden your objectives, achieve fulfillment, lay the basis for a rewarding new life after you leave your company.

Brief as this guide is, it's loaded. And it also has given you one of the most significant job hints of your entire career if it challenges you merely to find your answers to those two deceptively simple questions:

What do you want out of life?

What do you want to do?

WHAT MOVES TO MAKE

Now let's say you are in your thirties—into the decade during which you should be preparing yourself for what you want to do and be.

Let's say, too, that you have found a new job as a well-paid middle executive in an aggressive fast-growing corporation. The promise of rapid promotion into the upper corporate ranks was part of the deal— as long as management believes you deserve a promotion because of your superior performance in your starting position.

What moves can you make at this stage to boost your chances of stepping up the corporate ladder as rapidly as possible? Here are nine— drawn up by a top authority in the field of executive behavior:

(1) *Keep open the widest possible set of options* or of future opportunities to alter your behavior. It is less important to know exactly where you are going than to keep your options open. When you see that you are being stereotyped, make a move either within or outside the company to break the stereotype.

(2) *Avoid loss of career time.* Do not waste this precious commodity by working for an immobile superior. The chances are greater that you will be blocked by such a boss, for a shelf-sitter is more likely to stay than be replaced.

(3) *Become a crucial subordinate to a mobile superior.* When he moves you'll move, since you are as important to him as he is to you.

(4) *Aim for increased exposure and visibility,* and make sure you are traveling the right kind of "route" in your company. If manufacturing men tend to inherit the presidency and you are in sales, think very

hard about whether or not you have gone as far as you can go up the management ladder.

(5) *Practice "self-nomination" for top jobs.* Let those who do the nominating for key posts know that you want a bigger job or at least want to learn how to qualify for it.

(6) *Make sure that if you leave your company* you do so on your own terms, and always leave on the best of terms.

(7) *If after long and serious deliberation you decide to quit, rehearse the move ahead of time.* Avoid being counted among the executives who have fired their corporation in the afternoon and rehired it the next day. Instead, write out your resignation, put it in a safe place in your desk, and let at least a week go by before you submit it.

(8) *Look upon the corporation as a market* rather than a place in which you simply work for a living. The market is for skills, and skill is best determined by your real achievements and performance.

(9) *Have faith* that if you can succeed in one thing you can probably succeed in another, even without having climbed a single rung on a corporate ladder.

FIVE CLUES ON PROMOTIONS

Now study the following five clues on promotions offered by other experts on the subject of executive advancement:

(1) The great majority of promotions to top executive spots are made from within the firm; significant numbers of these, however, were employed by their companies for only a relatively few years.

(2) The average age of newly promoted company presidents and chief executive officers is now in the early to mid-forties.

(3) Virtually all newly promoted company executives are college graduates and more than one in three holds an advanced degree. Among those holding B.A. degrees, most majored in business or engineering and among those with masters' degrees, most are in business.

(4) The top four rungs of the corporate ladder from which executives are being promoted today are: operations-division management; finance; marketing; administration.

(5) The least likely corporate specialties from which businessmen are now promoted to top jobs are: public relations; manufacturing; international; research and development.

SHOULD YOU QUIT YOUR JOB?

Here are fifteen questions which will reveal to you your own feelings about your job:

(1) In the last couple of months have you thought that you would like to quit or change jobs because you do not like the work itself?

(2) Do you feel that your work is monotonous, that the work itself provides no basic interest?

(3) Do you like the work itself that you are doing?

(4) Do you feel your work is checked too much?

(5) When you are away from work, do you think of your job as something you look forward to?

(6) Do you feel your job is a dead end as far as a work career is concerned?

(7) Do you find your work interesting enough to talk about it with people outside your work situation?

(8) Do you feel that your job is a place where you can continually learn something worth while?

(9) Do you find your job less interesting than, say, six months ago?

(10) How often are you fed back information about things that go wrong in a way embarrassing or awkward for you?

(11) How often do you feel that putting in effort to do your job well is not worth it because it really won't affect anything in the long run?

(12) How often do you feel that some parts of the job you do really do not make sense?

(13) How often do you find yourself wishing that you could take up another type of work because the work itself is not interesting?

(14) How often do you feel that you are just marking time, just putting in time at your work?

(15) How often do you feel that putting in extra effort is just looking for more problems?

Your answers just to these fifteen questions will indicate the scope of your dissatisfaction with your job.

And will your answers also determine whether you should switch

jobs? At the very least, they will give you something to ponder very, very hard.

DO'S AND DON'TS ON QUITTING

Say you are a young middle-management executive earning between $20,000 and $25,000 in a subsidiary of a giant corporation and say three men in your own age bracket are ahead of you. Say you have just made a New Year's resolution to get out of this box *now* and find another job with better prospects for advancement. What should you do?

• *Don't* quit! Keep your present job while you look for another, for in addition to giving you income and a sense of security it will prove to a would-be employer that you are making the move voluntarily.

• *Do* get firmly in your own mind that this job change may be just one link in a lifelong chain of job changes. For if you are a man twenty years old, you can expect to make more than six job changes during the remainder of your working life. Even at age forty you can still expect to make more than two job changes, and even at fifty you can expect at least one more job change.

Of course, these are only averages, calculated by the Labor Department. Some of us will work at one job all our lives, some will make many more than the average number of changes. Nevertheless, the averages underline the extraordinary degree of job mobility in this country—despite the holding power of fringe benefits, pensions, seniority rights. Executive "dropouts" have become almost as commonplace as high school dropouts.

We're changing and upgrading our jobs and careers as never before in history. We're shopping continually not only for higher pay but—often more importantly—for more fringe benefits such as better pension plans and longer vacations; for a better chance to advance; for a more appreciative boss; for a way out of the big city rat race; for greater on-the-job excitement and adventure; for a chance to learn more; for an opportunity to do our bit to better the troubled world in which we live.

• *Don't* answer in your own name any "blind" ad (one giving only a box number and not identifying the company). Instead, have a friend cover for you by signing a third-person letter describing your qualifications to help you remain anonymous if the ad was placed by your own company. Do not have a job counselor, recruiter, or employment agent

answer for you, for the recipient may get the impression that money is changing hands and this will destroy your letter's impact.

• *Do* prepare on your own—and with no professional help—a résumé of your career, your qualifications, your objectives. See earlier in this chapter for rules on résumés.

• *Don't* be thrown off base if your employer discovers you are job hunting and in fact *do* accept the fact that you are taking this risk and your employer is likely to find out. This emphasizes the importance of having your campaign planned in advance—so you will be well on your way to something new by the time your plans are discovered.

• *Do,* if you know of employment agencies which others have found responsible and effective, register with them and leave your résumé. The company hiring you probably will pay the fee. If yours is a highly specialized field, you may be able to locate an agency specializing in finding jobs in this field.

• *Do* register too with your nearest state employment agency, which offers free job finding and/or counseling. Many branches of this agency now have specialized job placement services for executives and professionals. They also can steer you to further job training opportunities if appropriate.

And you may find of vital help the U.S. computerized "job banks" listing job openings in your field in many nearby states or even throughout the country. Ultimately the job banks' computers will be linked nationally and the network will be able to provide comprehensive information on all major *national* job markets—for professionals, technicians, managers, and others.

• *Do* also send a covering letter and résumé to executive recruiters who work at your salary level. This is admittedly a long shot but certainly worth the price of a postage stamp. (You can get a list of responsible recruiting organizations from the Association of Executive Recruiting Consultants, 30 Rockefeller Plaza, New York, N.Y. 10020.)

WHAT IF YOU LOSE YOUR JOB?

"My husband is an advertising account executive in his early forties, earning $30,000 a year. We have a daughter halfway through college and a son who is a senior in high school and will be entering college next

fall. We have a large house in southern Connecticut and my husband commutes to New York City by his car or train. I am president of the local garden club.

"For the past year or so we have been spending every cent coming into this house and are just barely managing to scrape up $5,000 a year for our daughter's college tuition, fees, and expenses. A couple of months ago we committed my husband's next year-end bonus (usually $1,500 or more) to a skiing vacation in Switzerland in January and made a down payment on a charter flight.

"We had been planning to sell some of our mutual fund shares at a profit to pay our son's freshman-year college costs but the shares are now selling for much *less* than we paid for them and we hate to sell and take the loss.

"Last evening my husband came home and told me that, because of a sharp drop in his agency's profits, this year's bonus is being canceled and all executives are also being asked to accept a 20 per cent pay cut. Moreover, he said it would be only realistic for us to consider his job in serious jeopardy.

"What if hé loses his job? Where do we go for help? *What can we do?*"

Answer: *Don't panic!*

INTERVIEW YOURSELF

Many young executives are—or have been—in exactly this same bind. The bind may be in the form of a layoff, outright firing, a pay cut, a "vacation without pay," a merger, forced "early retirement," or corporate bankruptcy.

But in every case it means you (and here I'm writing to both and either of you) must at least think about finding a new job—sooner or later. In every case, also, it should mean taking a penetrating new look at yourselves—as a husband, as a wife, as partners—and at both of your ways of life.

Sure, it may have been years since you've pounded the pavement to find a job.

Sure, the threat of losing your job comes at a moment when you've become accustomed to spending to the hilt and even overspending, and when you're faced with an ever rising cost of living.

Sure, you may be confronted with a job market which is riddled with irrational prejudices against "older workers" in their fifties and even forties.

But why not turn this emergency to your own advantage?

Whether or not this is precisely the moment to make a job switch, at least ask yourself: is your job one which you find truly rewarding? Or do you feel trapped in it? Has it become overspecialized or too narrow in scope? Are you bored? Frustrated? How did you get into your present career in the first place—and do the reasons still make sense to you?

Think hard about *yourself*. Interview yourself: prepare a synopsis of your own past career, your qualifications, your goals. Decide whether or not you like this man who is you. In short, are you "doing your thing"?

A new, second career in mid-life can be a glorious adventure. In fact, many career counselors now are advising young Americans to expect and welcome the prospect of two or even three entirely different careers during the course of their working lifetimes.

For facts on your unemployment insurance *rights,* see Part IV, "Your Rights and How to Get Them."

"HIDDEN" RESERVE

But quite possibly you, the wife and marriage partner, are the biggest "hidden" financial reserve. If you, this non-working wife, are no more than average, you are entirely capable of earning a pay check from a part-time or full-time job. In fact, the threat of your husband's job loss easily could turn out to be a blessing for you, by forcing you to consider the benefits of going outside your home to work, particularly if your children are on their way out of your nest and the need for you to be at home during the daytime hours will soon disappear.

If you are like many of the women I know, you would like to return to work but you don't know how—and you're afraid.

Okay. Use your husband's crisis as your catalyst and with his blessing (if he's an understanding man, he'll be happy to give it) start moving back into the job world.

WHY?

In any event, and whatever financial resources you fall back on to ease the blow of being fired, you, the husband, should make a real effort to find out why *you* were the one (or among those) to be fired, laid off, sent on an unpaid vacation or whatever. Don't be unduly brutal with yourself, but be as honest as you can be. The answers and reasons could be valuable clues to help steer you into a new career direction or toward a different type of employer.

Were you really able to work smoothly and effectively with co-workers as well as your boss and those working under you?

Was your interest in the job really sincere and enthusiastic?

Were you flexible enough to welcome—and use—new facts and techniques affecting your bailiwick?

Were you willing to learn on the job?

Were you up to the demands of your job? And, on the other hand, was the job big enough for your talents and energies?

MERGER!

Or perhaps you were dismissed from your job because your company merged with another company and a certain number of heads inevitably had to roll.

For you who may face this prospect—and millions of men and women will indeed face it in coming years—here are profoundly important warnings which almost surely will startle you:

The more successful you may be as an executive in your present job the *less* likely you may be to advance in a new company created by a merger.

Higher-placed executives are *not* necessarily the ones who will be in on merger discussions *or* the ones who will necessarily come out on top.

Those top executives who have a basic sense of security and who are good leaders and administrators are *not* necessarily the most likely to exercise good business judgment on behalf of themselves when a merger occurs.

Nine out of ten executives are psychologically unprepared to cope with the aftermath of a merger.

A QUIZ TO PROTECT YOURSELF

How do you use this information to help yourself in a merger? Study this quiz. Use the answers to protect yourself against weakness in a future merger.

(1) Did the new owner buy your company for management talent, including yours?

(2) Are you the key executive in a profit center of vital interest to the new management?

(3) Are you flexible enough to: (a) report to a new group of executives; (b) function in a new organization setup; (c) do things "their" way?

(4) Are your executive skills transferable within the new structure?

(5) Was your company acquired for non-management reasons, special financial advantages, manufacturing facilities, distribution structure—of which you are a part?

(6) Is your salary high in relation to the compensation scale of the purchasing company?

(7) Is your salary high relative to the market place for your job outside the company?

(8) Is your function duplicated in the parent company?

(9) Were you publicly against the merger?

(10) Are you in a staff position?

(11) Are you a "self-made" man with long tenure?

If you answer "yes" to the first five questions and "no" to the remaining six, you are in a strong position in a corporate merger. If your answers are off—on even three or four points—*look out!*

GUIDE FOR EXECUTIVE JOB HUNTERS

What's the difference between an "executive search firm," an "executive job counselor," and an employment agency? Who pays for each type of service—you, the executive seeking a new job, or your new employer?

These are vitally important questions to which you must have the correct answers if you are to avoid some perilous traps in the labor market today. To name just one: the unscrupulous "career counselor" who promises a high-paying job which he cannot deliver, but for which he still charges a fee amounting to thousands of dollars.

Therefore, following is your guide to . . .

WHO DOES WHAT IN EXECUTIVE SEARCH

Management consultants: In some cases, find new executives for client companies. The employer always pays for this service, and the fee is often based on the time needed to conduct the search. You, the job seeker, never pay.

Note to executives: Thus, if you are looking for a new or better job, and if you know of a consulting firm which recruits executives, let this firm know that you are available.

Executive search firms: Also are always paid by the companies for which they find new talent. These firms, known too as executive recruiters, search out, screen, and assess the talents of prospective executive employees and charge fees amounting to one fourth or more of the new executive's first year's pay. (Some charge a flat fee.) Although, normally, executive search firms are interested in knowing about qualified executives looking for jobs, they do *not* normally assist in the job hunt.

Executive career counselors: Work for the *executive,* who pays for services ranging from appraisal interviewing to aptitude and psychological tests. (In some cases, an employer wanting to assist a laid-off executive may pick up the tab.) However, job counseling firms are *not* employment agencies and are not in any position to guarantee you employment.

The fee you pay an executive counselor can range all the way from $50 for a couple of hours of consultation to $1,000 or more. Get this fee spelled out in detail *before* you sign any contract and check all details in advance with your lawyer. Also check carefully the reputation of any job counselor you are considering with your local Better Business Bureau—as a protection against worthless tests, empty mailings to would-be employers, other traps. The "psychological appraisals," for example, may simply be designed to flatter you into buying more services than you want or need.

Employment agencies: Normally are state-licensed, the job placement fees also regulated by the state. The maximum fee for executives may be up to 20 to 30 per cent of your first year's salary, usually payable *after* you get a job. The employer seeking you will often pay the fee, but if he does not you, the executive, must. So get this point clear before you accept a new position.

Here is a summary of who pays—and how much—for key types of executive career and job counseling, prepared by a large New York international management consulting firm:

TYPE OF SERVICE	WHO PAYS?	HOW MUCH
Management consultants	Corporation	Per hour or per diem
Executive search firms	Corporation	25% and up of first year's salary
Executive career counselors	Executive	Per hour, per diem, % or flat fee
Manufacturers' representatives search services	Corporation	Per hour, per diem, flat fee
Personnel psychological testing services	Corporation	Per hour, per diem, flat fee
Do-it-yourself career counselors	Executive	Usually flat amount
Employment agencies	Either may pay if job is accepted; if corporation does not pay, executive does	A % of base salary depending on state law

BEWARE: JOB-FINDING TRAPS

You, the job-hunting executive, answer a "career counselor's" newspaper ad which claims there will be no "initial charge." After a brief interview at the firm's office, in which a smooth salesman name-drops you into confiding in him, the salesman says, "Why don't you go home and bring your wife back for the next interview? After all, this is a family affair."

Your wife accompanies you on the next visit and the salesman now aims a special pitch appealing to her desire (blatant or buried) for her husband to earn more money.

"Mr. A., like your husband," the spiel goes, "was fired just a few weeks ago from a $25,000 job. But we managed to find him a $50,000 job in no time."

You, who have just lost your job, now lose your resistance. You're like the victim of an unscrupulous fast-talking funeral director just after a member of the family has died. You sign a lengthy contract. Job interviews are set up—although there is no realistic chance of employment. Expensive résumés are prepared and mailed out indiscriminately to dozens of companies.

The résumés and interviews may—or may not—result in a job or better salary. The "counseling" may be next to useless. In the words of one victim, "The psychological evaluation was a farce. The counseling amounted to bull sessions."

If you do get a job, you'll probably have to get it on your own and it won't be at anything like the salary level you have been led to believe you'll achieve.

But you are presented with a bill for $2,000 or more—far above the typical $500 to $1,000 which most reputable firms charge for job counseling, testing, and referral services.

To avoid such a trap:

Steer clear of any job counseling firm which leads you to believe it is also an employment agency or makes extravagant claims or promises. Use your cold judgment.

Check out the reputations of any firms with which you are considering a relationship and ask for, then follow through on references from former clients similar to yourself.

Do not sign a contract before you have asked a lawyer to read it and before you are satisfied that the firm is reputable and will actually provide you with services you need at a fair price.

Get those definitions and the facts straight on this whole befuddling subject of job assistance so you know where you're going and what to expect.

Shop with care for job advice. Consult friends or others who have dealt with the agency or firm whose advice you would like to buy. Also ask officers of your former employer for guidance.

Write to The Association of Executive Recruiting Consultants, 30 Rockefeller Plaza, New York, N.Y. 10020, for its membership list and/or send $2.00 to the American Management Association, 135 West Fiftieth Street, New York, N.Y. 10020, for its Executive Employment Guide.

TEN QUESTIONS TO ASK

You will protect yourself if you get satisfactory answers to these ten key questions about any career counseling firm with which you are considering doing business:

(1) Just what obligation are you incurring?

(2) How long has the firm been in business?

(3) How competent is its staff in executive guidance—and what are the qualifications?

(4) What is the firm's record of success or placements and what are the names of satisfied client-executives? Can you check them yourself?

(5) What are the names of satisfied employers with whom it has placed personnel? Can you verify this?

(6) Has the firm's advertising been proper and accurate as to the services offered?

(7) Does the contract cover *all* aspects of the agreement?

(8) Are additional promises in writing and signed by an officer of the firm?

(9) What service period is covered by contract?

(10) What provisions are there, if any, for a refund?

JOB-HUNTING TIPS FOR THE OVER-FORTY-FIVE

You're out of a job. You are in your late forties or older. You are being turned down by employer after employer as "overqualified" or "inexperienced" in whatever the specialty is. You're told over and over again that you "shouldn't have any trouble finding a job," as you're ushered out the door of your interviewer. But in your heart you know the towering obstacle is your age alone.

For your rights if you are hit by job discrimination because of your age, see Part IV, "Your Rights and How to Get Them." But always, no matter what, remember these do's and don'ts for improving your job-getting chances.

Don't apologize for your age or for minor disabilities or insignificant physical limitations.

Don't dwell on your need for a job.

Don't underrate yourself in your résumé or interview. Shoot as high as you think reasonable in your pay and status.

Don't hesitate to remind a prospective employer who may throw the old myths at you—for instance, older workers are slower workers, less flexible, weaker, more prone to absence and illness—that numerous objective studies prove precisely the opposite. Older workers' attendance and motivation records are likely to be better than those of younger workers; older workers are less likely to job-hop; the productivity of older workers compares favorably with that of younger workers; the learning ability of an individual in his or her fifties is approximately the same as that of a sixteen-year-old. Do the reminding in terms of your own work history.

Don't fail to register with your state employment office. Many of these offices have specially trained counselors to help those in your position. And even if your local office does not offer such services, it is still required to give you an equal crack at any job opening listed.

Do check the nearest federal Job Information Center (these centers are located in dozens of U.S. cities) for advice and information on federal job opportunities. Another good public source of help: your state Agency on Aging.

Do inquire about any federal government programs through which you might find appropriate training, leading to a good-paying job.

Do check whether there is any private employment agency in your area specializing in helping middle-aged and older workers find jobs. One such agency, Mature Temps, Inc., is backed by the non-profit American Association of Retired Persons, based in Washington with offices in several other major cities. Check into whether there is a "Forty-Plus Club" in your area and whether it has anything to offer you. Also touch base with such organizations as the Chamber of Commerce, YWCA, and private temporary employment agencies.

Do ask your trade association or professional association for job advice, and look into professional journals in your field for job leads. Ask your former business colleagues for guidance.

Do approach *all* employers who you think might have use for your services and go straight to the top people in these companies or agencies or organizations to present your qualifications.

It's easier said, I know. It's even somewhat unrealistic, I admit. But *do,* above all, keep your confidence!

SHOULD YOU GO INTO BUSINESS FOR YOURSELF?

WHY BUSINESSES FAIL

If you go into business for yourself, even when the United States is in a period of major prosperity, the odds that you'll survive for even two years are only fifty-fifty.

Although there were 8.8 million small businesses in the United States in the middle of this decade—the vast majority of them in the black—each year hundreds of thousands of them closed their doors.

Why?

The answer underlying the failure in an overwhelming nine cases out of ten is: the manager's incompetence, inexperience, ineptitude.

The apparent causes may appear entirely different: a slump in sales because of economic recession, heavy operating expenses, a poor location, a rise in competition, excessive fixed assets, etc. But why did sales slump or why were operating expenses so out of balance or why was the firm in a poor location? Because of the boss's incompetence or inexperience. All the other explanations for business failures can be bunched into that minor 10 per cent—including neglect, fraud, disaster.

Should this discourage you from realizing the American dream of going into business for yourself, of being your own boss? *No!* But surely it shouts a warning to you to take all the proper steps in advance to avoid the obvious pitfalls, to make sure that you have prepared yourself to win. That's merely elementary common sense.

A QUIZ TO SUCCESS

As a guide to success, ask yourself and honestly answer these questions:

Have you worked before in a business like the one you want to start and do you want this venture badly enough to keep working long hours without knowing how much money you'll end up with?

Do you know how much money you will need to get your business started and have you a precise idea of how much money of your own you can put into the business?

Do you know how much credit you can get initially from your suppliers, the people you will buy from—and where you can borrow the rest you need to start?

Have you made an educated estimate of the net yearly income you can expect to get from this enterprise (count your salary and your profit on the money you put into the business) and can you live on less than this amount so you can use some of it to help your business grow?

Do you know the good and bad points about going it alone, having a partner, or incorporating your business?

Have you talked to both a lawyer and a banker about legal and financial aspects of your plans?

Have you tried to find out whether businesses like the one you want to open are doing well in your area and elsewhere?

Do you know what kind of people will want to buy what you plan to sell? Do people like that live in your neighborhood and do they need an outlet like yours?

If you're planning to buy a business someone else has started, are you sure you know the real reason why the owner wants to sell?

Have you talked with other businessmen in the area to see what they think of the type of business you want to start?

Are you timing your move right, thus giving yourself every chance to succeed financially—in terms of demand for the goods and services you want to sell, availability and cost of credit, quantity and quality of competition already lined up against you?

Do you have a real interest in people—both the prospective employees who will be working for and with you and the customers who will buy from you?

Are you a good, sensible planner—financially and otherwise—since your profits will depend largely on your capacity for advance planning, timing the introduction of new products, etc.?

Are you capable of delegating authority and responsibility to those capable of handling it?

Do you know the local zoning and licensing rules covering the type and size of business you want to launch?

Have you answered "yes" to every question? If so, okay, you seem a good risk.

If you have answered even one "no," back up and think again. For this suggests you have a lot more preparing to do.

Whatever your answers to this sampling, write for the Small Business Administration's pamphlet, "Checklist for Going into Business." Available from the Superintendent of Documents, Washington, D.C. 20402, or the SBA, 1030 15th Street N.W., Washington, D.C. 20417. (Free.)

Study the pamphlet with great care.

FUNDAMENTAL RULES

Now, ask your friends and objective observers—a lawyer, banker, casual acquaintance at your office—to judge you too, against the following fundamental rules for success in launching any new business:

Know thoroughly the line you're going into and don't kid yourself about your own know-how.

Be sure you have well-rounded experience—in selling, purchasing, producing, whatever—or that you can get others to fill in your gaps.

Provide yourself with ample cash and access to credit to carry your business through the first, most vulnerable years. Be sure to budget ample sums for start-up advertising and promotion costs, for buying stocks, for extending credit to your customers.

If you are buying an existing business, study the "Business Opportunities" section of your local newspaper. See if alternate possibilities to the plan you already have in mind seem worth checking through. Also, compare the prices asked for businesses in the field which interests you with the price being asked for the business you think you want to purchase.

Ask the appropriate trade association in the field in which you want to work for ideas and leads on companies which may be for sale. One catalogue of these associations, which you may be able to find in your library, is the *Directory of National Trade Associations*.

Go to the nearest branch of the Small Business Administration for further guidance on buying a business. The SBA publishes several vitally important booklets, available free or for little cost.

Do not even attempt to buy *or* launch a business without the help of a competent lawyer, a competent accountant—and the appropriate officer at the bank with which you do business.

IS FRANCHISING FOR YOU?

ANOTHER WAY TO GO INTO BUSINESS

By the mid-1970s, the total of franchises in the United States had soared to between 400,000 and 700,000. In 1974 alone, Americans bought local franchises which sold an enormous $140 to $150 billion of goods and services—more than 10 per cent of our country's total yearly output.

Among the hundreds of different areas in which franchises were available in the mid-seventies:

anti-smoking clinics	computer programing schools
art galleries	laundromats
auto transmission and brake repairs	miniature golf courses
	mobile classrooms
beauty salons	nursing homes
bridal salons	pet grooming establishments
burglar and fire alarms	portable toilets
campgrounds	roadside ice cream stands
computer dating schemes	

Among the most rapidly-growing areas of franchising in this decade have been:

automotive products and services	educational products and services
business aids and services	fast food establishments
construction and remodeling businesses	recreation, travel, and entertainment
convenience grocery stores	rental and leasing services
	tax preparation services

Among the most eager and most vulnerable investors in franchises are: financially strapped family breadwinners needing to supplement their regular income; unemployed men in their forties and fifties who are suffering from job discrimination; elderly individuals and couples seeking to boost their meager retirement incomes; college students needing a means to help pay today's high college costs.

Is franchising a business for *you*—the man or woman whose experience has been limited until now to working for others?

The answer is a resounding *"No!"*

unless you realize it's easier to lose money than to make it in a franchise operation;

unless you choose a reputable, solid operation;

unless you have enough capital to cover your initial investment and carry you through at least the first six months;

unless you first do a lot of "homework" about yourself as well as the business;

and *unless* you are on the alert for the fraudulent operators who have in the past infested franchising.

QUESTION AND ANSWER GUIDE FOR POTENTIAL INVESTORS

Q. *Exactly what is a franchise?*

A. A franchise is a contractual right and a license to sell a product or service produced by a parent (usually national) company, and advertised and promoted by that company. For this right you usually pay a fee.

Q. *What type of operation should an amateur choose?*

A. Only one in which you have some experience. If you are a bookkeeper, for instance, don't go into an auto transmission overhaul operation which demands a mechanical skill you probably don't possess. Instead, choose a direct mail business or a personnel service. Also, as an unsophisticated franchisee, choose an area with a proven record of success and avoid areas which play on fads. As one illustration: several years ago, trampoline franchises were hot businesses. But the fad died quickly and most of the franchises flopped.

A key point never to forget: a franchise will *not* magically endow you with abilities you do not already have or are not willing to learn. There's just no way for a retired letter carrier to become an entrepreneur in two weeks. And a degree in physics is *not* necessarily a passport to a successful art gallery or nursing home.

Q. *How failure-prone are franchises—as compared to your own small business?*

A. Statistically speaking, franchising is a lot safer than starting your own independent business—on average, many times safer, in fact, according to the U. S. Department of Commerce.

Q. *What sort of investigation should you make?*

A. As thorough as you can. Check basic sources of information on available franchises—e.g., the *Wall Street Journal* and New York *Times,* journals in your field of interest (you will find the names listed in a directory available in most libraries, entitled Standard Rate and Data).

Get the 1974 *Directory of Franchising Opportunities* (Pilot Books, 347 Fifth Avenue, New York, N.Y. 10016, $2.50).

Collect advice on both the parent company and the type of business from friends, bankers, brokers, trade associations, the Small Business Administration, lawyers, accountants, the local Better Business Bureau.

Get a detailed, certified profit and loss statement from the franchiser on one or more existing firms—and check the figures yourself with the owners of those firms.

Have your bank check the franchiser's bank and its Dun & Bradstreet rating.

Dig out—from other franchisees—full details on weekly sales, selling costs, rent and utility bills, advertising and promotion costs, labor and tax bills, insurance, as well as profits.

Ask each about traffic, hours, seasonal business, personal involvement, and also about one experience each has had in dealing with the franchiser.

Beware of any franchise firm that is unwilling to supply you with the names and addresses of other franchisees.

Take a month to make your decision, and under *no* circumstances sign up under pressure from a franchise salesman.

Have your lawyer go over details of the franchise agreement before you sign anything.

If you decide to engage (and pay for) the services of a franchise consultant, check thoroughly into his or her reputation and make *sure* the consultant is not working with the enfranchiser to whom he may refer you.

Q. *What about the franchise fee?*

A. Virtually all franchising operations require an initial fee, or "front money." The average requirement in the mid-seventies was between $500 and $25,000 (although some ran up into six- or even seven-figure levels).

You *must* have a sufficient pool of liquid capital not only to buy the franchise but also to keep you going for several months. Don't expect to be in the black from the beginning. No new business, franchise or non-franchise, ever is.

Q. *What about the profit potentials?*

A. A franchise operation should eventually give you a net profit of at least $15,000 a year—just to make the investment worth while. But don't expect a big annual income from a small franchise investment. The franchisers have a good idea of what their kind of operation will gross and net and they scale their franchise fee accordingly.

Q. *What will a legitimate franchiser do for you that you couldn't do for yourself?*

A. Give you a name built up by national advertising; proven selling, advertising, and public relations techniques; experts who will help you get started; a line of credit which you may tap or advice on how to establish your own credit; trouble shooters through the year to help you too; guidance on where you should (and should not) locate; equipment at a fair price because the franchiser bought the equipment in volume at discount prices; training you might need to make a success from your franchise; an employee training program.

If a franchiser you're considering doesn't offer you most of these fundamentals in return for the fee, *beware!*

FRANCHISING CHECK LISTS

Here are check lists, developed by the Council of Better Business Bureaus, designed to lead you, the prudent investor, into collecting sufficient background information on which to base an informed decision and commitment.

The Company

1. How long has the firm been in business?
2. Does it have a past record of accomplishment?
3. Are its principals well regarded? Experienced?
4. What is its financial strength?
5. What are its plans for future development?
6. How does it stand with your Better Business Bureau or Chamber of Commerce?
7. How selective is it in choosing franchisees?

The Product or Source

8. What is the product's quality?
9. Is it a staple, a fad, a luxury item?
10. Is it seasonal?
11. How well is it selling now, and has it sold in the past?
12. Would the franchisee buy it on its merits?
13. Is it priced competitively?
14. Is it packaged attractively?
15. How long has it been on the market?
16. Where is it sold?

The Sales Area

17. Is the territory well defined?
18. Is it exclusive?
19. Is it large enough to offer good sales potential?
20. What are its growth possibilities?
21. What is its income level?
22. Are there fluctuations in income?
23. What is the competition in this area?
24. How are nearby franchisees doing?

The Contract

25. Does the contract cover all aspects of the agreement?
26. Does it benefit both parties?
27. Can it be renewed, terminated, transferred?
28. What are the conditions for obtaining a franchise?
29. Under what conditions can the franchise be lost?
30. Is a certain size and type of operation specified?

31. Is there an additional fixed payment each year?
32. Is there a per cent of gross sales payment?
33. Must a certain amount of merchandise be purchased? From whom?
34. Is there an annual sales quota?
35. Can the franchisee return merchandise for credit?
36. Can the franchisee engage in other business activities?
37. Is there a franchise fee? Is it equitable?
38. Has your lawyer examined it?

Continuing Assistance

39. Does the franchiser provide continuing assistance?
40. Is there training for franchisees and key employees?
41. Are manuals, sales kits, accounting system supplied?
42. Does the franchiser select store locations? Is there a fee?
43. Does he handle lease arrangements?
44. Does he design store layout and displays?
45. Does he select opening inventory?
46. Does he provide inventory control methods?
47. Does he provide market surveys?
48. Does he help analyze financial statements?
49. Does he provide purchasing guides?

SOURCES FOR ADVICE ON JUDGING A FRANCHISE

Here are the names and addresses of the organizations most likely to be able to give you practical advice or assistance in judging a franchise today:

International Franchise Association
7315 Wisconsin Avenue
Bethesda, Md. 20014

Council of Better Business Bureaus, Inc.
1150 17th Street, N.W.
Washington, D.C. 20036

Small Business Administration
1030 15th Street, N.W.
Washington, D.C. 20417—or any of the SBA's field offices

Small Business Guidance and Development Center
Howard University
1420 N Street, N.W., Suite 5A
Washington, D.C. 20005

Office of Minority Business Enterprise
U. S. Department of Commerce
Washington, D.C. 20230—or any of the Commerce
Department's field offices

CRIME INSURANCE FOR SMALL BUSINESSMEN

A PROGRAM TO INVESTIGATE

If you are a small businessman in a high-crime-risk area in city or suburb, you are probably eager for crime insurance at "affordable rates."

But you may not even be aware that low-cost federal crime insurance up to a stated maximum exists. The insurance came into being in mid-1971 under a program of the Department of Housing and Urban Development. The objective of the program is to make crime insurance available at tolerable rates in states where it has been especially hard to come by. Since 1971 the law has been liberalized twice to make it much easier and also cheaper for you to obtain the federal crime insurance coverage. This is a program which you should investigate at once.

To give you key details:

• If you are the owner of a small business (liquor store, jewelry store, grocery store, restaurant, clothing store, beauty shop, etc.) you can buy either burglary coverage or robbery coverage. Burglary coverage pays off on visible signs of entry, while robbery insurance pays for holdups or observed theft.

• There are specific provisions requiring you to use protective devices—ranging from window grates to central and local alarm systems.

• There are favorable provisions on deductibles. The deductible depends on your annual gross receipts.

• If you are interested and eligible, go to any licensed insurance agent or broker, ask for an application, and complete it. Your application will then be forwarded to an insurance company acting under contract with the Federal Insurance Administration. The policies are not available directly from any federal agency but are sold through licensed agents and brokers and through a servicing company designated by the FIA for each participating state. Your policy will go into effect after the servicing company has inspected your premises and approved the protective devices.

Rates vary depending on your geographic location, crime statistics compiled by the FBI, and the amount of your gross receipts.

BEWARE: "BUSINESS OPPORTUNITIES" SWINDLES

RACK ROUTES

"PART-TIME/FULL-TIME . . . P/T 5–6 hours weekly nets to $700 monthly . . . F/T 50 hours weekly nets to $7,000 monthly. . . .

"$2,800 part-time investment secured by inventory fully refundable has unlimited growth opportunity with potential earnings to $100,000 per year. This national public company has outstanding success record since 1954 and is seeking reliable individuals to service company secured routes. An opportunity to own your own business and become part of a multi-million dollar market. This is no get rich quick scheme or a pyramid but a solid year-round business. . . .

"NO SELLING, NO OVERHEAD, IMMEDIATE INCOME . . . No experience necessary; we train . . . Simply check stores weekly and restock what has been sold . . . LIMITED OPENINGS AVAILABLE. MAKE THE AMERICAN DREAM A REALITY. OWN YOUR OWN BUSINESS TODAY . . . Write or call. . . ."

An ad of this sort—the above is a composite for a "rack route"—shouts "Fraud!" It has, though, deep appeal to men and women searching for ways to solve their income problems by going into business for themselves. Business opportunities rackets are, in fact, heading into the top ranks of all lists of swindles in the latter half of this decade.

Thus, beware these earmarks of a "rack route" gyp:

• Inconsistencies. The ad says that one can realize an immediate income and advertises that, while no experience is required, earnings can go up to $100,000. How can this be if "no selling is required" and the investor isn't paid a wage or a salary?

A "business" is a going concern, an active enterprise, but what's really involved in this case is a static inventory of goods for resale—and you're the only one to do the selling.

• Appeal to flattery. This usually comes in the initial letter you get from the company in which there are flattering references to "your talent and your experience in your job" plus your capacity to "bring profit to your company way above your own present pay." Few people who have just lost their jobs will stop to consider how presumptuous are these statements by an unknown correspondent who doesn't know them personally.

• Pressure to act quickly. This is evident in the phrases "limited openings available" and "own your own business today."

• Claims of ease of operation of business. All you need do is "check stores weekly and restock." That's ridiculous.

• Exaggeration. The ad is saturated with impressions of instant wealth, and the promotional literature when it arrives also suggests almost automatic acquisition of this wealth. "A few hours each week and you are on your way to a whole chain. . . ."

What's wrong with this operation?

The earnings are simply not there—and it's not because you're not working hard enough. They're just not there.

The product is frequently inferior. For instance, if you're selling cosmetics, you may have been stuck with last year's colors or antiquated packages. While the claim is that no selling is involved, the product doesn't sell itself and your income is dependent on the sale of the product.

The service you get from the promoting company is inferior: late delivery or no delivery, no maintenance when you need it.

The misrepresentations begin to manifest themselves. The implication that the promoter is connected with, or endorsed by, a nationally known company just isn't true.

To avoid being taken in by this racket:

• Ignore the flattery. Be honest about your own qualifications. Do you really know anything about merchandising? Are you really a good enough salesman to develop and maintain successful relationships with twenty or more retail merchants in widely separated, distinct businesses?

• Verify the claims made to you with at least two independent sources. Call the local Better Business Bureau. Frequently the BBB will have a report on the company.

• Talk to the man behind the operation, not the front man or a salesman. There are hundreds of salesmen for these schemes and they move from one scheme to the next, not caring what they sell or what they say. Give the BBB not only the company's name but the promoter's name. Promotions come and go but the promoters remain the same.

TRAVEL

"Do you want to get into travel? Make money? You can. Right now! . . . No experience necessary. Immediate sales force.

"We are offering an exclusive area and some incomparable advantages including a marketing force of at least 25 travel ambassadors, professionally trained to sell big ticket travel programs in their neighborhoods and bring business to you!

"Our company is organized and operated by experts in every phase of the travel business. We assist you in the operation of your business. In addition you get a bonus—a going advertising and promotional campaign!

"PLUS! Since you must enjoy travel to be in this business, as a franchise owner with us you see the world—premiere classe! . . . If you are interested in PROFITS AND FUN, call . . ."

This too is a composite ad which illustrates a "business opportunities" fraud in the giant travel field.

Here are the earmarks of fraud in this ad:

• Lack of clarity. An "exclusive" area is promised, but how an area could be protected from other travel agencies is not explained. The American Society of Travel Agents, in warning against phony travel agencies that offer "round trips to nowhere," has condemned this very feature as reprehensible.

• Exaggeration. You get a bonus—"a going advertising and promotional campaign." If there really is such a campaign, it's designed to lure new suckers like you, not customers for you. "Operated by experts." Anybody can call himself an expert. "See the world premiere classe." Hardly. "Travel benefits do not flow automatically to travel agents," warns ASTA. As for those twenty-five professionals hunting out prospects for you alone, the promise strains all credulity.

• Inconsistency. The travel business is a highly complex business, as any thoughtful person must realize. It requires years of experience for success. That "no experience is necessary" simply cannot be reconciled with realities in this area.

The pitch is all too simple. You pay the promoters from a few hundred dollars to $20,000 and they'll put you in the travel business. But no matter what you're led to believe, you cannot become a successful travel agent overnight—and this highly competitive business arena is no place for the rank amateur.

As for the training programs, they are often no more than short lectures—as valuable in real life as those "exclusive" territories which may be described but not delivered.

How do you avoid being lured into this racket?

• Before responding to an ad such as this, learn something on your own about the travel business. There are plenty of courses available to you. Also talk to travel agents running their own agencies or employed by airlines and steamship companies to get the facts and a believable appraisal of opportunities.

• Ask the American Society of Travel Agents (360 Lexington Avenue, New York, N.Y. 10017) for literature describing the nature of the industry and for any other literature it says would be of help to you.

• Call the local Better Business Bureau for a report on the company behind this promotion. Give the name of the promoters, too.

• Ask the company itself for substantiation of its claims. For instance, will it show you the advertising campaign that is supposed to be available to you? Say that you want to study it before making a decision. Surely, if the program is so successful, the ads must have appeared in print or been seen on TV or heard on the radio by the time you show up.

• Be honest with yourself in evaluating your own qualifications. If in fact the full "25 travel ambassadors" would become available to you as your sales force, would you have the expert knowledge to use them properly and keep them busy? Have you the qualities essential to run a business of your own?

• Do not underestimate the part that any current unfortunate circumstances—loss of a job, difficulty in getting employment at a level you want, sinking profits in your present business—may be playing in your eagerness to become a "franchise owner" in this glamorous "see the world" industry. Be extra conservative.

PYRAMID SELLING

"Help Wanted Male/Female . . . College Graduate 15 M to 25 M Caliber . . . Executives/Managers On the Way Up . . .

"Our company has openings in mgt. positions recently created through our northeast expansion. Must be self-starter and have leadership capabilities. No exp. necessary. We will train . . .

"For interview, call . . ."

This apparent route to a successful venture of your own sounds so attractive, seems a way to avoid ever again being dependent on someone else's fortunes for a pay check.

But don't fall for it! It's a composite ad that highlights still another "business opportunities" fraud. Here are the major earmarks of this one:

• Inconsistencies. What "college graduate" with "no experience" will be handed a $20,000 pay check? What "management position" requires "no experience"? Any man or woman intelligent enough to have completed college will be unable to reconcile the claims. And any thoughtful person will wonder why any successful company has to advertise this way for executives and managers.

• Incongruities. Legitimate $20,000 management positions usually aren't advertised in the general help-wanted male/female columns but in the business sections of newspapers and specialized business publications.

• Appeal to flattery and to status. That's implicit in the "college graduate" lure and in the "must be self-starter and have leadership capabilities" requirements. Don't we all think we are self-starters and potential leaders?

What are the pitfalls?

The ad is simply bait for a pyramid scheme, among the most vicious and pervasive of all "business opportunities" swindles flourishing in the United States today.

The prospective investor is pressured to invest on the spot. The "opportunity" meeting the investor attends is so emotionally charged that if he hasn't left his checkbook at home he may sign away his savings right there.

The investor can never make the money predicted by the advertiser, because in fact there are never enough people in a community to sustain the pyramid, or the chain-selling method, indefinitely. One would-be investor characterized this ad as "an invitation to cheat my friends" (see Chapter 13, "A Roof Over Your Head," for mathematical proof of the giant pitfall of this scheme—which is the required number of "qualified" prospects).

Millions of dollars have been lost on these pyramid or chain schemes in this decade, and government regulations against certain pyramid operators have been tightened. But the pyramid selling racket continues to flourish and the promoters continue to lure victims through ads that slip into every medium. So, to protect yourself:

• Get the details on this type of ad over the phone, and if the details are sketchy, just forget it. If this were a valid help wanted offer, the person answering the phone would want to discourage unqualified applicants, not intrigue you. Don't even bother going to the personal "interview."

• If you do go to a personal interview, leave your checkbook—and your enthusiasm—at home. Don't sign anything, no matter how pressured you are.

• Be suspicious at once of any help-wanted ad which does not pay a wage or salary, which does not disclose selling is involved, and which does require an investment. This is all wrong! The advertiser is deceiving the medium as well as you.

VENDING MACHINES

"$500 PART-TIME $5,000 FULL-TIME per month . . . Fast growing international company. No selling. Huge profits . . .

"Opportunity for persons looking for good income in field of coin-operated vending machines. Secured investment of $3,000 required. We secure locations.

"Financing available to those who qualify. Call . . ."

Beware! The telltale signs that this is a racket are in the ad:

• Lack of clarity. Again, is this $500 to $5,000 a month a wage, salary, profits, what? Where is that money to come from? The company calls itself "international." What does international mean? In the case of one company, it became international because one investor sent his machine to Madrid.

• Flattery, hint of exclusivity. "Financing available to those who qualify," says the ad. How many, if any, are actually rejected when they apply?

• Inconsistency. The mutually exclusive "no selling required" and "huge profits."

• Exaggeration. The ad mentions a "secured investment." What's the security in an inventory of broken vending machines?

The earmarks of this fraud also show up during the interview—which actually is the focal point of the deception.

• Verbal promises that don't appear in the contract. For instance, the salesman promises help with establishing routes for the vending machines. He also may promise that the company will buy back the machines if the investor changes his or her mind or that the territory is exclusive. None of these conditions and promises appears in the contract, however. Here's the way a complainant described her meeting with a salesman:

"Even before I mailed the card back authorizing a visit from a salesman, one called . . . He did not seem pleased when I told him that my husband and father would be present; he wanted to know if I had authority to close the deal. He arrived an hour early. . . . He evaded our questions, I had to ask some questions two or three times. My husband asked to see the machines in operation at some locations but he wouldn't give specific addresses. When we told him we wanted to check out his company with the Better Business Bureau he became very quiet and nervously put his papers together."

The major pitfalls in this operation are:

The machines are of such poor quality they frequently break down as soon as they are put into use. One disenchanted investor wrote: "I bought two machines at $550 each. They were supposed to vend a toy and play a tune at the same time. I had mechanical problems every other day—the toy would not come out and the music kept on playing. In six months I had to move my machines around to six different locations. I've had virtually no return."

The quality of goods to be dispensed is often very poor. Unknown or inferior brands have frequently been supplied by the promoter, sometimes at exorbitant prices.

You can't get the company to answer your service calls and no local servicing is available.

• To protect yourself, be alert to such claims in the sales pitch as "laboratory tested," "location tested," "non-competitive." What laboratory, what locations, what results? If you're told the machine is "patented," check that out. A patent number touted by one company in its literature turned out to be fictitious; the company supplied another which the Patent Office said had expired. There was nothing at all exclusive about the machine.

• If the company mentions a nationally known manufacturer in its sales pitch, check whether the manufacturer does in fact endorse the company. Probably not. Don't be impressed by such words in names of the companies as "U.S." or "International" or "American" or "Nationwide," "General," the like.

• Ignore the flattery.

• Talk to the people behind the operation.

DISTRIBUTORSHIPS

"Make big profits! Become an authorized distributor. Sell Special Formula gasoline additive—the hottest selling item in the automotive direct selling field. Manufacturer endorsed.

"Guaranteed free luxury motor car if appointed state franchise director . . . Free samples available. Send $10.35 . . .

"Good only for orders received in next 10 days. Bigger discounts if order rushed."

Then appears a table showing that your cost for six units is $24.50, on which you make a profit of $7.00. But if you buy three dozen units at a cost of $92.50, you make a profit of $90.

The telltale signs of fraud, as exemplified by this ad, are:

• "Creative" accounting. That table is very clever, for who's going to buy $24.50 of goods to make a $7.00 profit when he can make approximately 100 per cent if he goes up to $92.50?

• Exaggerations. A "free luxury motor car" if one sells enough cans of gasoline additive? Even a cockeyed optimist should have trouble believing that one. "Manufacturer endorsed"? Who? "The hottest selling item in the field of automotive direct selling"? Hardly. . . .

• Pressure. The implication is that you must act at once or you're barred. The offer will last for only ten days. The pressure is intensified in follow-up letters to the sucker.

• Duplicity. There are "free samples" offered to the skeptical—but the "free" samples cost $10.35.

• Ease of operation. This is not in the composite ad, but it is in the letter the potential investor receives, assuring him that "you don't have to be a salesman in order to rake in those profits. Those unique formulas, together with the endorsement from the luxury motor car, practically sell themselves."

How do you avoid being taken by this business opportunities swindle—as in the others preceding?

• Verify the claims for the product. Check out the endorsements from manufacturers referred to in the literature. Ask the company representative for the name of a person at the manufacturer's office to whom you can talk and with whom you can discuss your doubts. Do not permit yourself to be turned away.

• Ask the promoter for names and addresses of other distributors. Contact them to find out how much money they have made selling these products under current market conditions.

• Find out how many of these distributors have been in operation for more than a year. A year should be long enough to determine whether or not the business can be a success.

• Discuss the investment and operation of the business with your own family, your lawyer, your local banker.

• Never forget that a written guarantee is only as good as the company behind it. If the company offering "full refund" isn't in business, the offer is worthless.

From these five illustrations, you can carry away the guides to protect you from all other variations of business opportunities rackets.

WHAT ABOUT WORKING AT HOME?

A POWERFUL TREND

Still another way to "be your own boss" is to work at home—even if you're working for some relatively distant employer. And there is now a powerful and grossly underestimated trend in this country toward doing just that.

You well may be among the millions who *could* do so if you really wanted to. The switch could be a real boon if, say, you are a young mother who can't leave the house but still have plenty of spare time; if you are a businessman who could easily switch your office to your home and who detests the daily commute to the big city; if you are a shut-in for any reason; if in your work you spend virtually the whole day on the telephone and could easily use the phone just as well at home as at the office.

Today, millions of Americans work at home, part or full time, and the list of jobs which you can perform without going to an office is lengthening daily. Some work from elaborate home offices, fitted with typewriters, electric calculators, dictating machines, filing cabinets, and other office equipment. Others manage to earn a living from a bedroom card table.

Of course, some people simply can't work at home. Your job, for instance, may involve the use of expensive specialized equipment available only in an office. You may need to confer frequently—and face to face—with others in your office. Or you might be subject to destructive distractions at home from children, social telephoning, visiting neighbors. Or you might not have the essential discipline to set up and stick to a productive work schedule. Or you may be unproductive without the stimulus of a busy office.

But for many of you the advantages far outweigh the disadvantages. Anybody who works at home can save substantial sums of money by not having to pay commuting costs, eat lunches out, keep up an office wardrobe, lose hours of work time battling traffic.

If you are a working mother, a job at home may save substantial sums on baby-sitting fees—which when combined with other typical expenses of working mothers often chew up 40¢ to 50¢ or more of your pay dollar. For pregnant women, there are obvious reasons for working at home.

A further advantage lies in the substantial income tax deductions that can be claimed for the bona fide costs associated with the portion of your house you use as an office, the cost of business equipment, business telephone calls, etc.

SAMPLING OF "AT HOME" CAREERS

Following are some of the jobs which are being performed, at least in part, at home. Study them carefully to see if this could spark a desired new trend in your own life.

In journalism-publishing: foreign language translation, proofreading, copy editing, technical writing, art work, copy writing—and, of course, the usual writing of books, magazine articles, feature stories.

In education: many assistant teaching jobs such as correcting test papers, tutoring in remedial reading and other key subjects, music and art instruction, child day care, vocational counseling, speech therapy.

In scientific and technical fields: inventing, engineering and scientific consulting, computer programing, a wide assortment of individual projects in chemistry, mathematics, and other disciplines, appliance repair.

In health and medicine: physical and occupational therapy, the practice of medicine, dentistry, psychiatry.

In radio and TV: disc jockeying, film editing, film making, script writing.

In advertising: Literally thousands of small ad agencies are operating out of private homes in this country today.

Also: architecture, art, law, insurance and real estate, interior decorating, investment management, sewing, cake baking, public relations, many kinds of research, accounting and drafting. And this is only a random selection. There are dozens of others.

If the idea of working at home appeals to you, analyze your interests and/or your present job. *You* can tell as well as anyone what the potentials are.

Before you decide to go ahead, check the local zoning rules and also any restrictions which may be included in your own deed (or rental lease) against at-home business operations. These limitations could be a temporary obstacle—but that's all they can be *if* "working at home" is what you really want.

BEWARE: "EARN MONEY AT HOME" SWINDLES!

But precisely because so huge a number of you secretly wish you could work at home, the crooks and gypsters can make fortunes exploiting your yearnings.

As an illustration, let's say you are a young mother who is staying at home to care for your infants. Let's say, too, that you're finding it increasingly tough to get by on your young husband's pay check, quarrels about money are starting to undermine your marriage, and thus you're desperately seeking ways to supplement your family's income.

You are now a perfect setup for the "work at home" swindlers.

Here is a sampling of the most common forms making the rounds—along with the catch in each case and rules for spotting outright gyps.

Scheme: Address postcards at home. Promoter furnishes everything. Earn $50 a week.

Catch: Promoter is selling "instructions"—not offering employment—despite the fact that he lures you through the help-wanted columns. If you're a "double victim," you'll pay for postcards as well as instructions. You make money only if the cards you send actually bring in orders. In a typical case, a home worker spent a total of $25 for instruction, 250 postcards, and for postage. Total revenue from two orders: $2.50. Loss: $22.50.

Scheme: Assemble at home anything from bow ties to garters, fish lures to artificial flowers. And reap enormous piecework profits.

Catch: Promoter offers no employment. Again, he's selling instructions and in all probability overpriced equipment and precut materials. He has no intention of buying the goods you make unless they're "up to standards" and, of course, they never are. Often, victims spend hundreds of dollars on heavy equipment at grossly inflated prices in the belief that the promoter will furnish enough work to cover the equipment costs. Such work never materializes and you're left with a heartache and a debt payable to a finance company.

Scheme: Clip newspapers at home. Earn $75 a week selling local press mentions to individuals and companies at $1.00 to $5.00 a piece.

Catch: "Instructions" cost up to $15 (often shoddy, badly mimeographed, unprofessional), and you must subscribe to the newpapers yourself. You also must find your own markets for your clips.

Scheme: Raise animals—bullfrogs, chinchillas, foxes, minks, muskrats, etc.—at home and sell them for fabulous profits. Typical ad says: "There is Big Money in raising bullfrogs. Start in your back yard. We furnish breeders and instructions and buy what you raise."

Catch: Breeders are excessively priced, potential profits are grossly exaggerated, and animals bought back must be "in a healthy and marketable condition." Of course, they never are so judged by a gypster, and frequently the fine print you never read stipulates the animals must be skinned and butchered before they will be bought.

Scheme: Test consumer products in your own home, in your spare time. We pay up to $10 for each opinion you give us on the products we send you.

Catch: To get on this gravy train, you must send in a $10 "registration fee." Legitimate market researchers do not operate in this manner and do not ask you for any "registration fees" in exchange for your supposedly unbiased opinion of their products or services. You're lucky if you get so much as a couple of dollars for whatever opinions you send in—much less a refund of your registration fee.

Scheme: Go into the mail order business at home. Earn huge sums by mailing out, for example, catalogues.

Catch: The cost of such a "distributorship": $10 a year. The point to remember about this gimmick is that any firm wishing to employ your services to help mail out catalogues will not charge you a fee for this privilege.

Scheme: Be a "Personal Shopper." Buy clothes and other products from a list of parent firms, then sell the products to consumers in your exclusive marketing area. Guaranteed: short-term financing, instructions on selling, collection of past due accounts, credit for unsold merchandise, *and* substantial earnings.

Catch: Earnings are *not* substantial. Help for the supplies is minimal. In many cases collection is not possible on delinquent accounts.

OBVIOUS EARMARKS OF A FRAUDULENT SCHEME

There are many, many more—all the frauds feeding on your need and on the fact that there are legitimate deals for making money at home.

Here are the most obvious earmarks of the fraudulent scheme:

• Ads slanted to imply the offer of home employment when in fact the advertiser is selling something, not hiring.

• A promise of huge profits or big part-time earnings.

• A profusion of vague "testimonials" to the deal.

• A requirement that you buy expensive instructions and equipment—even before the promoter gives you details of the deal.

KEY QUESTIONS ABOUT ADS

Here are the key questions to ask about any ad you see in your local newspaper or which comes to you through the mails regarding home work deals.

• Will you be paid by the firm and, if so, how much? If you will not be paid by the firm, where will the promised earnings come from?

• Are you expected to pay any significant sum to buy "instructions"

—before you can get into business? (If so, consider this a warning signal to stay away from the deal.)

• Who will be your customers and who will be responsible for lining them up—the company or you?

• Is the product or service in which you are supposed to invest—either time or money or both—one for which you will manage to find a market close to your home?

• If commissions are promised as payments for your efforts, what assurance do you have that such commissions actually will be paid? A vague promise which comes through the mail from a company unknown to you is hardly adequate insurance.

• Is the company willing to give you names and phone numbers of other people who have invested in its instructions or products so that you can query them about their experience in the real market place? How much money did *these* people make on the deal? (Disregard any and all "testimonials" quoted in ads if you cannot check them out personally.)

Finally, and especially if "fantastic profits" for "easy work" are offered, in combination with a requirement that *you* invest substantial sums of money for instructions, materials etc., find out whether the firm is trying to buy your services, or—much more likely—sell you a bill of goods. Get in touch with your nearest Better Business Bureau, Federal Trade Commission office, or consumer protection agency. Do not take one further step toward the deal without informed assurance it is legitimate.

P.S. A good source of legitimate and often original ideas for working at home is the monthly "Home Office Report" published by Leon Henry, Jr. A full list of occupations covered by this publication is available free upon request. Address: 17 Scarsdale Farm Road, Scarsdale, N.Y. 10583.

NEEDED: VOLUNTEERS

THE GREAT NON-PAID PRODUCER

Across the land are close to 2 million of you who are working as American Red Cross trained volunteers in community activities—in the blood and youth programs, in safety, nursing, and health programs, in hospitals, clinics, disaster relief, in helping members of the armed forces and their families, and in raising funds to support all of these services.

On average, you are putting in 150 hours a year at your volunteer jobs. But that's just average: many of you are putting in 150 hours a month. Many of you certainly are contributing twice, three, four times 150 hours a year.

All of you give your time, training, devotion, and dedication for *zero* pay in dollars. All of you fall into one of the enormous categories of non-paid producers in the U.S. economy. On top of this, hundreds of thousands of you also contribute cash and property.

If you were paid merely $2.00 an hour, your contribution of only 150 hours a year would amount to an annual output well over $500 million, an impressive sum by any yardstick.

If you were paid what your skills—as a nurse, a first aid or swimming instructor, a teacher—could easily bring in the job market place, your contribution of only 150 hours a year would easily mount to $1 billion or more. And if there were a more accurate estimate of the number of hours you actually work, the total would go zooming again—would add billions of dollars to our annual output of goods and services, give a far more realistic picture of what is our true Gross National Product.

Of course the contribution of the volunteer goes far beyond this. There are now more than 43 million volunteers working for 22 national and local agencies in the U.S. Put a dollar total on that production, I defy you!

But because I have been so close to the Red Cross in past years I have had a unique chance to see how its volunteers work. And I haven't included in the volunteer total the millions who donate blood each year or the millions of students who participate in the Red Cross programs in schools.

The economic story of the volunteer in America never has been told—and perhaps it never can be. But just because we cannot put a precise dollar tag on the volunteer's contribution must not lead us into downgrading the magnificent size of that contribution.

WHERE THE VOLUNTEER JOBS ARE

"Long hours, hard work, low pay . . ."
"Dirt and rats, crowded rooms . . . headaches, frustration."

"$50 a month."

This was one of the come-ons blared across the nation a few years back to launch Volunteers in Service to America—VISTA, the "domestic Peace Corps." Tens of thousands responded from every age group, background, political stripe, and tax bracket—and tackled some of the hardest, dirtiest, most thankless jobs imaginable.

Most federal voluntary programs have since been merged into an agency called Action, including:

the Peace Corps, which puts volunteer nurses, mechanics, organic farmers, teachers, and many others to work in dozens of countries on every continent; VISTA; the Teacher Corps, part of the U. S. Office of Education—HEW; Foster Grandparents; and the Service Corps of Retired Executives (SCORE) who help small businesses.

And outside Action:

• Boy Scouts, Girl Scouts, Boys Clubs, Campfire Girls, 4-H Clubs, YMCA, YWCA, YMHA and YWHA groups, American Youth Hostels and many other organized youth groups have needed volunteers for years and still do.

• In schools and child care programs, thousands of volunteers of all ages are acting as teaching assistants, helping individual children in music and art programs, tutoring dropouts, taking youngsters on field and camping trips. In poverty areas, more thousands are serving and recruiting in a wide variety of programs, helping in Neighborhood Health Centers and drug addiction centers, working with alcoholics in rehabilitation programs.

• Church-related groups, such as American Friends Service Committee, co-ordinate thousands of volunteers to help other people.

• In Neighborhood Legal Centers across the land, young lawyers and law students are helping to provide free legal advice and services to the poor.

• In consumer agencies, "action lines," and similar organizations, thousands of young volunteers and semivolunteers are answering phones, handling consumer complaints, tracking down the sources of various problems.

• Also across the land, environment-minded citizens—young and old—are investigating complaints on forms of pollution, organizing "pollution tours" for local citizens to view the area's offenders, launching recycling programs, and in a heartening percentage of cases earning money in the recycling process.

• But nowhere can volunteers find a more fascinating array of jobs and responsibility than in hospitals, outpatient clinics, emergency rooms, drug addiction programs, physical therapy programs.

Blood bank aides are needed to call on patients who have received blood to ask them to sign forms for their friends or families to replace the blood they have used and to arrange donations. Translators are needed to interpret for non-English-speaking hospital or outpatient clinic patients. Maternity-room aides are needed to accompany maternity patients to labor and delivery rooms to give aid and comfort.

Other hospital volunteer areas range from assistants in children's wards to recreational therapy helpers. In city hospitals alone, it's estimated that 300,000 additional volunteers are needed right now. Gone forever are the days when volunteers worked only in the gift shop or hospital library. Desperately in demand are volunteers in just about every phase and at every level of health care.

Similarly, there is a relentless demand for volunteers to track down and look after the desperate needs of many elderly Americans: to see that these citizens are fed, make sure they're getting Social Security and welfare benefits to which they're entitled, to run errands, arrange to have plumbing problems solved, just to take them out for a Sunday drive.

As for the kids, here are just a couple of hints on the opportunities which have sprung up for helping youngsters:

In Philadelphia, HELP was launched by the young, for the young, to answer calls around the clock, deal with problems ranging from homelessness to drugs, pregnancy, and suicide.

In San Rafael, California, the YMCA launched a Dropout Prevention Program in which college students work with second- through fifth-graders who show early indications that they might later drop out of school.

Big Brothers of America matches fatherless young boys with male volunteers who stick with their charges (and their problems) year after year, on a one-to-one basis.

And of course, volunteers work in the offices of political candidates and elected officials such as state senators, congressmen, etc. —at many different types of jobs.

Yet broad as this sampling is, it still gives you only an idea of the variety of volunteer jobs actually open to you today.

"MOST WANTED"

Professionals are among the "most wanted" of all volunteers—for obvious reasons of skills and scarcity.

Semiprofessionals, including just about anybody with specialized education or professional training, are in great demand to help the pros. There are simply not enough professionals to go around, and there won't be enough for years.

Retired citizens with special skills, talents, or training are finding jobs in the Action program, doing everything from helping to clean up city slums to teaching Alaskan Eskimo school children.

Shut-ins are being invited to volunteer for telephone and desk work at home.

The poor are being welcomed as a vital link with other poor.

Even twelve- to fifteen-year-olds are helping in preschool classes. As a former anti-poverty leader remarked: "We need millions of 'extra mothers,' because millions of children simply don't have them. The crying need still is for warm sensitive human beings with a willingness to spend time on another human being, with the diligence and perseverance not to wash their hands of a problem when things get tough and grimy."

HOW DO YOU VOLUNTEER?

Volunteer work no longer is strictly summer, strictly unpaid, or strictly private. Many volunteers just cannot afford to work without pay. Instead, they may be part-time, part-paid, part-reimbursed, part-government-financed.

In contrast to the old concept of "busy work" for volunteers, today you can count on assuming as much responsibility as you are capable of handling and of becoming involved in a broad range of demanding tasks.

Volunteer jobs in recent years have spread to all income, age, and ethnic brackets, and a volunteer job well may be a major assist to you when you apply for a full-time permanent job later.

(1) If you want to volunteer for any of the major federal volunteer programs, get in touch directly with the Washington headquarters

of these programs. Or get in touch with the National Center for Voluntary Action, 1785 Massachusetts Avenue, Washington, D.C. 20036, which acts as a referral agency for local volunteer placement organizations.

(2) If you have had training in a field related to environmental protection and if you're interested in working on a volunteer program abroad, contact the Smithsonian-Peace Corps Environmental Program based in Washington (Office of Ecology, Smithsonian Institution, Washington, D.C. 20560). Some of the areas where volunteers were needed in the mid-seventies were fish biology, ornithology, entomology, zoology, marine biology, plant pathology, plant ecology. The program operates in 55 countries, with length of tours ranging from twenty-four to twenty-seven months. All volunteers are paid modest in-country living allowances plus a small stipend per month, held in the United States. Many of the jobs give volunteers an opportunity to carry out research that could be used to complete requirements for an advanced degree.

(3) If you are interested in working through a private charity, you will find that major private charities participating in anti-poverty and other programs have telephone listings in all sizable cities and towns. The Service Corps of Retired Executives, for example, has chapters in cities from coast to coast. To find the closest one to you, contact SCORE's national headquarters at 1030 15th Street, N.W., Washington, D.C. 20417.

(4) If you are a student, check the National Student Volunteer Program, which oversees student volunteer efforts now under way at more than four out of five U.S. colleges and universities. Involved are hundreds of thousands of students, many in state-wide student volunteer programs. Simply inquire at nearby colleges for details.

(5) Investigate whether your community is among the cities and communities which have set up Voluntary Action Centers or Volunteers Bureaus to ease the red tape and to guide volunteers in best applying their talents and individual circumstances to meet the most urgent demands.

(6) Also inquire about volunteer jobs and sources of actual jobs in *your* city at: City Hall; local youth organizations; the public school system headquarters; the welfare department; juvenile court.

(7) Look into a publication entitled *Invest Yourself*. This is a catalog of service opportunities in the United States and abroad compiled by the Commission on Voluntary Service and Action, a council of

roughly 150 private organizations in the United States and Canada which sponsor and/or support voluntary service projects all over the world (no connection between this council and the federal Action agency). CVSA's address is 475 Riverside Drive, Room 830, New York, N.Y. 10027.

(8) Or simply pin down your own community's most urgent unmet needs and start up your own volunteer program to help fill these needs.

The central point is that *if* you want to volunteer and *if* you are willing to work you are wanted, you are needed. And your contribution to our economy will run into incalculable tens of billions of dollars a year—helping us as individuals, helping us as a nation.

12

HOW TO SAVE
ON VACATIONS

TIME YOUR VACATION OFF SEASON	601
SAVE BY GOING WHERE THE CROWDS ARE NOT	602
SAVE ON A PACKAGE PLAN	602
SHOPPING	604
HOW TO SHOP FOR A VACATION TOUR	605
WHAT A TRAVEL AGENT CAN (AND CANNOT) DO FOR YOU	607
DO-IT-YOURSELF TRAVEL PLANNING	610
DO'S AND DON'TS FOR CUTTING YOUR HOTEL BILLS	612
WHOM AND HOW TO TIP	614
AND TIPPING ON WINTER CRUISES	615
SAVE BY HOSTELING	616
BUS PASSES AND BIKE TRAILS	617
MONEYSAVING GUIDES FOR CAMPING TRIPS	619
TOURISM AND ENERGY SHORTAGES	622

TIME YOUR VACATION OFF SEASON

If you take a trip to Rome during the Thanksgiving holidays, you well may save 20 per cent on a double room at one well-known luxury hotel as against the price you would pay during the packed, pushy, peak tourist summer days.

If you rent a car for an Irish holiday in October, you'll save even larger percentages as against the sum you would pay for the same car during the summer—and you'd enjoy additional savings on plane and boat fares, hotel rooms, meals, local transportation, entertainment.

If you take a three-week package tour of eight European countries starting in October, you well might pay $100 less than the same tour would cost you in June–August.

And if you are planning a week's skiing vacation this winter, you'll save 20 per cent or more on hotel accommodations just by waiting until late in the ski season, when the snow will be just as skiable, but the influx of skiers and après skiers will have slowed to a snowplow's pace.

Timing is at the very core of saving money on your vacation—either in the United States or abroad. What's more, since millions of you now have the privilege of taking your vacation whenever you wish during the year, this is a major moneysaving weapon you can use at your discretion and to whatever extent you want to.

You even might split your vacation into two holidays, taking advantage of bargain off-season rates at traditional summer resorts, then repeating your move and taking advantage of off-season rates at traditional winter resorts.

A key fact is that in many resort areas across the United States the weather is far more trustworthy in off season than it is at the season's height. May and October are particularly glorious months in many foreign lands.

As a general rule, the expensive "high season" in the Caribbean runs from mid-December until mid-March. In Europe, it's more or less the reverse: the high season begins with June and runs to (or, in some cases and places, *through*) September. A short "shoulder season" with intermediate prices sits between the high and low seasons.

SAVE BY GOING WHERE THE CROWDS ARE NOT

But even if you *must* take your vacation during the peak weeks of summer, you can save by heading for the less-crowded areas and by avoiding the well-known paths.

Don't squeeze yourself into the popular national parks, or visit a jammed resort. Head for one of the less crowded western Canadian provinces, or the wide-open spaces of Montana or Idaho, or a remote section of Upper Michigan. Or go to New York City while New Yorkers are off summer vacationing themselves. Miami and the Florida Keys offer reduced summer rates (though increasing numbers of tourists are discovering the fact). The ski towns of Colorado don't have as many summer visitors as winter skiers, yet their year-round weather and accommodations are delightful.

You also will be extra smart in midsummer if you avoid day-by-day travel, and instead find a single resort or hotel which can accept your reservation for a week or two.

SAVE ON A PACKAGE PLAN

Another key way to save is by buying a vacation "package." Many hotels in resort areas advertise special rates for stays of a weekend or a week or more. Often these are part of a transportation package with the airline or railroad serving the resort. Travel agents can suggest literally hundreds of good, moneysaving packages.

Or if you are buying a tour, consider a package, too, on unescorted standard-itinerary tours sold by tour operators. Included in the flat, low price will be your air ticket, hotel room, and certain sightseeing expeditions. You pay only for meals and extras and *you* decide how you'll spend most of your time.

Here's a sampling of the many other ways you can cut your vacation costs today:

• If you can, hook into an "inclusive tour charter" arranged by a travel agent. By doing so, you'll slash your air fare. For more details on air travel bargains, see Chapter 9, "Your Transportation."

• Inquire about other air fare bargain deals: excursion fares (good for 14- to 21- or 22- to 45-day trips); reserve-in-advance packages (which include a minimum payment for land arrangements); special fares.

• Look into the "stopover." Any time you travel outside the continental United States, your ticket probably entitles you to stop at additional cities (not shown on the ticket) without extra charge or at a very low charge.

• Investigate the Home Exchange Service, affiliated with Pan American World Airways, which publishes an annual directory of thousands of homes around the world whose owners want to exchange with other members in other countries. Members work out their own arrangements, pay a specified moderate total in dues per year. Address of HES: 119 Fifth Avenue, New York, N.Y. 10003.

• Or, as a poor man's alternative, get a copy of the "Travelers Directory," a listing throughout the United States and abroad of hundreds of people and places which will put you up for free (51-02 39th Avenue, Woodside, N.Y. 11377). You must offer your hospitality to others to get the directory, and a "donation" of a few dollars is requested to cover printing costs.

• If you're a student more than twelve years old, get for a small cost an International Student Identity Card from the Council on International Educational Exchange, 777 United Nations Plaza, New York, N.Y. 10017. This card gives you significant price reductions in a wide variety of student (not youth) hotels, restaurants, transportation, and cultural events abroad.

• Buy a cut-rate Eurailpass—giving you unlimited rail travel in thirteen continental countries on Western Europe's vast, subsidized railway system. Cost of a first-class rail pass in 1976: $180 for three weeks, $220 for one month, $300 for two months, or $360 for three months. If you're a foreign student (e.g., American) under age twenty-six, you can get a thirteen-country, two-month second-class Student-Railpass for only $195. (Of course, prices will go up from time to time but the bargain aspects will remain.) No Eurailpasses are available in Europe; all must be bought in the United States.

The Eurailpass in some instances entitles you to steamship or bus travel in addition to rail travel—either to facilitate surface connections or simply as an "extra."

For full details on the Eurailpass, ask your travel agent or write to Eurailpass, c/o French National Railroad, 610 Fifth Avenue, New York, N.Y. 10020, or Box 90, Lindenhurst, N.Y. 11757. (Information also available from the Austrian, German, Italian, Scandinavian, and Swiss railroad offices in the United States.)

• Avoid renting cars or buying goods and services in airports. Prices usually range 10 to 40 per cent above prices off the airport premises.

SHOPPING

Do your Christmas shopping at cut-rate duty-free shops. Take advantage of your quota of duty-free liquor, tobacco, etc. U. S. Customs permits you to bring back to the United States $100 worth of goods* you bought outside the country—retail value—if you were away at least forty-eight hours. (No minimum time applies to Mexico or U. S. Virgin Islands.) If you bring back more than $100 worth, you pay duty on the wholesale value, or about 40 per cent of the retail value. Special rules cover liquor and tobacco. You may include a quart of liquor duty- and tax-free, in your $100 exemption. If you're returning from the American Virgin Islands, Guam, or Samoa a *gallon* is duty-free under your exemption from duty, which increases to $200. Duty on wines, even expensive wines, is low.

You pay no duty at all on original oil paintings, stamps, or coins, books, or on antiques more than a hundred years old. Trademark restrictions limit the number or amounts of certain items you may bring home—particularly watches, perfumes, clocks, and cameras.

If you buy an automobile abroad and want to bring it back with you, you'll have to pay duty, of course—although under most circumstances you and other members of the family may use all your $100 exemptions to reduce the value of the car for duty purposes. In 1974 the rate of duty on a passenger car was 3 per cent of the "dutiable value," as determined by the customs inspector. To use the $100 exemption, the key rules for a returning U.S. resident are that:

the auto is imported for your personal use or for use of members of your household;

* 1974.

the auto has been acquired abroad as an incident of the journey from which you are returning;

the auto accompanies you at the time of your return on the same carrier.

Customs agents normally apply your $100 exemptions to the items with highest duty to give you the maximum savings, but it's wise to check yourself to be sure this is being done.

For more details on customs regulations, request the following pamphlets from the Bureau of Customs, Treasury Department, Washington, D.C. 20226:

"U. S. Customs Trademark Information," "Know Before You Go," "Customs Hints for Returning U. S. Residents," and "Importing a Car."

HOW TO SHOP FOR A VACATION TOUR

In recent years scandal after scandal has erupted across the front pages of the nation about "bargain" vacation tours. If you were a victim, you found many real costs hidden in the small print; or your costs were vastly increased when omitted essentials were included; or your de luxe accommodations were marginal at best; or you, a single, discovered too late that you had been booked into a double room with a stranger. Or many, many times your departure was at an abysmally "off" off hour.

But in strictly economic terms, the package tour *is* the least expensive way to take a vacation, particularly a vacation abroad, today.

Just what is a package tour? It is not, as you might think, always a highly organized, closely time-tabled tour during which the tour members eat, tour, sightsee, practically sleep together, and are herded in and out of places and countries with stopwatch precision.

Some travelers, primarily older couples, single persons, and inexperienced travelers may prefer the security of the traditional escorted group tour. But most of today's tour packages allow you to travel on your own and require only that the relatively small group fly together to and from their destinations.

A tour package does have, though, a predetermined price, number of features, and period of time. Within those limits, you, the traveler, can do whatever you please when you please. The greatest advantage to the traveler is that the cost of the land tour arrangements and air fare in the package is far less than the costs the traveler would otherwise pay for each item separately.

But, how do *you* avoid the traps? How do *you* shop for a tour?

Obviously, the prime rule—which I cannot repeat too often—is to deal only with an airline or tour operator or travel agent you have checked thoroughly and are confident is honest, reliable, and well established.

Obviously, it's no more than common sense to phone a couple of airlines, car rental firms, and the like to double-check whether the price of the tour you want really represents a saving over booking your vacation yourself or through a travel agent.

Now, use this check list to help you decide what you want from a vacation tour, to compare one tour against another, and to alert you to possible hidden costs.

Price: What's the total, including taxes and other extras, for the accommodations you want? If the tag says "from $198," will this minimum give you the comforts you need?

What's included: How many meals are provided each day? Fixed menu—or à la carte? Who pays tips for porters and tour guides? Who pays the hotel bills? For sight-seeing buses and guides? For theater tickets? For transfers between airports, train stations, and midtown? For transportation to your hotel? Is air fare included? If a rented car is part of the package, who pays for gas, a very costly item in most foreign lands? Typical *exclusions:* one or two meals a day, porters' tips, airport taxes, laundry and valet costs, taxi fares, snacks, excess baggage costs.

Accommodations: What type and class of hotel rooms are offered? Are the hotels named? Is there a clause permitting the tour operator to book you into substitute hotels for those named? Is the stated price for double occupancy? If you're traveling alone, is there a supplementary charge for a single room? Are such basic amenities as a bathroom included? Is the hotel's location convenient to where you're likely to be spending your time?

You'll save a lot of money by not bolting from the "package" to higher-cost hotel rooms. But if you prefer fancier surroundings, find out from the airline or tour operator the conditions and costs of trading up, if you so desire.

Terms: When do you have to pay for the tour? Is a deposit required and, if so, how much? What are the conditions for getting a refund if you cancel out or change your vacation plans? If you're paying on the installment plan, what annual interest rate is charged on the outstanding balance and how does this rate compare with the rate you might get on a loan from your bank or savings institution?

Your companions: How many other people will be along? Will they be interesting company for you—if you must be in close quarters (such as a bus) for long periods? Is there a theme for the tour to attract people with interests similar to yours?

Timing: How far in advance must you sign up? Choose a departure date and itinerary? Make a deposit? Pay in full?

Free time: How much will you have in each place you visit? Can you duck out for an afternoon or a day or two without being left behind, if you so wish? What's the likely pace of the tour? Will you be up to it? (As a general rule, if you travel more than nine or ten hours a day or more than 250 miles a day, you well might find your trip exhausting.) Will local guides shepherd you on certain legs of your trip and supplement your regular guide?

Find out these details *before* you sign up!

WHAT A TRAVEL AGENT CAN (AND CANNOT) DO FOR YOU

Let's say you are planning your first major vacation trip—either in the United States or abroad—and you have a general idea where you want to go and what you want to do. But you know absolutely nothing about costs, schedules, hotel accommodations. Just what could a travel agent do for you at what (if any) cost? How and where do you find a suitable travel agency?

A good travel agent should be well supplied with air and boat schedules; rates and costs for various types of travel; details on tours and group arrangements, schedules of festivals and other special events, hotel-motel room rates, cruise information.

A knowledgeable travel agent can:

guide you in applying for a passport and/or visa, alert you on immunizations you'll need for travel abroad, fill you in on customs rules and regulations;

sign you up for almost any kind of group tour (including tours the travel agency itself is putting together and selling);

make almost any kind of reservation or buy any kind of tickets for you—hotel, motel, plane, train, theater, ballet, bullfight, etc.—although many travel agencies do not sell bus and train tickets or short-haul air tickets or freighter accommodations;

sell you traveler's checks and counsel you on how to get the best deal when you change money abroad;

steer you to bargain vacation packages—including transportation, hotel rooms, car rentals, meals, etc., off-season deals, places which cater to and offer cut rates to families traveling with children;

tell you what are the "on" seasons, the "off" seasons and the "shoulder" seasons in between—in various parts of the world;

advise on tipping customs, what kind of clothes to take, what kind of weather to expect, good restaurants;

"tailor-make" a trip or tour for you and your family—to fit *your* tastes, *your* interests, *your* budget. This type of trip is known in the travel trade as an "Independent Inclusive Tour" (IIT) and this category is further divided into the Domestic Independent Tour (DIT) and the Foreign Independent Tour (FIT).

How much do travel agents' services cost you, the traveler? How and by whom are these costs paid?

The bulk of travel agents' costs are paid by the airlines, steamship lines, railroads, hotels and resorts, tour operators, in the form of commissions. But you, the customer, well may be charged for such extras as:

certain telegrams and long-distance telephone calls;

reticketing;

making reservations in certain foreign hotels;

short-stay hotel reservations.

Many travel agents also charge you for arranging a special, fancy custom-designed trip abroad.

Okay, now that you know what travel agents do—and don't do—how do you find a good one?

Get recommendations from friends and others who have been

customers of a travel agency with which you are considering doing business.

Try to find a travel agent who has himself (or herself) traveled in the area where *you* intend to go—and ask just how extensive the travel was.

Take the time to *visit* the travel agency. How thorough and "personal" is the agent's interview with you to discover your travel needs and wants? What "extras" are offered—i.e., a reading list on the countries you intend to visit?

Discuss your budget as well as your travel tastes frankly.

Ask if the agency is a member of the American Society of Travel Agents. (This is only a clue, since many reputable travel agencies are *not* members.)

Do not be misled by the size of a travel agency, for this is *not* necessarily an indication of the quality of its services. Good ones come both large and small.

Note whether the agent seems genuinely interested in steering you to travel bargains or whether he or she tries to push you into more expensive ways to "get there" than you can afford (remember, travel agents are paid commissions based on the cost of the accommodations). If the latter, go to another agency.

If you are booking a tour being sold by the travel agency, nail down details on deposits you'll be required to make, policies on refunds and cancellation fees. Each agency sets its own rules in this area and if the agent fails voluntarily to spell out the rules, *ask* what they are. (You may lose 100 per cent of whatever amount you have paid toward a tour —if this is the written policy of the tour operator and/or travel agency selling the deal. The loss could include even air fares you've paid for overseas tours. Also, when you sign a contract with a travel agent it's a legally binding piece of paper—both ways.)

If a travel agency promises to make refunds for cancellations you have made for valid reasons, find out just what constitutes valid reasons.

If a "slight" penalty is to be imposed in the event you cancel, check just how slight is "slight."

If you ask a travel agent to draw up a special itinerary for you, find out in advance what the costs will be, whether you'll be required to make a deposit, and, if so, how much. The charge for a custom-planned trip can be as high as 25 to 50 per cent of the value of the package—if the planning involves a lot of the agent's time, thought, and expertise.

If you have any suspicions about a travel agent with whom you're considering doing any substantial amount of business, check the agency's reputation with the local Better Business Bureau.

DO-IT-YOURSELF TRAVEL PLANNING

If you are booking on your own into one of the large hotels and hotel chains, use their toll-free telephone reservations number. You'll get an instant answer by phone or a letter more or less by return mail to confirm your reservation.

If you are making your own airline reservations, ask any major airline to advise you on other airline schedules as well as on special rates offered by all airlines. Most will freely do so.

Call Amtrak for most U.S. rail travel. (The toll-free number throughout the United States for reservations and information: (800) 523-5720.) More than 5,000 travel agents around the world also are authorized to sell Amtrak tickets. In Canada, the two key lines are: Canadian National Railways, 630 Fifth Avenue, New York, N.Y. 10020 (or CN System, Rail Travel Bureau, Central Station, Montreal, Quebec); and the Canadian Pacific Railway, 581 Fifth Avenue, New York, N.Y. 10017 (or CP Rail, Windsor Station, Montreal 101, Quebec).

The two best-known domestic bus lines are Greyhound and Trailways. Both have offices located at Eighth Avenue and Forty-first Street, New York, N.Y. 10014 (the New York Port Authority bus terminal).

Most of the key steamship lines have headquarters offices in New York City.

Look into the wide array of overseas travel information available from each major country's government travel office in New York (and, in some cases, in other cities as well).

Write the state Tourist Information Bureaus in the states you want to visit within our borders or the U. S. National Park Service, Department of the Interior, Eighteenth and E streets, Washington, D.C. 20240.

Go to the nearest Passport Office for guidance on how to apply for a passport. In some cities and towns which have no Passport Office, this information is now available at the U. S. Post Office along with passport application forms; elsewhere, get the information and application forms from the clerk of a federal or state court or from your county clerk's office.

For details on international auto registration certificates and International Drivers' Licenses, check the American Automobile Association, 28 East Seventy-eighth Street, New York, N.Y. 10021. And if you're a member of this organization, use its facilities to help plan your trip—including information on roads under construction and speed traps; maps; itinerary recommendations; regional guides to motels, restaurants (with ratings and tourist attractions).

Check your automobile insurance to be sure it covers you in all states you will visit. (Failure to take care of this could be very costly in the event of an accident.) If you will be traveling in Canada, ask your insurance company for a Canada Non-Resident Inter-Province Motor Vehicle Liability Insurance Card, required to prove your coverage to provincial officials. In Mexico, auto insurance laws are very strict. U.S. insurance is usually not valid for more than forty-eight hours after entry and you will need a more expensive Mexican policy for longer stays. *Be sure* to look into the car insurance problem *before* you leave home.

Study at least a couple of travel guides and books which you can borrow from your library or buy at a bookstore. (Some have coupons which will buy you discounts for various tourist services.) Among the best ones:

Fielding's Travel Guide to Europe and many other Fielding guides (William Morrow).

Frommer's *Europe on $5 and $10 a Day* and other "$5-a-Day" guides (Simon & Schuster).

Fodor's *Europe* and other Fodor guides (McKay).

Let's Go: Europe, a Student Guide (Harvard Student Agencies, Inc., distributed through E. P. Dutton & Co.).

The Mobil Travel Guides (Simon & Schuster).

Writers' Guides to the various states of the United States.

Rand McNally Guidebooks: *Road Atlas, Travel Trailer Guide, Guidebook to Campgrounds, Campground and Trailering Guide, National Park Guide, Ski Guide*.

Woodall's *Parks and Campgrounds* (Woodall Publishing).

The Michelin Guides to France and other European countries and Michelin's *Green Guide to New York City* (Simon & Schuster).

A to Z Guides by Robert S. Kane (Doubleday).

Blue Guides (Rand McNally).

AAA Tour Book, one for each region of the United States; also *Eastern and Western AAA Campground Guide*—all available to AAA members only.

The Official Student Travel Guide (International Student Travel Conference, 1560 Broadway, New York).

Whole World Handbook—Six Continents on a Student Budget (Council on International Educational Exchange, 777 United Nations Plaza, New York, N.Y. 10017).

PanAm's New Horizons World Guide and other PanAm guides to the United States, Canada, South America, European countries, Africa, Asia, the Middle East, and the Caribbean.

And finally the most important rule for all do-it-yourselfers: *plan ahead,* just as far ahead as you possibly can.

DO'S AND DON'TS FOR CUTTING YOUR HOTEL BILLS

If you're a typical American today, your spending for hotel and/or motel bills will run into hundreds of dollars a year. So will your spending for food and drink away from home—on long weekends, holidays, vacations.

If you're typical, you'll also "waste" as much as $2.00 of every $10 you spend simply because you do not know the basic do's and don'ts for saving on your hotel and motel bills:

Do, when you make a room reservation, ask for a room by price category. (Most hotels have three categories: economy, standard, and luxury.) If you want the minimum rate, ask for it. Virtually all good hotels now provide radio, TV, phone, air conditioning—and, if the hotel isn't full, many will give you better than minimum room accommodations even though you pay the lowest rate.

Don't underestimate the cost of room service. There usually is a room-service charge added to the bill the waiter gives you and the prices on the room-service menu usually are higher than prices for the same or similar items in the hotel coffee shop. Room service is a luxury which makes sense when you're on a special vacation, but it can add many dollars to your bills if you are a frequent traveler.

Do be careful about check-out time. If you want to stay an hour or two after check-out time, notify the manager or assistant manager directly, and unless your room is needed at once, he'll probably allow you to stay without charge. But if you stay as long as three hours after check-out time, the hotel may charge you $5.00 extra, and if you stay into the evening hours, you may be charged for a full extra day.

Don't, if you're traveling with your family, fail to inquire about the "family plan" that many hotels feature. It's ridiculous to pay for an extra room when—for no charge or for at most a nominal fee—the hotel will provide a folding bed which can be set up in your room. And this rule may apply to kids into their teens. Also, many hotels have special meal-ticket programs which will cut down on your family's dining bills.

Do take advantage of the toll-free electronic reservations systems which most large chains provide. By doing so, you can save the expense of a phone call or of a wire ahead to hotels in other cities you are planning to visit.

Don't, if you are driving your own car, ignore the extent to which overnight parking fees can throw your budget out of line. Make sure the midtown hotel you choose offers free parking either on the premises or nearby. Even in New York City, major hotel chains park cars without charge. Frequently, however, a charge is made each time you take your car out of the garage.

Do find out in advance if the hotel at which you're planning to stay is on the regular route of an airport bus or limousine. If it isn't at one of the regular stops, you'll have the added expense of a taxi to get you to your destination.

Do take another look at famed old downtown hotels which you may by-pass because you assume they're too expensive. To meet the competition of motor inns, airport and suburban hotels, many of these great establishments have cut their rates. You may be concentrating on saving a tip or two by staying in a motel, but as one great hotel man remarked, "I could never understand why anybody would want to spend $2.00 more for a room to save 25¢ on a tip."

Don't pay for the use of a hotel or motel swimming pool, sauna, gym, etc. (which may add $1.00 to $2.00 to daily room rates) if you don't intend to use the facilities.

And *do,* finally, try to plan your travels around the hotel package deals—off-season bargains, weekend plans, family specials—I've underlined in the preceding pages.

WHOM AND HOW TO TIP

The old guideline for restaurants, resort hotels, taxis, etc.—tip 15 per cent of the bill—has been firmly upped to 15 to 20 per cent of the total if you want to be known as generous.

The old rule for *porters* carrying your luggage also has been upped from 25¢ a bag to a minimum of 50¢, and frequently $1.00 is the minimum if you want to avoid scowls and recriminations from the porter.

The minimum tip for *taxi drivers* in big cities is 25¢—which works out to 25 per cent of a $1.00 fare.

Of course, many travelers still tip well below these levels—and a surprising number of skinflints don't tip *anyone any* percentage at all. But tipping remains an economic institution in this land and so:

The hotel doorman: Tip him 50¢ when you arrive, if he carries your baggage to the registration desk, $1.00 if you have three or more bags. Give him 25¢ each time he finds you a taxi—but give him no more than a "thank you" if he does no more than wave forward a cab waiting in line in front of the hotel.

The bellhop: Tip him as you tipped the doorman, increasing your tips if your luggage is especially heavy and/or cumbersome. Whenever he delivers anything you have ordered, give him at least 25¢, even if it is only a newspaper costing 10¢. Of course, if he has paid for the item you requested, also reimburse him.

The wine steward: Tip him 10 to 15 per cent of the cost of the wine, at the end of the meal.

Room service: Tip 50¢ each time an item is delivered. But tip $1.00 if the waiter brings ice and drink mixers and $1.50 to $2.00 if he brings a whole tray full of soda, glasses, ice, and other drinking equipment. When you have a meal sent to your room, tip as you would in a restaurant—15 to 20 per cent of the check.

Valet: Tip 50¢ per delivery. If you give the valet a rush order, though, or ask for extraordinary service—say a suit pressed and back within the hour—give him $1.00.

Chambermaid: You need not tip her if you spend only a night or two at a regular commercial hotel, but it's increasingly recommended that you leave her 50¢ a day if you stay longer. Leave the money in an envelope addressed "For the Chambermaid in Room—" at the reception desk the last day of your stay and tell the housekeeping department you left it. Tip her $1.00 to $2.00 if you have a cocktail party in your room or suite, involving a big cleanup job for her. In a resort hotel, the standard minimum tip for the chambermaid is 50¢ per day for a single person, $1.00 a day for a couple, more for special service.

Travel abroad: Even if a substantial service charge has already been added to your hotel or restaurant bill, the trend today is toward adding another 10 per cent to the total rather than just leaving the small change. The trend also is toward personal distribution of the money to make sure the chambermaid, doorman, waiter, or others who have served you actually get the tips. And the trend too is for tipping above and beyond these percentages for any extra special services—for tips frequently are the sole source of income for service personnel in Europe and elsewhere abroad.

At a resort hotel—including those operating on the American plan (all meals included) or modified American plan (breakfast and dinner included)—a service charge of 15 per cent or more may be added to your total bill. If it isn't, tip your dining-room waiter 15 per cent of your restaurant bill. You'll probably find details on how much of your daily room rate is for your meals in the hotel directory in the dresser drawer of your room but, if not, ask the assistant manager or social director for pertinent facts. Tip bellboys 50¢ for each bag they carry and tip your chambermaid and pool boy 50¢ each per day per person, as you leave. Tip your resort's hairdresser 15 to 20 per cent.

Visiting friends: If there is a housekeeper or cook who helps make your stay more gracious and comfortable, you, as a visiting couple, might properly tip $1.00 to $2.00 a day as a "thank you."

P.S.: Perhaps as you grumble and struggle over whether to tip 10 per cent or 15 per cent or 20 per cent or whatever, you might remember that, by one definition, "TIPS" were originally intended as a means "To Insure Prompt Service." This reminder might help guide you to the right amount for the right persons.

AND TIPPING ON WINTER CRUISES

Let's say you are now making plans for your first winter vacation on a cruise ship. You've read all the brochures on what to wear, what to see, what to do. But one angle I'll wager you've missed is: whom to tip how much. Even if you already have been on every type of winter holiday, I'll bet you have made plenty of inadvertent tipping blunders.

Here, too, tipping expectations are being revised sharply upward in many instances from the old 10 to 15 per cent range to a new 15 to 20 per cent range—and employees who never were considered eligible for tips suddenly are turning up on the lists. Following, therefore, you will find up-to-date rules for cruise-ship tipping:

• Tip your dining-room steward and your room steward or steward-ess a minimum of $1.00 each per day per person. Thus, if you are a cou-ple on a two-week cruise, tip a total of about $30. If your cruise lasts a week or less, tip at least $10 for each steward—at the end of the trip.

• Tip the deck steward 50¢ a day or about $2.50 to $3.00 a week. Tip the headwaiter in the dining room a couple of dollars, plus $1.00 or $2.00 each time he performs some special service for you. Tip the bartender 15 to 20 per cent each time you are served a new drink. Tip the telephone operator $1.00 or $2.00 if she puts through complicated ship-to-shore calls for you.

• On shore, tip tour guides 50¢ or 15 per cent of the cost of the tour if it's a half-day tour, $1.00 if it's a full-day tour. Tip the men who carry your luggage in U.S. ports at least 35¢ per bag—even if the dock is plastered with "no tipping" signs.

• Don't tip the cruise's social director; or the person who leads calis-thenics; or the purser or other ship's officers; or customs men in port. If you are in doubt, ask for guidelines from your travel agent, the cruise director, or the ship's purser. The excursion agent on board your ship can tell you if tipping is expected anywhere ashore.

SAVE BY HOSTELING

One of the least expensive ways to "see the world" is to use the world's extraordinary network of youth hostels. These are inexpensive dormitory-style accommodations providing shelter, bunks or beds, and often some sort of kitchen facilities. Fees in the United States are typically $2.50 in summer and $3.25 in winter per day for lodging; abroad, fees are lower.

There are some 4,400 hostels today in 48 different countries, and the youth hosteling organizations offer a long list of special bargains to hostelers. You can go hosteling by foot, canoe, bike, public transportation, or car. You can go alone, or with friends, or with a group and trained leader.

Typical cost of a thirty-day American Youth Hostel tour within the United States in 1976 was in the $350 to $400 range and in the $550 to $650 range for tours abroad. Included were: transportation from a specified departure point; all costs of accommodations and food; insurance; leadership; and transportation back to the original departure point. *Not* included in this price were: equipment you must have (generally simple camping gear); spending money; cost of passports; bicycle shipping; transportation to or from trip starting point; AYH membership dues; and an emergency fund which must be deposited with the trip leader for unexpected expenses (unused amounts are returned).

Hostelers on a National Group Trip must be at least fourteen years old or must have completed ninth grade. On International Trips campers must be at least sixteen years old or have previously completed a National Trip. There is no upper age limit, but most trips are intended for young travelers in good physical condition. A few, however, are for adults only.

As an alternative to a youth hostel tour, you can travel on your own, staying at youth hostels along the way. American Youth Hostels also has a bargain car-leasing plan in Europe. Or you can rent a car and tent and camp where there are no hostels.

Your passport to hostels throughout the world is a pass issued by AYH.

A junior pass in 1976 (for people under age eighteen) cost $5.00; a senior pass for older hostelers cost $10; a family membership covering children up to age eighteen cost $11. Only individual passes—junior and senior—can be used outside the United States.

For detailed information on trips and applications for passes, write American Youth Hostels, AYH National Campus, Delaplane, Va. 22025.

BUS PASSES AND BIKE TRAILS

Another way to cover a large territory on your vacation—at very low cost—is to go by bus. You can now get a special type of bus ticket, similar to the well-known Eurailpass, which will give you virtually unlimited bus travel in the United States and Canada for sixty days. Greyhound calls its version Ameripass and Continental Trailways calls its ticket Eaglepass, but in 1976 both cost about $175 for thirty days and about $250 for sixty days. This worked out to $4.00 to $6.00 a day—a clue to how great a bargain the passes really are.

Your only limitations in using either pass are: you may not take more than four round trips between any two points; neither pass is valid during the peak summer travel months.

More than 150,000 miles of routes in forty-eight states and Canada are yours to choose from, and Greyhound's pass also gives you a variety of discounts up to 20 per cent on hotels, car rentals, tours, and other services. Greyhound's pass may be used on the Trailways system where Greyhound does not provide service and vice versa. But it is most convenient to buy your pass from the line which serves your travel plans best.

An increasingly popular way to go camping—or just to sight-see at your vacation destination—is by bicycle. You can even combine it with bus travel. Bicycles are proliferating and it is becoming easier all the time to find places to combine this sport with camping. The Bureau of Outdoor Recreation, U. S. Department of Interior, estimates that there will be more than 200,000 miles of bike routes in the United States by the end of this decade. Ohio, for instance, has more than a half dozen biking routes running through the most scenic areas of the state, and more are being laid out all the time. The average length of these routes is about 30 miles and all are marked by standard bikeway signs. ("Ohio Is Happening Along Bikeways" from the Ohio Department of Development, Box 1011, Columbus, O. 43216, describes the trails.)

Or you can ride through Indiana's covered-bridge country on a bikeway running through Parke County. A longer trail is the towpath of the old Chesapeake and Ohio Canal from Georgetown, D.C. to Cumberland, Md.—184 miles. Or you can ride 320 miles on the Wisconsin State Bikeway from the Mississippi River to Lake Michigan.

Many more trails are being planned for the future; most spurred locally, but some of them with financial help from the federal government. But you don't have to wait for official designation of trails. With a little help from cycling clubs and friends, plus some practice and experience on your own, you'll be able to choose the most enjoyable routes yourself from highway maps and government topographic maps.

Also, send for "The AYH North American Bike Atlas," which describes 60 one-day trips throughout the United States and 100 one-week to one-month trips in Canada, Mexico, and the Caribbean ($2.45; American Youth Hostels, Inc., AYH National Campus, Delaplane, Va. 22025).

Try combining hostels, state and private campgrounds, perhaps a friendly farmer or two, and even an occasional motel. You'll surely find you can work out literally hundreds of real cycling adventures almost anywhere in the country—at astonishingly low cost. (The rules on how to *buy* a bicycle are in Chapter 9, "Your Transportation," on pages 430–33.)

MONEYSAVING GUIDES FOR CAMPING TRIPS

During most of the summer weeks each summer, tens of millions of you go off on camping trips and in the process spend more than $1 billion on travel trailers alone, plus hundreds of millions on camping equipment, plus millions more on getting to and from the camping grounds, on overnight fees, and on other expenses.

Until recently, camping in the United States meant stuffing a sleeping bag, some warm clothes, a few cooking utensils and first-aid equipment into a rucksack, slinging it over your back, and heading for the hills. But today the typical camper travels in a fully equipped trailer or motor home, cooks on gas stoves instead of campfires, watches TV instead of beavers. Today's typical campsite provides creature comforts ranging from hot showers to hair dryers, clothes washers to canteens.

Obviously, camping has become a significant factor in the outdoor recreation industry and also a potentially whopping expense to the individual camper or camping family.

As one measure of camping's spectacular growth just in this decade, the Rand McNally *Guidebook to Campgrounds* listed more than 15,000 campgrounds in the United States and Canada in 1974 (with more than 550,000 individual campsites), up from only 5,000 campgrounds listed in 1961. Rand McNally also counted thousands of camping areas specifically set up to accommodate travel trailers, with more than 400,000 separate sites for trailers.

If you're the back-to-nature type and really prefer to rough it, you and your family can go on a camping trip by foot or by canoe in any one of thousands of national and state parks for as little as $75 a week,* as-

* All of these figures prevailed in 1974.

suming you don't go too far from home and you already own basic equipment such as cooking utensils, sleeping bags, and back packs. Even if you have to rent these basics, the total cost for a family of three or four needn't run over $100 a week. But if you prefer the "motel in the wilderness" type of camping, involving rented travel trailers, overnight fees at private campgrounds, electricity and gas bills, etc., costs can rise to $300 or more a week.

If you're considering taking your first camping expedition, your best bet is to avoid an outlay of hundreds of dollars to buy trailers, tents, etc. Rent them instead. Buy just as little as possible until you find out whether or not you like the whole idea of camping and, if so, what style of camping you enjoy most.

If you decide to go the recreational vehicle route, you can choose from a wide range of travel trailers, campers, motor homes, etc.—at an even wider array of prices. (You will find the money saving guides on buying recreational vehicles in Chapter 9, "Your Transportation," pages 426–28.)

Another possibility is a U.S.- or foreign-made small camper which you can rent for about the price of renting a car at an airport. This type of camper will sleep four people and has the full range of kitchen equipment and other camping gear. The vehicles are available in many major U.S. cities and throughout Europe.

Here are more tips if you prefer to rough it:

• The federal government offers a $10 Golden Eagle Passport card which will admit you and any passengers in your car to all areas of the national park system and give you the use of most facilities and services provided by the National Park Service during the year. (A free version, available to citizens more than sixty-two years old, also gives a 50 per cent discount on all special user fees on all federal lands—not just the national parks.)

Get your pass at any national park, at most national forests, or from any first- or second-class post office. Also write the U. S. Superintendent of Documents, Washington, D.C. 20402, for brochures entitled "Camping in the National Park System," "Fishing in the National Park System" and "Boating in the National Park System" (modest cost for each).

• If you're inclined toward a really "wild" camping experience, full of educational information about the wild areas you visit and the ways to get there, it is hard to beat the package wilderness tours offered on a non-profit basis by several large conservation and other outdoor sport associations. Examples:

The Wilderness Society operates dozens of tours ranging from hiking, back-packing, and canoeing to horseback riding in wilderness areas throughout the United States. Emphasis is on getting to know the wilderness in a non-destructive way. (For information, write to the Wilderness Society, Western Regional Office, 4260 Evans Avenue, Denver, Colo. 80222.)

The American River Touring Association runs an extensive program of river touring in many distant parts of the world as well as in the United States. Prices in 1974 ranged from under $100 for weekend trips to up to $2,000 and more for month-long semi-expeditions. (Write ARTA, 1016 Jackson Street, Oakland, Calif. 94607.)

The Sierra Club, the oldest and one of the largest (137,000 members) wilderness conservation club in the United States, sponsors hundreds of wilderness outings each year, including river trips (by raft or canoe), hiking/back-packing trips, and saddle trips. You may be continuously moving or operate in a more leisurely fashion from a base camp. Many trips are specifically designed as family trips. You can write the Sierra Club for a publication describing the entire year's trips at 1050 Mills Tower, 220 Bush Street, San Francisco, Calif. 94104. Chapters also organize a regular schedule of local trips throughout the year at very low cost.

• If you are camping in a national park, choose your campsites carefully. Each year, more than 50 million people somehow squeeze themselves into fewer than a million campsites. In the process, many areas become overused, while some are underused. The name of the game, of course, is to find the latter.

• Be on the lookout for the creation of new national parks on the very edges of major cities. The current proposal of the Interior Department is to make 1 million park acres easily accessible near every city of 250,000 or more people.

• But even before these new areas are created, study the areas close to your home carefully. Often you'll find little gems of wilderness in the midst of urban areas, unfrequented by the crowds whose urge to escape leads them to overlook their immediate neighborhood and to travel as far as possible. If you find one of these, restful camping may be yours for very little money and travel time.

• If your interest extends beyond camping to the more exacting sports—such as mountaineering, rock climbing, white-water canoeing, or scuba diving—you'll need special instruction as well as special gear. First-aid courses are also valuable if you plan to do much camping. You can get this training most economically from experienced friends or from local clubs, who usually share their knowledge willingly and without charge.

Nationally known groups, such as the Sierra Club or the Red Cross, are sound non-profit alternatives though they may charge for direct expenses. There also are dozens of commercial schools, whose reputations and costs are usually easy to check through knowledgeable devotees of the sport.

TOURISM AND ENERGY SHORTAGES

Tourism is defined as travel fifty miles or more one way, in any form of transport, for any purpose other than commuting for work. It is a vital part of our country's life style, employing 4 million people and accounting for $60 to $65 billion of spending each year (food, lodging, public transportation, fuel, auto operating costs, entertainment, sightseeing). It is a labor-intensive, service industry, and in every state tourism is vital to our economic well-being (we take in each other's washing). In three states—Florida, Hawaii, and Nevada—tourism is the leading industry. In six others—California, Texas, Pennsylvania, Illinois, Michigan, Ohio—tourism brings in more than $1 billion annually. In seven other areas—Maine, Alaska, Arizona, Washington, D.C., the Virgin Islands, Puerto Rico, and Guam—the dependence on the travel dollar is extremely heavy.

Not only for your own physical and mental well-being, but also for your nation's welfare, the thing to do in this era of energy shortages is to plan your vacation so that, with the use of 75 per cent of the energy you consumed before the shortages emerged, you can enjoy 100 per cent of your life style.

Here, therefore, are tips on travel designed specifically to help you conserve energy:

• Investigate with much more care than you formerly did fly/drive, bus/drive, rail/drive, fly/sight-see packages. Be as flexible on dates and routing as you can and use public transportation where feasible.

• Fly/drive vacations now come in all types and sizes, involving rental cars and hotels. Nearly all the airlines have them. Check with a reputable travel agent for pertinent details.

• "Take me along" vacations are booming. For the very simple reason that it saves money, families are planning their vacations around convention and business trips.

• If you like national parks, you'll have no trouble getting to the park by bus these days as well as rail. And buses within the parks have been vastly improved too. There are 200 park systems located within 100 miles of a metropolitan center—involving the use of bus rather than a tankful of gas.

• Hotels and motels are offering minivacations and "escape weekends" to people within 100 miles at up to 50 per cent discounts. Most major attractions are within 100 miles of airports or rail terminals or can be reached by bus.

• When traveling by air, be much more flexible on dates, avoiding Fridays and Sundays if possible. On routing, adjust your schedule if need be and don't insist on non-stop.

• Let your travel agent make one booking, and have a confirmed reservation. Avoid double booking—which means you are depriving someone else of a seat.

• Investigate Amtrak, especially for family travel and short-haul business travel. Railroads and motorcoaches are the most economical users of fuel.

• Discover your own area close to home by motorcoach. Travel in groups. Avoid congested areas by private auto. On these trips, you really waste gas because of traffic tie-ups and idling motors.

• Take buses to the airport, get there early, avoid gas-eating traffic jams, try not to meet friends at airports.

• Forget haphazard touring. Do not plan an auto trip without a plan. Know where you want to go, when. Buy guides, know your wayside itinerary, make reservations.

• Now the universities are trying to lure us with vacation and travel opportunities on college campuses and surrounding areas. Mort's "Guide to Low-Cost Vacations & Lodgings on College Campuses" ($2.95 in bookstores or $3.50 from CMG Publications, Box 630, Princeton, N.J. 08540), describes the great recreational and cultural facilities of 144 colleges in the United States and Canada which formerly have been enjoyed mostly by students but now are open to all of us at a fraction of commercial recreational, food, and lodging prices.

You need only make relatively easy adjustments. Try them, you'll even like them.